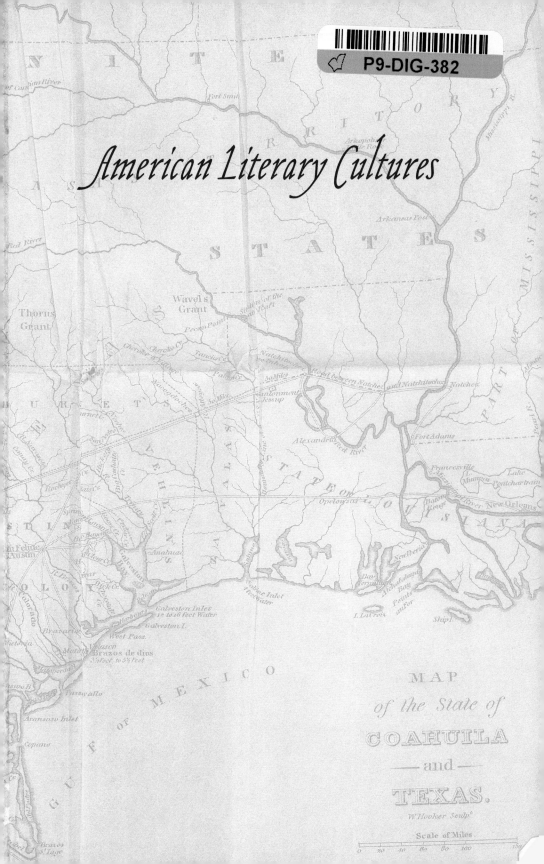

American Literary Cultures

MAP

of the State of

COAHUILA

— and —

TEXAS.

W. Hooker Sculp.

Scale of Miles

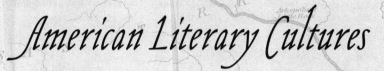

American Literary Cultures

A Reader

Elizabeth J. Dell and Joe B. Fulton

editors

BAYLOR UNIVERSITY PRESS

Cover and book design by Kasey McBeath

Cover and front matter image: *Map of the State of Coahuila and Texas* (c. 1833),
by William Hooker (1782–1856), included in Mary Austin Holley, *Texas:
Observations, Historical, Geographical and Descriptive: in a series of letters,
written during a visit to Austin's colony, with a view to a permanent settlement
in that country, in the Autumn of 1831. 31 × 26 cm.* Courtesy of the Texas
Collection, Baylor University, Waco, Texas.

Paperback ISBN: 978-1-4813-1263-9
Library of Congress Control Number: 2020936973

Printed in the United States of America on acid-free paper.

Contents

2 :: Colonial Literature and the Road to Revolution

3 :: Romanticism

4 :: Realism

5 :: Naturalism

6 :: Early Modernism

Acknowledgments

The editors would like to thank Baylor University's College of Arts and Sciences for initiating this reader as a supplement to the new core course American Literary Cultures. We are grateful to Dean of the College Lee Nordt and to Associate Dean for Humanities and Social Sciences Kim Kellison, for their support; and to Associate Dean for Undergraduate Studies Blake Burleson, who spearheaded the Common Core Reader Initiative. We would like to thank the committee that formed the Common Core Reader Initiative—those who offered us advice along the way, Drs. Derek Dodson and Doug Weaver of the Religion Department; those who worked alongside us on their core reader, Drs. Julie deGraffenried and Stephen Sloan of the History Department; and those who offered leadership, Dr. Christopher Richmann, Assistant Director for the Academy for Teaching and Learning, and Dr. Lauren Poor, Director of the Core.

We would also like to express our gratitude to Dr. Kevin Gardner, Chair of the English Department, for his wisdom and leadership; to Ms. Lois E. Avey, Office Manager of the English Department, for her assistance in problem-solving; to Dr. Richard Russell, Graduate Program Director of English, for providing a graduate assistant; to Vice Provost and Dean of the Graduate School Larry Lyon for his generosity; and to our colleagues in the English Department for their recommendations.

We would especially like to acknowledge our many student workers: Jonathan Scruggs, master's in English, who assisted with editing and proofreading; Elena Pappas, a recent graduate of Baylor who served as our editorial assistant; Kendall Elliott, also a recent graduate of Baylor who proofed early drafts; and Graham Gardner, a Baylor undergraduate, who gave office assistance.

We would like to thank the following University Librarians: Eileen Bentsen, Reference Librarian, Research and Engagement; Becky Parton, Instructional Designer, Library and Academic Technology Services; and Rachel DeShong, Map Curator, Texas Collection.

Our thanks to Professor Hannah M. Dyar, Lecturer in Modern Languages and Cultures, for her excellent translations from Spanish.

We would like to thank Baylor University Press, most especially, Jenny Hunt, Associate Director of Digital Publishing and Production Manager, for shepherding this project through; Kasey McBeath, Design Manager, for the cover and interior design; David Aycock, Interim Director, for financial support and assistance with marketing and publicity; Juliana Mudd, for her excellent work in editing and proofing the manuscript; and the many students who assisted with the clean-up and transcription of texts, including Brooke Hill, Katherine McClellan, Lindsey Keller, Celsie Moseley, and Maya Adams.

All royalties received from the sale of this reader benefit the English Department's Excellence Fund.

Introduction

"To read these or any foreign works fairly, the reader must
understand the national circumstances under which they were
written. To use them worthily, he must know how to interpret them
for the use of the universe."

—Margaret Fuller, 1845

American Transcendentalist Margaret Fuller penned these high-minded
sentiments in her essay "French Novelists of the Day" in 1845, arguing that
to read well one must know something of the text's context—its cultural
history—not only to interpret but to make use of its ideas.* Fuller speaks to
a newly identified American audience to read with intention and perspective, to read both within and without a text, both the thing itself and the
context in which the text lives, words still applicable today.† The selections
in this reader are by writers of indigenous, African, Tejano, Spanish, Mexican, French, and English descent; they are about America, by and about
literary cultures that have forged an American literature. Like other readers,
this reader begins with literature from indigenous oral traditions and earliest
recorded European exploration, stopping with the early twentieth century,
but with a twist. Designed with Baylor University's Common Core in mind,
with its emphasis on globalism, diversity, and dialogue, and its connection
to the core virtues, the reader is particularly strong in indigenous, Latinx,
Southwestern, and Texan cultural influences. Emphasizing the variety of

---

* Margaret Fuller, "French Novelists of the Day," *The Writings of Margaret Fuller*, ed. Mason
Wade (New York: Viking, 1941), 311.

† Not *all* of the words are acceptable today, though understanding American history and
literature requires understanding the use of the language. As students read through
the texts in this reader, they will notice occasional examples of racial epithets, racially
charged language, or insensitive characterizations. Such elements reveal much about the
past and call us to remember: while such language and characterizations do not reflect
who we are today, these challenging texts may deepen our desire to further diversity and
civil discourse as citizens of this region, this nation, and this world. Readers may find
much to discuss productively and sensitively about who we wish to be and become.

1

American literary cultures, as well as less frequently anthologized texts, the reader offers context—engaging regional, national, and global concerns even while speaking to the universal and eternal themes Fuller championed.*

While tracing diverse heritages and global impulses shaping America from Contact to World War I, this reader spotlights literature by regional writers about Texas and the Southwest, literature that reflects this state's culturally rich, global, and heterogeneous heritage—indigenous, Latinx, European, African. These narratives and counternarratives join a conversation with equally diverse narratives, addressing cultures in dialogue with and cultures in conflict with one another. The reader, then, seeks to challenge its audience to reflect upon the diversity of literary voices of those near and far, familiar and foreign; to engage texts critically, creatively, and empathetically; to question and sometimes unsettle; to read into and against American literary cultures: in short, to discover and, as Fuller encourages, make use of ideas that become a part of one's own personal narrative.

This reader is predicated on the assumption that a college education ought to deepen our understanding of our country, its diversity and complexity, along with its place in the global literary conversation. Original explanatory footnotes offer additional context and are distinguished by brackets and our initials (E.J.D. and J.B.F.). The texts within this reader reflect the creative abundance that American literature has to offer—its different experiences, backgrounds, ideas, and assumptions as well as its diverse genres and styles. Further, these texts illustrate the dynamic world that is the English classroom at Baylor, a venue where we champion writing of different types and from different perspectives, where we illustrate the imaginative breadth of American literature. Indeed, the great American poet Emily Dickinson might have imagined Baylor students engaged in reading when she wrote,

> There is no frigate like a book
> To take us lands away,
> Nor any coursers like a page
> Of prancing poetry.
> This traverse may the poorest take
> Without oppress of toll;
> How frugal is the chariot
> That bears a human soul.†

---

* Because no one reader could do justice to all literary cultures, the editors have designed this as a supplemental reader, rather than an encyclopedic one; as such, it complements texts currently in use by Baylor faculty.

† Emily Dickinson, "XCIX," *The Complete Poems of Emily Dickinson* (Boston: Little, Brown, and Company, 1924): 53–54.

Books, as we know, inspire curiosity, invite intellectual thought, encourage moral growth, and even inspire us spiritually as we strive to discern and become our best selves. Books take us on a journey. So, too, this book invites readers to traverse a literary landscape at once local and global—that may "take us lands away": Alexis de Tocqueville critiques American literature from the point of view of the European, while Mark Twain counters with humor, delightfully describing the American "Back from 'Yurrup.'" The memoirs of frontiersmen Davy Crockett and Bigfoot Wallace exemplify Texas' literary role in Southwest humor, while ex-slave and cowboy Nat Love and John Rollin Ridge (Cheesquatalawny) explore complex racial relations in their narratives of the Old West. In their memoirs of the nineteenth-century West, Rachel Plummer and Sarah Winnemucca (Thocmentony) offer opposing views of the violence of native against white, white against native. Writers as diverse as regionalist Sarah Orne Jewett of Maine and naturalist Mary Hunter Austin of California speak across the continent as protofeminist environmental protectors of the land.

Contact, imperialism, and exchange are present in the early American texts: as cultures encounter one another, texts confront one another with varying perspectives on the landscape and peoples they face. Lost Spanish explorer Álvar Núñez Cabeza de Vaca, given hospitality by the coastal peoples of south Texas, shares his surprise at their compassion and generosity given scarce resources yet disdains their (to him) primitive cultures. In contrast, founding father Ben Franklin counters the common nomenclature of indigenous peoples as "savage" by praising instances of hospitality and civility. Brother Matías Sáenz of San Antonio, father of Spanish Catholic missions in south Texas, argues that the indigenous peoples are barbarous but "docile," "sheep" ready for conversion, while Red Jacket of the New York Seneca politely rejects missionaries evangelizing among his people. His people, Red Jacket argues, are content with their culture, and he reminds his audience of the value of religious liberty and the natural right of freedom of conscience. Where then might this reader take us? What moral and intellectual travels? Present in these selections alone we discover themes of nature, culture, boundaries, moving frontiers, the West, religious diversity, memory, slavery, individualism, community, and freedom. Where else might we journey?

Reading draws us into a cultural conversation that is at once regional, national, global, and universal. At times it is individual and specific, a meeting of the minds where we engage with other lives. Books truly are, as Wayne Booth aptly put it, "the company we keep," and he marveled that readers tend to view characters as "more like people" than as "textual puzzles to be deciphered." For students using this reader, the company you will keep during your college years ranges from fellow students, friends, and professors to the books you read. "These are not books, lumps of lifeless paper," Gilbert Highet once said of the library, "but *minds* alive on the shelves." In his influential speech against censorship, *Areopagitica*, English poet John Milton asserted that "books are not absolutely dead things" but retain the spirit of the author. He then radically declared, "As good almost kill a man as kill a good book: who kills a man kills a reasonable creature, God's image; but he who destroys a good book, kills reason itself, kills the image of God." Throughout your college career and after, books and writing will influence you right along with friends, family, and others. You will be living life but also writing the story of your life, crafting a narrative in which you are the protagonist, your story a part of overlapping cultures from local to global.*

Above the entrance to the library of Alexandria, the greatest library of the ancient world, was imprinted the motto "Place of the cure of the soul." The twentieth-century Austrian writer Franz Kafka put it differently when he commented, "A book must be the axe for the frozen sea inside us."† Reading the works in this reader allows us to participate in a larger conversation, one that spans recorded human history, about the formation of human consciousness and community. Reading today, we acquire facts about the past and skills for understanding American literary cultures, American identity, and America's place in a global world even while empathizing with other lives and becoming part of larger communities. Reading in this sense is far from an idle pastime. The poet Walt Whitman wrote, "Books are to be call'd for, and supplied, on the assumption that the process of reading is not a half-sleep, but, in highest sense, an exercise, a gymnast's struggle; that the reader is to do something for himself, must be on the alert, must himself or herself construct indeed the poem, argument, history, metaphysical essay—the text furnishing the hints, the clue, the start or frame-work."‡ This energized, engaged reading is an important part of how we become the person we hope to be as we walk across the stage to receive a diploma, a recognition that we have become, not just skilled at a craft, but a better version of ourselves. Literature is part of the road map. Literature helps us "Dream other dreams, and better!" as Mark Twain exhorted.§

---

* Wayne C. Booth, *The Company We Keep: An Ethics of Fiction* (Berkeley: University of California Press, 1988), x; Gilbert Highet, *The Immortal Profession: The Joys of Teaching and Learning* (New York: Weybright and Talley, 1976), 4; John Milton, "Areopagitica, A Speech for the Liberty of Unlicensed Printing," *The Complete Prose Works of John Milton*, ed. Rufus Wilmot Griswold, 2 vols. (Philadelphia: Herman Hooker, 1845), 1:168.

† Alberto Manguel, *The Library at Night* (New Haven: Yale University Press, 2008), 26; Franz Kafka, *Letters to Friends, Family, and Editors* (New York: Schocken, 1977), 16.

‡ Walt Whitman, "Democratic Vistas," *Complete Prose Works of Walt Whitman*, 7 vols. (New York: G. P. Putnam's Sons, 1902), 2:148.

§ Mark Twain, *No. 44, The Mysterious Stranger* (Berkeley: University of California Press, 1982), 186.

1 :: Contact and Conflict

1—1

Southwestern Native American Poetry and Song

The songs and poems in this section are of ancient origin and were transmitted as part of oral cultures. In most cases, they were committed to paper by American anthropologists of the late nineteenth and early twentieth centuries who sought to record and preserve them. Notable among those involved in collecting and translating songs for *The Path on the Rainbow* was Carl Sandburg, an established poet and biographer of Abraham Lincoln, and Mary Hunter Austin, whose *Land of Little Rain* figures in a later section on Realism. Selections from these sources focus on indigenous tribes of the Southwest and West.

Nahuatl is the language of the Aztecs and remains the first language of many people in Mexico. The destruction of the great libraries of the Aztecs was a historical tragedy, and few books have survived. ANCIENT NAHUATL POETRY represents some of the oral culture that was preserved, with selections below gathered in 1887 by pioneering linguist and anthropologist Daniel G. Brinton. In his introduction, Brinton expounds on the value of song and the importance of the singer for Ancient Nahuas, a tradition so powerful that it later concerned Spanish colonial authorities:

> The profession of the poet stood in highest honor. It was the custom before the Conquest for every town, every ruler and every person of importance to maintain a company of singers and dancers, paying them fixed salaries, and the early writer, Duran,* tells us that this custom continued in his own time, long after the Conquest. He sensibly adds, that he can see nothing improper in it, although it was condemned by some of the Spaniards. (9–10)

≈≈ ≈≈ ≈≈

* [Father Diego Duran was a Spaniard (1537–1588) who lived in Mexico and became an expert in Nahuatl language and culture—*E.J.D. and J.B.F.*]

From *Traditional Songs of the Zuñi Indians*

"Sunset Song: Ceremonial Thanks Offering to the Sun"[*]

Note: The "Sunset Ceremonial" was the first song I listened to and witnessed on my arrival and introduction into Zuñiland. I was very much impressed with the earnestness and fervor of the Sun-worshipers and immediately joined the Exercises with them. This however created quite a surprise and displeasure, when a sub-chief reproved me for bowing to the Sun, with a *white man's hat on*, and *noisy heel boots*, instead of *moccasins*; and proclaimed I was a Wasitoni-man,[†] and should be expelled from the Ceremony. I immediately removed my hat, breathed on the Chief's hand,[‡] which he courteously responded by breathing on mine. He then took off his turbaned headgear with golden tassels attached, and tied it around my head, and motioned me to join again in the Ceremonial, which I did.

This created at once a very friendly feeling towards me, and a cordial welcome in their midst.

It was also my first opportunity to display my Violin, as they never had seen or heard one before, and marvelled at my playing the "Sunset Song" for them, after the Ceremonial.

At the instance of the Sun touching the border of the horizon at Sunset, the Zuñis assembled upon the highest cliffs and housetops to sing their Song of Praise.

They face the sun with uplifted hands (palms outwards) and bow with graceful rhythmic motion—upward and downward at every measure of the song in the manner of a "Salaam" which they repeat continuously, until the Sun sinks out of sight. They then prostrate themselves in adoration of the Sun. The chant takes about a minute to sing, and the Sun-worshippers repeat it five times, which is the limit the Sun occupies in its downward course after its first contact on the horizon.

---

[*] Recorded and harmonized by Carlos Troyer.

[†] A "Wasitoni" man, is what they call a person claiming authority from Washington, often an agent or land grabbers whom they look upon with distrust and fear.

[‡] *"Breathing on the hand"* of another, is an act of courtesy of special significance, which prevails among the cliffdwellers of the occult clan or sacred order of Brotherhood. It is a "sign" of the highest esteem, fidelity and eternal friendship conferred upon a person, which the latter is expected to return in like manner, to show the honor is accepted and mutual. It symbolizes: *"My breath is my life"* (to you).

During the first four repetitions of the song, the worshippers remain *standing*; in the last repetition, they are *kneeling* (on one knee;) and in the *Finale*, prostrate themselves towards the Sun, in silence.

SUNSET SONG
Ceremonial Thanks Offering to the Sun

In a public Recital this song, if *repeated once*, will be sufficiently effective.

Recorded and harmonized by
CARLOS TROYER

From *The Path on The Rainbow*[*]

"Early Moon"[†]

The baby moon, a canoe, a silver papoose canoe, sails and sails in the
Indian West.
A ring of silver foxes, a mist of silver foxes, sit and sit around the
Indian moon.
One yellow star for a runner, and rows of blue stars for more runners,
keep a line of watchers.
O foxes, baby moon, runners, you are the panel of memory, fire-white
writing tonight of the Red Man's dreams.
Who squats, legs crossed, and arms folded, matching its look against
the moon-face, the star-faces, of the West?
Who are the Mississippi Valley ghosts, of copper foreheads, riding wiry
ponies in the night?—no bridles, love arms on the pony necks, riding
in the night, a long old trail?
Why do they always come back when the silver foxes sit around the
early moon, a silver papoose, in the Indian West?

"Hunting Songs"
(Dakota)

I

Something I've killed, and I lift up my voice;
Something I've killed, and I lift up my voice;
The northern buffalo I've killed, and I lift up my voice;
Something I've killed, and I lift up my voice.

II

The saddle bind:
Children dear.
For half a day,
I will kill.

---

[*] *The Path on the Rainbow* was edited by George W. Cronyn. The book's dedication reads,
"To those who have labored faithfully in the collection and transcription of the Art
Forms of a Vanishing Race this book is respectfully dedicated. Many of the songs and
chants herein translated are very ancient; a number are modern, but none exhibit the
slightest traces of European influence; they are genuine American Classics."
[†] Translated by Carl Sandburg.

"Songs of the Ghost-Dance Religion"
(Arapaho)

Disillusion
I

My children, when at first I liked the Whites,
My children, when at first I liked the Whites,
I gave them fruits,
I gave them fruits.

Ecstasy
II

My children, my children,
The wind makes the head-feathers sing—
The wind makes the head-feathers sing.
My children, my children.

Labors of the Spirit
III

My children, my children,
I take pity on those who have been taught,
Because they push on hard,
Says our Father.

Wonder
IV

How bright is the moonlight!
Tonight as I ride with my load of buffalo beef.

The Whirlwind (Power of Change) Speaks
V

I circle around
The boundaries of earth,
Wearing the long wing feathers as I fly.

Vision
VI

My children, my children,
Look! the earth is about to move.
My Father tells me so.

Spirit-Joy
VII

I fly around yellow,
I fly with the wild rose on my head,
On high—He'e'e'!

Revelation
VIII

My children, my children,
It is I who wear the morning star on my head;
I show it to my children,
Says the Father.

Travail of Spirit
IX

Father, have pity on me,
Father, have pity on me;
I am crying for thirst;
All is gone—I have nothing to eat.

Invocation
IX

Father, the Morning Star!
Father, the Morning Star!
Look on us, we have danced until daylight,
Take pity on us—Hi'i'i!

"Songs of Life Returning"
(Paiute)

I

The wind stirs the willows.
The wind stirs the grasses.

II

The cottonwoods are growing tall,
They are growing tall and verdant.

III

A slender antelope,
A slender antelope
He is wallowing upon the ground.

IV

Fog! Fog!
Lightning! Lightning!
Whirlwind! Whirlwind!

V

Whirlwind! Whirlwind!
The snowy earth comes gliding, the snowy earth comes gliding.

VI

There is dust from the whirlwind,
There is dust from the whirlwind,
The whirlwind on the mountain.

VII

The rocks are ringing,
The rocks are ringing,
They are ringing in the mountains.

Song of the Path of Souls
VIII

The snow lies there—ro'rani!
The snow lies there—ro'rani!
The milky way lies there!

"Judgment"
(Kiowa)

I

The Father will descend.
Everybody will arise.
Stretch out your hands.
The earth will tremble.

Visitation
II

The spirit army is approaching,
The whole world is moving onward.
See! Everybody is standing watching.
Let us all pray.

The Secret of Humanity
III

Because I am poor,
I pray for every living creature.

The God-Man
IV

My Father has had pity on me.
I have eyes like my Father's,
I have hands like my Father's,
I have legs like my Father's,
I have a form like my Father's.

The Spirit Hunters
V

The spirit host is advancing, they say.
They are coming with the buffalo, they say.
They are coming with the new earth, they say.

Mystic
VI

That wind, that wind
Shakes my tipi, shakes my tipi,
And sings a song for me,
And sings a song for me.

"War Songs"
(Zuñi)

To you of the six regions
Whose homes cover the earth
I give shells.
Yellow ant, blue ant, red ant, all color ant
U—hu—we—u—hu—we—
U—hu—we—u—hu—we.
To you whose homes
Are covered with mountain tops
I give shells
Yellow, blue, red, white, all color, black.
When we meet the enemy
A little arrow storm will arise.

When we meet him on the road near by
He will never more inhale the sacred breath of day.
I inhale the sacred breath of day.
All come quickly,
The enemy comes from ambush.
A Navajo is killed,
We inhale the sacred breath of day.

You have met the enemy.
He will never more inhale the sacred breath of day.
The enemy is destroyed.
Who will be our great Bow priest?
Who is to become a Bow priest?
Well! who will kick the scalp?
His younger mother, his elder sister.
Who will wash the scalp?
His younger father, his elder brother.
Well!
Good!

"Rain Song of the Giant Society"
(Sia)

We, the Ancient Ones,
Who ascended from the middle of the world below,
Our medicine is precious,
It is as our hearts precious to us,
Arrow of lightning
Come to us
Echo.
Spruce of the north
And all your people;
Your thoughts come to us.
Who is it?
White floating clouds.
May your thoughts come to us
And all your people,
May their thoughts come to us.
Who is it?
Clouds like the plains,
May your thoughts come to us.

Who is it?
Arrow of lightning,
May your thoughts come to us.
Who is it?
Earth horizon
And all your people,
May your thoughts come to us.

"Magpie Song"
(Navajo)

The Magpie! The Magpie! Here underneath
In the white of his wings are the footsteps of morning.
It dawns! It dawns!

"Protection Song (To Be Sung on Going into Battle)"
(Navajo)

I

Now, Slayer of the Alien Gods, among men am I.
Now among the alien gods with weapons of magic am I.
Rubbed with the summits of the mountains,
Now among the alien gods with weapons of magic am I.
Now upon the beautiful trail of old age,
Now among the alien gods with weapons of magic am I.

II

Now, Offspring of the Water, among men am I.
Now among the alien gods with weapons of magic am I.
Rubbed with the water of the summits,
Now among the alien gods with weapons of magic am I.
Now upon the beautiful trail of old age,
Now among the alien gods with weapons of magic am I.

III

Now, Lightning of the Thunder, among men am I.
Now among the alien gods with weapons of magic am I.
Rubbed with the summit of the sky,
Now among the alien gods with weapons of magic am I.
Now upon the beautiful trail of old age,
Now among the alien gods with weapons of magic am I.

IV

Now, Altsodoniglehi, among men am I.
Now among the alien gods with weapons of magic am I.
Rubbed with the summits of the earth,
Now among the alien gods with weapons of magic am I.
Now upon the beautiful trail of old age,
Now among the alien gods with weapons of magic am I.

"Songs of Spirits"
(Wintu)

I
Lightning

I bear the sucker-torch to the western tree-ridge.
Behold me! first born and greatest.

II
Olelbis (The Creator)

I am great above.
I tan the black cloud.

III
Hau (Red Fox)

On the stone ridge east I go.
On the white road I, Hau, crouching go.
I, Hau, whistle on the road of stars.

IV
Polar Star

The circuit of earth which you see,
The scattering of stars in the sky which you see,
All that is the place for my hair.

"Songs of Kumastamxo"
(Yuma)

I
When the Spirit-Wind Approached

"The Wind is wandering, is wandering;
The Wind is wandering, is wandering."

II
When He Burnt the Unclean House

"The house will burn, will burn.
The house will be crackling, will be crackling.
It will blaze.
We are going to dance.
It is going to be lighted.
It is going to be lighted.
It will blaze.
We are going to dance.
Something bird-like is coming.
Bird-like tracks will be about the place.
We are going to light this unclean house.
It will blaze, blaze."*

III
When He Made the River

"This is my water, my water.
This is my river, my river.
We love its water.
We love its foamwood.
It shall flow forever.
It shall flow forever.
When the weather grows hot, it shall rise and overflow its banks.
It shall flow forever."

IV
After He Had Finished His Creating

"Into the earth I go down, go down.
Nothing but earth will I be seeing, will I be seeing.
I sink down into the old river-bed,
Down into the interior."

V
When He Became the Eagle

"I am springing, springing.
Wing-feathers!
Body-feathers!
On my hands wing-feathers.
On my body body-feathers."

* Note.—Where a house had been burnt seeds were scattered, for the birds to devour.

"Song to the Mesa"
(The Hako Ceremony)

I

The mesa see; its flat top like a straight line cuts across the sky;
It blocks our path, and we must climb, the mesa climb.

II

More mesas see; their flat tops rise against the sky, they bar our path;
We reach their base, and we must climb, the mesas climb.

III

The mesas' side we now ascend, the sharp ridge pass, its flat top reach;
There lies their base that we must take, and forward go.

IV

The mesas rise around us still, their flat tops cut across the sky;
They block our way, yet still we climb, the mesas climb.

"Mother Corn Reasserts Leadership"
The Search for the Children

I

Here we give our thanks, led by Mother Corn,
As our eyes dwell upon the borders of the land
Where dwell the Children we are seeking.

II

Now our eyes look on people walking to.
Soon our eyes catch the print of footsteps on the ground,
Made by the Children we are seeking.

III

Still we travel on, led by Mother Corn.
Now our eyes look on people walking to and fro;
They the Children are, we are seeking.

> *As we move on and enter the land of the Children we sing, in the second stanza, about their footprints, the marks of their moccasins where they have walked to and fro on the ground.*

> *We may not actually see these marks, but the song represents us as seeing them; Mother Corn has seen them, and she is leading us.*

From *Ancient Nahuatl Poetry*

"Song at the Beginning"

1. I am wondering where I may gather some pretty, sweet flowers. Whom shall I ask? Suppose that I ask the brilliant humming-bird, the emerald trembler; suppose that I ask the yellow butterfly; they will tell me, they know, where bloom the pretty, sweet flowers, whether I may gather them here in the laurel woods where dwell the tzinitzcan birds, or whether I may gather them in the flowery forests where the tlauquechol lives. There they may be plucked sparkling with dew, there they come forth in perfection. Perhaps there I shall see them if they have appeared; I shall place them in the folds of my garment, and with them I shall greet the children, I shall make glad the nobles.

2. Truly as I walk along I hear the rocks as it were replying to the sweet songs of the flowers; truly the glittering, chattering water answers, the bird-green fountain, there it sings, it dashes forth, it sings again; the mocking bird answers; perhaps the coyol bird answers, and many sweet singing birds scatter their songs around like music. They bless the earth pouring out their sweet voices.

3. I said, I cried aloud, may I not cause you pain ye beloved ones, who are seated to listen; may the brilliant humming-birds come soon. Whom do we seek, O noble poet? I ask, I say: Where are the pretty, fragrant flowers with which I may make glad you my noble compeers? Soon they will sing to me, "Here we will make thee to see, thou singer, truly wherewith thou shalt make glad the nobles, thy companions."

4. They led me within a valley to a fertile spot, a flowery spot, where the dew spread out in glittering splendor, where I saw various lovely fragrant flowers, lovely odorous flowers, clothed with the dew, scattered around in rainbow glory, there they said to me, "Pluck the flowers, whichever thou wishest, mayest thou the singer be glad, and give them to thy friends, to the nobles, that they may rejoice on the earth."

5. So I gathered in the folds of my garment the various fragrant flowers, delicate scented, delicious, and I said, may some of our people enter here, may very many of us be here; and I thought I should go forth to announce to our friends that here all of us should rejoice in the different lovely, odorous flowers, and that we should cull the various sweet songs with which we might rejoice our friends here on earth, and the nobles in their grandeur and dignity.

6. So I the singer gathered all the flowers to place them upon the nobles, to clothe them and put them in their hands; and soon I lifted my voice in a

worthy song glorifying the nobles before the face of the Cause of All, where there is no servitude.

7. Where shall one pluck them? Where gather the sweet flowers? And how shall I attain that flowery land, that fertile land, where there is no servitude, nor affliction? If one purchases it here on earth, it is only through submission to the Cause of All; here on earth grief fills my soul as I recall where I the singer saw the flowery spot.

8. And I said, truly there is no good spot here on earth, truly in some other bourne there is gladness; For what good is this earth? Truly there is another life in the hereafter. There may I go, there the sweet birds sing, there may I learn to know those good flowers, those sweet flowers, those delicious ones, which alone pleasurably, sweetly intoxicate, which alone pleasurably, sweetly intoxicate.

"Another Plain Song, to the Same Tune"

1. I, the singer, entered into the house strewn with flowers, where stood upright the emerald drum, where awaiting the Giver of Life the nobles strewed flowers around, the place where the head is bowed for lustration, the house of corrupt odors, where the burning fragrant incense spreads and penetrates, intoxicating our souls in the presence of the Cause of All.

2. Where shall we obtain the fragrance which intoxicates our souls? We do not yet know the various flowersongs with which we may rejoice the Cause of All, however desirous we are; thou my friend, would that thou bring to my instrument various flowers, that thou shouldst clothe it in brilliant oco flowers, that thou shouldst offer them, and lift thy voice in a new and worthy song to rejoice the Cause of All.

3. Wherefore should we recall while the soul is in life that our souls must be scattered hither and thither, and that wherever we go we are to be destroyed on earth? Rather let us hide it, turn from it, and listen to some worthy new song; delight thy soul with the pervading fragrance of flowers, as I the singer lift my voice in a new song that I may rejoice the Cause of All.

4. Come hither, thou my friend, to where stands the drum, decked with flowers, gleaming with brightness, green with the outspread plumes of the quetzal bird, where are looked for and cared for the seats near the Cause of All; leave the place of night and clouds, turn hither with us, lift thy voice in the new song I sing so that I may rejoice the Cause of All, as the dawn approaches in the house of thy heart.

5. Of what use is it that I frame my sad songs, that I recall to mind the youths, the beloved children, the precious relatives, the dear friends, famous

and celebrated as they were on earth? Who now hears their fame, their deeds? Where can they find them? All of us are but mortal, and our home is there in the Hereafter, where there is life without end.

"An Otomi Song of the Mexicans"

1. I, the singer, polished my noble new song like a shining emerald, I arranged it like the voice of the tzinitzcan bird, I called to mind the essence of poetry, I set it in order like the chant of the zacuan bird, I mingled it with the beauty of the emerald, that I might make it appear like a rose bursting its bud, so that I might rejoice the Cause of All.

2. I skillfully arranged my song like the lovely feathers of the zacuan bird, the tzinitzcan and the quechol; I shall speak forth my song like the tinkling of golden bells; my song is that which the miaua bird pours forth around him; I lifted my voice and rained down flowers of speech before the face of the Cause of All.

3. In the true spirit of song I lifted my voice through a trumpet of gold, I let fall from my lips a celestial song, I shall speak notes precious and brilliant as those of the miaua bird, I shall cause to blossom out a noble new song, I lifted my voice like the burning incense of flowers, so that I the singer might cause joy before the face of the Cause of All.

4. The divine quechol bird answers me as I, the singer, sing, like the coyol bird, a noble new song, polished like a jewel, a turquoise, a shining emerald, darting green rays, a flower song of spring, spreading celestial fragrance, fresh with the dews of roses, thus have I the poet sung.

5. I colored with skill, I mingled choice roses in a noble new song, polished like a jewel, etc. (as in v. 4).

6. I was glorified, I was enriched, by the flower-sweet song as by the smoke of the poyomatl, my soul was contented, I trembled in spirit, I inhaled the sweetness, my soul was intoxicated, I inhaled the fragrance of delicious flowers in the place of riches, my soul was drunken with the flowers.

"XIV"

1. Only the tzinitzcan is in power, the tzinitzcan arouses me in my affliction, letting fall its songs like sad flowers.

2. Wherever it wanders, wherever it lives, one awaits it here with the drum, in affliction, in distress, here in the house of spring.

3. Who is the royal son? Is not the royal son, the son of God, Jesus Christ, as was written in your writings, as was written in your songs?

4. Is not the flowery writing within the house of flowers that he shall come there from heaven?

5. Look around and wonder at this scene of many colored houses which God has created and endowed with life.

6. They make us who are miserable to see the light among the flowers and songs of the fertile fields, they cause us to see those things which God has created and endowed with life.

7. They dwell in the place of spring, in the place of spring, here within the broad fields, and only for our sakes does the turquoise-water fall in broken drops on the surface of the lake.

8. Where it gleams forth in fourfold rays, where the fragrant yellow flowers bud, there live the Mexicans, the youths.

"XIX"

Tico, toco, toco, tiquiti, quiti, quiti, quito; where it is to turn back again.

1. Resting amid parti-colored flowers I rejoiced; the many shining flowers came forth, blossomed, burst forth in honor of our mother Holy Mary.

2. They sang as the beauteous season grew, that I am but a creature of the one only God, a work of his hands that he has made.

3. Mayst thy soul walk in the light, mayst thou sing in the great book, mayst thou join the dance of the rulers as our father the bishop speaks in the great temple.

4. God created thee, he caused thee to be born in a flowery place, and this new song to Holy Mary the bishop wrote for thee.

"XXV"

Tico, toco, tocoto, and then it ends, ticoto, ticoto.

1. The sweet voiced quechol there, ruling the earth, has intoxicated my soul.

2. I am like the quetzal bird, I am created in the house of the one only God; I sing sweet songs among the flowers; I chant songs and rejoice in my heart.

3. The fuming dew-drops from the flowers in the field intoxicate my soul.

4. I grieve to myself that ever this dwelling on earth should end.

5. I foresaw, being a Mexican, that our rule began to be destroyed, I went forth weeping that it was to bow down and be destroyed.

6. Let me not be angry that the grandeur of Mexico is to be destroyed.

7. The smoking stars gather together against it; the one who cares for flowers is about to be destroyed.

8. He who cared for books wept, he wept for the beginning of the destruction.

1–2

Vinland Sagas (10th–11th c.)

Hundreds of years before the *Niña*, the *Pinta*, and the *Santa Maria* headed toward North America, an expedition to colonize "Vinland" was made
by an Icelandic Viking, Thorfinn Karlsefne (fl. 1000–1015). Leif Erikson
had discovered the new land in 1001, but according to the Vinland
Sagas it was Thorfinn who left Erik the Red's Greenland to lead the expedition around 1010 to establish a colony in North America. Archae-
ological evidence in Newfoundland does confirm that the Vikings had
in fact attempted a colony. Evidence also suggests that the failure of the
colony may have been due to their violent interactions with the native
population, whom they called "Skraelings," a derogatory Old Norse term
of uncertain etymology but possibly meaning "savages." Conflict is also
apparent in this reading; while Thorfinn and his wife Gudrid will raise
many sons in the new faith, Thorhall the Hunter, a believer in traditional
Norse gods, casts doubt on the power of the Christian God.

≈ ≈ ≈

From *Voyages of the Northmen to America*

The Vinland Voyage

In Brattahlid began people to talk much about, that Vinland the Good should
be explored, and it was said that a voyage thither would be particularly profitable by reason of the fertility of the land; and it went so far that Karlsefne and
Snorri made ready their ship to explore the land in the spring. With them went
also the before-named men called Bjarni and Thorhall, with their ship. There
was a man called Thorvard; he married Freydis, a natural daughter of Erik the
Red; he went also with them, and Thorvald the son of Erik*, and Thorhall who
was called the hunter; he had long been with Erik, and served him as huntsman in summer, and steward in winter; he was a large man, and strong, black,

---

* Here is again evidently some confusion of names, as Thorvald Erikson's death has been
previously related in the Saga of Erik the Red, and Karlsefne was now married to his
widow Gudrid: it seems probable that some other Thorvald accompanied Karlsefne on
this voyage.—See *Antiq. Amer., Præfatio*, p. xiv.

In the preceding section it is stated that Thorfinn married Thurid: she was sometimes also called Gudrid. Professor Rafn thinks it probable that she was called by the
former in childhood, which was a pagan name derived from the god Thor, but afterward for religious reasons Gudrid was adopted in its place.—*Vide Beamish.*

and like a giant, silent and foul-mouthed in his speech, and always egged on Erik to the worst: he was a bad Christian: he was well acquainted with uninhabited parts: he was in the ship with Thorvard and Thorvald. They had the ship which Thorbjörn had brought out [from Iceland]. They had in all one hundred and sixty men* when they sailed to the western settlement, and from thence to Bjanney. Then sailed they two days to the south; then saw they land, and put off boats, and explored the land, and found there great flat stones, many of which were twelve ells broad: foxes were there. They gave the land a name, and called it Helluland.† Then sailed they two days, and turned from the south to the south-east, and found a land covered with wood, and many wild beasts upon it: an island lay there out from the land to the south-east; there killed they a bear, and called the place afterwards Bear island,‡ but the land Markland. Thence sailed they far to the southward along the land, and came to a ness; the land lay upon the right; there were long and sandy strands. They rowed to land, and found there upon the ness the keel of a ship, and called the place Kjalarness,§ and the strands they called Furdustrands, for it was long to sail by them. Then became the land indented with coves; they ran the ship into a cove. King Olaf Tryggvason had given Leif two Scotch people, a man called

---

* Literally "40 men and a hundred" [40 manna oh hundrad], but the great or long hundred must be understood, consisting of 12 decades, or 120.—*Antiq. Amer.*, p. 137, note *b*. Thus Tegner, describing the drinking hall of Frithiof:—

"Ei femhundrade män [til *tio tolfter* på hundrat] Fyllde den rymliga fal, när de famlats att dricka om Julen." *Frithiofs Saga* III., p. 18.

Not five hundred men (though *ten twelves* you count to the hundred) Could fill that wide hall, when they gathered to banquet at Yule.—*Beamish.*

† The whole of the northern coast of America, west of Greenland, was called by the ancient Icelandic geographers *Helluland it Mikla*, or Great Helluland; and the Island of Newfoundland simply Helluland, or *Litla Helluland.—Beamish.* Helluland, ita dictam aut ob ingentes planos, qui ibi funt, lapides [*hella*, gen. *hellu*, pl. *hellur*], aut ea ratione, quod terræ illius litora plana fuerint et dura. Reperimus apud antiquos duas terras hoc nomine insignitas, quarum una appellata est *Helluland hit mikla*, Hellulandia Major, altera *Litla Helluland*, Hellulandia Minor.—*Antiq. Amer.*, p. 419. *Vide* Tab. XVI.—*Idem.*

‡ Bjanney, from *Björn*, a bear, gen. bjarnar, and *ey*, island: hence Bjarney contracted from Bjarnarey; but the common pronunciation of the latter is Bjadney or Bjanney.—*Antiq. Amer.*, p. 138, note *c.—Beamish.*

§ In the visit of Thorvald, the son of Erik the Red, to Vinland, in 1002, four years before this present voyage, the keel of his ship had been broken off on a ness, where he remained some time to repair it. Was not the keel found by Karlsefne the same which had been broken off in the voyage of Thorvald? Does not the accident to the keel, and the repairs upon it at this place, furnish sufficient reason for naming it Kjalarness? Indeed it had been so named in the previous voyage. *Vide antea*, p. 38.

Haki, and a woman called Hekja; they were swifter than beasts. These people were in the ship with Karlsefne; but when they had sailed past Furdustrands, then set they the Scots on shore, and bade them run to the southward of the land, and explore its qualities, and come back again within three days. They had a sort of clothing which they called kjafal, which was so made that a hat was on the top, and it was open at the sides, and no arms to it; fastened together between the legs with buttons and clasps, but in other places it was open. They stayed away the appointed time; but when they came back, the one had in the hand a bunch of grapes, and the other, a new sowen ear of wheat: these went on board the ship, and after that sailed they farther. They sailed into a frith; there lay an island before it, round which there were strong currents, therefore called they it Stream island. There were so many eider ducks on the island, that one could scarcely walk in consequence of the eggs. They called the place Stream frith.* They took their cargo from the ship, and prepared to remain there. They had with them all sorts of cattle. The country there was very beautiful. They undertook nothing but to explore the land. They were there for the winter without having provided food beforehand. In the summer the fishing declined, and they were badly off for provisions; then disappeared Thorhall the huntsman. They had previously made prayers to God for food, but it did not come so quick as they thought their necessities required. They searched after Thorhall for three days,† and found him on the top of a rock; there he lay, and looked up in the sky, and gaped both with nose and mouth, and murmured something; they asked him why he had gone there; he said it was no business of theirs; they bade him come home with them, and he did so. Soon after came there a whale and they went thither, and cut it up, and no one knew what sort of whale it was; and when the cook dressed it, then ate they,

---

* Straumfjord and Straumey, from *straumr*, a current; *ey*, island; and *fjord*, frith: also, Furdustrandir, from *furda*, gen. furdu, wonderful and *strönd*, pl. strandir, beach.—*Beamish.*

† 3 dægr. There seems to be considerable ambiguity about the Icelandic words *dagr* and *dægr*, which are arbitrarily used to express either the natural day of 24 hours or the artificial day of 12 hours. Throughout this and the preceding narrative, *dægr* is considered by the editor to mean the artificial day, and *dagr* the natural day, hence 2 *dægr* is rendered "a day and night" [Dan. "en Dag og en Nat,"—Lat. "noctem diemque,"]—and 3 *dægr*, "three half natural days" (36 hours) [Dan. "tre halve Dögn,"—Lat. "tria nychthemerium"]. But in a subsequent narrative (De Ario Mario Filii, Antiq. Amer., p. 211) we find VI. *dægr* rendered, in the Danish version, "6 Dögn," and, in the Latin, "sex dierum," thus applying the word *dægr* to the natural day of 24 hours. Finn Magnusen, also, expressly states that the artificial day was called *dagr*, and the natural day *dægr*.—See *Mem. de la Soc. Roy. des Antiq. du Nord*, 1836, 1837, p. 165.—*Beamish.*

and all became ill in consequence.* Then said Thorhall: "The red-bearded† was more helpful than your Christ; this have I got now for my verses that I sung of Thor, my protector; seldom has he deserted me." But when they came to know this, they cast the whole whale into the sea, and resigned their case to God. Then the weather improved, and it was possible to row out fishing; and they were not then in want of provisions, for wild beasts were caught on the land, and fish in the sea, and eggs collected on the island.

Of Karlsefne and Thorhall

So is said that Thorhall would go to the northward along Furdustrands, to explore Vinland, but Karlsefne would go southwards along the coast. Thorhall got ready, out under the island, and there were no more together than nine men; but all the others went with Karlsefne. Now when Thorhall bore water to his ship, and drank, then sung he this song:—

> People told me when I came
> Hither, all would be so fine;
> The good Vinland, known to fame,
> Rich in fruits, and choicest wine;
> Now the water pail they send;
> To the fountain I must bend,
> Nor from out this land divine
> Have I quaffed one drop of wine.

And when they were ready, and hoisted sail, then chaunted Thorhall:—

---

* This whale was probably a species of the *Balæna physalis* of Linnæus, which was not edible, and, being rarely seen in the Greenland and Iceland seas, was unknown to the Northmen. A kind of whale called *Balæna mysticetus* is mentioned by Ebeling, as having been formerly found on the coasts of Rhode Island and Massachusetts, revisiting the more southern latitudes in winter, and returning northwards in the spring; in after times, however, they disappeared altogether from the coasts; and in the present day the number of whales in northern latitudes has much diminished.—*Idem.*

† Thor, the eldest son of Odin and Frigga, the strongest of the Aser, and next to Odin in rank.
"There sits on golden throne Aloft the god of war, Save Odin, yields to none 'Mongst gods great Aser, Thor." *Oehlenschläger, Pigott's Translation.*
The introduction of Christianity being but recent in Iceland, many of the Northmen still believed in Thor, or, embracing the new religion with a wavering faith, applied to the Aser gods in cases of difficulty. "The remains of the worship of Thor lingered longer in the North than those of any of the other Scandinavian deities. In Nial's Saga, a female skald says to a Christian, 'Do you not know that Thor has challenged your Christ to single combat, and that he dares not fight him?'"—*Pigott's Scandinavian Mythology*, p. 101.—*Idem.*

Let our trusty band
Haste to Fatherland;
Let our vessel brave
Plough the angry wave,
While those few who love
Vinland, here may rove,
Or, with idle toil,
Fetid whales may boil,
Here on Ferdustrand,
Far from Fatherland.*

After that, sailed they northwards past Furdustrands and Kjalarness, and would cruise to the westward; then came against them a strong west wind, and they were driven away to Ireland, and were there beaten, and made slaves, according to what the merchants have said.

Now is to be told about Karlsefne, that he went to the southward along the coast, and Snorri and Bjarni, with their people. They sailed a long time, and until they came to a river, which ran out from the land, and through a lake, out into the sea. It was very shallow, and one could not enter the river without high water. Karlsefne sailed, with his people, into the mouth, and they called the place Hóp.† They found there upon the land self-sown fields of wheat, there where the ground was low, but vines there where it rose somewhat. Every stream there was full of fish. They made holes there where the land commenced, and the waters rose highest; and when the tide fell, there were sacred fish‡ in the holes. There were a great number of all kinds of wild beasts in the woods. They remained there a half month, and amused themselves, and did not perceive any thing [new]: they had their cattle with them. And one morning early, when they looked round, saw they

---

* Omnes hæ strophæ antiquitatem et genium sapiunt seculi 10^{mi} et 11^{mi}, tam quod attinet ad metaphoras, quam ceteram indolem.—*Rafn, Antiq. Amer.*, p. 144, note *a*. [The Latin translates roughly to the following: "All of these stanzas have the feel of antiquity and the spirit of the 10th and 11th centuries, which applies as much to their metaphors as to the rest of their character."—*E.J.D. and J.B.F.*]

† I Hópi, from the Icelandic word *hópa*, to recede, and may signify here either the recess formed by the confluence of a river and the sea, or the mouth of the river, or merely the inlet of the sea into which the river falls.—*Beamish*

‡ Helgir fiskar. This is supposed to have been the species of flounder or flat fish, called by the English *halibut* (*Pleuronectes hippoglossus* Linn., *Hippoglossus vulgaris* Cuv.), and which is still called in Iceland "holy fish" (*heilagfiski*), a name given, according to Pliny, in consequence of the presence of these fish being considered to denote safe water. Speaking of the danger to be apprehended from the dog-fish, he adds: "Certissima est securitas vidisse *planos pisces*, quia nunquam sunt, ubi maleficæ bestiæ: qua de causa urinantes *sacros* appellant eos."—*Hist. Nat.*, Lib. ix.—*Beamish*.

a great many canoes, and poles were swung upon them, and it sounded like the wind in a straw-stack, and the swinging was with the sun. Then said Karlsefne: "What may this denote?" Snorri Thorbrandson answered him: "It may be that this is a sign of peace, so let us take a white shield, and hold it towards them"; and so did they. Upon this the others rowed towards them, and looked with wonder upon those that they met, and went up upon the land. These people were black, and ill favored, and had coarse hair on the head; they had large eyes and broad cheeks. They remained there for a time, and gazed upon those that they met, and rowed afterwards away to the southward, round the ness.

Karlsefne and his people had made their dwellings above the lake, and some of the houses were near the water, others more distant. Now were they there for the winter; there came no snow, and all their cattle fed themselves on the grass. But when spring* approached, saw they one morning early that a number of canoes rowed from the south round the ness; so many, as if the sea were sowen with coal: poles were also swung on each boat. Karlsefne and his people then raised up the shield, and when they came together, they began to barter; and these people would rather have red cloth [than any thing else]; for this they had to offer skins and real furs. They would also purchase swords and spears, but this Karlsefne and Snorri forbade. For an entire fur skin the Skrælings took a piece of red cloth, a span long, and bound it round their heads. Thus went on their traffic for a time; then the cloth began to fall short among Karlsefne and his people, and they cut it asunder into small pieces, which were not wider than the breadth of a finger, and still the Skrælings gave just as much for that as before, and more.†

It happened that a bull, which Karlsefne had, ran out from the wood and roared aloud; this frightened the Skrælings, and they rushed to their canoes, and rowed away to the southward, round the coast: after that they were not seen for three entire weeks. But at the end of that time, a great number of Skrælings' ships were seen coming from the south like a rushing torrent; all the poles were turned from the sun, and they all howled very loud. Then took Karlsefne's people a red shield, and held it towards them. The Skrælings jumped out of their ships, and after this went they against each other, and fought. There was a sharp shower of weapons, for the Skrælings had slings. Karlsefne's people saw

---

* A.D. 1009.

† The Saga of Erik the Red, in giving an account of this transaction, adds that Karlsefne, on the cloth being expended, hit upon the expedient of making the women take out milk porridge to the Skrælings, who, as soon as they saw this new article of commerce, would buy the porridge and nothing else. "Thus," says the Saga, "the traffic of the Skrælings was wound up by their bearing away their purchases in their stomachs, but Karlsefne and his companions retained their goods and skins."—*Antiq. Amer.*, pp. 59, 60.—*Beamish.*

that they raised up on a pole an enormous large ball something like a sheep's paunch, and of a blue color; this swung they from the pole over Karlsefne's men, upon the ground, and it made a frightful crash as it fell down.* This caused great alarm to Karlsefne and all his people, so that they thought of nothing but running away, and they fell back along the river, for it appeared to them that the Skrælings pressed upon them from all sides; and they did not stop until they came to some rocks, where they made a stout resistance. Freydis came out and saw that Karlsefne's people fell back, and she cried out: "Why do ye run, stout men as ye are, before these miserable wretches, whom I thought ye would knock down like cattle? and if I had weapons, methinks I could fight better than any of ye." They gave no heed to her words. Freydis would go with them, but she was slower, because she was pregnant; however she followed after them into the wood. The Skrælings pursued her; she found a dead man before her: it was Thorbrand Snorrason, and there stood a flat stone stuck in his head; the sword lay naked by his side; this took she up, and prepared to defend herself. Then came the Skrælings towards her; she drew out her breasts from under her clothes, and dashed them against the naked sword; by this the Skrælings became frightened, and ran off to their ships, and rowed away. Karlsefne and his people then came up, and praised her courage. Two men fell on Karlsefne's side, but a number of the Skrælings. Karlsefne's band was over-matched, and they now drew home to their dwellings, and bound their wounds; and they thought over what crowd that could have been, which had pressed upon them from the land side, and it now appeared to them that it could scarcely have been real people from the ships, but that these must have been optical illusions. The Skrælings found also a dead man, and an axe lay by him; one of them took up the axe, and cut wood with it, and now one after another did the same, and thought it was an excellent thing, and bit well; after that one took it, and cut at a stone, so that the axe broke, and then thought they it was of no use, because it would not cut stone, and they threw it away.

Karlsefne and his people now thought they saw, that although the land had many good qualities, still would they be always exposed there to the fear of hostilities from the earlier inhabitants. They proposed, therefore, to depart, and return to their own country. They sailed northwards along the coast, and found five Skrælings clothed in skins, sleeping near the sea. They had with

---

* The nature of this missile does not exactly appear, but it probably had some affinity with the harpoon used by the Esquimaux in fishing, and to which is attached a bladder, as well for the purpose of directing the weapon as of marking its position after having been thrown. In the present instance, stones would appear to have been added to this contrivance.—*Antiq. Amer.*, p. 152, note *b.*—*Beamish.*

them vessels containing animal marrow mixed with blood. Karlsefne's people thought they understood that these men had been banished from the land: they killed them. After that came they to a ness, and many wild beasts were there; and the ness was covered all over with dung, from the beasts which had lain there during the night. Now came they back to Straumfjord, and there was abundance of every thing that they wanted to have. It is some men's say, that Bjarni and Gudrid remained behind, and a hundred men with them, and did not go further; but that Karlsefne and Snorri went southwards, and forty men with them, and were not longer in Hope than barely two months, and the same summer came back.* Karlsefne went then with one ship to seek after Thorhall the hunter, but the rest remained behind, and they sailed northwards past Kjalarness, and thence westwards, and the land was upon their larboard hand; there were wild woods over all, as far as they could see, and scarcely any open places. And when they had long sailed, a river fell out of the land from east to west; they put in to the mouth of the river, and lay by its southern bank.

1–3

Álvar Núñez Cabeza de Vaca (1490–1558)

Sometimes called the "first historian of Texas," ÁLVAR NÚÑEZ CABEZA DE VACA (1490–1559) was the first European to contact Native Americans in what would become Texas, New Mexico, and Arizona. Born near Cadiz, Spain, CABEZA DE VACA joined the ill-fated Narváez Expedition of 1527 that sought to colonize the region between Florida and modern-day Tampico, Mexico. Shipwrecks, starvation, attacks by Native Americans, and exposure to the cold left only four survivors of the original 300. By the time he arrived in Mexico City in 1536, Cabeza de Vaca had traveled some 2,400 miles on foot. In 1542, he published the account of his adventures. This selection, translated by Fanny Bandelier, an ethnologist of Southwest Native American cultures, in 1905, focuses on the Spaniard's time in Texas, in the Galveston area, and the reception he received from indigenous peoples.

≈≈ ≈≈ ≈≈

---

* This passage is evidently the statement of an imperfect tradition, to which the writer of the Saga gave no credit; and, although only involving a question of *time*, it must be rejected as inconsistent with the previous details; its insertion, however, is strongly characteristic of the candor and honesty of the writer, who is obviously desirous of stating all that he has heard upon the subject.—*Beamish.*

Early contact literature

From *The Journey of Álvar Núñez Cabeza de Vaca and His Companions from Florida to the Pacific* (1542)

[November 1528, Cabeza de Vaca and his men, separated from Captain Narváez once leaving Florida, arrive off the coast of what is now believed to be Galveston. The surviving Spaniards would dub this the Isle of Ill Fate.—*E.J.D. and J.B.F.*]

The next day, at sunrise, which was the hour the Indians had given us to understand, they came as promised and brought us plenty of fish and some roots which they eat that taste like nuts, some bigger, some smaller, most of which are taken out of the water with much trouble.

In the evening they returned and brought us more fish and some of the same roots, and they brought their women and children to look at us. They thought themselves very rich with the little bells and beads we gave them, and thereafter visited us daily with the same things as before. As we saw ourselves provided with fish, roots, water and the other things we had asked for, we concluded to embark again and continue our voyage.

We lifted the barge out of the sand into which it had sunk (for which purpose we all had to take off our clothes) and had great work to set her afloat, as our condition was such that much lighter things would have given us trouble.

Then we embarked. Two crossbow shots from shore a wave swept over us, we all got wet, and being naked and the cold very great, the oars dropped out of our hands. The next wave overturned the barge. The inspector and two others clung to her to save themselves, but the contrary happened; they got underneath the barge and were drowned.

The shore being very rough, the sea took the others and thrust them, half dead, on the beach of the same island again, less the three that had perished underneath the barge.

The rest of us, as naked as we had been born, had lost everything, and while it was not worth much, to us it meant a great deal. It was in November, bitterly cold, and we in such a state that every bone could easily be counted, and we looked like death itself. Of myself I can say that since the month of May I had not tasted anything but toasted maize, and even sometimes had been obliged to eat it raw. Although the horses were killed during the time the barges were built, I never could eat of them, and not ten times did I taste fish. This I say in order to explain and that any one might guess how we were off. On top of all this, a north wind arose, so that we were nearer death than life. It pleased Our Lord that, searching for the remnants of our former fire, we found wood with which we built big fires and then with many tears begged Our Lord for mercy and forgiveness of our sins. Every one of us pitied not only himself, but all the others whom he saw in the same condition.

At sunset the Indians, thinking we had not left, came to bring us food, but when they saw us in such a different attire from before and so strange-looking, they were so frightened as to turn back. I went to call them, and in great fear they came. I then gave them to understand by signs how we had lost a barge and three of our men had been drowned, while before them there lay two of our men dead, with the others about to go the same way.

Upon seeing the disaster we had suffered, our misery and distress, the Indians sat down with us and all began to weep out of compassion for our misfortune, and for more than half an hour they wept so loud and so sincerely that it could be heard far away.

Verily, to see beings so devoid of reason, untutored, so like unto brutes, yet so deeply moved by pity for us, it increased my feelings and those of others in my company for our own misfortune. When the lament was over, I spoke to the Christians and asked them if they would like me to beg the Indians to take us to their homes. Some of the men, who had been to New Spain, answered that it would be unwise, as, once at their abode, they might sacrifice us to their idols.

Still, seeing there was no remedy and that in any other way death was surer and nearer, I did not mind what they said, but begged the Indians to take us to their dwellings, at which they showed great pleasure, telling us to tarry yet a little, but that they would do what we wished. Soon thirty of them loaded themselves with firewood and went to their lodges, which were far away, while we stayed with the others until it was almost dark. Then they took hold of us and carried us along hurriedly to where they lived.

Against the cold, and lest on the way some one of us might faint or die, they had provided four or five big fires on the road, at each one of which they warmed us. As soon as they saw we had regained a little warmth and strength they would carry us to the next fire with such haste that our feet barely touched the ground.

So we got to their dwellings, where we saw they had built a hut for us with many fires in it. About one hour after our arrival they began to dance and to make a great celebration (which lasted the whole night), although there was neither pleasure, feast nor sleep in it for us, since we expected to be sacrificed. In the morning they again gave us fish and roots, and treated us so well that we became reassured, losing somewhat our apprehension of being butchered.

That same day I saw on one of the Indians a trinket he had not gotten from us, and asking from where they had obtained it they answered, by signs, that other men like ourselves and who were still in our rear, had given it to them. Hearing this, I sent two Christians with two Indians to guide them to those people. Very near by they met them, and they also were looking for us, as the Indians had told them of our presence in the neighborhood. These were the Captains Andrés Dorantes and Alonso del Castillo, with all of their crew. When they came near us they were much frightened at our appearance and grieved at being unable to give us anything, since they had nothing but their clothes. And they stayed with us there, telling how, on the fifth of that same month, their barge stranded a league and a half from there, and they escaped without anything being lost.

All together, we agreed upon repairing their barge, and that those who had strength and inclination should proceed in it, while the others should remain until completely restored and then go as best they could along the coast, following it till God would be pleased to get us all together to a land of Christians.

So we set to work, but ere the barge was afloat Tavera, a gentleman in our company, died, while the barge proved not to be seaworthy and soon sank. Now, being in the condition which I have stated—that is, most of us naked and the weather so unfavorable for walking and for swimming across rivers and coves, and we had neither food nor any way to carry it, we determined upon submitting to necessity and upon wintering there, and we also agreed that four men, who were the most able-bodied, should go to Pánuco, which we believed to be nearby, and that, if it was God, Our Lord's will to take them there, they should tell of our remaining on the island and of our distress. One of them was a Portuguese, called Alvaro Fernandez, a carpenter and sailor; the second was Mendez; the third, Figueroa, a native of Toledo; the fourth, Astudillo, from Zafra. They were all good swimmers and took with them an Indian from the island.

A few days after these four Christians had left, the weather became so cold and tempestuous that the Indians could no longer pull roots, and the cane-brake in which they used to fish yielded nothing more. As the lodges afforded so little shelter, people began to die, and five Christians, quartered on the coast, were driven to such an extremity that they ate each other up until but one remained, who being left alone, there was nobody to eat him. Their names are: Sierra, Diego, Lopez, Corral, Palacios and Gonzalo Ruiz. At this the Indians were so startled, and there was such an uproar among them, that I verily believe if they had seen this at the beginning they would have killed them, and we all would have been in great danger. After a very short time, out of eighty men who had come there in our two parties only fifteen remained alive.

Then the natives fell sick from the stomach, so that one-half of them died also, and they, believing we had killed them, and holding it to be certain, they agreed among themselves to kill those of us who survived.

But when they came to execute it an Indian who kept me told them not to believe we were the cause of their dying, for if we had so much power we would not have suffered so many of our own people to perish without being able to remedy it ourselves. He also told them there remained but very few of us, and none of them did any harm or injury, so that the best was to let us alone. It pleased Our Lord they should listen to his advice and counsel and give up their idea.

To this island we gave the name of the *Island of Ill Fate.** The people on it are tall and well formed; they have no other weapons than bows and arrows with which they are most dextrous. The men have one of their nipples perforated from side to side and sometimes both; through this hole is thrust a reed as long as two and a half hands and as thick as two fingers; they also have the under lip perforated and a piece of cane in it as thin as the half of a finger. The women do the hard work. People stay on this island from October till the end of February, feeding on the roots I have mentioned, taken from under the water in November and December. They have channels made of reeds and get fish only during that time; afterwards they subsist on roots. At the end of February they remove to other parts in search of food, because the roots begin to sprout and are not good any more.

Of all the people in the world, they are those who most love their children and treat them best, and should the child of one of them happen to die, parents and relatives bewail it, and the whole settlement, the lament lasting a full year, day after day. Before sunrise the parents begin to weep, after them the tribe, and the same they do at noon and at dawn. At the end of the year of mourning they celebrate the anniversary and wash and cleanse themselves of all their paint. They mourn all their dead in this manner, old people excepted, to whom they do not pay any attention, saying that these have had their time and are no longer of any use, but only take space, and food from the children.

Their custom is to bury the dead, except those who are medicine men among them, whom they burn, and while the fire is burning, all dance and make a big festival, grinding the bones to powder. At the end of the year, when they celebrate the anniversary, they scarify themselves and give to the relatives the pulverized bones to drink in water. Every man has a recognized wife, but the medicine men enjoy greater privileges, since they may have two or three, and among these wives there is great friendship and harmony.

When one takes a woman for his wife, from the day he marries her, whatever he may hunt or fish, she has to fetch it to the home of her father, without

---

* In *Relacion* (p. 277) Cabeza de Vaca says the island was called by them *"Mal Fondo,"* which seems a misprint.

daring to touch or eat of it, and from the home of the father-in-law they bring the food to the husband. All the while neither the wife's father nor her mother enter his abode, nor is he allowed to go to theirs, or to the homes of his brothers-in-law, and should they happen to meet they go out of each other's way a crossbow's shot or so, with bowed heads and eyes cast to the ground, holding it to be an evil thing to look at each other or speak. The women are free to communicate with their parents-in-law or relatives and speak to them. This custom prevails from that island as far as about fifty leagues inland.

There is another custom, that when a son or brother dies no food is gathered by those of his household for three months, preferring rather to starve, but the relatives and neighbors provide them with victuals. Now, as during the time we were there so many of them died, there was great starvation in most of the lodges, due to their customs and ceremonials, as well as to the weather, which was so rough that such as could go out after food brought in but very little, withal working hard for it. Therefore the Indians by whom I was kept forsook the island and in several canoes went over to the mainland to some bays where there were a great many oysters and during three months of the year they do not eat anything else and drink very bad water. There is lack of firewood, but great abundance of mosquitoes. Their lodges are made of matting and built on oyster shells, upon which they sleep in hides, which they only get by chance. There we remained to the end of April, when we went to the seashore, where we ate blackberries for a whole month, during which time they danced and celebrated incessantly.

. . .

Nearly six years I spent thus in the country, alone among them and naked, as they all were themselves . . . *

On the opposite shore we saw Indians who had come to meet those in our company. They informed us that further on there were three men like ourselves and told us their names. . . . We asked them about those who remained alive, and they said they were in a very sorry condition, as the boys and other Indians, idlers and roughs, kicked them, slapped their faces and beat them with sticks, and such was the life they had to lead.

We inquired about the country further on and the sustenance that might be found in it. They said it was very thinly settled, with nothing to eat, and the people dying from cold, as they had neither hides nor anything else to protect

* [At this point, Cabeza de Vaca reunites with several other men remaining from the original fleet that left Cuba. Perhaps eighty men of the original three hundred reached Galveston; fifteen survived the winter. In the following passages the remaining men will recount what has occurred to the other Spaniards.—E.J.D. and J.B.F.]

their bodies. They also told us that, if we wished to meet the three Christians about two days hence, the Indians would come to a place about a league from there on the shore of that river to feed on nuts. And to show us that what they said of the ill-treatment of our people was true the Indians with whom we were kicked and beat my companion. Neither did I remain without my share of it. They threw mud at us, and put arrows to our chests every day, saying they would kill us in the same way as our other companions. And fearing this, Lope de Oviedo, my companion, said he preferred to go back, with some women of the Indians in whose company we had forded the cove and who had remained behind. I insisted he should not go and did all I could to prevail upon him to remain, but it was in vain. He went back and I remained alone among these Indians, who are named *Guevenes*, whereas those with whom he went away were called *Deaguanes*.

Two days after Lope de Oviedo had gone the Indians who kept Alonso del Castillo and Andrés Dorantes came to the very spot we had been told of to eat the nuts upon which they subsist for two months in the year, grinding certain small grains with them, without eating anything else. Even of that they do not always have, since one year there may be some and the next year not. They (the nuts) are of the size of those of Galicia, and the trees are very big and numerous.

An Indian told me that the Christians had come and that if I wished to see them I should run away to hide on the edge of a grove to which he pointed, as he and some of his relatives were to visit these Indians and would take me along to the Christians. I confided in them and determined to do it because they spoke a different language from that of my Indians. So the next day they took me along. When I got near the site where they had their lodges, Andrés Dorantes came out to look who it was, because the Indians had informed him also that a Christian was coming, and when he saw me he was much frightened, as for many days they believed me to be dead, the Indians having told them so. We gave many thanks to God for being together again, and that day was one of the happiest we enjoyed in our time, and going to where was Castillo they asked me whither I went. I told him my purpose was to go to a country of Christians and that I followed this direction and trail. Andrés Dorantes said that for many days he had been urging Castillo and Estevanico to go further on, but they did not risk it, being unable to swim and afraid of the rivers and inlets that had to be crossed so often in that country.

Still, as it pleased God, Our Lord, to spare me after all my sufferings and sickness and finally let me rejoin them, they at last determined upon fleeing, as I would take them safely across the rivers and bays we might meet. But they advised me to keep it secret from the Indians (as well as my own departure) lest they would kill me forthwith, and that to avoid this it was necessary to remain with them for six months longer, after which time they would remove to another section in order to eat prickly pears. These are a fruit of the size of eggs, red and black, and taste very good. For three months they subsist upon them exclusively, eating nothing else.

Now, at the time they pluck this fruit, other Indians from beyond come to them with bows for barter and exchange, and when those turn back we thought of joining them and escaping in this way. With this understanding I remained, and they gave me as a slave to an Indian with whom Dorantes stayed. This Indian, his wife, their son and another Indian who was with them were all cross-eyed. These are called *Mariames*, and Castillo was with others, who were their neighbors, called *Iguaces*.

And so, being here with them, they told me that after leaving the Island of Ill-Fate they met on the coast the boat in which the purser and the monks were going adrift, and that crossing the rivers, of which there were four, all very large and very swift, the barges in which they crossed were swept out into the sea, where four of their number were drowned. Thus they went ahead until they had crossed the inlet, which they did by dint of great efforts. Fifteen leagues from there they met another of our parties, and when they reached there, already two of their companions had died in sixty leagues of travel. The survivors also were very near death. On the whole trip they ate nothing but crawfish and *yerba pedrera.*[*]

At this, the last cove, they said they saw Indians eating blackberries, who, upon perceiving the Christians, went away to another promontory. While seeking a way to cross the cove an Indian and a Christian came towards them, and they recognized Figueroa, one of the four we had sent ahead from the Island of Ill-Fate, who there told them how he and his companions had gotten to that place, where two of their number and one Indian had died from cold and hunger, because they had come and remained in the worst weather known. He also said the Indians took him and Mendez.

While with them Mendez fled, going in the direction of Pánuco[†] as best he might, but the Indians pursued and killed him. So, as he (Figueroa) was with these same Indians he learned (from them) that with the *Mariames* there was a Christian who had come over from the other side and had met him[‡] with those called *Guevenes*; and that this Christian was Hernando de Esquivel, from

---

[*] I have been unable to find, as yet, any reference that might serve to explain this term.

[†] [In Mexico—*E.J.D. and J.B.F.*]

[‡] Thus in original, although it seems unclear. I do not venture to make or suggest a change.

Badajoz, a companion of the commissary. From Esquivel he learned how the Governor, the purser and the others had ended.

The purser, with the friars, had stranded with their barge among the rivers, and, while they were proceeding along the coast, the barge of the Governor and his men came to land also. He (the Governor) then went with his barge as far as the big cove, whence he returned and took his men across to the other side, then came back for the purser, the monks and the rest. He further told him that after disembarking, the Governor revoked the powers he had given to the purser as his lieutenant, giving the office to a captain that was with him called Pantoja.

The Governor did not land that night, but remained on his barge with a pilot and a page who was sick. They had neither water nor anything to eat aboard, and at midnight a northerner set in with such violence that it carried the barge out into the sea, without anybody noticing it. They had for an anchor only a stone, and never more did they hear of him. Thereupon the people who had remained on land proceeded along the coast, and, being much impeded by water, built rafts with great trouble, in which they passed to the other side.

Going ahead, they reached a point of timber on the beach, where they found Indians, who, upon seeing them approach, placed their lodges on the canoes and crossed over to the other side of the coast, and the Christians, in view of the season and weather, since it was in the month of November, remained in this timber, because they found water and firewood, some crawfish and other sea-food, but from cold and hunger they began to die.

Moreover, Pantoja, who remained as lieutenant, ill-treated them. On this Sotomayor, brother of Vasco Porcallo (the one from the Island of Cuba, who had come in the fleet as Maestro de Campo), unable to stand it longer, quarrelled with Pantoja and struck him a blow with a stick, of which he died. Thus they perished one after another, the survivors slicing the dead for meat. The last one to die was Sotomayor, and Esquivel cut him up and fed on his body until the first of March, when an Indian, of those who had taken to flight previously, came to look if they were dead and took Esquivel along with him.

Once in the hands of this Indian, Figueroa spoke to Esquivel, learning from him what we have told here, and he entreated him to go in his company towards Pánuco. But Esquivel refused, saying he had heard from the monks that Pánuco was in their rear, and so he remained, while Figueroa went back to the coast where he formerly had been.[*]

---

[*] This is substantially corroborated in Oviedo.

All this account Figueroa gave after Esquivel's narrative, and thus, from one to the other, it came to me. Through it the fate of the whole fleet will be learned and known, and what happened to every one in particular. And he said furthermore that if the Christians would go about there for some time they might possibly meet Esquivel, because he knew that he had run away from the Indian with whom he was and gone to others called *Mariames*, who were their neighbors. And, as I have just said, he and the Asturian wished to go to other Indians further on, but when those with whom they were found it out, they beat them severely, undressed the Asturian and pierced one of his arms with an arrow.

At last the Christians escaped through flight, and remained with the other Indians, whose slaves they agreed to become. But, although serving them, they were so ill-treated, that no slaves, nor men in any condition of life, were ever so abused. Not content with cuffing and beating them and pulling out their beards for mere pastime, they killed three out of the six only because they went from one lodge to another. These were Diego Dorantes, Valdivieso and Diego de Huelva. The three remaining ones expected to meet the same fate in the end.

To escape from that life Andrés Dorantes fled to the *Mariames*, and they were the ones with whom Esquivel had been. They told him how Esquivel stayed with them and how he fled because a woman dreamt he would kill her son, and the Indians pursued and killed him. They also showed Andrés Dorantes his sword, his rosary, his prayer book and other things of his.

It is a custom of theirs to kill even their own children for the sake of dreams, and the girls when newly born they throw away to be eaten by dogs. The reason why they do it is (as they say) that all the others of that country are their enemies with whom they are always at war, and should they marry their daughters they might multiply so much as to be able to overcome them and reduce them to slavery. Hence they prefer to kill the girls rather than see them give birth to children who would become their foes.

We asked them why they did not wed the girls among themselves. They replied it was bad to marry them to their own kin, and much better to do away with their daughters than to leave them to relatives or to enemies. This custom they have in common with their neighbors, the *Iguaces*, and no other tribe of that country has it. When they want to get married they buy their wives from their enemies. The price paid for a woman is a bow, the best to be had, with two arrows, and if he has no bow he gives a net as much as a fathom in width and one in length. They kill their own children and buy those of strangers. Marriage only lasts as long as they please. For a mere nothing they break up wedlock.

Dorantes remained only a few days with those Indians and then escaped. Castillo and Estevanico went inland to the *Iguaces*. All those people are archers and well built, although not as tall as those we had left behind us, and they have the nipple and lip perforated. Their principal food are two or three kinds of roots, which they hunt for all over the land; they are very unhealthy, inflating, and it takes two days to roast them. Many are very bitter, and with all that they are gathered with difficulty. But those people are so much exposed to starvation that these roots are to them indispensable and they walk two and three leagues to obtain them. Now and then they kill deer and at times get a fish, but this is so little and their hunger so great that they eat spiders and ant eggs,* worms, lizards and salamanders and serpents, also vipers the bite of which is deadly. They swallow earth and wood, and all they can get, the dung of deer and more things I do not mention; and I verily believe, from what I saw, that if there were any stones in the country they would eat them also. They preserve the bones of the fish they eat, of snakes and other animals, to pulverize them and eat the powder. . . . †

Early the next day many Indians came and brought five people who were paralyzed and very ill, and they came for Castillo to cure them. Every one of the patients offered him his bow and arrows, which he accepted, and by sunset he made the sign of the cross over each of the sick, recommending them to God, Our Lord, and we all prayed to Him as well as we could to restore them to health. And He, seeing there was no other way of getting those people to help us so that we might be saved from our miserable existence, had mercy upon us, and in the morning all woke up well and hearty and went away in such good health as if they never had had any ailment whatever. This caused them great admiration and moved us to thanks to Our Lord and to greater faith in His goodness and the hope that He would save us, guiding us to where we could serve Him. For myself I may say that I always had full faith in His mercy and in that He would liberate me from captivity, and always told my companions so.

When the Indians had gone and taken along those recently cured, we removed to others that were eating tunas also, called *Cultalchulches* and *Malicones*, which speak a different language, and with them were others, called *Coayos* and *Susolas*, and on another side those called *Atayos*, who were at war with the *Susolas*, and exchanging arrow shots with them every day.

Nothing was talked about in this whole country but of the wonderful cures which God, Our Lord, performed through us, and so they came from many

* The pupas.
† [In this section, Cabeza de Vaca describes how he came to be a faith healer.—*E.J.D. and J.B.F.*]

places to be cured, and after having been with us two days some Indians of the *Susolas* begged Castillo to go and attend to a man who had been wounded, as well as to others that were sick and among whom, they said, was one on the point of death. Castillo was very timid, especially in difficult and dangerous cases, and always afraid that his sins might interfere and prevent the cures from being effective. Therefore the Indians told me to go and perform the cure. They liked me, remembering that I had relieved them while they were out gathering nuts, for which they had given us nuts and hides. This had happened at the time I was coming to join the Christians. So I had to go, and Dorantes and Estevanico went with me.

When I came close to their ranches I saw that the dying man we had been called to cure was dead, for there were many people around him weeping and his lodge was torn down, which is a sign that the owner has died. I found the Indian with eyes upturned, without pulse and with all the marks of lifelessness. At least so it seemed to me, and Dorantes said the same. I removed a mat with which he was covered, and as best I could prayed to Our Lord to restore his health, as well as that of all the others who might be in need of it, and after having made the sign of the cross and breathed on him many times they brought his bow and presented it to me, and a basket of ground tunas, and took me to many others who were suffering from vertigo. They gave me two more baskets of tunas, which I left to the Indians that had come with us. Then we returned to our quarters.

Our Indians to whom I had given the tunas remained there, and at night returned telling, that the dead man whom I attended to in their presence had resuscitated, rising from his bed, had walked about, eaten and talked to them, and that all those treated by me were well and in very good spirits. This caused great surprise and awe, and all over the land nothing else was spoken of. All who heard it came to us that we might cure them and bless their children, and when the Indians in our company (who were the *Cultalchulches*) had to return to their country, before parting they offered us all the tunas they had for their journey, not keeping a single one, and gave us flint stones as long as one and a-half palms, with which they cut and that are greatly prized among them. They begged us to remember them and pray to God to keep them always healthy, which we promised to do, and so they left, the happiest people upon earth, having given us the very best they had.

We remained with the *Avavares* Indians for eight months, according to our reckoning of the moons. During that time they came for us from many places and said that verily we were children of the sun. Until then Dorantes and the negro had not made any cures, but we found ourselves so pressed by the Indians coming from all sides, that all of us had to become medicine men. I was the most daring and reckless of all in undertaking cures. We never treated anyone that did not afterwards say he was well, and they had such confidence in our skill as to believe that none of them would die as long as we were among them.

These Indians and the ones we left behind told us a very strange tale. From their account it may have occurred fifteen or sixteen years ago. They said there wandered then about the country a man, whom they called "Bad Thing," of small stature and with a beard, although they never could see his features clearly, and whenever he would approach their dwellings their hair would stand on end and they began to tremble. In the doorway of the lodge there would then appear a firebrand. That man thereupon came in and took hold of anyone he chose, and with a sharp knife of flint, as broad as a hand and two palms in length, he cut their side, and, thrusting his hand through the gash, took out the entrails, cutting off a piece one palm long, which he threw into the fire. Afterwards he made three cuts in one of the arms, the second one at the place where people are usually bled, and twisted the arm, but reset it soon afterwards. Then he placed his hands on the wounds, and they told us that they closed at once. Many times he appeared among them while they were dancing, sometimes in the dress of a woman and again as a man, and whenever he took a notion to do it he would seize the hut or lodge, take it up into the air and come down with it again with a great crash. They also told us how, many a time, they set food before him, but he never would partake of it, and when they asked him where he came from and where he had his home, he pointed to a rent in the earth and said his house was down below.[*]

We laughed very much at those stories, making fun of them, and then, seeing our incredulity they brought to us many of those whom, they said, he had taken, and we saw the scars of his slashes in the places and as they told. We told them he was a demon and explained as best we could that if they would believe in God, Our Lord, and be Christians like ourselves, they would not have to fear that man, nor would he come and do such things unto them, and they might be sure that as long as we were in this country he would not dare to appear again. At this they were greatly pleased and lost much of their apprehension.

The same Indians told us they had seen the Asturian and Figueroa with other Indians further along on the coast, which we had named of the figs. All those people had no reckoning by either sun or moon, nor do they count by months and years; they judge of the seasons by the ripening of fruits, by the

---

[*] There is no mention of this story in Oviedo. What may be the basis for it is impossible to conjecture. It may have been a tradition, but completely misunderstood, hence misreported, by the Spaniards.

time when fish die and by the appearance of the stars, in all of which they are very clever and expert. While with them we were always well treated, although our food was never too plentiful, and we had to carry our own water and wood. Their dwellings and their food are like those of the others, but they are much more exposed to starvation, having neither maize nor acorns or nuts. We always went about naked like they and covered ourselves at night with deer skins.

During six of the eighteen months we were with them we suffered much from hunger, because they do not have fish either. At the end of that time the tunas began to ripen, and without their noticing it we left and went to other Indians further ahead, called *Maliacones*, at a distance of one day's travel. Three days after I and the negro reached there I sent him back to get Castillo and Dorantes, and after they rejoined me we all departed in company of the Indians, who went to eat a small fruit of some trees. On this fruit they subsist for ten or twelve days until the tunas are fully ripe. There they joined other Indians called *Arbadaos*, whom we found to be so sick, emaciated and swollen that we were greatly astonished. The Indians with whom we had come went back on the same trail, and we told them that we wished to remain with the others, at which they showed grief. So we remained with the others in the field near their dwellings.

When the Indians saw us they clustered together, after having talked among themselves, and each one of them took the one of us whom he claimed by the hand and they led us to their homes. While with those we suffered more from hunger than among any of the others. In the course of a whole day we did not eat more than two handfuls of the fruit, which was green and contained so much milky juice that our mouths were burnt by it. As water was very scarce, whoever ate of them became very thirsty. And we finally grew so hungry that we purchased two dogs, in exchange for nets and other things, and a hide with which I used to cover myself. I have said already that through all that country we went naked, and not being accustomed to it, like snakes we shed our skin twice a year. Exposure to the sun and air covered our chests and backs with big sores that made it very painful to carry the big and heavy loads, the ropes of which cut into the flesh of our arms.

The country is so rough and overgrown that often after we had gathered firewood in the timber and dragged it out, we would bleed freely from the thorns and spines which cut and slashed us wherever they touched. Sometimes it happened that I was unable to carry or drag out the firewood after I had gathered it with much loss of blood. In all that trouble my only relief or consolation was to remember the passion of our Saviour, Jesus Christ, and the blood He shed for me, and to ponder how much greater His sufferings had been from the thorns, than those I was then enduring. I made a contract with the Indians to make combs, arrows, bows and nets for them. Also we made matting of which their lodges are constructed and of which they are in very great need, for, although they know how to make it, they do not like to do any work, in order to be able to go in quest of food. Whenever they work they suffer greatly from hunger.

Again, they would make me scrape skins and tan them, and the greatest luxury I enjoyed was on the day they would give me a skin to scrape, because I scraped it very deep in order to eat the parings, which would last me two or three days. It also happened to us, while being with these Indians and those before mentioned, that we would eat a piece of meat which they gave us, raw, because if we broiled it the first Indian coming along would snatch and eat it; it seemed useless to take any pains, in view of what we might expect; neither were we particular to go to any trouble in order to have it broiled and might just as well eat it raw. Such was the life we led there, and even that scanty maintenance we had to earn through the objects made by our own hands for barter.

After we had eaten the dogs it seemed to us that we had enough strength to go further on, so we commended ourselves to the guidance of God, our Lord, took leave of these Indians, and they put us on the track of others of their language who were nearby. While on our way it began to rain and rained the whole day. We lost the trail and found ourselves in a big forest, where we gathered plenty of leaves of tunas which we roasted that same night in an oven made by ourselves, and so much heat did we give them that in the morning they were fit to be eaten. After eating them we recommended ourselves to God again, and left, and struck the trail we had lost.

1—4

Pedro Reyes de Castañeda (1510?–1554)

PEDRO REYES DE CASTAÑEDA (1510?–1554) was born in northern Spain and was stationed in Mexico when he joined Francisco Vázquez de Coronado's expedition to discover the "Seven Cities of Cibola," reputed to be "cities of gold." The full title of the work gives an idea of the geographical scope of the expedition, as recorded by Castañeda: *The Journey of Coronado, 1540–1542, from the City of Mexico to the Grand*

Canyon of the Colorado and the Buffalo Plains of Texas, Kansas, and Nebraska. Although Coronado's expedition failed to find gold, it discovered such treasures as the Grand Canyon. These selections describe Coronado's journey through the Panhandle to Quivira and the lands of the Great Plains Wichita and Caddo.

≈≈ ≈≈ ≈≈

From *The Journey of Coronado* (1540–1542)

Chapter 7. Which Treats of the Plains That Were Crossed, of the Cows, and of the People Who Inhabit Them*

We have spoken of the settlements of high houses which are situated in what seems to be the most level and open part of the mountains, since it is 150 leagues across before entering the level country between the two mountain chains which I said were near the North sea and the South sea, which might better be called the Western sea along this coast. This mountain series is the one which is near the South sea.[†] In order to show that the settlements are in the middle of the mountains, I will state that it is 80 leagues from Chichilticalli, where we began to cross this country, to Cibola; from Cibola, which is the first village, to Cicuye, which is the last on the way across, is 70 leagues; it is 30 leagues from Cicuye to where the plains begin. It may be we went across in an indirect or roundabout way, which would make it seem as if there was more country than if it had been crossed in a direct line, and it may be more difficult and rougher. This cannot be known certainly, because the mountains change their direction above the bay at the mouth of the Firebrand (Tizon) river.

Now we will speak of the plains. The country is spacious and level, and is more than 400 leagues wide in the part between the two mountain ranges—one, that which Francisco Vazquez Coronado crossed, and the other that which the force under Don Fernando de Soto crossed, near the North sea, entering the country from Florida. No settlements were seen anywhere on these plains.

In traversing 250 leagues, the other mountain range was not seen, nor a hill nor a hillock which was three times as high as a man. Several lakes were found at intervals; they were round as plates, a stone's throw or more across, some fresh and some salt. The grass grows tall near these lakes; away from them it is

---

* [The land described below is believed to be Blanco Canyon, Crosby County, Texas—*E.J.D. and J.B.F.*]

† More than once Castañeda seems to be addressing those about him where he is writing in Culiacan.

very short, a span or less. The country is like a bowl, so that when a man sits down, the horizon surrounds him all around at the distance of a musket shot. There are no groves of trees except at the rivers, which flow at the bottom of some ravines where the trees grow so thick that they were not noticed until one was right on the edge of them. They are of dead earth. There are paths down into these, made by the cows when they go to the water, which is essential throughout these plains.

As I have related in the first part, people follow the cows, hunting them and tanning the skins to take to the settlements in the winter to sell, since they go there to pass the winter, each company going to those which are nearest, some to the settlements at Cicuye, others toward Quivira, and others to the settlements which are situated in the direction of Florida. These people are called Querechos and Teyas. They described some large settlements, and judging from what was seen of these people and from the accounts they gave of other places, there are a good many more of these people than there are of those at the settlements. They have better figures, are better warriors, and are more feared. They travel like the Arabs, with their tents and troops of dogs loaded with poles* and having Moorish pack saddles with girths. When the load gets disarranged, the dogs howl, calling some one to fix them right. These people eat raw flesh and drink blood. They do not eat human flesh. They are a kind people and not cruel. They are faithful friends. They are able to make themselves very well understood by means of signs. They dry the flesh in the sun, cutting it thin like a leaf, and when dry they grind it like meal to keep it and make a sort of sea soup of it to eat. A handful thrown into a pot swells up so as to increase very much. They season it with fat, which they always try to secure when they kill a cow.† They empty a large gut and fill it with blood, and carry this around the neck to drink when they are thirsty. When they open the belly of a cow, they squeeze out the chewed grass and drink the juice that remains behind, because they say that this contains the essence of the stomach. They cut the hide open at the back and pull it off at the joints, using a flint as large as a finger, tied in a little stick, with as much ease as if working with a good iron tool. They give it an edge with their own teeth. The quickness with which they do this is something worth seeing and noting.

There are very great numbers of wolves on these plains, which go around with the cows. They have white skins. The deer are pied with white. Their skin is loose, so that when they are killed it can be pulled off with the hand while warm, coming off like pigskin. The rabbits, which are very numerous, are so

---

* The well known travois of the plains tribes.
† Pemmican.

foolish that those on horseback killed them with their lances. This is when they are mounted among the cows. They fly from a person on foot.

Chapter 13. Of Quivira, of Where It Is and Some Information about It[*]

Quivira is to the west of those ravines, in the midst of the country, somewhat nearer the mountains toward the sea, for the country is level as far as Quivira, and there they began to see some mountain chains. The country is well settled. Judging from what was seen on the borders of it, this country is very similar to that of Spain in the varieties of vegetation and fruits. There are plums like those of Castile, grapes, nuts, mulberries, oats, pennyroyal, wild marjoram, and large quantities of flax, but this does not do them any good, because they do not know how to use it.[†] The people are of almost the same sort and appearance as the Teyas. They have villages like those in New Spain. The houses are round, without a wall, and they have one story like a loft, under the roof, where they sleep and keep their belongings. The roofs are of straw. There are other thickly settled provinces around it containing large numbers of men. A friar named Juan de Padilla remained in this province, together with a Spanish-Portuguese and a negro and a half-blood and some Indians from the province of Capothan, in New Spain. They killed the friar because he wanted to go to the province of the Guas, who were their enemies. The Spaniard escaped by taking flight on a mare, and afterward reached New Spain, coming out by way of Panuco. The Indians from New Spain who accompanied the friar were allowed by the murderers to bury him, and then they followed the Spaniard and overtook him. This Spaniard was a Portuguese, named Campo.

The great river of the Holy Spirit (Espiritu Santo),[‡] which Don Fernando de Soto discovered in the country of Florida, flows through this country. It passes through a province called Arache, according to the reliable accounts which were obtained here. The sources were not visited, because, according to what they said, it comes from a very distant country in the mountains of the South sea, from the part that sheds its waters onto the plains. It flows across all the level country and breaks through the mountains of the North sea, and comes out where the people with Don Fernando de Soto navigated it. This is more than 300 leagues from where it enters the sea. On account of this, and also

---

* [Quivira, thought by Coronado to be a lost city of gold, is possibly in Kansas.—*E.J.D. and J.B.F.*]

† Mr. Savage, in the Transactions of the Nebraska Historical Society, vol. i., p. 198, shows how closely the descriptions of Castañeda, Jaramillo, and the others on the expedition, harmonize with the flora and fauna of his State.

‡ The Mississippi and Missouri rivers.

because it has large tributaries, it is so mighty when it enters the sea that they lost sight of the land before the water ceased to be fresh.[*]

This country of Quivira was the last that was seen, of which I am able to give any description or information. Now it is proper for me to return and speak of the army, which I left in Tiguex, resting for the winter, so that it would be able to proceed or return in search of these settlements of Quivira, which was not accomplished after all, because it was God's pleasure that these discoveries should remain for other peoples and that we who had been there should content ourselves with saying that we were the first who discovered it and obtained any information concerning it, just as Hercules knew the site where Julius Cæsar was to found Seville or Hispales. May the all-powerful Lord grant that His will be done in everything. It is certain that if this had not been His will Francisco Vazquez would not have returned to New Spain without cause or reason, as he did, and that it would not have been left for those with Don Fernando de Soto to settle such a good country, as they have done, and besides settling it to increase its extent, after obtaining, as they did, information from our army.[†]

1—5
Luís Lazo de la Vega (fl. 1600s)

ST. JUAN DIEGO (1474–1548) or CUAUHTLATOATZIN [TALKING EAGLE] converted to Roman Catholicism from his native religion. The Virgin Mary appeared to him twice, on both occasions speaking to him in his native language, Nahuatl. The original accounts of the apparition were written in that language and then translated into Spanish. The depictions of Our Lady of Guadalupe blend native and Roman Catholic elements; most notable is that Mary is depicted as "somewhat dark," like Juan Diego and other indigenous people, a feature that caused some to question the authenticity of the experience. Juan Diego built the original shrine to the Virgin Mary; today, the Basilica of Our Lady of Guadalupe is the most-visited Catholic shrine in the world. St. Juan Diego was

---

[*] This is probably a reminiscence of Cabeza de Vaca's narrative.

[†] Mota Padilla, cap. xxxiii., 4, p. 166, gives his reasons for the failure of the expedition: "It was most likely the chastisement of God that riches were not found on this expedition, because, when this ought to have been the secondary object of the expedition, and the conversion of all those heathen their first aim, they bartered with fate and struggled after the secondary; and thus the misfortune is not so much that all those labors were without fruit, but the worst is that such a number of souls have remained in their blindness."

canonized in 2002, becoming the first indigenous saint in the Americas. This full account was penned by Father Luis Lazo de Vega, a Mexican priest, more than one hundred years after the apparition, in 1649.

≈≈ ≈≈ ≈≈

"History of the Miraculous Apparition" (1649)

History of the Miraculous Apparition, according to the text published in 1649 by Lazo de la Vega. Lessons of the new Office, granted and approved by His Holiness Leon XIII, wherein is described the tradition and worship of the Virgin of Guadalupe. Life of Juan Diego.

Herein is the account of how once again the renowned Holy Virgin Mary Mother of God, Our Lady, miraculously appeared in the place called Tepeyacac.

She appeared first to a native named Juan Diego, and later her divine image appeared before the first bishop Brother Juan de Zumárraga. The many miracles she has done are described as well. About ten years after water began to be brought down from the mountain of Mexico, when the arrow and the shield had been stilled, when peace was beginning to shine forth everywhere, the faith and knowledge of Him by whose favor we live, the true God, were already being proclaimed.

In the year 1531 at the beginning of December, a poor native named Juan Diego, as it is said, had a house in Quahutítlan. One Saturday very early in the morning, he was coming to participate in divine worship, for which everyone came to *Tlatilolco*, as well as to tend to his own errands. Having arrived at the hill called Tepeyacac near dawn, he heard the sound of singing upon the hill, like that of many choice birds singing, their voices echoing against the hill, which greatly rejoiced in response, spreading joy with its song, completely surpassing the cascabel bird and all the others.

Juan Diego stopped to reflect and said to himself: *Is it by chance my joy I'm hearing? Perhaps I'm only dreaming? Where am I? Is it perhaps the flowery land, the fruitful land of which our ancient ancestors, our grandparents told us? Is it perhaps the earthly paradise?*

He was looking in the direction of the hill, toward the east from which came the celestial song. The song having ceased, he heard someone calling to him from over the hill: *Juan.* Juan Diego didn't dare to go beyond to where he was called; he didn't even move. Perhaps he was surprised by something; nevertheless, he became joyful and happy, began climbing the hill to which he was called and, as he approached, at the peak of the hill he saw a woman standing there. She called him to her and, having arrived in her presence, he watched her very carefully, her beauty excellent and her garments shining like the radiant sun. The stones and the caves shone like precious gold where her brightness struck them, like the rainbow sending its gleams on the earth. The cacti and the rest of the plants there seemed like celestial plants, their leaves and thorns shining like gold in her presence. He genuflected and heard her voice, her words which made him exceedingly joyful; affectionately, as though she loved him, she said:

Listen, Juan my child, where are you going? He responded: *My Goddess, my Lady, my Maiden, I am going to your house—Mexico-Tlatilolco, I am going to attend divine worship, as our priests taught us.*

Then she made known to him her divine will, saying: *Know this; may your heart be very assured, my child: that I am to the highest degree forever the Holy Virgin Mother of the true God, by whose favor we live, the creator, the master of the sky and master of the earth. I desire very much that here a temple be built for me wherein will be shown, revealed, and given all that there is of my love, my mercy, my help and protection, for truly I am your compassionate mother, yours and all the rest of my dear people who call upon me, seek me, and trust in me. There I will hear their cry, their words, that I may make perfect and heal all their ills, their labors and their miseries, and that my will and my mercy may be confirmed. Go to the palace of the Bishop of Mexico and tell him that I am sending you to make known to him how much I desire that a temple be made for me here; and tell him all that you have seen and heard. May your heart be assured that I will be thankful and will repay you with glory, and you will be well-deserving of the reward I give you for the exertion, the labor you suffer in fulfilling this errand I am sending you on. You have heard my words, my child; go now and fulfill your errand.*

Then he knelt before her and said: *My Goddess, my Lady, I go to fulfill your command.*

Then he descended the hill to fulfill his charge, taking the path that goes straight to Mexico. Having arrived in the city, he went straight toward the palace of the Lord Bishop, whose name was Brother Juan de Zumárraga, a priest from San Francisco who was the first to come to this town. Having arrived, Juan Diego endeavored to see the Lord Bishop, begging his servants to notify their master. After a good while, when the Lord Bishop gave the command to have him enter, they came to call him. Having come in before him, Juan Diego knelt, bowed down, and told him the words of the Queen of Heaven, and also everything he saw and heard. Having heard all Juan Diego's words and his errand, the Lord Bishop was not completely persuaded and responded in this way:

My son, you shall come another time less hastily. I will hear you from the beginning; I will see why you came, your will, your desire. Juan Diego left with great sadness, because the Lord Bishop did not at that time consider his errand truthful.

He returned that very day and went straight up the hill where he had seen the Queen of Heaven who, still there where he had first seen her, was waiting for him. Seeing her, he bowed down before her, yielded himself on the ground, saying: *My Goddess, my most noble person, my lady, my child, my maiden, I went to do what you sent me for. Although with great difficulty I entered the Lord Bishop's chamber, I saw him at last. I put your words before him as you commanded me. He received me kindly and heard me attentively, but he responded as if he did not consider it true, did not believe it. He told me I should come another time less hastily, that he will hear me from the root, and see why I came, what I want, what I desire. I perceived, according to what he said to me, that it seems to him that the temple that you want him to make for you here, that perhaps I have made it up, that perhaps it is not your will. I beg you, my Goddess, my Lady, my daughter, that you leave this charge with some gentlemen that are well known, respected, and credible so that they may bring your words and be believed. Certainly, because I am poor, I am not worthy to do what you have commanded me, I am not worthy to go where you have sent me. Forgive me, my child, lest I cast a shadow over your renowned heart, lest I fall under your wrath.*

The Virgin of eternal renown responded, saying: *Hear me, my child, be assured that I am not lacking in servants, ambassadors that can carry my words and thus verify my will; but it is important that you speak; despite your weariness, it is through your hands that my desire, my will must be verified. But I beg you, my child, and advise you with great care, to go again to the Bishop tomorrow and make him understand my desire, my will, and request that he make the temple that I ask him for; and tell him again that I am the ever Virgin Holy Mary, the Mother of God who sends you there.* And Juan Diego responded, saying: *Queen of Heaven, my Goddess, my maiden, let not your heart be afflicted, for with all my heart I will go to deliver your words with all sincerity; in no way will I neglect them for lack of desire or because the path is difficult, but only because perhaps I will not be heard and I may not be believed if I am by chance heard; I will go and follow your words and tomorrow in the afternoon as the sun sets I will bring the answer to your words that the Lord Bishop gives me. I leave you now, my child, my maiden, my Lady. Rest in the meantime.*

With that he went to his house to rest. The following day, Sunday, he left his house in the morning and came straight to Tlatilulco for Mass and the homily. He was determined to see the Lord Bishop at ten when he finished hearing the Mass and the homily and all the natives in attendance had gone out. Juan Diego then went to the Bishop's palace and, upon arriving, made every attempt to see him. With much difficulty he saw him, knelt at his feet, and cried, deeply moved as he delivered the words of the Queen of Heaven, hoping that perhaps his charge—the will of the most renowned Virgin that they make for her the desired temple which he had mentioned—would be believed.

But the Lord Bishop asked Juan Diego many things to ascertain the event. He asked: *Where did you see her? What is the woman that you saw like?* And he told the Lord Bishop everything he saw; but although he declared everything as it was so that it seemed very likely that she was the immaculate Virgin, the dear Mother of our Lord Jesus Christ, even that did not make him certain. He said: *What you ask cannot be done, cannot be accomplished only with your words. Some sign is very necessary so that it may be believed that she that sends you is indeed the Queen of Heaven.*

And having heard the Lord Bishop, Juan Diego said: *Sir, consider what must be the sign that you request, and I will go immediately and ask the Queen of Heaven who sent me for it.* And the Lord Bishop, seeing that he was in agreement, and that with nothing was he confounded or disturbed, told him to leave and ordered some of his highly trusted servants to follow him and see where he was going and whom he was going to see or speak to. Thus, then, it was done, and Juan Diego immediately took the royal path, and those who followed him there lost track of him on the bridge over the river that passes next to the hill. Though they searched for him everywhere, they found him nowhere. Thus they returned, not only weary of him but also angry with him. They returned and told the Lord Bishop more than what had happened so that he wouldn't believe Juan Diego: they told him that he was only deceiving them and pretending what he had come to tell, that perhaps he dreamed it, and they agreed together and said if he came here again they would detain him and punish him in order that he may not lie again.

The following day, Monday, when Juan Diego was supposed to bring some sign that he might be believed, he did not return because when he arrived at his house, one of his uncles that was staying with him, called Juan Bernardino, was very sick with typhus. First he went to call the doctor and ensure his health, but there was no longer time because he was already very sick. Early in the morning his uncle begged him to call one of the priests in Tlatilulco to come hear his confession, because he was very certain that it was his time to die, that he would never rise from his bed, that he would not recover.

On Tuesday, early in the morning, Juan Diego left his house to summon the priest in Tlatilulco and when he came close to the hill, on the path that passes by the foot of the blessed hill toward the east, his usual path, he said: *If I go straight I will surely see the lady and she will enjoin me again to bring the sign to the Lord Bishop. Let's first relieve our concern; I will go first to call the priest. Isn't my poor uncle waiting for him?*

With that he went round the path of the hill near the sandbanks, climbed, and aimed to come out on the other side toward the west to arrive more quickly in Mexico. (He thought that by going this way he would not see the Queen of Heaven, who is watching everywhere.) He saw how from the peak of the hill the lady had come down from where he always saw her, took a shortcut down the side of the hill, and said to him: *My child, where are you going?* And he was frightened; it is not known whether he was bothered, ashamed, or astonished. He bowed down before her, greeted her, and said: *My daughter, my Child, may God protect you, Lady. How did you wake up; by chance do you feel your immaculate body to be well? My Goddess, I will add sorrow to your heart. Know, my Virgin, that my uncle, your servant, is very sick; a grave illness has come upon him, overpowered him, that will undoubtedly kill him. I go quickly to your house in Mexico to call one of those loved by our God, our priests, that he may hear my uncle's confession, after having fulfilled which, I will return again to carry your message. My Virgin, my Lady, forgive me, suffer me, until I fulfill my errand, for I will come here tomorrow to be at your service.*

Having heard Juan Diego's words, the merciful and immaculate Virgin responded: *Hear, be assured, my child, that I will protect you, do not be afraid, do not be sorrowful; let not your heart be troubled, though the illness of which you speak be great. Am I not here, I who am your mother? Are you not safe under my shelter? Do I not share your nature? Let not this sickness of your uncle worry you, for he will not die; be assured that he is already healed. Shall you be offered another thing?* (And in that very hour his uncle was healed, as he found out afterwards.)

Having heard the words of the Queen of Heaven, Juan Diego became very happy and was persuaded and begged her to again send him to the Lord Bishop with some sign that he may believe what he'd already been told. The Queen of Heaven then commanded him to ascend to the peak of the hill where he always saw her and said to him: *Go up, my child, to the peak of the hill, where you saw me. There you will see many flowers; cut them and gather them, then bring them down here to me.*

Juan Diego climbed the hill and, arriving at the peak, was amazed to see several beautiful flowers of Castile blossoming, though it wasn't the season for them, because the ground was quite frozen. He was surprised by their scent. Then he began to cut them, gathered them very carefully, and wrapped them in his blanket, then brought down all the flowers that he had gone to cut to the Queen of Heaven. She, seeing them, took them in her immaculate hands, then put them back in his blanket and said: *My child, all these flowers are the sign that you must take to the Bishop. In my name you shall tell him that with this he may see and acknowledge my will and do what I desire and that you are my trustworthy ambassador. I warn you with all care that only before the Bishop must you stretch out your blanket, and you must make known to him what you carry and tell him that I told you to climb to the peak of the hill to cut these flowers. You shall also tell him all that you saw, so that you may convince the Lord Bishop, that he may then arrange to build the temple that I asked of him.*

The Queen of Heaven having counseled him, he continued on the royal path that goes straight to Mexico. He went happily because he was persuaded that his errand would turn out well. He went bearing with great care what he had wrapped in his blanket and rejoicing at the fragrance of the beautiful flowers. Upon arriving at the Bishop's palace, he found his butler and other servants of his and begged them to notify the Bishop that he desired to see him, but they all refused, perhaps because it was early in the morning, or because when they recognized him he made them angry, or because they remembered how their other companions had lost him when they went to follow him on the path. He waited there a long time, standing very hunched over to see if perhaps they would call him. Seeing that it was already getting late, they came up to him to see what he had brought with him, to confirm what he had said. Juan Diego, seeing that he could no longer hide from them what he had brought and that they would torment him and push him or beat him, to free himself he showed them that they were roses. Seeing that they were all very fresh and fragrant Castilian roses and it was not the season for them, they were astonished and tried to grab a few. They lunged three times to grab them, but they couldn't because when they went to grab them, it was no longer roses they saw but painted or embroidered flowers. Then they went to tell the Lord Bishop what they had seen, and how the Indian who had come to see him many times wanted to see him and had been waiting for him for some time.

Upon hearing this, the Lord Bishop recognized it as the sign to persuade him that what the Indian said was true. He immediately sent for Juan Diego to come before him. Having entered into his presence, Juan Diego bowed down (as he had always done) and again told him at length, happily and wonderingly, everything he had seen, saying: *Sir, I did what you commanded. I went to tell my Goddess, the Queen of Heaven, the dear Holy Mary, Mother of God, that you requested some sign that you might believe that she wanted you to build the temple already mentioned. Thus, I told her how I gave my word that I would bring you some sign that you might believe what she left to my charge, and she heard with pleasure your thought and received it favorably. And now very early in the morning, she told me to come see you again, and I asked her for the sign that she told me she would give to me. Then she sent me to the peak of the hill where I had always seen her, to go cut the flowers I saw there. And having cut them, I brought them to her at the foot of the hill where I had left her, and she took them in her immaculate hands and again wrapped them in my blanket so that I might bring them here to you, although I knew very well that the peak of the hill was no place for flowers because it was a thorny place with cacti, caves, and mesquite trees. I was not for that reason confounded or doubtful. When I arrived at the summit of the hill, I saw that there was a garden of flowers with many fragrant flowers like those found in Castile; I cut them and brought them to the Queen of Heaven, and she told me I must give them to you yourself and here I am doing so, that you may see the sign that you ask for and that her will might be done. Receive them.* And immediately he spread out his cloak where he had wrapped the flowers. After he spilled out all the roses of Castile, there appeared suddenly the immaculate image of the renowned Virgin Holy Mary, Mother of God, just like the one that is now kept in her holy house, in her temple that is called Guadalupe. Upon seeing her, the Lord Bishop and all that were there immediately knelt down and looked upon her with admiration, grew sad, and wept and were left distraught, and the Lord Bishop with tenderness and mourning begged her forgiveness because he didn't do her will when she had made it known. Standing up, he untied the cloak on which the Queen of Heaven was emblazoned from around Juan Diego's neck, then took it to his chapel. Juan Diego remained the whole day in the Bishop's house, for the latter had detained him and told him the next day: *You shall show me where the Queen of Heaven wants me to build her temple.* Having shown it, Juan Diego told him that he wished to go to his house to see his uncle Juan Bernardino, who had been very sick when he came to Tlatilulco to call one of the priests to hear his confession, and whom the Queen of Heaven had said was already made well.

They did not let him go alone but brought him to his house. Upon arriving, they saw his uncle already well, nothing ailing him any longer. The uncle, greatly amazed when he saw how they brought his nephew with such courtesy, asked him why he was treated thus. Juan Diego told him how when he had left his house to call a confessor to hear his uncle's confession he had seen the Queen of Heaven there on the hill that is called Tepeyacac, and she had sent him to Mexico to bid the Lord Bishop build her a temple. She also told him not to be sorrowful, for his uncle was already well. At this, the uncle was very cheered and told him it was true he had been healed at that moment, and that he had seen her exactly as Juan Diego had seen her. He said she told him how she had sent him to Mexico to see the Lord Bishop and that, when he went to see him, he should make known all that he saw, how she had miraculously healed his uncle, and that the Most Holy Image of the Immaculate Virgin must be called Holy Mary of Guadalupe.

Then they brought Juan Bernardino into the presence of the Lord Bishop to tell him under oath all that had happened. Both (that is, Juan Diego and Juan Bernardino) were lodged in his house for some days, until the temple of the Queen of Heaven was built in the place Juan Diego indicated. The Lord Bishop moved the sacred image of the Queen of Heaven that he had in his chapel to the cathedral so all the people could see it.

The whole city crowded around to see her most holy image; they saw how it miraculously appeared and that no one in the world had painted it on Juan Diego's cloak. The cloak on which the holy image of the Queen of Heaven miraculously appeared was of a fabric made from the agave plant, somewhat thick and of a fine weave. In those days all the indigenous people wore that fabric; only nobles, educated men, and war captains wore cotton or wool cloaks.

The venerated cloak on which the Immaculate Virgin, our sovereign Queen, appeared is of two pieces, sewn together with cotton thread. The most holy image from the sole of the foot to the crown of the head is six spans tall (a woman's span). Her most holy face is very beautiful, serious, and somewhat swarthy. Her precious figure, as it appears, is unassuming, her hands at her breast. Her belt is purple. The tip of her right foot, with its earth-colored shoe, shows slightly on the right side. Her robe is of a rosy hue; in the shadows it appears dark red and is embroidered with diverse flowers gilded around the edges; the pendant at her neck is a little golden wheel with a black outline and a cross in the middle. Another white cotton robe is visible underneath, having what seem to be laced cuffs and extending to her wrists. The outer robe, reaching from head to feet, is sky blue, is folded in the middle, and has a wide golden border. It is covered all over with golden stars (forty-six altogether). Her most holy head is inclined toward the right, and on her head above her robe she wears a beaming golden crown. At her feet is the crescent moon with its two tips facing upward, in the midst of which the Immaculate Virgin stands. She also appears to be standing in the middle of the sun, its beams surrounding her; there are one hundred of them, some big and others small, twelve of them surrounding her most holy face and head, fifty altogether on each side. The edge of the cloak forms a circle of white clouds. This divine image with all that has been described is poised above an angel nestled up to its waist among the clouds. He is grasping both sides of the Queen of Heaven's outer robes where they fall in generous folds around her most holy feet. The angel's robe is of a rosy hue with a golden collar. His wings have many sizes of feathers, and he appears to be very happy to be carrying the Queen of Heaven.

The text of the preceding account, as has been said, was published in the Na-huatl tongue by Luis Lazo de la Vega, Chaplain of the Sanctuary of Our Lady of Guadalupe in Mexico in the year 1649, which was commanded to be translated literally and word for word by Don Lorenzo Boturini.

The preceding pages come from the authorized copy located in the archive of the Council of the Collegiate Church.

1–6

Roger Williams (1603–1683)

Founder of the Rhode Island Colony, ROGER WILLIAMS (1603–1683) came to the new land as a Puritan preacher and leader. Quickly, however, he sparred with important Puritans like John Winthrop and John Cotton who labeled him a dissenter. Suffering exile from the Massachusetts Bay Colony for promoting "tolerance," Williams established his colony on that very idea. Williams was more accepting of those with religious views diverging from his own (he allowed Catholics, Baptists, Muslims, pagans, and even atheists into the colony); he also held a more enlightened attitude toward Native Americans. *A Key into the Language of America* (1643) reveals Williams' interest in native languages, both for propagating the gospel and for their intrinsic interest. This selection offers his introduction to the volume and an excerpt from his lexicon.

≈ ≈ ≈

From *A Key into the Language of America* (1643)

To My Deare and Welbeloved Friends and Countreymen, in Old and New England.

I present you with a Key; I have not heard of the like, yet framed, since it pleased God to bring that mighty continent of America to light: others of my Countreymen, have often and excellently, and lately written of the Countrey (and none that I know beyond the goodnesse and worth of it.)

This Key, respects the native language of it, and happily may unlocke some Rarities concerning the natives themselves, not yet discovered.

I drew the materialls in a rude lumpe at Sea, as a private helpe to my owne memory, that I might not by my present absence lightly lose what I had so dearely bought in some few yeares hardship and charges among the Barbarians; yet being reminded by some, what pitie it were to bury those Materialls in my Grave at land or sea; and withall, remembring how oft I have been importun'd by worthy friends of all sorts, to afford them some helps this way.

I resolved (by the assistance of the most High) to cast those Materials into this Key, pleasant and profitable for All, but specially for my friends residing in those parts:

A little Key may open a Box, where lies a bunch of Keyes.

With this I have entred into the secrets of those Countries, where ever English dwel about two hundred miles, betweene the French and Dutch Plantations; for want of this, I know what grosse mistakes my selfe and others, have run into.

There is a mixture of this Language North and South, from the place of my abode, about six hundred miles; yet within the two hundred miles (aforementioned) their Dialects doe exceedingly differ; yet not so, but (within that compasse) a man may by this helpe, converse with thousands of Natives all over the Countrey: and by such converse it may please the Father of Mercies to spread civilitie (and in his owne most holy season) Christianitie; for one Candle will light ten thousand, and it may please God to blesse a little Leaven to season the mightie lump of those Peoples and Territories.

It is expected, that having had so much converse with these Natives, I should write some little of them.

Concerning them (a little to gratifie expectation) I shall touch upon foure Heads:

First, by what Names they are distinguished.

Secondly, Their Originall and Descent.

Thirdly, their Religion, Manners, Customes, &c.

Fourthly, That great Point of their Conversion.

To the first, their Names are of two Sorts:

First, those of the English giving: as Natives, Salvages, Indians, Wild-men, (so the Dutch call them Wilden) Abergeny men, Pagans, Barbarians, Heathen.

Secondly, their names, which they give themselves.

I cannot observe, that they ever had (before the comming of the English, French, or Dutch amongst them) any Names to difference themselves from strangers, for they knew none; but two sorts of names they had, and have amongst themselves.

First, generall, belonging to all Natives, as Nínnuock, Ninnimissinûwock, Eniskeetompaûwog, which signifies Men, Folke or People.

Secondly, particular names, peculiar to severall Nations of them amongst themselves, as Nanhigganèuck, Massachusêuck, Cawasumséuck, Cowwesêuck, Quintikóock, Quinnipiéuck, Pequttóog, &c.

They have often asked mee, why wee call them Indians, Natives, &c. and understanding the reason, they will call themselves Indians in opposition to English &c.

For the second Head proposed, their Originall and Descent.

From Adam and Noah that they spring, it is granted on all hands

But for their later Descent and whence they came into those parts, it seemes as hard to finde, as to finde the well head of some fresh Streame, which running many miles out of the Countrey to the salt Ocean, hath met with many mixing Streames by the way. They say themselves, that they have sprung and growne up in that very place, like the very trees of the wildernesse.

They say that their Great God Cowtantowwit created those parts, as I observed in the Chapter of their Religion. They have no Clothes, Bookes, nor Letters, and conceive their Fathers never had; and therefore they are easily perswaded that the God that made Englishmen is a greater God, because Hee hath so richly endowed the English above themselves: But when they heare that about sixteen hundred yeeres agoe, England and the Inhabitants thereof were like unto themselves, and since have received from God, Clothes, Bookes, &c. they are greatly affected with a secret hope concerning themselves.

Wise and judicious men with whom I have discoursed, maintaine their originall to be Northward from Tartaria: and at my now taking ship, at the Dutch Plantation, it pleased the Dutch Governour (in some discourse with mee about the natives) to draw their Line from Iceland, because the name Sackmakan (the name for an Indian Prince, about the Dutch) is the name for a Prince in Iceland.

Other opinions I could number up: under favour I shall present (not mine opinion, but) my observations to the judgement of the wise.

First, others (and myselfe) have conceived some of their words to hold affinitie with the Hebrew.

Secondly, they constantly anoint their heads as the Jewes did.

Thirdly, they give Dowries for their wives as the Jewes did.

Fourthly (and which I have not so observed amongst other nations as amongst the Jewes, and these) they constantly seperate their women (during the time of their monthly sicknesse) in a little house alone by themselves foure or five dayes, and hold it an Irreligious thing for either Father or Husband or any Male to come neere them.

They have often asked me if it bee so with women of other nations, and whether they are so separated: and for their practice they plead Nature and tradition. Yet againe I have found a greater affinity of their language with the Greek tongue.

2. As the Greekes and other nations, and our selves call the seven starres (or Charles Waine, the beare,) so doe they Mosk, or Paukunnawaw the beare.*

3. They have many strange Relations of one Wétucks, a man that wrought great Miracles amongst them, and walking upon the waters, &c. with some kind of broken resemblance to the Sonne of God.

Lastly, it is famous that the Sowwest (Sowaniu) is the great subject of their discourse. From thence their Traditions. There they say (at the South west) is the Court of their Great God Cautántouwit: at the South-west are their fore-fathers soules: to the South west they goe themselves when they dye; From the South west came their Corne, and Beanes out of their great God Caután-towwits field: and indeed the further Northward and Westward from us their Corne will not grow, but to the Southward better and better. I dare not conjec-ture in these Uncertainties, I believe they are lost, and yet hope (in the Lords holy season) some of the wildest of them shall be found to share in the blood of the son of God. To the third head, concerning their Religion, Customes, Man-ners &c. I shall here say nothing, because in those 32 chapters of the whole book, I have briefly touched those of all sorts, from their birth to their burialls, and have endeavoured (as the nature of the worke would give way) to bring some short observations and applications home to Europe from America.

Therefore fourthly, to that great point of their conversion so much to bee longed for, and by all New-English so much pretended, and I hope in Truth.

For my selfe I have uprightly laboured to suite my endeavours to my pre-tences: and of later times (out of desire to attaine their Language) I have run through varieties of Intercourses with them Day and Night, Summer and Win-ter, by Land and Sea, particular passages tending to this, I have related divers, in the Chapter of their Religion.

Many solemne discourses I have had with all sorts of nations of them, from one end of the Countrey to another (so farre as opportunity, and the little lan-guage I have could reach.)

---

* [Williams means that linguistically there is a point of similarity; both Greeks and Natives of Rhode Island call the seven-star constellation "the bear."—*E.J.D. and J.B.F.*]

I know there is no small preparations in the hearts of multitudes of them. I know their many solemne confesions to my self; and one to another of their lost wandring conditions.

I know strong Convictions upon the Consciences of many of them, and their desires uttred that way.

I know not with how little Knowledge and Grace of Christ the Lord may save, and therefore neither will despair or report much.

But since it hath pleased some of my worthy Countrymen to mention (of late in print) Wequash, the Pequt Captaine, I shall be bold so farre to second their relations, as to relate mine own hope of him (though I dare not be so confident as others.)

Two dayes before his death, as I past up to Quinnihticut River it pleased my worthy friend Mr. Fenwick whom I visited at his house in Say-Brook Fort at the mouth of that River, to tell me that my old friend Wequash lay very sick: I desired to see him, and Himselfe was pleased to be my Guide two mile where Wequash lay.

Amongst other discourse concerning his sicknesse and Death (in which hee freely bequeathed his son to Mr. Fenwick) I closed with him concerning his Soule: Hee told me that some two or three yeare before he had lodged at my House, where I acquainted him with the Condition of all mankind, and his own in particular, how God created Man and All things: how Man fell from God, and of his present Enmity against God, and the wrath of God against Him until Repentance: said he, "your words were never out of my heart to this present"; and said hee "me much pray to Jesus Christ." I told him so did many English, French and Dutch, who had never turned to God, nor loved Him: He replyed in broken English: "me so big naughty Heart, me heart all one stone!" Savory expressions using to breath from compunct and broken Hearts, and a sence of inward hardnesse and unbrokennesse. I had many discourses with him in his Life, but this was the summe of our last parting untill our generall meeting.

Now because this is the great Inquiry of all men what Indians have been converted? what have the English done in those parts? what hopes of the Indians receiving the knowledge of Christ!

And because to this Question some put an edge from the boast of the Jesuits in Canada and Maryland, and especially from the wonderfull conversions made by the Spaniards and Portugalls in the West-Indies, besides what I have here written, as also, besides what I have observed in the Chapter of their Religion; I shall further present you with a brief additionall discourse concerning this Great Point, being comfortably perswaded that that Father of Spirits, who was graciously pleased to perswade Japhet (the Gentiles) to dwell in the Tents of Shem (the Jewes) will in his holy season (I hope approaching) perswade these Gentiles of America to partake of the mercies of Europe, and then shall bee fulfilled what is written by the Prophet Malachi, from the rising of the Sunne (in Europe) to the going down of the same (in America) my name shall be great among the Gentiles. So I desire to hope and pray,

Your unworthy Country-man,
Roger Williams

Directions for the Use of the Language

1. A dictionary or Grammer way I had consideration of, but purposely avoided, as not so accommodate to the benefit of all, as I hope, this forme is.

2. A Dialogue also I had thoughts of, but avoided for brevities sake, and yet (with no small paines) I have so framed every Chapter and the matter of it, as I may call it an implicite Dialogue.

3. It is framed chiefly after the Narrogánset Dialect, because most Spoken in the Countrey, and yet (with attending to the variation of peoples and Dialects) it will be of great use in all parts of the Countrey.

4. Whatever your occasion bee either of Travell, Discourse, Trading &c. turne to the Table which will direct you to the Proper Chapter.

5. Because the Life of all Language is in the Pronuntiation, I have been at the paines and charges to Cause the Accents, Tones or sounds to be affixed, (which some understand according to the Greeke Language, Acutes, Graves, Circumflexes) for example, in the second Leafe in the word Ewò He: the Sound or tone must not be put on E, but Wò, where the grave accent is.

In the same leafe, in the word *Ascowequássin*, the sound must not be on any of the Syllables, but on *quáss*, where the Acute or Sharp sound is.

In the same leafe, in the word Anspaumpmaûntam, the Sound must not be on any other Syllable but Màun where the Circumflex or long sounding Accent is.

6. The *English* for every *Indian* word or phrase stands in a straight line directly against the *Indian*: yet sometimes there are two words for the same thing (for their Language is exceeding copious, and they have five or six words sometimes for one thing) and then the English stands against them both; for example in the second leafe.

| Cowáuncakmish and Cuckquénamish | I pray your favour. |

An Helpe to the Native Language of That Part of America Called New-England

Chapter 1. Of Salutation—Observation

The natives are of two sorts (as the English are) some more rude and clownish, who are not so apt to salute, but upon salutation resalute lovingly. Others, and the generall, are sober and grave, and yet cheerfull in a meane, and as ready to begin a salutation as to resalute, which yet the English generally begin, out of desire to civilize them.

What cheare *Nétop* is the general salutation of all English toward them. *Nétop* is friend. *Netompaûog*, Friends.

They are exceedingly delighted with Salutations in their own Language.

Neèn, Keèn, Ewò,	I, you, he
Keénkaneen	You and I
Ascowequássin Ascowequassunnúmmis,	Good morrow,
Askuttaaquompsín,	Hou doe you?
Asnpaumpmaúntam,	I am very well.
Taubút paump maúntaman,	I am glad you are well.
Cowaúnckamish,	My service to you.

Observation

This word upon speciall Salutations they use, and upon some offence conceived by the *Sachim* or Prince against any; I have seen the party reverently doe obeysance, by stroking the Prince upon both his shoulders, and using this word,

Cowaúnckamish and Cuckquénamish	I pray your favour
Cowaúnkamuck,	He salutes you
Aspaumpmáuntam Sachim,	How doth the Prince?
Aspaumpmáuntam committamus	How doth your wife?

Aspaumpmaúntamwock cummuckiaûg?	How doth your children?
Konkeeteâug,	They are well.
Táubot ne paump maunthéttit,	I am glad they are well.
Túnna Cowâum?	Whence came you?
Tuckôteshana, Yò nowaùm,	I came that way.
Náwwatucknóteshem,	I came from farre.
Mattaâsu nóteshem,	I came from hard by. . . .

Observation

As commonly a single person hath no house, so after the death of a Husband or Wife, they often break up house, and live here and there a while with Friends to allay their excessive sorrowes.

Tou wuttûin?	Where lives he?
Awânickûchick,	Who are these?
Awaùn ewò?	Who is that?
Túnna úmwock, Tunna Wutshaûock,	Whence come they?
Yo nowékin,	I dwell here.
Yo ntiîn,	I live here.
Eîu or Nnîu?	Is it so?
Nux,	Yea.
Mat-nippompitámmen,	I have heard nothing.
Wésuonck,	A name.
Tocketussawêitch,	What is your name?
Taantússawese?	Doe you aske my name.
Ntússawese,	I am called, &c.
Matnowesuónckane,	I have no name.

Observation

Obscure and meane persons amongst them have no names: *nullius numeri* &c. as the Lord Jesus foretells his followers that their names should be cast out, Luk. 6.22. as not worthy to be named &c. Againe, because they abhorre to name the dead (Death being the King of Terrours to all naturall men: and though the natives hold the Soule to live ever, yet not holding a Resurrection they die and mourn without Hope.) In that respect I say, if any of their Sáchims or neighbours die who were of their names, they lay down those Names as dead.

Now ánnehick nowésuonck—I have forgot my name. Which is common amongst some of them, this being one Incivilitie amongst the more rusticall sort, not to call each other by their names, but Keen, You, Ewo, He &c.

Tahéna	What is his name?
Tahossowêtam,	What is the name of it?
Tahéttamen,	What call you this?
Teáqua,	What is this?
Yò néepoush,	Stay or stand here
Máttapsh,	Sit down.
Noónshem, Non ânum,	I cannot.
Tawhitch Kuppee Yaúmen,	What come you for?
Téaqua Kunnaúnta men,	What doe you fetch?
Chenock cuppeeyâu mis?	When came you?
Maish-Kitummâyi,	Just even now.
Kitummâyi nippeéam,	I came just now.
Yò commíttamus,	Is this your wife?
Yò cuppáppoos,	Is this your child?
Yò cummúckquachucks,	Is this your son?
Yò cuttaûnis,	Is this your daughter?
Wunnêtu,	It is a fine child. . . .
Tawhítch mat pe titeáyean?	Why come you not in?

Observ.

In this respect they are remarkably free and courteous, to invite all strangers in; and if any come to them upon any occasion, they request them to come in, if they come not in of themselves.

Awássish,	Warme you.
Máttapsh yóteg,	Sit by the fire.
Tocketúnnawem,	What say you?

Keén nétop,	Is it you friend.
Peeyàush nétop,	Come hither friend.
Pétitees,	Come in.
Kunnúnni,	Have you seene me?
Kunnúnnous,	I have seen you.
Taubot mequaun naméan,	I thank you for your kind remembrance.
Taûbotneanawáyean,	I thank you.
Taûbotne aunana méan,	I thank you for your love.

Observ.

I have acknowledged amongst them an heart sensible of kindnesses and have reaped kindnesse again from many, seaven yeares after, when I myselfe had forgotten &c. Hence the Lord Jesus exhorts his followers to doe good for evill; for otherwise sinners will do good for good, kindnesse for kindnesse. &c.

Cowàmmaunsh,	I love you.
Cowammaunûck,	He loves you.
Cowámmaus,	You are loving.
Cowáutam,	Understand you.
Nowautam,	I understand.
Cowawtam tawhitche nippeeyaûmen,	Doe you know why I come.
Cowannántam,	Have you forgotten?
Awanagusàntowosh,	Speake English.
Eenàntowash,	Speake Indian. . . .
Nippenowàntawem,	I am of another language.
Penowantowawhettûock,	They are of a divers Language.
Matnowawtauhettémina,	We understand not each other.
Nummaûchenèm,	I am sicke.
Cummaúchenem,	Are you sicke?
Tashúckunne cummauchenaúmis,	How long have you been sicke?
Nummauchêmin or Ntannetéimmin,	I will be going

Saûop cummauchêmin.	You shall goe to-morrow.
Maúchish or Anakish,	Be going.
Kuttannâwshesh,	Depart.
Mauchié or Annittui,	He is gone.
Kautanaûshant,	He being gone.
Mauchéhettit or Kautanawshàwhettit,	When are they gone?
Kukkowètous	I will lodge with you.
Yó Còwish,	Do lodge here.
Hawûnshech,	Farewell.
Chénock wonck cup peeyeâumen,	When will you be here againe?
Nétop tattà,	My friend, I cannot tell.

From these courteous Salutations, observe in generall; There is a savour of civility and courtesie even amongst these wild Americans, both amongst themselves and towards strangers.

More particular:

> 1. The courteous Pagan shall condemne
> Uncourteous Englishmen,
> Who live like Foxes, Beares and Wolves,
> Or Lyon in his Den.

> 2. Let none sing blessings to their soules,
> For that they courteous are:
> The wild Barbarians with no more
> Then nature, goe so farre:

> 3. If natures Sons both wild and tame,
> Humane and courteous be:
> How ill becomes it Sonnes of God
> To want Humanity?

1–7

Anne Bradstreet (1612–1672)

Like Winthrop and Williams, ANNE BRADSTREET (1612–1672) was born and educated in England. A committed Puritan, she became the first woman in the American colonies to publish a book of poetry, *The Tenth Muse Lately Sprung up in America* (London 1650). Her classical education (literature, history, language, and religion) is visible in her poetry, both in form and substance. While her poetry could include the political and historical, such as her "A Dialogue between Old England and New; Concerning their Present Troubles, Anno. 1642," a detailed analysis of the effect of the English Civil War on England and its American colony, Bradstreet is most famous for her personal poetry, included here. Bradstreet's years of sickness, isolation, and child birthing (she had eight children) are reflected in her "errand into the wilderness"— the Christian's spiritual journey and the colonist's lived reality of that experience—and heard in her conflict between her attachment to the secular world and her Puritan desire for the sacred.

≋ ≋ ≋

"By Night When Others Soundly Slept" (1657?)

1

By night when others soundly slept,
And hath at once both ease and Rest,
My waking eyes were open kept,
And so to lye I found it best.

2

I sought him whom my Soul did Love,
With tears I sought him earnestly;
He bow'd his ear down from Above,
In vain I did not seek or cry.

3

My hungry Soul he fill'd with Good;
He in his Bottle putt my teares,*

---

* "Put thou my tears into thy bottle: *are they* not in thy book?"—Psalm lvi. 8.

My smarting wounds washt in his blood,
And banisht thence my Doubts and feares.

4

What to my Saviour shall I give,
Who freely hath done this for me?
I'll serve him here whilst I shall live,
And Love him to Eternity.

"Before the Birth of One of Her Children" (1678)

All things within this fading world hath end,
Adversity doth still our joyes attend;
No tyes so strong, no friends so dear and sweet,
But with death's parting blow is sure to meet.
The sentence past is most irrevocable,
A common thing, yet oh, inevitable;
How soon, my Dear, death may my steps attend,
How soon't may be thy Lot to lose thy friend,
We both are ignorant, yet love bids me
These farewell lines to recommend to thee,
That when that knot's untied that made us one,
I may seem thine, who in effect am none.
And if I see not half my dayes that's due,
What nature would, God grant to yours and you;
The many faults that well you know I have,
Let be interr'd in my oblivious grave;
If any worth or virtue were in me,
Let that live freshly in thy memory
And when thou feel'st no grief, as I no harms,
Yet love thy dead, who long lay in thine arms:
And when thy loss shall be repaid with gains
Look to my little babes my dear remains.
And if thou love thy self, or loved'st me,
These O protect from step Dame's injury.
And if chance to thine eyes shall bring this verse,
With some sad sighs honour my absent Hearse;
And kiss this paper for thy love's dear sake,
Who with salt tears this last Farewel did take.

"To My Dear and Loving Husband" (1678)

If ever two were one, then surely we.
If ever man were lov'd by wife, then thee;
If ever wife was happy in a man,
Compare with me ye women if you can.
I prize thy love more than whole Mines of gold,
Or all the riches that the East doth hold.
My love is such that Rivers cannot quench,
Nor ought but love from thee, give recompence.
Thy love is such I can no way repay,
The heavens reward thee manifold I pray.
Then while we live, in love let's so persever,
That when we live no more, we may live ever.

2 :: Colonial Literature and the Road to Revolution

Brother Matías Sáenz of San Antonio (?–1754)

BROTHER MATÍAS SÁENZ OF SAN ANTONIO (?–1754) was one of the "Zacotecan Missionaries" sent to the Mexican province of Texas. He traveled through much of Texas, was a Franciscan Friar at Nuestra Señora de Guadalupe de los Nacogdoches Mission near modern-day Nacogdoches, and was appointed to leadership roles in several Mexican colonial universities. He ardently promoted the cause of the missions in Texas, arguing eloquently for them in his writing and during stays at the Vatican and in Spain. Historian Stafford Poole has credited him with helping to popularize devotion to the Our Lady of the Virgin of Guadalupe beyond Mexico City. In "Lord, if the Shepherd Does Not Give Heed" (1724), a letter to the Spanish king, in which he begs for more Spanish families to settle the mission, more funds, and better military and political support, one can see the priest's literary and rhetorical skills as well as his humanity.

≈ ≈ ≈

"Lord, if the Shepherd Does Not Give Heed" (1724)
("Señor, si el pastor no escucha")

Lord,

If the Shepherd does not give heed to the bleating of the sheep; if the Father does not hear the weeping of his sons; if the Lord does not attend to the cry of his vassals, he will not be able to feel his loving obligation in their times of need, as Saint Bernard says with the common people: "Eyes that don't see, heart that doesn't break."*

The urgent needs of the inhabitants of the New Philippines, province of Texas Indians, newly conquered during the timely government of the Marquis of Valero in New Spain, are placed today before the nobles and Your Catholic Majesty's devout men, so that You may hear them as their Pastor, encourage them as their Father, and protect and provide for them as their King and natural Lord, considering the love with which they ask for it in their need, and Your Majesty's obligation to intervene; and so that Your Majesty may become more informed about the nature of this difficulty, I should first put briefly before Your royal consideration what this province is, its situation, and who its inhabitants are, as well as the time of its acquisition.

In the year 1716, it had been about one hundred years since those kingdoms gained an inch of land. Divine Providence decreed that with twenty-five men I enter (against all risks) with forty religious companions of the Apostolic College of our Lady of Guadalupe of Zacatecas and another five from the College of the Holy Cross of Queretaro. With immense effort we penetrated almost three hundred leagues, from the last stronghold of Christianity as far as the aforementioned province of Texas Indians, in whose district are innumerable barbarous mountain-dwelling nations, and there we erected six missions, which are still maintained today. The last mission lies in view of a garrison of Frenchmen. Receiving news of this, I went to sound out their line, that it might not pass forward until I gave notice to the Crowns.

This province, Lord, is so rich in minerals that there is no hill that is not a treasure; it is so lush in flowers and plants, rivers, and fountains, that it is a paradise. It is so fertile in fruits that it is a wonder. For there is no one that the land does not receive, yielding more than a hundred percent; it abounds with wild fruit, such as grapes, plums, Chinese pomegranates, loquats, nuts, and chestnuts, and many others in abundance, such as indigo plants and diverse medicinal plants. There is an abundance of substantial foods, admirable grasses for all kind of cattle, turkeys, partridges, and other birds. The rivers and fountains have rich waters endowed with many kinds of fish. Its inhabitants are barbarous Gentiles, idolaters without discipline or government, whose homes are small thatched huts, as well as some caves. They move from time to time to other places to seek out the wild fruits from which they live, roots, and hunting ground for bears, wild boars, and deer. They go about naked from head to foot, and only in the winter do they fight off the cold with animal skins, having no artful design beyond that afforded by the natural shape of the

* ["Out of sight, out of mind."—*translator's note*]

wild beast skinned for the purpose. Notwithstanding, they are docile, naturally inclined to the Spaniards that treat them well, because they sense in them
protection and defense against their enemies. They are located near the north,
at thirty-two degrees. They have a healthy constitution, like a Castilian. From
the center of this province, looking toward the north, New Mexico lies at a distance of three hundred leagues, as prudence dictates. Toward the south lies the
province of Tampico at a distance of about two hundred leagues. Toward the
east, it runs into the Port of Holy Mary of Galvez, on the coast of the Gulf of
Mexico, with its neighboring Port of Movila, occupied by the French, probably
at a distance of two hundred or more leagues from the Line of the Nachitoos,
neighbors of our Texas Indians, as far as the aforementioned Movila, a district
with settled towns and garrisons of Frenchmen. The French capital is New
Orleans, located on the River of the Fence, opening into the sea. This river
is very wide, because the Missouri River, the Mississippi River, and the Red
Shore—all large rivers—run into it. To the northeast are the English and the
sea pirates, whom we have not reached because of the opposition these nations
present along with their Indian allies. To the west is the new kingdom of Leon,
through whose border we entered. The barbarous nations that occupy these
areas are innumerable and abundant. Having described in brief the province—
its setting and inhabitants—I venture to present before Your Majesty's compassionate gaze the necessities of our new sons and vassals, who appeal to you for
Your help and providence as Shepherd, Father, King, and natural Lord.

First, they need economic and doctrinal policy, which requires neighbors
of Christian customs, hardworking like the Galicians or Islanders, who can
teach, instruct, and encourage them in profiting from the land, in making
homes and wool fabrics, and in the other trades befitting a well-organized
Republic. The Creoles of America cannot serve this purpose because, for the
most part, they are men too delicate for work due to their physique; the rest
are weak and lazy due to the fecundity and abundance of their countries, and
most of them lack customs befitting such principles. Since these infidels, in
their savage roughness, receive the Holy Faith and Christian doctrine more
through the eyes than through the ear, they need approved exemplars for the
teaching of doctrine, the Holy Sacrifice of the Mass, obedience, and reverence
of priests and evangelical ministers, as the early inhabitants of those kingdoms
had. Thus will be achieved here (as was achieved there) much good effect. By
such measures, those lost souls, Christ's scattered sheep, may be gathered to
the pasture of life and forsake death's morbid fare, to which the Demon has
them blindly bound. Likewise, with such company they may defend and secure themselves against their enemies, by reason of whom they live dispersed
even during peacetime in order to protect themselves from sudden assaults of

war, for which they only gather at specified times and places, where they die like ants, giving the Demon an abundant harvest. It is a shame that in Catholic hearts there is little room for pain at the thought of so many lost souls; it is a disgrace to the precious blood of our Redeemer, of whom Your Majesty is the substitute, before whom as before a Compassionate Father these wretches and forsaken children manifest their need.

As to a King and Lord, they make plain the loss that threatens, not only those lands and provinces, but also all the kingdoms of New Spain, within view of the French, English, and sea pirates that approach them, having power over many Indian nations, which are quite skillful in the use of firearms, pikes, machetes, spears, and sickles, with which they are already supplied. There is no force that can resist them when they break out in war, and if (may God forbid) there is no peace, or there is a discontinuation of arms within the European powers, any of them will be able to enter through those areas as if through their own house as far as Mexico because they are all firm and open lands presenting no resistance at all beyond the three hundred men (in the Bay of the Holy Spirit, on the San Antonio River, and among the Texas Indians) that Your Majesty has distributed along a distance of more than two hundred leagues, which serve more to hold possession of the dominions than to act as a defense in emergencies.

Here, my Lord, is where Your Majesty's attention is needed. These nations of French, English, and sea pirates are made up of Huguenots and various heretics, which proclaim freedom of conscience wherever they go, a powerful attraction for individuals—content with the protection of weapons—to maintain their evil customs and false religions, which with the Demon's help come about spontaneously. If such a misfortune ended here, it would be a hard thing, but not the greatest cruelty. But at the heart, in the kingdom of the Mexican provinces, our Holy Faith is so sick, and the palates of most of their inhabitants are so insensible of the sweetness and tenderness of the Law of Christ that if this word of freedom of conscience settles among them they would run quickly to the enemies, these being more numerous. For if the few faithful Spaniards—vassals surrendered to Your Majesty—were withdrawn, the greater part of the body consists of Negroes, mulattos, half-breeds, Indians, and mestizos, so many that there are five hundred of them for every Spaniard. This, my Lord, is cause for great concern, and so public and notorious that there is no one who has been in those kingdoms that would not say so. As an esteemed witness, the Marquis of Valero can attest to it. His witness should be heeded without qualms or difficulty, so that a remedy may be instituted before more harm is done. Besides being swift, the remedy is easy and not costly to the Royal Reserve. Rather, if well considered, it will result in the increase of Your

Majesty's Royal Profits (incentive enough for it to be carried out) and likewise the dissemination of our Holy Faith and the preservation and expansion of Your Majesty's dominions, as I will here make evident.

If Your Majesty sends (as you should) 500 families (from Galicia if possible; if not, from the Islands), settling 150 in the Bay of the Holy Spirit and the garrison of San Antonio, 250 in the appropriate places belonging to the Texas Indians, these families will be the first to occupy the pasture of the foreign nations dwelling in those regions, and the following year 200 military positions within their populations may be discontinued, out of the 300 that Your Majesty maintains among the aforementioned Texas Indians, the garrison of San Antonio, and the Bay of the Holy Spirit. And from the 1354 pesos required for the settlement of these 300, soldiers will lower their expenses 904 pesos each year. Considering subsequent years, many millions will be saved for the Royal Treasury. And these same retired soldiers will be able to remain neighbors with the help of the settlers' income. The results of this will be the fructification of those lands, the acquisition of the nations, an increase in royal taxes, tributes, and the rest of the royal laws, with the greatest increase of Christianity, whose exemplar we have in the Island of Havana, with the product of its treaties and tobacco, just as also in the other provinces of the American Empire, which has maintained and still maintains the Spanish Peninsula and filled all the European powers with wealth.

With these measures, my Lord, the foreign nations will be contained, Your Majesty's dominions and the rule of Jesus Christ will be expanded in the aggregation of the countless nations that will come under the Spaniards' protection, and Your Majesty will obtain the glory of Your predecessors, from the undefeated Charles V, Hercules I of the New World, up until Your Majesty, all of whom endeavored to exude Catholic zeal for God's interests. Even Your Majesty's Kingly Father, whose tenderness softens the very stones, manifests it clearly in the Golden Letter, which he writes to You in his courageous and inimitable retirement.

In short, my Lord, what is requested is very little, but Your interest in it is great, and everything will be put at risk if You do not take an interest because, of all the things that make up a monarchy like this one, the lifeblood of this body is that which flows through the mineral veins of that American kingdom. A body—maintained with flesh and blood—must not neglect its own preservation. If (may God forbid) You come to be in need, it would be due to the ruin of America, with the inexplicable misfortune of an insult against the faith of God and the dwelling place of Jesus Christ, the Demon remaining enthroned and our God poorly served. To this end, my Lord, God has brought me from those coarse regions to Your Majesty's royal feet, escorted by the Marquis of

Valero, who can attest to this truth with more elegant and effective arguments, as one who has assessed the difficulties.

Also, my Lord, I should put before Your Majesty's royal consideration the very grave need for spiritual nourishment that the vassals in the two kingdoms of Leon and New Biscay suffer. One is the boundary of the Texas Indians, and the other is New Mexico. Thus because of the lack of regulations in the ecclesiastical sphere and the excesses of governors in the political and military spheres who look only to their own interests, Your Majesty's vassals suffer detriment, and damage is done to the service of both You and Your Father. In the two kingdoms of Leon and New Biscay, most die without the Holy Sacrament of Confirmation because no bishops have arrived in these places. This is not the bishops' fault, because the bishopric of Durango and that of Guadalajara, to whom it belongs, are 350 leagues in breadth, the space in between mostly unpopulated, having no houses for 40 or 50 leagues, and in many of them unbelieving enemy Indians are a threat that has imperiled travelers in the past and imperils them each day. The bishops send visitors—usually strong young men—to check on their parishioners. Of these visitors, none can confirm and many of them, instead of cleansing the sheep of their sicknesses and filth, dress them with holy documents, strip them, and make their sicknesses worse with the new contingencies that they bring about, which it is not my place to recount. In New Mexico, until now no bishop or visitor has arrived, such that the people there and in the surrounding areas live like sheep without a Shepherd, although they have priests. I can only lament so much misery. Plants deprived of the Sun's beams cannot bear ripe fruit. Your Catholic Majesty is the firmament of those lights from which these blessings come.

What follows this is that the governors exalt their power, flaunting it as more than royal and pontifical through their tyrannies, intimidating the clergy and the laypeople beyond measure, not holding fast to the laws of God and of Your Majesty, but to their own interests and whims. The viceroys of Mexico can do nothing because of the delay in appeals for their patients, for the tribunal is almost five hundred leagues away; neither can these poor people get to their tribunal, for lack of means, and because afterward those who expressed their piteous complaint are strongly oppressed. And if anyone has the courage to go and deliver the information, the judges will not sympathize because they themselves are not persecuted or because, wishing to maintain advantageous friendships and the governors' favor, they serve as false witnesses against reason. Some person or other facilitates the false oath in such remote regions, and all this causes the land to end up unpopulated, because many poor people leave it and go elsewhere.

Furthermore, these governors usually employ soldiers in the service of their estates, their herds, and perhaps in Your Majesty's postal services, taking for themselves the money that should be paid to them. As a result, the governors being few and occupied with such cases, the borders are not patrolled, and the land is not monitored for dangers. The enemy Indians take advantage of this to steal cattle and to kill people on the ranches as well as unsuspecting travelers, a circumstance which obliges them to leave the area. This, my Lord, is a point that could not be verified by some investigating judge, for the reasons already given. But I have witnessed it firsthand while carrying out my apostolic duties in these areas. And I, as Your loyal vassal and evangelical minister, must inform Your Majesty of it, guaranteeing (as I do) that I am not persuaded by anything but service to both You and Your Father and the unburdening of my conscience upon Yours, to which God alone is my witness.

In addition, my Lord, the soldiers are starving, most of them naked, and many unarmed, because the governors and captains receive their salaries and pay them with tent fabrics, so highly priced that what is worth six is given for twenty, such that the soldiers lose two-thirds of their salary and thus go about always indebted and lacking what they need. As a result, they run away, in many cases because they can't pay their dues. When soldiers die, their replacements are charged with the debt of the dead. Not wishing to take the position under this condition, they leave it vacant until the governors and captains are paid what they have no right to demand. Thus, the soldiers being fewer, the royal service finds itself very defective.

I know not, my Lord, what might rectify this problem. But if we latch onto the experience of our ancient exemplars, it seems to me best that Your Majesty provide bishops for the vineyard of New Biscay, New Mexico, the kingdom of Leon, and people zealous in the service of God, of souls, and of Your Majesty. The presence of unselfish apostolic men will allow the inhabitants of those places to apply themselves to their work with pleasure, being content with those scarcities or the mediocrity that those jurisdictions offer at present, such that they might endure it with decorum. And if Your Majesty determined to confer upon these bishops the civil and military governments, with the same salary that those in charge at present receive, many other benefits would follow from this relief of the bishops. First, the parishioners and soldiers, being watched over as by fathers, would be schooled in charity (not forcibly compelled): if they accept their duty to give alms to those in need, they will not take work away from the poor. Second, in the shadow and company of similar prelates, the lands would be populated, as was the Diocese of Durango, which before found itself in similar circumstances until a bishop was placed there. Third, the Holy Gospel would shine more brightly, Christian doctrine would be practiced more, and the priests and justices would be more respected. Fourth, Your Majesty and the viceroys of Mexico would have more esteemed witnesses of news and cases of urgency. Fifth, and most remarkable, an evil that is a great impediment to the propagation of our Holy Faith would be avoided, namely, that until now the governors and captains, having warrant to monitor the land, enter the Infidels' land to steal children and women to give as gifts to their friends, relatives, and comrades and to sell them multiple times as slaves, against all decrees and divine and royal laws. These insults make it inevitable that some be injured, others killed, and the poor frightened Indians deterred from our Holy Faith. Grieving like lions robbed of their cubs, they run enraged to the mountains, hills, and passes, gathering nations together for vengeance. Hence the land is always in disorder. With a charitable and zealous bishop, an apostolic governor, these problems would be avoided because he would seek them out carefully and affectionately and give them those things they find appealing, such as trinkets, glass beads, corals, sashes, mirrors, combs, knives, tobacco leaves, wool, cloths, and other things, to which they come like lambs in droves. Experience with the Indians of Texas has taught me all this. To seek them out and attract them, one should give alms, for this is the only gunpowder with which these innocents can be conquered, and their swords and weapons surrendered. And it is not much; such small gifts break down their resistance, accustomed as they are to stark living.

If Your Majesty wishes more authentic and general news to testify to this truth I've expressed, the Marquis of Valero can satisfy You, for I am certain that he has kept Your Majesty's Kingly Father informed from Mexico about the matters of his government. This very day he has papers, minutes, and instructions for the aforementioned bishops with all the grounds necessary for their elevation and the cogent rationale for the advantage to be gained by it. Your Majesty can learn from said marquis what the most prudent resolution is. If it seems wisest to Your Majesty to appoint a minister of intelligence over those regions, so that he might hear me out and I might answer for any difficulties that he identifies, I will carry it out in a godly fashion. I am ready to execute everything Your Majesty decrees, for I consider such action to be of great service to God, to the people, and to Your Majesty. May Your years be many. Madrid, April 7, 1724.

Brother Matías Sáenz of San Antonio

Apostolic Missionary

2–2

Benjamin Franklin (1706–1790)

Printer, businessperson, writer, politician, revolutionary leader, philosopher, and inventor, BENJAMIN FRANKLIN (1706–1790) embodied the American success story. Like many other American writers, Franklin began writing while working as a printer's devil, setting type for a newspaper. His role in the newspaper business grew, and he became a publisher of the *Pennsylvania Gazette*, placing him in an excellent position to shape public opinion with his noted wit. He achieved fame and influence, too, with his *Poor Richard's Almanack*, which featured useful information along with homely adages and apothegms as well as humorous commentary. His autobiography with its list of virtues and rags-to-riches story has influenced American writers from Frederick Douglass to F. Scott Fitzgerald. Franklin's cartoon "Join or Die," featuring the rattlesnake cut in pieces, published in 1754, is considered the first political cartoon; in 1775, as the American Revolution began, he revived the rattlesnake as a symbol of American character. Two other selections here, from the 1780s, address American character. In his "Remarks Concerning the Savages," Franklin argues that indigenous peoples are anything but "savages," and recommends their civility, honesty, and tolerance. In his "Information to Those Who Would Remove," he reminds Europeans settling in America that opportunity necessitates industry.

"The Rattle-Snake as a Symbol of America" (1775)

Messrs. Printers,

I observed on one of the drums belonging to the marines now raising, there was painted a Rattle-Snake, with this modest motto under it, "Don't tread on me." As I know it is the custom to have some device on the arms of every country, I supposed this may have been intended for the arms of America; and as I have nothing to do with public affairs, and as my time is perfectly my own, in order to divert an idle hour, I sat down to guess what could have been intended by this uncommon device—I took care, however, to consult on this occasion a person who is acquainted with heraldry, from whom I learned, that it is a rule among the learned in that science "That the worthy properties of the animal, of the crest-born, shall be considered," and, "That the base ones cannot have been intended"; he likewise informed me that the ancients considered the serpent as an emblem of wisdom, and in a certain attitude of endless duration—both which circumstances I suppose may have been had in view.—Having gained this intelligence, and recollecting that countries are sometimes represented by animals peculiar to them, it occurred to me that the Rattle-Snake is found in no other quarter of the world besides America, and may therefore have been chosen, on that account, to represent her.

But then "the worthy properties" of a Snake I judged would be hard to point out—This rather raised than suppressed my curiosity, and having frequently seen the Rattle-Snake, I ran over in my mind every property by which she was distinguished, not only from other animals, but from those of the same genus or class of animals, endeavouring to fix some meaning to each, not wholly inconsistent with common sense.

I recollected that her eye excelled in brightness that of any other animal, and that she has no eye-lids—She may therefore be esteemed an emblem of vigilance.—She never begins an attack, nor, when once engaged, ever surrenders: She is therefore an emblem of magnanimity and true courage.—As if anxious to prevent all pretentions of quarrelling with her, the weapons with which nature has furnished her, she conceals in the roof of her mouth, so that, to those who are unacquainted with her, she appears to be a most defenceless animal; and even when those weapons are shewn and extended for her defence, they appear weak and contemptible; but their wounds however small, are decisive and fatal:—Conscious of this, she never wounds till she has generously given notice, even to her enemy, and cautioned him against the danger of treading on her.—Was I wrong, Sir, in thinking this a strong picture of the temper and conduct of America? The poison of her teeth is the necessary means of digesting her food, and at the same time is certain destruction to her enemies—This may be understood to intimate that those things which are destructive to our enemies, may be to us not only harmless, but absolutely necessary to our existence.—I confess I was wholly at a loss what to make of the rattles, till I went back and counted them and found them just thirteen, exactly the number of the Colonies united in America; and I recollected too that this was the only part of the snake that increased in numbers—Perhaps it might be only fancy, but, I conceited the painter had shown a half formed additional rattle, which, I suppose, may have been intended to represent the province of Canada.—'Tis curious and amazing to observe how distinct and independent of each other the rattles of this animal are, and yet how firmly they are united together, so as never to be separated but by breaking them to pieces.—One of those rattles singly, is incapable of producing sound, but the ringing of thirteen together, is sufficient to alarm the boldest man living. The Rattle-Snake is solitary, and associates with her kind only when it is necessary for their preservation—In winter, the warmth of a number together will preserve their lives, while singly, they would probably perish—The power of fascination attributed to her, by a generous construction, may be understood to mean, that those who consider the liberty and blessings America affords, and once come over to her, never afterwards leave her, but spend their lives with her.—She strongly resembles America in this, that she is beautiful in youth and her beauty increaseth with her age, "her tongue also is blue and forked as the lightning, and her abode is among impenetrable rocks."

Having pleased myself with reflections of this kind, I communicated my sentiments to a neighbor of mine, who has a surprising readiness at guessing at every thing which relates to publick affairs, and indeed I should be jealous of his reputation, in that way, was it not that the event constantly shews that he has guessed wrong—He instantly declared it as his sentiments, that the Congress meant to allude to Lord North's declaration in the House of Commons, that he never would relax his measures until he had brought America to his feet, and to intimate to his Lordship, that were she brought to his feet, it would be dangerous treading on her.—But, I am positive he has guessed wrong, for I am sure the Congress would not condescend, at this time of day, to take the least notion of his Lordship in that or any other way.—In which opinion, I am determined to remain your humble servant,

An American Guesser

"Information to Those Who Would Remove to America"* (1782)

Many persons in Europe, having directly or by letters, express'd to the writer of this, who is well acquainted with North America, their desire of transporting and establishing themselves in that country; but who appear to have formed, thro' ignorance, mistaken ideas and expectations of what is to be obtained there; he thinks it may be useful, and prevent inconvenient, expensive, and fruitless removals and voyages of improper persons, if he gives some clearer and truer notions of that part of the world, than appear to have hitherto prevailed.

He finds it is imagined by numbers, that the inhabitants of North America are rich, capable of rewarding, and dispos'd to reward, all sorts of ingenuity; that they are at the same time ignorant of all the sciences, and, consequently, that strangers, possessing talents in the Belles-Lettres, fine arts, &c., must be highly esteemed, and so well paid, as to become easily rich themselves; that there are also abundance of profitable offices to be disposed of, which the natives are not qualified to fill; and that, having few persons of family among them, strangers of birth must be greatly respected, and of course easily obtain the best of those offices, which will make all their fortunes; that the governments too, to encourage emigrations from Europe, not only pay the expence of personal transportation, but give lands gratis to strangers, with Negroes to work for them, utensils of husbandry, and stocks of cattle. These are all wild imaginations; and those who go to America with expectations founded upon them will surely find themselves disappointed.

The truth is, that though there are in that country few people so miserable as the poor of Europe, there are also very few that in Europe would be called rich; it is rather a general happy mediocrity that prevails. There are few great proprietors of the soil, and few tenants; most people cultivate their own lands, or follow some handicraft or merchandise; very few rich enough to live idly upon their rents or incomes, or to pay the high prices given in Europe for paintings, statues, architecture, and the other works of art, that are more curious than useful. Hence the natural geniuses, that have arisen in America with such talents, have uniformly quitted that country for Europe, where they can be more suitably rewarded. It is true, that letters and mathematical knowledge are in esteem there, but they are at the same time more common than is apprehended; there being already existing nine colleges or universities, viz. four in New England, and one in each of the provinces of New York, New Jersey, Pensilvania, Maryland, and Virginia, all furnish'd with learned professors; besides

* Believed to have been written in September, 1782.—Ed.

a number of smaller academies; these educate many of their youth in the languages, and those sciences that qualify men for the professions of divinity, law, or physick. Strangers indeed are by no means excluded from exercising those professions; and the quick increase of inhabitants everywhere gives them a chance of employ, which they have in common with the Natives. Of civil offices, or employments, there are few; no superfluous ones, as in Europe; and it is a rule establish'd in some of the states, that no office should be so profitable as to make it desirable. The 36th article of the Constitution of Pennsilvania, runs expressly in these words; "As every freeman, to preserve his independence, (if he has not a sufficient estate) ought to have some profession, calling, trade, or farm, whereby he may honestly subsist, there can be no necessity for, nor use in, establishing offices of profit; the usual effects of which are dependance and servility, unbecoming freemen, in the possessors and expectants; faction, contention, corruption, and disorder among the people. Wherefore, whenever an office, thro' increase of fees or otherwise, becomes so profitable, as to occasion many to apply for it, the profits ought to be lessened by the lagislature."

These ideas prevailing more or less in all the United States, it cannot be worth any man's while, who has a means of living at home, to expatriate himself, in hopes of obtaining a profitable civil office in America; and, as to military offices, they are at an end with the war, the armies being disbanded. Much less is it adviseable for a person to go thither, who has no other quality to recommend him but his birth. In Europe it has indeed its value; but it is a commodity that cannot be carried to a worse market than that of America, where people do not inquire concerning a stranger, *What is he?* but, *What can he do?* If he has any useful art, he is welcome; and if he exercises it, and behaves well, he will be respected by all that know him; but a mere man of quality, who, on that account, wants to live upon the public, by some office or salary, will be despis'd and disregarded. The husband-man is in honor there, and even the mechanic, because their employments are useful. The people have a saying, that God Almighty is himself a mechanic, the greatest in the univers; and he is respected and admired more for the variety, ingenuity, and utility of his handyworks, than for the antiquity of his family. They are pleas'd with the observation of a negro, and frequently mention it, that *Boccarorra* (meaning the white men) *make de black man workee, make de horse workee, make de ox workee, make ebery ting workee; only de hog. He, de hog, no workee; he eat, he drink, he walk about, he go to sleep when he please, he libb like a gentleman.* According to these opinions of the Americans, one of them would think himself more oblig'd to a genealogist, who could prove for him that his ancestors and relations for ten generations had been ploughmen, smiths, carpenters, turners, weavers, tanners, or even shoemakers, and consequently that they were useful members of society; than if he could only prove that they were gentlemen, doing nothing of value, but living idly on the labour of others, mere *fruges consumere nati*,* and otherwise *good for nothing*, till by their death their estates, like the carcass of the negro's gentleman-hog, come to be *cut up*.

With regard to encouragements for strangers from government, they are really only what are derived from good laws and liberty. Strangers are welcome, because there is room enough for them all, and therefore the old inhabitants are not jealous of them; the laws protect them sufficiently, so that they have no need of the patronage of great men; and every one will enjoy securely the profits of his industry. But, if he does not bring a fortune with him, he must work and be industrious to live. One or two years' residence gives him all the rights of a citizen; but the government does not at present, whatever it may have done in former times, hire people to become settlers, by paying their passages, giving land, negroes, utensils, stock, or any other kind of emolument whatsoever. In short, America is the land of labour, and by no means what the English call *Lubberland*, and the French *Pays de Cocagne*, where the streets are said to be pav'd with half-peck loaves, the houses til'd with pancakes, and where the fowls fly about ready roasted, crying, *Come eat me!*

Who then are the kind of persons to whom an emigration to America may be advantageous? And what are the advantages they may reasonably expect?

Land being cheap in that country, from the vast forests still void of inhabitants, and not likely to be occupied in an age to come, insomuch that the propriety of an hundred acres of fertile soil full of wood may be obtained near the frontiers, in many places, for eight or ten guineas, hearty young labouring men, who understand the husbandry of corn and cattle, which is nearly the same in that country as in Europe, may easily establish themselves there. A little money sav'd of the good wages they receive there, while they work for others, enables them to buy the land and begin their plantation, in which they are assisted by the good-will of their neighbours, and some credit. Multitudes of poor people from England, Ireland, Scotland, and Germany, have by this means in a few years become wealthy farmers, who, in their own countries, where all the lands are fully occupied, and the wages of labour low, could never have emerged from the poor condition wherein they were born.

From the salubrity of the air, the healthiness of the climate, the plenty of good provisions, and the encouragement to early marriages by the certainty of subsistence in cultivating the earth, the increase of inhabitants by natural

---

* "..... born / Merely to eat up the corn."—Watts.

generation is very rapid in America, and becomes still more so by the accession of strangers; hence there is a continual demand for more artisans of all the necessary and useful kinds, to supply those cultivators of the earth with houses, and with furniture and utensils of the grosser sorts, which cannot so well be brought from Europe. Tolerably good workmen in any of those mechanic arts are sure to find employ, and to be well paid for their work, there being no restraints preventing strangers from exercising any art they understand, nor any permission necessary. If they are poor, they begin first as servants or journeymen; and if they are sober, industrious, and frugal, they soon become masters, establish themselves in business, marry, raise families, and become respectable citizens.

Also, persons of moderate fortunes and capitals, who, having a number of children to provide for, are desirous of bringing them up to industry, and to secure estates for their posterity, have opportunities of doing it in America, which Europe does not afford. There they may be taught and practise profitable mechanic arts, without incurring disgrace on that account, but on the contrary acquiring respect by such abilities. There small capitals laid out in lands, which daily become more valuable by the increase of people, afford a solid prospect of ample fortunes thereafter for those children. The writer of this has known several instances of large tracts of land, bought, on what was then the frontier of Pensilvania, for ten pounds per hundred acres, which after 20 years, when the settlements had been extended far beyond them, sold readily, without any improvement made upon them, for three pounds per acre. The acre in America is the same with the English acre, or the acre of Normandy.

Those, who desire to understand the state of government in America, would do well to read the constitutions of the several states, and the Articles of Confederation that bind the whole together for general purposes, under the direction of one assembly, called the Congress. These constitutions have been printed, by order of Congress, in America; two editions of them have also been printed in London; and a good translation of them into French has lately been published at Paris.

Several of the princes of Europe having of late years, from an opinion of advantage to arise by producing all commodities and manufactures within their own dominions, so as to diminish or render useless their importations, have endeavoured to entice workmen from other countries by high salaries, privileges, &c. Many persons, pretending to be skilled in various great manufactures, imagining that America must be in want of them, and that the Congress would probably be dispos'd to imitate the princes above mentioned, have proposed to go over, on Condition of having their passages paid, lands given, salaries appointed, exclusive privileges for terms of years, &c. Such persons, on reading the Articles of Confederation, will find, that the Congress have no power committed to them, or money put into their hands, for such purposes; and that if any such encouragement is given, it must be by the government of some separate state. This, however, has rarely been done in America; and, when it has been done, it has rarely succeeded, so as to establish a manufacture, which the country was not yet so ripe for as to encourage private persons to set it up; labour being generally too dear there, and hands difficult to be kept together, every one desiring to be a master, and the cheapness of lands inclining many to leave trades for agriculture. Some indeed have met with success, and are carried on to advantage; but they are generally such as require only a few hands, or wherein great part of the work is performed by machines. Things that are bulky, and of so small value as not well to bear the expence of freight, may often be made cheaper in the country than they can be imported; and the manufacture of such things will be profitable wherever there is a sufficient demand. The farmers in America produce indeed a good deal of wool and flax; and none is exported, it is all work'd up; but it is in the way of domestic manufacture, for the use of the family. The buying up quantities of wool and flax, with the design to employ spinners, weavers, &c., and form great establishments, producing quantities of linen and woollen goods for sale, has been several times attempted in different provinces; but those projects have generally failed, goods of equal value being imported cheaper. And when the governments have been solicited to support such schemes by encouragements, in money, or by imposing duties on importation of such goods, it has been generally refused, on this principle, that, if the country is ripe for the manufacture, it may be carried on by private persons to advantage; and if not, it is a folly to think of forcing nature. Great establishments of manufacture require great numbers of poor to do the work for small wages; these poor are to be found in Europe, but will not be found in America, till the lands are all taken up and cultivated, and the excess of people, who cannot get land, want employment. The manufacture of silk, they say, is natural in France, as that of cloth in England, because each country produces in plenty the first material; but if England will have a manufacture of silk as well as that of cloth, and France one of cloth as well as that of silk, these unnatural operations must be supported by mutual prohibitions, or high duties on the importation of each other's goods; by which means the workmen are enabled to tax the home consumer by greater prices, while the higher wages they receive makes them neither happier nor richer, since they only drink more and work less. Therefore the governments in America do nothing to encourage such projects. The people, by this means, are not impos'd on, either by the merchant or mechanic. If the merchant demands too much profit on imported shoes, they buy of the shoemaker; and if he asks too high a price, they take them of the merchant; thus the two professions are checks on each other. The shoemaker, however, has, on the whole, a considerable profit upon his labour in America, beyond what he had in Europe, as he can add to his price a sum nearly equal to all the expences of freight and commission, risque or insurance, &c., necessarily charged by the merchant. And the case is the same with the workmen in every other mechanic art. Hence it is, that artisans generally live better and more easily in America than in Europe; and such as are good œconomists make a comfortable provision for age, and for their children. Such may, therefore, remove with advantage to America.

In the long-settled countries of Europe, all arts, trades, professions, farms, &c., are so full, that it is difficult for a poor man, who has children, to place them where they may gain, or learn to gain, a decent livelihood. The artisans, who fear creating future rivals in business, refuse to take apprentices, but upon conditions of money, maintenance, or the like, which the parents are unable to comply with. Hence the youth are dragg'd up in ignorance of every gainful art, and oblig'd to become soldiers, or servants, or thieves, for a subsistence. In America, the rapid increase of inhabitants takes away that fear of rivalship, and artisans willingly receive apprentices from the hope of profit by their labour, during the remainder of the time stipulated, after they shall be instructed. Hence it is easy for poor families to get their children instructed; for the artisans are so desirous of apprentices, that many of them will even give money to the parents, to have boys from ten to fifteen years of age bound apprentices to them till the age of twenty-one; and many poor parents have, by that means, on their arrival in the country, raised money enough to buy land sufficient to establish themselves, and to subsist the rest of their family by agriculture. These contracts for apprentices are made before a magistrate, who regulates the agreement according to reason and justice, and, having in view the formation of a future useful citizen, obliges the master to engage by a written indenture, not only that, during the time of service stipulated, the apprentice shall be duly provided with meat, drink, apparel, washing, and lodging; and, at its expiration, with a compleat new suit of cloaths, but also that he shall be taught to read, write, and cast accompts; and that he shall be well instructed in the art or profession of his master, or some other, by which he may afterwards gain a livelihood, and be able in his turn to raise a family. A copy of this indenture is given to the apprentice or his friends, and the magistrate keeps a record of it, to which recourse may be had, in case of failure by the master in any point of performance. This desire among the masters, to have more hands employ'd in working for them, induces them to pay the passages of young persons, of both sexes, who, on their arrival, agree to serve them one, two, three, or four years; those, who have already learnt a trade, agreeing for a shorter term, in proportion to their skill, and the consequent immediate value of their service; and those, who have none, agreeing for a longer term, in consideration of being taught an art their poverty would not permit them to acquire in their own country.

The almost general mediocrity of fortune that prevails in America obliging its people to follow some business for subsistence, those vices, that arise usually from idleness, are in a great measure prevented. Industry and constant employment are great preservatives of the morals and virtue of a nation. Hence bad examples to youth are more rare in America, which must be a comfortable consideration to parents. To this may be truly added, that serious religion, under its various denominations, is not only tolerated, but respected and practised. Atheism is unknown there; infidelity rare and secret; so that persons may live to a great age in that country, without having their piety shocked by meeting with either an atheist or an infidel. And the divine being seems to have manifested his approbation of the mutual forbearance and kindness with which the different sects treat each other, by the remarkable prosperity with which He has been pleased to favour the whole country.

"Remarks Concerning the Savages of North America"* (1784)

Savages we call them, because their manners differ from ours, which we think the perfection of civility; they think the same of theirs.

Perhaps, if we could examine the manners of different nations with impartiality, we should find no people so rude, as to be without any rules of politeness; nor any so polite, as not to have some remains of rudeness.

The Indian men, when young, are hunters and warriors; when old, counsellors; for all their government is by counsel of the sages; there is no force, there are no prisons, no officers to compel obedience, or inflict punishment. Hence they generally study oratory, the best speaker having the most influence. The Indian women till the ground, dress the food, nurse and bring up the children, and preserve and hand down to posterity the memory of public transactions. These employments of men and women are accounted natural and honourable. Having few artificial wants, they have abundance of leisure for improvement by conversation. Our laborious manner of life, compared

---

* This paper was published in a separate pamphlet in England, in the year 1784; and afterwards, in 1787, formed a part of the edition printed for Dilly. The draft in L. C. is undated, and it is uncertain when it was written.—Ed.

with theirs, they esteem slavish and base; and the learning, on which we value ourselves, they regard as frivolous and useless. An instance of this occurred at the Treaty of Lancaster, in Pennsylvania, *anno* 1744, between the Government of Virginia and the Six Nations. After the principal business was settled, the commissioners from Virginia acquainted the Indians by a speech, that there was at Williamsburg a college, with a fund for educating Indian youth; and that, if the Six Nations would send down half a dozen of their young lads to that college, the government would take care that they should be well provided for, and instructed in all the learning of the white people. It is one of the Indian rules of politeness not to answer a public proposition the same day that it is made; they think it would be treating it as a light matter, and that they show it respect by taking time to consider it, as of a matter important. They therefore deferr'd their answer till the day following; when their speaker began, by expressing their deep sense of the kindness of the Virginia Government, in making them that offer; "for we know," says he, "that you highly esteem the kind of learning taught in those colleges, and that the maintenance of our young men, while with you, would be very expensive to you. We are convinc'd, therefore, that you mean to do us good by your proposal; and we thank you heartily. But you, who are wise, must know that different nations have different conceptions of things; and you will therefore not take it amiss, if our ideas of this kind of education happen not to be the same with yours. We have had some experience of it; several of our young people were formerly brought up at the colleges of the Northern Provinces; they were instructed in all your sciences; but, when they came back to us, they were bad runners, ignorant of every means of living in the woods, unable to bear either cold or hunger, knew neither how to build a cabin, take a deer, or kill an enemy, spoke our language imperfectly, were therefore neither fit for hunters, warriors, nor counsellors; they were totally good for nothing. We are however not the less oblig'd by your kind offer, tho' we decline accepting it; and, to show our grateful sense of it, if the gentlemen of Virginia will send us a dozen of their sons, we will take great care of their education, instruct them in all we know, and make *men* of them."

Having frequent occasions to hold public councils, they have acquired great order and decency in conducting them. The old men sit in the foremost ranks, the warriors in the next, and the women and children in the hindmost. The business of the women is to take exact notice of what passes, imprint it in their memories (for they have no writing), and communicate it to their children. They are the records of the council, and they preserve traditions of the stipulations in treaties 100 years back; which, when we compare with our writings, we always find exact. He that would speak, rises. The rest observe a profound silence. When he has finish'd and sits down, they leave him 5 or 6 minutes to recollect, that, if he has omitted any thing he intended to say, or has any thing to add, he may rise again and deliver it. To interrupt another, even in common conversation, is reckon'd highly indecent. How different this is from the conduct of a polite British House of Commons, where scarce a day passes without some confusion, that makes the speaker hoarse in calling *to order*; and how different from the mode of conversation in many polite companies of Europe, where, if you do not deliver your sentence with great rapidity, you are cut off in the middle of it by the impatient loquacity of those you converse with, and never suffer'd to finish it!

The politeness of these savages in conversation is indeed carried to excess, since it does not permit them to contradict or deny the truth of what is asserted in their presence. By this means they indeed avoid disputes; but then it becomes difficult to know their minds, or what impression you make upon them. The missionaries who have attempted to convert them to Christianity, all complain of this as one of the great difficulties of their mission. The Indians hear with patience the truths of the Gospel explain'd to them, and give their usual tokens of assent and approbation; you would think they were convinc'd. No such matter. It is mere civility.

A Swedish minister, having assembled the chiefs of the Susquehanah Indians, made a sermon to them, acquainting them with the principal historical facts on which our religion is founded; such as the fall of our first parents by eating an apple, the coming of Christ to repair the mischief, his miracles and suffering, &c. When he had finished, an Indian orator stood up to thank him. "What you have told us," says he, "is all very good. It is indeed bad to eat apples. It is better to make them all into cyder. We are much oblig'd by your kindness in coming so far, to tell us these things which you have heard from your mothers. In return, I will tell you some of those we have heard from ours. In the beginning, our fathers had only the flesh of animals to subsist on; and if their hunting was unsuccessful, they were starving. Two of our young hunters, having kill'd a deer, made a fire in the woods to broil some part of it. When they were about to satisfy their hunger, they beheld a beautiful young woman descend from the clouds, and seat herself on that hill, which you see yonder among the blue mountains. They said to each other, it is a spirit that has smelt our broiling venison, and wishes to eat of it; let us offer some to her. They presented her with the tongue; she was pleas'd with the taste of it, and said, 'Your kindness shall be rewarded; come to this place after thirteen moons, and you shall find something that will be of great benefit in nourishing you and your children to the latest generations.' They did so, and, to their surprise, found plants they had never seen before; but which, from that ancient time, have been constantly cultivated among us, to our great advantage. Where her right hand had touched the ground, they found maize; where her left hand had touch'd it, they found kidney-beans; and where her backside had sat on it, they found tobacco." The good missionary, disgusted with this idle tale, said, "What I delivered to you were sacred truths; but what you tell me is mere fable, fiction, and falshood." The Indian, offended, reply'd, "My brother, it seems your friends have not done you justice in your education; they have not well instructed you in the rules of common civility. You saw that we, who understand and practise those rules, believ'd all your stories; why do you refuse to believe ours?"

When any of them come into our towns, our people are apt to crowd round them, gaze upon them, and incommode them, where they desire to be private; this they esteem great rudeness, and the effect of the want of instruction in the rules of civility and good manners. "We have," say they, "as much curiosity as you, and when you come into our towns, we wish for opportunities of looking at you; but for this purpose we hide ourselves behind bushes, where you are to pass, and never intrude ourselves into your company."

Their manner of entring one another's village has likewise its rules. It is reckon'd uncivil in travelling strangers to enter a village abruptly, without giving notice of their approach. Therefore, as soon as they arrive within hearing, they stop and hollow, remaining there till invited to enter. Two old men usually come out to them, and lead them in. There is in every village a vacant dwelling, called *the Strangers' House.* Here they are plac'd, while the old men go round from hut to hut, acquainting the inhabitants, that strangers are arriv'd, who are probably hungry and weary; and every one sends them what he can spare of victuals, and skins to repose on. When the strangers are refresh'd, pipes and tobacco are brought; and then, but not before, conversation begins, with enquiries who they are, whither bound, what news, &c.; and it usually ends with offers of service, if the strangers have occasion of guides, or any necessaries for continuing their journey; and nothing is exacted for the entertainment.

The same hospitality, esteem'd among them as a principal virtue, is practis'd by private persons; of which Conrad Weiser, our interpreter, gave me the following instance. He had been naturaliz'd among the Six Nations, and spoke well the Mohock language. In going thro' the Indian country, to carry a message from our governor to the council at Onondaga, he call'd at the Habitation of Canassatego, an old Acquaintance, who embrac'd him, spread furs for him to sit on, plac'd before him some boil'd beans and venison, and mix'd some rum and water for his drink. When he was well refresh'd, and had lit his pipe, Canassatego began to converse with him; ask'd how he had far'd the many years since they had seen each other; whence he then came; what occasion'd the journey, &c. Conrad answered all his questions; and when the discourse began to flag, the Indian, to continue it, said, "Conrad, you have lived long among the white people, and know something of their customs; I have been sometimes at Albany, and have observed, that once in seven days they shut up their shops, and assemble all in the great house; tell me what it is for? What do they do there?" "They meet there," says Conrad, "to hear and learn *good things*." "I do not doubt," says the Indian, "that they tell you so; they have told me the same; but I doubt the truth of what they say, and I will tell you my reasons. I went lately to Albany to sell my skins and buy blankets, knives, powder, rum, &c. You know I us'd generally to deal with Hans Hanson; but I was a little inclin'd this time to try some other merchant. However, I call'd first upon Hans, and asked him what he would give for beaver. He said he could not give any more than four shillings a pound; 'but,' says he, 'I cannot talk on business now; this is the day when we meet together to learn *good things*, and I am going to the meeting.' So I thought to myself, 'Since we cannot do any business to-day, I may as well go to the meeting too,' and I went with him. There stood up a man in black, and began to talk to the people very angrily. I did not under-stand what he said; but, perceiving that he look'd much at me and at Hanson, I imagin'd he was angry at seeing me there; so I went out, sat down near the house, struck fire, and lit my pipe, waiting till the meeting should break up. I thought too, that the man had mention'd something of beaver, and I suspected it might be the subject of their meeting. So, when they came out, I accosted my merchant. 'Well, Hans,' says I, 'I hope you have agreed to give more than four shillings a pound.' 'No,' says he, 'I cannot give so much; I cannot give more than three shillings and sixpence.' I then spoke to several other dealers, but they all sung the same song,—Three and sixpence,—Three and sixpence. This made it clear to me, that my suspicion was right; and, that whatever they pretended of meeting to learn *good things*, the real purpose was to consult how to cheat Indians in the price of beaver. Consider but a little, Conrad, and you must be of my opinion. If they met so often to learn *good things*, they would certainly have learnt some before this time. But they are still ignorant. You know our practice. If a white man, in travelling thro' our country, enters one of our cabins, we all treat him as I treat you; we dry him if he is wet, we warm him if he is cold, we give him meat and drink, that he may allay his thirst and hun-ger; and we spread soft furs for him to rest and sleep on; we demand nothing in return. But, if I go into a white man's house at Albany, and ask for victuals and drink, they say, 'Where is your money?' and if I have none, they say, 'Get out, you Indian dog.' You see they have not yet learned those little *good things*, that

we need no meetings to be instructed in, because our mothers taught them to us when we were children; and therefore it is impossible their meetings should be, as they say, for any such purpose, or have any such effect; they are only to contrive *the cheating of Indians in the price of beaver*."[*]

2–3
Thomas Paine (1737–1809)

Author of America's first bestseller, the political pamphlet *Common Sense* (1776), THOMAS PAINE (1737–1809) was born and educated in England before emigrating to the colonies in 1774 to agitate for natural rights for all. His political writings in this country and abroad had considerable influence. In addition to *Common Sense*, he penned *The Crisis* (1776–1783), *The Rights of Man* (1791–1792), and *The Age of Reason* (1794, 1796). His poem "The Liberty Tree" (1775) champions the elm tree that for more than a decade had served as a meeting place near the Boston Common for the Sons of Liberty and others opposing British rule. It was intended to be sung to the tune "Gods of the Greeks." Liberty trees were planted in all thirteen colonies.

〜〜 〜〜 〜〜

"The Liberty Tree" (1775)

> In a chariot of light from the regions of day,
>   The Goddess of Liberty came;
> Ten thousand celestials directed the way,
>   And hither conducted the dame.
> A fair budding branch from the gardens above,
>   Where millions with millions agree,
> She brought in her hand as a pledge of her love,
>   And the plant she named *Liberty Tree*.
>
> The celestial exotic struck deep in the ground,
>   Like a native it flourished and bore;

---

[*] Note.—It is remarkable that in all ages and countries hospitality has been allow'd as the virtue of those whom the civiliz'd were pleas'd to call Barbarians. The Greeks celebrated the Scythians for it. The Saracens possess'd it eminently, and it is to this day the reigning virtue of the wild Arabs. St. Paul, too, in the relation of his voyage and shipwreck on the island of Melita says the barbarous people shewed us no little kindness; for they kindled a fire, and received us every one, because of the present rain, and because of the cold.—P.

The fame of its fruit drew the nations around,
    To seek out this peaceable shore.
Unmindful of names or distinctions they came,
    For freemen like brothers agree;
With one spirit endued, they one friendship pursued,
    And their temple was *Liberty Tree.*

Beneath this fair tree, like the patriarchs of old,
    Their bread in contentment they ate
Unvexed with the troubles of silver and gold,
    The cares of the grand and the great.
With timber and tar they Old England supplied,
    And supported her power on the sea;
Her battles they fought, without getting a groat,
    For the honor of *Liberty Tree.*

But hear, O ye swains, 'tis a tale most profane,
    How all the tyrannical powers,
Kings, Commons and Lords, are uniting amain,
    To cut down this guardian of ours;
From the east to the west blow the trumpet to arms,
    Through the land let the sound of it flee,
Let the far and the near, all unite with a cheer,
    In defence of our *Liberty Tree.*

2—4

Olaudah Equiano (1745–1797)

According to most accounts, including his own, OLAUDAH EQUIANO (1745–1797) was born of the Igbo peoples in what is today Nigeria, was captured and enslaved as a child, and was sold to a British naval officer serving in Virginia. *The Interesting Narrative of the Life of Olaudah Equiano* (1789) recounts the story of his enslavement, life as a slave in the American South and elsewhere, and his purchase of his own freedom. The book went through many editions, was published in America, England, and other countries, and helped to establish the slave narrative as a genre of substantial power. Equiano became an abolitionist, belonging to the group "The Sons of Africa," which in time helped abolish slavery in British territory (Slave Abolition Act of 1833). The selections here are from the first two chapters; the first describes Equiano's early life in

Africa, the laws and customs, the wars between peoples, and the culture which he finds analogous to that of the Jews in the Old Testament. The second chapter describes how he and his sister were abducted, forced to travel, sold and sold again, and separated until Equiano was put aboard a slave ship and crossed the Middle Passage to the New World.

≈ ≈ ≈

From *The Interesting Narrative of the Life of Olaudah Equiano* (1789)

Chapter 1

I believe it is difficult for those who publish their own memoirs to escape the imputation of vanity; nor is this the only disadvantage under which they labor: it is also their misfortune, that what is uncommon is rarely, if ever, believed, and what is obvious we are apt to turn from with disgust, and to charge the writer with impertinence. People generally think those memoirs only worthy to be read or remembered which abound in great or striking events; those, in short, which in a high degree excite either administration or pity: all others they consign to contempt and oblivion. It is therefore, I confess, not a little hazardous in a private and obscure individual, and a stranger too, thus to solicit the indulgent attention of the public; especially when I own I offer here the history of neither a saint, a hero, nor a tyrant. I believe there are few events in my life, which have not happened to many: it is true the incidents of it are numerous; and, did I consider myself an European, I might say my sufferings were great: but when I compare my lot with that of most of my countrymen, I regard myself as a *particular favorite of heaven* and acknowledge the mercies of Providence in every occurrence of my life. If, then, the following narrative does not appear sufficiently interesting to engage general attention, let my motive be some excuse for its publication. I am not so foolishly vain as to expect from it either immortality or literary reputation. If it affords any satisfaction to my numerous friends, at whose request it has been written, or in the smallest degree promotes the interests of humanity, the ends for which it was undertaken will be fully attained, and every wish of my heart gratified. Let it therefore be remembered, that, in wishing to avoid censure, I do not aspire to praise.

That part of Africa, known by the name of Guinea, to which the trade for slaves is carried on, extends along the coast above 3400 miles, from Senegal to Angola, and includes a variety of kingdoms. Of these the most considerable is the kingdom of Benin, both as to extent and wealth, the richness and cultivation of the soil, the power of its king, and the number and warlike disposition of the inhabitants. It is situated nearly under the line, and extends along the coast about 170 miles, but runs back into the interior part of Africa to a distance hitherto, I believe, unexplored by any traveller; and seems only terminated at length by the empire of Abyssinnia, near 1500 miles from its beginning. This kingdom is divided into many provinces or districts: in one of the most remote and fertile of which I was born, in the year 1745, situated in a charming fruitful vale, named Essaka. The distance of this province from the capital of Benin and the sea coast must be very considerable: for I had never heard of white men or Europeans, nor of the sea; and our subjection to the king of Benin was little more than nominal; for every transaction of the government, as far as my slender observation extended, was conducted by the chief or elders of the place. The manners and government of a people who have little commerce with other countries, are generally very simple; and the history of what passes in one family or village, may serve as a specimen of the whole nation. My father was one of those elders or chiefs I have spoken of, and was styled Embrenche; a term, as I remember, importing the highest distinction, and signifying in our language a *mark* of grandeur. This mark is conferred on the person entitled to it, by cutting the skin across at the top of the forehead, and drawing it down to the eye-brows: and while it is in this situation applying a warm hand, and rubbing it until it shrinks up into a thick *weal* across the lower part of the forehead. Most of the judges and senators were thus marked; my father had long borne it: I had seen it conferred on one of my brothers, and I also was *destined* to receive it by my parents. . . .

Our manner of living is entirely plain; for as yet the natives are unacquainted with those refinements in cookery which debauch the taste: bullocks, goats, and poultry, supply the greatest part of their food.—These constitute likewise the principal wealth of the country, and the chief articles of its commerce.— The flesh is usually stewed in a pan; to make it savory we sometimes use also pepper, and other spices, and we have salt made of wood ashes. Our vegetables are mostly plantains, eadas, yams, beans, and Indian corn. The head of the family usually eats alone; his wives and slaves have also their separate tables. Before we taste food we always wash our hands: indeed our cleanliness on all occasions is extreme; but on this it is an indispensable ceremony. After washing, libation is made, by pouring out a small portion of the drink on the floor and tossing a small quantity of the food in a certain place, for the spirits of departed relations, which the natives suppose to preside over their conduct, and guard them from evil. . . .

As we live in a country where nature is prodigal of her favors, our wants are few and easily supplied; of course we have few manufactures. They consist for the most part of calicoes, earthen ware, ornaments, and instruments of war and husbandry.—But these make no part of our commerce, the principal articles of which, as I have observed, are provisions. In such a state, money is of little use; however, we have some small pieces of coin, if I may call them such. They are made something like an anchor; but I do not remember either their value or denomination. We have also markets, at which I have been frequently with my mother. These are sometimes visited by stout mahogany-colored men from the south-west of us: we call them *Oye-Eboe*, which term signifies red men living at a distance.—They generally bring us fire-arms, gunpowder, hats, beads, and dried fish. The last we esteemed a great rarity, as our waters were only brooks and springs. These articles they barter with us for odoriferous woods and earth, and our salt of wood ashes. They always carry slaves through our land; but the strictest account is exacted of their manner of procuring them before they are suffered to pass. Sometimes indeed, we sold slaves to them, but they were only prisoners of war, or such among us as had been con- victed of kidnapping, or adultery, and some other crimes, which we esteemed heinous. This practice of kidnapping induces me to think, that, notwithstand- ing all our strictness, their principal business among us was to trepan our peo- ple. I remember too, they carried great sacks along with them, which not long after, I had an opportunity of fatally seeing applied to that infamous purpose.

Our land is uncommonly rich and fruitful, and produces all kinds of vege- tables in great abundance.—We have plenty of Indian corn, and vast quantities of cotton and tobacco. Our pine apples grow without culture; they are about the size of the largest sugar-loaf, and finely flavored. We have also spices of different kinds, particularly pepper; and a variety of delicious fruits which I have never seen in Europe; together with gums of various kinds, and honey in abundance. All our industry is exerted to improve these blessings of nature. Agriculture is our chief employment; and every one, even the children and women, are engaged in it. Thus we are all habituated to labor from our earliest years. Everyone contributes something to the common stock; and, as we are unacquainted with idleness, we have no beggars. The benefits of such a mode of living are obvious. The West India planters prefer the slaves of Benin or Eboe, to those of any other part of Guinea, for their hardiness, intelligence, integrity, and zeal. Those benefits are felt by us in the general healthiness of the people, and in their vigor and activity; I might have added, too, in their comeliness. . . .

. . . Our women, too, were in my eye at least, uncommonly graceful, alert, and modest to a degree of bashfulness; nor do I remember to have heard of an instance of incontinence amongst them before marriage.—They are also remarkably cheerful. Indeed, cheerfulness and affability are two of the leading characteristics of our nation.

. . . From what I can recollect of these battles, they appear to have been irruptions of one little state or district on the other, to obtain prisoners or booty. Perhaps they were incited to this, by those traders who brought the European goods I mentioned, amongst us. Such a mode of obtaining slaves in Africa is common; and I believe more are procured this way, and by kidnapping, than any other.* When a trader wants slaves, he applies to a chief for them, and tempts him with his wares. It is not extraordinary, if on this occasion he yields to the temptation with as little firmness, and accepts the price of his fellow creatures' liberty, with as little reluctance as the enlightened merchant.—Accordingly he falls on his neighbors, and a desperate battle ensues. If he prevails and takes prisoners, he gratifies his avarice by selling them; but, if his party be vanquished, and he falls into the hands of the enemy, he is put to death; for, as he has been known to foment their quarrels, it is thought dangerous to let him survive, and no ransom can save him, though all other prisoners may be redeemed. . . . I was once a witness to a battle in our common. We had been all at work in it one day as usual, when our people were suddenly attacked. I climbed a tree at some distance, from which I beheld the fight. There were many women as well as men on both sides; among others my mother was there, and armed with a broad sword. After fighting for a considerable time with great fury, and many had been killed, our people obtained the victory, and took their enemy's Chief a prisoner. He was carried off in great triumph, and, though he offered a large ransom for his life, he was put to death. A virgin of note among our enemies, had been slain in the battle, and her arm was exposed in our marketplace, where our trophies were always exhibited. The spoils were divided according to the merit of the warriors. Those prisoners which were not sold or redeemed, we kept as slaves: but how different was their condition from that of the slaves in the West Indies! With us, they do no more work than other members of the community, even their master; their food, clothing and lodging were nearly the same as theirs, (except that they were not permitted to eat with those who were free-born;) and there was scarce any other difference between them, than a superior degree of importance which the head of a family possesses in our state, and that authority which, as such, he exercises over every part of his household. Some of these slaves have even slaves under them as their own property, and for their own use.

. . .

---

* See Benezet's 'Account of Africa' throughout.

We practiced circumcision like the Jews, and made offerings and feasts on that occasion, in the same manner as they did. Like them also, our children were named from some event, some circumstance, or fancied foreboding, at the time of their birth. I was named *Olaudah*, which in our language signifies vicissitude, or fortunate; also, one favored, and having a loud voice and well spoken. I remember we never polluted the name of the object of our adoration; on the contrary, it was always mentioned with the greatest reverence; and we were totally unacquainted with swearing, and all those terms of abuse and reproach which find their way so readily and copiously into the language of more civilized people. The only expressions of that kind I remember were, 'May you rot, or may you swell, or may a beast take you.' . . .

Chapter 2

I hope the reader will not think I have trespassed on his patience in introducing myself to him, with some account of the manners and customs of my country. They had been implanted in me with great care, and made an impression on my mind, which time could not erase, and which all the adversity and variety of fortune I have since experienced, served only to rivet and record; for, whether the love of one's country be real or imaginary, or a lesson of reason, or an instinct of nature, I still look back with pleasure on the first scenes of my life, though that pleasure has been for the most part mingled with sorrow.

I have already acquainted the reader with the time and place of my birth. My father, besides many slaves, had a numerous family, of which seven lived to grow up, including myself and a sister, who was the only daughter. As I was the youngest of the sons, I became, of course, the greatest favorite with my mother, and was always with her; and she used to take particular pains to form my mind. I was trained up from my earliest years in the art of war: my daily exercise was shooting and throwing javelins; and my mother adorned me with emblems, after the manner of our greatest warriors. In this way I grew up till I was turned the age of eleven, when an end was put to my happiness in the following manner:—generally when the grown people in the neighborhood were gone far in the fields to labor, the children assembled together in some of the neighboring premises to play; and commonly some of us used to get up a tree to look out for any assailant, or kidnapper, that might come upon us—for they sometimes took those opportunities of our parents' absence, to attack and carry off as many as they could seize. One day as I was watching at the top of a tree in our yard, I saw one of those people come into the yard of our next neighbor but one to kidnap, there being many stout young people in it. Immediately on this I gave the alarm of the rogue, and he was surrounded by the stoutest of them, who entangled him with cords, so that he could not escape till some of the grown people came and secured him. But, alas! ere long it was my fate to be thus attacked, and to be carried off, when none of the grown people were nigh. One day, when all our people were gone out to their works as usual, and only I and my dear sister were left to mind the house, two men and a woman got over our walls, and in a moment seized us both, and, without giving us time to cry out, or make resistance, they stopped our mouths, and ran off with us into the nearest wood. Here they tied our hands, and continued to carry us as far as they could, till night came on, when we reached a small house, where the robbers halted for refreshment, and spent the night. We were then unbound, but were unable to take any food; and, being quite overpowered by fatigue and grief, our only relief was some sleep, which allayed our misfortune for a short time. The next morning we left the house, and continued travelling all the day. For a long time we had kept the woods, but at last we came into a road which I believed I knew. I had now some hopes of being delivered; for we had advanced but a little way before I discovered some people at a distance, on which I began to cry out for their assistance; but my cries had no other effect than to make them tie me faster and stop my mouth, and then they put me into a large sack. They also stopped my sister's mouth, and tied her hands; and in this manner we proceeded till we were out of sight of these people. When we went to rest the following night, they offered us some victuals, but we refused it; and the only comfort we had was in being in one another's arms all that night, and bathing each other with our tears. But alas! we were soon deprived of even the small comfort of weeping together. The next day proved a day of greater sorrow than I had yet experienced; for my sister and I were then separated, while we lay clasped in each other's arms. It was in vain that we besought them not to part us; she was torn from me, and immediately carried away, while I was left in a state of distraction not to be described. I cried and grieved continually; and for several days did not eat any thing but what they forced into my mouth. At length, after many days travelling, during which I had often changed masters, I got into the hands of a chieftain, in a very pleasant country. This man had two wives and some children, and they all used me extremely well, and did all they could to comfort me; particularly the first wife, who was something like my mother. Although I was a great many days' journey from my father's house, yet these people spoke exactly the same language with us. This first master of mine, as I may call him, was a smith, and my principal employment was working his bellows, which were the same kind as I had seen in my vicinity. . . .

From the time I left my own nation, I always found somebody that understood me till I came to the sea coast. The languages of different nations did not totally differ, nor were they so copious as those of the Europeans, particularly the English. They were therefore, easily learned; and, while I was journeying thus through Africa, I acquired two or three different tongues. In this manner I had been travelling for a considerable time, when, one evening, to my great surprise, whom should I see brought to the house where I was but my dear sister! As soon as she saw me, she gave a loud shriek, and ran into my arms—I was quite overpowered: neither of us could speak; but, for a considerable time, clung to each other in mutual embraces, unable to do any thing but weep. Our meeting affected all who saw us; and, indeed, I must acknowledge, in honor of those sable destroyers of human rights, that I never met with any ill treatment, or saw any offered to their slaves, except tying them, when necessary, to keep them from running away. When these people knew we were brother and sister, they indulged us to be together; and the man, to whom I supposed we belonged, lay with us, he in the middle, while she and I held one another by the hands across his chest all night; and thus for a while we forgot our misfortunes, in the joy of being together; but even this small comfort was soon to have an end; for scarcely had the fatal morning appeared when she was again torn from me forever! I was now more miserable, if possible, than before. The small relief which her presence gave me from pain, was gone, and the wretchedness of my situation was redoubled by my anxiety after her fate, and my apprehensions lest her sufferings should be greater than mine, when I could not be with her to alleviate them. . . .

I did not long remain after my sister. I was again sold, and carried through a number of places, till after travelling a considerable time, I came to a town called Tinmah, in the most beautiful country I had yet seen in Africa. It was extremely rich, and there were many rivulets which flowed through it, and supplied a large pond in the centre of the town, where the people washed. Here I first saw and tasted cocoa nuts, which I thought superior to any nuts I had ever tasted before; and the trees which were loaded, were also interspersed among the houses, which had commodious shades adjoining, and were in the same manner as ours, the insides being neatly plastered and whitewashed. Here I also saw and tasted for the first time, sugar-cane. Their money consisted of little white shells, the size of the fingernail. I was sold here for one hundred and seventy-two of them, by a merchant who lived and brought me there. I had been about two or three days at his house, when a wealthy widow, a neighbor of his, came there one evening, and brought with her an only son, a young gentleman about my own age and size. Here they saw me; and, having taken a fancy to me, I was bought of the merchant, and went home with them. Her house and premises were situated close to one of those rivulets I have mentioned, and were the finest I ever saw in Africa: they were very extensive, and she had a number of slaves to attend her. The next day I was washed and perfumed, and when meal time came, I was led into the presence of my mistress, and ate and drank before her with her son. This filled me with astonishment; and I could scarce help expressing my surprise that the young gentleman should suffer me, who was bound, to eat with him who was free; and not only so, but that he would not at any time either eat or drink till I had taken first, because I was the eldest, which was agreeable to our custom. Indeed, everything here, and all their treatment of me, made me forget that I was a slave. The language of these people resembled ours so nearly, that we understood each other perfectly. They had also the very same customs as we. There were likewise slaves daily to attend us, while my young master and I, with other boys, sported with our darts and bows and arrows, as I had been used to do at home. In this resemblance to my former happy state, I passed about two months; and I now began to think I was to be adopted into the family, and was beginning to be reconciled to my situation, and to forget by degrees my misfortunes, when all at once the delusion vanished; for, without the least previous knowledge, one morning early, while my dear master and companion was still asleep, I was awakened out of my reverie to fresh sorrow and hurried away even amongst the uncircumcised.

Thus, at the very moment I dreamed of the greatest happiness, I found myself most miserable; and it seemed as if fortune wished to give me this taste of joy only to render the reverse more poignant.—The change I now experienced, was as painful as it was sudden and unexpected. It was a change indeed, from a state of bliss to a scene which is inexpressible by me, as it discovered to me an element I had never before beheld, and till then had no idea of, and wherein such instances of hardship and cruelty continually occurred, as I can never reflect on but with horror.

All the nations and people I had hitherto passed through, resembled our own in their manners, customs, and language: but I came at length to a country, the inhabitants of which differed from us in all those particulars. I was very much struck with this difference, especially when I came among a people who did not circumcise, and ate without washing their hands. They cooked also in iron pots, and had European cutlasses and cross bows, which were unknown to us, and fought with their fists among themselves. Their women were not so modest as ours, for they ate, and drank, and slept with their men. But above all, I was amazed to see no sacrifices or offerings among them. In some of those places the people ornamented themselves with scars, and likewise filed their teeth very sharp. They wanted sometimes to ornament me in the same manner, but I would not suffer them; hoping that I might some time be among a people who did not thus disfigure themselves, as I thought they did. . . . Thus I continued to travel, sometimes by land, sometimes by water, through different countries and various nations, till, at the end of six or seven months after I had been kidnapped, I arrived at the sea coast. . . .

The first object which saluted my eyes when I arrived on the coast, was the sea, and a slave ship, which was then riding at anchor, and waiting for its cargo. These filled me with astonishment, which was soon converted into terror, when I was carried on board. I was immediately handled, and tossed up to see if I were sound, by some of the crew; and I was now persuaded that I had gotten into a world of bad spirits, and that they were going to kill me. Their complexions, too, differing so much from ours, their long hair, and the language they spoke, (which was very different from any I had ever heard) united to confirm me in this belief. Indeed, such were the horrors of my views and fears at the moment, that, if ten thousand worlds had been my own, I would have freely parted with them all to have exchanged my condition with that of the meanest slave in my own country. When I looked round the ship too, and saw a large furnace of copper boiling, and a multitude of black people of every description chained together, every one of their countenances expressing dejection and sorrow, I no longer doubted of my fate; and, quite overpowered with horror and anguish, I fell motionless on the deck and fainted. When I recovered a little, I found some black people about me, who I believed were some of those who had brought me on board, and had been receiving their pay; they talked to me in order to cheer me, but all in vain. I asked them if we were not to be eaten by those white men with horrible looks, red faces, and long hair. They told me I was not: and one of the crew brought me a small portion of spirituous liquor in a wine glass, but, being afraid of him, I would not take it out of his hand. One of the blacks, therefore, took it from him and gave it to me, and I took a little down my palate, which, instead of reviving me, as they thought it would, threw me into the greatest consternation at the strange feeling it produced, having never tasted any such liquor before. Soon after this, the blacks who brought me on board went off, and left me abandoned to despair.

I now saw myself deprived of all chance of returning to my native country, or even the least glimpse of hope of gaining the shore, which I now considered as friendly; and I even wished for my former slavery in preference to my present situation, which was filled with horrors of every kind, still heightened by my ignorance of what I was to undergo. I was not long suffered to indulge my grief; I was soon put down under the decks, and there I received such a salutation in my nostrils as I had never experienced in my life: so that, with the loathsomeness of the stench, and crying together, I became so sick and low that I was not able to eat, nor had I the least desire to taste any thing. I now wished for the last friend, death, to relieve me; but soon, to my grief, two of the white men offered me eatables; and, on my refusing to eat, one of them held me fast by the hands, and laid me across, I think the windlass, and tied my feet, while the other flogged me severely. I had never experienced any-thing of this kind before, and although not being used to the water, I naturally feared that element the first time I saw it, yet, nevertheless, could I have got over the nettings, I would have jumped over the side, but I could not; and besides, the crew used to watch us very closely who were not chained down to the decks, lest we should leap into the water; and I have seen some of these poor African prisoners most severely cut, for attempting to do so, and hourly whipped for not eating. This indeed was often the case with myself. In a little time after, amongst the poor chained men, I found some of my own nation, which in a small degree gave ease to my mind. I inquired of these what was to be done with us? they gave me to understand, we were to be carried to these white people's country to work for them. I then was a little revived, and thought, if it were no worse than working, my situation was not so desperate; but still I feared I should be put to death, the white people looked and acted, as I thought, in so savage a manner; for I had never seen among any people such instances of brutal cruelty; and this not only shown towards us blacks, but also to some of the whites themselves. One white man in particular I saw, when we were permitted to be on deck, flogged so unmercifully with a large rope near the foremast, that he died in consequence of it; and they tossed him over the side as they would have done a brute. This made me fear these people the more; and I expected nothing less than to be treated in the same manner. I could not help expressing my fears and apprehensions to some of my coun-trymen; I asked them if these people had no country, but lived in this hollow place? (the ship) they told me they did not, but came from a distant one. 'Then,' said I, 'how comes it in all our country we never heard of them?' They told me because they lived so very far off. I then asked where were their women? had they any like themselves? I was told they had. 'And why,' said I, 'do we not see them?' They answered, because they were left behind. I asked how the vessel could go? they told me they could not tell; but that there was cloth put upon the masts by the help of the ropes I saw, and then the vessel went on; and the white men had some spell or magic they put in the water when they liked, in order to stop the vessel. I was exceedingly amazed at this account, and really thought they were spirits. I therefore wished much to be from amongst them, for I expected they would sacrifice me; but my wishes were vain—for we were so quartered that it was impossible for any of us to make our escape.

. . .

. . . The stench of the hold while we were on the coast was so intolerably loathsome, that it was dangerous to remain there for any time, and some of us had been permitted to stay on the deck for the fresh air; but now that the whole ship's cargo were confined together, it became absolutely pestilential. The closeness of the place, and the heat of the climate, added to the number in the ship, which was so crowded that each had scarcely room to turn himself, almost suffocated us. This produced copious perspirations, so that the air soon became unfit for respiration, from a variety of loathsome smells, and brought on a sickness among the slaves, of which many died—thus falling victims to the improvident avarice, as I may call it, of their purchasers. This wretched situation was again aggravated by the galling of the chains, now became in-supportable; and the filth of the necessary tubs, into which the children often fell, and were almost suffocated. The shrieks of the women, and the groans of the dying, rendered the whole a scene of horror almost inconceivable. Happily perhaps, for myself, I was soon reduced so low here that it was thought neces-sary to keep me almost always on deck; and from my extreme youth I was not put in fetters. In this situation I expected every hour to share the fate of my companions, some of whom were almost daily brought upon deck at the point of death, which I began to hope would soon put an end to my miseries. Often did I think many of the inhabitants of the deep much more happy than myself. I envied them the freedom they enjoyed, and as often wished I could change my condition for theirs. Every circumstance I met with, served only to render my state more painful, and heightened my apprehensions, and my opinion of the cruelty of the whites.

. . .

. . . At last, we came in sight of the island of Barbadoes, at which the whites on board gave a great shout, and made many signs of joy to us. We did not know what to think of this; but as the vessel drew nearer, we plainly saw the harbor, and other ships of different kinds and sizes, and we soon anchored amongst them, off Bridgetown. Many merchants and planters now came on board, though it was in the evening. They put us in separate parcels, and exam-ined us attentively. They also made us jump, and pointed to the land, signifying we were to go there. We thought by this, we should be eaten by these ugly men, as they appeared to us; and, when soon after we were all put down under the deck again, there was much dread and trembling among us, and nothing but bitter cries to be heard all the night from these apprehensions, insomuch, that at last the white people got some old slaves from the land to pacify us. They told us we were not to be eaten, but to work, and were soon to go on land, where we should see many of our country people. This report eased us much. And sure enough, soon after we were landed, there came to us Africans of all languages.

We were conducted immediately to the merchant's yard, where we were all pent up together, like so many sheep in a fold, without regard to sex or age. As every object was new to me, every thing I saw filled me with surprise. What struck me first was that the houses were built with bricks and stories, and in every other respect different from those I had seen in Africa; but I was still more astonished on seeing people on horseback. I did not know what this could mean; and, indeed, I thought these people were full of nothing but magical arts. While I was in this astonishment, one of my fellow-prisoners spoke to a countryman of his, about the horses, who said they were the same kind they had in their country. I understood them, though they were from a distant part of Africa; and I thought it odd I had not seen any horses there; but afterwards, when I came to converse with different Africans, I found they had many horses amongst them, and much larger than those I then saw.

We were not many days in the merchant's custody before we were sold after their usual manner, which is this:—On a signal given, (as the beat of a drum,) the buyers rush at once into the yard where the slaves are confined, and make choice of that parcel they like best. The noise and clamor with which this is attended, and the eagerness visible in the countenances of the buyers, serve not a little to increase the apprehension of terrified Africans, who may well be supposed to consider them as the ministers of that destruction to which they think themselves devoted. In this manner, without scruple, are relations and friends separated, most of them never to see each other again. I remember, in the vessel in which I was brought over, in the men's apartment, there were several brothers, who, in the sale, were sold in different lots; and it was very moving on this occasion, to see and hear their cries at parting. O, ye nominal Christians! might not an African ask you— Learned you this from your God, who says unto you, Do unto all men as you would men should do unto you? Is it not enough that we are torn from our country and friends, to toil for your luxury and lust of gain? Must every tender feeling be likewise sacrificed to your avarice? Are the dearest friends and relations, now rendered more dear by their separation from their kindred, still to be parted from each other, and thus prevented from cheering the gloom of slavery, with the small comfort of being together, and mingling their sufferings and sorrows? Why are parents to lose their children, brothers their sisters, or husbands their wives? Surely this is a new refinement in cruelty, which, while it has no advantage to atone for it, thus aggravates distress, and adds fresh horrors even to the wretchedness of slavery.

2—5
Red Jacket (Sa-Go-Ye-Wat-Ha) (1750–1830)

RED JACKET (c. 1750s–1830) or SAGOYEWATHA (roughly, "he keeps them awake") was a Seneca chief famed for his oratorical abilities. His English name refers to his typical attire as chief, wearing a red jacket given to him by British troops during the American Revolution. Although Red Jacket was responsible for the Seneca siding with the British and maintained an attitude of resistance toward Americans and the influence of their culture, he used his influence to convince the Seneca to side with the Americans during the War of 1812. "Red Jacket's Speech" (1805), addressed to missionaries, illustrates the Chief's rhetorical abilities and also the resistance that characterized his career. The Seneca lands to which he refers were in and around Buffalo, in western New York State.

≈ ≈ ≈

From *Life and Times of Red-Jacket or Sa-Go-Ye-Wat-Ha* (1805)

"Brothers: I wish to talk with you as one friend talks with another; and if you have any objections to receive the religion which I preach, I wish you to state them; and I will endeavor to satisfy your minds and remove the objections.

"Brothers: I want you to speak your minds freely: for I wish to reason with you on the subject, and, if possible, remove all doubts, if there be any on your minds. The subject is an important one, and it is of consequence that you give it an early attention while the offer is made you. Your friends the Boston Missionary Society will continue to send you good and faithful ministers, to instruct and strengthen you in religion, if, on your part, you are willing to receive them.

"Brothers: Since I have been in this part of the country, I have visited some of your small villages, and talked with your people. They appear willing to receive instruction, but as they look up to you as their older brothers in council, they want first to know your opinion on the subject. You have now heard what I have to propose at present. I hope you will take it into consideration, and give me an answer before we part."

After about two hours consultation among themselves, Red-Jacket rose and spoke as follows:—

"Friend and Brother: It was the will of the Great Spirit that we should meet together this day. He orders all things, and has given us a fine day for our Council. He has taken his garment from before the sun, and caused it to shine with brightness upon us. Our eyes are opened, that we see clearly; our ears are unstopped, that we have been able to hear distinctly the words you have spoken. For all these favors we thank the Great Spirit; and Him *only*.

"Brother: This council fire was kindled by you. It was at your request that we came together at this time. We have listened with attention to what you have said. You requested us to speak our minds freely. This gives us great joy; for we now consider that we stand upright before you, and can speak what we think. All have heard your voice, and all speak to you now as one man. Our minds are agreed.

"Brother: You say you want an answer to your talk before you leave this place. It is right you should have one, as you are a great distance from home, and we do not wish to detain you. But we will first look back a little, and tell you what our fathers have told us, and what we have heard from the white people.

"Brother: Listen to what we say. There was a time when our forefathers owned this great island. Their seats extended from the rising to the setting sun. The Great Spirit had made it for the use of Indians. He had created the buffalo, the deer, and other animals for food. He had made the bear and the beaver. Their skins served us for clothing. He had scattered them over the country, and taught us how to take them. He had caused the earth to produce corn for bread. All this He had done for his red children, because He loved them. If we had some disputes about our hunting ground, they were generally settled without the shedding of much blood. But an evil day came upon us. Your forefathers crossed the great water and landed on this island. Their numbers were small. They found friends and not enemies. They told us they had fled from their own country for fear of wicked men, and had come here to enjoy their religion. They asked for a small seat. We took pity on them, granted their request; and they sat down amongst us. We gave them corn and meat; they gave us poison* in return.

"The white people, Brother, had now found our country. Tidings were carried back, and more came amongst us. Yet we did not fear them. We took them to be friends. They called us brothers. We believed them and gave them a larger seat. At length their numbers had greatly increased. They wanted more

---

* Rum.

land; they wanted our country. Our eyes were opened, and our minds became uneasy. Wars took place. Indians were hired to fight against Indians, and many of our people were destroyed. They also brought strong liquor amongst us. It was strong and powerful, and has slain thousands.

"Brother: Our seats were once large and yours were small. You have now become a great people, and we have scarcely a place left to spread our blankets. You have got our country, but are not satisfied; you want to force your religion upon us.

"Brother: Continue to listen. You say that you are sent to instruct us how to worship the Great Spirit agreeably to his mind, and, if we do not take hold of the religion which you white people teach, we shall be unhappy hereafter. You say that you are right and we are lost. How do we know this to be true? We understand that your religion is written in a book. If it was intended for us as well as you, why has not the Great Spirit given to us, and not only to us, but why did he not give to our forefathers, the knowledge of that book, with the means of understanding it rightly? We only know what you tell us about it. How shall we know when to believe, being so often deceived by the white people?

"Brother: You say there is but one way to worship and serve the Great Spirit. If there is but one religion, why do you white people differ so much about it? Why not all agreed, as you can all read the book?

"Brother: We do not understand these things. We are told that your religion was given to your forefathers, and has been handed down from father to son. We also have a religion, which was given to our forefathers, and has been handed down to us their children. We worship in that way. It teaches us to be thankful for all the favors we receive; to love each other, and to be united. We never quarrel about religion.

"Brother: The Great Spirit has made us all, but He has made a great difference between his white and red children. He has given us different complexions and different customs. To you He has given the arts. To those He has not opened our eyes. We know these things to be true. Since He has made so great a difference between us in other things, why may we not conclude that He has given us a different religion according to our understanding? The Great Spirit does right. He knows what is best for his children; we are satisfied.

"Brother: We do not wish to destroy your religion, or take it from you. We only want to enjoy our own.

"Brother: You say you have not come to get our land or our money, but to enlighten our minds. I will now tell you that I have been at your meetings, and saw you collect money from the meeting. I cannot tell what this money was intended for, but suppose that it was for your minister, and if we should conform to your way of thinking, perhaps you may want some from us.[*]

"Brother: We are told that you have been preaching to the white people in this place. These people are our neighbors. We are acquainted with them. We will wait a little while, and see what effect your preaching has upon them. If we find it does them good, makes them honest and less disposed to cheat Indians, we will then consider again of what you have said.

"Brother: You have now heard our answer to your talk, and this is all we have to say at present. As we are going to part, we will come and take you by the hand, and hope the Great Spirit will protect you on your journey, and return you safe to your friends."

2–6

Phillis Wheatley (1753?–1784)

PHILLIS WHEATLEY (1753?–1784), the first African American woman to publish a collection of poems, was enslaved in West Africa at about age seven and sold to a wealthy Bostonian, John Wheatley. While she was expected to perform domestic work, the family provided Phillis with an education, unusual at the time. An assiduous reader of the Bible and excellent student of the classics, her efforts at verse were recognized by the Wheatleys and became known to other Bostonians. At age eighteen she traveled to London, where *Poems on Various Subjects, Religious and Moral* was published (1773). One can clearly see the neoclassical influences on her poetry, particularly of the great English poet Alexander Pope. Her attention to neoclassicism may help to account for a palpable tension between a desire for order and a recognition that all is not right with the world as it is, elements visible in the selections printed below. In 1838, an American abolitionist published her work to highlight the intellectual accomplishments of an African American woman; more recently, scholars have discovered sources that show Wheatley was indeed committed to the cause of freedom.

≈ ≈ ≈

---

[*] This paragraph is not contained in the first edition of the speech, as published by James D. Bemis, in 1811; but I find it in the speech as given by Drake, in his Book of the Indians, and also in Thatcher's Indian Biography. Still, it appears to me to be an interpolation.

Published according to Act of Parliament, Sept. 1. 1773 by Arch.ᵈ Bell,
Bookseller N.⁰ 8 near the Saracens Head Aldgate.

"On Being Brought from Africa to America" (1773)

'Twas mercy brought me from my pagan land,
Taught my benighted soul to understand
That there's a God—that there's a Saviour too;
Once I redemption neither sought nor knew.
Some view our sable race with scornful eye—
'Their color is a diabolic dye.'
Remember, Christians, Negroes black as Cain,
May be refined, and join the angelic train.

"To the University of Cambridge, in New-England" (1773)

While an intrinsic ardor prompts to write,
The Muses promise to assist my pen.
'Twas not long since I left my native shore,
The land of errors and Egyptian gloom:
Father of mercy! 'twas thy gracious hand
Brought me in safety from those dark abodes.

Students, to you 'tis given to scan the heights
Above, to traverse the etherial space,
And mark the systems of revolving worlds.
Still more, ye sons of science, ye receive
The blissful news by messengers from heaven,
How Jesus' blood for your redemption flows.
See him, with hands out-stretched upon the cross!
Immense compassion in his bosom glows;
He hears revilers, nor resents their scorn.
What matchless mercy in the Son of God!
He deigned to die, that they might rise again,
And share with him, in the sublimest skies,
Life without death, and glory without end.

Improve your privileges while they stay,
Ye pupils; and each hour redeem, that bears
Or good or bad report of you to heaven.
Let sin, that baneful evil to the soul,
By you be shunned; nor once remit your guard:
Suppress the deadly serpent in its egg,
Ye blooming plants of human race divine,
An Ethiop tells you, 'tis your greatest foe;
Its transient sweetness turns to endless pain,
And in immense perdition sinks the soul.

"On the Death of the Rev. Mr. George Whitefield—1770"* (1773)

Hail, happy saint! on thine immortal throne,
Possest of glory, life, and bliss unknown:
We hear no more the music of thy tongue,
Thy wonted auditories cease to throng.
Thy sermons in unequalled accents flowed,
And ev'ry bosom with devotion glowed;
Thou didst, in strains of eloquence refined,
Inflame the heart, and captivate the mind.
Unhappy, we the setting sun deplore,
So glorious once, but ah! it shines no more.

---

* [George Whitefield, an Englishman and Anglican, was the founder of Methodism and the evangelical movement, visiting and preaching in America many times. His position on slavery was complex.—E.J.D and J.B.F.]

Behold the prophet in his towering flight!
He leaves the earth for heaven's unmeasured height,
And worlds unknown receive him from our sight.
There Whitefield wings with rapid course his way,
And sails to Zion through vast seas of day.
Thy prayers, great saint, and thine incessant cries
Have pierced the bosom of thy native skies.
Thou moon hast seen, and all the stars of light,
How he has wrestled with his God by night.
He prayed that grace in ev'ry heart might dwell;
He longed to see America excel;
He charged its youth that ev'ry grace divine
Should with full lustre in their conduct shine.
That Saviour, which his soul did first receive,
The greatest gift that ev'n a God can give,
He freely offered to the numerous throng,
That on his lips with list'ning pleasure hung.

"Take him, ye wretched for your only good,
"Take him, ye starving sinners, for your food;
"Ye thirsty, come to this life-giving stream,
"Ye preachers, take him for your joyful theme;
"Take him, my dear Americans, he said,
"Be your complaints on his kind bosom laid:
"Take him, ye Africans, he longs for you;
"Impartial Saviour is his title due:
"Washed in the fountain of redeeming blood,
"You shall be sons, and kings, and priests to God."

Great Countess,* we Americans revere
Thy name, and mingle in thy grief sincere;
New-England deeply feels, the orphans mourn,
Their more than father will no more return.

But though arrested by the hand of death,
Whitefield no more exerts his lab'ring breath,
Yet let us view him in the eternal skies,
Let ev'ry heart to this bright vision rise;
While the tomb, safe, retains its sacred trust,
Till life divine reanimates his dust.

---

* The Countess of Huntingdon, to whom Mr. Whitefield was chaplain.

3 :: Romanticism

3–1
Mary Austin Holley (1784–1846)

Cousin of Stephen F. Austin, the "Father of Texas," MARY AUSTIN HOLLEY (1784–1846) was a New Englander who did not visit Texas until a grown woman. To promote the Austin family legacy, earn needed money, and create interest in the new lands of Texas, she wrote the first English-language book about the state, *Texas: Observations, Historical, Geographical and Descriptive, in a Series of Letters Written during a Visit to Austin's Colony*. She later expanded this into the first full-length English-language history of Texas, including a recounting of the Texas Revolution. By writing the lyrics to "Brazos Boat Glee" (c. 1838), she also wrote what may have been the first English-language song written in Texas. Her views of race and gender are representative of her time and place, and the section below reflects Holley's ardent support of the Texas Republic.

≈ ≈ ≈

From *Texas: Observations, Historical, Geographical, and Descriptive, in a Series of Letters Written during a Visit to Austin's Colony* (1836)

Chapter 7. Inhabitants—Society and Manners

The population of Texas, exclusive of the Indian tribes, is estimated at fifty thousand souls. Of these about five thousand are Mexicans, and the remainder mostly Anglo-Americans, with a small number of Europeans. The principal settlements of Mexicans are the old Spanish towns of Bexar and Goliad (formerly called La Bahia).

The former was the capital of Texas, under the Spanish and Mexican dominions, and contains about twenty-five hundred inhabitants. The latter is a village whose inhabitants do not exceed eight hundred. There is, also, a small village of Mexicans on the Guadalupe, at Victoria, near which there was also formerly a military post. At Nacogdoches and in the vicinity of the town, there is a Mexican population of about five hundred souls. A few families are also dispersed among the American settlers, particularly in Austin's colony; but the addition of one thousand to those already mentioned, would include the total Mexican population in Texas. The Mexicans, in the colonies, are employed by the settlers mostly as herdsmen, and are universally acknowledged to be the best hands that can be procured, for the management of cattle, horses, and other live stock. Their occupation indeed, generally, is raising live stock, and agriculture on a limited scale. Many of them make a business of catching and taming *mustangs* or wild horses, which they sell to the American settlers. They are also frequently employed in the conduct of trade, by caravans, with the neighboring Mexican States. They are very ignorant and degraded, and generally speaking, timid and irresolute; and a more brutal and, at the same time, more cowardly set of men does not exist than the Mexican soldiery. They are held in great contempt by the American settlers, who assert that five Indians will chase twenty Mexicans, but five Anglo-Americans will chase twenty Indians. This savors rather of a "half horse and half alligator" origin, but the experience of the late revolution has confirmed its truth in the main. The Mexicans are commonly very indolent, of loose morals, and, if not infidels of which there are many, involved in the grossest superstition. This view exhibits why it is by no means wonderful that this people have been the dupes and slaves of so many masters, or that the plans of intelligent and patriotic men, for the political regeneration of Mexico, have heretofore entirely failed. The moral education of this people must be improved, before their political condition can be ameliorated. There are many honorable and signal exceptions to this statement, it is true; but we believe the general character of the Mexicans in Texas and her vicinity has been pretty accurately drawn. Fortunately however, as we have seen, there are but few of the race within her confines.

The great majority of the population of Texas, and the most valuable portion of it, consists of emigrants from the United States. The active and enterprising New Englander—the bold and hardy western hunter—the high-spirited southern planter—meet here upon common ground, divested of all sectional influence, to lend their combined energies to the improvement of this infant but delightful and prosperous country. It has been said and published by certain individuals, for what cause we know not without it is in sheer enmity to this country, that Texas is the great penitentiary of America, where outlaws, murderers, thieves, and vagabonds resort, after having been compelled to flee from the judgments of offended laws, or the scorn and detestation of society. This is a gross misrepresentation, and unworthy of any man who has the least regard for truth. That cases have existed and are yet occasionally found of this description we will not pretend to deny. They are unavoidable evils to which every new country is liable. We know indeed that a considerable portion of the United States was settled by transported convicts, and the evil increased to such a degree, as to become one of the primary matters of complaint, by the colonies to the mother country. Such is not the case however in Texas. It is true that there are found, here and there, refugees from justice; but they cannot be properly called colonists; they are here, as in their own country, the marks of public contempt and abhorrence, holding no influence in society, nor honored with the confidence or regard of any citizen. They are considered as pests, and avoided as such. Never has any cis-Atlantic* State been peopled by a more honest, industrious, intelligent, and respectable emigration than Texas, and especially Austin's colony. Sturdy mechanics, substantial farmers, able professional men, and, not unfrequently, wealthy planters, have sought and found a home in the Brazos valley; while the great body of settlers, though commonly poor, have been of the most respectable and enterprising character. The empresario, Gen. Austin, has never admitted into his colony any man known to be of disreputable standing, and has always, as far as practicable, made diligent inquiries in order to ascertain, if possible, the conduct and reputation of each applicant. Facts—eloquent facts—in the rapid growth of this country, the state of public sentiment manifest in their present struggle, the success which has attended her arms, and the sympathy which she has universally excited, loudly proclaim how false and slanderous have been such imputations upon the honor of her citizenship, as that cited above. The tide of emigration now flowing in from the United States is of a character most desirable for any new country. The present American population is about fifty thousand and is augmenting daily.

Of trans-Atlantic emigrants, the principal are Germans, French, English, and Irish; but chiefly the last.

The colonies of McMullen & McGloin, and Powers, were contracted for, with the special purpose of settling an Irish population on their lands. These

---

* [The same side of the Atlantic—*E.J.D. and J.B.F.*]

grants embrace the greater portion of the region situated between the Nueces and San Antonio rivers. This is a very valuable part of Texas, and there can be no doubt but that many thousands of the oppressed sons of Erin, if they possessed the information and means of emigration, would joyfully exchange their "cow's grass" and "potatoe lots" for rich farms in this colony. Here are no tithes, no poor rates, no burthensome exactions, nor vexatious restrictions. Here enterprise and energy may unfold themselves to their fullest extent, in all the various pursuits of honest industry, without fear and without reproach. The colony has already commenced operations under favorable auspices, and will doubtless succeed and ultimately flourish. Nothing is now wanting to insure its immediate success, but a sufficient supply of industrious emigrants; and these are fast coming in. A number of Irish families have already established themselves in the upper grant of San Patrick, charmed with the country and animated with the certain prospect of plenty and independence, and the lower grant is constantly receiving accessions. Never was there a more inviting asylum for Irish emigrants, than is presented by the Irish colonies on the Nueces, and it is to be hoped that large numbers of them will avail themselves of the advantages here presented in the event of their becoming settlers.

There are a considerable number of Negroes in Texas who, though slavery is prohibited, by an evasion of the law are "bound" for life, and are, *de facto*, the property of their masters. They are however, from the restraints of law, invested with more liberty and less liable to abuse than the slaves of the Southern United States. The question of negro slavery in connexion with the settlement of this country, is one of great importance, and perhaps may hereafter present a serious difficulty. The former constitution and laws totally prohibited this worst of evils. Should this wise policy be abandoned and Texas become, what Louisiana now is, the receptacle of the redundant and jail-delivered slaves of other countries, all its energies would be paralyzed, and whatever oppressions may hereafter arise either from abroad or at home, must be endured, for the country would require a prop to lean upon, and, from necessity, would be forever dependant.*

---

* [Holley expresses some of the complexity of the slavery issue in Texas. Banned by the Mexican government, favored by some Texans, slavery was an issue before, during, and after the Revolution, and the issue continued to divide Texans during the Annexation debate as well as the later debate over Secession. Many northerners (Thoreau among them) opposed Texas Annexation because of the spread of slavery, but Sam Houston, the first president of the Republic of Texas, voted against the spread of slavery into new territories.—E.J.D. and J.B.F.]

Various Indian tribes are resident in Texas; but we reserve a notice of them for the succeeding chapter, which will be specially devoted to their history and manners.

The character of Leather Stocking is not uncommon in Texas. Many persons employ an individual of this class in the business of hunting, in all its branches; and thus are constantly supplied with provisions of every description, even to eggs, which are furnished by the immense number of wild fowl. These hunters are very profitable to their employers, and much cherished in the family, and often become spoiled by familiarity and indulgence. A roughness of manners, and a rudeness of speech are tolerated in them, which would not be brooked in other servants. They are a sort of privileged character. Indians and Mexicans are considered the best qualified for this important office. But it sometimes happens that a white man from the *States*, who has become some what decivilized, (to coin a word,) is substituted. The dress of these hunters is usually of deer-skin; hence the appropriate name of *Leather Stocking*. Their generic name, for they form a distinct class, is *Frontiers-men*.*

The use of the rifle, however, is not confined to the Leather Stockings, or to the ruder sex exclusively; as the following anecdote, the subject of which is still living, will testify. Mrs. M—, the Texas Diana, has killed with the rifle eighty deer and one buffalo. Her canting husband wanting industry and capacity, she was compelled thus to support him and her children. She now lives alone with her children, in the prairie near Chocolate Bayou. She was an illiterate woman, having never been to school in her life; but the same independent spirit which placed the rifle in her hand for the support of her family, prompted her to study and improve herself by learning to read, after which she taught the same to her children; a great blessing for a poor family, where schools were formerly so very rare. The mode of her education, in the use of the rifle, will show how natural it is that we should find, in a wild unsettled country, many females in her circumstances and of a daring spirit, who are acquainted with its use. The same bold mind which, in different circumstances, would make such a female a polished lady, would lead her, here, to acquire the accomplishments

---

* The family of Dust who reside on the "mound," noticed in this work as situated on the road between Brazoria and San Felipe, are perhaps the most illiterate and decivilized of any in Texas. The children are totally uneducated, wild, and rude, and flee from any association with strangers. They are, literally, "wild men of the woods," with the exception of one daughter, who married an intelligent and industrious yankee, with whom she now resides on the mound, and has become a very tidy woman, and quite respectable. Mrs. Dust, the mother of the family, is a grand daughter of the Kentucky patriarch, Daniel Boone, and does no discredit to her lineage, as far as a disposition for a roving and solitary life can testify.

of "wood-craft"; so much are we the creatures of circumstances. Her father came from Mississippi with his family in a keel-boat. Having to "put in" along shore frequently on the way, and to go hunting in order to provide food for the party, she, then a young girl, took, at last, the habit of carrying the rifle, and thus learned the use of it. She is a strong active woman not yet thirty. When she hunts, not being able to lift a whole deer, she divides the animal with a "tomahawk" into quarters, tying two of them together, and thus suspending them on each side of her horse.

It must not be supposed from the characters we have named here as existing in Texas, that such constitute the body of her population, and give tone to her society. These are a distinct class of people, who are invariably found among the pioneers of every new country, and are such as alone would be able to encounter the hardships, to endure the privations, and enjoy the solitude of the wilderness around them. Such as these form the *avant couriers* of civilization, and prepare the way for the less hardy but more refined colonist. Many of these who first penetrated into this then wild and uninhabited region, are still living to see the face of nature and society almost wholly changed by the rapid march of improvement, and are themselves solitary monuments, thinly scattered through her territory, to show how great that change has been. Though rude and unfit for the common avocations of social life, they are not however an useless or troublesome class. They are brave, generous, and hospitable; though generally careless and unreflecting. Never having felt the various artificial wants of society, they regard not those luxuries which are required to supply them. Having lived mostly free from the restraints of law, they are not apt to pay implicit obedience to its dictates, when contrary to their own views and feelings. The descendants of this class reared in the midst of civilized society, combine the noble daring and independence of the one, with the refinement of the other; and, thus, frequently form the most intelligent, enterprising, and, altogether, the most valuable portion of a community.

With regard to the state of society here, from what we have seen, it is natural to expect some incongruities. It will take some time for people gathered from the north and from the south, from east and from the west, to assimilate and adopt themselves to new situations. But there is one redeeming quality which is universal, and which will exert a most beneficial influence upon the manners of the people; that is the virtue of hospitality. Every body's house is open, and table spread to accommodate the traveller; the best of every thing is presented freely, not indeed with the refinement and courtesy of a polished European community, but with the honest, blunt, but hearty welcome of a Texas back-woodsman. There are a few here of the higher class, whose manners are more courtly but not less sincere. Nature has lavished her treasures upon all, and they seem imbued with the spirit of liberality which such abundance should create. Though there are a few who may be styled *nabobs*, as far as wealth is concerned, and others who are worthless and wretched: yet, as a general remark, there are no poor people here, and none rich; that is, none who have much money. The poor and the rich, to use the correlatives where distinction there is none, get the same quantity of land on arrival; and if they do not continue equal, it is for want of good management on the one part, or superior industry and sagacity on the other. All are happy, because busy; and none meddle with the affairs of their neighbors, because they have enough to do to take care of their own. They are bound together, by a common interest, by sameness of purpose and hopes. Artificial wants are entirely forgotten in the view of real ones; and self, eternal self, does not alone fill up the round of life. Delicate ladies find they can be useful, and need not be vain. Even privations become pleasures; people grow ingenious in overcoming difficulties. Many latent faculties are developed. They discover in themselves powers which they did not suspect themselves of possessing, and, equally surprised and delighted with the discovery, they apply to their labors with all that energy and spirit, which new hope and conscious strength inspire. This state of things may be changed, and society probably advanced a grade higher in the scale, by the events of the present war.[*]

. . .

There is no aristocracy observable here except such as nature herself demands; the only distinction is that which always should obtain between virtue and vice. All are contented; all are happy. Each thinks himself, with a pardonable vanity, the most highly favored of men. Each has in his own opinion the best land, the best water courses, the finest timber, and the most judicious mode of operation; proving at least that each is satisfied with his own lot, and not disposed to envy his neighbor. There are exceptions to this tone of feeling it is true; but we are merely tracing the general complexion of society, which is such as we have described it, at present, whatever changes may be wrought in it hereafter.

Many foreigners, well educated, and of polished manners, have found a home in the Brazos valley; and the higher requisites of social intercourse are not totally absent here. Great attention is beginning to be paid to education and the spread of useful knowledge among the people. Two newspapers are already established in Austin's colony—the Texas Republican at Brazoria; and the Telegraph at San Felipe. Several schools with competent instructors are

---

[*] [The Texas Revolution—*E.J.D. and J.B.F.*]

well supported, and the "knights of the birch" will find a broad and profitable field for labor in the numerous settlements here, where all are more or less wealthy, and anxious to bestow upon their children a good education.

Public instruction, by the confederated state of Coahuila and Texas was predicated upon the following basis: "In all the towns of the State, there shall be established a competent number of common schools, in which there shall be taught reading, writing, and cyphering; the catechism of the Christian religion, a short and simple explanation of the constitution, and the general one of the Republic; the rights and duties of man in Society, and that which can conduce to the better education of youth."

"The method of instruction shall be uniform throughout the State, and in those places where it may be necessary, there shall be institutions of learning more suitable for disseminating public instruction in the useful arts and sciences."

So wise an act of legislation, we are confidently assured, will not be altered by the free and independent State of Texas, should she attain to independence; but, on the contrary, new and improved facilities will be extended for the promotion of the interests of education.

With regard to the language of the Texans, you *hear* nothing but English. This is to be expected, inasmuch as the great body of settlers is composed of emigrants from the United States. It is owing to this cause that the laws and all public proceedings, which were formerly published in Spanish, are by a late act, required to be promulgated in the English language. It is about as great an accomplishment to speak Spanish there, as it is French in our own States. It is however convenient to know it; and all who *can*, try to attain it. Lawyers who know it, will hereafter have a great advantage over others who are ignorant of it; all deeds, conveyances, &c. being written in the Spanish. Those acquainted with this language find a profitable business as translators: this shows how few there are who are adepts in it. As to language, idioms, &c. as well as many customs, it would be unnecessary for us to go into a detail. Let the reader only fancy himself in Kentucky or any *new* State, listening to their conversation and observing their manners, and he will have an accurate idea of such things in Texas. Indeed it is very probable that we have already wasted too much time in our description of Texans and their manners, and that it would have been fully sufficient to have said, with regard to many things, that the inhabitants differ but very little from those of the recently settled western and southern States of our country.

A few remarks upon some peculiarities in Texas customs, and we shall conclude this chapter.

We have heretofore spoken of the wild daring of this people, even of the females; and cited a case which was rather an extreme one—of rare occurrence.

But necessity has taught many of a more elevated rank in life, a hardihood and courage which is truly surprising in the gentle sex. We shall now make a few remarks upon a great class, of which the example we shall give is a just one, who were formed to be remarkable women in any sphere, and whose characters have been moulded by the circumstances of the country, in which their lots have been cast. At the same time it will be recollected that the state of the country is fast changing the character of society, and that this class is yielding to one of a different description, such as improvement and refinement in any country naturally gives birth to.

Living in a wild country under circumstances requiring constant exertion, forms the character to great and daring enterprise. Women thus situated are known to perform exploits, which the effeminate men of populous cities might tremble at. Hence there are more Dianas and *Esther Stanhopes* than one in Texas. It is not uncommon for ladies to mount their mustangs and hunt with their husbands, and with them to camp out for days on their excursions to the sea shore for fish and oysters. All visiting is done on horseback, and they will go fifty miles to a ball with their silk dresses, made perhaps in Philadelphia or New Orleans, in their saddle-bags. Hardy, vigorous constitutions, free spirits, and spontaneous gaiety are thus induced, and continued a rich legacy to their children, who, it is to be hoped, will sufficiently value the blessing not to squander it away, in their eager search for the luxuries and refinements of polite life. Women have capacity for greatness, but they require occasions to bring it out. They require, perhaps, stronger motives than men—they have stronger barriers to break through of indolence and habit—but, when roused, they are quick to discern and unshrinking to act. *Lot was unfortunate in his wife.* Many a wife in Texas has proved herself the better half, and many a widow's heart has prompted her to noble daring.

Mrs. — left her home in Kentucky with her six sons, and *no other jewels.* There was good land and room in Texas. Hither she came with the first settlers, at a time when the Indians were often troublesome by coming in large companies and encamping near an isolated farm, demanding of its helpless proprietors, not then too well provided for, whatever of provisions or other things struck their fancies. One of these *foraging* parties, not over nice in their demands, stationed themselves in rather too near proximity to the dwelling of this veteran lady. They were so well satisfied with their position, and scoured the place so completely, that she ventured to remonstrate, gently at first, then more vehemently. All would not do: the *pic-nics* would not budge an inch; and moreover threatened life if she did not forbear from further expressions of impatience. The good woman was *armed*. She buckled on her *breastplate* of *courage*, if not of *righteousness*, and with her children and women servants, all her household around her, sent for the chief, and very boldly expostulating with him, *commanded* him to depart on the instant at the peril of his tribe; or by a signal she would call in her whole *people*, numerous and formidable, and exterminate his race. She was no more troubled with the Indians. She lives comfortably with her thriving family and thriving fortune, and with great credit to herself, on the road between Brazoria and San Felipe, in the same house now famed for its hospitality and comfort. It is the usual stopping place for travellers on that route, who are not a little entertained with the border stories and characteristic jests, there related, by casual companies meeting for the night and sharing the same apartment. It was thus that the above incident, much more exemplified, was drawn from the hostess herself. A volume of *reminiscences* thus collected, racy with the marvellous, would not be *unapt* to modern taste, and the modern science of book-making.

The ladies of Texas during the *passing* struggle—more *patriots* even than the men—have displayed much of the Roman virtue, encouraging the citizens, and keeping up the chivalry of the volunteers by expressions of enthusiasm and by fétes as well as by a careful attention to their wants. They have not yet been called upon to shoulder the rifle and mount the war-steed, but with the occasion will come the spirit to do so. Their present duty is to *guard* the domicil.

The early settlers are much given to boasting of their exploits—especially with the Indians—considering such achievements as a sort of title to nobility. Noble deeds certainly are the best claim to the best species of nobility. Hence all good governments—except our own America—are liberal in their gifts of titles as well as of money to their statesmen, heroes, artists, and all who distinguish themselves.

These enterprising and proud pioneers are not half pleased that persons coming in at the *eleventh hour*, should share the benefits of the colony equally with those who have borne the *heat and burthen of the day.* They should reflect, however, that there are other claims to the privileges of good citizenship, besides fighting Indians—*or Mexicans.*

3–2

Poetry of Early Texas, authors unknown (1835–1850)

The newspaper poems collected by PHILIP GRAHAM (1898–1967) in *Early Texas Verse, 1835–1850* were generally unsigned but all charted "the gradual but steady growth of environmental influences on Texas verse" (v).

≈ ≈ ≈

"Lines to the San Antonio River"* (1838)

Sweet Western stream, thy waters long
Have murmured to the 'desert air,'
Thy lovely self unknown among
The lauded, beautiful and fair;
Wild plains have circled thee around,
And locked thee in their dear embrace;
Wild beasts and wilder men have found
Upon thy banks a hiding place;
But yet thou wert not quite alone,
For on thy margin Bexar stood,
And still she stands, encased in stone,†
The mistress of the mighty wood.

The desert Queen—but dark the tale
That her historic pages state;
Strange legends consecrate the vale
That lies about her city gate.
Bexar! the very sound conveys
A thought of blood and murderous strife,
Of evil War's most gloomy days,
The secret dagger and the knife;
'Tis past, thou art accursed no more.
Behold improvement's sun appear,
Thy moral darkness flies before,
And leaves thy sky forever clear;
Henceforth, fair stream, thy silver wave
No more shall blush with human gore.
The tyrant and the treacherous slave
Shall war upon thy banks no more.
Peace to thy beauty! May she reign,
The Goddess of the sunny vale,
And mayst thou never hear again
The battle's rage or widow's wail.

* Published in *The Telegraph and Texas Register* (Houston), August 11, 1838.
† The Alamo.

"Storm on the Prairie"* (1841)

Clouds are gathering, fierce and black,
O'er the trader's prairie track.
Night is closing, dark and fast,
Round the desert wild and vast.
Sudden stops the caravan
As the sky the traders scan.
Down the west the sun is dashing,
O'er the head are thunders pealing,
Round the sky are lightnings flashing,
Wild sublimity revealing!

Down upon the prairie land,
Like an angry spirit band,
Press the thunder laden vapors,
Quenching even starry tapers.
While the far-off mutter comes,
Louder still and nearer swelling,
Like the battle call of drums
From the storm fiend's misty dwelling.
By the lightning's fitful lamp
Soon is formed the trader's camp.

Now above the fearful yell
Of the tempest, wildly shrieking,
In successive roar and swell,
Jove is heard in terror speaking!
Lurid lightnings, far and nigh,
Flash and quiver round the sky.
Mute the desert pilgrim stands,
Awe-struck and with clasped hands,
While above his shrinking form
Breaks at last the prairie storm!

Now like hail-stones on the plain
Heavy beats the pelting rain,
Driven far before the blast
That goes howling on its course
O'er the lonely region vast

* Published in *The Telegraph and Texas Register* (Houston), May 5, 1841.

With a voice so wild and hoarse,
Darkness like the pall of death
Yields an instant to the flash
Of the lightning; human breath
Pauses for the coming crash!

Like a phantom through the sky
Hear the peal go rattling by,—
Sharp and loud, and wildly clear,
Ringing on the trader's ear,
Rending earth, and bursting near,
Like a thing of death and fear!
O, how brightly morning beams
Over plains and over streams
When the prairie storm is gone,
"When the hurly burly's done!"

3–3
John James Audubon (1785–1851)

Born in Haiti, the illegitimate son of a French Captain and his maid, JOHN JAMES AUDUBON (1785–1851) came to America at the age of eighteen. While Audubon is most famous for his collection of paintings, *Birds of America* (1831–1838), this ornithologist and naturalist achieved popularity for his writings as well. Taken together, Audubon's paintings and writings provide a view into the social and natural world in the years of the early republic. His essay "The Prairie" is from his *Delineations of American Scenery and Character*, a work in which his love of adventure is as apparent as his love for the landscape.

≈ ≈ ≈

"The Prairie" (1832)

On my return from the Upper Mississippi, I found myself obliged to cross one of the wide Prairies, which, in that portion of the United States, vary the appearance of the country. The weather was fine, all around me was as fresh and blooming as if it had just issued from the bosom of nature. My knapsack, my gun, and my dog, were all I had for baggage and company. But, although well moccassined, I moved slowly along, attracted by the brilliancy of the flowers,

and the gambols of the fawns around their dams, to all appearance as thoughtless of danger as I felt myself.

My march was of long duration; I saw the sun sinking beneath the horizon
long before I could perceive any appearance of woodland, and nothing in the
shape of man had I met with that day. The track which I followed was only an
old Indian trace, and as darkness overshaded the prairie, I felt some desire to
reach at least a copse, in which I might lie down to rest. The Night-hawks were
skimming over and around me, attracted by the buzzing wings of the beetles
which form their food, and the distant howling of wolves gave me some hope
that I should soon arrive at the skirts of some woodland.

I did so, and almost at the same instant a fire-light attracting my eye, I
moved towards it, full of confidence that it proceeded from the camp of some
wandering Indians. I was mistaken:—I discovered by its glare that it was from
the hearth of a small log cabin, and that a tall figure passed and repassed between it and me, as if busily engaged in household arrangements.

I reached the spot, and presenting myself at the door, asked the tall figure, which proved to be a woman, if I might take shelter under her roof for
the night. Her voice was gruff, and her attire negligently thrown about her.
She answered in the affirmative. I walked in, took a wooden stool, and quietly
seated myself by the fire. The next object that attracted my notice was a finely
formed young Indian, resting his head between his hands, with his elbows on
his knees. A long bow rested against the log wall near him, while a quantity of
arrows and two or three raccoon skins lay at his feet. He moved not; he apparently breathed not. Accustomed to the habits of the Indians, and knowing that
they pay little attention to the approach of civilized strangers (a circumstance
which in some countries is considered as evincing the apathy of their character), I addressed him in French, a language not unfrequently partially known
to the people in that neighbourhood. He raised his head, pointed to one of his
eyes with his finger, and gave me a significant glance with the other. His face
was covered with blood. The fact was, that an hour before this, as he was in
the act of discharging an arrow at a raccoon in the top of a tree, the arrow had
split upon the cord, and sprung back with such violence into his right eye as
to destroy it for ever.

Feeling hungry, I inquired what sort of fare I might expect. Such a thing as
a bed was not to be seen, but many large untanned bear and buffalo hides lay
piled in a corner. I drew a fine time-piece from my breast, and told the woman
that it was late, and that I was fatigued. She had espyed my watch, the richness of which seemed to operate upon her feelings with electric quickness. She
told me that there was plenty of venison and jerked buffalo meat, and that on

removing the ashes I should find a cake. But my watch had struck her fancy, and her curiosity had to be gratified by an immediate sight of it. I took off the gold chain that secured it from around my neck, and presented it to her. She was all ecstasy, spoke of its beauty, asked me its value, and put the chain round her brawny neck, saying how happy the possession of such a watch should make her. Thoughtless, and, as I fancied myself, in so retired a spot, secure, I paid little attention to her talk or her movements. I helped my dog to a good supper of venison, and was not long in satisfying the demands of my own appetite.

The Indian rose from his seat, as if in extreme suffering. He passed and repassed me several times, and once pinched me on the side so violently, that the pain nearly brought forth an exclamation of anger. I looked at him. His eye met mine; but his look was so forbidding, that it struck a chill into the more nervous part of my system. He again seated himself, drew his butcher-knife from its greasy scabbard, examined its edge, as I would do that of a razor suspected dull, replaced it, and again taking his tomahawk from his back, filled the pipe of it with tobacco, and sent me expressive glances whenever our hostess chanced to have her back towards us.

Never until that moment had my senses been awakened to the danger which I now suspected to be about me. I returned glance for glance to my companion, and rested well assured that, whatever enemies I might have, he was not of their number.

I asked the woman for my watch, wound it up, and under pretence of wishing to see how the weather might probably be on the morrow, took up my gun, and walked out of the cabin. I slipped a ball into each barrel, scraped the edges of my flints, renewed the primings, and returning to the hut, gave a favourable account of my observations. I took a few bear-skins, made a pallet of them, and calling my faithful dog to my side, lay down, with my gun close to my body, and in a few minutes was, to all appearance, fast asleep.

A short time had elapsed, when some voices were heard, and from the corner of my eyes I saw two athletic youths making their entrance, bearing a dead stag on a pole. They disposed of their burden, and asking for whisky, helped themselves freely to it. Observing me and the wounded Indian, they asked who I was, and why the devil that rascal (meaning the Indian, who, they knew, understood not a word of English) was in the house. The mother—for so she proved to be, bade them speak less loudly, made mention of my watch, and took them to a corner, where a conversation took place, the purport of which it required little shrewdness in me to guess. I tapped my dog gently. He moved his tail, and with indescribable pleasure I saw his fine eyes alternately fixed on me and raised towards the trio in the corner. I felt that he perceived danger in my situation. The Indian exchanged a last glance with me.

The lads had eaten and drunk themselves into such condition, that I already looked upon them as *hors de combat*; and the frequent visits of the whisky bottle to the ugly mouth of their dam I hoped would soon reduce her to a like state. Judge of my astonishment, reader, when I saw this incarnate fiend take a large carving-knife, and go to the grindstone to whet its edge. I saw her pour the water on the turning machine, and watched her working away with the dangerous instrument, until the sweat covered every part of my body, in despite of my determination to defend myself to the last. Her task finished, she walked to her reeling sons, and said, "There, that'll soon settle him! Boys, kill you—, and then for the watch."

I turned, cocked my gun-locks silently, touched my faithful companion, and lay ready to start up and shoot the first who might attempt my life. The moment was fast approaching, and that night might have been my last in this world, had not Providence made preparations for my rescue. All was ready. The infernal hag was advancing slowly, probably contemplating the best way of despatching me, whilst her sons should be engaged with the Indian. I was several times on the eve of rising and shooting her on the spot:—but she was not to be punished thus. The door was suddenly opened, and there entered two stout travellers, each with a long rifle on his shoulder. I bounced up on my feet, and making them most heartily welcome, told them how well it was for me that they should have arrived at that moment. The tale was told in a minute. The drunken sons were secured, and the woman, in spite of her defence and vociferations, shared the same fate. The Indian fairly danced with joy, and gave us to understand that, as he could not sleep for pain, he would watch over us. You may suppose we slept much less than we talked. The two strangers gave me an account of their once having been themselves in a somewhat similar situation. Day came, fair and rosy, and with it the punishment of our captives.

They were now quite sobered. Their feet were unbound, but their arms were still securely tied. We marched them into the woods off the road, and having used them as Regulators were wont to use such delinquents, we set fire to the cabin, gave all the skins and implements to the young Indian warrior, and proceeded, well pleased towards the settlements.

During upwards of twenty-five years, when my wanderings extended to all parts of our country, this was the only time at which my life was in danger from my fellow creatures. Indeed, so little risk do travellers run in the United States, that no one born there ever dreams of any to be encountered on the road; and I can only account for this occurrence by supposing that the inhabitants of the cabin were not Americans.

Will you believe, reader, that not many miles from the place where this adventure happened, and where fifteen years ago, no habitation belonging to civilized man was expected, and very few ever seen, large roads are now laid out, cultivation has converted the woods into fertile fields, taverns have been erected, and much of what we Americans call comfort is to be met with. So fast does improvement proceed in our abundant and free country.

3–4
George Catlin (1796–1872)

It would be hard to find a painter who better created the iconography of the American West than GEORGE CATLIN (1796–1872). Catlin left the eastern United States, vowing to record in his paintings every native tribe west of the Mississippi. His many expeditions West resulted in thousands of sketches and paintings of the Western tribes. He painted individuals but also tribal feasts, war councils, and celebrations. Catlin was a popular lecturer, painter, and writer, and his descriptions of native life in *Letters and Notes on the Manners, Customs and Conditions of the North American Indians* are as sensitively accomplished as his paintings, though occasionally touched with racist language and depictions. The chapter included here is of the Comanche his party met on their travels along the Oklahoma-Texas border; note the mention of the "Wico," understood by scholars to be the Waco.

≈ ≈ ≈

From *Letters and Notes on the Manners, Customs and Conditions of the North American Indians* (1842)

Letter—No. 42

Great Camanchee Village[*]

The village of the Camanchees by the side of which we are encamped, is composed of six or eight hundred skin-covered lodges, made of poles and buffalo skins, in the manner precisely as those of the Sioux and other Missouri tribes, of which I have heretofore given some account. This village with its thousands

---

[*] [Near Wichita Mountains, southwestern Oklahoma—*E.J.D. and J.B.F.*]

164

165

of wild inmates, with horses and dogs, and wild sports and domestic occupations, presents a most curious scene; and the manners and looks of the people, a rich subject for the brush and the pen.

In the view I have made of it (plate 164), but a small portion of the village is shewn; which is as well as to shew the whole of it, inasmuch as the wigwams, as well as the customs, are the same in every part of it. In the foreground is seen the wigwam of the chief; and in various parts, crotches and poles, on which the women are drying meat, and "*graining*" buffalo robes. These people, living in a country where buffaloes are abundant, make their wigwams more easily of their skins, than of anything else; and with them find greater facilities of moving about, as circumstances often require; when they drag them upon the poles attached to their horses, and erect them again with little trouble in their new residence.

We white men, strolling about amongst their wigwams, are looked upon with as much curiosity as if we had come from the moon; and evidently create a sort of chill in the blood of children and dogs, when we make our appearance. I was pleased to-day with the simplicity of a group which came out in front of the chief's lodge to scrutinize my faithful friend Chadwick and I, as we were strolling about the avenues and labyrinths of their village; upon which I took out my book and sketched as quick as lightning, whilst "Joe" rivetted their attention by some ingenious trick or other, over my shoulders, which I did not see, having no time to turn my head (plate 165). These were the juvenile parts of the chief's family, and all who at this moment were at home; the venerable old man, and his three or four wives, making a visit, like hundreds of others, to the encampment.

In speaking just above, of the mode of moving their wigwams, and changing their encampments, I should have said a little more, and should also have given to the reader, a sketch of one of these extraordinary scenes, which I have had the good luck to witness (plate 166); where several thousands were on the march, and furnishing one of those laughable scenes which daily happen, where so many dogs, and so many squaws, are travelling in such a confused mass; with so many conflicting interests, and so many local and individual rights to be pertinaciously claimed and protected. Each horse drags his load, and each dog, *i.e.* each dog that *will* do it (and there are many that will *not*), also dragging his wallet on a couple of poles; and each squaw with her load, and all together (notwithstanding their burthens) cherishing their pugnacious feelings, which often bring them into general conflict, commencing usually amongst the dogs, and sure to result in fisticuffs of the women; whilst the men, riding leisurely on the right or the left, take infinite pleasure in overlooking these desperate conflicts, at which they are sure to have a laugh, and in which, as sure never to lend a hand.

The Camanchees, like the Northern tribes, have many games, and in pleasant weather seem to be continually practicing more or less of them, on the prairies, back of, and contiguous to, their village.

In their ball-plays, and some other games, they are far behind the Sioux and others of the Northern tribes; but, in racing horses and riding, they are not equalled by any other Indians on the Continent. Racing horses, it would seem, is a constant and almost incessant exercise, and their principal mode of gambling; and perhaps, a more finished set of jockeys are not to be found. The exercise of these people, in a country where horses are so abundant, and the country so fine for riding, is chiefly done on horseback; and it "stands to reason," that such a people, who have been practicing from their childhood, should become exceedingly expert in this wholesome and beautiful exercise. Amongst their feats of riding, there is one that has astonished me more than anything of the kind I have ever seen, or expect to see, in my life:—a stratagem of war, learned and practiced by every young man in the tribe; by which he is able to drop his body upon the side of his horse at the instant he is passing, effectually screened from his enemies' weapons (plate 167) as he lays in a horizontal position behind the body of his horse, with his heel hanging over the horse's back; by which he has the power of throwing himself up again, and changing to the other side of the horse if necessary. In this wonderful condition, he will hang whilst his horse is at fullest speed, carrying with him his bow and his shield, and also his long lance of fourteen feet in length, all or either of which he will wield upon his enemy as he passes; rising and throwing his arrows over the horse's back, or with equal ease and equal success under the horse's neck.˙ This astonishing feat which the young men have been repeatedly playing off to our surprise as well as amusement, whilst they have been galloping about in front of our tents, completely puzzled the whole of us; and appeared to be the result of magic, rather than of skill acquired by practice. I had several times great curiosity to approach them, to ascertain by what means their bodies could be suspended in this manner, where nothing could be seen but the heel hanging over the horse's back. In these endeavors I was continually frustrated, until one day I coaxed a young fellow up within a little

---

* Since writing the above, I have conversed with some of the young men of the Pawnees, who practice the same feat, and who told me they could throw the arrow from under the horse's belly, and elevate it upon an enemy with deadly effect!

This feat I did not see performed, but from what I did see, I feel inclined to believe that these young men were boasting of no more than they were able to perform.

166

167

distance of me, by offering him a few plugs of tobacco, and he in a moment solved the difficulty, so far as to render it apparently more feasible than before: yet leaving it one of the most extraordinary results of practice and persevering endeavors. I found on examination, that a short hair halter was passed around under the neck of the horse, and both ends tightly braided into the mane, on the withers, leaving a loop to hang under the neck, and against the breast, which, being caught up in the hand, makes a sling into which the elbow falls, taking the weight of the body on the middle of the upper arm. Into this loop the rider drops suddenly and fearlessly, leaving his heel to hang over the back of the horse, to steady him, and also to restore him when he wishes to regain his upright position on the horse's back.

Besides this wonderful art, these people have several other feats of horsemanship, which they are continually showing off; which are pleasing and extraordinary, and of which they seem very proud. A people who spend so very great a part of their lives, actually on their horses' backs, must needs become exceedingly expert in every thing that pertains to riding—to war, or to the chase; and I am ready, without hesitation, to pronounce the Camanchees the most extraordinary horsemen that I have seen yet in all my travels, and I doubt very much whether any people in the world can surpass them.

The Camanchees are in stature, rather low, and in person, often approaching to corpulency. In their movements, they are heavy and ungraceful; and on their feet, one of the most unattractive and slovenly-looking races of Indians that I have ever seen; but the moment they mount their horses, they seem at once metamorphosed, and surprise the spectator with the ease and elegance of their movements. A Camanchee on his feet is out of his element . . . but the moment he lays his hand upon his horse, his *face*, even, becomes handsome, and he gracefully flies away like a different being.

Our encampment is surrounded by continual swarms of old and young—of middle aged—of male and female—of dogs, and every moving thing that constitutes their community; and our tents are lined with the chiefs and other worthies of the tribe. So it will be seen there is no difficulty of getting subjects enough for my brush, as well as for my pen, whilst residing in this place.

The head chief of this village, who is represented to us here, as the head of the nation, is a mild and pleasant looking gentleman, without anything striking or peculiar in his looks (plate 168); dressed in a very humble manner, with very few ornaments upon him, and his hair carelessly falling about his face, and over his shoulders. The name of this chief is Ee-shah-ko-nee (the bow and quiver). The only ornaments to be seen about him were a couple of beautiful shells worn in his ears, and a boar's tusk attached to his neck, and worn on his breast.

For several days after we arrived at this place, there was a huge mass of flesh (plate 169), Ta-wah-que-nah (the mountain of rocks), who was put forward as head chief of the tribe; and all honors were being paid to him by the regiment of dragoons, until the above-mentioned chief arrived from the country, where it seems he was leading a war-party; and had been sent for, no doubt, on the occasion. When he arrived, this huge monster, who is the largest and fattest Indian I ever saw, stepped quite into the background, giving way to this admitted chief, who seemed to have the confidence and respect of the whole tribe.

This enormous man, whose flesh would undoubtedly weigh three hundred pounds or more, took the most wonderful strides in the exercise of his temporary authority; which, in all probability, he was lawfully exercising in the absence of his superior, as second chief of the tribe.

A perfect personation of Jack Falstaff, in size and in figure, with an African face, and a beard on his chin of two or three inches in length. His name, he tells me, he got from having conducted a large party of Camanchees through a secret and subterraneous passage, entirely through the mountain of granite rocks, which lies back of their village; thereby saving their lives from their more powerful enemy, who had "cornered them up" in such a way, that there was no other possible mode for their escape. The mountain under which he conducted them, is called *Ta-wah-que-nah* (the mountain of rocks), and from this he has received his name, which would certainly have been far more appropriate if it had been a *mountain of flesh*.

Corpulency is a thing exceedingly rare to be found in any of the tribes, amongst the men, owing, probably, to the exposed and active sort of lives they lead; and that in the absence of all the spices of life, many of which have their effect in producing this disgusting, as well as unhandy and awkward extravagance in civilized society.

Ish-a-ro-yeh (he who carries a wolf, plate 170); and Is-sa-wah-tam-ah (the wolf tied with hair, plate 171); are also chiefs of some standing in the tribe, and evidently men of great influence, as they were put forward by the head chiefs, for their likenesses to be painted in turn, after their own. The first of the two seemed to be the leader of the war-party which we met, and of which I have spoken; and in escorting us to their village, this man took the lead and piloted us the whole way, in consequence of which Colonel Dodge presented him a very fine gun.

His-oo-san-ches (the Spaniard, plate 172), a gallant little fellow, is represented to us as one of the leading warriors of the tribe; and no doubt is one

172

of the most extraordinary men at present living in these regions. He is half Spanish, and being a half-breed, for whom they generally have the most contemptuous feelings, he has been all his life thrown into the front of battle and danger; at which posts he has signalized himself, and commanded the highest admiration and respect of the tribe, for his daring and adventurous career. This is the man of whom I have before spoken, who dashed out so boldly from the war-party, and came to us with the white flag raised on the point of his lance. I have here represented him as he stood for me, with his shield on his arm, with his quiver slung, and his lance of fourteen feet in length in his right hand. This extraordinary little man, whose figure was light, seemed to be all bone and muscle, and exhibited immense power, by the curve of the bones in his legs and his arms. We had many exhibitions of his extraordinary strength, as well as agility; and of his gentlemanly politeness and friendship, we had as frequent evidences. As an instance of this, I will recite an occurrence which took place but a few days since, when we were moving our encampment to a more desirable ground on another side of their village. We had a deep and powerful stream to ford, when we had several men who were sick, and obliged to be carried on litters. My friend "Joe" and I came up in the rear of the regiment, where the litters with the sick were passing, and we found this little fellow up to his chin in the muddy water, wading and carrying one end of each litter on his head, as they were in turn, passed over. After they had all passed, this gallant little fellow beckoned to me to dismount, and take a seat on his shoulders, which I declined; preferring to stick to my horse's back, which I did, as he took it by the bridle and conducted it through the shallowest ford. When I was across, I took from my belt a handsome knife and presented it to him, which seemed to please him very much.

Besides the above-named chiefs and warriors, I painted the portrait of *Kots-o-ko-ro-ko* (the hair of the bull's neck); and *Hah-nee* (the beaver); the first, a chief, and the second, a warrior of terrible aspect, and also of considerable distinction. These and many other paintings, as well as manufactures from this tribe, may be always seen in my museum, if I have the good luck to get them safe home from this wild and remote region.

From what I have already seen of the Camanchees, I am fully convinced that they are a numerous and very powerful tribe, and quite equal in numbers and prowess, to the accounts generally given of them.

It is entirely impossible at present to make a correct estimate of their numbers; but taking their own account of villages they point to in such numbers, South of the banks of the Red River, as well as those that lie farther West, and undoubtedly North of its banks, they must be a very numerous tribe; and I think I am able to say, from estimates that these chiefs have made me, that they number some 30 or 40,000—being able to shew some 6 or 7000 warriors, well-mounted and well-armed. This estimate I offer not as conclusive, for so little is as yet known of these people, that no estimate can be implicitly relied upon other than that, which, in general terms, pronounces them to be a very numerous and warlike tribe.

We shall learn much more of them before we get out of their country; and I trust that it will yet be in my power to give something like a fair census of them before we have done with them.

They speak much of their allies and friends, the Pawnee Picts, living to the West some three or four days' march, whom we are going to visit in a few days, and afterwards return to this village, and then "bend our course" homeward, or, in other words, back to Fort Gibson. Besides the Pawnee Picts, there are the Kiowas and Wicos; small tribes that live in the same vicinity, and also in the same alliance, whom we shall probably see on our march. Every preparation is now making to be off in a few days—and I shall omit further remarks on the Camanchees, until we return, when I shall probably have much more to relate of them and their customs. So many of the men and officers are getting sick, that the little command will be very much crippled, from the necessity we shall be under, of leaving about thirty sick, and about an equal number of well to take care of and protect them; for which purpose, we are constructing a fort, with a sort of breastwork of timbers and bushes, which will be ready in a day or two; and the sound part of the command prepared to start with several Camanchee leaders, who have agreed to pilot the way.

3–5

Sojourner Truth (1797–1883)

> Born Isabella Baumfree, Sojourner Truth (1797–1883) adopted her speaking name in response to a profound sense of religious calling. Held in bondage in New York State until she was nearly thirty years old, she escaped slavery with her daughter and later went to court to free her son. After becoming a Christian, she set out to tell her truth that slavery was an abomination. Truth never received a formal education, but her highly effective extemporaneous speeches were legendary. Truth and Harriet Beecher Stowe, the abolitionist, were contemporaries, one speaking with ethos, the other writing with pathos, but both using rhetoric and imagination to fight for freedom. Truth delivered the following brief speech at the Women's Rights Convention in Akron, Ohio, in 1851. Ohio native, abolitionist, and women's rights activist Frances D. Gage would record her memory, notable for describing Truth's delivery and the audience's enthusiasm, and for recalling the now-famous refrain "Ain't I a Woman?"

SOJOURNER TRUTH.

≋ ≋ ≋

Speech to the Women's Rights Convention (1851), from *History of Woman Suffrage*

Sojourner Truth, Mrs. Stowe's "Lybian Sibyl," was present at this Convention. Some of our younger readers may not know that Sojourner Truth was once a slave in the State of New York, and carries to-day as many marks of the diabolism of slavery, as ever scarred the back of a victim in Mississippi. Though she can neither read nor write, she is a woman of rare intelligence and common-sense on all subjects. She is still living, at Battle Creek, Michigan, though now 110 years old. Although the exalted character and personal appearance of this noble woman have been often portrayed, and her brave deeds and words many times rehearsed, yet we give the following graphic picture of Sojourner's appearance in one of the most stormy sessions of the Convention, from reminiscences by Frances D. Gage. . . .

There were very few women in those days who dared to "speak in meeting"; and the august teachers of the people were seemingly getting the better of us, while the boys in the galleries, and the sneerers among the pews, were hugely enjoying the discomfiture, as they supposed, of the "strong-minded." Some of the tender-skinned friends were on the point of losing dignity, and the atmosphere betokened a storm. When, slowly from her seat in a corner rose Sojourner Truth, who, till now, had scarcely lifted her head. "Don't let her speak!"

gasped half a dozen in my ear. She moved slowly and solemnly to the front, laid her old bonnet at her feet, and turned her great speaking eyes to me. There was a hissing sound of disapprobation above and below. I rose and announced "Sojourner Truth," and begged the audience to keep silence for a few moments.

The tumult subsided at once, and every eye was fixed on this almost Amazon form, which stood nearly six feet high, head erect, and eyes piercing the upper air like one in a dream. At her first word there was a profound hush. She spoke in deep tones, which, though not loud, reached every ear in the house, and away through the throng at the doors and windows.

"Wall, chilern, whar dar is so much racket dar must be somethin' out o' kilter. I tink dat 'twixt de niggers of de Souf and de womin at de Norf, all talkin' 'bout rights, de white men will be in a fix pretty soon. But what's all dis here talkin' 'bout?

"Dat man ober dar say dat womin needs to be helped into carriages, and lifted ober ditches, and to hab de best place everywhar. Nobody eber helps me into carriages, or ober mud-puddles, or gibs me any best place!" And raising herself to her full height, and her voice to a pitch like rolling thunder, she asked. "And a'n't I a woman? Look at me! Look at my arm! (and she bared her right arm to the shoulder, showing her tremendous muscular power). I have ploughed, and planted, and gathered into barns, and no man could head me! And a'n't I a woman? I could work as much and eat as much as a man—when I could get it—and bear de lash as well! And a'n't I a woman? I have borne thirteen chilern, and seen 'em mos' all sold off to slavery, and when I cried out with my mother's grief, none but Jesus heard me! And a'n't I a woman?

"Den dey talks 'bout dis ting in de head; what dis dey call it?" ("Intellect," whispered some one near.) "Dat's it, honey. What's dat got to do wid womin's rights or nigger's rights? If my cup won't hold but a pint, and yourn holds a quart, wouldn't ye be mean not to let me have my little half-measure full?" And she pointed her significant finger, and sent a keen glance at the minister who had made the argument. The cheering was long and loud.

"Den dat little man in black dar, he say women can't have as much rights as men, 'cause Christ wasn't a woman! Whar did your Christ come from?" Rolling thunder couldn't have stilled that crowd, as did those deep, wonderful tones, as she stood there with outstretched arms and eyes of fire. Raising her voice still louder, she repeated, "Whar did your Christ come from? From God and a woman! Man had nothin' to do wid Him." Oh, what a rebuke that was to that little man.

Turning again to another objector, she took up the defense of Mother Eve. I can not follow her through it all. It was pointed, and witty, and solemn; eliciting at almost every sentence deafening applause; and she ended by asserting: "If de fust woman God ever made was strong enough to turn de world upside down all alone, dese women togedder (and she glanced her eye over the platform) ought to be able to turn it back, and get it right side up again! And now dey is asking to do it, de men better let 'em." Long-continued cheering greeted this. "'Bleeged to ye for hearin' on me, and now ole Sojourner han't got nothin' more to say."

Amid roars of applause, she returned to her corner, leaving more than one of us with streaming eyes, and hearts beating with gratitude. She had taken us up in her strong arms and carried us safely over the slough of difficulty turning the whole tide in our favor. I have never in my life seen anything like the magical influence that subdued the mobbish spirit of the day, and turned the sneers and jeers of an excited crowd into notes of respect and admiration. Hundreds rushed up to shake hands with her, and congratulate the glorious old mother, and bid her God-speed on her mission of "testifyin' agin concerning the wickedness of this 'ere people."

3–6
William Apess (1798–1839)

Methodist preacher and early Indian activist, WILLIAM APESS (1798–1839) experienced much of the tragic history of Native American-European relations in his own family. A descendant of Metacomet (King Philip), Apess was born into a family that had experienced the destruction of Pequot cultural life, enslavement, and threats of removal West. Apess became a Methodist circuit rider and evangelist, using his position to promote Christian salvation and Native American rights. In the 1830s, he lived and preached among the Mashpee, and successfully took up their cause against the state of Massachusetts. Apess published the first autobiography written by a Native American, *A Son of the Forest* (1829), as well as his later work *The Experiences of Five Christian Indians of the Pequod Tribe* (1833), from which this memorable selection below is taken.

≈ ≈ ≈

"An Indian's Looking-Glass for the White Man" (1833)
Having a desire to place a few things before my fellow creatures who are travelling with me to the grave, and to that God who is the maker and preserver both of the white man and the Indian, whose abilities are the same, and who are to

be judged by one God, who will show no favor to outward appearances, but will judge righteousness. Now I ask if degradation has not been heaped long enough upon the Indians? And if so, can there not be a compromise; is it right to hold and promote prejudices? If not, why not put them all away? I mean here amongst those who are civilized. It may be that many are ignorant of the situation of many of my brethren within the limits of New England. Let me for a few moments turn your attention to the reservations in the different states of New England, and, with but few exceptions, we shall find them as follows: The most mean, abject, miserable race of beings in the world—a complete place of prodigality and prostitution.

Let a gentleman and lady, of integrity and respectability visit these places, and they would be surprised; as they wandered from one hut to the other they would view with the females who are left alone, children half starved, and some almost as naked as they came into the world. And it is a fact that I have seen them as much so—while the females are left without protection, and are seduced by white men, and are finally left to be common prostitutes for them, and to be destroyed by that burning, fiery curse, that has swept millions, both of red and white men, into the grave with sorrow and disgrace—Rum. One reason why they are left so is, because their most sensible and active men are absent at sea. Another reason is, because they are made to believe they are minors and have not the abilities given them from God, to take care of themselves, without it is to see to a few little articles, such as baskets and brooms. Their land is in common stock, and they have nothing to make them enterprising.

Another reason is because those men who are Agents, many of them are unfaithful, and care not whether the Indians live or die; they are much imposed upon by their neighbors who have no principle. They would think it no crime to go upon Indian lands and cut and carry off their most valuable timber, or any thing else they chose; and I doubt not but they think it clear gain. Another reason is because they have no education to take care of themselves; if they had, I would risk them to take care of their own property.

Now I will ask, if the Indians are not called the most ingenious people amongst us? And are they not said to be men of talents? And I would ask, could there be a more efficient way to distress and murder them by inches than the way they have taken? And there is no people in the world but who may be destroyed in the same way. Now if these people are what they are held up in our view to be, I would take the liberty to ask why they are not brought forward and pains taken to educate them? to give them all a common education, and those of the brightest and first-rate talents put forward and held up to office. Perhaps some unholy, unprincipled men would cry out, the skin was not good enough; but stop friends—I am not talking about the skin, but about the principles. I would ask if there cannot be as good feelings and principles under a red skin as there can be under a white? And let me ask, is it not on the account of a bad principle, that we who are red children have had to suffer so much as we have? And let me ask, did not this bad principle proceed from the whites or their forefathers? And I would ask, is it worth while to nourish it any longer? If not, then let us have a change; although some men no doubt will spout their corrupt principles against it, that are in the halls of legislation and elsewhere. But I presume this kind of talk will seem surprising and horrible. I do not see why it should so long as they (the whites) say that they think as much of us as they do of themselves.

This I have heard repeatedly, from the most respectable gentlemen and ladies—and having heard so much precept, I should now wish to see the example. And I would ask who has a better right to look for these things than the naturalist himself—the candid man would say none.

I know that many say that they are willing, perhaps the majority of the people, that we should enjoy our rights and privileges as they do. If so, I would ask why are not we protected in our persons and property throughout the Union? Is it not because there reigns in the breast of many who are leaders, a most unrighteous, unbecoming and impure black principle, and as corrupt and unholy as it can be—while these very same unfeeling, self-esteemed characters pretend to take the skin as a pretext to keep us from our unalienable and lawful rights? I would ask you if you would like to be disfranchised from all your rights, merely because your skin is white, and for no other crime? I'll venture to say, these very characters who hold the skin to be such a barrier in the way, would be the first to cry out, injustice! awful injustice!

But, reader, I acknowledge that this is a confused world, and I am not seeking for office; but merely placing before you the black inconsistency that you place before me—which is ten times blacker than any skin that you will find in the Universe. And now let me exhort you to do away that principle, as it appears ten times worse in the sight of God and candid men, than skins of color—more disgraceful than all the skins that Jehovah ever made. If black or red skins, or any other skin of color is disgraceful to God, it appears that he has disgraced himself a great deal—for he has made fifteen colored people to one white, and placed them here upon this earth.

Now let me ask you, white man, if it is a disgrace for to eat, drink and sleep with the image of God, or sit, or walk and talk with them? Or have you the folly to think that the white man, being one in fifteen or sixteen, are the only beloved images of God? Assemble all nations together in your imagination, and then let the whites be seated amongst them, and then let us look for the whites, and I doubt not it would be hard finding them; for to the rest of the nations, they are still but a handful. Now suppose these skins were put together, and each skin had its national crimes written upon it—which skin do you think would have the greatest? I will ask one question more. Can you charge the Indians with robbing a nation almost of their whole Continent, and murdering their women and children, and then depriving the remainder of their lawful rights, that nature and God require them to have? And to cap the climax, rob another nation to till their grounds, and welter out their days under the lash with hunger and fatigue under the scorching rays of a burning sun? I should look at all the skins, and I know that when I cast my eye upon that white skin, and if I saw those crimes written upon it, I should enter my protest against it immediately, and cleave to that which is more honorable. And I can tell you that I am satisfied in the manner of my creation, fully— whether others are or not.

But we will strive to penetrate more fully into the conduct of those who profess to have pure principles, and who tell us to follow Jesus Christ and imitate him and have his Spirit. Let us see if they come any where near him and his ancient disciples. The first thing we are to look at, are his precepts, of which we will mention a few. 'Thou shalt love the Lord thy God with all thy heart, with all thy soul, with all thy mind, and with all thy strength. The second is like unto it. Thou shalt love thy neighbor as thyself. On these two precepts hang all the law and the prophets.—Matt. xxii. 37, 38, 39, 40. By this shall all men know that they are my disciples, if ye have love one to another.'—John xiii. 35. Our Lord left this special command with his followers, that they should love one another.

Again, John in his Epistles says, 'He who loveth God, loveth his brother also.'—iv 21. 'Let us not love in word but in deed.'—iii. 18. 'Let your love be without dissimulation. See that ye love one another with a pure heart fervently.'—1. Peter, viii. 22. 'If any man say, I love God, and hateth his brother, he is a liar.'—John iv. 20. 'Whosoever hateth his brother is a murderer, and no murderer hath eternal life abiding in him.' The first thing that takes our attention, is the saying of Jesus, 'Thou shalt love,' &c. The first question I would ask my brethren in the ministry, as well as that of the membership, What is love, or its effects? Now if they who teach are not essentially affected with pure love, the love of God, how can they teach as they ought? Again, the holy teachers of old said, 'Now if any man have not the spirit of Christ, he is none of his.'— Rom. viii. 9. Now my brethren in the ministry, let me ask you a few sincere questions. Did you ever hear or read of Christ teaching his disciples that they ought to despise one because his skin was different from theirs? Jesus Christ being a Jew, and those of his Apostles certainly were not whites,—and did not he who completed the plan of salvation complete it for the whites as well as for the Jews, and others? And were not the whites the most degraded people on the earth at that time, and none were more so; for they sacrificed their children to dumb idols! And did not St. Paul labor more abundantly for building up a Christian nation amongst you than any of the Apostles. And you know as well as I that you are not indebted to a principle beneath a white skin for your religious services, but to a colored one.

What then is the matter now; is not religion the same now under a colored skin as it ever was? If so I would ask why is not a man of color respected; you may say as many say, we have white men enough. But was this the spirit of Christ and his Apostles? If it had been, there would not have been one white preacher in the world—for Jesus Christ never would have imparted his grace or word to them, for he could forever have withheld it from them. But we find that Jesus Christ and his Apostles never looked at the outward appearances. Jesus in particular looked at the hearts, and his Apostles through him being discerners of the spirit, looked at their fruit without any regard to the skin, color or nation; as St. Paul himself speaks, 'Where there is neither Greek nor Jew, circumcision nor uncircumcision, Barbarian nor Scythian, bond nor free—but Christ is all and in all.' If you can find a spirit like Jesus Christ and his Apostles prevailing now in any of the white congregations, I should like to know it. I ask, is it not the case that every body that is not white is treated with contempt and counted as barbarians? And I ask if the word of God justifies the white man in so doing? When the prophets prophesied, of whom did they speak? When they spoke of heathens, was it not the whites and others who were counted Gentiles? And I ask if all the nations with the exception of the Jews were not counted heathens? and according to the writings of some, it could not mean the Indians, for they are counted Jews. And now I would ask, why is all this distinction made among these Christian societies? I would ask what is all this ado about Missionary Societies, if it be not to christianize those who are not Christians? And what is it for? To degrade them worse, to bring them into society where they must welter out their days in disgrace merely because their skin is a different complexion. What folly it is to try to make the state of human society worse than it is. How astonished some may be at this—but let me ask, is it not so? Let me refer you to the churches only. And my brethren, is there any agreement? Do brethren and sisters love one another?—Do they not rather hate one another. Outward forms and ceremonies, the lusts of the flesh, the lusts of the eye and pride of life is of more value to many professors, than the love of God shed abroad in their hearts, or an attachment to his altar, to his ordinances or to his children. But you may ask who are the children of God? perhaps you may say none but white. If so, the word of the Lord is not true.

I will refer you to St. Peter's precepts—Acts 10. 'God is no respecter of persons'—&c. Now if this is the case, my white brother, what better are you than God? And if no better, why do you who profess his gospel and to have his spirit, act so contrary to it? Let me ask why the men of a different skin are so dispised, why are not they educated and placed in your pulpits? I ask if his services well performed are not as good as if a white man performed them? I ask if a marriage or a funeral ceremony, or the ordinance of the Lord's house would not be as acceptable in the sight of God as though he was white? And if so, why is it not to you? I ask again, why is it not as acceptable to have men exercise their office in one place as well as in another? Perhaps you will say that if we admit you to all of these privileges you will want more. I expect that I can guess what that is—Why, say you, there would be intermarriages. How that would be I am not able to say—and if it should be, it would be nothing strange or new to me; for I can assure you that I know a great many that have intermarried, both of the whites and the Indians—and many are their sons and daughters—and people too of the first respectability. And I could point to some in the famous city of Boston and elsewhere. You may now look at the disgraceful act in the statute law passed by the Legislature of Massachusetts,* and behold the fifty pound fine levied upon any Clergyman or Justice of the Peace that dare to encourage the laws of God and nature by a legitimate union in holy wedlock between Indians and whites. I would ask how this looks to your law makers. I would ask if this corresponds with your sayings—that you think as much of the Indians as you do of the whites. I do not wonder that you blush many of you while you read; for many have broken the ill-fated laws made by man to hedge up the laws of God and nature. I would ask if they who have made the law have not broken it—but there is no other state in New England that has this law but Massachusetts; and I think as many of you do not, that you have done yourselves no credit.

But as I am not looking for a wife, having one of the finest cast, as you no doubt would understand while you read her experience and travail of soul in the way to heaven, you will see that it is not my object. And if I had none, I should not want any one to take my right from me and choose a wife for me; for I think that I or any of my brethren have a right to choose a wife for themselves as well as the whites—and as the whites have taken the liberty to choose

* [Anti-miscegenation laws were not struck down until 1967, in *Loving vs. the State of Virginia*—E.J.D. and J.B.F.]

my brethren, the Indians, hundreds and thousands of them as partners in life, I believe the Indians have as much a right to choose their partners amongst the whites if they wish. I would ask you if you can see any thing inconsistent in your conduct and talk about the Indians? And if you do, I hope you will try to become more consistent. Now if the Lord Jesus Christ, who is counted by all to be a Jew, and it is well known that the Jews are a colored people, especially those living in the East, where Christ was born—and if he should appear amongst us, would he not be shut out of doors by many, very quickly? and by those too, who profess religion?

By what you read, you may learn how deep your principles are. I should say they were skin deep. I should not wonder if some of the most selfish and ignorant would spout a charge of their principles now and then at me. But I would ask, how are you to love your neighbors as yourself? Is it to cheat them? is it to wrong them in any thing? Now to cheat them out of any of their rights is robbery. And I ask, can you deny that you are not robbing the Indians daily, and many others? But at last you may think I am what is called a hard and uncharitable man. But not so. I believe there are many who would not hesitate to advocate our cause; and those too who are men of fame and respectability—as well as ladies of honor and virtue. There is a Webster, an Everett, and a Wirt, and many others who are distinguished characters—besides an host of my fellow citizens, who advocate our cause daily. And how I congratulate such noble spirits—how they are to be prized and valued; for they are well calculated to promote the happiness of mankind. They well know that man was made for society, and not for hissing stocks and outcasts. And when such a principle as this lies within the hearts of men, how much it is like its God—and how it honors its Maker—and how it imitates the feelings of the good Samaritan, that had his wounds bound up, who had been among thieves and robbers.

Do not get tired, ye noble-hearted—only think how many poor Indians want their wounds done up daily; the Lord will reward you, and pray you stop not till this tree of distinction shall be levelled to the earth, and the mantle of prejudice torn from every American heart—then shall peace pervade the Union.

3–7

Richard Penn Smith, supposed author (1799–1854)

DAVID CROCKETT (1786–1836), often simply known as "Davy," was a native Tennessean who served in the state legislature and was elected to Congress in 1827, 1829, and 1833. Even during his lifetime, his frontier exploits were exaggerated (by him and others) into tall tales. His motto was in some ways a motto for the entire nation, "Be sure you're right, then go ahead!" Upon defeat for a fourth term in Congress, Crockett famously declared, "You may all go to hell, and I will go to Texas." Crockett died heroically at the Alamo, further adding to his already mythic status. The selections that follow are from an 1836 work published after Crockett's death. The work drew freely on previously published works, the tall tale tradition, and the imagination of the supposed author Richard Penn Smith (1799–1854). The selection accurately reflects Crockett's antagonism toward Andrew Jackson and his political allies.

≋ ≋ ≋

From *Col. Crockett's Exploits and Adventures in Texas* (1836)

Chapter 2

August 11, 1835. I am now at home in Weakley county.* My canvass is over, and the result is known. Contrary to all expectation, I am beaten two hundred and thirty votes, from the best information I can get; and in this instance, I may say, bad is the best. My mantle has fallen upon the shoulders of Adam, and I hope he may wear it with becoming dignity, and never lose sight of the welfare of the nation, for the purpose of elevating a few designing politicians to the head of the heap. The rotten policy pursued by "the Government" cannot last long; it will either work its own downfall, or the downfall of the republic, soon, unless the people tear the seal from their eyes, and behold their danger time enough to avert the ruin.

I wish to inform the people of these United States what I had to contend against, trusting that the exposé I shall make will be a caution to the people not to repose too much power in the hands of a single man, though he should be "the greatest and the best."—I had, as I have already said, Mr. Adam Huntsman for my competitor, aided by the popularity of both Andrew Jackson and governor Carroll and the whole strength of the Union Bank at Jackson. I have been told by good men, that some of the managers of the bank on the days of the election were heard say, that they would give twenty-five dollars a vote for votes enough to elect Mr. Huntsman. This is a pretty good price for a vote, and in ordinary times a round dozen might be got for the money.

* [Tennessee—*E.J.D. and J.B.F.*]

I have always believed, since Jackson removed the deposites,[*] that his whole object was to place the treasury where he could use it to influence elections; and I do believe he is determined to sacrifice every dollar of the treasury to make the Little Flying Dutchman[†] his successor. If this is not my creed I wish I may be shot. For fourteen years since I have been a candidate I never saw such means used to defeat any candidate, as were put in practice against me on this occasion. There was a disciplined band of judges and officers to hold the elections at almost every poll. Of late years they begin to find out that there's an advantage in this, even in the west. Some officers held the election, and at the same time had nearly all they were worth bet on the election. Such judges I should take it are like the handle of a jug, all on one side; and I am told it doesn't require much schooling to make the tally list correspond to a notch with the ballot box, provided they who make up the returns have enough loose tickets in their breeches pockets. I have no doubt that I was completely rascalled out of my election, and I do regret that duty to myself and to my country compels me to expose such villany. . . . [‡]

. . . He stated that I had charged mileage for one thousand miles and that it was but seven hundred and fifty miles, and held out the idea that I had taken pay for the same mileage that Mr. Fitzgerald had taken, when it was well known that he charged thirteen hundred miles from here to Washington, and he and myself both live in the same county. It is somewhat remarkable how this fact should have escaped the keen eye of "the Government."

. . .

I come within two hundred and thirty votes of being elected, notwithstanding I had to contend against "the greatest and the best," with the whole power of the Treasury against me. . . . I am gratified that I have spoken the truth to the people of my district regardless of consequences. I would not be compelled to bow down to the idol for a seat in Congress during life. I have never known what it was to sacrifice my own judgment to gratify any party, and I have no doubt of the time being close at hand when I will be rewarded for letting my tongue speak what my heart thinks. I have suffered myself to be politically sacrificed to save my country from ruin and disgrace, and if I am never again elected, I will have the gratification to know that I have done my duty.—Thus much I say in relation to the manner in which my downfall was effected, and

[*] [Crockett strongly disagreed with Jackson's decision to divert government money from the National Bank—E.J.D. and J.B.F.]

[†] [Reference to Martin Van Buren, a Jackson ally and successor to the presidency—E.J.D. and J.B.F.]

[‡] [Here Crockett continues to charge Andrew Jackson and several others for false claims and for stealing his election.—E.J.D. and J.B.F.]

in laying it before the public, "I take the responsibility." I may add in the words of the man in the play, "Crockett's occupation's gone."—

Two weeks and more have elapsed since I wrote the foregoing account of my defeat, and I confess the thorn still rankles, not so much on my own account as the nation's, for I had set my heart on following up the travelling deposites until they should be fairly gathered to their proper nest, like young chickens, for I am aware of the vermin that are on the constant look-out to pounce upon them, like a cock at a blackberry, which they would have done long since, if it had not been for a few such men as Webster, Clay,* and myself. It is my parting advice, that this matter be attended to without delay, for before long the little chickens will take wing, and even the powerful wand of the magician of Kinderhook will be unable to point out the course they have flown.

As my country no longer requires my services, I have made up my mind to go to Texas. My life has been one of danger, toil, and privation, but these difficulties I had to encounter at a time when I considered it nothing more than right good sport to surmount them; but now I start anew upon my own hook, and God only grant that it may be strong enough to support the weight that may be hung upon it. I have a new row to hoe, a long and a rough one, but come what will I'll go ahead.

A few days ago I went to a meeting of my constituents. . . .

I told them to keep a sharp look-out for the deposites, for it requires an eye as insinuating as a dissecting knife to see what safety there is in placing one million of the public funds in some little country shaving shop with no more than one hundred thousand dollars capital. This bank, we will just suppose, without being too particular, is in the neighbourhood of some of the public lands, where speculators, who have every thing to gain and nothing to lose, swarm like crows about carrion. They buy the United States' land upon a large scale, get discounts from the aforesaid shaving shop, which are made upon a large scale also, upon the United States' funds; they pay the whole purchase money with these discounts, and get a clear title to the land, so that when the shaving shop comes to make a Flemish account of her transactions, "the Government" will discover that he has not only lost the original deposite, but a large body of the public lands to boot. So much for taking the responsibility.

I told them that they were hurrying along a broad M'Adamized road to make the Little Flying Dutchman the successor, but they would no sooner accomplish that end, than they would be obliged to buckle to, and drag the Juggernaut through many narrow and winding and out-of-the-way paths, and

* [Daniel Webster, Senator from Massachusetts; Henry Clay, Senator from Kentucky—*E.J.D. and J.B.F.*]

hub deep in the mire. That they reminded me of the Hibernian, who bet a glass of grog with a hod carrier, that he could not carry him in his hod up a ladder to the third story of a new building. He seated himself in the hod, and the other mounted the ladder with his load upon his shoulder. He ascended to the second story pretty steadily, but as he approached the third his strength failed him, he began to totter, and Pat was so delighted at the prospect of winning his bet, that he clapped his hands and shouted, "By the powers the grog's mine," and he made such a stir in the hod, that I wish I may be shot if he didn't win it, but he broke his neck in the fall. And so I told my constituents that they might possibly gain the victory, but in doing so, they would ruin their country.

I told them moreover of my services, pretty straight up and down, for a man may be allowed to speak on such subjects when others are about to forget them; and I also told them of the manner in which I had been knocked down and dragged out, and that I did not consider it a fair fight any how they could fix it. I put the ingredients in the cup pretty strong I tell you, and I concluded my speech by telling them that I was done with politics for the present, and that they might all go to hell, and I would go to Texas.

When I returned home I felt a sort of cast down at the change that had taken place in my fortunes, and sorrow, it is said, will make even an oyster feel poetical. I never tried my hand at that sort of writing, but on this particular occasion such was my state of feeling, that I began to fancy myself inspired; so I took pen in hand, and as usual I went ahead. When I had got fairly through, my poetry looked as zigzag as a worm fence; the lines wouldn't tally, no how; so I showed them to Peleg Longfellow, who has a first-rate reputation with us for that sort of writing, having some years ago made a carrier's address for the Nashville Banner, and Peleg lopped off some lines, and stretched out others; but I wish I may be shot if I don't rather think he has made it worse than it was when I placed it in his hands. It being my first, and no doubt last piece of poetry, I will print it in this place, as it will serve to express my feelings on leaving my home, my neighbours, and friends and country, for a strange land, as fully as I could in plain prose.

> Farewell to the mountains whose mazes to me
> Were more beautiful far than Eden could be;
> No fruit was forbidden, but Nature had spread
> Her bountiful board, and her children were fed.
> The hills were our garners—our herds wildly grew,
> And Nature was shepherd and husbandman too.
> I felt like a monarch, yet thought like a man,
> As I thank'd the Great Giver, and worshipp'd his plan.

The home I forsake where my offspring arose:
The graves I forsake where my children repose.
The home I redeem'd from the savage and wild;
The home I have loved as a father his child;
The corn that I planted, the fields that I clear'd,
The flocks that I raised, and the cabin I rear'd;
The wife of my bosom—Farewell to ye all!
In the land of the stranger I rise—or I fall.

Farewell to my country!—I fought for thee well,
When the savage rush'd forth like the demons from hell.
In peace or in war I have stood by thy side—
My country, for thee I have lived—would have died!
But I am cast off—my career now is run,
And I wander abroad like the prodigal son—
Where the wild savage roves, and the broad prairies spread,
The fallen—despised—will again go ahead!

Chapter 6

There was a considerable number of passengers on board the boat,[*] and our assortment was somewhat like the Yankee merchant's cargo of notions, pretty particularly miscellaneous, I tell you. I moved through the crowd from stem to stern, to see if I could discover any face that was not altogether strange to me; but after a general survey, I concluded that I had never seen one of them before. There were merchants and emigrants and gamblers, but none who seemed to have embarked in the particular business that for the time being occupied my mind—I could find none who were going to Texas. All seemed to have their hands full enough of their own affairs, without meddling with the cause of freedom. The greater share of glory will be mine, thought I, so go ahead, Crockett.

I saw a small cluster of passengers at one end of the boat, and hearing an occasional burst of laughter, thinks I, there's some sport started in that quarter, and having nothing better to do, I'll go in for my share of it. Accordingly I drew nigh to the cluster, and seated on a chest was a tall lank sea sarpent looking blackleg, who had crawled over from Natchez under the hill, and was amusing the passengers with his skill at thimblerig; at the same time he was picking up their shillings just about as expeditiously as a hungry gobbler would a pint of corn. He was doing what might be called an average business in a small way, and lost no time in gathering up the fragments.

---

[*] [To Texas—*E.J.D. and J.B.F.*]

I watched the whole process for some time, and found that he had adopted the example set by the old tempter himself, to get the weathergage of us poor weak mortals. He made it a point to let his victims win always the first stake, that they might be tempted to go ahead; and then, when they least suspected it, he would come down upon them like a hurricane in a cornfield, sweeping all before it.

I stood looking on, seeing him pick up the chicken feed from the green horns, and thought if men are such darned fools as to be cheated out of their earnings by a fellow who had just brains enough to pass a pea from one thimble to another, with such slight of hand, that you could not tell under which he had deposited it; it is not astonishing that the magician of Kinderhook* should play thimblerig upon the big figure, and attempt to cheat the whole nation. I thought that " the Government" was playing the same game with the deposites, and with such address too, that before long it will be a hard matter to find them under any of the thimbles where it is supposed they have been originally placed.

The thimble conjurer saw me looking on, and eyeing me as if he thought I would be a good subject, said carelessly, "Come, stranger, won't you take a chance?" the whole time passing the pea from one thimble to the other, by way of throwing out a bait for the gudgeons to bite at. "I never gamble, stranger," says I, "principled against it; think it a slippery way of getting through the world at best." "Them are my sentiments to a notch," says he; "but this is not gambling by no means. A little innocent pastime, nothing more. Better take a hack by way of trying your luck at guessing." All this time he continued working with his thimbles; first putting the pea under one, which was plain to be seen, and then uncovering it, would show that the pea was there; he would then put it under the second thimble, and do the same, and then under the third; all of which he did to show how easy it would be to guess where the pea was deposited, if one would only keep a sharp look-out.

"Come, stranger," says he to me again, "you had better take a chance. Stake a trifle, I don't care how small, just for fun of the thing."

"I am principled against betting money," says I, "but I don't mind going in for drinks for the present company, for I'm as dry as one of little Isaac Hill's regular set speeches."

"I admire your principles," says he, "and to show that I play with these here thimbles just for the sake of pastime, I will take that bet, though I'm a whole hog temperance man. Just say when, stranger."

---

* [Reference to Martin Van Buren—*E.J.D. and J.B.F.*]

He continued all the time slipping the pea from one thimble to another; my eye was as keen as a lizard's, and when he stopped, I cried out, "Now; the pea is under the middle thimble." He was going to raise it to show that it wasn't there, when I interfered, and said, "Stop, if you please," and raised it myself, and sure enough the pea was there; but it mought have been otherwise if he had had the uncovering of it.

"Sure enough you've won the bet," says he. "You've a sharp eye, but I don't care if I give you another chance. Let us go fifty cents this bout; I'm sure you'll win."

"Then you're a darned fool to bet, stranger," says I; "and since that is the case, it would be little better than picking your pocket to bet with you; so I'll let it alone."

"I don't mind running the risk," said he.

"But I do," says I; "and since I always let well enough alone, and I have had just about glory enough for one day, let us all go to the bar and liquor."

This called forth a loud laugh at the thimble conjurer's expense; and he tried hard to induce me to take just one chance more, but he mought just as well have sung psalms to a dead horse, for my mind was made up; and I told him, that I looked upon gambling as about the dirtiest way that a man could adopt to get through this dirty world; and that I would never bet any thing beyond a quart of whisky upon a rifle shot, which I considered a legal bet, and gentlemanly and rational amusement. "But all this cackling," says I, "makes me very thirsty, so let us adjourn to the bar and liquor."

He gathered up his thimbles, and the whole company followed us to the bar, laughing heartily at the conjurer; for, as he had won some of their money, they were sort of delighted to see him beaten with his own cudgel. He tried to laugh too, but his laugh wasn't at all pleasant, and rather forced. The barkeeper placed a big-bellied bottle before us; and after mixing our liquor, I was called on for a toast, by one of the company, a chap just about as rough hewn as if he had been cut out of a gum log with a broad axe, and sent into the market without even being smoothed off with a jack plane,—one of them chaps who, in their journey through life, are always ready for a fight or a frolic, and don't care the toss of a copper which.

"Well, gentlemen," says I, "being called upon for a toast, and being in a slave-holding state, in order to avoid giving offence, and running the risk of being Lynched, it may be necessary to premise that I am neither an abolitionist nor a colonizationist, but simply Colonel Crockett, of Tennessee, now bound for Texas." When they heard my name they gave three cheers for Colonel Crockett; and silence being restored, I continued, "Now, gentlemen, I will offer you a toast, hoping, after what I have stated, that it will give offence to no one present; but should I be mistaken, I must imitate the 'old Roman,' and take the responsibility. I offer, gentlemen, The abolition of slavery: Let the work first begin in the two houses of Congress. There are no slaves in the country more servile than the party slaves in Congress. The wink or the nod of their masters is all sufficient for the accomplishment of the most dirty work."

They drank the toast in a style that satisfied me, that the Little Magician might as well go to a pigsty for wool, as to beat round in that part for voters; they were all either for Judge White or Old Tippecanoe.* The thimble conjurer having asked the barkeeper how much to pay, was told there were sixteen smallers, which amounted to one dollar. He was about to lay down the blunt, but not in Benton's metallic currency, which I find has already become as shy as honesty with an office holder, but he planked down one of Biddle's notes, when I interfered, and told him that the barkeeper had made a mistake.

"How so?" demanded the barkeeper.

"How much do you charge," says I, "when you retail your liquor?"

"A fip a glass."

"Well, then," says I, "as Thimblerig here, who belongs to the temperance society, took it in wholesale, I reckon you can afford to let him have it at half price?"

Now, as they had all noticed that the conjurer went what is called the heavy wet, they laughed outright, and we heard no more about temperance from that quarter. When we returned to the deck the blackleg set to work with his thimbles again, and bantered me to bet; but I told him that it was against my principle, and as I had already reaped glory enough for one day, I would just let well enough alone for the present. . . .

One of the passengers, hearing that I was on board of the boat, came up to me, and began to talk about the affairs of the nation, and said a good deal in favour of "the Magician," and wished to hear what I had to say against him. He talked loud, which is the way with all politicians educated in the Jackson school; and by his slang-whanging, drew a considerable crowd around us. Now, this was the very thing I wanted, as I knew I should not soon have another opportunity of making a political speech; he no sooner asked to hear what I had to say against his candidate, than I let him have it, strong and hot as he could take, I tell you.

"What have I to say against Martin Van Buren? He is an artful, cunning, intriguing, selfish, speculating lawyer, who, by holding lucrative offices for more than half his life, has contrived to amass a princely fortune, and is now seeking the presidency, principally for sordid Gain, and to gratify the most selfish

* [William Henry Harrison, the ninth U.S. President—*E.J.D. and J.B.F.*]

ambition. His fame is unknown to the history of our country, except as a most adroit political manager and successful office hunter. He never took up arms in defence of his country, in her days of darkness and peril. He never contributed a dollar of his surplus wealth to assist her in her hours of greatest want and weakness. Office and Money have been the gods of his idolatry; and at their shrines has the ardent worship of his heart been devoted, from the earliest days of his manhood to the present moment. He can lay no claim to pre-eminent services as a statesman; nor has he ever given any evidences of superior talent, except as a political electioneerer and intriguer. As a politician he is 'all things to all men.' He is for internal improvement, and against it; for the tariff, and against it; for the bank monopoly, and against it; for abolition of slavery, and against it; and for any thing else, and against any thing else; just as he can best promote his popularity and subserve his own private interest. He is so totally destitute of moral courage, that he never dares to give an opinion upon any important question until he first finds out whether it will be popular, or not. He is celebrated as the 'Little Non Committal Magician,' because he enlists on no side of any question until he discovers which is the strongest party; and then always moves in so cautious, sly, and secret a manner, that he can change sides at any time, as easily as a juggler or a magician can play off his arts of legerdemain. . . . *

". . . Mr. Van Buren became himself a member of the United States Senate, and, while there, *opposed* every proposition to improve the west or to add to her numerical strength.

"He voted *against* the continuance of the national road through Ohio, Indiana, Illinois, and *against* appropriations for its preservation.

"He voted *against* the graduation of the price of the public lands.

"He voted *against* ceding the refuse lands to the states in which they lie.

"He voted *against* making donations of the lands to actual settlers.

"He again voted *against* ceding the refuse lands, not worth twenty-five cents per acre, to the new states for purposes of education and internal improvement.

"He voted *against* the bill providing 'settlement and pre-emption rights' to those who had assisted in opening and improving the western country, and thus deprived many an honest poor man of a home.

"He voted *against* donations of land to Ohio, to prosecute the Miami Canal; and, although a member of the Senate, he was not present when the vote was taken upon the engrossment of the bill giving land to Indiana for her Wabash and Erie Canal, and was known to have opposed it in all its stages.

---

* [Crockett lists the misdeeds of Martin Van Buren—*E.J.D. and J.B.F.*]

"He voted *in favour* of erecting toll gates on the national road; thus demanding a tribute from the west for the right to pass upon her own highways, constructed out of her own money—a thing never heard of before.

"After his term of service had expired in the Senate, he was elected Governor of New York, by a plurality of votes. He was afterward sent to England as minister plenipotentiary, and upon his return was elected Vice President of the United States, which office he now holds, and from which the office holders are seeking to transfer him to the presidency."

My speech was received with great applause, and the politician, finding that I was better acquainted with his candidate than he was himself, for I wrote his life, shut his fly trap, and turned on his heel without saying a word. He found that he had barked up the wrong tree. I afterward learnt that he was a mail contractor in those parts, and that he also had large dealings in the Land office, and therefore thought it necessary to chime in with his penny whistle, in the universal chorus. There's a large band of the same description, but I'm thinking Uncle Sam will some day find out that he has paid too much for the piper.

Chapter 7

After my speech, and setting my face against gambling, poor Thimblerig was obliged to break off conjuring for want of customers, and call it half a day. He came and entered into conversation with me, and I found him a good-natured intelligent fellow, with a keen eye for the main chance. He belonged to that numerous class, that it is perfectly safe to trust as far as a tailor can sling a bull by the tail—but no farther. He told me that he had been brought up a gentleman; that is to say, he was not instructed in any useful pursuit by which he could obtain a livelihood, so that when he found he had to depend upon himself for the necessaries of life, he began to suspect, that dame nature would have conferred a particular favour if she had consigned him to the care of any one else. She had made a very injudicious choice when she selected him to sustain the dignity of a gentleman.

The first bright idea that occurred to him as a speedy means of bettering his fortune, would be to marry an heiress. Accordingly he looked about himself pretty sharp, and after glancing from one fair object to another, finally his hawk's eye rested upon the young and pretty daughter of a wealthy planter. Thimblerig run his brazen face with his tailor for a new suit, for he abounded more in that metallic currency than he did in either Benton's mint drops or in Biddle's notes; and having the gentility of his outward Adam thus endorsed by his tailor—an important endorsement, by-the-way, as times go—he managed to obtain an introduction to the planter's daughter.

Our worthy had the principle of going ahead strongly developed. He was possessed of considerable address, and had brass enough in his face to make a wash-kettle; and having once got access to the planter's house, it was no easy matter to dislodge him. In this he resembled those politicians who commence life as office holders; they will hang on tooth and nail, and even when death shakes them off, you'll find a commission of some kind crumpled up in their clenched fingers. Little Van appears to belong to this class—there's no beating his snout from the public crib. He'll feed there while there's a grain of corn left, and even then, from long habit, he'll set to work and gnaw at the manger.

Thimblerig got the blind side of the planter, and every thing to outward appearances went on swimmingly. Our worthy boasted to his cronies that the business was settled, and that in a few weeks he should occupy the elevated station in society that nature had designed him to adorn. He swelled like the frog in the fable, or rather like Johnson's wife, of Kentucky, when the idea occurred to her of figuring away at Washington. But there's many a slip 'twixt the cup and the lip, says the proverb, and suddenly Thimblerig discontinued his visits at the planter's house. His friends inquired of him the meaning of this abrupt termination of his devotions.

"I have been treated with disrespect," replied the worthy, indignantly.

"Disrespect! in what way?"

"My visits, it seems, are not altogether agreeable."

"But how have you ascertained that?"

"I received a hint to that effect; and I can take a hint as soon as another."

"A hint!—and have you allowed a hint to drive you from the pursuit? For shame. Go back again."

"No, no, never! a hint is sufficient for a man of my gentlemanly feelings. I asked the old man for his daughter."

"Well, what followed? what did he say?"

"Didn't say a word."

"Silence gives consent all the world over."

"So I thought. I then told him to fix the day."

"Well, what then?"

"Why, then he kicked me down stairs, and ordered his slaves to pump upon me. That's hint enough for me, that my visits are not properly appreciated; and blast my old shoes if I condescend to renew the acquaintance, or notice them in any way until they send for me."

As Thimblerig's new coat became rather too seedy to play the part of a gentleman much longer in real life, he determined to sustain that character upon the stage, and accordingly joined a company of players. He began, according to custom, at the top of the ladder, and was regularly hissed and pelted through every gradation until he found himself at the lowest rowel. "This," said he, "was a dreadful check to proud ambition"; but he consoled himself with the idea of peace and quiet in his present obscure walk; and though he had no prospect of being elated by the applause of admiring multitudes, he no longer trod the scene of mimic glory in constant dread of becoming a target for rotten eggs and oranges.—"And there was much in that," said Thimblerig. But this calm could not continue for ever.

The manager, who, like all managers who pay salaries regularly, was as absolute behind the scenes as the "old Roman" is in the White House, had fixed upon getting up an eastern spectacle, called the Cataract of the Ganges. He intended to introduce a fine procession, in which an elephant was to be the principal feature. Here a difficulty occurred. What was to be done for an elephant? Alligators were plenty in those parts, but an elephant was not to be had for love or money. But an alligator would not answer the purpose, so he determined to make a pasteboard elephant as large as life, and twice as natural. The next difficulty was to find members of the company of suitable dimensions to perform the several members of the pasteboard star. The manager cast his eye upon the long gaunt figure of the unfortunate Thimblerig, and cast him for the hinder legs, the rump, and part of the back of the elephant. The poor player expostulated, and the manager replied, that he would appear as a star on the occasion, and would no doubt receive more applause than he had during his whole career. "But I shall not be seen," said the player. "All the better," replied the manager, "as in that case you will have nothing to apprehend from eggs and oranges."

Thimblerig, finding that mild expostulation availed nothing, swore that he would not study the part, and accordingly threw it up in dignified disgust. He said that it was an outrage upon the feelings of the proud representative of Shakespeare's heroes, to be compelled to play pantomime in the hinder parts of the noblest animal that ever trod the stage. If it had been the fore quarters of the elephant, it might possibly have been made a speaking part; at any rate he might have snorted through the trunk, if nothing more; but from the position he was to occupy, damned the word could he utter, or even roar with propriety. He therefore positively refused to act, as he considered it an insult to his reputation to tread the stage in such a character; and he looked upon the whole affair as a profanation of the legitimate drama. The result was, our worthy was discharged from the company, and compelled to commence hoeing another row.

3–8

José María Heredia (1803–1839)

JOSÉ MARÍA HEREDIA (1803–1839) is one of those literary figures fought over by many countries. Born in Cuba, he spent some of his childhood in Venezuela, was exiled from Cuba due to his pro-Independence activism, and spent nearly two years in the United States, before settling in Mexico. These experiences supplemented Heredia's classical education, which one can see in his poetry that combines neoclassical sense with a Romantic sensibility. Heredia's most famous work "Niagara," translated here by American Romantic poet William Cullen Bryant, led to a plaque placed at the falls in his honor. "Hurricane," like "Niagara," invests nature with intensity and feeling—both were written after a failed love affair!

≈≈ ≈≈ ≈≈

"Niagara" (1824)

My lyre! Give me my lyre! My bosom feels
The glow of inspiration. O, how long
Have I been left in darkness, since this light
Last visited my brow! Niagara!
Thou with thy rushing waters dost restore
The heavenly gift that sorrow took away.

Tremendous torrent! for an instant hush
The terrors of thy voice, and cast aside
Those wide-involving shadows, that my eyes
May see the fearful beauty of thy face!
I am not all unworthy of thy sight,
For from my very boyhood have I loved,
Shunning the meaner track of common minds,
To look on Nature in her loftier moods.
At the fierce rushing of the hurricane,
At the near bursting of the thunderbolt,
I have been touched with joy; and when the sea
Lashed by the wind hath rocked my bark, and showed
Its yawning caves beneath me, I have loved
Its dangers and the wrath of elements.

But never yet the madness of the sea
Hath moved me as thy grandeur moves me now.

Thou flowest on in quiet, till thy waves
Grow broken 'midst the rocks; thy current then
Shoots onward like the irresistible course
Of Destiny. Ah, terribly they rage,—
The hoarse and rapid whirlpools there! My brain
Grows wild, my senses wander, as I gaze
Upon the hurrying waters, and my sight,
Vainly would follow, as toward the verge
Sweeps the wide torrent. Waves innumerable
Meet there and madden,—waves innumerable
Urge on and overtake the waves before,
And disappear in thunder and in foam.

They reach, they leap the barrier,—the abyss
Swallows insatiable the sinking waves.
A thousand rainbows arch them, and woods
Are deafened with the roar. The violent shock
Shatters to vapor the descending sheets.
A cloudy whirlwind fills the gulf, and heaves
The mighty pyramid of circling mist
To heaven. The solitary hunter near
Pauses with terror in the forest shades.

What seeks my restless eye? Why are not here,
About the jaws of this abyss, the palms—
Ah, the delicious palms,—that on the plains
Of my own native Cuba spring and spread
Their thickly foliaged summits to the sun,
And, in the breathings of the ocean air,
Wave soft beneath the heaven's unspotted blue?

But no, Niagara,—thy forest pines
Are fitter coronal for thee. The palm,
The effeminate myrtle, and frail rose may grow
In gardens, and give out their fragrance there,
Unmanning him who breathes it. Thine it is
To do a nobler office. Generous minds
Behold thee, and are moved, and learn to rise

Above earth's frivolous pleasures; they partake
Thy grandeur, at the utterance of thy name.

God of all truth! in other lands I've seen
Lying philosophers, blaspheming men,
Questioners of thy mysteries, that draw
Their fellows deep into impiety;
And therefore doth my spirit seek thy face
In earth's majestic solitudes. Even here
My heart doth open all itself to thee.
In this immensity of loneliness,
I feel thy hand upon me. To my ear
The eternal thunder of the cataract brings
Thy voice, and I am humbled as I hear.

Dread torrent, that with wonder and with fear
Dost overwhelm the soul of him that looks
Upon thee, and dost bear it from itself,—
Whence hast thou thy beginning? Who supplies,
Age after age, thy unexhausted springs?
What power hath ordered, that when all thy weight
Descends into the deep, the swollen waves
Rise not and roll to overwhelm the earth?

The Lord has opened his omnipotent hand,
Covered thy face with clouds, and given voice
To thy down-rushing waters; he hath girt
Thy terrible forehead with his radiant bow.
I see thy never-resting waters run,
And I bethink me how the tide of time
Sweeps to eternity. So pass of man—
Pass, like a noonday dream—the blossoming days
And he awakes to sorrow. I, alas!
Feel that my youth is withered, and my brow
Ploughed early with the lines of grief and care.

Never have I so deeply felt as now
The hopeless solitude, the abandonment,
The anguish of a loveless life. Alas!
How can the impassioned, the unfrozen heart
Be happy without love? I would that one

Beautiful, worthy to be loved and joined
In love with me, now shared my lonely walk
On this tremendous brink. 'Twere sweet to see
Her sweet face touched with paleness, and become
More beautiful from fear, and overspread
With a faint smile while clinging to my side.
Dreams,—dreams! I am an exile, and for me
There is no country and there is no love.

Hear, dread Niagara, my latest voice!
Yet a few years, and the cold earth shall close
Over the bones of him who sings thee now
Thus feelingly. Would that this, my humble verse,
Might be, like thee, immortal! I, meanwhile,
Cheerfully passing to the appointed rest,
Might raise my radiant forehead in the clouds
To listen to the echoes of my fame.

"Hurricane" (1824?)

Hurricane, hurricane, I feel thee coming.
Lord of the winds! I feel thee nigh,
I know thy breath in the burning sky!
And I wait, with a thrill in every vein,
For the coming of the hurricane!

And lo! on the wing of the heavy gales,
Through the boundless arch of heaven he sails;
Silent and slow, and terribly strong,
The mighty shadow is borne along,
Like the dark eternity to come;
While the world below, dismayed and dumb,
Through the calm of the thick hot atmosphere,
Looks up at its gloomy folds with fear.

They darken fast; and the golden blaze
Of the sun is quenched in the lurid haze,
And he sends through the shade a funeral ray—
A glare that is neither night nor day,
A beam that touches, with hues of death,
The clouds above and the earth beneath.
To its covert glides the silent bird,
While the hurricane's distant voice is heard

Uplifted among the mountains round,
And the forests hear and answer the sound.

He is come! he is come! do ye not behold
His ample robes on the wind unrolled?
Giant of air! we bid thee hail!—
How his gray skirts toss in the whirling gale;
How his huge and writhing arms are bent
To clasp the zone of the firmament,
And fold at length, in their dark embrace,
From mountain to mountain the visible space.

Darker—still darker! the whirlwinds bear
The dust of the plains to the middle air:
And hark to the crashing, long and loud,
Of the chariot of God in the thunder-cloud!
You may trace its path by the flashes that start
From the rapid wheels where'er they dart,
As the fire-bolts leap to the world below,
And flood the skies with a lurid glow.

What roar is that?—'tis the rain that breaks
In torrents away from the airy lakes,
Heavily poured on the shuddering ground,
And shedding a nameless horror round.
Ah! well-known woods, and mountains, and skies,
With the very clouds!—ye are lost to my eyes.

I seek ye vainly, and see in your place
The shadowy tempest that sweeps through space,
A whirling ocean that fills the wall
Of the crystal heaven, and buries all,
And I, cut off from the world, remain
Alone with the terrible hurricane.

Sublime tempest! As if filled with thy solemn inspiration, I forget the
   vile and wretched world and raise my head full of delight. Where
   is the coward soul that fears thy roar? In thee I rise to the throne of
   the Lord; I hear in the clouds the echo of his voice; I feel the earth
   listen to him and tremble. Hot tears descend my pale cheeks and
   trembling, I adore his lofty majesty.*

* [The final stanza of Heredia's poem, which Bryant thought too racy to include, is added
here—E.J.D and J.B.F.]

3–9
Thomas Commuck (1804–1855)

THOMAS COMMUCK (1804–1855), a Rhode Island Narragansett, the same tribe whose language a century and a half before Roger Williams had studied and recorded, was educated by one of the Christian mission schools that Red Jacket had warned would defeat the culture of indigenous peoples. Commuck's writing syncretizes native and Christian cultures. After leaving the East Coast, Commuck and his wife headed west to Wisconsin to live among the Brothertown. The Brothertown were a community of Pequot, Mohegan, and other indigenous peoples of the Northeast who came to be called "praying" Indians. In 1839 they successfully negotiated with the U.S. government to keep their lands in Wisconsin, the first tribe to do so and not be removed to "Indian Territory." In 1845, Commuck published *Indian Melodies*, 120 Christian hymns harmonized by Thomas Hastings in "shape note" style to encourage congregational singing and titled after "the names of noted Indian chiefs, Indian females, Indian names of place, &c. . . . as a tribute of respect to the memory of some tribes that are now nearly if not quite extinct; also a mark of courtesy to some tribes with whom the author is acquainted" (Commuck, vi).

≈ ≈ ≈

From *Indian Melodies* (1845)

Preface

The author of the following original tunes wished to get some person better educated than himself to write a preface or introduction to his little work; but on reflection it occurred to him that he could tell the public all about it as well as any one else; so he concluded to make the attempt. He is, however, fully aware of the difficulties attendant upon an attempt to appear successfully as an author before a scrutinizing and discerning public, especially when unaided by the influence of wealth, or a long list of influential friends; and whatever may be the fate of this production, he feels that he must stem the current of public opinion alone. Add to this the circumstance of having been born, not only in obscurity, but being descended from that unfortunate and proscribed people, the Indians, with whose name a considerable portion of the enlightened American people are unwilling to associate even the shadow of anything like talent, virtue, or genius, and as being wholly incapable

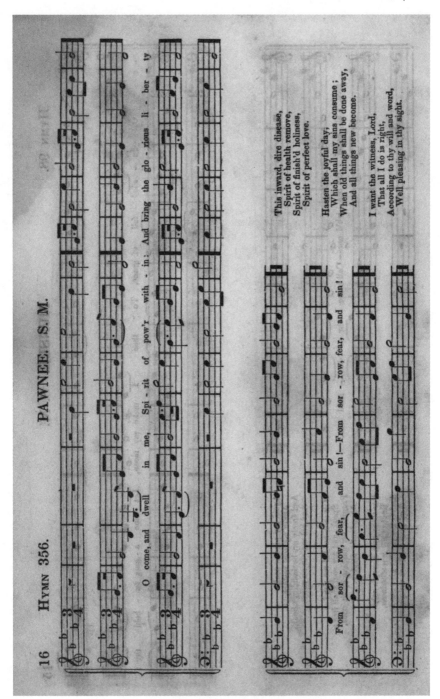

PAWNEE. S. M.

Hymn 356.

O come, and dwell in me, Spi - rit of pow'r with - in : And bring the glo - rious li - ber - ty

From sor - row, fear, and sin !—From sor - row, fear, and sin !

This inward, dire disease,
Spirit of health remove,
Spirit of finish'd holiness,
Spirit of perfect love.

Hasten the joyful day,
Which shall my sins consume ;
When old things shall be done away,
And all things new become.

I want the witness, Lord,
That all I do is right,
According to thy will and word,
Well pleasing in thy sight.

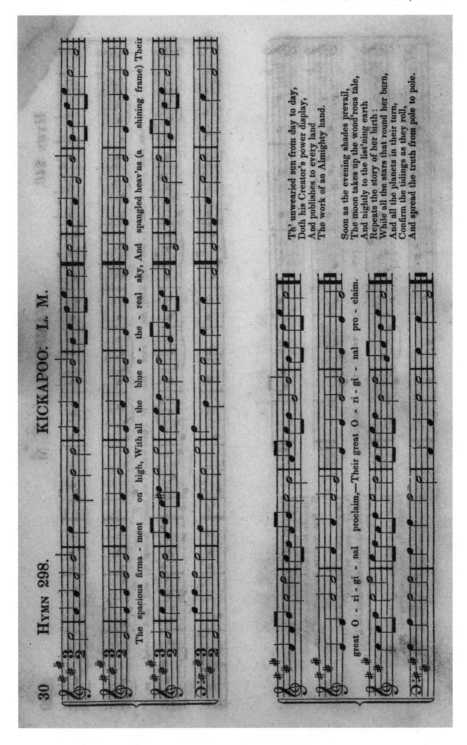

KICKAPOO. L. M.

HYMN 298.

The spacious firma-ment on high, With all the blue e-the-real sky, And spangled heav'ns (a shining frame) Their great O-ri-gi-nal proclaim,—Their great O-ri-gi-nal pro-claim.

Th' unwearied sun from day to day,
Doth his Creator's power display,
And publishes to every land
The work of an Almighty hand.

Soon as the evening shades prevail,
The moon takes up the wond'rous tale,
And nightly to the list'ning earth
Repeats the story of her birth:
While all the stars that round her burn,
And all the planets in their turn,
Confirm the tidings as they roll,
And spread the truth from pole to pole.

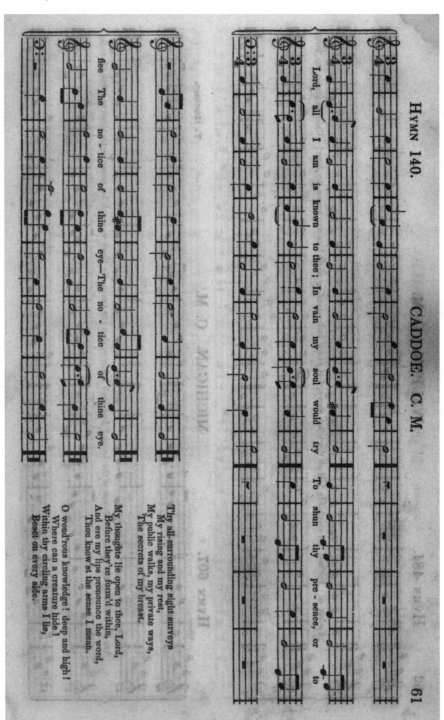

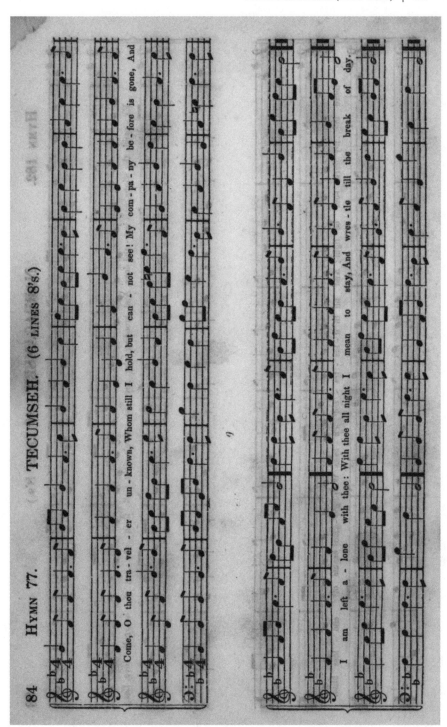

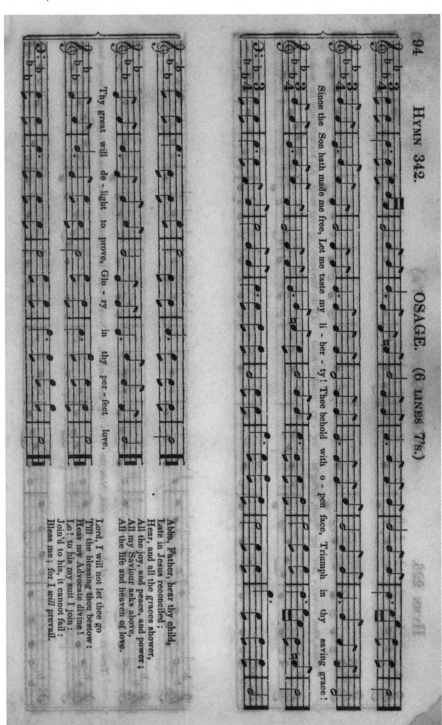

of any improvement, either moral, mental, or physical, and the wonder will cease to be a wonder. In view of all these disadvantages, it is not without great diffidence that he attempts to appear at the bar of public opinion, not knowing but Judge Prejudice may preside, and condemn his work to the deep and silent shades of everlasting oblivion, without even a hearing. Should this be its fate with the generality of the public, still he thinks he has a claim upon a certain portion of the Christian public, he means his brethren of the Methodist Episcopal Church: for if there be any meaning in that clause of our excellent Discipline which recommends the "employing of members in preference to others; helping each other in business, &c.," the author feels that he has a claim upon them, and he humbly trusts, judging from Christian feelings, that that claim will not be wholly disregarded. The work now offered to the public, small as it is, has occupied the attention of the author for the space of seven years; and it may not be amiss to state, that it was not until the year 1836 that he first commenced trying to learn, scientifically, the art of singing; in the acquirement of which, from that time to the present, he has had to encounter and overcome the difficulties attending the same alone, and unaided by any instruction, except what he could obtain by simply reading the rules contained in the few musical works to which he has had access. From these works he has been enabled, under the blessing of God, to obtain that amount of theoretical knowledge in music which has prompted him to offer this little volume to the public. . . .

The Author

Manchester, Wisconsin Ter., March 7, 1845

3–10

Nathaniel Hawthorne (1804–1864)

Born in Salem and descended from New England Puritans, including one of the judges in the Salem Witchcraft Trials, NATHANIEL HAWTHORNE (1804–1864) was deeply invested in Romanticism and questions of individual subjectivity within the larger culture. Hawthorne is beloved both as the author of *The Scarlet Letter* (1850) and *The House of the Seven Gables* (1851). He is also respected as one of earliest masters of the short story, for which he received praise even from the notoriously nettlesome Edgar Allan Poe. Among the classics of the genre is "The Birthmark" (1843). The protagonist Aylmer, more of an alchemist than a scientist, believes himself a modern-day Pygmalion. The sculptor in the classical myth, Pygmalion, carves a beautiful woman from marble, which Venus brings to life.

≈ ≈ ≈

"The Birthmark" (1843)

In the latter part of the last century there lived a man of science, an eminent proficient in every branch of natural philosophy, who not long before our story opens had made experience of a spiritual affinity more attractive than any chemical one. He had left his laboratory to the care of an assistant, cleared his fine countenance from the furnace smoke, washed the stain of acids from his fingers, and persuaded a beautiful woman to become his wife. In those days when the comparatively recent discovery of electricity and other kindred mysteries of Nature seemed to open paths into the region of miracle, it was not unusual for the love of science to rival the love of woman in its depth and absorbing energy. The higher intellect, the imagination, the spirit, and even the heart might all find their congenial aliment in pursuits which, as some of their ardent votaries believed, would ascend from one step of powerful intelligence to another, until the philosopher should lay his hand on the secret of creative force and perhaps make new worlds for himself. We know not whether Aylmer possessed this degree of faith in man's ultimate control over Nature. He had devoted himself, however, too unreservedly to scientific studies ever to be weaned from them by any second passion. His love for his young wife might prove the stronger of the two; but it could only be by intertwining itself with his love of science, and uniting the strength of the latter to his own.

Such a union accordingly took place, and was attended with truly remarkable consequences and a deeply impressive moral. One day, very soon after their marriage, Aylmer sat gazing at his wife with a trouble in his countenance that grew stronger until he spoke.

"Georgiana," said he, "has it never occurred to you that the mark upon your cheek might be removed?"

"No, indeed," said she, smiling; but perceiving the seriousness of his manner, she blushed deeply. "To tell you the truth it has been so often called a charm that I was simple enough to imagine it might be so."

"Ah, upon another face perhaps it might," replied her husband; "but never on yours. No, dearest Georgiana, you came so nearly perfect from the hand of Nature that this slightest possible defect, which we hesitate whether to term a defect or a beauty, shocks me, as being the visible mark of earthly imperfection."

"Shocks you, my husband!" cried Georgiana, deeply hurt; at first reddening with momentary anger, but then bursting into tears. "Then why did you take me from my mother's side? You cannot love what shocks you!"

To explain this conversation it must be mentioned that in the centre of Georgiana's left cheek there was a singular mark, deeply interwoven, as it were, with the texture and substance of her face. In the usual state of her complexion—a healthy though delicate bloom—the mark wore a tint of deeper crimson, which imperfectly defined its shape amid the surrounding rosiness. When she blushed it gradually became more indistinct, and finally vanished amid the triumphant rush of blood that bathed the whole cheek with its brilliant glow. But if any shifting motion caused her to turn pale, there was the mark again, a crimson stain upon the snow, in what Aylmer sometimes deemed an almost fearful distinctness. Its shape bore not a little similarity to the human hand, though of the smallest pygmy size. Georgiana's lovers were wont to say that some fairy at her birth hour had laid her tiny hand upon the infant's cheek, and left this impress there in token of the magic endowments that were to give her such sway over all hearts. Many a desperate swain would have risked life for the privilege of pressing his lips to the mysterious hand. It must not be concealed, however, that the impression wrought by this fairy sign manual varied exceedingly, according to the difference of temperament in the beholders. Some fastidious persons—but they were exclusively of her own sex—affirmed that the bloody hand, as they chose to call it, quite destroyed the effect of Georgiana's beauty, and rendered her countenance even hideous. But it would be as reasonable to say that one of those small blue stains which sometimes occur in the purest statuary marble would convert the Eve of Powers to a monster. Masculine observers, if the birthmark did not heighten their admiration, contented themselves with wishing it away, that the world might possess one living specimen of ideal loveliness without the semblance of a flaw. After his marriage,—for he thought little or nothing of the matter before,—Aylmer discovered that this was the case with himself.

Had she been less beautiful,—if Envy's self could have found aught else to sneer at,—he might have felt his affection heightened by the prettiness of this mimic hand, now vaguely portrayed, now lost, now stealing forth again and glimmering to and fro with every pulse of emotion that throbbed within her heart; but seeing her otherwise so perfect, he found this one defect grow more and more intolerable with every moment of their united lives. It was the fatal flaw of humanity which Nature, in one shape or another, stamps ineffaceably on all her productions, either to imply that they are temporary and finite, or that their perfection must be wrought by toil and pain. The crimson hand expressed the ineludible gripe in which mortality clutches the highest and purest of earthly mould, degrading them into kindred with the lowest, and even with the very brutes, like whom their visible frames return to dust. In this manner, selecting it as the symbol of his wife's liability to sin, sorrow, decay, and death, Aylmer's sombre imagination was not long in rendering the birthmark a frightful object, causing him more trouble and horror than ever Georgiana's beauty, whether of soul or sense, had given him delight.

At all the seasons which should have been their happiest, he invariably and without intending it, nay, in spite of a purpose to the contrary, reverted to this one disastrous topic. Trifling as it at first appeared, it so connected itself with innumerable trains of thought and modes of feeling that it became the central point of all. With the morning twilight Aylmer opened his eyes upon his wife's face and recognized the symbol of imperfection; and when they sat together at the evening hearth his eyes wandered stealthily to her cheek, and beheld, flickering with the blaze of the wood fire, the spectral hand that wrote mortality where he would fain have worshipped. Georgiana soon learned to shudder at his gaze. It needed but a glance with the peculiar expression that his face often wore to change the roses of her cheek into a deathlike paleness, amid which the crimson hand was brought strongly out, like a bas-relief of ruby on the whitest marble.

Late one night when the lights were growing dim, so as hardly to betray the stain on the poor wife's cheek, she herself, for the first time, voluntarily took up the subject.

"Do you remember, my dear Aylmer," said she, with a feeble attempt at a smile, "have you any recollection of a dream last night about this odious hand?"

"None! none whatever!" replied Aylmer, starting; but then he added, in a dry, cold tone, affected for the sake of concealing the real depth of his emotion, "I might well dream of it; for before I fell asleep it had taken a pretty firm hold of my fancy."

"And you did dream of it?" continued Georgiana hastily, for she dreaded lest a gush of tears should interrupt what she had to say. "A terrible dream! I wonder that you can forget it. Is it possible to forget this one expression?—'It is in her heart now; we must have it out!' Reflect, my husband; for by all means I would have you recall that dream."

The mind is in a sad state when Sleep, the all-involving, cannot confine her spectres within the dim region of her sway, but suffers them to break forth, affrighting this actual life with secrets that perchance belong to a deeper one. Aylmer now remembered his dream. He had fancied himself with his servant Aminadab, attempting an operation for the removal of the birthmark; but the deeper went the knife, the deeper sank the hand, until at length its tiny grasp appeared to have caught hold of Georgiana's heart; whence, however, her husband was inexorably resolved to cut or wrench it away.

When the dream had shaped itself perfectly in his memory, Aylmer sat in his wife's presence with a guilty feeling. Truth often finds its way to the mind close muffled in robes of sleep, and then speaks with uncompromising directness of matters in regard to which we practise an unconscious self-deception during our waking moments. Until now he had not been aware of the tyrannizing influence acquired by one idea over his mind, and of the lengths which he might find in his heart to go for the sake of giving himself peace.

"Aylmer," resumed Georgiana solemnly, "I know not what may be the cost to both of us to rid me of this fatal birthmark. Perhaps its removal may cause cureless deformity; or it may be the stain goes as deep as life itself. Again: do we know that there is a possibility, on any terms, of unclasping the firm gripe of this little hand which was laid upon me before I came into the world?"

"Dearest Georgiana, I have spent much thought upon the subject," hastily interrupted Aylmer, "I am convinced of the perfect practicability of its removal."

"If there be the remotest possibility of it," continued Georgiana, "let the attempt be made at whatever risk. Danger is nothing to me; for life, while this hateful mark makes me the object of your horror and disgust,—life is a burden which I would fling down with joy. Either remove this dreadful hand, or take my wretched life! You have deep science. All the world bears witness of it. You have achieved great wonders. Cannot you remove this little, little mark, which I cover with the tips of two small fingers? Is this beyond your power, for the sake of your own peace, and to save your poor wife from madness?"

"Noblest, dearest, tenderest wife," cried Aylmer rapturously, "doubt not my power. I have already given this matter the deepest thought—thought which might almost have enlightened me to create a being less perfect than yourself. Georgiana, you have led me deeper than ever into the heart of science. I feel myself fully competent to render this dear cheek as faultless as its fellow; and then, most beloved, what will be my triumph when I shall have corrected what Nature left imperfect in her fairest work! Even Pygmalion, when his sculptured woman assumed life, felt not greater ecstasy than mine will be."

"It is resolved, then," said Georgiana, faintly smiling. "And, Aylmer, spare me not, though you should find the birthmark take refuge in my heart at last."

Her husband tenderly kissed her cheek—her right cheek—not that which bore the impress of the crimson hand.

The next day Aylmer apprised his wife of a plan that he had formed whereby he might have opportunity for the intense thought and constant watchfulness which the proposed operation would require; while Georgiana, likewise, would enjoy the perfect repose essential to its success. They were to seclude themselves in the extensive apartments occupied by Aylmer as a laboratory, and where, during his toilsome youth, he had made discoveries in the elemental powers of Nature that had roused the admiration of all the learned societies in Europe. Seated calmly in this laboratory, the pale philosopher had investigated the secrets of the highest cloud region and of the profoundest mines; he had satisfied himself of the causes that kindled and kept alive the fires of the volcano; and had explained the mystery of fountains, and how it is that they gush forth, some so bright and pure, and others with such rich medicinal virtues, from the dark bosom of the earth. Here, too, at an earlier period, he had studied the wonders of the human frame, and attempted to fathom the very process by which Nature assimilates all her precious influences from earth and air, and from the spiritual world, to create and foster man, her masterpiece. The latter pursuit, however, Aylmer had long laid aside in unwilling recognition of the truth—against which all seekers sooner or later stumble—that our great creative Mother, while she amuses us with apparently working in the broadest sunshine, is yet severely careful to keep her own secrets, and, in spite of her pretended openness, shows us nothing but results. She permits us, indeed, to mar, but seldom to mend, and, like a jealous patentee, on no account to make. Now, however, Aylmer resumed these half-forgotten investigations,—not, of course, with such hopes or wishes as first suggested them, but because they involved much physiological truth and lay in the path of his proposed scheme for the treatment of Georgiana.

As he led her over the threshold of the laboratory, Georgiana was cold and tremulous. Aylmer looked cheerfully into her face, with intent to reassure her, but was so startled with the intense glow of the birthmark upon the whiteness of her cheek that he could not restrain a strong convulsive shudder. His wife fainted.

"Aminadab! Aminadab!" shouted Aylmer, stamping violently on the floor.

Forthwith there issued from an inner apartment a man of low stature, but bulky frame, with shaggy hair hanging about his visage, which was grimed with the vapors of the furnace. This personage had been Aylmer's underworker during his whole scientific career, and was admirably fitted for that office by his great mechanical readiness, and the skill with which, while incapable of comprehending a single principle, he executed all the details of his master's experiments. With his vast strength, his shaggy hair, his smoky aspect, and the indescribable earthiness that incrusted him, he seemed to represent man's physical nature; while Aylmer's slender figure, and pale, intellectual face, were no less apt a type of the spiritual element.

"Throw open the door of the boudoir, Aminadab," said Aylmer, "and burn a pastil."

"Yes, master," answered Aminadab, looking intently at the lifeless form of Georgiana; and then he muttered to himself, "If she were my wife, I'd never part with that birthmark."

When Georgiana recovered consciousness she found herself breathing an atmosphere of penetrating fragrance, the gentle potency of which had recalled her from her deathlike faintness. The scene around her looked like enchantment. Aylmer had converted those smoky, dingy, sombre rooms, where he had spent his brightest years in recondite pursuits, into a series of beautiful apartments not unfit to be the secluded abode of a lovely woman. The walls were hung with gorgeous curtains, which imparted the combination of grandeur and grace that no other species of adornment can achieve; and as they fell from the ceiling to the floor, their rich and ponderous folds, concealing all angles and straight lines, appeared to shut in the scene from infinite space. For aught Georgiana knew, it might be a pavilion among the clouds. And Aylmer, excluding the sunshine, which would have interfered with his chemical processes, had supplied its place with perfumed lamps, emitting flames of various hue, but all uniting in a soft, impurpled radiance. He now knelt by his wife's side, watching her earnestly, but without alarm; for he was confident in his science, and felt that he could draw a magic circle round her within which no evil might intrude.

"Where am I? Ah, I remember," said Georgiana faintly; and she placed her hand over her cheek to hide the terrible mark from her husband's eyes.

"Fear not, dearest!" exclaimed he. "Do not shrink from me! Believe me, Georgiana, I even rejoice in this single imperfection, since it will be such a rapture to remove it."

"Oh, spare me!" sadly replied his wife. "Pray do not look at it again. I never can forget that convulsive shudder."

In order to soothe Georgiana, and, as it were, to release her mind from the burden of actual things, Aylmer now put in practice some of the light and playful secrets which science had taught him among its profounder lore. Airy figures, absolutely bodiless ideas, and forms of unsubstantial beauty came and danced before her, imprinting their momentary footsteps on beams of light. Though she had some indistinct idea of the method of these optical phenomena, still the illusion was almost perfect enough to warrant the belief that her husband possessed sway over the spiritual world. Then again, when she felt a wish to look forth from her seclusion, immediately, as if her thoughts were answered, the procession of external existence flitted across a screen. The scenery and the figures of actual life were perfectly represented, but with that bewitching, yet indescribable difference which always makes a picture, an image, or a shadow so much more attractive than the original. When wearied of this, Aylmer bade her cast her eyes upon a vessel containing a quantity of earth. She did so, with little interest at first; but was soon startled to perceive the germ of a plant shooting upward from the soil. Then came the slender stalk; the leaves gradually unfolded themselves; and amid them was a perfect and lovely flower.

"It is magical!" cried Georgiana. "I dare not touch it."

"Nay, pluck it," answered Aylmer: "pluck it, and inhale its brief perfume while you may. The flower will wither in a few moments and leave nothing save its brown seed vessels; but thence may be perpetuated a race as ephemeral as itself."

But Georgiana had no sooner touched the flower than the whole plant suffered a blight, its leaves turning coal-black as if by the agency of fire.

"There was too powerful a stimulus," said Aylmer thoughtfully.

To make up for this abortive experiment, he proposed to take her portrait by a scientific process of his own invention. It was to be effected by rays of light striking upon a polished plate of metal. Georgiana assented; but, on looking at the result, was affrighted to find the features of the portrait blurred and indefinable; while the minute figure of a hand appeared where the cheek should have been. Aylmer snatched the metallic plate and threw it into a jar of corrosive acid.

Soon, however, he forgot these mortifying failures. In the intervals of study and chemical experiment he came to her flushed and exhausted, but seemed invigorated by her presence, and spoke in glowing language of the resources of his art. He gave a history of the long dynasty of the alchemists, who spent so many ages in quest of the universal solvent by which the golden principle might be elicited from all things vile and base. Aylmer appeared to believe that, by the plainest scientific logic, it was altogether within the limits of possibility to discover this long-sought medium; "but," he added, "a philosopher who should go deep enough to acquire the power would attain too lofty a wisdom to stoop to the exercise of it." Not less singular were his opinions in regard to the elixir vitæ. He more than intimated that it was at his option to concoct a liquid that should prolong life for years, perhaps interminably; but that it would produce a discord in Nature which all the world, and chiefly the quaffer of the immortal nostrum, would find cause to curse.

"Aylmer, are you in earnest?" asked Georgiana, looking at him with amazement and fear. "It is terrible to possess such power, or even to dream of possessing it."

"Oh, do not tremble, my love," said her husband. "I would not wrong either you or myself by working such inharmonious effects upon our lives; but I would have you consider how trifling, in comparison, is the skill requisite to remove this little hand."

At the mention of the birthmark, Georgiana, as usual, shrank as if a red-hot iron had touched her cheek.

Again Aylmer applied himself to his labors. She could hear his voice in the distant furnace-room giving directions to Aminadab, whose harsh, uncouth, misshapen tones were audible in response, more like the grunt or growl of a brute than human speech. After hours of absence, Aylmer reappeared and proposed that she should now examine his cabinet of chemical products and natural treasures of the earth. Among the former he showed her a small vial, in which, he remarked, was contained a gentle yet most powerful fragrance, capable of impregnating all the breezes that blow across a kingdom. They were of inestimable value, the contents of that little vial; and, as he said so, he threw some of the perfume into the air and filled the room with piercing and invigorating delight.

"And what is this?" asked Georgiana, pointing to a small crystal globe containing a gold-colored liquid. "It is so beautiful to the eye that I could imagine it the elixir of life."

"In one sense it is," replied Aylmer; "or rather, the elixir of immortality. It is the most precious poison that ever was concocted in this world. By its aid I could apportion the lifetime of any mortal at whom you might point your finger. The strength of the dose would determine whether he were to linger out years, or drop dead in the midst of a breath. No king on his guarded throne could keep his life if I, in my private station, should deem that the welfare of millions justified me in depriving him of it."

"Why do you keep such a terrific drug?" inquired Georgiana in horror.

"Do not mistrust me, dearest," said her husband, smiling; "its virtuous potency is yet greater than its harmful one. But see! here is a powerful cosmetic. With a few drops of this in a vase of water, freckles may be washed away as easily as the hands are cleansed. A stronger infusion would take the blood out of the cheek, and leave the rosiest beauty a pale ghost."

"Is it with this lotion that you intend to bathe my cheek?" asked Georgiana, anxiously.

"Oh, no," hastily replied her husband; "this is merely superficial. Your case demands a remedy that shall go deeper."

In his interviews with Georgiana, Aylmer generally made minute inquiries as to her sensations and whether the confinement of the rooms and the temperature of the atmosphere agreed with her. These questions had such a particular drift that Georgiana began to conjecture that she was already subjected to certain physical influences, either breathed in with the fragrant air or taken with her food. She fancied likewise, but it might be altogether fancy, that there was a stirring up of her system—a strange, indefinite sensation creeping through her veins, and tingling, half painfully, half pleasurably, at her heart. Still, whenever she dared to look into the mirror, there she beheld herself pale as a white rose and with the crimson birthmark stamped upon her cheek. Not even Aylmer now hated it so much as she.

To dispel the tedium of the hours which her husband found it necessary to devote to the processes of combination and analysis, Georgiana turned over the volumes of his scientific library. In many dark old tomes she met with chapters full of romance and poetry. They were the works of the philosophers of the middle ages, such as Albertus Magnus, Cornelius Agrippa, Paracelsus, and the famous friar who created the prophetic Brazen Head. All these antique naturalists stood in advance of their centuries, yet were imbued with some of their credulity, and therefore were believed, and perhaps imagined themselves to have acquired from the investigation of Nature a power above Nature, and from physics a sway over the spiritual world. Hardly less curious and imaginative were the early volumes of the Transactions of the Royal Society, in which the members, knowing little of the limits of natural possibility, were continually recording wonders or proposing methods whereby wonders might be wrought.

But to Georgiana the most engrossing volume was a large folio from her husband's own hand, in which he had recorded every experiment of his scientific career, its original aim, the methods adopted for its development, and its final success or failure, with the circumstances to which either event was attributable. The book, in truth, was both the history and emblem of his ardent, ambitious, imaginative, yet practical and laborious life. He handled physical details as if there were nothing beyond them; yet spiritualized them all, and redeemed himself from materialism by his strong and eager aspiration towards the infinite. In his grasp the veriest clod of earth assumed a soul. Georgiana, as she read, reverenced Aylmer and loved him more profoundly than ever, but with a less entire dependence on his judgment than heretofore. Much as he had accomplished, she could not but observe that his most splendid successes were almost invariably failures, if compared with the ideal at which he aimed. His brightest diamonds were the merest pebbles, and felt to be so by himself, in comparison with the inestimable gems which lay hidden beyond his reach. The volume, rich with achievements that had won renown for its author, was yet as melancholy a record as ever mortal hand had penned. It was the sad confession and continual exemplification of the shortcomings of the composite man, the spirit burdened with clay and working in matter, and of the despair that assails the higher nature at finding itself so miserably thwarted by the earthly part. Perhaps every man of genius in whatever sphere might recognize the image of his own experience in Aylmer's journal.

So deeply did these reflections affect Georgiana that she laid her face upon the open volume and burst into tears. In this situation she was found by her husband.

"It is dangerous to read in a sorcerer's books," said he with a smile, though his countenance was uneasy and displeased. "Georgiana, there are pages in that volume which I can scarcely glance over and keep my senses. Take heed less it prove as detrimental to you."

"It has made me worship you more than ever," said she.

"Ah, wait for this one success," rejoined he, "then worship me if you will. I shall deem myself hardly unworthy of it. But come, I have sought you for the luxury of your voice. Sing to me, dearest."

So she poured out the liquid music of her voice to quench the thirst of his spirit. He then took his leave with a boyish exuberance of gayety, assuring her that her seclusion would endure but a little longer, and that the result was already certain. Scarcely had he departed when Georgiana felt irresistibly impelled to follow him. She had forgotten to inform Aylmer of a symptom which for two or three hours past had begun to excite her attention. It was a sensation in the fatal birthmark, not painful, but which induced a restlessness throughout her system. Hastening after her husband, she intruded for the first time into the laboratory.

The first thing that struck her eye was the furnace, that hot and feverish worker, with the intense glow of its fire, which by the quantities of soot clustered above it seemed to have been burning for ages. There was a distilling apparatus in full operation. Around the room were retorts, tubes, cylinders, crucibles, and other apparatus of chemical research. An electrical machine stood ready for immediate use. The atmosphere felt oppressively close, and was tainted with gaseous odors which had been tormented forth by the processes of science. The severe and homely simplicity of the apartment, with its naked walls and brick pavement, looked strange, accustomed as Georgiana had become to the fantastic elegance of her boudoir. But what chiefly, indeed almost solely, drew her attention, was the aspect of Aylmer himself.

He was pale as death, anxious and absorbed, and hung over the furnace as if it depended upon his utmost watchfulness whether the liquid which it was distilling should be the draught of immortal happiness or misery. How different from the sanguine and joyous mien that he had assumed for Georgiana's encouragement!

"Carefully now, Aminadab; carefully, thou human machine; carefully, thou man of clay!" muttered Aylmer, more to himself than his assistant. "Now, if there be a thought too much or too little, it is all over."

"Ho! ho!" mumbled Aminadab. "Look, master! look!"

Aylmer raised his eyes hastily, and at first reddened, then grew paler than ever, on beholding Georgiana. He rushed towards her and seized her arm with a gripe that left the print of his fingers upon it.

"Why do you come hither? Have you no trust in your husband?" cried he impetuously. "Would you throw the blight of that fatal birthmark over my labors? It is not well done. Go, prying woman, go!"

"Nay, Aylmer," said Georgiana with the firmness of which she possessed no stinted endowment, "it is not you that have a right to complain. You mistrust your wife; you have concealed the anxiety with which you watch the development of this experiment. Think not so unworthily of me, my husband. Tell me all the risk we run, and fear not that I shall shrink; for my share in it is far less than your own."

"No, no, Georgiana!" said Aylmer, impatiently; "it must not be."

"I submit," replied she calmly. "And, Aylmer, I shall quaff whatever draught you bring me; but it will be on the same principle that would induce me to take a dose of poison if offered by your hand."

"My noble wife," said Aylmer, deeply moved, "I knew not the height and depth of your nature until now. Nothing shall be concealed. Know, then, that this crimson hand, superficial as it seems, has clutched its grasp into your being with a strength of which I had no previous conception. I have already administered agents powerful enough to do aught except to change your entire physical system. Only one thing remains to be tried. If that fail us we are ruined."

"Why did you hesitate to tell me this?" asked she.

"Because, Georgiana," said Aylmer, in a low voice, "there is danger."

"Danger? There is but one danger—that this horrible stigma shall be left upon my cheek!" cried Georgiana. "Remove it, remove it, whatever be the cost, or we shall both go mad!"

"Heaven knows your words are too true," said Aylmer sadly. "And now, dearest, return to your boudoir. In a little while all will be tested."

He conducted her back and took leave of her with a solemn tenderness which spoke far more than his words how much was now at stake. After his departure Georgiana became rapt in musings. She considered the character of Aylmer, and did it completer justice than at any previous moment. Her heart exulted, while it trembled, at his honorable love—so pure and lofty that it would accept nothing less than perfection nor miserably make itself contented with an earthlier nature than he had dreamed of. She felt how much more precious was such a sentiment than that meaner kind which would have borne with the imperfection for her sake, and have been guilty of treason to holy love by degrading its perfect idea to the level of the actual; and with her whole spirit she prayed that, for a single moment, she might satisfy his highest and deepest conception. Longer than one moment she well knew it could not be; for his spirit was ever on the march, ever ascending, and each instant required something that was beyond the scope of the instant before.

The sound of her husband's footsteps aroused her. He bore a crystal goblet containing a liquor colorless as water, but bright enough to be the draught of immortality. Aylmer was pale; but it seemed rather the consequence of a highly wrought state of mind and tension of spirit than of fear or doubt.

"The concoction of the draught has been perfect," said he, in answer to Georgiana's look. "Unless all my science have deceived me, it cannot fail."

"Save on your account, my dearest Aylmer," observed his wife, "I might wish to put off this birthmark of mortality by relinquishing mortality itself in preference to any other mode. Life is but a sad possession to those who have attained precisely the degree of moral advancement at which I stand. Were I weaker and blinder it might be happiness. Were I stronger, it might be endured hopefully. But, being what I find myself, methinks I am of all mortals the most fit to die."

"You are fit for heaven without tasting death!" replied her husband. "But why do we speak of dying? The draught cannot fail. Behold its effect upon this plant."

On the window seat there stood a geranium diseased with yellow blotches, which had overspread all its leaves. Aylmer poured a small quantity of the liquid upon the soil in which it grew. In a little time, when the roots of the plant had taken up the moisture, the unsightly blotches began to be extinguished in a living verdure.

"There needed no proof," said Georgiana quietly. "Give me the goblet. I joyfully stake all upon your word."

"Drink, then, thou lofty creature!" exclaimed Aylmer, with fervid admiration. "There is no taint of imperfection on thy spirit. Thy sensible frame, too, shall soon be all perfect."

She quaffed the liquid and returned the goblet to his hand.

"It is grateful," said she, with a placid smile. "Methinks it is like water from a heavenly fountain; for it contains I know not what of unobtrusive fragrance and deliciousness. It allays a feverish thirst that had parched me for many days. Now, dearest, let me sleep. My earthly senses are closing over my spirit like the leaves around the heart of a rose at sunset."

She spoke the last words with a gentle reluctance, as if it required almost more energy than she could command to pronounce the faint and lingering syllables. Scarcely had they loitered through her lips ere she was lost in slumber. Aylmer sat by her side, watching her aspect with the emotions proper to a man the whole value of whose existence was involved in the process now to be tested. Mingled with this mood, however, was the philosophic investigation characteristic of the man of science. Not the minutest symptom escaped him. A heightened flush of the cheek, a slight irregularity of breath, a quiver of the eyelid, a hardly perceptible tremor through the frame,—such were the details which, as the moments passed, he wrote down in his folio volume. Intense thought had set its stamp upon every previous page of that volume, but the thoughts of years were all concentrated upon the last.

While thus employed, he failed not to gaze often at the fatal hand, and not without a shudder. Yet once, by a strange and unaccountable impulse, he pressed it with his lips. His spirit recoiled, however, in the very act; and Georgiana, out of the midst of her deep sleep, moved uneasily and murmured as if in remonstrance. Again Aylmer resumed his watch. Nor was it without avail. The crimson hand, which at first had been strongly visible upon the marble paleness of Georgiana's cheek, now grew more faintly outlined. She remained not less pale than ever; but the birthmark, with every breath that came and went, lost somewhat of its former distinctness. Its presence had been awful; its departure was more awful still. Watch the stain of the rainbow fading out of the sky, and you will know how that mysterious symbol passed away.

"By Heaven! it is well-nigh gone!" said Aylmer to himself, in almost irrepressible ecstasy. "I can scarcely trace it now. Success! success! And now it is like the faintest rose color. The lightest flush of blood across her cheek would overcome it. But she is so pale!"

He drew aside the window curtain and suffered the light of natural day to fall into the room and rest upon her cheek. At the same time he heard a gross, hoarse chuckle, which he had long known as his servant Aminadab's expression of delight.

"Ah, clod! ah, earthly mass!" cried Aylmer, laughing in a sort of frenzy, "you have served me well! Matter and spirit—earth and heaven—have both done their part in this! Laugh, thing of the senses! You have earned the right to laugh."

These exclamations broke Georgiana's sleep. She slowly unclosed her eyes and gazed into the mirror which her husband had arranged for that purpose. A faint smile flitted over her lips when she recognized how barely perceptible was now that crimson hand which had once blazed forth with such disastrous brilliancy as to scare away all their happiness. But then her eyes sought Aylmer's face with a trouble and anxiety that he could by no means account for.

"My poor Aylmer!" murmured she.

"Poor? Nay, richest, happiest, most favored!" exclaimed he. "My peerless bride, it is successful! You are perfect!"

"My poor Aylmer," she repeated, with a more than human tenderness, "you have aimed loftily; you have done nobly. Do not repent that with so high and pure a feeling, you have rejected the best the earth could offer. Aylmer, dearest Aylmer, I am dying!"

Alas! it was too true! The fatal hand had grappled with the mystery of life, and was the bond by which an angelic spirit kept itself in union with a mortal frame. As the last crimson tint of the birthmark—that sole token of human imperfection—faded from her cheek, the parting breath of the now perfect woman passed into the atmosphere, and her soul, lingering a moment near her husband, took its heavenward flight. Then a hoarse, chuckling laugh was heard again! Thus ever does the gross fatality of earth exult in its invariable triumph over the immortal essence which, in this dim sphere of half development, demands the completeness of a higher state. Yet, had Aylmer reached a profounder wisdom, he need not thus have flung away the happiness which would have woven his mortal life of the selfsame texture with the celestial. The momentary circumstance was too strong for him; he failed to look beyond the shadowy scope of time, and, living once for all in eternity, to find the perfect future in the present.

3–11

Alexis de Tocqueville (1805–1859)

Alexis Charles-Henri Clérel, Viscount de Tocqueville has gone down in history by the shorter name, ALEXIS DE TOCQUEVILLE (1805–1859). The son of wealthy French aristocrats, Tocqueville lost many members of his extended family during the French Revolution and the ensuing Reign of Terror. This helps explain his dogged attempts to understand American democracy. From 1831–1832, Tocqueville traveled through the young country, taking voluminous notes. He also absorbed official governmental reports and hundreds of books as he engaged in the research for *Democracy in America* (1835–1840), a masterpiece of insight and acumen. The selection printed here outlines some difficulties facing American writers in the early national era. Tocqueville expresses faith that a national literature will arise, but that one cannot predict what it might look like. His analysis is particularly interesting given that the "American Renaissance," with writers like Fuller, Emerson, Thoreau, Douglass, Melville, Hawthorne, and others is on the immediate horizon.

≋ ≋ ≋

From *Democracy in America* (1835–1840)

"Literary Characteristics of Democratic Ages"

When a traveller goes into a bookseller's shop in the United States, and examines the American books upon the shelves, the number of works appears extremely great; whilst that of known authors appears, on the contrary, to be extremely small. He will first meet with a number of elementary treatises, destined to teach the rudiments of human knowledge. Most of these books are written in Europe; the Americans reprint them, adapting them to their own country. Next comes an enormous quantity of religious works, Bibles, sermons, edifying anecdotes, controversial divinity, and reports of charitable societies; lastly, appears the long catalogue of political pamphlets. In America, parties do not write books to combat each other's opinions, but pamphlets which are circulated for a day with incredible rapidity, and then expire. In the midst of all these obscure productions of the human brain are to be found the more remarkable works of that small number of authors, whose names are, or ought to be, known to Europeans.

Although America is perhaps in our days the civilized country in which literature is least attended to, a large number of persons are nevertheless to be found there who take an interest in the productions of the mind, and who make them, if not the study of their lives, at least the charm of their leisure hours. But England supplies these readers with the larger portion of the books which they require. Almost all important English books are republished in the United States. The literary genius of Great Britain still darts its rays into the recesses of the forests of the New World. There is hardly a pioneer's hut which does not contain a few odd volumes of Shakespeare. I remember that I read the feudal play of Henry V for the first time in a loghouse.

Not only do the Americans constantly draw upon the treasures of English literature, but it may be said with truth that they find the literature of England growing on their own soil. The larger part of that small number of men in the United States who are engaged in the composition of literary works are English in substance, and still more so in form. Thus they transport into the midst of democracy the ideas and literary fashions which are current amongst the aristocratic nation they have taken for their model. They paint with colors borrowed from foreign manners; and as they hardly ever represent the country they were born in as it really is, they are seldom popular there. The citizens of the United States are themselves so convinced that it is not for them that books are published, that before they can make up their minds upon the merit of one of their authors, they generally wait till his fame has been ratified in England, just as in pictures the author of an original is held to be entitled to judge of the merit of a copy. The inhabitants of the United States have then at present, properly speaking, no literature. The only authors whom I acknowledge as American are the journalists. They indeed are not great writers, but they speak the language of their countrymen, and make themselves heard by them. Other authors are aliens; they are to the Americans what the imitators of the Greeks and Romans were to us at the revival of learning—an object of curiosity, not of general sympathy. They amuse the mind, but they do not act upon the manners of the people.

I have already said that this state of things is very far from originating in democracy alone, and that the cases of it must be sought for in several peculiar circumstances independent of the democratic principle. If the Americans, retaining the same laws and social condition, had had a different origin, and had been transported into another country, I do not question that they would have had a literature. Even as they now are, I am convinced that they will ultimately have one; but its character will be different from that which marks the American literary productions of our time, and that character will be peculiarly its own. Nor is it impossible to trace this character beforehand.

I suppose an aristocratic people amongst whom letters are cultivated; the labors of the mind, as well as the affairs of state, are conducted by a ruling class in society. The literary as well as the political career is almost entirely confined to this class, or to those nearest to it in rank. These premises suffice to give me a key to all the rest. When a small number of the same men are engaged at the same time upon the same objects, they easily concert with one another, and agree upon certain leading rules which are to govern them each and all. If the object which attracts the attention of these men is literature, the productions of the mind will soon be subjected by them to precise canons, from which it will no longer be allowable to depart. If these men occupy a hereditary position in the country, they will be naturally inclined, not only to adopt a certain number of fixed rules for themselves, but to follow those which their forefathers laid down for their own guidance; their code will be at once strict and traditional. As they are not necessarily engrossed by the cares of daily life—as they have never been so, any more than their fathers were before them—they have learned to take an interest, for several generations back, in the labors of the mind. They have learned to understand literature as an art, to love it in the end for its own sake, and to feel a scholar-like satisfaction in seeing men conform to its rules. Nor is this all: the men of whom I speak began and will end their lives in easy or in affluent circumstances; hence they have naturally conceived a taste for choice gratifications, and a love of refined and delicate pleasures. Nay more, a kind of indolence of mind and heart, which they frequently contract in the midst of this long and peaceful enjoyment of so much welfare, leads them to put aside, even from their pleasures, whatever might be too startling or too acute. They had rather be amused than intensely excited; they wish to be interested, but not to be carried away.

Now let us fancy a great number of literary performances executed by the men, or for the men, whom I have just described, and we shall readily conceive a style of literature in which everything will be regular and prearranged. The slightest work will be carefully touched in its least details; art and labor will be conspicuous in everything; each kind of writing will have rules of its own, from which it will not be allowed to swerve, and which distinguish it from all others. Style will be thought of almost as much importance as thought; and the form will be no less considered than the matter: the diction will be polished, measured, and uniform. The tone of the mind will be always dignified, seldom very animated; and writers will care more to perfect what they produce than to multiply their productions. It will sometimes happen that the members of the literary class, always living amongst themselves and writing for themselves alone, will lose sight of the rest of the world, which will infect them with a false and labored style; they will lay down minute literary rules for their exclusive use, which will insensibly lead them to deviate from common-sense, and finally to transgress the bounds of nature. By dint of striving after a mode of parlance different from the vulgar, they will arrive at a sort of aristocratic jargon, which is hardly less remote from pure language than is the coarse dialect of the people. Such are the natural perils of literature amongst aristocracies.

Every aristocracy which keeps itself entirely aloof from the people becomes impotent—a fact which is as true in literature as it is in politics.*

Let us now turn the picture and consider the other side of it; let us transport ourselves into the midst of a democracy, not unprepared by ancient traditions and present culture to partake in the pleasures of the mind. Ranks are there intermingled and confounded; knowledge and power are both infinitely subdivided, and, if I may use the expression, scattered on every side. Here then is a motley multitude, whose intellectual wants are to be supplied. These new votaries of the pleasures of the mind have not all received the same education; they do not possess the same degree of culture as their fathers, nor any resemblance to them—nay, they perpetually differ from themselves, for they live in a state of incessant change of place, feelings, and fortunes. The mind of each member of the community is therefore unattached to that of his fellow-citizens by tradition or by common habits; and they have never had the power, the inclination, nor the time to concert together. It is, however, from the bosom of this heterogeneous and agitated mass that authors spring; and from the same source their profits and their fame are distributed. I can without difficulty understand that, under these circumstances, I must expect to meet in the literature of such a people with but few of those strict conventional rules which are admitted by readers and by writers in aristocratic ages. If it should happen that the men of some one period were agreed upon any such rules, that would prove nothing for the following period; for amongst democratic nations each new generation is a new people. Amongst such nations, then, literature will not easily be subjected to strict rules, and it is impossible that any such rules should ever be permanent.

In democracies it is by no means the case that all the men who cultivate literature have received a literary education; and most of those who have some tinge of *belles-lettres* are either engaged in politics, or in a profession which only allows them to taste occasionally and by stealth the pleasures of the mind. These pleasures, therefore, do not constitute the principal charm of their lives; but they are considered as a transient and necessary recreation amidst the serious labors

---

* All this is especially true of the aristocratic countries which have been long and peacefully subject to a monarchical government. When liberty prevails in an aristocracy, the higher ranks are constantly obliged to make use of the lower classes; and when they use, they approach them. This frequently introduces something of a democratic spirit into an aristocratic community. There springs up, moreover, in a privileged body, governing with energy and an habitually bold policy, a taste for stir and excitement which must infallibly affect all literary performances.

of life. Such men can never acquire a sufficiently intimate knowledge of the art of literature to appreciate its more delicate beauties; and the minor shades of expression must escape them. As the time they can devote to letters is very short, they seek to make the best use of the whole of it. They prefer books which may be easily procured, quickly read, and which require no learned researches to be understood. They ask for beauties, self-proffered and easily enjoyed; above all, they must have what is unexpected and new. Accustomed to the struggle, the crosses, and the monotony of practical life, they require rapid emotions, startling passages—truths or errors brilliant enough to rouse them up, and to plunge them at once, as if by violence, into the midst of a subject.

Why should I say more? or who does not understand what is about to follow, before I have expressed it? Taken as a whole, literature in democratic ages can never present, as it does in the periods of aristocracy, an aspect of order, regularity, science, and art; its form will, on the contrary, ordinarily be slighted, sometimes despised. Style will frequently be fantastic, incorrect, overburdened, and loose—almost always vehement and bold. Authors will aim at rapidity of execution, more than at perfection of detail. Small productions will be more common than bulky books; there will be more wit than erudition, more imagination than profundity; and literary performances will bear marks of an untutored and rude vigor of thought—frequently of great variety and singular fecundity. The object of authors will be to astonish rather than to please, and to stir the passions more than to charm the taste. Here and there, indeed, writers will doubtless occur who will choose a different track, and who will, if they are gifted with superior abilities, succeed in finding readers, in spite of their defects or their better qualities; but these exceptions will be rare, and even the authors who shall so depart from the received practice in the main subject of their works, will always relapse into it in some lesser details.

I have just depicted two extreme conditions: the transition by which a nation passes from the former to the latter is not sudden but gradual, and marked with shades of very various intensity. In the passage which conducts a lettered people from the one to the other, there is almost always a moment at which the literary genius of democratic nations has its confluence with that of aristocracies, and both seek to establish their joint sway over the human mind. Such epochs are transient, but very brilliant: they are fertile without exuberance, and animated without confusion. The French literature of the eighteenth century may serve as an example.

I should say more than I mean if I were to assert that the literature of a nation is always subordinate to its social condition and its political constitution. I am aware that, independently of these causes, there are several others which confer certain characteristics on literary productions; but these appear to me to be the chief. The relations which exist between the social and political condition of a people and the genius of its authors are always very numerous: whoever knows the one is never completely ignorant of the other.

3—12
Henry Wadsworth Longfellow (1807–1882)

Few American poets have ever matched the popularity of HENRY WADSWORTH LONGFELLOW (1807–1882). One of the "Fireside Poets" along with Holmes, Lowell, and Whittier, Longfellow was educated at Bowdoin College in Maine, where classmates included Nathaniel Hawthorne and Franklin Pierce. Longfellow became a professor of modern language at Harvard University, and in addition to writing such favorite poems as "A Psalm of Life" (1838) and "Paul Revere's Ride" (1861), he translated Dante's *The Divine Comedy* (1867), a translation still respected and read. One can also see his interest in foreign languages in his use of the Finnish national epic the *Kalevala* to provide the trochaic tetrameter meter for one of his most famous works, *The Song of Hiawatha* (1855), based on contemporary ethnographies of Native American legends, especially that of an Ojibwe warrior. Indeed, Longfellow's influences were international, and he is memorialized in Poet's Corner at Westminster Abbey.

≈ ≈ ≈

From *The Song of Hiawatha* (1855)

III
Hiawatha's Childhood

Downward through the evening twilight,
In the days that are forgotten,
In the unremembered ages,
From the full moon fell Nokomis,
Fell the beautiful Nokomis,
She a wife, but not a mother.

She was sporting with her women,
Swinging in a swing of grape-vines,
When her rival the rejected,
Full of jealousy and hatred,

Cut the leafy swing asunder,
Cut in twain the twisted grape-vines,
And Nokomis fell affrighted
Downward through the evening
    twilight,
On the Muskoday, the meadow,
On the prairie full of blossoms.
"See! a star falls!" said the people;
"From the sky a star is falling!"

There among the ferns and
    mosses,
There among the prairie lilies,
On the Muskoday, the meadow,
In the moonlight and the starlight,
Fair Nokomis bore a daughter.
And she called her name Wenonah,
As the first-born of her daughters.
And the daughter of Nokomis
Grew up like the prairie lilies,
Grew a tall and slender maiden,
With the beauty of the moonlight,
With the beauty of the starlight.

And Nokomis warned her often,
Saying oft, and oft repeating,
"Oh, beware of Mudjekeewis,
Of the West-Wind, Mudjekeewis;
Listen not to what he tells you;
Lie not down upon the meadow,
Stoop not down among the lilies,
Lest the West-Wind come and harm
    you!"

But she heeded not the warning,
Heeded not those words of wisdom,
And the West-Wind came at evening,
Walking lightly o'er the prairie,
Whispering to the leaves and blossoms,
Bending low the flowers and grasses,
Found the beautiful Wenonah,

Lying there among the lilies,
Wooed her with his words of sweetness,
Wooed her with his soft caresses,
Till she bore a son in sorrow,
Bore a son of love and sorrow.

Thus was born my Hiawatha,
Thus was born the child of wonder;
But the daughter of Nokomis,
Hiawatha's gentle mother,
In her anguish died deserted
By the West-Wind, false and faithless,
By the heartless Mudjekeewis.

For her daughter long and
    loudly
Wailed and wept the sad Nokomis;
"Oh that I were dead!" she murmured,
"Oh that I were dead, as thou art!
No more work, and no more weeping,
Wahonowin! Wahonowin!"

By the shores of Gitche Gumee,
By the shining Big-Sea-Water,
Stood the wigwam of Nokomis,
Daughter of the Moon, Nokomis.
Dark behind it rose the forest,
Rose the black and gloomy pine-trees
Rose the firs with cones upon them;
Bright before it beat the water,
Beat the clear and sunny water,
Beat the shining Big-Sea-Water.

There the wrinkled old
    Nokomis
Nursed the little Hiawatha,
Rocked him in his linden cradle,
Bedded soft in moss and rushes,
Safely bound with reindeer sinews;
Stilled his fretful wail by saying,
"Hush! the Naked Bear will hear thee!"

Lulled him into slumber, singing,
"Ewa-yea! my little owlet!
Who is this, that lights the wigwam?
With his great eyes lights the wigwam?
Ewa-yea! my little owlet!"

Many things Nokomis taught
    him
Of the stars that shine in heaven;
Showed him Ishkoodah, the comet,
Ishkoodah, with fiery tresses;
Showed the Death-Dance of the spirits,
Warriors with their plumes and war-
    clubs,
Flaring far away to northward
In the frosty nights of Winter;
Showed the broad white road in
    heaven,
Pathway of the ghosts, the shadows,
Running straight across the heavens,
Crowded with the ghosts, the shadows.

At the door on summer
    evenings
Sat the little Hiawatha;
Heard the whispering of the pine-trees,
Heard the lapping of the waters,
Sounds of music, words of wonder;
"Minne-wawa!" said the pine-trees,
"Mudway-aushka!" said the water.

Saw the fire-fly, Wah-wah-taysee,
Flitting through the dusk of evening,
With the twinkle of its candle
Lighting up the brakes and bushes,
And he sang the song of children,
Sang the song Nokomis taught him:
"Wah-wah-taysee, little fire-fly,
Little, flitting, white-fire insect,
Little, dancing, white-fire creature,
Light me with your little candle,

Ere upon my bed I lay me,
Ere in sleep I close my eyelids!"

Saw the moon rise from the
    water
Rippling, rounding from the water,
Saw the flecks and shadows on it,
Whispered, "What is that, Nokomis?"
And the good Nokomis answered:
"Once a warrior, very angry,
Seized his grandmother, and threw her
Up into the sky at midnight;
Right against the moon he threw her;
'Tis her body that you see there."

Saw the rainbow in the heaven,
In the eastern sky, the rainbow,
Whispered, "What is that, Nokomis?"
And the good Nokomis answered:
"'Tis the heaven of flowers you see
    there;
All the wild-flowers of the forest,
All the lilies of the prairie,
When on earth they fade and perish,
Blossom in that heaven above us."

When he heard the owls at
    midnight,
Hooting, laughing in the forest,
"What is that?" he cried in terror,
"What is that," he said, "Nokomis?"
And the good Nokomis answered:
"That is but the owl and owlet,
Talking in their native language,
Talking, scolding at each other."

Then the little Hiawatha
Learned of every bird its language,
Learned their names and all their
    secrets,
How they built their nests in Summer,

Where they hid themselves in Winter,
Talked with them whene'er he met
    them,
Called them "Hiawatha's Chickens."

Of all beasts he learned the
    language,
Learned their names and all their
    secrets,
How the beavers built their lodges,
Where the squirrels hid their acorns,
How the reindeer ran so swiftly,
Why the rabbit was so timid,
Talked with them whene'er he met
    them,
Called them "Hiawatha's Brothers."

Then Iagoo, the great boaster,
He the marvellous story-teller,
He the traveller and the talker,
He the friend of old Nokomis,
Made a bow for Hiawatha;
From a branch of ash he made it,
From an oak-bough made the arrows,
Tipped with flint, and winged with
    feathers,
And the cord he made of deer-skin.

Then he said to Hiawatha:
"Go, my son, into the forest,
Where the red deer herd together,
Kill for us a famous roebuck,
Kill for us a deer with antlers!"

Forth into the forest straightway
All alone walked Hiawatha
Proudly, with his bow and arrows;
And the birds sang round him, o'er
    him,
"Do not shoot us, Hiawatha!"
Sang the robin, the Opechee,

Sang the bluebird, the Owaissa,
"Do not shoot us, Hiawatha!"

Up the oak-tree, close beside
    him,
Sprang the squirrel, Adjidaumo,
In and out among the branches,
Coughed and chattered from the oak-
    tree,
Laughed, and said between his
    laughing,
"Do not shoot me, Hiawatha!"

And the rabbit from his
    pathway
Leaped aside, and at a distance
Sat erect upon his haunches,
Half in fear and half in frolic,
Saying to the little hunter,
"Do not shoot me, Hiawatha!"

But he heeded not, nor heard
    them,
For his thoughts were with the red
    deer;
On their tracks his eyes were fastened,
Leading downward to the river,
To the ford across the river,
And as one in slumber walked he.

Hidden in the alder-bushes,
There he waited till the deer came,
Till he saw two antlers lifted,
Saw two eyes look from the thicket,
Saw two nostrils point to windward,
And a deer came down the pathway,
Flecked with leafy light and shadow.
And his heart within him fluttered,
Trembled like the leaves above him,
Like the birch-leaf palpitated,
As the deer came down the pathway.

Then, upon one knee uprising,
Hiawatha aimed an arrow;
Scarce a twig moved with his motion,
Scarce a leaf was stirred or rustled,
But the wary roebuck started,
Stamped with all his hoofs together,
Listened with one foot uplifted,
Leaped as if to meet the arrow;
Ah! the singing, fatal arrow,
Like a wasp it buzzed and stung him!

Dead he lay there in the forest,
By the ford across the river;
Beat his timid heart no longer,
But the heart of Hiawatha
Throbbed and shouted and exulted,
As he bore the red deer homeward,
And Iagoo and Nokomis
Hailed his coming with applauses.

From the red deer's hide
  Nokomis
Made a cloak for Hiawatha,
From the red deer's flesh Nokomis
Made a banquet to his honor.
All the village came and feasted,
All the guests praised Hiawatha,
Called him Strong-Heart, Soan-ge-
  taha!
Called him Loon-Heart, Mahn-go-
  taysee!

XXI
The White Man's Foot

In his lodge beside a river,
Close beside a frozen river,
Sat an old man, sad and lonely.
White his hair was as a snow-drift;
Dull and low his fire was burning,
And the old man shook and trembled,
Folded in his Waubewyon,

In his tattered white-skin-wrapper,
Hearing nothing but the tempest
As it roared along the forest,
Seeing nothing but the snow-storm,
As it whirled and hissed and drifted.

All the coals were white with
  ashes,
And the fire was slowly dying,
As a young man, walking lightly,
At the open doorway entered.
Red with blood of youth his cheeks
  were,
Soft his eyes, as stars in Spring-time,
Bound his forehead was with grasses;
Bound and plumed with scented
  grasses,
On his lips a smile of beauty,
Filling all the lodge with sunshine,
In his hand a bunch of blossoms
Filling all the lodge with sweetness.

"Ah, my son!" exclaimed the old
  man,
"Happy are my eyes to see you.
Sit here on the mat beside me,
Sit here by the dying embers,
Let us pass the night together,
Tell me of your strange adventures,
Of the lands where you have travelled;
I will tell you of my prowess,
Of my many deeds of wonder."

From his pouch he drew his
  peace-pipe,
Very old and strangely fashioned;
Made of red stone was the pipe-head,
And the stem a reed with feathers;
Filled the pipe with bark of willow,
Placed a burning coal upon it,
Gave it to his guest, the stranger,

And began to speak in this wise:
"When I blow my breath about me,
When I breathe upon the landscape,
Motionless are all the rivers,
Hard as stone becomes the water!"

And the young man answered,
    smiling:
"When I blow my breath about me,
When I breathe upon the landscape,
Flowers spring up o'er all the meadows,
Singing, onward rush the rivers!"

"When I shake my hoary
    tresses,"
Said the old man darkly frowning,
"All the land with snow is covered;
All the leaves from all the branches
Fall and fade and die and wither,
For I breathe, and lo! they are not.
From the waters and the marshes
Rise the wild goose and the heron,
Fly away to distant regions,
For I speak, and lo! they are not.
And where'er my footsteps wander,
All the wild beasts of the forest
Hide themselves in holes and caverns,
And the earth becomes as flintstone!"

"When I shake my flowing
    ringlets,"
Said the young man, softly laughing,
"Showers of rain fall warm and
    welcome,
Plants lift up their heads rejoicing,
Back into their lakes and marshes
Come the wild goose and the heron,
Homeward shoots the arrowy swallow,
Sing the bluebird and the robin,
And where'er my footsteps wander,
All the meadows wave with blossoms,

All the woodlands ring with music,
All the trees are dark with foliage!"

While they spake, the night
    departed:
From the distant realms of Wabun,
From his shining lodge of silver,
Like a warrior robed and painted,
Came the sun, and said, "Behold me
Gheezis, the great sun, behold me!"

Then the old man's tongue was
    speechless
And the air grew warm and pleasant,
And upon the wigwam sweetly
Sang the bluebird and the robin,
And the stream began to murmur,
And a scent of growing grasses
Through the lodge was gently wafted.
And Segwun, the youthful stranger,
More distinctly in the daylight
Saw the icy face before him;
It was Peboan, the Winter!

From his eyes the tears were
    flowing,
As from melting lakes the streamlets,
And his body shrunk and dwindled
As the shouting sun ascended,
Till into the air it faded,
Till into the ground it vanished,
And the young man saw before him,
On the hearth-stone of the wigwam,
Where the fire had smoked and
    smouldered,
Saw the earliest flower of Spring-time,
Saw the Beauty of the Spring-time,
Saw the Miskodeed in blossom.

Thus it was that in the North-
    land

After that unheard-of coldness,
That intolerable Winter,
Came the Spring with all its splendor,
All its birds and all its blossoms,
All its flowers and leaves and grasses.

Sailing on the wind to
    northward,
Flying in great flocks, like arrows,
Like huge arrows shot through heaven,
Passed the swan, the Mahnahbezee,
Speaking almost as a man speaks;
And in long lines waving, bending
Like a bow-string snapped asunder,
Came the white goose, Waw-be-wawa;
And in pairs, or singly flying,
Mahng the loon, with clangorous
    pinions,
The blue heron, the Shuh-shuh-gah,
And the grouse, the Mushkodasa.

In the thickets and the meadows
Piped the bluebird, the Owaissa,
On the summit of the lodges
Sang the robin, the Opechee,
In the covert of the pine-trees
Cooed the pigeon, the Omemee;
And the sorrowing Hiawatha,
Speechless in his infinite sorrow,
Heard their voices calling to him,
Went forth from his gloomy doorway,
Stood and gazed into the heaven,
Gazed upon the earth and waters.

From his wanderings far to
    eastward,
From the regions of the morning,
From the shining land of Wabun,
Homeward now returned Iagoo,
The great traveller, the great boaster,
Full of new and strange adventures,

Marvels many and many wonders.

And the people of the village
Listened to him as he told them
Of his marvellous adventures,
Laughing answered him in this wise:
"Ugh! it is indeed Iagoo!
No one else beholds such wonders!"

He had seen, he said, a water
Bigger than the Big-Sea-Water,
Broader than the Gitche Gumee,
Bitter so that none could drink it!
At each other looked the warriors,
Looked the women at each other,
Smiled, and said, "It cannot be so!
Kaw!" they said, "it cannot be so!"

O'er it, said he, o'er this water
Came a great canoe with pinions,
A canoe with wings came flying,
Bigger than a grove of pine-trees,
Taller than the tallest tree-tops!
And the old men and the women
Looked and tittered at each other;
"Kaw!" they said, "we don't believe it!"

From its mouth, he said, to greet
    him,
Came Waywassimo, the lightning,
Came the thunder, Annemeekee!
And the warriors and the women
Laughed aloud at poor Iagoo;
"Kaw!" they said, "what tales you tell us!"

In it, said he, came a people,
In the great canoe with pinions
Came, he said, a hundred warriors;
Painted white were all their faces
And with hair their chins were covered!
And the warriors and the women

Laughed and shouted in derision,
Like the ravens on the tree-tops,
Like the crows upon the hemlocks.
"Kaw!" they said, "what lies you tell us!
Do not think that we believe them!"

Only Hiawatha laughed not,
But he gravely spake and answered
To their jeering and their jesting:
"True is all Iagoo tells us;
I have seen it in a vision,
Seen the great canoe with pinions,
Seen the people with white faces,
Seen the coming of this bearded
People of the wooden vessel
From the regions of the morning,
From the shining land of Wabun.

"Gitche Manito, the Mighty,
The Great Spirit, the Creator,
Sends them hither on his errand,
Sends them to us with his message.
Wheresoe'er they move, before them
Swarms the stinging fly, the Ahmo,
Swarms the bee, the honey-maker;
Wheresoe'er they tread, beneath them
Springs a flower unknown among us,
Springs the White-man's Foot in blossom.

"Let us welcome, then, the strangers,
Hail them as our friends and brothers,
And the heart's right hand of friendship
Give them when they come to see us.
Gitche Manito, the Mighty,
Said this to me in my vision.

"I beheld, too, in that vision
All the secrets of the future,
Of the distant days that shall be.
I beheld the westward marches

Of the unknown, crowded nations.
All the land was full of people,
Restless, struggling, toiling, striving,
Speaking many tongues, yet feeling
But one heart-beat in their bosoms.
In the woodlands rang their axes,
Smoked their towns in all the valleys,
Over all the lakes and rivers
Rushed their great canoes of thunder.

"Then a darker, drearier vision
Passed before me, vague and cloud-like;
I beheld our nation scattered,
All forgetful of my counsels,
Weakened, warring with each other:
Saw the remnants of our people
Sweeping westward, wild and woful,
Like the cloud-rack of a tempest,
Like the withered leaves of Autumn!"

3–13
Edgar Allan Poe (1809–1849)

EDGAR ALLAN POE (1809–1849) would still be remembered had he only written his poetry, his detective stories, or even his literary criticism and occasionally scorching book reviews. Poe's sometimes morbid themes in both poetry and fiction are often attributed to the loss of his parents at an early age, the poor relationship with his adoptive parents, the Allans, and, later, the illness and death of his young wife, Virginia Clemm, from tuberculosis. Poe's work often features a longing, a sense that this world is not one's true spiritual home, and frequently a feeling of dread. Such traits are visible in "To Helen" (1845), "The Raven" (1845), and "The Masque of the Red Death" (1842). Poe's astounding mastery of the English language and his wealth of classical allusions have made this writer popular worldwide: for example, Helen refers to the Greek Helen, about whom Homer wrote in the *Iliad*; "The Raven" alludes to Pallas Athena, Pluto of the underworld, and nepenthe, the drug of forgetting.

≋ ≋ ≋

"To Helen" (1845)

Helen, thy beauty is to me
Like those Nicæan barks of yore,
That gently, o'er a perfumed sea,
The weary, wayworn wanderer bore
To his own native shore.

On desperate seas long wont to roam,
Thy hyacinth hair, thy classic face,
Thy Naiad airs, have brought me home
To the glory that was Greece
And the grandeur that was Rome.

Lo! in yon brilliant window-niche
How statue-like I see thee stand,
The agate lamp within thy hand!
Ah, Psyche! from the regions which
Are Holy Land!

"The Raven" (1845)

Once upon a midnight dreary, while I pondered, weak and weary,
Over many a quaint and curious volume of forgotten lore,—
While I nodded, nearly napping, suddenly there came a tapping,
As of some one gently rapping, rapping at my chamber door.
"'Tis some visitor," I muttered, "tapping at my chamber door:
                    Only this and nothing more."

Ah, distinctly I remember it was in the bleak December,
And each separate dying ember wrought its ghost upon the floor.
Eagerly I wished the morrow;—vainly I had sought to borrow
From my books surcease of sorrow—sorrow for the lost Lenore,
For the rare and radiant maiden whom the angels name Lenore:
                    Nameless here for evermore.

And the silken sad uncertain rustling of each purple curtain
Thrilled me—filled me with fantastic terrors never felt before;
So that now, to still the beating of my heart, I stood repeating
"'Tis some visitor entreating entrance at my chamber door,
Some late visitor entreating entrance at my chamber door:
                    This it is and nothing more."

Presently my soul grew stronger; hesitating then no longer,
"Sir," said I, "or Madam, truly your forgiveness I implore;
But the fact is I was napping, and so gently you came rapping,
And so faintly you came tapping, tapping at my chamber door,
That I scarce was sure I heard you"—here I opened wide the door:—
                    Darkness there and nothing more.

Deep into that darkness peering, long I stood there wondering, fearing,
Doubting, dreaming dreams no mortal ever dared to dream before;
But the silence was unbroken, and the stillness gave no token,
And the only word there spoken was the whispered word, "Lenore?"
This I whispered, and an echo murmured back the word, "Lenore":
                    Merely this and nothing more.

Back into the chamber turning, all my soul within me burning,
Soon again I heard a tapping somewhat louder than before.
"Surely," said I, "surely that is something at my window lattice;
Let me see, then, what thereat is, and this mystery explore;
Let my heart be still a moment and this mystery explore:
                    'Tis the wind and nothing more."

Open here I flung the shutter, when, with many a flirt and flutter,
In there stepped a stately Raven of the saintly days of yore.
Not the least obeisance made he; not a minute stopped or stayed he;
But, with mien of lord or lady, perched above my chamber door,
Perched upon a bust of Pallas just above my chamber door:
                              Perched, and sat, and nothing more.

Then this ebony bird beguiling my sad fancy into smiling
By the grave and stern decorum of the countenance it wore,—
"Though thy crest be shorn and shaven, thou," I said, "art sure no
    craven,
Ghastly grim and ancient Raven wandering from the Nightly shore:
Tell me what thy lordly name is on the Night's Plutonian shore!"
                        Quoth the Raven, "Nevermore."

Much I marvelled this ungainly fowl to hear discourse so plainly,
Though its answer little meaning—little relevancy bore;
For we cannot help agreeing that no living human being
Ever yet was blessed with seeing bird above his chamber door,
Bird or beast upon the sculptured bust above his chamber door,
                      With such name as "Nevermore."

But the Raven, sitting lonely on the placid bust, spoke only
That one word, as if his soul in that one word he did outpour,
Nothing further then he uttered, not a feather then he fluttered,
Till I scarcely more than muttered,—"Other friends have flown before;
On the morrow *he* will leave me, as my Hopes have flown before."
                      Then the bird said, "Nevermore."

Startled at the stillness broken by reply so aptly spoken,
"Doubtless," said I, "what it utters is its only stock and store,
Caught from some unhappy master whom unmerciful Disaster
Followed fast and followed faster till his songs one burden bore:
Till the dirges of his Hope that melancholy burden bore
                  Of 'Never—nevermore.'"

But the Raven still beguiling all my fancy into smiling,
Straight I wheeled a cushioned seat in front of bird and bust and door;
Then, upon the velvet sinking, I betook myself to linking
Fancy unto fancy, thinking what this ominous bird of yore,
What this grim, ungainly, ghastly, gaunt, and ominous bird of yore
                  Meant in croaking "Nevermore."

This I sat engaged in guessing, but no syllable expressing
To the fowl whose fiery eyes now burned into my bosom's core;
This and more I sat divining, with my head at ease reclining
On the cushion's velvet lining that the lamp-light gloated o'er,
But whose velvet violet lining with the lamplight gloating o'er
She shall press, ah, nevermore!

Then, methought, the air grew denser, perfumed from an unseen
    censer
Swung by seraphim whose foot-falls tinkled on the tufted floor.
"Wretch," I cried, "thy God hath lent thee—by these angels he hath sent
    thee
Respite—respite and nepenthe from thy memories of Lenore!
Quaff, oh, quaff this kind nepenthe, and forget this lost Lenore!"
Quoth the Raven, "Nevermore."

"Prophet!" said I, "thing of evil! prophet still, if bird or devil!
Whether Tempter sent, or whether tempest tossed thee here ashore,
Desolate yet all undaunted, on this desert land enchanted—
On this home by Horror haunted—tell me truly, I implore:
Is there—*is* there balm in Gilead?—tell me—tell me, I implore!"
Quoth the Raven, "Nevermore."

"Prophet!" said I, "thing of evil—prophet still, if bird or devil!
By that Heaven that bends above us, by that God we both adore,
Tell this soul with sorrow laden if, within the distant Aidenn,
It shall clasp a sainted maiden whom the angels name Lenore:
Clasp a rare and radiant maiden whom the angels name Lenore!"
Quoth the Raven, "Nevermore."

"Be that word our sign of parting, bird or fiend!" I shrieked, upstarting:
"Get thee back into the tempest and the Night's Plutonian shore!
Leave no black plume as a token of that lie thy soul hath spoken!
Leave my loneliness unbroken! quit the bust above my door!
Take thy beak from out my heart, and take thy form from off my door!"
Quoth the Raven, "Nevermore."

And the Raven, never flitting, still is sitting, still is sitting
On the pallid bust of Pallas just above my chamber door;
And his eyes have all the seeming of a demon's that is dreaming,
And the lamp-light o'er him streaming throws his shadow on the floor:
And my soul from out that shadow that lies floating on the floor
Shall be lifted—nevermore!

"The Masque of the Red Death" (1842)

The "Red Death" had long devastated the country. No pestilence had ever been so fatal, or so hideous. Blood was its avatar and its seal—the redness and the horror of blood. There were sharp pains, and sudden dizziness, and then profuse bleeding at the pores, with dissolution. The scarlet stains upon the body, and especially upon the face, of the victim were the pest ban which shut him out from the aid and from the sympathy of his fellow-men. And the whole seizure, progress, and termination of the disease were the incidents of half an hour.

But the Prince Prospero was happy and dauntless and sagacious. When his dominions were half depopulated, he summoned to his presence a thousand hale and light-hearted friends from among the knights and dames of his court, and with these retired to the deep seclusion of one of his castellated abbeys. This was an extensive and magnificent structure, the creation of the Prince's own eccentric yet august taste. A strong and lofty wall girdled it in. This wall had gates of iron. The courtiers, having entered, brought furnaces and massy hammers, and welded the bolts. They resolved to leave means neither of ingress or egress to the sudden impulses of despair or of frenzy from within. The abbey was amply provisioned. With such precautions the courtiers might bid defiance to contagion. The external world could take care of itself. In the meantime it was folly to grieve, or to think. The Prince had provided all the appliances of pleasure. There were buffoons, there were improvisatori, there were ballet-dancers, there were musicians, there was Beauty, there was wine. All these and security were within. Without was the "Red Death."

It was toward the close of the fifth or sixth month of his seclusion, and while the pestilence raged most furiously abroad, that the Prince Prospero entertained his thousand friends at a masked ball of the most unusual magnificence.

It was a voluptuous scene, that masquerade. But first let me tell of the rooms in which it was held. There were seven—an imperial suite. In many palaces, however, such suites form a long and straight vista, while the folding-doors slide back nearly to the walls on either hand, so that the view of the whole extent is scarcely impeded. Here the case was very different, as might have been expected from the Prince's love of the bizarre. The apartments were so irregularly disposed that the vision embraced but little more than one at a time. There was a sharp turn at every twenty or thirty yards, and at each turn a novel effect. To the right and left, in the middle of each wall, a tall and narrow Gothic window looked out upon a closed corridor which pursued the windings of the suite. These windows were of stained glass, whose color varied in accordance with the prevailing hue of the decorations of the chamber into which it opened. That at the eastern extremity was hung, for example, in blue—and vividly blue were its windows. The second chamber was purple in its ornaments and tapestries, and here the panes were purple. The third was green throughout, and so were the casements. The fourth was furnished and lighted with orange, the fifth with white, the sixth with violet. The seventh apartment was closely shrouded in black velvet tapestries that hung all over the ceiling and down the walls, falling in heavy folds upon a carpet of the same material and hue. But, in this chamber only, the color of the windows failed to correspond with the decorations. The panes here were scarlet—a deep blood-color. Now in no one of the seven apartments was there any lamp or candelabrum, amid the profusion of golden ornaments that lay scattered to and fro or depended from the roof. There was no light of any kind emanating from lamp or candle within the suite of chambers. But in the corridors that followed the suite there stood, opposite to each window, a heavy tripod, bearing a brazier of fire, that projected its rays through the tinted glass and so glaringly illumined the room. And thus were produced a multitude of gaudy and fantastic appearances. But in the western or black chamber the effect of the firelight that streamed upon the dark hangings through the blood-tinted panes was ghastly in the extreme, and produced so wild a look upon the countenances of those who entered that there were few of the company bold enough to set foot within its precincts at all.

It was in this apartment, also, that there stood against the western wall a gigantic clock of ebony. Its pendulum swung to and fro with a dull, heavy, monotonous clang; and when the minute-hand made the circuit of the face, and the hour was to be stricken, there came from the brazen lungs of the clock a sound which was clear and loud and deep and exceedingly musical, but of so peculiar a note and emphasis that, at each lapse of an hour, the musicians of the orchestra were constrained to pause, momentarily, in their performance, to hearken to the sound; and thus the waltzers perforce ceased their evolutions; and there was a brief disconcert of the whole gay company; and, while the chimes of the clock yet rang, it was observed that the giddiest grew pale, and the more aged and sedate passed their hands over their brows as if in confused revery or meditation. But when the echoes had fully ceased, a light laughter at once pervaded the assembly; the musicians looked at each other and smiled as if at their own nervousness and folly, and made whispering vows, each to the other, that the next chiming of the clock should produce in them no similar emotion; and then, after the lapse of sixty minutes (which embrace three thousand and six hundred seconds of the Time that flies) there came yet another chiming of the clock, and then were the same disconcert and tremulousness and meditation as before.

But, in spite of these things, it was a gay and magnificent revel. The tastes of the Prince were peculiar. He had a fine eye for colors and effects. He disregarded the *decora* of mere fashion. His plans were bold and fiery, and his conceptions glowed with barbaric lustre. There were some who would have thought him mad. His followers felt that he was not. It was necessary to hear and see and touch him to be *sure* that he was not.

He had directed, in great part, the movable embellishments of the seven chambers, upon occasion of this great *fête*; and it was his own guiding taste which had given character to the masqueraders. Be sure they were grotesque. There were much glare and glitter and piquancy and phantasm—much of what has been since seen in *Hernani*. There were arabesque figures with unsuited limbs and appointments. There were delirious fancies such as the madman fashions. There was much of the beautiful, much of the wanton, much of the bizarre, something of the terrible, and not a little of that which might have excited disgust. To and fro in the seven chambers there stalked, in fact, a multitude of dreams. And these—the dreams—writhed in and about, taking hue from the rooms, and causing the wild music of the orchestra to seem as the echo of their steps. And, anon, there strikes the ebony clock which stands in the hall of the velvet. And then, for a moment, all is still, and all is silent save the voice of the clock. The dreams are stiff-frozen as they stand. But the echoes of the chime die away—they have endured but an instant—and a light, half-subdued laughter floats after them as they depart. And now again the music swells, and the dreams live, and writhe to and fro more merrily than ever, taking hue from the many tinted windows through which stream the rays from the tripods. But to the chamber which lies most westwardly of the seven, there are now none of the maskers who venture; for the night is waning away, and there flows a ruddier light through the blood-colored panes; and the blackness of the sable drapery appalls; and to him whose foot falls upon the sable carpet, there comes from the near clock of ebony a muffled peal more solemnly emphatic than any which reaches *their* ears who indulge in the more remote gayeties of the other apartments.

But these other apartments were densely crowded, and in them beat feverishly the heart of life. And the revel went whirlingly on, until at length there commenced the sounding of midnight upon the clock. And then the music ceased, as I have told; and the evolutions of the waltzers were quieted; and there was an uneasy cessation of all things as before. But now there were twelve strokes to be sounded by the bell of the clock; and thus it happened, perhaps, that more of thought crept, with more of time, into the meditations of the thoughtful among those who revelled. And thus, too, it happened, perhaps, that before the last echoes of the last chime had utterly sunk into silence, there were many individuals in the crowd who had found leisure to become aware of the presence of a masked figure which had arrested the attention of no single individual before. And the rumor of this new presence having spread itself whisperingly around, there arose at length from the whole company a buzz, or murmur, expressive of disapprobation and surprise—then, finally, of terror, of horror, and of disgust.

In an assembly of phantasms such as I have painted, it may well be supposed that no ordinary appearance could have excited such sensation. In truth the masquerade license of the night was nearly unlimited; but the figure in question had out-Heroded Herod, and gone beyond the bounds of even the Prince's indefinite decorum. There are chords in the hearts of the most reckless which cannot be touched without emotion. Even with the utterly lost, to whom life and death are equally jests, there are matters of which no jest can be made. The whole company, indeed, seemed now deeply to feel that in the costume and bearing of the stranger neither wit nor propriety existed. The figure was tall and gaunt, and shrouded from head to foot in the habiliments of the grave. The mask which concealed the visage was made so nearly to resemble the countenance of a stiffened corpse that the closest scrutiny must have had difficulty in detecting the cheat. And yet all this might have been endured, if not approved, by the mad revellers around. But the mummer had gone so far as to assume the type of the Red Death. His vesture was dabbled in *blood*— and his broad brow, with all the features of the face, was besprinkled with the scarlet horror.

When the eyes of Prince Prospero fell upon this spectral image (which with a slow and solemn movement, as if more fully to sustain its *rôle*, stalked to and fro among the waltzers) he was seen to be convulsed, in the first moment, with a strong shudder either of terror or distaste; but, in the next, his brow reddened with rage.

"Who dares?" he demanded hoarsely of the courtiers who stood near him—"who dares insult us with this blasphemous mockery? Seize him and unmask him—that we may know whom we have to hang at sunrise, from the battlements!"

It was in the eastern or blue chamber in which stood the Prince Prospero as he uttered these words. They rang throughout the seven rooms loudly and clearly—for the Prince was a bold and robust man, and the music had become hushed at the waving of his hand.

It was in the blue room where stood the Prince, with a group of pale courtiers by his side. At first, as he spoke, there was a slight rushing movement of this group in the direction of the intruder, who at the moment was also near at hand, and now, with deliberate and stately step, made closer approach to the speaker. But from a certain nameless awe with which the mad assumptions of the mummer had inspired the whole party, there were found none who put forth hand to seize him; so that, unimpeded, he passed within a yard of the Prince's person; and while the vast assembly, as if with one impulse, shrank from the centres of the rooms to the walls, he made his way uninterruptedly, but with the same solemn and measured step which had distinguished him from the first, through the blue chamber to the purple—through the purple to the green—through the green to the orange—through this again to the white—and even thence to the violet, ere a decided movement had been made to arrest him. It was then, however, that the Prince Prospero, maddening with rage and the shame of his own momentary cowardice, rushed hurriedly through the six chambers, while none followed him on account of a deadly terror that had seized upon all. He bore aloft a drawn dagger, and had approached, in rapid impetuosity, to within three or four feet of the retreating figure, when the latter, having attained the extremity of the velvet apartment, turned suddenly and confronted his pursuer. There was a sharp cry—and the dagger dropped gleaming upon the sable carpet, upon which, instantly afterwards, fell prostrate in death the Prince Prospero. Then, summoning the wild courage of despair, a throng of the revellers at once threw themselves into the black apartment, and, seizing the mummer, whose tall figure stood erect and motionless within the shadow of the ebony clock, gasped in unutterable horror at finding the grave cerements and corpse-like mask, which they handled with so violent a rudeness, untenanted by any tangible form.

And now was acknowledged the presence of the Red Death. He had come like a thief in the night. And one by one dropped the revellers in the blood-bedewed halls of their revel, and died each in the despairing posture of his fall. And the life of the ebony clock went out with that of the last of the gay. And the flames of the tripods expired. And Darkness and Decay and the Red Death held illimitable dominion over all.

3–14
Oliver Wendell Holmes, Sr. (1809–1894)

OLIVER WENDELL HOLMES (1809–1894) was a medical doctor and professor of anatomy who achieved success for his chatty essays, gathered first in *The Autocrat of the Breakfast Table* (1860). He also wrote medical works and biographies but is best known today for his poetry. Among his most familiar poems are "The Deacon's Masterpiece: or the Wonderful One-Hoss Shay" (1858). Holmes is also remembered as the father of the Supreme Court justice of the same name, and is consequently frequently referred to as "Oliver Wendell Holmes, Sr."

≈ ≈ ≈

"The Chambered Nautilus" (1858)

This is the ship of pearl, which, poets feign,
   Sails the unshadowed main,—
   The venturous bark that flings
On the sweet summer wind its purpled wings
In gulfs enchanted, where the Siren sings,
   And coral reefs lie bare,
Where the cold sea-maids rise to sun their streaming hair.

Its webs of living gauze no more unfurl;
   Wrecked is the ship of pearl!
   And every chambered cell,
Where its dim dreaming life was wont to dwell,
As the frail tenant shaped his growing shell,
   Before thee lies revealed,—
Its irised ceiling rent, its sunless crypt unsealed!

Year after year beheld the silent toil
   That spread his lustrous coil;
   Still, as the spiral grew,
He left the past year's dwelling for the new,
Stole with soft step its shining archway through,
   Built up its idle door,
Stretched in his last-found home, and knew the old no more.

Thanks for the heavenly message brought by thee,
   Child of the wandering sea,
   Cast from her lap, forlorn!
From thy dead lips a clearer note is born
Than ever Triton blew from wreathèd horn!
   While on mine ear it rings,
Through the deep caves of thought I hear a voice that sings:—

Build thee more stately mansions, O my soul,
   As the swift seasons roll!

Leave thy low-vaulted past!
Let each new temple, nobler than the last,
Shut thee from heaven with a dome more vast,
    Till thou at length art free,
Leaving thine outgrown shell by life's unresting sea!

3–15
Harriet Beecher Stowe (1811–1896)

"The little woman who wrote the book that started this great war," as President Abraham Lincoln is alleged to have said, HARRIET BEECHER STOWE (1811–1896) was a staunch abolitionist whose *Uncle Tom's Cabin* (1852) influenced many to consider views they had before resisted. Stowe was born into a reform-minded, deeply religious family. Her father Lyman was an evangelical preacher who moved his large family from Litchfield, Connecticut, to Cincinnati when she was in her early twenties. Just across the Ohio River from Kentucky, Cincinnati offered refuge for fugitive slaves who crossed over and climbed the banks to freedom. In the 1830s and 1840s, while in Ohio, Stowe met her future husband, Calvin Stowe, a professor at the seminary where her father taught, and she was introduced to fugitive slaves for the first time. She and her husband supported the Underground Railroad; slavery became the burning issue of her life and led to her seminal novel. The following story, a response to the Fugitive Slave Law of 1850 that required the return of fugitive slaves to their owners, frames the issue of slavery alongside the fight for liberty from colonial rule.

≈ ≈ ≈

"The Two Altars; or, Two Pictures in One" (1851)

1. The Altar of Liberty, Or 1776

The well-sweep of the old house on the hill was relieved dark and clear, against the reddening sky, as the early winter sun was going down in the west. It was a brisk, clear, metallic evening; the long drifts of snow blushed crimson red on their tops, and lay in shades of purple and lilac in the hollows; and the old wintry wind brushed shrewdly along the plain, tingling people's noses, blowing open their cloaks, puffing in the back of their necks, and showing other unmistakable indications that he was getting up steam for a real roistering night.

"Hurrah! How it blows!" said little Dick Ward, from the top of the mossy wood-pile.

Now Dick had been sent to said wood-pile, in company with his little sister Grace, to pick up chips, which, everybody knows, was in the olden time considered a wholesome and gracious employment, and the peculiar duty of the rising generation. But said Dick, being a boy, had mounted the wood-pile, and erected there a flagstaff, on which he was busily tying a little red pocket-handkerchief, occasionally exhorting Grace "to be sure and pick up fast."

"Oh, yes, I will," said Grace; "but you see the chips have got ice on 'em, and make my hands so cold!"

"Oh, don't stop to suck your thumbs! Who cares for ice? Pick away, I say, while I set up the flag of liberty."

So Grace picked away as fast as she could, nothing doubting but that her cold thumbs were in some mysterious sense an offering on the shrine of liberty; while soon the red handkerchief, duly secured, fluttered and snapped in the brisk evening wind.

"Now you must hurrah, Gracie, and throw up your bonnet," said Dick, as he descended from the pile.

"But won't it lodge down in some place in the woodpile?" suggested Grace thoughtfully.

"Oh, never fear; give it to me, and just holler now, Gracie, 'Hurrah for liberty!' and we'll throw up your bonnet and my cap; and we'll play, you know, that we are a whole army and I'm General Washington."

So Grace gave up her little red hood, and Dick swung his cap, and up they both went into the air; and the children shouted, and the flag snapped and fluttered, and altogether they had a merry time of it. But then the wind—good-for-nothing, roguish fellow!—made an ungenerous plunge at poor Grace's little hood, and snipped it up in a twinkling, and whisked it off, off, off,— fluttering and bobbing up and down, quite across a wide, waste, snowy field,— and finally lodged it on the top of a tall, strutting rail, that was leaning, very independently, quite another way from all the other rails of the fence.

"Now see, do see!" said Grace; "there goes my bonnet! What will Aunt Hitty say?" and Grace began to cry.

"Don't you cry, Gracie; you offered it up to liberty, you know: it's glorious to give up everything for liberty."

"Oh, but Aunt Hitty won't think so."

"Well, don't cry, Gracie, you foolish girl! Do you think I can't get it? Now, only play that that great rail is a fort, and your bonnet is a prisoner in it, and see how quick I'll take the fort and get it!" and Dick shouldered a stick, and started off.

"What upon *airth* keeps those children so long? I should think they were *making* chips!" said Aunt Mehetabel; "the fire's just a-going out under the tea-kettle."

By this time Grace had lugged her heavy basket to the door, and was stamping the snow off her little feet, which were so numb that she needed to stamp, to be quite sure they were yet there. Aunt Mehetabel's shrewd face was the first that greeted her as the door opened.

"Gracie—What upon *airth!*—wipe your nose, child; your hands are frozen. Where alive is Dick?—and what's kept you out all this time?—and where's your bonnet?"

Poor Grace, stunned by this cataract of questions, neither wiped her nose nor gave any answer, but sidled up into the warm corner where grandmamma was knitting, and began quietly rubbing and blowing her fingers, while the tears silently rolled down her cheeks, as the fire made the former ache intolerably.

"Poor little dear!" said grandmamma, taking her hands in hers; "Hitty sha'n't scold you. Grandma knows you've been a good girl,—the wind blew poor Gracie's bonnet away"; and grandmamma wiped both eyes and nose, and gave her, moreover, a stalk of dried fennel out of her pocket, whereat Grace took heart once more.

"Mother always makes fools of Roxy's children," said Mehetabel, puffing zealously under the tea-kettle. "There's a little maple sugar in that saucer up there, mother, if you will keep giving it to her," she said, still vigorously puffing. "And now, Gracie," she said, when, after a while, the fire seemed in tolerable order, "will you answer my question? Where is Dick?"

"Gone over in the lot to get my bonnet."

"How came your bonnet off?" said Aunt Mehetabel. "I tied it on firm enough."

"Dick wanted me to take it off for him, to throw up for liberty," said Grace.

"Throw up for fiddlestick! Just one of Dick's cut-ups; and you was silly enough to mind him!"

"Why, he put up a flagstaff on the wood-pile, and a flag to liberty, you know, that papa's fighting for," said Grace more confidently, as she saw her quiet, blue-eyed mother, who had silently walked into the room during the conversation.

Grace's mother smiled, and said encouragingly, "And what then?"

"Why, he wanted me to throw up my bonnet and he his cap, and shout for liberty; and then the wind took it and carried it off, and he said I ought not to be sorry if I did lose it,—it was an offering to liberty."

"And so I did," said Dick, who was standing as straight as a poplar behind the group; "and I heard it in one of father's letters to mother that we ought to offer up everything on the altar of liberty and so I made an altar of the wood-pile."

"Good boy!" said his mother; "always remember everything your father writes. He has offered up everything on the altar of liberty, true enough; and I hope you, son, will live to do the same."

"Only, if I have the hoods and caps to make," said Aunt Hitty, "I hope he won't offer them up every week,—that's all!"

"Oh, well, Aunt Hitty, I've got the hood; let me alone for that. It blew clear over into the Daddy Ward pasture lot, and there stuck on the top of the great rail; and I played that the rail was a fort, and besieged it, and took it."

"Oh, yes! you're always up to taking forts, and anything else that nobody wants done. I'll warrant, now, you left Gracie to pick up every blessed one of them chips."

"Picking up chips is girls' work," said Dick; "and taking forts and defending the country is men's work."

"And pray, Mister Pomp, how long have you been a man?" said Aunt Hitty.

"If I ain't a man, I soon shall be; my head is 'most up to my mother's shoulder, and I can fire off a gun, too. I tried, the other day, when I was up to the store. Mother, I wish you'd let me clean and load the old gun, so that, if the British should come"—

"Well, if you are so big and grand, just lift me out that table, sir," said Aunt Hitty; "for it's past supper-time."

Dick sprang, and had the table out in a trice, with an abundant clatter, and put up the leaves with quite an air. His mother, with the silent and gliding motion characteristic of her, quietly took out the table-cloth and spread it, and began to set the cups and saucers in order, and to put on the plates and knives, while Aunt Hitty bustled about the tea.

"I'll be glad when the war's over, for one reason," said she. "I'm pretty much tired of drinking sage tea, for one, I know."

"Well, Aunt Hitty, how you scolded that peddler, last week, that brought along that real tea!"

"To be sure I did. S'pose I'd be taking any of his old tea, bought of the British?—fling every teacup in his face first."

"Well, mother," said Dick, "I never exactly understood what it was about the tea, and why the Boston folks threw it all overboard."

"Because there was an unlawful tax laid upon it, that the government had no right to lay. It wasn't much in itself; but it was a part of a whole system of oppressive meanness, designed to take away our rights, and make us slaves of a foreign power."

"Slaves!" said Dick, straightening himself proudly. "Father a slave!"

"But they would not be slaves! They saw clearly where it would all end, and they would not begin to submit to it in ever so little," said the mother.

"I wouldn't, if I was they," said Dick.

"Besides," said his mother, drawing him towards her, "it wasn't for themselves alone they did it. This is a great country, and it will be greater and greater; and it's very important that it should have free and equal laws, because it will by and by be so great. This country, if it is a free one, will be a light of the world,—a city set on a hill, that cannot be hid; and all the oppressed and distressed from other countries shall come here to enjoy equal rights and freedom. This, dear boy, is why your father and uncles have gone to fight, and why they do stay and fight, though God knows what they suffer and"—And the large blue eyes of the mother were full of tears; yet a strong, bright beam of pride and exultation shone through those tears.

"Well, well, Roxy, you can always talk, everybody knows," said Aunt Hitty, who had been not the least attentive listener of this little patriotic harangue; "but, you see, the tea is getting cold, and yonder I see the sleigh is at the door, and John's come; so let's set up our chairs for supper."

The chairs were soon set up, when John, the eldest son, a lad of about fifteen, entered with a letter. There was one general exclamation, and stretching out of hands towards it. John threw it into his mother's lap; the tea-table was forgotten, and the tea-kettle sang unnoticed by the fire, as all hands crowded about mother's chair to hear the news. It was from Captain Ward, then in the American army at Valley Forge. Mrs. Ward ran it over hastily, and then read it aloud. A few words we may extract.

"There is still," it said, "much suffering. I have given away every pair of stockings you sent me, reserving to myself only one; for I will not be one whit better off than the poorest soldier that fights for his country. Poor fellows! it makes my heart ache sometimes to go round among them, and see them with their worn clothes and torn shoes, and often bleeding feet, yet cheerful and hopeful, and every one willing to do his very best. Often the spirit of discouragement comes over them, particularly at night, when, weary, cold, and hungry, they turn into their comfortless huts, on the snowy ground.

Then sometimes there is a thought of home, and warm fires, and some speak of giving up; but next morning out come Washington's general orders,—little short note, but's wonderful the good it does; and then they all resolve to hold on, come what may. There are commissioners going all through the country to pick up supplies. If they come to you, I need not to tell you what to do. I know all that will be in your hearts."

"There, children, see what your father suffers," said the mother, "and what it costs these poor soldiers to gain our liberty."

"Ephraim Scranton told me that the commissioners had come as far as the Three Mile Tavern, and that he rather 'spected they'd be along here to-night," said John, as he was helping round the baked beans to the silent company at the tea-table.

"To-night?—do tell, now!" said Aunt Hitty. "Then it's time we were awake and stirring. Let's see what can be got."

"I'll send my new overcoat, for one," said John. "That old one isn't cut up yet, is it, Aunt Hitty?"

"No," said Aunt Hitty; "I was laying out to cut it over next Wednesday, when Desire Smith could be here to do the tailoring."

"There's the south room," said Aunt Hitty, musing; "that bed has the two old Aunt Ward blankets on it, and the great blue quilt, and two comforters. Then mother's and my room, two pair—four comforters—two quilts—the best chamber has got"—

"Oh, Aunt Hitty, send all that's in the best chamber! If any company comes, we can make it up off from our beds," said John. "I can send a blanket or two off from my bed, I know,—can't but just turn over in it, so many clothes on, now."

"Aunt Hitty, take a blanket off from our bed," said Grace and Dick at once.

"Well, well, we'll see," said Aunt Hitty, bustling up.

Up rose grandmamma, with great earnestness, now, and going into the next room, and opening a large cedar-wood chest, returned, bearing in her arms two large snow-white blankets, which she deposited flat on the table, just as Aunt Hitty was whisking off the table-cloth.

"Mortal! mother, what are you going to do?" said Aunt Hitty.

"There," she said, "I spun those, every thread of 'em, when my name was Mary Evans. Those were my wedding-blankets, made of real nice wool, and worked with roses in all the corners. I've got *them* to give!" and grandmamma stroked and smoothed the blankets, and patted them down, with great pride and tenderness. It was evident she was giving something that lay very near her heart; but she never faltered.

"La! mother, there's no need of that," said Aunt Hitty. "Use them on your own bed, and send the blankets off from that; they are just as good for the soldiers."

"No, I sha'n't!" said the old lady, waxing warm; "'tisn't a bit too good for 'em. I'll send the very best I've got, before they shall suffer. Send 'em the *best*!" and the old lady gestured oratorically.

They were interrupted by a rap at the door, and two men entered, and announced themselves as commissioned by Congress to search out supplies for the army. Now the plot thickens. Aunt Hitty flew in every direction,—through entry passage, meal-room, milk-room, down cellar, up chamber,—her cap border on end with patriotic zeal; and followed by John, Dick, and Grace, who eagerly bore to the kitchen the supplies that she turned out, while Mrs. Ward busied herself in quietly sorting and arranging, in the best possible traveling order, the various contributions that were precipitately launched on the kitchen floor.

Aunt Hitty soon appeared in the kitchen with an armful of stockings, which, kneeling on the floor, she began counting and laying out.

"There," she said, laying down a large bundle on some blankets, "that leaves just two pair apiece all round."

"La!" said John, "what's the use of saving two pair for me? I can do with one pair, as well as father."

"Sure enough," said his mother; "besides, I can knit you another pair in a day."

"And I can do with one pair," said Dick.

"Yours will be too small, young master, I guess," said one of the commissioners.

"No," said Dick; "I've got a pretty good foot of my own, and Aunt Hitty will always knit my stockings an inch too long, 'cause she says I grow so. See here,— these will do"; and the boy shook his triumphantly.

"And mine, too," said Grace, nothing doubting, having been busy all the time in pulling off her little stockings.

"Here," she said to the man who was packing the things into a wide-mouthed sack; "here's mine," and her large blue eyes looked earnestly through her tears.

Aunt Hitty flew at her. "Good land! the child's crazy. Don't think the men could wear your stockings,—take 'em away!"

Grace looked around with an air of utter desolation, and began to cry. "I wanted to give them something," said she. "I'd rather go barefoot on the snow all day than not send 'em anything."

"Give me the stockings, my child," said the old soldier tenderly. "There, I'll take 'em, and show 'em to the soldiers, and tell them what the little girl said that sent them. And it will do them as much good as if they could wear them. They've got little girls at home, too." Grace fell on her mother's bosom completely happy, and Aunt Hitty only muttered,—

"Everybody does spile that child; and no wonder, neither!"

Soon the old sleigh drove off from the brown house, tightly packed and heavily loaded. And Grace and Dick were creeping up to their little beds.

"There's been something put on the altar of Liberty to-night, hasn't there, Dick?"

"Yes, indeed," said Dick; and, looking up to his mother, he said, "But, mother, what did you give?"

"I?" said the mother musingly.

"Yes, you, mother; what have you given to the country?"

"All that I have, dears," said she, laying her hands gently on their heads,— "my husband and my children!"

2. The Altar of ——, Or 1850

The setting sun of chill December lighted up the solitary front window of a small tenement on —— Street, in Boston, which we now have occasion to visit. As we push gently aside the open door, we gain sight of a small room, clean as busy hands can make it, where a neat, cheerful young mulatto woman is busy at an ironing-table. A basket full of glossy-bosomed shirts, and faultless collars and wristbands, is beside her, into which she is placing the last few items with evident pride and satisfaction. A bright black-eyed boy, just come in from school, with his satchel of books over his shoulder, stands, cap in hand, relating to his mother how he has been at the head of his class, and showing his school tickets, which his mother, with untiring admiration, deposits in the little real china teapot, which, as being their most reliable article of gentility, is made the deposit of all the money and most especial valuables of the family.

"Now, Henry," says the mother, "look out and see if father is coming along the street"; and she begins filling the little black tea-kettle, which is soon set singing on the stove.

From the inner room now daughter Mary, a well-grown girl of thirteen, brings the baby, just roused from a nap, and very impatient to renew his acquaintance with his mamma.

"Bless his bright eyes!—mother will take him," ejaculates the busy little woman, whose hands are by this time in a very floury condition, in the incipient stages of wetting up biscuit,—"in a minute"; and she quickly frees herself from the flour and paste, and, deputing Mary to roll out her biscuit, proceeds to the consolation and succor of young master.

"Now, Henry," says the mother, "you'll have time, before supper, to take that basket of clothes up to Mr. Sheldin's; put in that nice bill that you made out last night. I shall give you a cent for every bill you write out for me. What a comfort it is, now, for one's children to be gettin' learnin' so!"

Henry shouldered the basket and passed out the door, just as a neatly dressed colored man walked up with his pail and whitewash brushes.

"Oh, you've come, father, have you? Mary, are the biscuits in? You may as well set the table now. Well, George, what's the news?"

"Nothing, only a pretty smart day's work. I've brought home five dollars, and shall have as much as I can do, these two weeks"; and the man, having washed his hands, proceeded to count out his change on the ironing-table.

"Well, it takes you to bring in the money," said the delighted wife; "nobody but you could turn off that much in a day."

"Well, they do say—those that's had me once—that they never want any other hand to take hold in their rooms. I s'pose it's a kinder practice I've got, and kinder natural!"

"Tell ye what," said the little woman, taking down the family strong box,— to wit, the china teapot aforenamed,—and pouring the contents on the table, "we're getting mighty rich now! We can afford to get Henry his new Sunday cap, and Mary her mousseline-de-laine dress—Take care, baby, you rogue!" she hastily interposed, as young master made a dive at a dollar bill, for his share in the proceeds.

"He wants something, too, I suppose," said the father; "let him get his hand in while he's young."

The baby gazed, with round, astonished eyes, while mother, with some difficulty, rescued the bill from his grasp; but, before any one could at all anticipate his purpose, he dashed in among the small change with such zeal as to send it flying all over the table.

"Hurrah! Bob's a smasher!" said the father, delighted; "he'll make it fly, he thinks"; and, taking the baby on his knee, he laughed merrily as Mary and her mother pursued the rolling coin all over the room.

"He knows now, as well as can be that he's been doing mischief," said the delighted mother, as the baby kicked and crowed uproariously; "he's such a forward child, now, to be only six months old! Oh, you've no idea, father, how mischievous he grows"; and therewith the little woman began to roll and tumble the little mischief-maker about, uttering divers frightful threats, which appeared to contribute, in no small degree, to the general hilarity.

"Come, come, Mary," said the mother at last, with a sudden burst of recollection; "you mustn't be always on your knees fooling with this child! Look in the oven at them biscuits."

"They're done exactly, mother,—just the brown!" and, with the word, the mother dumped baby on to his father's knee, where he sat contentedly munching a very ancient crust of bread, occasionally improving the flavor thereof by rubbing it on his father's coat-sleeve.

"What have you got in that blue dish there?" said George, when the whole little circle were seated around the table.

"Well, now, what do you suppose?" said the little woman, delighted; "a quart of nice oysters,—just for a treat, you know. I wouldn't tell you till this minute," said she, raising the cover.

"Well," said George, "we both work hard for our money, and we don't owe anybody a cent; and why shouldn't we have our treats, now and then, as well as rich folks?"

And gayly passed the supper hour; the tea-kettle sung, the baby crowed, and all chatted and laughed abundantly.

"I'll tell you," said George, wiping his mouth; "wife, these times are quite another thing from what it used to be down in Georgia. I remember then old mas'r used to hire me out by the year; and one time, I remember, I came and paid him in two hundred dollars,—every cent I'd taken. He just looked it over, counted it, and put it in his pocketbook, and said, 'You are a good boy, George,'—and he gave me half a dollar!"

"I want to know, now!" said his wife.

"Yes, he did, and that was every cent I ever got of it; and, I tell you, I was mighty bad off for clothes, them times."

"Well, well, the Lord be praised, they're over, and you are in a free country now!" said the wife, as she rose thoughtfully from the table, and brought her husband the great Bible. The little circle were ranged around the stove for evening prayers.

"Henry, my boy, you must read—you are a better reader than your father—thank God, that let you learn early!"

The boy, with a cheerful readiness, read, "The Lord is my Shepherd," and the mother gently stilled the noisy baby to listen to the holy words. Then all kneeled, while the father, with simple earnestness, poured out his soul to God.

They had but just risen—the words of Christian hope and trust scarce died on their lips—when, lo! the door was burst open, and two men entered; and one of them, advancing, laid his hand on the father's shoulder. "This is the fellow," said he.

"You are arrested in the name of the United States!" said the other.

"Gentlemen, what is this?" said the poor man, trembling.

"Are you not the property of Mr. B., of Georgia?" said the officer.

"Gentlemen, I've been a free, hard-working man these ten years."

"Yes; but you are arrested, on suit of Mr. B., as his slave."

Shall we describe the leave-taking,—the sorrowing wife, the dismayed children, the tears, the anguish, that simple, honest, kindly home, in a moment so desolated? Ah, ye who defend this because it is law, think for one hour what if this that happens to your poor brother should happen to you!

It was a crowded court-room, and the man stood there to be tried—for life?—no; but for the life of life—for liberty!

Lawyers hurried to and fro, buzzing, consulting, bringing authorities,—all anxious, zealous, engaged,—for what? To save a fellow man from bondage? No; anxious and zealous lest he might escape; full of zeal to deliver him over to slavery. The poor man's anxious eyes follow vainly the busy course of affairs, from which he dimly learns that he is to be sacrificed—on the altar of the Union; and that his heart-break and anguish, and the tears of his wife, and the desolation of his children are, in the eyes of these well-informed men, only the bleat of a sacrifice, bound to the horns of the glorious American altar!

Again it is a bright day, and business walks brisk in this market. Senator and statesman, the learned and patriotic, are out, this day, to give their countenance to an edifying and impressive and truly American spectacle,—the sale of a man! All the preliminaries of the scene are there: dusky-browed mothers, looking with sad eyes while speculators are turning round their children, looking at their teeth, and feeling of their arms; a poor, old, trembling woman, helpless, half blind, whose last child is to be sold, holds on to her bright boy with trembling hands. Husbands and wives, sisters and friends, all soon to be scattered like the chaff of the threshing-floor, look sadly on each other with poor nature's last tears; and among them walk briskly glib, oily politicians, and thriving men of law, letters, and religion, exceedingly sprightly and in good spirits—for why?—it isn't *they* that are going to be sold; it's only somebody else. And so they are very comfortable, and look on the whole thing as quite a matter-of-course affair, and, as it is to be conducted to-day, a decidedly valuable and judicious exhibition.

And now, after so many hearts and souls have been knocked and thumped this way and that way by the auctioneer's hammer, comes the *instructive* part of the whole; and the husband and father, whom we saw in his simple home, reading and praying with his children, and rejoicing in the joy of his poor ignorant heart that he lived in a free country, is now set up to be admonished of his mistake.

Now there is great excitement, and pressing to see, and exultation and approbation; for it is important and interesting to see a man put down that has tried to be a *free man.*

"That's he, is it? Couldn't come it, could he?" says one.

"No; and he will never come it, that's more," says another triumphantly.

"I don't generally take much interest in scenes of this nature," says a grave representative; "but I came here today for the sake of the principle!"

"Gentlemen," says the auctioneer, "we've got a specimen here that some of your Northern abolitionists would give any price for; but they sha'n't have him! no! we've looked out for that. The man that buys him must give bonds never to sell him to go North again!"

"Go it!" shout the crowd; "good! good! hurrah!" "An impressive idea!" says a Senator; "a noble maintaining of principle!" and the man is bid off, and the hammer falls with a last crash on his heart, his hopes, his manhood, and he lies a bleeding wreck on the altar of Liberty!

Such was the altar in 1776; such is the altar in 1850!

3–16

Harriet Jacobs (1813–1897)

Born into slavery in North Carolina, Harriet Jacobs (1813–1897) learned to write from an early mistress. After her escape to the North in 1842, she used that skill to tell her story first in anonymous letters in newspapers and later in *Incidents in the Life of a Slave Girl* (1861). These works revealed the sexual exploitation of slave women and provided powerful ammunition for the abolitionist cause. Jacobs was reunited with her children in the North and worked in an abolitionist reading room and bookstore in Rochester, New York, in the same building where Frederick Douglass ran his newspaper *The North Star*. Jacobs gave herself and all characters in the autobiography pseudonyms. Thus she becomes Linda Brent; her white master, Dr. Flint.

≈ ≈ ≈

From *Incidents in the Life of a Slave Girl* (1861)

Preface by the Author

Reader, be assured this narrative is no fiction. I am aware that some of my adventures may seem incredible; but they are, nevertheless, strictly true. I have not exaggerated the wrongs inflicted by Slavery; on the contrary, my descriptions fall far short of the facts. I have concealed the names of places, and given persons fictitious names. I had no motive for secrecy on my own account, but I deemed it kind and considerate towards others to pursue this course.

I wish I were more competent to the task I have undertaken. But I trust my readers will excuse deficiencies in consideration of circumstances. I was born and reared in Slavery; and I remained in a Slave State twenty-seven years. Since I have been at the North, it has been necessary for me to work diligently for my own support, and the education of my children. This has not left me much leisure to make up for the loss of early opportunities to improve myself; and it has compelled me to write these pages at irregular intervals, whenever I could snatch an hour from household duties.

When I first arrived in Philadelphia, Bishop Paine advised me to publish a sketch of my life, but I told him I was altogether incompetent to such an undertaking. Though I have improved my mind somewhat since that time, I still remain of the same opinion; but I trust my motives will excuse what might otherwise seem presumptuous. I have not written my experiences in order to attract attention to myself; on the contrary, it would have been more pleasant to me to have been silent about my own history. Neither do I care to excite sympathy for my own sufferings. But I do earnestly desire to arouse the women of the North to a realizing sense of the condition of two millions of women at the South, still in bondage, suffering what I suffered, and most of them far worse. I want to add my testimony to that of abler pens to convince the people of the Free States what Slavery really is. Only by experience can any one realize how deep, and dark, and foul is that pit of abominations. May the blessing of God rest on this imperfect effort in behalf of my persecuted people!

Linda Brent

Introduction by the Editor

The author of the following autobiography is personally known to me, and her conversation and manners inspire me with confidence. During the last seventeen years, she has lived the greater part of the time with a distinguished family in New York, and has so deported herself as to be highly esteemed by them. This fact is sufficient, without further credentials of her character. I believe those who know her will not be disposed to doubt her veracity, though some incidents in her story are more romantic than fiction.

At her request, I have revised her manuscript; but such changes as I have made have been mainly for purposes of condensation and orderly arrangement. I have not added any thing to the incidents, or changed the import of her very pertinent remarks. With trifling exceptions, both the ideas and the language are her own. I pruned excrescences a little, but otherwise I had no reason for changing her lively and dramatic way of telling her own story. The names of both persons and places are known to me; but for good reasons I suppress them.

It will naturally excite surprise that a woman reared in Slavery should be able to write so well. But circumstances will explain this. In the first place, nature endowed her with quick perceptions. Secondly, the mistress, with whom she lived till she was twelve years old, was a kind, considerate friend, who taught her to read and spell. Thirdly, she was placed in favorable circumstances after she came to the North; having frequent intercourse with intelligent persons, who felt a friendly interest in her welfare, and were disposed to give her opportunities for self-improvement.

I am well aware that many will accuse me of indecorum for presenting these pages to the public; for the experiences of this intelligent and much-injured woman belong to a class which some call delicate subjects, and others indelicate. This peculiar phase of Slavery has generally been kept veiled; but the public ought to be made acquainted with its monstrous features, and I willingly take the responsibility of presenting them with the veil withdrawn. I do this for the sake of my sisters in bondage, who are suffering wrongs so foul, that our ears are too delicate to listen to them. I do it with the hope of arousing conscientious and reflecting women at the North to a sense of their duty in the exertion of moral influence on the question of Slavery, on all possible occasions. I do it with the hope that every man who reads this narrative will swear solemnly before God that, so far as he has power to prevent it, no fugitive from Slavery shall ever be sent back to suffer in that loathsome den of corruption and cruelty.

L. Maria Child *

I. Childhood

I was born a slave; but I never knew it till six years of happy childhood had passed away. My father was a carpenter, and considered so intelligent and skilful in his trade, that, when buildings out of the common line were to be erected, he was sent for from long distances, to be head workman. On condition of paying his mistress two hundred dollars a year, and supporting himself, he was allowed to work at his trade, and manage his own affairs. His strongest wish was to purchase his children; but, though he several times offered his hard earnings for that purpose, he never succeeded. In complexion my parents were a light shade of brownish yellow, and were termed mulattoes. They lived

---

* [Lydia Maria Child was a well-known women's rights activist, writer, and abolitionist. —E.J.D and J.B.F.]

together in a comfortable home; and, though we were all slaves, I was so fondly shielded that I never dreamed I was a piece of merchandise, trusted to them for safe keeping, and liable to be demanded of them at any moment. I had one brother, William, who was two years younger than myself—a bright, affectionate child. I had also a great treasure in my maternal grandmother, who was a remarkable woman in many respects. She was the daughter of a planter in South Carolina, who, at his death, left her mother and his three children free, with money to go to St. Augustine, where they had relatives. It was during the Revolutionary War; and they were captured on their passage, carried back, and sold to different purchasers. Such was the story my grandmother used to tell me; but I do not remember all the particulars. She was a little girl when she was captured and sold to the keeper of a large hotel. I have often heard her tell how hard she fared during childhood. But as she grew older she evinced so much intelligence, and was so faithful, that her master and mistress could not help seeing it was for their interest to take care of such a valuable piece of property. She became an indispensable personage in the household, officiating in all capacities, from cook and wet nurse to seamstress. She was much praised for her cooking; and her nice crackers became so famous in the neighborhood that many people were desirous of obtaining them. In consequence of numerous requests of this kind, she asked permission of her mistress to bake crackers at night, after all the household work was done; and she obtained leave to do it, provided she would clothe herself and her children from the profits. Upon these terms, after working hard all day for her mistress, she began her midnight bakings, assisted by her two oldest children. The business proved profitable; and each year she laid by a little, which was saved for a fund to purchase her children. Her master died, and the property was divided among his heirs. The widow had her dower in the hotel, which she continued to keep open. My grandmother remained in her service as a slave; but her children were divided among her master's children. As she had five, Benjamin, the youngest one, was sold, in order that each heir might have an equal portion of dollars and cents. There was so little difference in our ages that he seemed more like my brother than my uncle. He was a bright, handsome lad, nearly white; for he inherited the complexion my grandmother had derived from Anglo-Saxon ancestors. Though only ten years old, seven hundred and twenty dollars were paid for him. His sale was a terrible blow to my grandmother; but she was naturally hopeful, and she went to work with renewed energy, trusting in time to be able to purchase some of her children. She had laid up three hundred dollars, which her mistress one day begged as a loan, promising to pay her soon. The reader probably knows that no promise or writing given to a slave is legally binding;

for, according to Southern laws, a slave, *being* property, can *hold* no property. When my grandmother lent her hard earnings to her mistress, she trusted solely to her honor. The honor of a slaveholder to a slave!

To this good grandmother I was indebted for many comforts. My brother Willie and I often received portions of the crackers, cakes, and preserves, she made to sell; and after we ceased to be children we were indebted to her for many more important services.

Such were the unusually fortunate circumstances of my early childhood. When I was six years old, my mother died; and then, for the first time, I learned, by the talk around me, that I was a slave. My mother's mistress was the daughter of my grandmother's mistress. She was the foster sister of my mother; they were both nourished at my grandmother's breast. In fact, my mother had been weaned at three months old, that the babe of the mistress might obtain sufficient food. They played together as children; and, when they became women, my mother was a most faithful servant to her whiter foster sister. On her death-bed her mistress promised that her children should never suffer for any thing; and during her lifetime she kept her word. They all spoke kindly of my dead mother, who had been a slave merely in name, but in nature was noble and womanly. I grieved for her, and my young mind was troubled with the thought who would now take care of me and my little brother. I was told that my home was now to be with her mistress; and I found it a happy one. No toilsome or disagreeable duties were imposed upon me. My mistress was so kind to me that I was always glad to do her bidding, and proud to labor for her as much as my young years would permit. I would sit by her side for hours, sewing diligently, with a heart as free from care as that of any free-born white child. When she thought I was tired, she would send me out to run and jump; and away I bounded, to gather berries or flowers to decorate her room. Those were happy days—too happy to last. The slave child had no thought for the morrow; but there came that blight, which too surely waits on every human being born to be a chattel.

When I was nearly twelve years old, my kind mistress sickened and died. As I saw the cheek grow paler, and the eye more glassy, how earnestly I prayed in my heart that she might live! I loved her; for she had been almost like a mother to me. My prayers were not answered. She died, and they buried her in the little churchyard, where, day after day, my tears fell upon her grave.

I was sent to spend a week with my grandmother. I was now old enough to begin to think of the future; and again and again I asked myself what they would do with me. I felt sure I should never find another mistress so kind as the one who was gone. She had promised my dying mother that her children should never suffer for any thing; and when I remembered that, and recalled her many proofs of attachment to me, I could not help having some hopes that she had left me free. My friends were almost certain it would be so. They thought she would be sure to do it, on account of my mother's love and faithful service. But, alas! we all know that the memory of a faithful slave does not avail much to save her children from the auction block.

After a brief period of suspense, the will of my mistress was read, and we learned that she had bequeathed me to her sister's daughter, a child of five years old. So vanished our hopes. My mistress had taught me the precepts of God's Word: "Thou shalt love thy neighbor as thyself." "Whatsoever ye would that men should do unto you, do ye even so unto them." But I was her slave, and I suppose she did not recognize me as her neighbor. I would give much to blot out from my memory that one great wrong. As a child, I loved my mistress; and, looking back on the happy days I spent with her, I try to think with less bitterness of this act of injustice. While I was with her, she taught me to read and spell; and for this privilege, which so rarely falls to the lot of a slave, I bless her memory.

She possessed but few slaves; and at her death those were all distributed among her relatives.* Five of them were my grandmother's children, and had shared the same milk that nourished her mother's children. Notwithstanding my grandmother's long and faithful service to her owners, not one of her children escaped the auction block. These God-breathing machines are no more, in the sight of their masters, than the cotton they plant, or the horses they tend.

V. The Trials of Girlhood

During the first years of my service in Dr. Flint's family, I was accustomed to share some indulgences with the children of my mistress. Though this seemed to me no more than right, I was grateful for it, and tried to merit the kindness by the faithful discharge of my duties. But I now entered on my fifteenth year—a sad epoch in the life of a slave girl. My master began to whisper foul words in my ear. Young as I was, I could not remain ignorant of their import. I tried to treat them with indifference or contempt. The master's age, my extreme youth, and the fear that his conduct would be reported to my grandmother, made him bear this treatment for many months. He was a crafty man, and resorted to many means to accomplish his purposes. Sometimes he had stormy, terrific ways, that made his victims tremble; sometimes he assumed a gentleness that he thought must surely subdue. Of the two, I preferred his

* [The author becomes the slave of Dr. Flint's underage daughter.—E.J.D. and J.B.F.]

stormy moods, although they left me trembling. He tried his utmost to corrupt the pure principles my grandmother had instilled. He peopled my young
mind with unclean images, such as only a vile monster could think of. I turned
from him with disgust and hatred. But he was my master. I was compelled to
live under the same roof with him—where I saw a man forty years my senior
daily violating the most sacred commandments of nature. He told me I was
his property; that I must be subject to his will in all things. My soul revolted
against the mean tyranny. But where could I turn for protection? No matter
whether the slave girl be as black as ebony or as fair as her mistress. In either
case, there is no shadow of law to protect her from insult, from violence, or
even from death; all these are inflicted by fiends who bear the shape of men.
The mistress, who ought to protect the helpless victim, has no other feelings
towards her but those of jealousy and rage. The degradation, the wrongs, the
vices, that grow out of slavery, are more than I can describe. They are greater
than you would willingly believe. Surely, if you credited one half the truths that
are told you concerning the helpless millions suffering in this cruel bondage,
you at the north would not help to tighten the yoke. You surely would refuse
to do for the master, on your own soil, the mean and cruel work which trained
bloodhounds and the lowest class of whites do for him at the south.

Every where the years bring to all enough of sin and sorrow; but in slavery
the very dawn of life is darkened by these shadows. Even the little child, who
is accustomed to wait on her mistress and her children, will learn, before she
is twelve years old, why it is that her mistress hates such and such a one among
the slaves. Perhaps the child's own mother is among those hated ones. She
listens to violent outbreaks of jealous passion, and cannot help understanding what is the cause. She will become prematurely knowing in evil things.
Soon she will learn to tremble when she hears her master's footfall. She will be
compelled to realize that she is no longer a child. If God has bestowed beauty
upon her, it will prove her greatest curse. That which commands admiration
in the white woman only hastens the degradation of the female slave. I know
that some are too much brutalized by slavery to feel the humiliation of their
position; but many slaves feel it most acutely, and shrink from the memory of
it. I cannot tell how much I suffered in the presence of these wrongs, nor how I
am still pained by the retrospect. My master met me at every turn, reminding
me that I belonged to him, and swearing by heaven and earth that he would
compel me to submit to him. If I went out for a breath of fresh air, after a day
of unwearied toil, his footsteps dogged me. If I knelt by my mother's grave,
his dark shadow fell on me even there. The light heart which nature had given
me became heavy with sad forebodings. The other slaves in my master's house

noticed the change. Many of them pitied me; but none dared to ask the cause. They had no need to inquire. They knew too well the guilty practices under that roof; and they were aware that to speak of them was an offence that never went unpunished.

I longed for some one to confide in. I would have given the world to have laid my head on my grandmother's faithful bosom, and told her all my troubles. But Dr. Flint swore he would kill me, if I was not as silent as the grave. Then, although my grandmother was all in all to me, I feared her as well as loved her. I had been accustomed to look up to her with a respect bordering upon awe. I was very young, and felt shamefaced about telling her such impure things, especially as I knew her to be very strict on such subjects. Moreover, she was a woman of a high spirit. She was usually very quiet in her demeanor; but if her indignation was once roused, it was not very easily quelled. I had been told that she once chased a white gentleman with a loaded pistol, because he insulted one of her daughters. I dreaded the consequences of a violent outbreak; and both pride and fear kept me silent. But though I did not confide in my grandmother, and even evaded her vigilant watchfulness and inquiry, her presence in the neighborhood was some protection to me. Though she had been a slave, Dr. Flint was afraid of her. He dreaded her scorching rebukes. Moreover, she was known and patronized by many people; and he did not wish to have his villany made public. It was lucky for me that I did not live on a distant plantation, but in a town not so large that the inhabitants were ignorant of each other's affairs. Bad as are the laws and customs in a slaveholding community, the doctor, as a professional man, deemed it prudent to keep up some outward show of decency.

O, what days and nights of fear and sorrow that man caused me! Reader, it is not to awaken sympathy for myself that I am telling you truthfully what I suffered in slavery. I do it to kindle a flame of compassion in your hearts for my sisters who are still in bondage, suffering as I once suffered.

I once saw two beautiful children playing together. One was a fair white child; the other was her slave, and also her sister. When I saw them embracing each other, and heard their joyous laughter, I turned sadly away from the lovely sight. I foresaw the inevitable blight that would fall on the little slave's heart. I knew how soon her laughter would be changed to sighs. The fair child grew up to be a still fairer woman. From childhood to womanhood her pathway was blooming with flowers, and overarched by a sunny sky. Scarcely one day of her life had been clouded when the sun rose on her happy bridal morning.

How had those years dealt with her slave sister, the little playmate of her childhood? She, also, was very beautiful; but the flowers and sunshine of love were not for her. She drank the cup of sin, and shame, and misery, whereof her persecuted race are compelled to drink.

In view of these things, why are ye silent, ye free men and women of the north? Why do your tongues falter in maintenance of the right? Would that I had more ability! But my heart is so full, and my pen is so weak! There are noble men and women who plead for us, striving to help those who cannot help themselves. God bless them! God give them strength and courage to go on! God bless those, every where, who are laboring to advance the cause of humanity!

X. A Perilous Passage in the Slave Girl's Life

After my lover went away, Dr. Flint contrived a new plan. He seemed to have an idea that my fear of my mistress was his greatest obstacle. In the blandest tones, he told me that he was going to build a small house for me, in a secluded place, four miles away from the town. I shuddered; but I was constrained to listen, while he talked of his intention to give me a home of my own, and to make a lady of me. Hitherto, I had escaped my dreaded fate, by being in the midst of people. My grandmother had already had high words with my master about me. She had told him pretty plainly what she thought of his character, and there was considerable gossip in the neighborhood about our affairs, to which the open-mouthed jealousy of Mrs. Flint contributed not a little. When my master said he was going to build a house for me, and that he could do it with little trouble and expense, I was in hopes something would happen to frustrate his scheme; but I soon heard that the house was actually begun. I vowed before my Maker that I would never enter it. I had rather toil on the plantation from dawn till dark; I had rather live and die in jail, than drag on, from day to day, through such a living death. I was determined that the master, whom I so hated and loathed, who had blighted the prospects of my youth, and made my life a desert, should not, after my long struggle with him, succeed at last in trampling his victim under his feet. I would do any thing, every thing, for the sake of defeating him. What *could* I do? I thought and thought, till I became desperate, and made a plunge into the abyss.

And now, reader, I come to a period in my unhappy life, which I would gladly forget if I could. The remembrance fills me with sorrow and shame. It pains me to tell you of it; but I have promised to tell you the truth, and I will do it honestly, let it cost me what it may. I will not try to screen myself behind the plea of compulsion from a master; for it was not so. Neither can I plead ignorance or thoughtlessness. For years, my master had done his utmost to pollute my mind with foul images, and to destroy the pure principles inculcated by my grandmother, and the good mistress of my childhood. The influences of slavery had had the same effect on me that they had on other young girls; they had made me prematurely knowing, concerning the evil ways of the world. I knew what I did, and I did it with deliberate calculation.

But, O, ye happy women, whose purity has been sheltered from childhood, who have been free to choose the objects of your affection, whose homes are protected by law, do not judge the poor desolate slave girl too severely! If slavery had been abolished, I, also, could have married the man of my choice; I could have had a home shielded by the laws; and I should have been spared the painful task of confessing what I am now about to relate; but all my prospects had been blighted by slavery. I wanted to keep myself pure; and, under the most adverse circumstances, I tried hard to preserve my self-respect; but I was struggling alone in the powerful grasp of the demon Slavery; and the monster proved too strong for me. I felt as if I was forsaken by God and man; as if all my efforts must be frustrated, and I became reckless in my despair.

I have told you that Dr. Flint's persecutions and his wife's jealousy had given rise to some gossip in the neighborhood. Among others, it chanced that a white unmarried gentleman had obtained some knowledge of the circumstances in which I was placed.* He knew my grandmother, and often spoke to me in the street. He became interested for me, and asked questions about my master, which I answered in part. He expressed a great deal of sympathy, and a wish to aid me. He constantly sought opportunities to see me, and wrote to me frequently. I was a poor slave girl, only fifteen years old.

So much attention from a superior person was, of course, flattering; for human nature is the same in all. I also felt grateful for his sympathy, and encouraged by his kind words. It seemed to me a great thing to have such a friend. By degrees, a more tender feeling crept into my heart. He was an educated and eloquent gentleman; too eloquent, alas, for the poor slave girl who trusted in him. Of course I saw whither all this was tending. I knew the impassable gulf between us; but to be an object of interest to a man who is not married and who is not her master, is agreeable to the pride and feelings of a slave, if her miserable situation has left her any pride or sentiment. It seems less degrading to give one's self, than to submit to compulsion. There is something akin to freedom in having a lover who has no control over you, except that which he gains by kindness and attachment. A master may treat you as rudely as he pleases, and you dare not speak; moreover, the wrong does not seem so great with an unmarried man, as with one who has a wife to be made unhappy.

---

* [Linda Brent has two children, Benny and Ellen, by Mr. Sands, an unmarried white man of high social standing in the community.—*E.J.D. and J.B.F.*]

There may be sophistry in all this; but the condition of a slave confuses all principles of morality, and, in fact, renders the practice of them impossible.

When I found that my master had actually begun to build the lonely cottage, other feelings mixed with those I have described. Revenge, and calculations of interest, were added to flattered vanity and sincere gratitude for kindness. I knew nothing would enrage Dr. Flint so much as to know that I favored another; and it was something to triumph over my tyrant even in that small way. I thought he would revenge himself by selling me, and I was sure my friend, Mr. Sands, would buy me. He was a man of more generosity and feeling than my master, and I thought my freedom could be easily obtained from him. The crisis of my fate now came so near that I was desperate. I shuddered to think of being the mother of children that should be owned by my old tyrant. I knew that as soon as a new fancy took him, his victims were sold far off to get rid of them; especially if they had children. I had seen several women sold, with his babies at the breast. He never allowed his offspring by slaves to remain long in sight of himself and his wife. Of a man who was not my master I could ask to have my children well supported; and in this case, I felt confident I should obtain the boon. I also felt quite sure that they would be made free. With all these thoughts revolving in my mind, and seeing no other way of escaping the doom I so much dreaded, I made a headlong plunge. Pity me, and pardon me, O virtuous reader! You never knew what it is to be a slave; to be entirely unprotected by law or custom; to have the laws reduce you to the condition of a chattel, entirely subject to the will of another. You never exhausted your ingenuity in avoiding the snares, and eluding the power of a hated tyrant; you never shuddered at the sound of his footsteps, and trembled within hearing of his voice. I know I did wrong. No one can feel it more sensibly than I do. The painful and humiliating memory will haunt me to my dying day. Still, in looking back, calmly, on the events of my life, I feel that the slave woman ought not to be judged by the same standard as others.

The months passed on. I had many unhappy hours. I secretly mourned over the sorrow I was bringing on my grandmother, who had so tried to shield me from harm. I knew that I was the greatest comfort of her old age, and that it was a source of pride to her that I had not degraded myself, like most of the slaves. I wanted to confess to her that I was no longer worthy of her love; but I could not utter the dreaded words.

As for Dr. Flint, I had a feeling of satisfaction and triumph in the thought of telling *him*. From time to time he told me of his intended arrangements, and I was silent. At last, he came and told me the cottage was completed, and ordered me to go to it. I told him I would never enter it. He said, "I have heard enough of such talk as that. You shall go, if you are carried by force; and you shall remain there."

I replied, "I will never go there. In a few months I shall be a mother."

He stood and looked at me in dumb amazement, and left the house without a word. I thought I should be happy in my triumph over him. But now that the truth was out, and my relatives would hear of it, I felt wretched. Humble as were their circumstances, they had pride in my good character. Now, how could I look them in the face? My self-respect was gone! I had resolved that I would be virtuous, though I was a slave. I had said, "Let the storm beat! I will brave it till I die." And now, how humiliated I felt!

I went to my grandmother. My lips moved to make confession, but the words stuck in my throat. I sat down in the shade of a tree at her door and began to sew. I think she saw something unusual was the matter with me. The mother of slaves is very watchful. She knows there is no security for her children. After they have entered their teens she lives in daily expectation of trouble. This leads to many questions. If the girl is of a sensitive nature, timidity keeps her from answering truthfully, and this well-meant course has a tendency to drive her from maternal counsels. Presently, in came my mistress, like a mad woman, and accused me concerning her husband. My grandmother, whose suspicions had been previously awakened, believed what she said. She exclaimed, "O Linda! has it come to this? I had rather see you dead than to see you as you now are. You are a disgrace to your dead mother." She tore from my fingers my mother's wedding ring and her silver thimble. "Go away!" she exclaimed, "and never come to my house, again." Her reproaches fell so hot and heavy, that they left me no chance to answer. Bitter tears, such as the eyes never shed but once, were my only answer. I rose from my seat, but fell back again, sobbing. She did not speak to me; but the tears were running down her furrowed cheeks, and they scorched me like fire. She had always been so kind to me! *So* kind! How I longed to throw myself at her feet, and tell her all the truth! But she had ordered me to go, and never to come there again. After a few minutes, I mustered strength, and started to obey her. With what feelings did I now close that little gate, which I used to open with such an eager hand in my childhood! It closed upon me with a sound I never heard before.

Where could I go? I was afraid to return to my master's. I walked on recklessly, not caring where I went, or what would become of me. When I had gone four or five miles, fatigue compelled me to stop. I sat down on the stump of an old tree. The stars were shining through the boughs above me. How they mocked me, with their bright, calm light! The hours passed by, and as I sat there alone a chilliness and deadly sickness came over me. I sank on the ground. My mind was full of horrid thoughts. I prayed to die; but the prayer was not answered. At last, with great effort I roused myself, and walked some distance further, to the house of a woman who had been a friend of my mother. When I told her why I was there, she spoke soothingly to me; but I could not be comforted. I thought I could bear my shame if I could only be reconciled to my grandmother. I longed to open my heart to her. I thought if she could know the real state of the case, and all I had been bearing for years, she would perhaps judge me less harshly. My friend advised me to send for her. I did so; but days of agonizing suspense passed before she came. Had she utterly forsaken me? No. She came at last. I knelt before her, and told her the things that had poisoned my life; how long I had been persecuted; that I saw no way of escape; and in an hour of extremity I had become desperate. She listened in silence. I told her I would bear any thing and do any thing, if in time I had hope of obtaining her forgiveness. I begged of her to pity me, for my dead mother's sake. And she did pity me. She did not say, "I forgive you"; but she looked at me lovingly, with her eyes full of tears. She laid her old hand gently on my head, and murmured, "Poor child! Poor child!"

XXI. The Loophole of Retreat

A small shed had been added to my grandmother's house years ago. Some boards were laid across the joists at the top, and between these boards and the roof was a very small garret, never occupied by any thing but rats and mice. It was a pent roof, covered with nothing but shingles, according to the southern custom for such buildings. The garret was only nine feet long and seven wide. The highest part was three feet high, and sloped down abruptly to the loose board floor. There was no admission for either light or air. My uncle Phillip, who was a carpenter, had very skilfully made a concealed trap-door, which communicated with the storeroom. He had been doing this while I was waiting in the swamp. The storeroom opened upon a piazza. To this hole I was conveyed as soon as I entered the house. The air was stifling; the darkness total. A bed had been spread on the floor. I could sleep quite comfortably on one side; but the slope was so sudden that I could not turn on the other without hitting the roof. The rats and mice ran over my bed; but I was weary, and I slept such sleep as the wretched may, when a tempest has passed over them. Morning came. I knew it only by the noises I heard; for in my small den day and night were all the same. I suffered for air even more than for light. But I was not comfortless. I heard the voices of my children. There was joy and there was sadness in the sound. It made my tears flow. How I longed to speak to them! I was eager to look on their faces; but there was no hole, no crack, through which I could peep. This continued darkness was oppressive. It seemed horrible to sit or lie in a cramped position day after day, without one gleam of light. Yet I would have chosen this, rather than my lot as a slave, though white people considered it an easy one; and it was so compared with the fate of others. I was never cruelly over-worked; I was never lacerated with the whip from head to foot; I was never so beaten and bruised that I could not turn from one side to the other; I never had my heel-strings cut to prevent my running away; I was never chained to a log and forced to drag it about, while I toiled in the fields from morning till night; I was never branded with hot iron, or torn by blood-hounds. On the contrary, I had always been kindly treated, and tenderly cared for, until I came into the hands of Dr. Flint. I had never wished for freedom till then. But though my life in slavery was comparatively devoid of hardships, God pity the woman who is compelled to lead such a life!

My food was passed up to me through the trap-door my uncle had contrived; and my grandmother, my uncle Phillip, and aunt Nancy would seize such opportunities as they could, to mount up there and chat with me at the opening. But of course this was not safe in the daytime. It must all be done in darkness. It was impossible for me to move in an erect position, but I crawled about my den for exercise. One day I hit my head against something, and found it was a gimlet. My uncle had left it sticking there when he made the trap-door. I was as rejoiced as Robinson Crusoe could have been at finding such a treasure. It put a lucky thought into my head. I said to myself, "Now I will have some light. Now I will see my children." I did not dare to begin my work during the daytime, for fear of attracting attention. But I groped round; and having found the side next the street, where I could frequently see my children, I stuck the gimlet in and waited for evening. I bored three rows of holes, one above another; then I bored out the interstices between. I thus succeeded in making one hole about an inch long and an inch broad. I sat by it till late into the night, to enjoy the little whiff of air that floated in. In the morning I watched for my children. The first person I saw in the street was Dr. Flint. I had a shuddering, superstitious feeling that it was a bad omen. Several familiar faces passed by. At last I heard the merry laugh of children, and presently two sweet little faces were looking up at me, as though they knew I was there, and were conscious of the joy they imported. How I longed to *tell* them I was there!

My condition was now a little improved. But for weeks I was tormented by hundreds of little red insects, fine as a needle's point, that pierced through my skin, and produced an intolerable burning. The good grandmother gave me herb teas and cooling medicines, and finally I got rid of them. The heat of my den was intense, for nothing but thin shingles protected me from the scorching summer's sun. But I had my consolations. Through my peeping-hole I could watch the children, and when they were near enough, I could hear their talk. Aunt Nancy brought me all the news she could hear at Dr. Flint's. From her I learned that the doctor had written to New York to a colored woman, who had been born and raised in our neighborhood, and had breathed his contaminating atmosphere. He offered her a reward if she could find out any thing about me. I know not what was the nature of her reply; but he soon after started for New York in haste, saying to his family that he had business of importance to transact. I peeped at him as he passed on his way to the steamboat. It was a satisfaction to have miles of land and water between us, even for a little while; and it was still greater satisfaction to know that he believed me to be in the Free States. My little den seemed less dreary than it had done. He returned, as he did from his former journey to New York, without obtaining any satisfactory information. When he passed our house next morning, Benny* was standing at the gate. He had heard them say that he had gone to find me, and he called out, "Dr. Flint, did you bring my mother home? I want to see her." The doctor stamped his foot at him in a rage, and exclaimed, "Get out of the way, you little damned rascal! If you don't, I'll cut off your head."

Benny ran terrified into the house, saying, "You can't put me in jail again. I don't belong to you now." It was well that the wind carried the words away from the doctor's ear. I told my grandmother of it, when we had our next conference at the trap-door; and begged of her not to allow the children to be impertinent to the irascible old man.

Autumn came, with a pleasant abatement of heat. My eyes had become accustomed to the dim light, and by holding my book or work in a certain position near the aperture I contrived to read and sew. That was a great relief to the tedious monotony of my life. But when winter came, the cold penetrated through the thin shingle roof, and I was dreadfully chilled. The winters there are not so long, or so severe, as in northern latitudes; but the houses are not built to shelter from cold, and my little den was peculiarly comfortless. The kind grandmother brought me bed-clothes and warm drinks. Often I was obliged to lie in bed all day to keep comfortable; but with all my precautions, my shoulders and feet were frostbitten. O, those long, gloomy days, with no object for my eye to rest upon, and no thoughts to occupy my mind, except the dreary past and the uncertain future! I was thankful when there came a day sufficiently mild for me to wrap myself up and sit at the loophole to watch the passers by. Southerners have the habit of stopping and talking in the streets, and I heard many conversations not intended to meet my ears. I heard slave-hunters planning how to catch some poor fugitive. Several times I heard

---

* [Her son by Mr. Sands—*E.J.D. and J.B.F.*]

allusions to Dr. Flint, myself, and the history of my children, who, perhaps, were playing near the gate. One would say, "I wouldn't move my little finger to catch her, as old Flint's property." Another would say, "I'll catch *any* nigger for the reward. A man ought to have what belongs to him, if he *is* a damned brute." The opinion was often expressed that I was in the Free States. Very rarely did any one suggest that I might be in the vicinity. Had the least suspicion rested on my grandmother's house, it would have been burned to the ground. But it was the last place they thought of. Yet there was no place, where slavery existed, that could have afforded me so good a place of concealment.

Dr. Flint and his family repeatedly tried to coax and bribe my children to tell something they had heard said about me. One day the doctor took them into a shop, and offered them some bright little silver pieces and gay handkerchiefs if they would tell where their mother was. Ellen shrank away from him, and would not speak; but Benny spoke up, and said, "Dr. Flint, I don't know where my mother is. I guess she's in New York; and when you go there again, I wish you'd ask her to come home, for I want to see her; but if you put her in jail, or tell her you'll cut her head off, I'll tell her to go right back."

3–17
John C. Duval (1816–1897)

As with such figures as Davy Crockett and Mike Fink, it is often difficult to tease truth from fact when discussing BIGFOOT WALLACE (1817–1899), whose given name was William Alexander Anderson Wallace. Descended from legendary Scotsmen William Wallace and Robert Bruce, Bigfoot Wallace was born in Virginia but came to Texas during the Texas Revolution after his brother's death at Goliad. He fought in the Mexican War and joined the Texas Rangers. Afterwards, he fought in the Civil War, served as a mail carrier, and fought in the Comanche War. Later in life, he settled near the Frio River, where the town of Bigfoot, Texas, was named in his honor. In *The Adventures of Big-Foot Wallace* (1870), John C. Duval wrote of his friend from notes and many interviews. He praised Wallace's "go-a-headativeness," a reference to Crockett's motto, but admitted that Wallace's tales were occasionally a bit tall and that he "stretched his blanket" upon occasion. Wallace exemplifies Texas' role in Southwest Humor, providing realistic details of pioneer life and western landscape alongside tall tale elements that sometimes strain credulity.

≈ ≈ ≈

From *The Adventures of Big-Foot Wallace* (1870)

Chapter 11. Black Wolf's Indian Legend—Determination to Escape—Back in the Settlements

"A great many years ago," said Black Wolf, "a young chief, belonging to one of the most powerful tribes of Arkansas, concluded that he would visit one of the nearest white settlements, and see some of the people of whom he had heard so much. So he took his gun and dog, crossed the 'father of waters' in his canoe, and travelled for many days toward the rising of the sun, through a dense forest that had never echoed to the sound of the white man's axe. One day, just as the sun was setting, he came to the top of a high hill, and four or five miles away, in the valley below, he saw the smoke curling up from the chimneys of the most western settlement, at that time, east of the Mississippi river.

"As it was too late to reach the settlement before dark, the chief sought out the thickest part of the woods, where he spread his blanket upon the ground, and laid himself down upon it, with the intention of passing the night there. He had scarcely settled himself to rest, when he heard a 'halloo' a long way off among the hills. Supposing that some one had got lost in the woods, he raised himself up and shouted as loud as he could. Again he heard the 'halloo' apparently a little nearer, but it sounded so mournful and wild, and so unlike the voice of any living being, that he became alarmed, and did not shout in return. After awhile, however, the long mournful 'halloo-o-o' was repeated, and this time much nearer than before. The chief's heart beat loudly in his bosom, and a cold sweat broke out upon his forehead; for he knew that the unearthly sounds that met his ears never came from mortal lips. His very dog, too, seemed to understand this, for he whined and cowered down at his feet, seemingly in the greatest dread. Again the prolonged and mournful 'halloo-o-o' was heard, and this time close at hand, and in a few moments an Indian warrior stalked up and took a seat near the chief, and gazed mournfully at him out of his hollow eyes, without uttering a word.

"He was dressed in a different garb from anything the chief had ever seen worn by the Indians, and he held a bow in his withered hand, and a quiver, filled with arrows, was slung across his shoulders. As the chief looked more closely at him, he saw that his unearthly visitor was, in fact, a grinning skeleton; for his white ribs showed plainly through the rents in his robe, and though seemingly he looked at the chief, there were no eyes in the empty sockets he turned toward him. Presently the figure rose up, and, in a hollow voice, spoke to the chief, and told him to return from whence he came, for their race was doomed—that they would disappear before the white people like dew before the morning sun—that he was the spirit of one of his forefathers, and that he came to warn him of the fate that awaited him and his people—that he could remember when the Indians were as numerous as the leaves on the trees, and the white people were few and weak, and shut up in their towns upon the sea-shore—now they are strong, and their number cannot be counted, and before many years they will drive the last remnant of the red race into the waters of the great western ocean. 'Go back,' said the figure, advancing toward the chief, and waving his withered hand, 'and tell your people to prepare themselves for their doom, and to meet me in the "happy hunting grounds," where the white man shall trouble them no more.'

"As he said this he came up close to the chief, and placed his skeleton fingers on his head, and glared at him out of the empty sockets in his fleshless skull! 'Son of a fading race, the last hour of your unfortunate people is fast approaching, and soon not a vestige of them will be left on all this wide continent. They and their forests, their hunting grounds, their villages and wigwams, will disappear forever, and the white man's cities and towns will rise up in the places where once they chased the buffalo, the elk, and the deer.'

"The chief was as fearless a warrior as ever went to battle; but when he felt the cold touch of that skeleton hand, a horrible dread took possession of him, and he remembered nothing of what happened afterward. In the morning, when he woke up, the sun was shining brightly over head, and the birds were whistling and chirping in the trees above him. He looked around for his gun, and was surprised beyond reason when he picked it up and found that the barrel was all eaten up with rust, and the stock so decayed and rotten that it fell to pieces in his hand. His dog was nowhere to be seen, and he whistled and called to him in vain; but at his feet he saw a heap of white bones, among which there was a skeleton of a neck, with the collar his dog had worn still around it! He then noticed that his buckskin hunting-shirt was decayed and mildewed, and hung in tatters upon him, and that his hair had grown so long that it reached down nearly to his waist. Bewildered by all these sudden and curious changes, he took his way toward the top of the hill, from which, the evening before, he had seen the smoke rising up from the cabins of the frontier settlement, and what was his astonishment when he saw, spread out in the valley below him, a great city, with its spires and steeples rising up as far as his eye could extend; and in place of the dense, unbroken forests that covered the earth when he came, a wide, open country presented itself to his view, fenced up into fields and pastures, and dotted over with the white man's stately houses and buildings.

"As he gazed at all this in surprise and wonder, he could distinctly hear, from where he stood, the distant hum of the vast multitude who were laboring and trafficking and moving about in the great city below him. Sad and dispirited, he turned his course homeward, and after travelling many days through farms and villages and towns, he at length reached once more the banks of the mighty Mississippi. But the white people had got there before him, and in place of a silent and lonely forest, he found a large town built up where it had once stood, and saw a huge steamboat puffing and paddling along right where he had crossed the 'father of waters' in his little canoe. When he had crossed the river, he found that the white settlements had gone on a long ways beyond it, but at length he came to the wilderness again, and after wandering about for many moons, he at last came up with the remnant of his people, but now no longer a powerful tribe, such as he had left them, for they had dwindled down to a mere handful. His father and mother were dead, his brothers and sisters were all dead, and no one knew the poor old warrior that had appeared so suddenly among them. For a while he staid with them, and talked, in the strangest way, about things that had happened long before the oldest people in the tribe were born; but one day, after telling the story I have told you, he took his way toward the setting sun, and was never seen more."

When I had been about three months with the tribe, I began to long exceedingly to be once more with my own people. I lost all relish for "forays" and "hunting expeditions," and thought only of effecting my escape, and making my way back to the "settlements." I became moody and discontented to such a degree that Black Wolf and his mother at length took notice of it. One day, when Black Wolf and myself were alone together in the lodge, he said to me, "My brother, what is it that makes you so unhappy and discontented; for I have seen for some time that you have had something on your mind? Has any one mistreated my brother?"

"No," said I, "every one has treated me well; but I tell you frankly, my brother," (for I knew he would not betray me,) "I am pining to see my own people again, and I am determined to attempt to make my escape into the settlements, if it should cost me my life."

"My brother," said Black Wolf, "I shall be very sorry if you leave us, and so will my old mother; but it is not strange you should wish to see your own people again, and you must go. I will help you all that I can to reach the settlements in safety. But be careful," said he, "not to say a word about this to anybody, for if you should attempt to escape and be recaptured, nothing could save your life, and I should be put to death for having aided you."

As Black Wolf advised me, I said nothing to any one of my intention of leaving, except to his old mother. She tried very hard to dissuade me from going, but finding I was resolute in my purpose, she gave up the point, and sang two or three more of her "bumble-bee" ditties over me at parting, which seemed to lighten her grief considerably. She also made me a present of a dried terrapin's tail, which she said would protect me from all danger from bullets in battle. I have kept the terrapin's tail, out of respect for the old squaw, but I must say, in the many "scrimmages" I have been in since then with the Mexicans and Indians, I have had more faith in the efficacy of a tree or a stump to protect me from bullets, than in the charm she gave me. She also gave me a necklace made of the claws of the grisly bear and porcupine quills, and a large copper ring to wear in my nose.

Black Wolf and I made our preparations quietly for the journey, but without exciting any suspicions on the part of the other Indians that I had any intention of quitting the tribe, as we told them we were going into the "hills" to take a bear hunt, and would be absent possibly several days. Black Wolf led the way, and Comanche and I followed, and the first day we travelled at least thirty miles from the village, and camped together that night for the last time. In the morning, before we separated, Black Wolf traced out upon the ground a map of the route I had to go, marking down upon it accurately all the ranges of hills and watercourses I would pass on the way. He then bade me good-by, and shouldering his gun, sorrowfully took his course back toward the village, and was soon lost to sight among the hills.

During my stay with the Indians I had acquired considerable knowledge of the woods, and how to steer my course through them even when the sun was not visible, and, in eight days after parting from Black Wolf, I arrived safely at the "settlements," and thus ended my first expedition into the "wilderness." Comanche lived with me till he died of old age, and left a progeny behind him, that, for trailing and fighting "varmints" and "sucking eggs," can't be beat by any dogs in the State of Texas. . . .

Chapter 25. Another Rattlesnake—How to Manage Rattlesnakes—Terrific Adventure with a Grape-vine Rattlesnake

The next day I rode along with our author, knowing if there was a rattlesnake on the road he would be sure to find it; and in fact he soon stirred up one, and I got down and killed it, and pulled off its rattles, which I slipped into my pocket, unnoticed by our author. "Captain," said he, as I remounted, "how in the world have you managed to live so long and camp out so much at night in this wilderness without ever having been bitten by a rattlesnake?"

"Why, you see," I answered, "if you don't lose your presence of mind, there's very little danger of a rattlesnake's biting you, even when he crawls to bed with you at night. When you discover one crawling under your blankets, all you've got to do is to lie still and let him fix himself to his notion (and they always pick out the warmest places), and as soon as he is fast asleep, you can jump up without the least danger of being bitten; but if you should move a peg before he has settled himself, he'll 'nip you' to a certainty."

"Yes," replied our author, "but who could lie still under such circumstances?"

"I have," said I, "a hundred times. One dark night, about a year ago, when I was camping near the edge of a thick chaparral, I felt a fellow crawling under my blanket. I lay perfectly still, and let him select his own locality, and nothing would do him but a place right along side of my face. I tell you it was pretty hard work to keep quiet when I felt his scaly sides rubbing up against my neck and face, as he slowly wound himself in his coil. After he had fixed himself to his notion, I lay perfectly still a few moments longer, to make sure he was asleep, and then sprang up suddenly, and striking a light, soon had the gentleman's head mashed as flat as a pancake. Remember, Mr. Author," I continued, "there's no danger at all of a rattlesnake's biting you at night, if you only lie still and keep quiet until he settles himself."

"Yes," said our author; "but who could lie still and keep quiet (unless he was made out of cast-iron) while a rattlesnake was slowly coiling itself up in his bosom? Ugh! the bare idea makes me shudder from head to foot."

I saw that my "snake story" had produced the desired effect upon him, and for the time I dropped the subject. The next night we encamped in a very snaky-looking locality, and I cut off a piece of grape-vine about as thick as an ordinary rattlesnake, which I slyly slipped under the edge of our blanket just before we "turned in." About half an hour after we had lain down, I drew out the slip of grape-vine and ran it slowly along the author's back, at the same time gently shaking my rattles, which I held in the other hand. He was just on the eve of dropping off to sleep, but the crawling motion and the "rattling" aroused him in an instant.

"Oh! murder, captain," said he, "there's a rattlesnake crawling along my back! What in the world am I to do?"

"I know it," I answered, "I hear him rattling now (and I gently shook the rattles I held in my hand). Lie still, and don't move a muscle until he coils up."

"Oh, yes," said the poor fellow (and his teeth fairly chattered from fright), "it's easy enough for you to say lie still when I am between you and the snake, but it isn't so easy for me, for I can feel him squirming along my back now."

"I know that," said I, "but you must lie still, for the first motion you make, he will have his fangs into you, sure."

"Oh!" said the poor fellow, as I gave the vine another serpentine twist along his back, "this is more than human nature can bear—ugh! ugh! Captain, can't you do anything for me?"

"There's no danger at all," I said, "if you will only keep still; he will soon settle himself, and then you can jump up without the least risk of being bitten. When he quits rattling altogether," said I, shaking the rattles in my hand, "you will know that he's asleep."

"Captain," he replied, in a faint and husky voice, as I gave the vine another twist and shook the rattles, "this is past endurance. I *must* get out of this at all hazards."

"Unless you want to die," said I, "don't do it, but lie as still as a mouse when puss is about. By the way, Mr. Author," said I, "can you tell me whether the rattlesnake is confined to the American continent, or if he is to be found also in other countries? I have heard a great many opposite opinions on the subject, and some pretend to think," I continued, giving the vine another twist, "that they are a species of the Cobra di Capello, the most poisonous serpent in the world."

"Captain," said our author, getting the better of his fright for the moment, in his indignation at being asked such an untimely question, "I like an inquiring mind, but I must say that you select the strangest occasions imaginable for obtaining information upon such subjects. Why, man," he continued, in a rage, and totally unsuspicious that I was playing upon him, "do you suppose a man is in a condition to answer any question rationally with a rattlesnake spooning up to his back?"

"There is no doubt," said I, pretending not to notice what he had said, and giving the vine another rake along his back, "that if they are not a species of the Cobra, they are just as poisonous, for I have seen a man die in twenty minutes after he had been bitten by one of them. There was Jake Thompson, who was bit on the foot by one, when we were scouting a year or two ago on the Nueces, and he didn't live long enough to say 'Jack Robinson, Junior'; and yet in that little time he turned as black in the face as a negro, and his body swelled up till he was as big as a 'skinned horse.'"

"Captain," said he, "will you do me the favor to postpone the balance of that interesting story for another occasion? I'll back you against the world for picking out the most unsuitable times for telling your yarns."

"Oh! I beg your pardon," said I, "I forgot you wasn't broke into the ways of the wilderness yet. When you have 'bunked' with a hundred rattlesnakes, as I have done, you won't mind it a bit. I recollect about six years ago, when Bill Hankins and me were out hunting on the head-waters of the Leon, we camped one night—"

"Oh! good gracious," said our author, "Bill Hankins again, and the head-waters of the Leon! Captain, I want you to distinctly understand that I've heard just as much as I desire of Bill Hankins and the head-waters of Leon, and—"

"Oh! very well," I said, interrupting him in turn, and shaking my rattles, and screwing the vine into the small of his back, "I've no wish at all to force my stories upon you."

"Ugh!" said the poor fellow, "this is past all endurance. Captain, remember me to all inquiring friends, and don't forget that the manuscript of the 'Wayworn Wanderer' is in my saddle-bags. Give it to the world with all its imperfections!"

"Hold on just one minute longer," I said, giving the rattles a vicious shake, "and you will be all right."

"Not another second," he cried, "it's no use talking, I may just as well die one way as another," and he made a desperate bound from under the blanket, and pitched head foremost on the ground ten or twelve paces off.

I seized a bottle of "Chili pepper-sauce" and ran to where he was lying. "Here, Mr. Author," I said, "drink this quick!" He took it, and in the hurry and excitement of the moment, hastily swallowed about a pint of the contents.

"Gracious," said I, "you have made another wonderful escape."

"I don't know so well about that," said he, sputtering and gasping for breath. "I'm afraid I'm bit."

"Do you feel," I asked, "as if you were up to your waist in a kettle of melted lead?"

"Not exactly," he replied, drawing his breath through his teeth, "but I feel as though I had swallowed a quart or so of it."

"Then," said I, "you are all safe, and you have made the most wonderful escape on record. No one before has ever missed being bit, who sprang off as you did, before the snake had coiled himself up. A most extraordinary escape, truly," I continued.

"What in the world," said he, "was that stuff you gave me just now?"

"That," replied I, "is an antidote I always keep for the bite of snakes. I got it from 'Puppy's Foot,' the Tonkawa chief, and if taken in time it will kill the poison of the most venomous snake."

"I have no doubt of it," said our author; "it would kill old Satan himself. It is hot enough to scald the throat out of a brass monkey. For mercy's sake, give me some water to cool my coppers."

I handed over the gourd to him, and he took a long swig at it, then seating himself on a log by the fire, in spite of my remonstrances, he persisted in sitting up the balance of the night . . .

Chapter 43. Wallace in Trouble—Leaves New Orleans—On the Mississippi—A Boat Race—Wallace Roars like a Mexican Lion—He "Sells" a Dandy—"Running Against a Snag"—Anchored on a Sand-bank—Damage Repaired, and Arrival at Cincinnati

In the morning when I woke up, I found myself lying on the floor of a room with little grated windows to it, and two or three policemen walking backward and forward before the door. There were at least a couple of dozen besides myself in the room, all looking very much the worse for wear: an hour or so afterward, the police came in, and took us all before the justice of the peace. He fined some of us considerably, especially those that seemed to be old acquaintances, and sent off all that couldn't pay to the "calaboose." When he came to me, and found that I was a stranger in the city, he only fined me five dollars, and gave me lots of good advice gratis, which I forgot ten minutes afterward.

This scrape rather sickened me with New Orleans, and after dinner I paid my bill at the St. Charles tavern, and hired a porter to take my trunk to a steamboat that was to start up the river that evening for Cincinnati, and in an hour or two after I went aboard she raised steam and put out.

She was a splendid boat, and everything belonging to her was of the finest sort, just as if the owners had no idea she would ever "bust up," or run into a snag or a sawyer, which I believe is the end, sooner or later, (generally sooner,) of all Mississippi steamboats. There was a crowd of passengers aboard, and the ladies' cabin was filled with women and children. Such eating and drinking as there was on that boat I never saw before! They weren't satisfied with three meals a day, but had to have another, between breakfast and dinner, they called "lunch." I thought of the times when I was a ranger, and used to ride hard all day, and then breakfast, lunch, dine, and sup, at night, on a little dried beef and a cake of "hard-tack," and I wondered how these city-folks would make out on such fare!

The river was very high, and had overflowed all the bottom lands, and it looked strange to see people going from one house to another in pirogues and yawl-boats. I thought I would rather live on one of the high-and-dry prairies of Texas, where I had to haul my drinking-water five miles, than in such a place, where I could neither ride nor walk, nor do anything but paddle about in a "dug-out." Water is a good thing in moderation, but it can be "overdid" like everything else, just as it is in the Gulf of Mexico, and in most of the liquors we get in Texas!

The next morning after leaving New Orleans, we noticed a large steamboat come puffing on behind us. She appeared to be rapidly gaining on us, and it was soon reduced to a certainty that if we didn't "hurry up the cakes" she would pass us before long. I saw the captain of our boat and the mate with their heads together, and shortly afterward three or four old tar-barrels and half a dozen sides of bacon were thrown into the furnace by the firemen. Pretty soon the black smoke began to rise out of the chimneys, and the old steamer quivered and shook like a green hunter with the "buck-ague." By this time the other steamer had got nearly opposite to us, and everybody on it and on our boat hurraed and waved their hats and handkerchiefs.

The captain of our boat walked up and down the guards, and tried to look as unconcerned as if he didn't know there was another boat in ten miles of him, but I saw plainly enough that he wasn't easy in his mind. The mate ran up and down the stairs every five minutes, till his face was as red as a turkey-gobbler's snout, and the firemen poked everything into the furnace they could lay their hands on. I do believe if we had taken the bran-new piano out of the ladies' cabin and handed it over to them, they would have shoved it in along with the tar-barrels, and never thought anything strange of it! Some of the passengers were afraid the boat would blow up, but they soon got over their scare, and "hurraed" as loud as the rest. And such a fizzing and whizzing and sputtering of steam you never heard. I tell you it was almost as exciting as a running fight on the prairies with the Comanche Indians!

At last we began slowly to gain on the other boat, and as soon as the passengers noticed it, they "hurraed" louder than ever, and I was just as crazy as the balance. I do believe, if I had known positively that our boat would have blown up the next minute, I would have yelled out, "A little more grape, Captain Bragg," to the fellows that were poking the fuel into the furnaces. I danced the "war dance," gave the Comanche death-yell, and then roared like a Mexican lion; and as soon as I saw that we were fairly leaving the other boat behind us, I ran up to the captain and grabbed him by the hand. The captain tried to look as if he thought the whole affair a small matter, but I could see well enough that he was tickled to the backbone. However, he was "sensible to the last," for the first words he said to me were, "Let's go and take something," and we went.

After we had taken a horn, the captain said to me, "See here, my friend, what sort of a yell do you call that you gave just now as we passed the other boat?"

"That," said I, "was the *bona fide* screech of the genuine Mexican lion."

"Well," said he, "I wouldn't begrudge five hundred dollars if I had a steam whistle on my boat that would blow in that style." From that time the captain seemed to take a great fancy to me, and always asked me to "liquor" whenever he went up to the bar, which was about every half-hour on a "low average," for he wasn't a hard drinker by any means.

One day, we stopped a little while at a place called Vicksburg, in Mississippi, where the gamblers were all hung some years ago. Pity we haven't got half a dozen Vicksburgs in Texas! At this place a fellow came on board and took passage for somewhere up the river. He was a dandified-looking little fellow, dressed up in the height of the fashion. How he kept his shirt-bosom and his clothes so smooth, was a mystery to me. He looked as slick and as shiny all over as a newly varnished cupboard. He had a great many rings on his fingers, (and on his toes too, for all I know,) and wore a big gold chain looped up in his vest pocket, and the half of a pair of spectacles hung round his neck by a black ribbon. Every now and then he would put this up to his eye, and take a sight through it at the ladies in the cabin. He was evidently laboring under a disease which we call in Texas the "swell-head," and I saw plain enough if something wasn't done for him pretty soon, there would be no chance for him ever to get over it; for it's a hard complaint to get rid of, anyhow!

The first time he dined on the boat, he happened to take his seat at the table right opposite to where I sat; and what do you think he did? He took out a silver knife and fork from a little morocco case he had brought along with him, and ate his dinner with them, instead of the knife and fork by his plate, which were good enough for anybody. Thinks I, old fellow, here's a fine chance to do something for your case, and I'll see if I can't take advantage of it.

The next day we stopped at a wood-yard to take in fuel, and I went on shore, and, while the deck-hands were getting in the wood, I whittled out a wooden case-knife about three feet long, and a fork in proportion. When I had finished them, I hid them under my coat, and carried them to my stateroom without anybody seeing them. There was a gentleman occupying the state-room with me, and I had to let him into the secret, but he was mightily tickled at the idea of "doing the dandy," and lent me the case of his double-barrel gun, which was just about long enough to hold my knife and fork.

When the dinner-bell rang, I took my seat at the table right opposite the chap with the "swell head," with my "gun-case" hid away under my frock coat, and waited for him to begin operations. He carefully laid the knife and fork by his plate to one side, and took out his own silver ones from the little morocco case, and began to eat in a "finniken" sort of way! I followed suit precisely, laid my knife and fork to one side, placed my "gun-case" on the table, and drew out my three-foot butcher-knife and "pitchfork," and began eating with them as sober as a judge. As soon as the folks at table saw what I was up to, the ladies all "tittered," and the gentlemen "haw, hawed," right out—the captain especially laughed till the tears ran down his cheeks; but I never cracked a smile, and kept on eating as "solemn" as a parson at a funeral.

After dinner, the captain came up to me, and says he, "Texas," (for that was what he always called me,) "you are a trump, sure," and he made me a present of a fine bowie-knife, which I have got yet, but it don't lift hair like "Old Butch"; and besides, when I went to settle for my passage, he knocked off five dollars, just for the effectual way in which he said I had "done for" the dandy. What went with "Swell Head" nobody knows, for he disappeared from the boat that day, and we never saw him afterward.

The next day, as we were going along "full clatter" against the swift current of the Mississippi, we ran head on against a snag, and stove a hole in the bottom of the boat as big as a flour barrel. I had often heard of running against a snag, and I understood the meaning of it pretty well after I tackled an old she-bear once, and got three hugs and a bite from her before "Old Butch" had the least show; but this was the first time I ever actually came in contact with the *bona fide* article! I tell you it made everything hop, and the old boat quivered from stem to stern like a dying buffalo! The ladies all came pouring out of the cabin, screaming like wild-cats, and some crying out, "Oh! we are lost! we are lost!" "The boat is sinking"; and some of the men, I noticed, were worse scared than the women. Such a "hubbub" and "to do" you never saw!

I wasn't the least bit frightened myself, for I learned to swim—like a puppy or an Indian papoose—before my eyes were open; and I stood on the guards, quietly waiting for the boat to sink, when I intended to strike out for the nearest shore. Most of the women screamed, and prayed, and wrung their hands, as if they thought it was the best way to keep the boat from going down; but I noticed one young woman that never "took on" at all the whole time; and a mighty good-looking one she was too! She was as pale as a lily, but as calm and quiet as a morning in May, and didn't seem the least bit frightened for herself, but only on account of a lame old gentleman, who, I suppose, was her father. She held on to his hand all the while, and looked up at him so lovingly and affectionately, I wouldn't have minded being her "pa" myself for a short time.

I determined, when the time came to "strike out," to take that young woman and the old gentleman into my especial keeping, and see 'em safe to shore; but just then a fat old lady, who weighed perhaps about two hundred and fifty pounds gross, came waddling by in a great fright, and grabbed me by the arm; and then another woman came along and hitched on to my other arm, while another clinched my coat tail, and they hung on to me like leeches till the alarm was over! If the boat had gone down I wouldn't have had a chance even to kick when I was drowning—they "hampered" me so!

The minute the boat struck the snag, the pilot backed her off, and steered for the nearest shore; but she filled so fast, we never could have made half the distance. Luckily for us, though, and particularly for me, with three women hanging on to me, we hadn't gone more than two or three hundred yards before we ran on to a sandbar in the middle of the river, and settled down on it hard and fast! and that was all that saved us. We laid there two days and nights, pumping out the boat and stopping up the hole the snag had made in the bottom. When everything was put to rights, we raised steam up to the high-pressure point and backed off, and once more went on our way rejoicing. Two or three days afterward we landed at Cincinnati, without any further accident.

3–18
Henry David Thoreau (1817–1862)

In his eulogy of fellow Transcendentalist HENRY DAVID THOREAU (1817–1862), Emerson said that his friend "did not feel himself except in opposition." That trait is visible in many aspects of his life. From his refusal to pay his poll tax, leading to his brief imprisonment, to his removal from society to Walden Pond, Thoreau was part of the separatist streak in American culture. Thoreau's essay "Resistance to Civil Government" (1849), often published under the title "On Civil Disobedience," takes its place with the "Declaration of Independence" as one of the most influential American documents, influencing resistance movements all around the globe. But his call for preserving the distinctive American wilderness in "Walking," delivered as a lecture many times in his life and published posthumously in 1862, and excerpted here, remains an enduring presence in modern environmental awareness and activism.

≈ ≈ ≈

From "Walking" (1862)

I wish to speak a word for Nature, for absolute freedom and wildness, as contrasted with a freedom and culture merely civil,—to regard man as an inhabitant, or a part and parcel of Nature, rather than a member of society. I wish to make an extreme statement, if so I may make an emphatic one, for there are enough champions of civilization: the minister and the school committee and every one of you will take care of that.

I have met with but one or two persons in the course of my life who understood the art of Walking, that is, of taking walks,—who had a genius, so to speak, for *sauntering*, which word is beautifully derived "from idle people who roved about the country, in the Middle Ages, and asked charity, under pretense of going *à la Sainte Terre*," to the Holy Land, till the children exclaimed, "There goes a *Sainte-Terrer*," a Saunterer, a Holy-Lander. They who never go to the Holy Land in their walks, as they pretend, are indeed mere idlers and vagabonds; but they who do go there are saunterers in the good sense, such as I mean. Some, however, would derive the word from *sans terre*, without land or a home, which, therefore, in the good sense, will mean, having no particular home, but equally at home everywhere. For this is the secret of successful sauntering. He who sits still in a house all the time may be the greatest vagrant of all; but the saunterer, in the good sense, is no more vagrant than the meandering river, which is all the while sedulously seeking the shortest course to the sea. But I prefer the first, which, indeed, is the most probable derivation. For every walk is a sort of crusade, preached by some Peter the Hermit in us, to go forth and reconquer this Holy Land from the hands of the Infidels.

It is true, we are but faint-hearted crusaders, even the walkers, nowadays, who undertake no persevering, never-ending enterprises. Our expeditions are but tours, and come round again at evening to the old hearth-side from which we set out. Half the walk is but retracing our steps. We should go forth on the shortest walk, perchance, in the spirit of undying adventure, never to return,—prepared to send back our embalmed hearts only as relics to our desolate kingdoms. If you are ready to leave father and mother, and brother and sister, and wife and child and friends, and never see them again,—if you have paid your debts, and made your will, and settled all your affairs, and are a free man, then you are ready for a walk.

To come down to my own experience, my companion and I, for I sometimes have a companion, take pleasure in fancying ourselves knights of a new, or rather an old, order,—not Equestrians or Chevaliers, not Ritters or Riders, but Walkers, a still more ancient and honorable class, I trust. The chivalric and heroic spirit which once belonged to the Rider seems now to reside in, or perchance to have subsided into, the Walker,—not the Knight, but Walker, Errant. He is a sort of fourth estate, outside of Church and State and People.

We have felt that we almost alone hereabouts practiced this noble art; though, to tell the truth, at least if their own assertions are to be received, most of my townsmen would fain walk sometimes, as I do, but they cannot.

No wealth can buy the requisite leisure, freedom, and independence which are the capital in this profession. It comes only by the grace of God. It requires a direct dispensation from Heaven to become a walker. You must be born into the family of the Walkers. *Ambulator nascitur, non fit.* Some of my townsmen, it is true, can remember and have described to me some walks which they took ten years ago, in which they were so blessed as to lose themselves for half an hour in the woods; but I know very well that they have confined themselves to the highway ever since, whatever pretensions they may make to belong to this select class. No doubt they were elevated for a moment as by the reminiscence of a previous state of existence, when even they were foresters and outlaws.

> "When he came to grene wode,
> In a mery mornynge,
> There he herde the notes small
> Of byrdes mery syngynge.
>
> "It is ferre gone, sayd Robyn
> That I was last here;
> Me lyste a lytell for to shote
> At the donne dere."

I think that I cannot preserve my health and spirits, unless I spend four hours a day at least—and it is commonly more than that—sauntering through the woods and over the hills and fields, absolutely free from all worldly engagements. You may safely say, A penny for your thoughts, or a thousand pounds. . . .

Living much out of doors, in the sun and wind, will no doubt produce a certain roughness of character,—will cause a thicker cuticle to grow over some of the finer qualities of our nature, as on the face and hands, or as severe manual labor robs the hands of some of their delicacy of touch. So staying in the house, on the other hand, may produce a softness and smoothness, not to say thinness of skin, accompanied by an increased sensibility to certain impressions. Perhaps we should be more susceptible to some influences important to our intellectual and moral growth, if the sun had shone and the wind blown on us a little less; and no doubt it is a nice matter to proportion rightly the thick and thin skin. But methinks that is a scurf that will fall off fast enough,—that the natural remedy is to be found in the proportion which the night bears to the day, the winter to the summer, thought to experience. There will be so much the more air and sunshine in our thoughts. The callous palms of the laborer are conversant with finer tissues of self-respect and heroism, whose touch thrills the heart, than the languid fingers of idleness. That is mere sentimentality that lies abed by day and thinks itself white, far from the tan and callus of experience.

When we walk, we naturally go to the fields and woods: what would become of us, if we walked only in a garden or a mall? Even some sects of philosophers have felt the necessity of importing the woods to themselves, since they did not go to the woods. "They planted groves and walks of Platanes," where they took *subdiales ambulationes* in porticos open to the air. Of course it is of no use to direct our steps to the woods, if they do not carry us thither. I am alarmed when it happens that I have walked a mile into the woods bodily, without getting there in spirit. In my afternoon walk I would fain forget all my morning occupations and my obligations to society. But it sometimes happens that I cannot easily shake off the village. The thought of some work will run in my head and I am not where my body is,—I am out of my senses. In my walks I would fain return to my senses. What business have I in the woods, if I am thinking of something out of the woods? I suspect myself, and cannot help a shudder, when I find myself so implicated even in what are called good works,—for this may sometimes happen.

My vicinity affords many good walks; and though for so many years I have walked almost every day, and sometimes for several days together, I have not yet exhausted them. An absolutely new prospect is a great happiness, and I can still get this any afternoon. Two or three hours' walking will carry me to as strange a country as I expect ever to see. A single farmhouse which I had not seen before is sometimes as good as the dominions of the King of Dahomey. There is in fact a sort of harmony discoverable between the capabilities of the landscape within a circle of ten miles' radius, or the limits of an afternoon walk, and the threescore years and ten of human life. It will never become quite familiar to you.

Nowadays almost all man's improvements, so called, as the building of houses and the cutting down of the forest and of all large trees, simply deform the landscape, and make it more and more tame and cheap. A people who would begin by burning the fences and let the forest stand! I saw the fences half consumed, their ends lost in the middle of the prairie, and some worldly miser with a surveyor looking after his bounds, while heaven had taken place around him, and he did not see the angels going to and fro, but was looking for an old post-hole in the midst of paradise. I looked again, and saw him standing in the middle of a boggy Stygian fen, surrounded by devils, and he had found his bounds without a doubt, three little stones, where a stake had been driven, and looking nearer, I saw that the Prince of Darkness was his surveyor.

I can easily walk ten, fifteen, twenty, any number of miles, commencing at my own door, without going by any house, without crossing a road except where the fox and the mink do: first along by the river, and then the brook, and then the meadow and the woodside. There are square miles in my vicinity which have no inhabitant. From many a hill I can see civilization and the abodes of man afar. The farmers and their works are scarcely more obvious than woodchucks and their burrows. Man and his affairs, church and state and school, trade and commerce, and manufactures and agriculture, even politics, the most alarming of them all,—I am pleased to see how little space they occupy in the landscape. Politics is but a narrow field, and that still narrower highway yonder leads to it. I sometimes direct the traveler thither. If you would go to the political world, follow the great road,—follow that market-man, keep his dust in your eyes, and it will lead you straight to it; for it, too, has its place merely, and does not occupy all space. I pass from it as from a bean-field into the forest, and it is forgotten. In one half-hour I can walk off to some portion of the earth's surface where a man does not stand from one year's end to another, and there, consequently, politics are not, for they are but as the cigar-smoke of a man.

. . .

Some do not walk at all; others walk in the highways; a few walk across lots. Roads are made for horses and men of business. I do not travel in them much, comparatively, because I am not in a hurry to get to any tavern or grocery or livery-stable or depot to which they lead. I am a good horse to travel, but not from choice a roadster. The landscape-painter uses the figures of men to mark a road. He would not make that use of my figure. I walk out into a nature such as the old prophets and poets, Menu, Moses, Homer, Chaucer, walked in. You may name it America, but it is not America; neither Americus Vespucius, nor Columbus, nor the rest were the discoverers of it. There is a truer account of it in mythology than in any history of America, so called, that I have seen.

. . .

At present, in this vicinity, the best part of the land is not private property; the landscape is not owned, and the walker enjoys comparative freedom. But possibly the day will come when it will be partitioned off into so-called pleasure-grounds, in which a few will take a narrow and exclusive pleasure only,—when fences shall be multiplied, and man-traps and other engines invented to confine men to the *public* road, and walking over the surface of God's earth shall be construed to mean trespassing on some gentleman's grounds. To enjoy a thing exclusively is commonly to exclude yourself from the true enjoyment of it. Let us improve our opportunities, then, before the evil days come.

What is it that makes it so hard sometimes to determine whither we will walk? I believe that there is a subtle magnetism in Nature, which, if we unconsciously yield to it, will direct us aright. It is not indifferent to us which way we walk. There is a right way; but we are very liable from heedlessness and stupidity to take the wrong one. We would fain take that walk, never yet taken by us through this actual world, which is perfectly symbolical of the path which we love to travel in the interior and ideal world; and sometimes, no doubt, we find it difficult to choose our direction, because it does not yet exist distinctly in our idea.

When I go out of the house for a walk, uncertain as yet whither I will bend my steps, and submit myself to my instinct to decide for me, I find, strange and whimsical as it may seem, that I finally and inevitably settle southwest, toward some particular wood or meadow or deserted pasture or hill in that direction. My needle is slow to settle,—varies a few degrees, and does not always point due southwest, it is true, and it has good authority for this variation, but it always settles between west and south-southwest. The future lies that way to me, and the earth seems more unexhausted and richer on that side. The outline which would bound my walks would be, not a circle, but a parabola, or rather like one of those cometary orbits which have been thought to be non-returning curves, in this case opening westward, in which my house occupies the place of the sun. I turn round and round irresolute sometimes for a quarter of an hour, until I decide, for a thousandth time, that I will walk into the southwest or west. Eastward I go only by force; but westward I go free. Thither no business leads me. It is hard for me to believe that I shall find fair landscapes or sufficient wildness and freedom behind the eastern horizon. I am not excited by the prospect of a walk thither; but I believe that the forest which I see in the western horizon stretches uninterruptedly toward the setting sun, and there are no towns nor cities in it of enough consequence to disturb me. Let me live where I will, on this side is the city, on that the wilderness, and ever I am leaving the city more and more, and withdrawing into the wilderness. I should not lay so much stress on this fact, if I did not believe that something like this is the prevailing tendency of my countrymen. I must walk toward Oregon, and not toward Europe. And that way the nation is moving, and I may say that mankind progress from east to west. Within a few years we have witnessed the phenomenon of a southeastward migration, in the settlement of Australia; but this affects us as a retrograde movement, and, judging from the moral and physical character of the first generation of Australians, has not yet proved a successful experiment. The eastern Tartars think that there is nothing west beyond Thibet. "The world ends there," say they; "beyond there is nothing but a shoreless sea." It is unmitigated East where they live.

We go eastward to realize history and study the works of art and literature, retracing the steps of the race; we go westward as into the future, with a spirit of enterprise and adventure. The Atlantic is a Lethean stream, in our passage over which we have had an opportunity to forget the Old World and its institutions. If we do not succeed this time, there is perhaps one more chance for the race left before it arrives on the banks of the Styx; and that is in the Lethe of the Pacific, which is three times as wide.

. . .

Every sunset which I witness inspires me with the desire to go to a West as distant and as fair as that into which the sun goes down. He appears to migrate westward daily, and tempt us to follow him. He is the Great Western Pioneer whom the nations follow. We dream all night of those mountain-ridges in the horizon, though they may be of vapor only, which were last gilded by his rays. The island of Atlantis, and the islands and gardens of the Hesperides, a sort of terrestrial paradise, appear to have been the Great West of the ancients, enveloped in mystery and poetry. Who has not seen in imagination, when looking into the sunset sky, the gardens of the Hesperides, and the foundation of all those fables?

Columbus felt the westward tendency more strongly than any before. He obeyed it, and found a New World for Castile and Leon. The herd of men in those days scented fresh pastures from afar.

> "And now the sun had stretched out all the hills,
> And now was dropped into the western bay;
> At last *he* rose, and twitched his mantle blue;
> To-morrow to fresh woods and pastures new."

Where on the globe can there be found an area of equal extent with that occupied by the bulk of our States, so fertile and so rich and varied in its productions, and at the same time so habitable by the European, as this is? Michaux, who knew but part of them, says that "the species of large trees are much more numerous in North America than in Europe; in the United States there are more than one hundred and forty species that exceed thirty feet in height; in France there are but thirty that attain this size." Later botanists more than confirm his observations. Humboldt came to America to realize his youthful dreams of a tropical vegetation, and he beheld it in its greatest perfection in the primitive forests of the Amazon, the most gigantic wilderness on the earth, which he has so eloquently described. The geographer Guyot, himself a European, goes farther,—farther than I am ready to follow him; yet not when he says: "As the plant is made for the animal, as the vegetable world is made for the animal world, America is made for the man of the Old World. . . . The man of the Old World sets out upon his way. Leaving the highlands of Asia, he descends from station to station towards Europe. Each of his steps is marked by a new civilization superior to the preceding, by a greater power of development. Arrived at the Atlantic, he pauses on the shore of this unknown ocean, the bounds of which he knows not, and turns upon his footprints for an instant." When he has exhausted the rich soil of Europe, and reinvigorated himself, "then recommences his adventurous career westward as in the earliest ages." So far Guyot.

From this western impulse coming in contact with the barrier of the Atlantic sprang the commerce and enterprise of modern times. . . .

. . . If the moon looks larger here than in Europe, probably the sun looks larger also. If the heavens of America appear infinitely higher, and the stars brighter, I trust that these facts are symbolical of the height to which the philosophy and poetry and religion of her inhabitants may one day soar. At length, perchance, the immaterial heaven will appear as much higher to the American mind, and the intimations that star it as much brighter. For I believe that climate does thus react on man,—as there is something in the mountain air that feeds the spirit and inspires. Will not man grow to greater perfection intellectually as well as physically under these influences? Or is it unimportant how many foggy days there are in his life? I trust that we shall be more imaginative, that our thoughts will be clearer, fresher, and more ethereal, as our sky,—our understanding more comprehensive and broader, like our plains,—our intellect generally on a grander scale, like our thunder and lightning, our rivers and mountains and forests,—and our hearts shall even correspond in breadth and depth and grandeur to our inland seas. Perchance there will appear to the traveler something, he knows not what, of *laeta* and *glabra*, of joyous and serene, in our very faces. Else to what end does the world go on, and why was America discovered?

To Americans I hardly need to say,—

"Westward the star of empire takes its way."

As a true patriot, I should be ashamed to think that Adam in paradise was more favorably situated on the whole than the backwoodsman in this country.

. . .

Some months ago I went to see a panorama of the Rhine. It was like a dream of the Middle Ages. I floated down its historic stream in something more than imagination, under bridges built by the Romans, and repaired by later heroes, past cities and castles whose very names were music to my ears, and each of which was the subject of a legend. There were Ehrenbreitstein and Rolandseck and Coblentz, which I knew only in history. They were ruins that interested me chiefly. There seemed to come up from its waters and its vine-clad hills and valleys a hushed music as of Crusaders departing for the Holy Land. I floated along under the spell of enchantment, as if I had been transported to an heroic age, and breathed an atmosphere of chivalry.

Soon after, I went to see a panorama of the Mississippi, and as I worked my way up the river in the light of to-day, and saw the steamboats wooding up, counted the rising cities, gazed on the fresh ruins of Nauvoo, beheld the Indians moving west across the stream, and, as before I had looked up the Moselle, now looked up the Ohio and the Missouri and heard the legends of Dubuque and of Wenona's Cliff,—still thinking more of the future than of the past or present,—I saw that this was a Rhine stream of a different kind; that the foundations of castles were yet to be laid, and the famous bridges were yet to be thrown over the river; and I felt that *this was the heroic age itself*, though we know it not, for the hero is commonly the simplest and obscurest of men.

The West of which I speak is but another name for the Wild; and what I have been preparing to say is, that in Wildness is the preservation of the World. Every tree sends its fibres forth in search of the Wild. The cities import it at any price. Men plow and sail for it. From the forest and wilderness come the tonics and barks which brace mankind. Our ancestors were savages. The story of Romulus and Remus being suckled by a wolf is not a meaningless fable. The founders of every state which has risen to eminence have drawn their nourishment and vigor from a similar wild source. It was because the children of the Empire were not suckled by the wolf that they were conquered and displaced by the children of the northern forests who were.

I believe in the forest, and in the meadow, and in the night in which the corn grows. We require an infusion of hemlock spruce or arbor-vitæ in our tea. There is a difference between eating and drinking for strength and from mere gluttony. The Hottentots eagerly devour the marrow of the koodoo and other antelopes raw, as a matter of course. Some of our northern Indians eat raw the marrow of the Arctic reindeer, as well as various other parts, including the summits of the antlers, as long as they are soft. And herein, perchance, they have stolen a march on the cooks of Paris. They get what usually goes to feed the fire. This is probably better than stall-fed beef and slaughter-house pork to make a man of. Give me a wildness whose glance no civilization can endure,— as if we lived on the marrow of koodoos devoured raw. . . .

. . . Life consists with wildness. The most alive is the wildest. Not yet subdued to man, its presence refreshes him. One who pressed forward incessantly and never rested from his labors, who grew fast and made infinite demands on life, would always find himself in a new country or wilderness, and surrounded by the raw material of life. He would be climbing over the prostrate stems of primitive forest-trees.

Hope and the future for me are not in lawns and cultivated fields, not in towns and cities, but in the impervious and quaking swamps. When, formerly, I have analyzed my partiality for some farm which I had contemplated purchasing, I have frequently found that I was attracted solely by a few square rods of impermeable and unfathomable bog,—a natural sink in one corner of it. That was the jewel which dazzled me. I derive more of my subsistence from the swamps which surround my native town than from the cultivated gardens in the village. . . .

Yes, though you may think me perverse, if it were proposed to me to dwell in the neighborhood of the most beautiful garden that ever human art contrived, or else of a Dismal Swamp, I should certainly decide for the swamp. How vain, then, have been all your labors, citizens, for me!

My spirits infallibly rise in proportion to the outward dreariness. Give me the ocean, the desert, or the wilderness! In the desert, pure air and solitude compensate for want of moisture and fertility. The traveler Burton says of it: "Your *morale* improves; you become frank and cordial, hospitable and singleminded. . . . In the desert, spirituous liquors excite only disgust. There is a keen enjoyment in a mere animal existence." They who have been traveling long on the steppes of Tartary say, "On reëntering cultivated lands, the agitation, perplexity, and turmoil of civilization oppressed and suffocated us; the air seemed to fail us, and we felt every moment as if about to die of asphyxia." When I would recreate myself, I seek the darkest wood, the thickest and most interminable and, to the citizen, most dismal, swamp. I enter a swamp as a sacred place, a *sanctum sanctorum*. There is the strength, the marrow, of Nature. The wildwood covers the virgin mould, and the same soil is good for men and for trees. A man's health requires as many acres of meadow to his prospect as his farm does loads of muck. There are the strong meats on which he feeds. A town is saved, not more by the righteous men in it than by the woods and swamps that surround it. A township where one primitive forest waves above while another primitive forest rots below,—such a town is fitted to raise not only corn and potatoes, but poets and philosophers for the coming ages. In such a soil grew Homer and Confucius and the rest, and out of such a wilderness comes the Reformer eating locusts and wild honey.

To preserve wild animals implies generally the creation of a forest for them to dwell in or resort to. So it is with man. A hundred years ago they sold bark in our streets peeled from our own woods. In the very aspect of those primitive and rugged trees there was, methinks, a tanning principle which hardened and consolidated the fibres of men's thoughts. Ah! already I shudder for these comparatively degenerate days of my native village, when you cannot collect a load of bark of good thickness, and we no longer produce tar and turpentine.

The civilized nations—Greece, Rome, England—have been sustained by the primitive forests which anciently rotted where they stand. They survive as long as the soil is not exhausted. Alas for human culture! little is to be expected of a nation, when the vegetable mould is exhausted, and it is compelled to make manure of the bones of its fathers. There the poet sustains himself merely by his own superfluous fat, and the philosopher comes down on his marrow-bones.

It is said to be the task of the American "to work the virgin soil," and that "agriculture here already assumes proportions unknown everywhere else." I think that the farmer displaces the Indian even because he redeems the meadow, and so makes himself stronger and in some respects more natural. I was surveying for a man the other day a single straight line one hundred and thirty-two rods long, through a swamp at whose entrance might have been written the words which Dante read over the entrance to the infernal regions, "Leave all hope, ye that enter,"—that is, of ever getting out again; where at one time I saw my employer actually up to his neck and swimming for his life in his property, though it was still winter. He had another similar swamp which I could not survey at all, because it was completely under water, and nevertheless, with regard to a third swamp, which I did *survey* from a distance, he remarked to me, true to his instincts, that he would not part with it for any consideration, on account of the mud which it contained. And that man intends to put a girdling ditch round the whole in the course of forty months, and so redeem it by the magic of his spade. I refer to him only as the type of a class.

. . .

In literature it is only the wild that attracts us. Dullness is but another name for tameness. It is the uncivilized free and wild thinking in Hamlet and the Iliad, in all the scriptures and mythologies, not learned in the schools, that delights us. As the wild duck is more swift and beautiful than the tame, so is the wild—the mallard—thought, which 'mid falling dews wings its way above the fens. A truly good book is something as natural, and as unexpectedly and unaccountably fair and perfect, as a wild-flower discovered on the prairies of the West or in the jungles of the East. Genius is a light which makes the darkness visible, like the lightning's flash, which perchance shatters the temple of knowledge itself,—and not a taper lighted at the hearth-stone of the race, which pales before the light of common day.

English literature, from the days of the minstrels to the Lake Poets,— Chaucer and Spenser and Milton, and even Shakespeare, included,—breathes no quite fresh and, in this sense, wild strain. It is an essentially tame and civilized literature, reflecting Greece and Rome. Her wilderness is a greenwood, her wild man a Robin Hood. There is plenty of genial love of Nature, but not so much of Nature herself. Her chronicles inform us when her wild animals, but not when the wild man in her, became extinct.

The science of Humboldt is one thing, poetry is another thing. The poet to-day, notwithstanding all the discoveries of science, and the accumulated learning of mankind, enjoys no advantage over Homer.

Where is the literature which gives expression to Nature? He would be a poet who could impress the winds and streams into his service, to speak for him; who nailed words to their primitive senses, as farmers drive down stakes in the spring, which the frost has heaved; who derived his words as often as he used them,—transplanted them to his page with earth adhering to their roots; whose words were so true and fresh and natural that they would appear to expand like the buds at the approach of spring, though they lay half smothered between two musty leaves in a library,—aye, to bloom and bear fruit there, after their kind, annually, for the faithful reader, in sympathy with surrounding Nature.

I do not know of any poetry to quote which adequately expresses this yearning for the Wild. Approached from this side, the best poetry is tame. I do not know where to find in any literature, ancient or modern, any account which contents me of that Nature with which even I am acquainted. You will perceive that I demand something which no Augustan nor Elizabethan age, which no *culture*, in short, can give. Mythology comes nearer to it than anything. How much more fertile a Nature, at least, has Grecian mythology its root in than English literature! Mythology is the crop which the Old World bore before its soil was exhausted, before the fancy and imagination were affected with blight; and which it still bears, wherever its pristine vigor is unabated. All other literatures endure only as the elms which overshadow our houses; but this is like the great dragon-tree of the Western Isles, as old as mankind, and, whether that does or not, will endure as long; for the decay of other literatures makes the soil in which it thrives.

The West is preparing to add its fables to those of the East. The valleys of the Ganges, the Nile, and the Rhine having yielded their crop, it remains to be seen what the valleys of the Amazon, the Plate, the Orinoco, the St. Lawrence, and the Mississippi will produce. Perchance, when, in the course of ages, American liberty has become a fiction of the past,—as it is to some extent a fiction of the present,—the poets of the world will be inspired by American mythology.

The wildest dreams of wild men, even, are not the less true, though they may not recommend themselves to the sense which is most common among Englishmen and Americans to-day. It is not every truth that recommends itself to the common sense. Nature has a place for the wild clematis as well as for the cabbage. Some expressions of truth are reminiscent,—others merely *sensible*, as the phrase is,—others prophetic. Some forms of disease, even, may prophesy forms of health. The geologist has discovered that the figures of serpents, griffins, flying dragons, and other fanciful embellishments of heraldry, have their prototypes in the forms of fossil species which were extinct before man was created, and hence "indicate a faint and shadowy knowledge of a previous state of organic existence." The Hindoos dreamed that the earth rested on an elephant, and the elephant on a tortoise, and the tortoise on a serpent; and though it may be an unimportant coincidence, it will not be out of place here to state, that a fossil tortoise has lately been discovered in Asia large enough to support an elephant. I confess that I am partial to these wild fancies, which transcend the order of time and development. They are the sublimest recreation of the intellect. The partridge loves peas, but not those that go with her into the pot.

In short, all good things are wild and free. There is something in a strain of music, whether produced by an instrument or by the human voice,—take the sound of a bugle in a summer night, for instance,—which by its wildness, to speak without satire, reminds me of the cries emitted by wild beasts in their native forests. It is so much of their wildness as I can understand. Give me for my friends and neighbors wild men, not tame ones. The wildness of the savage is but a faint symbol of the awful ferity with which good men and lovers meet.

. . .

Here is this vast, savage, howling mother of ours, Nature, lying all around, with such beauty, and such affection for her children, as the leopard; and yet we are so early weaned from her breast to society, to that culture which is exclusively an interaction of man on man,—a sort of breeding in and in, which produces at most a merely English nobility, a civilization destined to have a speedy limit.

In society, in the best institutions of men, it is easy to detect a certain precocity. When we should still be growing children, we are already little men. Give me a culture which imports much muck from the meadows, and deepens the soil,—not that which trusts to heating manures, and improved implements and modes of culture only!

. . .

We have heard of a Society for the Diffusion of Useful Knowledge. It is said that knowledge is power, and the like. Methinks there is equal need of a Society for the Diffusion of Useful Ignorance, what we will call Beautiful Knowledge, a knowledge useful in a higher sense: for what is most of our boasted so-called knowledge but a conceit that we know something, which robs us of the advantage of our actual ignorance? What we call knowledge is often our positive ignorance; ignorance our negative knowledge. By long years of patient industry and reading of the newspapers,—for what are the libraries of science but files of newspapers?—a man accumulates a myriad facts, lays them up in his memory, and then when in some spring of his life he saunters abroad into the Great Fields of thought, he, as it were, goes to grass like a horse and leaves all his harness behind in the stable. I would say to the Society for the Diffusion of Useful Knowledge, sometimes,—Go to grass. You have eaten hay long enough. The spring has come with its green crop. The very cows are driven to their country pastures before the end of May; though I have heard of one unnatural farmer who kept his cow in the barn and fed her on hay all the year round. So, frequently, the Society for the Diffusion of Useful Knowledge treats its cattle.

A man's ignorance sometimes is not only useful, but beautiful,—while his knowledge, so called, is oftentimes worse than useless, besides being ugly. Which is the best man to deal with,—he who knows nothing about a subject, and, what is extremely rare, knows that he knows nothing, or he who really knows something about it, but thinks that he knows all?

My desire for knowledge is intermittent, but my desire to bathe my head in atmospheres unknown to my feet is perennial and constant. The highest that we can attain to is not Knowledge, but Sympathy with Intelligence. I do not know that this higher knowledge amounts to anything more definite than a novel and grand surprise on a sudden revelation of the insufficiency of all that we called Knowledge before,—a discovery that there are more things in heaven and earth than are dreamed of in our philosophy. It is the lighting up of the mist by the sun. Man cannot *know* in any higher sense than this, any more than he can look serenely and with impunity in the face of the sun: Ὡς τὶ νοῶν, οὐ κεῖνον νοήσεις, "You will not perceive that, as perceiving a particular thing," say the Chaldean Oracles.

There is something servile in the habit of seeking after a law which we may obey. We may study the laws of matter at and for our convenience, but a successful life knows no law. It is an unfortunate discovery certainly, that of a law which binds us where we did not know before that we were bound. Live free, child of the mist,—and with respect to knowledge we are all children of the mist. The man who takes the liberty to live is superior to all the laws, by virtue of his relation to the lawmaker. "That is active duty," says the Vishnu Purana, "which is not for our bondage; that is knowledge which is for our liberation: all other duty is good only unto weariness; all other knowledge is only the cleverness of an artist."

. . .

While almost all men feel an attraction drawing them to society, few are attracted strongly to Nature. In their reaction to Nature men appear to me for the most part, notwithstanding their arts, lower than the animals. It is not often a beautiful relation, as in the case of the animals. How little appreciation of the beauty of the landscape there is among us! We have to be told that the Greeks called the world Κόσμος, Beauty, or Order, but we do not see clearly why they did so, and we esteem it at best only a curious philological fact.

For my part, I feel that with regard to Nature I live a sort of border life, on the confines of a world into which I make occasional and transient forays only, and my patriotism and allegiance to the state into whose territories I seem to retreat are those of a moss-trooper. Unto a life which I call natural I would gladly follow even a will-o'-the-wisp through bogs and sloughs unimaginable, but no moon nor firefly has shown me the causeway to it. Nature is a personality so vast and universal that we have never seen one of her features. The walker in the familiar fields which stretch around my native town sometimes finds himself in another land than is described in their owners' deeds, as it were in some faraway field on the confines of the actual Concord, where her jurisdiction ceases, and the idea which the word Concord suggests ceases to be suggested. These farms which I have myself surveyed, these bounds which I have set up, appear dimly still as through a mist; but they have no chemistry to fix them; they fade from the surface of the glass, and the picture which the painter painted stands out dimly from beneath. The world with which we are commonly acquainted leaves no trace, and it will have no anniversary.

I took a walk on Spaulding's Farm the other afternoon. I saw the setting sun lighting up the opposite side of a stately pine wood. Its golden rays straggled into the aisles of the wood as into some noble hall. I was impressed as if some ancient and altogether admirable and shining family had settled there in that part of the land called Concord, unknown to me,—to whom the sun was servant,—who had not gone into society in the village,—who had not been called on. I saw their park, their pleasure-ground, beyond through the wood, in Spaulding's cranberry-meadow. The pines furnished them with gables as they grew. Their house was not obvious to vision; the trees grew through it. I do not know whether I heard the sounds of a suppressed hilarity or not. They seemed to recline on the sunbeams. They have sons and daughters. They are quite well. The farmer's cart-path, which leads directly through their hall, does not in the least put them out, as the muddy bottom of a pool is sometimes seen through the reflected skies. They never heard of Spaulding, and do not know that he is their neighbor,—notwithstanding I heard him whistle as he drove his team through the house. Nothing can equal the serenity of their lives. Their coat-of-arms is simply a lichen. I saw it painted on the pines and oaks. Their attics were in the tops of the trees. They are of no politics. There was no noise of labor. I did not perceive that they were weaving or spinning. Yet I did detect, when the wind lulled and hearing was done away, the finest imaginable sweet musical hum,—as of a distant hive in May,—which perchance was the sound of their thinking. They had no idle thoughts, and no one without could see their work, for their industry was not as in knots and excrescences embayed.

But I find it difficult to remember them. They fade irrevocably out of my mind even now while I speak, and endeavor to recall them and recollect myself. It is only after a long and serious effort to recollect my best thoughts that I become again aware of their cohabitancy. If it were not for such families as this, I think I should move out of Concord.

. . .

We hug the earth,—how rarely we mount! Methinks we might elevate ourselves a little more. We might climb a tree, at least. I found my account in climbing a tree once. It was a tall white pine, on the top of a hill; and though I got well pitched, I was well paid for it, for I discovered new mountains in the horizon which I had never seen before,—so much more of the earth and the heavens. I might have walked about the foot of the tree for threescore years and ten, and yet I certainly should never have seen them. But, above all, I discovered around me,—it was near the end of June,—on the ends of the topmost branches only, a few minute and delicate red cone-like blossoms, the fertile flower of the white pine looking heavenward. I carried straightway to the village the topmost spire, and showed it to stranger jurymen who walked the streets,—for it was court week,—and to farmers and lumber-dealers and woodchoppers and hunters, and not one had ever seen the like before, but they wondered as at a star dropped down. Tell of ancient architects finishing their works on the tops of columns as perfectly as on the lower and more visible parts! Nature has from the first expanded the minute blossoms of the forest only toward the heavens, above men's heads and unobserved by them. We see only the flowers that are under our feet in the meadows. The pines have developed their delicate blossoms on the highest twigs of the wood every summer for ages, as well over the heads of Nature's red children as of her white ones; yet scarcely a farmer or hunter in the land has ever seen them.

Above all, we cannot afford not to live in the present. He is blessed over all mortals who loses no moment of the passing life in remembering the past. Unless our philosophy hears the cock crow in every barn-yard within our horizon, it is belated. That sound commonly reminds us that we are growing rusty and antique in our employments and habits of thought. His philosophy comes down to a more recent time than ours. There is something suggested by it that is a newer testament,—the gospel according to this moment. He has not fallen astern; he has got up early and kept up early, and to be where he is is to be in season, in the foremost rank of time. It is an expression of the health and soundness of Nature, a brag for all the world,—healthiness as of a spring burst forth, a new fountain of the Muses, to celebrate this last instant of time. Where he lives no fugitive slave laws are passed. Who has not betrayed his master many times since last he heard that note?

The merit of this bird's strain is in its freedom from all plaintiveness. The singer can easily move us to tears or to laughter, but where is he who can excite in us a pure morning joy? When, in doleful dumps, breaking the awful stillness of our wooden sidewalk on a Sunday, or, perchance, a watcher in the house of mourning, I hear a cockerel crow far or near, I think to myself, "There is one of us well, at any rate,"—and with a sudden gush return to my senses.

We had a remarkable sunset one day last November. I was walking in a meadow, the source of a small brook, when the sun at last, just before setting, after a cold, gray day, reached a clear stratum in the horizon, and the softest, brightest morning sunlight fell on the dry grass and on the stems of the trees in the opposite horizon and on the leaves of the shrub oaks on the hillside, while our shadows stretched long over the meadow eastward, as if we were the only motes in its beams. It was such a light as we could not have imagined a moment before, and the air also was so warm and serene that nothing was wanting to make a paradise of that meadow. When we reflected that this was not a solitary phenomenon, never to happen again, but that it would happen forever and ever, an infinite number of evenings, and cheer and reassure the latest child that walked there, it was more glorious still.

The sun sets on some retired meadow, where no house is visible, with all the glory and splendor that it lavishes on cities, and perchance as it has never set before,—where there is but a solitary marsh hawk to have his wings gilded by it, or only a musquash looks out from his cabin, and there is some little black-veined brook in the midst of the marsh, just beginning to meander, winding slowly round a decaying stump. We walked in so pure and bright a light, gilding the withered grass and leaves, so softly and serenely bright, I thought I had never bathed in such golden flood, without a ripple or a murmur to it. The west side of every wood and rising ground gleamed like the boundary of Elysium, and the sun on our backs seemed like a gentle herdsman driving us home at evening.

So we saunter toward the Holy Land, till one day the sun shall shine more brightly than ever he has done, shall perchance shine into our minds and hearts, and light up our whole lives with a great awakening light, as warm and serene and golden as on a bankside in autumn.

3–19
Rachel Parker Plummer (1819–1839)

RACHEL PARKER PLUMMER (1819–1839) was the daughter of Baptist pioneer minister James W. Parker. Rachel and Cynthia Ann Parker were taken captive by a large band of Comanche and Caddo Indians in the 1836 attack on Fort Parker, near present-day Mexia, Texas. Plummer's *Narrative* (1838) was the first captivity narrative to be published in Texas. It chronicles her almost two-year ordeal, as she traversed thousands of miles and endured the loss of children, beatings, and enslavement. Plummer's narrative is a powerful—and sometimes disturbing—example of an important American genre of literature that adds to Mary Rowlandson's and others with starkly graphic depictions of the West. A contrast to Plummer's narrative is provided later in the reader, with Sarah Winnemucca's *Life among the Piutes.*

≈≈ ≈≈ ≈≈

From *Narrative of the Capture and Subsequent Sufferings of Mrs. Rachel Plummer* (1838)

Preface

In my preface to the first edition of this narrative, I promised a second edition, should the first meet with public patronage. The patronage extended to it has far exceeded my most sanguine expectations, for which I embrace the present opportunity to return my most sincere thanks to my friends and the public in general. In redemption of my promise, I present this second edition, revised and corrected, confidently anticipating the favorable consideration and renewed patronage of a generous public. . . .

Rachel Plummer

City of Houston, Texas, Dec. 3, 1839

Narrative

On the 19th of May, 1836, I was living in Fort Parker, on the head waters of the river Favasott.* My father, (James W. Parker,) and my husband and brother-in-law were cultivating my father's farm, which was about a mile from the fort. In the morning, say 9 o'clock, my father, husband, brother-in-law, and brother, went to the farm to work. I do not think they had left the fort more than an hour before some one of the fort cried out, "Indians!" The inmates of the fort had retired to their farms in the neighborhood, and there were only six men in it, viz: my grandfather, Elder John Parker, my two uncles, Benjamin and Silas Parker, Samuel Frost and his son Robert, and Frost's son-in-law, G.E. Dwight. All appeared in a state of confusion, for the Indians (numbering something not far from eight hundred) had raised a white flag.

On the first sight of the Indians, my sister (Mrs. Nixon,) started to alarm my father and his company at the farm, whilst the Indians were yet more than a quarter of a mile from the fort, and I saw her no more. I was in the act of starting to the farm, but I knew I was not able to take my little son, (James Pratt Plummer.) The women were all soon gone from the fort, whither I did not know; but I expected towards the farm. My old grandfather and grandmother, and several others, started through the farm, which was immediately adjoining the fort. Dwight started with his family and Mrs. Frost and her little children. As he started, uncle Silas said, "Good Lord, Dwight, you are not going to run?" He said, "No, I am only going to try to hide the women and children in the woods." Uncle said, "Stand and fight like a man, and if we have to die we will sell our lives as dearly as we can."

The Indians halted; and two Indians came up to the fort to inform the inmates that they were friendly, and had come for the purpose of making a treaty with the Americans. This instantly threw the people off their guard, and uncle Benjamin went to the Indians, who had now got within a few hundred yards of the fort. In a few minutes he returned, and told Frost and his son and uncle Silas that he believed the Indians intended to fight, and told them to put every

---

*   [Navasota—*E.J.D. and J.B.F.*]

thing in the best order for defence. He said he would go back to the Indians and see if the fight could be avoided. Uncle Silas told him not to go, but to try to defend the place as well as they could; but he started off again to the Indians, and appeared to pay but little attention to what Silas said. Uncle Silas said, "I know they will kill Benjamin"; and said to me, "Do you stand here and watch the Indians' motions until I run into my house"—I think he said for his shot-pouch. I suppose he had got a wrong shot-pouch as he had four or five rifles. When uncle Benjamin reached the body of Indians they turned to the right and left and surrounded him. I was now satisfied they intended killing him. I took up my little James Pratt, and thought I would try to make my escape. As I ran across the fort, I met Silas returning to the place where he left me. He asked me if they had killed Benjamin. I told him, "No; but they have surrounded him." He said, "I know they will kill him, but I will be good for one of them at least." These were the last words I heard him utter.

I ran out of the fort, and passing the corner I saw the Indians drive their spears into Benjamin. The work of death had already commenced. I shall not attempt to describe their terrific yells, their united voices that seemed to reach the very skies, whilst they were dealing death to the inmates of the fort. It can scarcely be comprehended in the wide field of imagination. I know it is utterly impossible for me to give every particular in detail, for I was much alarmed.

I tried to make my escape, but alas, alas, it was too late, as a party of the Indians had got ahead of me. Oh! how vain were my feeble efforts to try to run to save myself and little James Pratt. A large sulky looking Indian picked up a hoe and knocked me down. I well recollect of their taking my child out of my arms, but whether they hit me any more I do not know, for I swooned away. The first I recollect, they were dragging me along by the hair. I made several unsuccessful attempts to raise to my feet before I could do it. As they took me past the fort, I heard an awful screaming near the place where they had first seized me.* I heard some shots. I then heard uncle Silas shout a triumphant huzza! I did, for one moment, hope the men had gathered from the neighboring farms, and might release me.

I was soon dragged to the main body of the Indians, where they had killed uncle Benjamin. His face was much mutilated, and many arrows were sticking in his body. As the savages passed by, they thrust their spears through him. I was covered with blood, for my wound was bleeding freely. I looked for my child but could not see him, and was convinced they had killed him, and every moment expected to share the same fate myself. At length I saw him. An

---

* I think Uncle Silas was trying to release me, and in doing this he lost his life; but not until he had killed four Indians.

Indian had him on his horse; he was calling, mother, oh, mother! He was just able to lisp the name of mother, being only about 18 months old. There were two Cumanche women with them, [their battles are always brought on by a woman,] one of whom came to me and struck me several times with a whip. I suppose it was to make me quit crying.

I now expected my father and husband, and all the rest of the men were killed. I soon saw a party of the Indians bringing my aunt Elizabeth Kellogg and uncle Silas' two oldest children, Cynthia Ann, and John; also some bloody scalps; among them I could distinguish that of my old grandfather by the grey hairs, but could not discriminate the balance.

Most of the Indians were engaged in plundering the fort. They cut open our bed ticks and threw the feathers in the air, which was literally thick with them. They brought out a great number of my father's books and medicines. Some of the books were torn up, and most of the bottles of medicine were broken; though they took on some for several days.[*]

I had but few minutes to reflect, for they soon started back the same way they came up. As I was leaving, I looked back at the place where I was one hour before, happy and free, and now in the hands of a ruthless, savage enemy.

They killed a great many of our cattle as they went along. They soon convinced me that I had no time to reflect upon the past, for they commenced whipping and beating me with clubs, &c., so that my flesh was never well from bruises and wounds during my captivity. To undertake to narrate their barbarous treatment would only add to my present distress, for it is with feelings of the deepest mortification that I think of it, much less to speak or write of it; for while I record this painful part of my narrative, I can almost feel the same heart-rending pains of body and mind that I then endured, my very soul becomes sick at the dreadful thought.

About midnight they stopped. They now tied a plaited thong around my arms, and drew my hands behind me. They tied them so tight that the scars can be easily seen to this day. They then tied a similar thong around my ankles, and drew my feet and hands together. They now turned me on my face and I was unable to turn over, when they commenced beating me over the head with their bows, and it was with great difficulty I could keep from smothering

---

[*] Among them was a bottle of pulverized arsenic, which the Indians mistook for a kind of white paint, with which they painted their faces and bodies all over, after dissolving it in their saliva. The bottle was brought to me to tell them what it was. I did not do it, though I knew it, for the bottle was labelled. Four of the Indians painted themselves with it as above described, and it did not fail to kill them.

in my blood; for the wound they gave me with the hoe, and many others, were bleeding freely.

I suppose it was to add to my misery that they brought my little James Pratt so near me that I could hear him cry. He would call for mother; and often was his voice weakened by the blows they would give him. I could hear the blows. I could hear his cries; but oh, alas, could offer him no relief. The rest of the prisoners were brought near me, but we were not allowed to speak one word together. My aunt called me once, and I answered her; but, indeed, I thought she would never call or I answer again, for they jumped with their feet upon us, which nearly took our lives. Often did the children cry, but were soon hushed by such blows that I had no idea they could survive. Then commenced screaming and dancing around the scalps; kicking and stamping the prisoners.

I now ask you, my christian reader, to pause. You who are living secure from danger—you who have read the sacred scriptures of truth—who have been raised in a land boasting of christian philanthropy—I say, I now ask you to form some idea of what my feelings were. Such dreadful savage yelling! enough to terrify the bravest hearts. Bleeding and weltering in my blood, and far worse, to think of my little darling Pratt! Will this scene ever be effaced from my memory? Not until my spirit is called to leave this tenement of clay; and may God grant me a heart to pray for them, for "they know not what they do."

Next morning, they started in a northern direction. They tied me every night, as before stated, for five nights. During the first five days, I never ate one mouthful of food, and had but a very scanty allowance of water. Notwithstanding my sufferings, I could not but admire the country—being prairie and timber, and very rich. I saw many fine springs. It was some 70 or 80 miles from the fort to the Cross Timbers. This is a range of timber-land from the waters of Arkansas, bearing a south-west direction, crossing the False Ouachita, Red River, the heads of Sabine, Angelina, Natchitoches, Trinity, Brazos, Colorado, &c., going on south-west, quite to the Rio Grande. This range of timber is of an irregular width, say from 5 to 35 miles wide, and is a very diversified country; abounding with small prairies, skirted with timber of various kinds—oak, of every description, ash, elm, hickory, walnut and mulberry. There is more post oak on the uplands than any other kind; and a great deal of this range of timber land is very rough, bushy, abounds with briers, and some of it poor. West, or S.W. of the Brazos, it is very mountainous. As this range of timber reaches the waters of the Rio Grande, (Big River,) it appears to widen out, and is directly adjoining the timber covering the table lands between Austin and Santa Fe. This country, particularly south-west of the Brazos, is a well watered country, and part of it will be densely inhabited. The purest atmosphere I ever breathed was that of these regions.

After we reached the Grand Prairie, we turned more to the east; that is, the party I belonged to. Aunt Elizabeth fell to the Kitchawas, and my nephew and niece to another portion of the Cumanches.

I must again call my reader to bear with me in rehearsing the continued barbarous treatment of the Indians. My child kept crying, and almost continually calling for "Mother," though I was not allowed even to speak to it. At the time they took off my fetters, they brought my child to me, supposing that I gave suck. As soon as it saw me, it, trembling with weakness, hastened to my embraces. Oh, with what feelings of love and sorrow did I embrace the mutilated body of my darling little James Pratt. I now felt that my case was much bettered, as I thought they would let me have my child; but oh, mistaken, indeed, was I; for as soon as they found that I had weaned him, they, in spite of all my efforts, tore him from my embrace. He reached out his hands towards me, which were covered with blood and cried, "Mother, Mother, oh, Mother!" I looked after him as he was borne from me, and I sobbed aloud. This was the last I ever heard of my little Pratt. Where he is, I know not.

Progressing farther and farther from my home, we crossed Big Red River, the head of Arkansas, and then turned more to the north-west. We now lost sight of timber entirely.

For several hundred miles after we had left the Cross Timber country, and on the Red River, Arkansas, &c., there is a fine country. The timber is scarce and scrubby. Some streams as salt as brine; and others, fine water. The land, in part, is very rich, and game plenty.

We would travel for weeks and not see a riding switch. Buffalo dung is all the fuel. This is gathered into a round pile; and when set on fire, it does very well to cook by, and will keep fire for several days.

In July, and in part of August, we were on the Snow Mountains. There it is perpetual snow; and I suffered more from cold than I ever suffered in my life before. It was very seldom I had any thing to put on my feet, but very little covering for my body. I had to mind the horses every night, and had a certain number of buffalo skins to dress every moon. This kept me employed all the time in day-light; and often would I have to take my buffalo skin with me, to finish it whilst I was minding the horses. My feet would be often frozen, even while I would be dressing skins, and I dared not complain; for my situation still grew more and more difficult.

In October, I gave birth to my second son. As to the months, &c., it was guess work with me, for I had no means of keeping the time. It was an interesting and beautiful babe. I had, as you may suppose, but a very poor chance to comfort myself with any thing suitable to my situation, or that of my little infant. The Indians were not as hostile now as I had feared they would be. I was still fearful they would kill my child; and having now been with them some six months, I had learned their language. I would often expostulate with my mistress* to advise me what to do to save my child; but all in vain. My child was some six or seven weeks old, when I suppose my master thought it too much trouble, as I was not able to go through as much labor as before. One cold morning, five or six large Indians came where I was suckling my infant. As soon as they came in I felt my heart sick; my fears agitated my whole frame to a complete state of convulsion; my body shook with fear indeed. Nor were my fears vain or ill-grounded. One of them caught hold of the child by the throat; and with his whole strength, and like an enraged lion actuated by its devouring nature, held on like the hungry vulture, until my child was to all appearance entirely dead. I exerted my whole feeble strength to relieve it; but the other Indians held me. They, by force, took it from me, and threw it up in the air, and let it fall on the frozen ground, until it was apparently dead.

They gave it back to me. The fountain of tears that had hitherto given vent to my grief, was now dried up. While I gazed upon the bruised cheeks of my darling infant, I discovered some symptoms of returning life. Oh, how vain was my hope that they would let me have it if I could revive it. I washed the blood from its face; and after some time, it began to breathe again; but a more heart-rending scene ensued. As soon as they found it had recovered a little, they again tore it from my embrace and knocked me down. They tied a plat-ted rope round the child's neck, and threw its naked body into the large ledges of prickly pears, which were from eight to twelve feet high. They would then pull it down through the pears. This they repeated several times. One of them then got on a horse, and tying the rope to his saddle, rode round a circuit of a few hundred yards, until my little innocent was not only dead, but literally torn to pieces. I stood horror-struck. One of them then took it up by the leg, brought it to me, and threw it into my lap. But in praise to the Indians, I must say, that they gave me time to dig a hole in the earth and bury it. After having performed this last service to the lifeless remains of my dear babe, I sat me down and gazed with joy on the resting place of my now happy infant; and I could, with old David, say, "You cannot come to me, but I must go to you"; and then, and even now, whilst I record the awful tragedy, I rejoice that it has passed from the sufferings and sorrows of this world. I shall hear its deathly

---

* Having fallen into the hands of an old man that had only his wife and one daughter, who composed his family, I was compelled to reverence both the women as mistresses.

cries no more; and fully and confidently believing, and solely relying on the imputed righteousness of God in Christ Jesus, I feel that my happy babe is now with its kindred spirits in that eternal world of joys. Oh! will my dear Saviour, by his grace, keep me through life's short journey, and bring me to dwell with my happy children in the sweet realms of endless bliss, where I shall meet the whole family of Heaven—those whose names are recorded in the Lamb's Book of Life.

I would have been glad to have had the pleasure of laying my little James Pratt with this my happy infant. I do really believe I could have buried him without shedding a tear; for, indeed, they had ceased to flow in relief of my grief. My heaving bosom could do no more than breathe deep sighs. Parents, you little know what you can bear. Surely, surely, my poor heart must break.

We left this place, as usual, and were again on a prairie. We soon discovered a large lake of water. I was very thirsty; and although we travelled directly towards it, we could never get any nearer to it. It did not appear to be more than forty or fifty steps off, and always kept the same distance. This astonished me beyond measure. Is there any thing like magic in this, said I. I never saw a lake, pond, or river, plainer in my life. My thirst was excessive, and I was panting for a drop of water; but I could get no nearer to it. I found it to be a kind of gas, as I supposed, and I leave the reader to put his own construction upon it. It is, by some, called water gas. It looks just like water, and appears even to show the waves. I have often seen large herds of Buffalo feeding in it. They appeared as if they were wading in the water; and their wakes looked as distinct as in real water.[*]

In those places, the prairies are as level as the surface of a lake, and can better be described by at once imagining yourself looking at a large lake. I have but a faint idea of the cause; but from the number of sea shells, (oysters', &c.,) I have no doubt that this great prairie was once a sea.

I was often on the salt plains. There the salt some little resembles dirty snow on a very cold day, being very light. The wind will blow it for miles. I have seen it in many places half leg deep; whilst other parts of the ground would be naked, owing to the strong winds drifting it.

I was at some of the salt lakes, which are very interesting to the view. Thousands of bushels of salt—yea, millions—resembling ice; a little on the muddy or milky order. It appears that there would not be consumption for

---

[*] This was the mirage, common to large deserts and prairies. Those travellers in the East, who have passed over the deserts of Asia and Africa, make frequent mention of these phenomena.

this immense amount of salt in all the world; for it forms anew when it is removed, so that it is inexhaustible.

These prairies abound with such a number and variety of beasts, that pages could not describe them.

1st. The little prairie dog is as large as a grey squirrel. Some of them are as spotted as a leopard; but they are mostly of a dark color, and live in herds. They burrow in the ground. As a stranger approaches them, they set up a loud barking; but will soon sink down into their holes. They are very fat, and fine to eat.

2d. The prairie fox is a curious animal. It is as tall as a small dog—its body not larger than a grey squirrel, but three times as long. Their legs are remarkably small; being but little larger than a large straw. They can run very fast. Seldom fat.

3d. The rabbit rivals the snow in whiteness, and is as large as a small dog. They are very active, and are delicious to eat. They can run very fast. I have thought they were the most beautiful animal I ever saw.

4th. The mountain sheep are smaller than the common sheep, and have long hair. They will feed on the brink of the steepest precipice, and are very active. They are very plenty about the mountains.

5th. Buffalo, the next largest animal known, except the elephant. Their number no one can tell. They are found in the prairies and seldom in the timber even when there is any. Their flesh is the most delicious of all the beef kind I have seen. I have often seen the ground covered with them as far as the eye could reach.

The Indians shoot them with their arrows from their horses. They kill them very fast, and will even shoot an arrow entirely through one of these large animals.

6th, The Elk, the largest of the deer species, with very large horns, and often more than six feet long. There are but few of them found in the same country with the buffalo; but they range along the Missouri river and in parts of the Rocky Mountains. Their flesh is like venison.

7th. The Antelope. This is, I believe, the fleetest animal in the world. They go in large flocks or herds. They will see the stranger a great way off, will run towards him till they get within twenty or thirty steps, and then the whole herd (perhaps some thousands) will wheel at the same moment, and are soon two or three miles off. They will again approach you, but not quite so near as at first, and then wheel again. They generally make about three or four of these visits, still wheeling from you at a greater distance. They will then leave you. They are much like the goat, and are by some called the wild goat.

8th. There are a great variety of wolves on the prairies: the large grey wolf, the large black wolf, the prairie wolf, and, I believe, the proper jackall. There is a large white wolf which will weigh 300 pounds, has very long hair of silvery white, and is very ferocious. They will kill a buffalo, and will not go out of the way of man or beast.

9th. There are four kinds of bears in the mountains; the white, grisley, red, and black bears. The grisley bear is the largest and most powerful. They will weigh 1200 or 1400 pounds. They cannot climb, but live in the valleys about the mountains. They are very delicious food. The white bear is very ferocious, and will attack either man or beast. They are hard to conquer. The Indians are very fearful of them, and will not attack them; and even if attacked by them, will try to make their escape. They are of a silvery white, and are found along the brows of the Rocky Mountains. They are very fat and delicious food. The common black bear is scarce, as is also the red bear. This last species of bear is alone heard of in the western part of the Rocky Mountains. They are the most beautiful beast I ever saw, being as red as vermillion.

10th. The common deer is in many places very plenty. In the mountains they grow much larger than they do in Texas.

11th. Turkies, on the heads of Columbia river, are very numerous. They do not range on the prairies nor about the Snow mountains.

12th. Wild horses (Mustangs) are very plenty on the prairies. Thousands of the very finest horses, mules, jacks, &c., may be seen in one day. They are very wild. The Indians often take them by running them on their horses and throwing the lasso over their heads. They are easily domesticated.

13th. Man-Tiger. The Indians say that they have found several of them in the mountains. They describe them as being of the feature and make of a man. They are said to walk erect, and are eight or nine feet high. Instead of hands, they have huge paws and long claws, with which they can easily tear a buffalo to pieces. The Indians are very shy of them, and whilst in the mountains, will never separate. They also assert that there is a species of human beings that live in the caves in the mountains. They describe them to be not more than three feet high. They say that these little people are alone found in the country where the man-tiger frequents, and that the former takes cognizance of them, and will destroy any thing that attempts to harm them.

14th. The beaver is found in great numbers in the ponds, which are very numerous on the heads of the Columbia, Missouri, Arkansas, Rio Grande, Platte, and all the country between; though it is very mountainous, and sometimes the ponds are on the highest ground.

These strange animals, in many instances, appear to possess the wisdom of human beings. They appear to have their family connections, and each family lives separate, sometimes numbering more than a hundred in a family. A stranger is not allowed to dwell with them. They burrow in the ground when they cannot get timber to build huts. In case they can get timber, they will cut down quite large trees with their teeth, then cut them off in lengths to suit their purposes; sometimes five or six feet long, and will then unite in hauling them to a chosen spot, and build up their houses in the edge of the water. The first story is some three feet high—one door under the water. The next story is not so high, has three doors, one next the water, one next the land, and one down through the floor into the first story. There is continually a sentinel at the door next the land, and on the approach of any thing that alarms them, they are soon in the water.

They will move from one pond to another, and it is strange to see what a large road they make in removing. Their fur and size need no description. They are generally very fat, but the tail only is fit to eat. The bait with which the traps are baited, is collected from this animal, and is difficult to prepare, as there has to be a precise amount of certain parts of the animal. If there is too much of any one ingredient they will become alarmed, and even leave the pond. In preparing the bait, no part of your flesh must touch it, or they will not come near it. The bait has to be changed every few days by adding something; a small piece of spignard or annis root may be dropped into it. It is kept close in bladders, or skin bags, and nothing that goes into it must be touched with the hands.

15th. Muskrats in those ponds are beyond number. They also build houses in the ponds. They are built of any kind of trash they can find.

The most abrupt range of the Rocky Mountains embraces a large tract of country, and so incredibly high, and perpendicular are they in many places, that it is impossible to ascend them. At some places the tall sharp peaks of mountains resemble much the steeple on a church. Probably you can see twenty of these high peaks at one sight; and in other places the steep rock bluff, perhaps 200 feet high, will extend ten miles perfectly strait and uniform. In some places you will find a small tract of level country on the tops of the mountains. These levels are generally very rich. This range of mountains crosses the heads of the Missouri, and bears in a south-westerly direction to, and beyond the Rio Grande, even as far as I have ever been; also, bearing north, down the Columbia river as far as I went, and the head waters of the Platte, (perhaps I may be mistaken in the names of some of the rivers.) They can better be described by saying they are a dreadful rough range of mountains, I suppose as high as any others in the world. The bottoms are very rich. It will be winter on the top of the mountains, and spring or summer in the valleys. There is a kind of wild flax that grows in these bottoms which yields a lint, out of which the Indians make ropes. It is very strong. As far as I was down on the tributaries of the Columbia, the bottoms were seldom more than one half mile wide; in some places a mile. The timber is indifferent in the bottoms, and more indifferent on the high land.

The buffalo sometimes finds it very difficult to ascend or descend these mountains. I have sometimes amused myself by getting on the top of one of these high pinnacles and looking over the country. You can see one mountain beyond another until they are lost in the misty air. Where you can see the valleys, you will often see them literally covered with the buffalo, sometimes the elk, wild horse, &c.

North-west of the head of the Rio Grande, which is some 150 miles N. W. of Santa Fe, the country becomes more level. Part of this country is inhabited by a nation of Indians, called Apatches, and another tribe called Ferbelows. In this section of country there are some farms where fine wheat is raised.

This region of country is but very little known by the American people, being infested with such numerous tribes of Indians that Americans are very unsafe to be there. If the timber was not so indifferent, this country would be densely inhabited. The soil would fully justify the idea. In point of health it certainly is not surpassed in the world; and although very far to the north, is not excessively cold. I do not think it is colder than the state of Tennessee. The present inhabitants say there is nothing like fevers known in that country.

. . .

About the middle of March, all the Indian bands—that is, the Cumanches, and all the hostile tribes, assembled and held a general war council. They met on the head waters of the Arkansas, and it was the largest assemblage I ever saw. The council was held upon a high eminence, descending every way. The encampments were as close as they could stand, and how far they extended I know not; for I could not see the outer edge of them with my naked eye.

I had now been with them so long that I had learned their language, and as the council was held in the Cumanche language, I determined, (for I yet entertained a faint hope that I would be released,) to know the result of their proceedings. It being contrary to their laws to permit their squaws to be present in their councils, I was several times repulsed with blows, but I cheerfully submitted to abuse and persevered in listening to their proceedings.

A number of traditionary ceremonies were performed, such as would be of but little interest to the reader. This ceremony occupied about three days, after which they come to a determination to invade and take possession of Texas. It was agreed that those tribes of Indians who were in the habit of raising corn, should cultivate the farms of the people of Texas; the prairie Indians were to have entire control of the prairies, each party to defend each other. After having taken Texas, killed and driven out the inhabitants, and the corn growing Indians had raised a good supply, they were to attack Mexico. There they expected to be joined by a large number of Mexicans who are disaffected with the government, as also a number that would or could be coerced into measures of subordination, they would soon possess themselves of Mexico. They would then attack the United States.

They said that the white men had now driven the Indian bands from the East to the West, and now they would work this plan to drive the whites out of the country; they said that the white people had got almost around them, and in a short time they would drive them again. I do believe that almost every band or nation of Indians was represented in that Council, and there was but one thing that was left unsettled, that was the time of attack—some said, the spring of 1838, and others said the spring of 1839; though this matter was to be left measurably to the Northern Indians, and to be communicated to the chiefs of the Cumanches. The Council continued in session seven days, and at the end of that period, they broke up. One Indian came to me on the prairie, and stated that he was a Beadie, that he lived on the San Jacinto river, and that they were determined to make servants of the white people, and cursed me in the English language, which were the only English words I had heard during my captivity.

. . .

One evening as I was at my work, (being north of the Rocky mountains,) I discovered some Mexican traders.* Hope instantly mounted the throne from whence it had long been banished. My tottering frame received fresh life and courage, as I saw them approaching the habitation of sorrow and grief where I dwelt. They asked for my master, and we were directly with him. They asked if he would sell me. No music, no sounds that ever reached my anxious ear, was half so sweet as *"ce senure,"* (yes, sir.) The trader made an offer for me. My owner refused. He offered more, but my owner still refused. Utter confusion hovers around my mind while I record this part of my history; and I can only ask my reader, if he can, to fancy himself in my situation; for language will fail to describe the anxious thoughts that revolved in my

---

* I had dreamed, the night before, that I saw an angel, the same I saw in the cave. He had four wings. He gave them to me, and immediately I was on the wing, and was soon with my father. But, when I awoke, behold! it was all a dream.

throbbing breast when I heard the trader say he could give no more. Oh! had I the treasures of the universe, how freely I would have given it; yea, and then consented to have been a servant to my countrymen. Would that my father could speak to him; but my father is no more. Or one of my dear uncles; yes, they would say "stop not for price." Oh! my good Lord, intercede for me. My eyes, despite my efforts, are swimming in tears at the very thought. I only have to appeal to the treasure of your hearts, my readers, to conceive the state of my desponding mind at this crisis. At length, however, the trader made another offer for me, which my owner agreed to take. My whole feeble frame was now convulsed in an extacy of joy, as he delivered the first article as an earnest of the trade. Memorable day!

. . .

Thousands of thoughts revolved through my mind as the trader was paying for me. My joy was full. Oh! shall I ever forget the time when my new master told me to go with him to his tent? As I turned from my prison, in my very soul I tried to return thanks to my God who always hears the cries of his saints:

> My God was with me in distress,
>> My God was always there;
> Oh! may I to my God address
>> Thankful and devoted prayer.

I was soon informed by my new master that he was going to take me to Santa Fe. That night, sleep departed from my eyes. In my fancy I surveyed the steps of my childhood, in company with my dear relations. It would, I suppose, be needless for me to say that I watched with eagerness the day spring, and that the night was long filled with gratitude to the Divine Conservator of the divine law of heaven and earth.

In the morning quite early, all things being ready, we started. We travelled very hard for seventeen days, when we reached Santa Fe. Then, my reader, I beheld some of my countrymen, and I leave you to conjecture the contrast in my feelings when I found myself surrounded by sympathising Americans, clad in decent attire. I was soon conducted to Col. William Donoho's residence. I found that it was him who had heard of the situation of myself and others, and being an American indeed, his manly and magnanimous bosom, heaved with sympathy characteristic of a christian, had devised the plan for our release.[*] Here I was at home. I hope that every American that reads this narrative may

---

[*] Mrs. Harris had also been purchased by his arrangements.

duly appreciate this amiable man, to whom, under the providence of God, I owe my release. . . .

The people of Santa Fe, by subscription, made me up $150 to assist me to my friends. This was put into the hands of Rev. C*******,* who kept it and never let me have it; and but for the kindness of Mr. and Mrs. Donoho, I could not have got along. Soon after I arrived in Santa Fe, a disturbance took place among the Mexicans. They killed several of their leading men. Mr. Donoho considered it unsafe for his family, and started with them to Missouri, and made me welcome as one of his family. The road led through a vast region of prairie, which is nearly one thousand miles across. This, to many, would have been a considerable undertaking, as it was all the way through an Indian country. But we arrived safely at Independence, in Missouri, where I received many signal favors from many of the inhabitants, for which I shall ever feel grateful. I staid at Mr. Donoho's, but I was impatient to learn something of my relatives.

My anxiety grew so great that I was often tempted to start on foot. I tried to pray, mingling my tears and prayers to Almighty God to intercede for me, and in his providence to devise some means by which I might get home to my friends. Despite of all the kind entreaties of that benevolent woman, Mrs. Donoho, I refused to be comforted; and who, I ask, under these circumstances, could have been reconciled?

One evening I had been in my room trying to pray, and on stepping to the door, I saw my brother-in-law, Mr. Nixon. I tried to run to him, but was not able. I was so much overjoyed I scarcely knew what to say or how to act. I asked, "Are my father and husband alive?" He answered affirmatively. "Are mother and the children alive?" He said they were. Every moment seemed an hour. It was very cold weather, being now the dead of winter.

Mr. Donoho furnished me a horse, and in a few days we started, Mr. Donoho accompanying us. We had a long and cold Journey of more than one thousand miles, the way we were compelled to travel, and that principally through a frontier country. But having been accustomed to hardships, together with my great anxiety, I thought I could stand any thing, and the nearer I approached my people, the greater my anxiety grew. Finally on the evening of the 19th day of February, 1838, I arrived at my father's house in Montgomery county, Texas. Here united tears of joy flowed from the eyes of father, mother, brothers and sisters; while many strangers, unknown to me, (neighbors to my father) cordially united in this joyful interview.

I am now not only freed from my Indian captivity, enjoying the exquisite pleasure that my soul has long panted for.

---

* At the request of my father I forbear publishing his name.

Oh! God of Love, with pitying eye
    Look on a wretch like me;
That I may on thy name rely,
    Oh, Lord! be pleased to see.

How oft have sighs unuttered flowed
    From my poor wounded heart,
Yet thou my wishes did reward,
    And sooth'd the painful smart.

Closing Address

I am compelled, by my fast declining physical strength, to stop short of what I had intended to write. I feel assured that soon, very soon, I shall enter upon a more serious and hazardous an adventure than that detailed in the foregoing pages—an adventure upon the things of eternity—and may I not indulge the hope that my kind readers will properly appreciate my feelings in these, my last moments, when the "king of terrors" is staring me in the face and bidding me to prepare to yield up my scarred and emaciated form to its mother earth, and my afflicted and immortal soul to Him who gave it.

When I indulge in a retrospect of the past, and all my trials and sufferings are brought in view to memories eye; whilst my heart bleeds anew over those scenes of sorrow and tribulation, through which it was the will of God I should pass, I feel a joyous hope, that they were the means my Heavenly Master, in his wisdom, thought proper to make use of in preparing me to meet the angels of glory in realms of eternal bliss. When I reflect back and live over again, as it were, my past life—when I see my dear children torn from me by the barbarous hands of the savage—one of whom was inhumanly killed before my eyes, and its lifeless and mangled corps thrown, with derision, into my arms—I feel rejoiced to think that all is well with it. Yes, with the eyes of faith, directed by a firm reliance on the promises of God, I can see its pure spirit mingling with those of the blessed around the eternal throne of the Most High God.

Where my dear child (James Pratt) is, I know not; but I sincerely hope, and have much consolation in believing that he too has been taken to his eternal home on high, where "the wicked cease from troubling and the weary are at rest." The firm hope I enjoy of meeting my dear babes in heaven, and of mingling with them and their kindred spirits, in eternal praises to "the Lamb of God, who taketh away the sins of the world," robs death of its sting and the grave of its victory. Yes—blessed be God—I feel a joy at the approach of death, which cannot be described—a joy which nothing earthly can impart, and none but pure spirits feel. I feel that my days of probation on this earth are fast drawing to a close; and I know, dear reader, that long before you shall read this, my closing address to my fellow-travellers to eternity, the mind that dictated it will have passed the just ordeal of a righteous and merciful God, and the hand that penned it, have become food for the worms of the grave.

. . .

There is, in these, my last hours, but one doubt in my mind that gives me pain; and that is, the uncertainty that hovers around the fate of my helpless child. I have said that I hoped and believed that God has cut short his sufferings, by the intervention of the hand of death. This is merely a hope, founded upon the supposition that his tender frame could not withstand the cruelties of his inhuman captors. He may yet live, and if so, he is now, whilst I am penning these lines, suffering all the horrors of Indian barbarity. Oh, God, have mercy on him, if it be so. Thou, who art a father to the fatherless, wilt, I know, deal with him, according to thy mercy and wisdom. When I suffer myself to indulge in doubt, and permit myself to believe that he still lives in bondage, my bosom heaves like the waves of the ocean, when lashed into madness by the furious tempest, and phrenzy seizes my brain. How gladly would I give the whole world, if it were mine—yea, my own life, were it in my power, to release him. But I have no hope of having this doubt removed. Soon, very soon, must I bid adieu to all the doubts, perplexities, and sorrows of this world; but I cannot nor shall cease to pray to God in his behalf. The fountain of my tears are dried up; I cannot weep for him—but may I not hope, that when I have passed into eternity, my dear parents and friends will breathe one prayer and shed one tear of sympathy for my poor lost child, James Pratt.

Rachel Plummer
January, 1839

NOTE.—The hand of Mrs. Plummer was stilled in death on the 19th day of February, 1839. She did not live to see her son recovered by his friends, and consequently died ignorant of his fate. . . .

3–20
Walt Whitman (1819–1892)

WALT WHITMAN (1819–1892) was, as he said in "Song of Myself" (1855), "a kosmos" and "untranslatable." He was born on Long Island and spent most of his formative years in Brooklyn, and, like Ben Franklin and Mark Twain, served as a printer's devil, typesetter, reporter, and finally newspaper editor. In 1855, Whitman published the first edition of *Leaves of Grass*. Powerfully influenced by Emerson and

Transcendentalism, Whitman was delighted when Emerson called it, "the most extraordinary piece of wit and wisdom that America has yet contributed," so delighted that he had the letter reprinted—without permission—in the 1856 edition of *Leaves of Grass*. Whitman continued to revise his work and to add to it, publishing multiple editions of *Leaves of Grass*, including the "Deathbed Edition" of 1892. In "To Foreign Lands" (1860) and "Passage to India" (1871), one sees Whitman's characteristic American bravado engaged in a global conversation. East has joined West as the Suez Canal and the Union Pacific Railroad, both completed in 1869, illustrate, but Whitman's journey to the East is more spiritual than geographical.

≈ ≈ ≈

"To Foreign Lands" (1860)

I heard that you ask'd for something to prove this puzzle, the New World,
And to define America, her athletic Democracy;
Therefore I send you my poems, that you behold in them what you wanted.

"Passage to India" (1871)

1

Singing my days,
Singing the great achievements of the present,
Singing the strong, light works of engineers,
Our modern wonders, (the antique ponderous Seven outvied,)
In the Old World, the east, the Suez canal,
The New by its mighty railroad spann'd,
The seas inlaid with eloquent, gentle wires,
I sound, to commence, the cry, with thee, O soul,
The Past! the Past! the Past!

The Past! the dark, unfathom'd retrospect!
The teeming gulf! the sleepers and the shadows!
The past! the infinite greatness of the past!
For what is the present, after all, but a growth out of the past?
(As a projectile, form'd, impell'd, passing a certain line, still keeps on,
So the present, utterly form'd, impell'd by the past.)

2

Passage, O soul, to India!
Eclaircise the myths Asiatic—the primitive fables.

Not you alone, proud truths of the world!
Nor you alone, ye facts of modern science!
But myths and fables of old—Asia's, Africa's fables!
The far-darting beams of the spirit!—the unloos'd dreams!
The deep diving bibles and legends;
The daring plots of the poets—the elder religions;
—O you temples fairer than lilies, pour'd over by the rising sun!
O you fables, spurning the known, eluding the hold of the known,
    mounting to heaven!
You lofty and dazzling towers, pinnacled, red as roses, burnish'd with gold!
Towers of fables immortal, fashion'd from mortal dreams!
You too I welcome, and fully, the same as the rest;
You too with joy I sing.

3

Passage to India!
Lo, soul! seest thou not God's purpose from the first?
The earth to be spann'd, connected by net-work,
The people to become brothers and sisters,
The races, neighbors, to marry and be given in marriage,
The oceans to be cross'd, the distant brought near,
The lands to be welded together.

(A worship new, I sing;
You captains, voyagers, explorers, yours!
You engineers! you architects, machinists, yours!
You, not for trade or transportation only,
But in God's name, and for thy sake, O soul.)

4

Passage to India!
Lo, soul, for thee, of tableaus twain,
I see, in one, the Suez canal initiated, open'd,
I see the procession of steamships, the Empress Eugenie's leading the
    van;
I mark, from on deck, the strange landscape, the pure sky, the level
    sand in the distance;

I pass swiftly the picturesque groups, the workmen gather'd,
The gigantic dredging machines.

In one, again, different, (yet thine, all thine, O soul, the same,)
I see over my own continent the Pacific Railroad, surmounting every
    barrier;
I see continual trains of cars winding along the Platte, carrying freight
    and passengers;
I hear the locomotives rushing and roaring, and the shrill steam-
    whistle,
I hear the echoes reverberate through the grandest scenery in the
    world;
I cross the Laramie plains—I note the rocks in grotesque shapes—the
    buttes;
I see the plentiful larkspur and wild onions—the barren, colorless,
    sage-deserts;
I see in glimpses afar, or towering immediately above me, the great
    mountains—I see the Wind River and the Wahsatch mountains;
I see the Monument mountain and the Eagle's Nest—I pass the
    Promontory—I ascend the Nevadas;
I scan the noble Elk mountain, and wind around its base;
I see the Humboldt range—I thread the valley and cross the river,
I see the clear waters of Lake Tahoe—I see forests of majestic pines,
Or, crossing the great desert, the alkaline plains, I behold enchanting
    mirages of waters and meadows;
Marking through these, and after all, in duplicate slender lines,
Bridging the three or four thousand miles of land travel,
Tying the Eastern to the Western sea,
The road between Europe and Asia.

(Ah Genoese, thy dream! thy dream!
Centuries after thou art laid in thy grave,
The shore thou foundest verifies thy dream!)

5

Passage to India!
Struggles of many a captain—tales of many a sailor dead!
Over my mood, stealing and spreading they come,
Like clouds and cloudlets in the unreach'd sky.

Along all history, down the slopes,
As a rivulet running, sinking now, and now again to the surface rising,

A ceaseless thought, a varied train—Lo, soul! to thee, thy sight, they rise,
The plans, the voyages again, the expeditions:
Again Vasco da Gama sails forth;
Again the knowledge gain'd, the mariner's compass,
Lands found, and nations born—thou born, America, (a hemisphere
    unborn,)
For purpose vast, man's long probation fill'd,
Thou, rondure of the world, at last accomplish'd.

6

O, vast Rondure, swimming in space!
Cover'd all over with visible power and beauty!
Alternate light and day, and teeming, spiritual darkness;
Unspeakable, high processions of sun and moon, and countless stars,
    above;
Below, the manifold grass and waters, animals, mountains, trees;
With inscrutable purpose—some hidden, prophetic intention;
Now, first, it seems, my thought begins to span thee.

Down from the gardens of Asia, descending, radiating,
Adam and Eve appear, then their myriad progeny after them,
Wandering, yearning, curious—with restless explorations,
With questionings, baffled, formless, feverish—with never-happy hearts,
With that sad, incessant refrain, *Wherefore, unsatisfied Soul?* and
    Whither, O mocking Life?

Ah, who shall soothe these feverish children?
Who justify these restless explorations?
Who speak the secret of impassive Earth?
Who bind it to us? What is this separate Nature, so unnatural?
What is this Earth, to our affections? (unloving earth, without a throb
    to answer ours;
Cold earth, the place of graves.)

Yet, soul, be sure the first intent remains—and shall be carried out;
(Perhaps even now the time has arrived.)

After the seas are all cross'd, (as they seem already cross'd,)
After the great captains and engineers have accomplish'd their work,
After the noble inventors—after the scientists, the chemist, the
    geologist, ethnologist,
Finally shall come the Poet, worthy that name;
The true Son of God shall come, singing his songs.

Then, not your deeds only, O voyagers, O scientists and inventors, shall
    be justified,
All these hearts, as of fretted children, shall be sooth'd,
All affection shall be fully responded to—the secret shall be told;
All these separations and gaps shall be taken up, and hook'd and link'd
    together;
The whole Earth—this cold, impassive, voiceless Earth, shall be
    completely justified;
Trinitas divine shall be gloriously accomplish'd and compacted by the
    true Son of God, the poet,
(He shall indeed pass the straits and conquer the mountains,
He shall double the Cape of Good Hope to some purpose;)
Nature and Man shall be disjoin'd and diffused no more,
The true Son of God shall absolutely fuse them.

7

Year at whose open'd, wide-flung door I sing!
Year of the purpose accomplish'd!
Year of the marriage of continents, climates and oceans!
(No mere Doge of Venice now, wedding the Adriatic;)
I see, O year, in you, the vast terraqueous globe, given, and giving all,
Europe to Asia, Africa join'd, and they to the New World;
The lands, geographies, dancing before you, holding a festival garland,
As brides and bridegrooms hand in hand.

8

Passage to India!
Cooling airs from Caucasus far, soothing cradle of man,
The river Euphrates flowing, the past lit up again.

Lo, soul, the retrospect, brought forward;
The old, most populous, wealthiest of Earth's lands,
The streams of the Indus and the Ganges, and their many affluents;
(I, my shores of America walking to-day, behold, resuming all,)
The tale of Alexander, on his warlike marches, suddenly dying,
On one side China, and on the other side Persia and Arabia,
To the south the great seas, and the Bay of Bengal;
The flowing literatures, tremendous epics, religions, castes,
Old occult Brahma, interminably far back—the tender and junior
    Buddha,
Central and southern empires, and all their belongings, possessors,

The wars of Tamerlane, the reign of Aurungzebe,
The traders, rulers, explorers, Moslems, Venetians, Byzantium, the
    Arabs, Portuguese,
The first travelers, famous yet, Marco Polo, Batouta the Moor,
Doubts to be solv'd, the map incognita, blanks to be fill'd,
The foot of man unstay'd, the hands never at rest,
Thyself, O soul, that will not brook a challenge.

9

The medieval navigators rise before me,
The world of 1492, with its awaken'd enterprise;
Something swelling in humanity now like the sap of the earth in spring,
The sunset splendor of chivalry declining,

And who art thou, sad shade?
Gigantic, visionary, thyself a visionary,
With majestic limbs, and pious, beaming eyes,
Spreading around, with every look of thine, a golden world,
Enhuing it with gorgeous hues.

As the chief historian,
Down to the footlights walks, in some great scena,
Dominating the rest, I see the Admiral himself,
(History's type of courage, action, faith;)
Behold him sail from Palos, leading his little fleet;
His voyage behold—his return—his great fame,
His misfortunes, calumniators—behold him a prisoner, chain'd,
Behold his dejection, poverty, death.

(Curious, in time, I stand, noting the efforts of heroes;
Is the deferment long? bitter the slander, poverty, death?
Lies the seed unreck'd for centuries in the ground? Lo! to God's due
    occasion,
Uprising in the night, it sprouts, blooms.
And fills the earth with use and beauty.)

10

Passage indeed, O soul, to primal thought!
Not lands and seas alone—thy own clear freshness,
The young maturity of brood and bloom;
To realms of budding bibles.

O soul, repressless, I with thee, and thou with me,
Thy circumnavigation of the world begin;
Of man, the voyage of his mind's return,
To reason's early paradise,
Back, back to wisdom's birth, to innocent intuitions,
Again with fair Creation.

11

O we can wait no longer!
We too take ship, O soul!
Joyous, we too launch out on trackless seas!
Fearless, for unknown shores, on waves of extasy to sail,
Amid the wafting winds, (thou pressing me to thee, I thee to me, O
    soul,)
Caroling free—singing our song of God,
Chanting our chant of pleasant exploration.

With laugh, and many a kiss,
(Let others deprecate—let others weep for sin, remorse, humiliation;)
O soul, thou pleasest me—I thee.

Ah, more than any priest, O soul, we too believe in God;
But with the mystery of God we dare not dally.

O soul, thou pleasest me—I thee;
Sailing these seas, or on the hills, or waking in the night,
Thoughts, silent thoughts, of Time, and Space, and Death, like waters
    flowing,
Bear me, indeed, as through the regions infinite,
Whose air I breathe, whose ripples hear—lave me all over;
Bathe me, O God, in thee—mounting to thee,
I and my soul to range in range of thee.

O Thou transcendant!
Nameless—the fibre and the breath!
Light of the light—shedding forth universes—thou centre of them!
Thou mightier centre of the true, the good, the loving!
Thou moral, spiritual fountain! affection's source! thou reservoir!
(O pensive soul of me! O thirst unsatisfied! waitest not there?
Waitest not haply for us, somewhere there, the Comrade perfect?)
Thou pulse! thou motive of the stars, suns, systems,

That, circling, move in order, safe, harmonious,
Athwart the shapeless vastnesses of space!
How should I think—how breathe a single breath—how speak—if, out
   of myself,
I could not launch, to those, superior universes?

Swiftly I shrivel at the thought of God,
At Nature and its wonders, Time and Space and Death,
But that I, turning, call to thee, O soul, thou actual Me,
And lo! thou gently masterest the orbs,
Thou matest Time, smilest content at Death,
And fillest, swellest full, the vastnesses of Space.

Greater than stars or suns,
Bounding, O soul, thou journeyest forth;
—What love, than thine and ours could wider amplify?
What aspirations, wishes, outvie thine and ours, O soul?
What dreams of the ideal? what plans of purity, perfection, strength?
What cheerful willingness, for others' sake, to give up all?
For others' sake to suffer all?

Reckoning ahead, O soul, when thou, the time achiev'd,
(The seas all cross'd, weather'd the capes, the voyage done,)
Surrounded, copest, frontest God, yieldest, the aim attain'd,
As, fill'd with friendship, love complete, the Elder Brother found,
The Younger melts in fondness in his arms.

12

Passage to more than India!
Are thy wings plumed indeed for such far flights?
O Soul, voyagest thou indeed on voyages like these?
Disportest thou on waters such as these?
Soundest below the Sanscrit and the Vedas?
Then have thy bent unleash'd.

Passage to you, your shores, ye aged fierce enigmas!
Passage to you, to mastership of you, ye strangling problems!
You, strew'd with the wrecks of skeletons, that, living, never reach'd you.

13

Passage to more than India!
O secret of the earth and sky!
Of you, O waters of the sea! O winding creeks and rivers!

Of you, O woods and fields! Of you, strong mountains of my land!
Of you, O prairies! Of you, gray rocks!
O morning red! O clouds! O rain and snows!
O day and night, passage to you!

O sun and moon, and all you stars! Sirius and Jupiter!
Passage to you!

Passage—immediate passage! the blood burns in my veins!
Away, O soul! hoist instantly the anchor!
Cut the hawsers—haul out—shake out every sail!
Have we not stood here like trees in the ground long enough?
Have we not grovell'd here long enough, eating and drinking like mere
    brutes?
Have we not darken'd and dazed ourselves with books long enough?
Sail forth! steer for the deep waters only!
Reckless, O soul, exploring, I with thee, and thou with me;
For we are bound where mariner has not yet dared to go,
And we will risk the ship, ourselves and all.

O my brave soul!
O farther, farther sail!
O daring joy, but safe! Are they not all the seas of God?
O farther, farther, farther sail!

3–21

John Rollin Ridge (Cheesquatalawny) (1827–1867)

Born in the Cherokee capital New Echota, Georgia, CHEESQUATA-
LAWNY ("YELLOW BIRD"), known by his English name, JOHN ROLLIN
RIDGE (1827–1867), is hailed today as an early Native American poet
and novelist. Following the Trail of Tears, he was educated in the North,
and later emigrated to California. Late in life he lobbied the American
government for the return of Cherokee lands. After emigrating West,
he wrote a novelistic and sometimes sympathetic treatment of the life
of a notorious Mexican American bandit in *The Life and Adventures of
Joaquin Murieta, The Celebrated California Bandit* (1854). Excerpts here
show the racism inflicted on this legendary character, resulting in his
shift from lover to outlaw.

≈ ≈ ≈

From *The Life and Adventures of Joaquín Murieta, the Celebrated California Bandit* (1854)

Chapter 1. His Boyhood, Early Education and Personal Appearance—His Acquaintance with Americans in Mexico—His Winning of the Beautiful Rosita—His Arrival in California—His Honest Occupation as a Miner—His Domicil Intruded upon by Lawless Men—Their Outrages upon Him and His Mistress—His Removal to a New Locality—New Intrusions and Oppressions.

Sitting down, as I now do, so give to the public such events of the life of Joaquin Murieta as have come into my possession, I am moved by no desire to administer to any depraved taste for the dark and horrible inhuman action, but rather by a wish to contribute my mite to those materials out of which the early history of California shall be composed. Aside from the interest naturally excited by the career of a man so remarkable in the annals of crime—for in deeds of daring and blood he has never been exceeded by any of the renowned robbers of the Old or New World who have preceded him—his character is well worth the scrutiny of the intelligent reader as being a product of the social and moral condition of the country in which he lived, while his individual record becomes a part of the most valuable, because it is a part of the earliest history of the State.

. . .

Joaquin Murieta was a Mexican of good blood, borne in the province of Sonora, of respectable parents, and educated to a degree sufficient for the common purposes of life in the schools of his native country. While growing up, he was remarkable for a very mild and peaceable disposition, and gave no sign of that indomitable and daring spirit which afterwards characterized him. Those who knew him in his school-boy days speak affectionately of his generous and noble nature at that period of his life, and can scarcely credit the fact, that the renowned and bloody bandit of California was one and the same being.

The first considerable interruption in the general smooth current of his existence, occurred in the latter portion of his seventeenth year. Near the rancho of his father resided a "packer," one Feliz, who, as ugly as sin itself, had a daughter named Rosita. Her mother was dead, and she, although but sixteen, was burdened with the responsibility of a house-keeper in their simple home, for her father and a younger brother, whose name will hereafter occasionally occur in the progress of this narration. Rosita, though in humble circumstances, was of Castilian descent, and showed her superior origin in the native royalty of her look and general dignity of her bearing. Yet she was of that voluptuous order to which so many of the dark-eyed daughters of Spain belong, and the rich blood of her race mounted to cheeks, lips and eyes. Her father doted upon and was proud of her, and it was his greatest happiness, on returning from occasional packing expeditions through the mountains of Sonora (he was simply employed by a more wealthy individual) to receive the gentle ministries of his gay and smiling daughter. Joaquin having nothing to do but ride his father's horses, and give a general superintendence to the herding of stock upon the rancho, was frequently a transient caller at the cabin of Feliz, more particularly when the old man was absent, making excuses for a drink of water or some such matter, and prolonging his stay for the purpose of an agreeable chit-chat with the by no means backward damsel. She had read of bright and handsome lovers, in the stray romances of the day, and well interpreted, no doubt, the mutual emotions of loving hearts. Indeed Nature herself is a sufficient instructor, without the aid of books, where tropic fire is in the veins, and glowing health runs hand in hand with the imagination. It was no wonder, then, that the youthful Joaquin and the precocious and blooming Rosita, in the absence, on each side, of all other like objects of attraction, should begin to feel the presence of each other as a necessity. They loved warmly and passionately. The packer being absent more than half of the time, there was every opportunity for the youthful pair to meet, and their intercourse was, with the exception of the occasional intrusion of her brother, Reyes, a mere boy, absolutely without restraint. Rosita was one of those beings who yield all for love, and, ere, she took time to consider her duties to society, to herself, or to her father, she found herself in the situation of a mere mistress to Joaquin. Old Feliz broke in at last, upon their felicity, by a chance discovery. Coming home one day from a protracted tour in the mountains, he found no one in the cabin but his son Reyes, who told him that Rosita and Joaquin had gone out together on the path leading up the little stream that ran past the dwelling. Following up the path indicated, the old man came upon the pair, in a position, as Byron has it in the most diabolical of his works, "loving, natural and Greek." His rage knew no bounds, but Joaquin did not tarry for its effects. On the contrary, he fled precipitately from the scene. Whether he showed a proper regard for the fair Rosita in so doing, it is not our province to discuss. All we have to do is to state what occurred, and leave moral discrepancies to be harmonized as they best may. At any rate, the loving girl never blamed him for his conduct, for she took the earliest opportunity of a moonlight night, to seek him at his father's rancho, and throw herself into his arms.

About this time, Joaquin had received a letter from a half brother of his, who had been a short time in California, advising him by all means to hasten to that region of romantic adventure and golden reward. He was not long in preparing for the trip. Mounted upon a valuable horse, with his mistress by his side upon another, and with a couple of packed mules before him, laden with provisions and necessaries, he started for the fields of gold. His journey was attended with no serious difficulties, and the trip was made with expedition.

The first that we hear of him in the Golden State is that in the spring of 1850, he is engaged in the honest occupation of a miner in the Stanislaus placers, then reckoned among the richest portions of the mines. He was then eighteen years of age, a little over the medium height, slenderly but gracefully built, and active as a young tiger. His complexion was neither very dark nor very light, but clear and brilliant, and his countenance is pronounced to have been at that time, exceedingly handsome and attractive. His large black eyes kindling with the enthusiasm of his earnest nature, his firm and well-formed mouth, his well-shaped head, from which the long, glossy black hair hung down over his shoulders, his silvery voice, full of generous utterance, and the frank and cordial manner which distinguished him, made him beloved by all with whom he came in contact. He had the confidence and respect of the whole community around him, and was fast amassing a fortune in his rich mining claim. He had built him a comfortable mining residence, in which he had domiciled his heart's treasure—the beautiful girl whom we have described.

The country then was full of careless and desperate men, who bore the name of Americans, but failed to support the honor and the dignity of that title. A feeling was prevalent among this class, of contempt for any and all Mexicans, whom they looked upon as conquered subjects of the United States, having no rights which could stand before a haughtier and superior race. They made no exceptions. If the proud blood of the Castilian, mounted to the cheek of a partial descendant of the Mexiques, showing that he had inherited the old chivalrous spirit of his Spanish ancestry, they looked upon it as a saucy presumption in one so inferior to them. The prejudice of color, the antipathy of races, which are always stronger and bitterer with the ignorant and unlettered, they could not overcome, or if they could, would not, because it afforded them a convenient excuse for their unmanly cruelty and oppression.

One pleasant evening, as Joaquin was sitting in his doorway, after a hard day's work, gazing forth upon the sparkling waters of the Stanislaus River, and listening to the musical voice of Rosita, who was singing a dreamy ditty of her native land, a band of the lawless men above alluded to approached the house and accosted its owner in a very insulting and supercilious manner, asking him by what means he, a d—d Mexican, presumed to be working a mining claim on American ground. Joaquin, who spoke very good English, having often met with Americans in Sonora, replied that, under the treaty of Guada-lupe Hidalgo, he had a right to become a citizen of the United States, and that as such he considered himself.

"Well, sir," said one of the party, "we allow no Mexicans to work in this region, and you have got to leave this claim."

As might have been expected, the young Mexican indignantly remonstrat-ed against such an outrage. He had learned to believe that to be an American was to be the soul of honor and magnanimity, and he could hardly realize that such a piece of meanness and injustice could be perpetrated by any portion of a race whom he had been led so highly to respect. His remonstrances only produced additional insult and insolence, and finally a huge fellow stepped forward and struck him violently in the face. Joaquin, with an ejaculation of rage, sprang toward his bowie-knife, which lay on the bed near by where he had carelessly thrown it on his arrival from work, when his affrighted mistress, fearing that his rashness, in the presence of such an overpowering force might be fatal to him, frantically seized and held him. At this moment his assailant again advanced, and, rudely throwing the young woman aside, dealt him a succession of blows which soon felled him, bruised and bleeding, to the floor. Rosita, at this cruel outrage, suddenly seemed transformed into a being of a different nature, and herself seizing the knife, she made a vengeful thrust at the American. There was fury in her eye and vengeance in her spring, but what could a tender female accomplish, against such ruffians? She was seized by her tender wrists, easily disarmed, and thrown fainting and helpless upon the bed. Meantime Joaquin had been bound hand and foot, by others of the party, and, lying in that condition he saw the cherished companion of his bosom deliberately violated by these very superior specimens of the much vaunted Anglo-Saxon race!

Leaving him in his agony, they gave him to understand that, if he was found in that cabin, or upon his claim after the expiration of the next ten days, they would take his life. The soul of the young man was from that moment dark-ened, and, as he himself related afterwards, he swore, with clenched hands, as his mistress unbound him, that he would live for revenge. She, weeping, implored him to live for *her*, as he knew she only lived for *him*, and try to for-get in some other and happier scene the bitter misery of the present. He was prevailed upon by her kindness and her tears, and soon after the young couple took their departure for a more northern portion of the mines.

The next we hear of them, they are located on a nice little farm on the banks of a beautiful stream that watered a fertile valley far out in the seclusion of the mountains of Calaveras. Here the somewhat saddened adventurer deemed that he might hope for peace and again be happy. But it was not so destined. One day, as he was engaged with an axe and mattock in clearing his ground, several Americans rode up to the fencing of his little retreat, and notified him that they allowed no infernal Mexican intruders, like him, to own land in that section. Joaquin's blood boiled in his veins, but he answered mildly that the valley was unoccupied save by himself, that he acknowledged allegiance to the American Government, that the treaty of peace between the United States and Mexico gave him his choice of citizenship either in California or in Mexico as he liked, that he had been already driven from the mines without any crime or offence on his part, and all he now asked was a very small patch of ground and the shelter of a humble home for himself and "wife." He was peremptorily told to leave, and, we blush to say it, compelled to abandon the spot he had selected and the fruits of his labor.

It is honorable to him to say that his spirit was still unbroken, nor had the iron so far entered his soul as to sear up the innate sensitiveness to honor and right which reigned in his bosom. Twice ruined in his honest pursuit of fortune, he resolved still to labor on with unflinching brow and with that true moral bravery which throws its redeeming light forward upon all his subsequently dark and criminal career. How deep must have been the anguish of that young heart, and how strongly rooted the native honesty of his soul, none can know or imagine but they that have been tried in like manner.

He bundled up his little moveable property, and again started forth to strike once more, like a brave and honest man, for fortune and for happiness. He arrived at Murphy's Diggings, in Calaveras County, in the month of April, 1850, and went again to mining, this time without interruption; but meeting with nothing like his former success, he soon abandoned that business, and devoted his time to dealing "monte," a game which is common in Mexico, and had been almost universally adopted by gamblers in Mexico. It is considered by the Mexican in no manner a disreputable employment, and many well-reared young men from the Atlantic States have resorted to it, in time past, as a "profession" in this land of luck and chances. It was once in much better odor than it is now, although it is at present a game which may be played on very fair and honest principles, provided anything can be strictly honest or fair which allows the taking of money without a valuable consideration in return. It was therefore looked upon as no departure from rectitude on the part of Joaquin, when he commenced the dealing of "monte." Having a very pleasing exterior and being, despite of all his sorrows, very gay and lively in his disposition, he attracted many persons to his table, and won their money with such skill and grace, or lost his own with such perfect good humor, that he was considered by all the very beau ideal of a gambler and the prince of clever fellows. His sky seemed clear and his prospects bright, but Fate was weaving her mysterious web around him, and fitting him by force of circumstances to become what nature never intended he should be.

His half brother, of whom we have spoken, resided on a small tract of land in the vicinity of Murphy's Diggings. Joaquin had paid him a visit, and returned to the Diggings on a horse borrowed from his brother. The animal, which his brother had bought and paid his money for, proved to have been originally stolen, and being recognized by a number of individuals in town, as well as by the owner, a stout rough-grained man, named J—s, an excitement was raised on the subject. Joaquin suddenly found himself surrounded by a furious mob, many of them strangers to him, who were by no means sparing of their threats and insults.

"So my covey," said J—s, laying his hand on Joaquin's shoulder, "you are the chap that's been a stealing horses and mules around here, for the last six months, are you?"

"You charge me unjustly," replied Joaquin. "I borrowed this horse of my half brother, who bought it from an American, which he can easily prove, as well as show a bill of sale besides."

"This is all gammon," said J—s "and you are nothing but a dirty thief."

"Hang him!" "Hang him!" cried out several voices from the crowd, and the young Mexican was at once seized and bound. Some one, more moderate than the rest, suggested that it would be better, before proceeding to extremities, to see what the half brother had to say for himself.

"Yes, nab him too!" exclaimed various persons in the mob, and they at once started for the half brother's house, taking their prisoner along with them.

"All I want you to do, gentlemen," said Joaquin, "is to give my brother a chance to prove his and my innocence. Let him have time to summon his witnesses."

This remark was only answered with jeers and contempt. Arriving at the place sought for, the brother of Joaquin being readily found, he was seized, with scarcely a word of explanation, hurried to a tree and swung by the neck, amid the hootings of the mob, until he was dead. Joaquin shed tears of agony at the sight, and begged that they would proceed at once to deal out the same fate to him. But the original intention, with regard to him, was changed by some sudden revulsion of feeling in the crowd, and a far more humiliating punishment inflicted. The unhappy young man was bound to the same tree upon which the lifeless form of his brother was swinging, and publicly disgraced with the lash. An eye-witness of this scene declared to the author that he never saw such an expression in all his life as at this moment passed over the face of Joaquin. He cast a look of unutterable scorn and scowling hate upon his torturers, and measured them from head to foot, as though he would imprint their likenesses upon his memory forever. In grim silence he received their blows, disdaining to utter a groan. The deed being over and his hands unbound, he resumed the garb which had been stripped from his shoulders, and was left alone with his dead brother.

Who can tell the piercing grief of his now desolate heart, and the tempest of mingled wrath and woe which swept over him as he lowered the dead form of his brother, and, with the few friends who came to his assistance, proceeded to pay him the last sad rites of rude and humble sepulture? Standing over the grave of his last and dearest relative, he swore an oath of the most awful solemnity, that his soul should never know peace until his hands were dyed deep in the blood of his enemies! Fearfully did he keep that oath, as the following pages will show.

Chapter 2. A Change in Joaquin's Character—Mysterious Disappearances—Murders upon the Highway—An Organized Banditti—Ranches Lose Their Stock—The Killing of the Deputy Sheriff of Santa Clara County— . . .

A change came over the character of Joaquin, suddenly and irrevocably. Wanton cruelty and the tyranny of prejudice had reached their climax. The soul of the injured man grew dark, and the barriers of honor, rocked into atoms by the strong passions which shook his heart like an earthquake, crumbled around him. He was no more the genial, generous, open-hearted Murieta, as of yore. He walked apart in moody silence, avoided intercourse with Americans and was seen to ride off into the mountains in company with such of his countrymen as he had never before condescended to be associated with.

It was not long before an American was found dead in the vicinity of Murphy's Diggings, having been almost literally cut to pieces with a knife. Although horribly mangled, he was recognized as one of the mob engaged in the whipping of Joaquin and the hanging of his brother.

A doctor, passing in the neighborhood of this murder, was met shortly afterward, by two men on horseback, who fired their revolvers at him, but, owing to his speed on foot, and the unevenness of the ground, he succeeded in escaping with no further injury than having a bullet shot through his hat, within an inch of the top of his head! A panic spread among the rash individuals who had composed that mob, and they were afraid to stir out on their ordinary business. Whenever any one of them strayed out of sight of his camp, or ventured to travel on the highway, he was shot down suddenly and mysteriously. Report after report came into the villages that Americans had been found dead on the highways, having been either shot or stabbed, and it was invariably discovered for many weeks, that the murdered men belonged to the mob that had outraged Joaquin. It was fearful and it was strange, to see how swiftly and mysteriously those men disappeared. J—s, the owner of the horse which had been the occasion of the mob, was among the missing, but whether he slid off for distant parts, in fear of his life, or fell a victim to the wrath of the avenger, I have never learned. Certain it is that Murieta's revenge was very nearly complete. Said an eye witness of these events, (an acquaintance of mine, named Burns,) in reply to an inquiry which I addressed him:

"I am inclined to think that Joaquin *wiped out* the most of those prominently engaged in whipping him."

Thus far, who can blame him? But the iron had entered too deeply into his soul for him to stop here. He had contracted a hatred for the whole American race, and was determined to shed their blood, whenever and wherever an opportunity occurred. It was no time now for him to retrace his steps. He had committed deeds which made him amenable to the law, and his only safety lay in a persistence in the unlawful course which he had begun. It was necessary that he should have horses, and that he should have money. These he could not obtain except by robbery and murder, and thus he became an outlaw and a bandit on the verge of his nineteenth year.

The year 1850 rolled away, marked with the eventful history of the young man's wrongs and trials, his bitter revenge on those who had perpetrated the crowning act of his deep injury and disgrace; and, as it closed, it shut him away forever from his peace of mind and purity of heart. He walked forth into the future a dark, determined criminal, and all his proud nobility of soul, save in fitful gleams, existed only in memory.

In 1851 it became generally known that an organized banditti were ranging the country; but it was not yet ascertained who was the leader. Travelers, laden with the produce of the mines, were met upon the roads by well dressed men who politely requested them to "stand and deliver"; persons riding alone in the many wild and lonesome regions, which form a large portion of this country, were skilfully noosed with the lasso, (which the Mexicans throw with great accuracy, being able thus to capture wild cattle, elk, and sometimes even grizzly bears, upon the plains,) dragged from their saddles and murdered in adjacent thickets. Horses of the finest mettle were stolen from the ranches, and, being tracked up, were found in the possession of a determined band of men, ready to retain them at all hazards, and fully able to stand their ground.

The scenes of murder and robbery shifted with the rapidity of lightning. At one time the northern counties would be suffering slaughters and depredations, at another the southern, and, before one would have imagined it possible, the east and the west and every point of the compass would be in trouble. There had been before this, neither in 1849 nor in 1850, any such thing as an organized banditti, and it had been a matter of surprise to every one, since the country was so well adapted to a business of this kind—the houses scattered at such distances along the roads, the plains so level and open in which to ride with speed, and the mountains so rugged with their ten thousand fastnesses, in which to hide! Grass was abundant in the far-off valleys which lay hidden in the rocky gorges, cool, delicious streams made music at the feet of the towering peaks, or came leaping down in gladness from their sides—game abounded on every hand, and nine unclouded months of the year made a climate so salubrious that nothing could be sweeter than a day's rest under the tall pines, or a night's repose under the open canopy of heaven. Joaquin knew his advantages. His superior intelligence and education gave him the respect of his comrades, and appealing to the prejudice against the "Yankees," which the disastrous results of the Mexican war had not tended to lessen in their minds, he soon assembled around him a powerful band of his countrymen, who daily increased, as he ran his career of almost magical success. Among the number was Manuel Garcia, more frequently known as "Three fingered Jack," from the fact of his having had one of his fingers shot off in a skirmish with an American party during the Mexican war. He was a man of unflinching bravery, but cruel and sanguinary. His form was large and rugged, and his countenance so fierce that few liked to look upon it. He was different from his more youthful leader, in possessing nothing of his generous, frank and cordial disposition, and in being utterly destitute of one merciful trait of humanity. His delight was in murder for its own diabolical sake, and he gloated over the agonies of his unoffending victims. He would sacrifice policy, the safety and interests of the band for the mere gratification of this murderous propensity, and it required all Joaquin's firmness and determination to hold him in check. The history of this monster was well known before he joined Joaquin. He was known to be the same man, who, in 1846, surrounded with his party two Americans, young men by the names of Cowie and Fowler, as they were traveling on the road between Sonoma and Bodega, stripped them entirely naked, and, binding them each to a tree, slowly tortured them to death. He began by throwing knives at their bodies, as if he were practicing at a target; he then cut out their tongues, punched out their eyes with his knife, gashed their bodies in numerous places, and, finally flaying them alive, left them to die. A thousand cruelties like these had he been guilty of, and long before Joaquin knew him he was a hardened, experienced and detestable monster. When it was necessary for the young chief to commit some peculiarly horrible and cold-blooded murder, some deed of hellish ghastliness at which his soul revolted, he deputed this man to do it; and well was it executed, with certainty and to the letter.

Another member was the boy, Reyes Feliz, whom I have before mentioned, as the brother of Rosita, and who was left by his fugitive sister a year or so before in the province of Sonora. The old father, the packer, was dead, and Reyes, having no ill-feeling whatever against Joaquin and his sister, had hastened with the remnant of his father's property, to join them, and had arrived in California a few weeks after the affair of the mob at Murphy's Diggings. He was now a mere youth of sixteen years, but he had read the wild romantic lines of the chivalrous robbers of Spain and Mexico, until his enthusiastic spirit had become imbrued with the same sentiments which actuated them, and he could conceive of nothing grander than to throw himself back upon the strictly natural rights of man and hurl defiance at society and its laws. There is many a villain nowadays, for the mere romance of the thing. Reyes Feliz was a devoted follower of his chief; like him, brave, impulsive, and generous.

A third member was Claudio, a man about thirty-five years of age, of a lean, but vigorous constitution, a dark complexion and possessing a somewhat savage but lively and expressive countenance. He was indisputably brave, but exceedingly cautious and cunning, springing upon his prey at an unexpected moment and executing his purposes with the greatest possible secrecy as well as precision. He was a deep calculator, a wise schemer, and could wear the appearance of an honest man with the same grace and ease that he would exhibit in throwing around his commanding figure the magnificent cloak in which he prided. In disposition he was revengeful, tenacious in his memory of a wrong, sly and secret in his windings as a serpent, and, with less nobility than the rattlesnake, he gave no warning before he struck. Yet, as I have said before, he was brave, when occasion called for courage, and although ever ready to take an advantage, he never flinched in the presence of danger. This extreme caution, united with a strong will and courage to do, made him an exceedingly formidable man.

A fourth member was Joaquin Valenzuela. . . . His chief threw upon him much responsibility in the government of the band, and entrusted him with important expeditions requiring in their execution a great amount of skill and experience. Valenzuela was a much older man than his leader, and had acted for many years in Mexico as a bandit under the famous guerilla chief, Padre Jurata.

Another distinguished member was Pedro Gonzales, less brave than many others, but a skillful spy and expert horse thief, and, as such, an invaluable adjunct to a company of mounted men who required a continual supply of fresh horses, as well as a thorough knowledge of the state of affairs around them.

There were many others belonging to this organization, whom it is not necessary to describe. It is sufficient to say they composed as formidable a force of outlaws as ever gladdened the eye of an acknowledged leader. Their number at this early period is not accurately known, but a fair estimate would not place it at a lower figure than fifty, with the advantage of a continual and steady increase, including a few renegade Americans, of desperate characters and fortunes.

. . .

Such was the unsettled condition of things, so distant and isolated were the different mining regions, so lonely and uninhabited the sections through which the roads and trails were cut, and so numerous the friends and acquaintances of the bandits themselves, that these lawless men carried on their operations with almost absolute impunity. It was a rule with them to injure no man who ever extended them a favor, and, whilst they plundered every one else, and spread devastation in every other quarter, they invariably left those ranches and houses unharmed, whose owners and inmates had afforded them shelter or assistance. Many persons who were otherwise honestly inclined, bought the safety of their lives and property by remaining scrupulously silent in regard to Joaquin, and neutral in every attempt to do him an injury. Further than this, there were many large rancheros who were secretly connected with the banditti, and stood ready to harbor them in times of danger, and to furnish them with the best animals that fed on their extensive pastures. The names of several of these wealthy and highly respectable individuals are well known, and will transpire in the course of this history.

At the head of this most powerful combination of men, Joaquin ravaged the State in various quarters during the year 1851, without at that time being generally known as the leader; his subordinates, Claudio, Valenzuela and Pedro Gonzalez, being alternately mistaken for the chief. Except to a few persons, even his name was unknown; and many were personally acquainted with him, and frequently saw him in the different towns and villages, without having the remotest idea that he stood connected with the bloody events which were then filling the country with terror and dismay. He resided for weeks at a time in different localities, ostensibly engaged in gambling, or employed as a vaquero, a packer, or in some other apparently honest avocation, spending much of his time in the society of that sweetest of all companions, the woman that he loved.

While living in a secluded part of the town of San Jose, sometime in the summer of '51, he one night became violently engaged in a row at a fandango, was arrested for a breach of the peace, brought up before a magistrate and fined twelve dollars. He was in charge of Mr. Clark, the Deputy Sheriff of Santa Clara county, who had made himself particularly obnoxious to the banditti, by his rigorous scrutiny into their conduct, and his determined attempts to arrest some of their number. Joaquin had the complete advantage of him, inasmuch as the Deputy was totally ignorant of the true character of the man with whom he had to deal. With the utmost frankness in his manner, Joaquin requested him to walk down to his residence in the skirts of the town, where he would pay him the money.

They proceeded together, engaged in a pleasant conversation, until they reached the edge of a thicket, when the young bandit suddenly drew a knife and informed Clark that he had brought him there to kill him, at the same instant stabbing him to the heart before he could draw his revolver. Though many persons knew the author of this most cool and bloody deed, by sight, yet it was a long time before it was ascertained that the escaped murderer was no less a personage than the leader of the daring cutthroats who were then infesting the country. . . .

3–22
Emily Dickinson (1830–1886)

Often considered reclusive, EMILY DICKINSON (1830–1886) was as intensely original as Emerson—and as religiously nonconformist. Her family was a prominent New England family (her grandfather had founded Amherst College), imbued with a stern Calvinism; Dickinson, by contrast, often questioned traditional pieties, creating a powerful religious dialogue in many of her eighteen hundred poems. In addition to religious themes, she frequently wrote about nature. Because she did not title her poems, many of them have the effect of riddles, with the reader grasping to find even the subject of the poem. Fascinated by language, Dickinson included wordplay and puns that unveil entirely new levels of meaning in her work. Meaning is further complicated by the publishing history. One of the first editors of Emily's work, her niece Martha Dickinson Bianchi (1866–1943), claimed authority with her "complete edition," sourced here, since challenged by many others.

I

Success is counted sweetest
By those who ne'er succeed.
To comprehend a nectar
Requires sorest need.

Not one of all the purple host
Who took the flag to-day

Can tell the definition,
So clear, of victory,

As he, defeated, dying,
On whose forbidden ear
The distant strains of triumph
Break, agonized and clear.

XV

A route of evanescence
With a revolving wheel;
A resonance of emerald,
A rush of cochineal;
And every blossom on the bush
Adjusts its tumbled head,—
The mail from Tunis, probably,
An easy morning's ride.

XIX

I started early, took my dog,
And visited the sea;
The mermaids in the basement
Came out to look at me,

And frigates in the upper floor
Extended hempen hands,
Presuming me to be a mouse
Aground, upon the sands.

But no man moved me till the tide
Went past my simple shoe,
And past my apron and my belt,
And past my bodice too,

And made as he would eat me up
As wholly as a dew
Upon a dandelion's sleeve—
And then I started too.

And he—he followed close behind;
I felt his silver heel
Upon my ankle,—then my shoes
Would overflow with pearl.

Until we met the solid town,
No man he seemed to know;
And bowing with a mighty look
At me, the sea withdrew.

XXXIV

Nature is what we see,
The Hill, the Afternoon—
Squirrel, Eclipse, the Bumble-bee,
Nay—Nature is Heaven.

Nature is what we hear,
The Bobolink, the Sea—
Thunder, the Cricket—
Nay,—Nature is Harmony.

Nature is what we know
But have no art to say,
So impotent our wisdom is
To Her simplicity.

XLIX

They dropped like flakes, they dropped like stars,
Like petals from a rose,
When suddenly across the June
A wind with fingers goes.

They perished in the seamless grass,—
No eye could find the place;
But God on his repealless list
Can summon every face.

LXIV

This is the land the sunset washes,
These are the banks of the Yellow Sea;
Where it rose, or whither it rushes,
These are the western mystery!

Night after night her purple traffic
Strews the landing with opal bales;
Merchantmen poise upon horizons,
Dip, and vanish with fairy sails.

4 :: Realism

4–1
Helen Hunt Jackson (1830–1885)

HELEN HUNT JACKSON (1830–1885) was a childhood friend of Emily Dickinson who shared her enthusiasm for poetry and free thinking. They corresponded as adults, Jackson encouraging her friend to publish her work. After the deaths of her two children and her husband, Jackson became a professional writer, supporting herself by publishing poetry, essays, stories, and novels. She married a Colorado financier and began writing more frequently about the West that became her home. "Cheyenne Mountain" (1879) depicts a peak outside of her new home in Colorado Springs. Her book *A Century of Dishonor* (1881) was a criticism of the American government's mistreatment of Native American tribes. Her novel *Ramona* (1884), set in California and featuring a mixed-race Native American heroine, became a bestseller.

"Cheyenne Mountain" (1879)

By easy slope to west as if it had
No thought, when first its soaring was begun,
Except to look devoutly to the sun,
It rises and has risen, until glad,
With light as with a garment, it is clad,
Each dawn, before the tardy plains have won
One ray; and after day has long been done
For us, the light doth cling reluctant, sad to leave its brow.

Beloved mountain, I
Thy worshipper as thou the sun's, each morn
My dawn, before the dawn, receive from thee;

And think, as thy rose-tinted peaks I see
That thou wert great when Homer was not born.
And ere thou change all human song shall die!

4–2
María Amparo Ruíz de Burton (1832–1895)

MARÍA AMPARO RUIZ DE BURTON (pseudonym C. LOYAL) (1832–1895) was the daughter of a prominent Mexican landowner who had been granted tens of thousands of acres of Baja California. Following the Mexican-American War and the surrender of Mexico to American troops, she married Captain Henry S. Burton, a Protestant, a Yankee, and an invading officer. Despite their differences, their marriage ushered her into American political circles as her husband rose in the ranks and was stationed in Washington. Ruiz de Burton became the first Mexican American woman to write a novel in English, and her most important works, *Who Would Have Thought It?* (1872) and *The Squatter and the Don* (1885), reflect her critical attitude toward the changing geopolitical world she inhabited. The 1848 Treaty of Guadalupe-Hidalgo, ceding large swaths of California, Colorado, Nevada, Arizona, New Mexico, and Utah, and the Rio Grande, to Texas, and the following 1851 Land Act shifted power structures and over time reduced the racial status of the Californios, or the Mexican elite, noted in Ruiz de Burton's historical critique.

From *The Squatter and the Don* (1885)

Chapter 5. The Don in His Broad Acres

"The one great principle of English law,"—Charles Dickens says, "is to make business for itself. There is no other principle distinctly, certainly and consistently maintained through all its narrow turnings. Viewed by this light, it becomes a coherent scheme, and not the monstrous maze the laity are apt to think it. Let them but once clearly perceive that its grand principle is to make business for itself at their expense, and surely they will cease to grumble."

The one great principle of American law is very much the same; our lawgivers keep giving us laws and then enacting others to explain them. The lawyers find plenty of occupation, but what becomes of the laity?

"No. 189. *An Act to ascertain and settle the private land claims in the State of California*," says the book.

And by a sad subversion of purposes, all the private land titles became *un-settled*. It ought to have been said, "An Act to *unsettle* land titles, and to upset the rights of the Spanish population of the State of the California."

It thus became not only necessary for the Spanish people to present their titles for revision, and litigate to maintain them (in case of any one contesting their validity, should the least irregularity be discovered, and others covet their possession), but to maintain them against the government before several tribunals; for the government, besides making its own laws, *appeals to itself* as against the land-owners, after their titles might have been *approved*. But this benign Act says (in "Sec. II"), "That the Commissioners, the District and Supreme Courts, in deciding on the validity of any claim, shall be governed by the treaty of Guadalupe Hidalgo; the law of nations; the laws, usages, and customs of the government *from which the claim is derived*; the principles of equity, and the decisions of the Supreme Court of the United States, etc., etc."

Thus the government washes its hands clean, liberally providing plenty of tribunals, plenty of crooked turnings through which to scourge the wretched land-owners.

Don Mariano had been for some years under the lash of the maternal government, whom he had found a cruel stepmother, indeed.

As it was arranged with Clarence, the meeting would take place that day on the broad piazza of John Gasbang's house, this being the most central point in the rancho.

The heads of families all came—the male heads, be it understood—as the squatters did not make any pretence to regard female opinion, with any more respect than other men.

All the benches and chairs that the house contained, with the exception of Mrs. Gasbang's sewing rocker, had been brought to the porch, which was quite roomy and airy.

At ten minutes before two, all the settlers were there, that is to say, all the old men, with their elder sons.

Clarence, Romeo, Tom and Jack, sat together in a corner, conversing in low tones, while Gasbang was entertaining his guests with some broad anecdotes, which brought forth peals of laughter.

At five minutes to two, Señor Alamar, accompanied by Mr. Mechlin, arrived in a buggy; his two sons followed on horseback.

Clarence had time to look at them leisurely, while they dismounted, and tied their horses to a hitching post.

"They are gentlemen, no doubt," observed Clarence.

"You bet they are," Romeo coincided. Evidently he admired and liked them.

"How much the boys look like the old man," Tom said.

"They look like Englishmen," was Clarence's next observation.

"Yes, particularly Victoriano; he is so light he looks more like a German, I think," said Romeo.

"I think Gabriel is very handsome," Tom said, "only of late he seems always so sad or thoughtful."

"That won't do for a man who is to marry soon," said Romeo. "I think he has always been rather reserved. He has only a cold salutation to give, while Victoriano will be laughing and talking to everybody. But, perhaps, you are right, and he is changed. I think he is less reconciled than the others, to have us, settlers, helping ourselves to what they consider their land. I used to work with them in ploughing and harvesting time, and both boys, and the Don, were always very kind to me, and I can't help liking them."

"The ladies, though, ain't so affable. They are very proud," said Tom; "they walk like queens."

"They didn't seem proud to me, but I never spoke to them," said Romeo.

Gasbang went forward to meet his guests, and all came into the porch.

"Good afternoon, gentlemen," said Don Mariano to the settlers, lifting his hat and bowing. His sons and Mr. Mechlin did the same. Clarence arose, and so did the other young men with him, returning their salutation. The elder Darrell, Pittikin and Hughes followed this example; the other settlers nodded only, and remained sitting with their hats on, looking with affected indifference at the trees beyond.

"I thank you for your courtesy in complying with my request to have this meeting," he said. Some nodded, others grinned and winked, others smiled silently.

"Take this chair, Señor, and you, Mr. Mechlin, take this one. They are the best in my establishment," said Gasbang. "The young gentlemen will find seats somewhere on the benches."

Clarence came forward and offered three chairs. Mr. Mechlin took his arm and presented him to the Alamars.

"I take pleasure in making your acquaintance, and I hope to have the opportunity to thank you for your kind co-operation more appropriately afterward," said Don Mariano. His sons shook hands with Clarence cordially, and accepted the proffered chairs.

Don Mariano excused himself for not speaking English more fluently.

"If you don't understand me I will repeat my words until I make my meaning clear, but I hope you will ask me to repeat them; or, perhaps, some one of these young gentlemen will do me the kindness to be my interpreter," said he.

"Romeo talks Spanish; he can interpret for you," said Victoriano.

"You talk English better," Romeo proudly replied, thinking he could tell his wife that the Don had asked him to be his interpreter.

"Perhaps Mr. Clarence Darrell would do me the favor," said Don Mariano.

"You speak very good English, señor. We understand you perfectly. You do not require an interpreter," Clarence said.

"That is so; you speak very well," said Mr. Mechlin.

Gasbang and Pittikin added: "Certainly, we understand him very well."

"Of course we do," said Darrell and others.

"You are very kind," said the Don, smiling, "and I will try to be brief, and not detain you long."

"We have all the afternoon," said Hughes.

"That's so, we ain't in a hurry," said several.

"Only let us out in time to bring the milch cows home, before night comes on," said old Miller, dryly.

"Exactly, we want to look after our cows, too," said the Don, laughing.

All saw the fine irony of the rejoinder, and laughed heartily. Miller scratched his ear, as if he had felt the retort there, knowing well, that with the exception of Mathews and Gasbang, he had killed and "*corraled*" more of the Don's cattle than any other settler.

"Speaking about cows, brings us at once to the object of this meeting,"— Don Mariano, still smiling, went on, saying: "You know that I have lost many, and that it is natural I should wish to save those I have left. To do this, and yet not ask that you give up your claims, I have one or two propositions to make to you. The reason why you have taken up land here is because you want homes. You want to make money. Isn't that the reason? Money! money!"

"That's it, exactly," said many voices, and all laughed.

"Well, I can show you how you may keep your homes and make more money than you can by your present methods, while at the same time, I also save my cattle. That little point, you know, I must keep in view."

All laughed again.

"To fence your fields, you have said, is too expensive, particularly as the rainy seasons are too uncertain to base upon them any calculations for getting crops to pay for fencing. I believe this is what most of you say; is it not?"

"We could have raised better crops if your cattle hadn't damaged them," said Mathews.

"I beg to differ; but supposing that you are right, do you think you could be sure of good crops if you killed all my stock, or if I took them all away to the mountains? No, most assuredly. The rainy season would still be irregular and unreliable, I think. Yes, I may say, I feel sure, it is a mistake to try to make San Diego County a grain-producing county. It is not so, and I feel certain it never will be, to any great extent. This county is, and has been, and will be always, a good grazing county—one of the best counties for cattle-raising on this coast, and the very best for fruit-raising on the face of the earth. God intended it should be. Why, then, not devote your time, your labor and your money to raising vineyards, fruits and cattle, instead of trusting to the uncertain rains to give you grain crops?"

"It takes a long time to get fruit trees to bearing. What are we to do for a living in the meantime?" asked Miller.

"Begin raising cattle—that will support you," the Don replied.

"Where is the capital to buy cattle with?" Gasbang asked.

"You don't require any more capital than you already have. I can let each of you have a number of cows to begin with, and give you four or five years' time to pay me. So you see, it will be with the increase of these cattle you will pay, for I shall charge you no interest."

"What do you expect us to do in return? To give back to you our home-steads?" asked Hughes.

"No, sir; I have said, and repeat again, you will retain your homesteads."

"And will you stop contesting our claims?" asked Mathews.

"I will, and will give each one a quit-claim deed."

"You will not fight our claims, but you don't want us to plant grain on our land," said Gasbang.

"You can plant grain, if you like, but to do so you must fence your land; so, as you all say, that fencing is expensive, I suggest your fencing orchards and vineyards only, but not grain fields—I mean large fields."

"Pshaw! I knew there was to be something behind all that display of gener-osity," muttered Mathews.

Don Mariano reddened with a thrill of annoyance, but quietly answered:

"You are too good business men to suppose that I should not reserve some slight advantage for myself, when I am willing you should have many more yourselves. All I want to do is to save the few cattle I have left. I am willing to quit-claim to you the land you have taken, and give you cattle to begin the stock business, and all I ask you in return is to put a fence around whatever land you wish to cultivate, so that my cattle cannot go in there. So I say, plant vineyards, plant olives, figs, oranges; makes wines and oil and raisins; export olives and dried and canned fruits. I had some very fine California canned fruit sent to me from San Francisco. Why could we not can fruits as well, or better? Our olives are splendid—the same our figs, oranges, apricots, and truly all semi-tropical fruits are of a superior quality. When this fact becomes generally known, I feel very sure that San Diego County will be selected for fruit and grape-growing. In two years grape vines begin to bear; the same with figs, peaches and other fruits. At three years old they bear quite well, and all without irrigation. So you would not have to wait so very long to begin getting a return from your labor and capital. Moreover, an orchard of forty acres or vineyard of twenty will pay better after three years' growth than one hundred and sixty acres of wheat or barley in good seasons, and more than three hundred acres of any grain in moderately good seasons, or one thousand acres in bad seasons. You can easily fence twenty or forty or sixty acres for a vineyard or orchard, but not so easily fence a field of one hundred and sixty, and the grain crop would be uncertain, depending on the rains, but not so the trees, for you can irrigate them, and after the trees are rooted that is not required."

"Where is the water to irrigate?" asked Miller.

"The water is in the sea now, for there we let it go every year; but if we were sensible, judicious men, we would not let it go to waste—we would save it. This rancho has many deep ravines which bring water from hills and sierras. These ravines all open into the valleys, and run like so many little rivers in the rainy season. By converting these ravines into reservoirs we could have more water than would be needed for irrigating the fruit trees on the foothills. In the low valleys no irrigation would be needed. If we all join forces to put up dams across the most convenient of these ravines, we will have splendid reservoirs. I will defray half the expense if you will get together and stand the other half. Believe me, it will be a great God-send to have a thriving, fruit-growing business in our county. To have the cultivated land well fenced, and the remainder left out for grazing. Then there would not be so many thousands upon thousands of useless acres as now have to be. For every ten acres of cultivated land (not fenced) there are ten thousand, yes, twenty thousand, entirely idle, useless. Why? Because those ten acres of growing grain must be protected, and the cattle which don't know the 'no fence' law, follow their inclination to go and eat the green grass. Then they are 'corralled' or killed. Is it not a pity to kill the poor dumb brutes, because we can't make them understand the law, and see the wisdom of our Sacramento legislators who enacted it? And is it not a pity to impoverish our county by making the bulk of its land useless? The foolishness of letting all of the rainfall go to waste, is an old time folly with us. Still, in old times, we had, at least, the good excuse that we raised all the fruits we needed for our use, and there was no market for any more. But we were not then, as now, guilty of the folly of making the land useless. We raised cattle and sold hides and tallow every year, and made money. When gold was discovered, we drove our stock north, got a good price for it, and made money. But now no money will be made by anybody out of cattle, if they are to be destroyed, and no money made out of land, for the grazing will be useless, when there will be no stock left to eat it. Thus, the county will have no cattle, and the crops be always uncertain. Believe me, in years to come, you will see that the county was impoverished by the 'no fence law,' unless we try to save our county, in spite of foolish legislation. If our wise legislators could enact a law obliging rain to come, so that we could have better chances to raise grain, then there would be some show of excuse for the '*no fence law,*' *perhaps*. I say PERHAPS, because, in my humble opinion, we ought to prefer cattle raising and fruit growing for our county. We should make these our specialty."

"I think it would be much more foolish to trust to a few cows to make out a living while trees grow," said Miller, "than to the seasons to give us grain crops."

"No, sir; because cattle are sure to increase, if they are not killed, and you could make cheese and butter, and sell your steers every year, while trees grow. You have been seven years a settler on this rancho. In these seven years you have raised two good crops; three poor, or only middling, and two, no crops at all."

"Yes, because your cattle destroyed them," said Mathews.

"No, sir; my cattle were not all over California; but the bad seasons were, and only in few places, moderately good crops were harvested; in the southern counties none at all. We had rains enough to get sufficiently good grazing, but not to raise grain."

"I think you are right about the uncertainty of our seasons, and I think a good dairy always pays well, also a good orchard and vineyard," said Darrell. "But the question is, whether we can adopt some feasible plan to put your idea into practice."

"Yes, how many cows will you let us have?" asked Hager.

"I will divide with you. Next week I shall have my '*rodeo.*' We can see then the number of cattle I have left. We shall count them. I shall take half, the other half you divide pro rata; each head of a family taking a proportionate number of cattle."

"That is fair," Darrell said.

"I don't want any cattle. I ain't no '*vaquero*' to go '*busquering*' around and *lassoing* cattle. I'll *lasso* myself; what do I know about whirling a *lariat*?" said Mathews.

"Then, don't take cattle. You can raise fruit trees and vineyards," said Darrell.

"Yes, and starve meantime," Mathews replied.

"You will not have to be a vaquero. I don't go '*busquering*' around *lassooing*, unless I wish to do so," said the Don. "You can hire an Indian boy to do that part. They know how to handle *la reata* and *echar el lazo* to perfection. You will not starve, either, for if you wish, you can make butter and cheese enough to help to pay expenses. I think this State ought to make and export as good cheese as it now imports, and some day people will see it, and do it, too. Thus, with the produce of your dairies, at first, and afterward with your fruits, you will do far better than with grain crops, and not work as hard. Let the northern counties raise grain, while we raise fruits and make wine, butter and cheese. You must not forget, either, that every year you can sell a number of cattle, besides keeping as many milch cows as you need."

"Where can we sell our cattle?" asked Hancock.

"Cattle-buyers will come to buy from you. But if you prefer it, you can drive your stock north yourselves, and make a good profit. Since 1850, I have sent nine times droves of cattle to the northern counties, and made a handsome profit every time. The first time we took stock north, was in '50; I took nearly six thousand head—three thousand were mine—and the others belonged to my brothers. We lost very few, and sold at a good price—all the way from eighteen to twenty-five dollars per head. About five hundred of mine I sold as high as thirty dollars per head. I made sixty thousand dollars by this operation. Then out of the next lot I made twenty-seven thousand dollars. Then I made twenty-two thousand, and so on, until my tame cows began to disappear, as you all know. In four years after my cows began to get shot, my cattle decreased more than half. Now I don't think I have many more than three thousand head. So you cannot blame me for wishing to save these few. But believe me, the plan I propose will be as beneficial to you as to me, and also to the entire county, for as soon as it is shown that we can make a success of the industries I propose, others will follow our example."

"If you have only three thousand head, you can't spare many to us, and it will hardly be worth while to stop planting crops to get a few cows," said Gasbang.

"I think I will be able to spare five or six hundred cows. I don't know how many I have left."

"We will buy from somebody else, if we want more," said Darrell. "We won't want many to begin with; it will be something of an experiment for some of us."

"For all of us here. Perhaps you understand *vaquering*; we don't," said Hancock; all laughed.

"Then fence your claim and plant grain," Darrell retorted.

"I am not so big a fool as to spend money in fences. The '*no fence*' law is better than all the best fences," Mathews said.

"But what if you make more money by following other laws that are more just, more rational?" said the Don.

"The 'no fence' law is rational enough for me," said Miller.

"And so say I," said Mathews.

"And I," said Gasbang.

Hughes nodded approvingly, but he was too much of a hypocrite to commit himself in words.

"We did not come to discuss the 'no fence' law, but only to propose something that will put more money in your pockets than killing dumb beasts," said Mr. Mechlin.

"Then propose something practicable," said Mathews.

"I think what has been proposed is practicable enough," Darrell said.

"Certainly it is," Mr. Mechlin added.

"I don't see it," said Mathews.

"Nor I, either," added Gasbang.

"Nor I, neither," said Hughes.

"Well, gentlemen," said Don Mariano, rising, "I shall leave you now; you know my views, and you perhaps prefer to discuss them, and discuss your own among yourselves, and not in my presence. Take your time, and when you come to a final decision let me know. Perhaps I can advance the money to those of you who do not have it ready to purchase fencing lumber. I shall charge no interest, and give you plenty of time to pay."

"I will do that, Señor Alamar," Clarence said; "if the settlers agree to fence their lands, I will advance the money to them to put up their fences."

"Yes, and if our crops fail, we will be in debt to the ears, with a chain around our necks," Mathews growled.

"I thought you said that if it were not for my cattle, your crops would not have failed," said Don Mariano, smiling.

"I said so, and it is so. But you see, that was before we had the '*no fence*' law," answered he, grinning.

Don Mariano shook hands with Clarence, whom he invited to call at his house—this invitation Clarence accepted with warm thanks—and followed by his sons and his friend Mr. Mechlin, Don Mariano took his leave, bowing to the settlers, who nodded and grinned in return.

"I suppose you, too, think the '*no fence*' law iniquitous, as you appear to favor the aristocracy," said Gasbang to Clarence.

"It is worse than that, it is stupid. Now it kills the cattle, afterwards it will kill the county," Clarence answered.

"Shall we plant no wheat, because the Spaniards want to raise cattle?" Mathews asked.

"Plant wheat, if you can do so without killing cattle. But do not destroy the larger industry with the smaller. If, as the Don very properly says, this is a grazing county, no legislation can change it. So it would be wiser to make laws to suit the county, and not expect that the county will change its character to suit absurd laws," Clarence replied.

4–3
Mark Twain (Samuel L. Clemens) (1835–1910)

SAMUEL LANGHORNE CLEMENS (1835–1910), better known by his "nom de guerre" (as he called it), MARK TWAIN, was born into a slaveholding family in the border state of Missouri. He became a steamboat pilot, but when river traffic was closed by the Civil War, he joined a Confederate militia before quickly deserting, fleeing West. Even in his youth, he had worked on newspapers, publishing his first work of fiction in 1852, but it was in the Nevada Territory that Sam Clemens became Mark Twain. His writing reveals a writer with roots deep in the American land yet at home abroad, too. Indeed, some of his best-known pieces of Americana were prompted by foreign travel, as when in *A Tramp Abroad* (1880), a visit to a German forest led to recounting one of his most memorable tall tales, "Jim Baker's Blue Jay Yarn," which was set in the Sierra Nevadas.

"The Celebrated Jumping Frog of Calaveras County" (1867)

In compliance with the request of a friend of mine, who wrote me from the East, I called on good-natured, garrulous old Simon Wheeler, and inquired after my friend's friend, *Leonidas W.* Smiley, as requested to do, and I hereunto append the result. I have a lurking suspicion that *Leonidas W.* Smiley is a myth; that my friend never knew such a personage; and that he only conjectured that, if I asked old Wheeler about him, it would remind him of his infamous *Jim* Smiley, and he would go to work and bore me nearly to death with some infernal reminiscence of him as long and tedious as it should be useless to me. If that was the design, it certainly succeeded.

I found Simon Wheeler dozing comfortably by the bar-room stove of the old, dilapidated tavern in the ancient mining camp of Angel's, and I noticed

FROM A PHOTOGRAPH TAKEN IN 1899
By H. W. Barnett, London

that he was fat and bald-headed, and had an expression of winning gentle-ness and simplicity upon his tranquil countenance. He roused up and gave me good-day. I told him a friend of mine had commissioned me to make some inquiries about a cherished companion of his boyhood named *Leonidas W. Smiley—Rev. Leonidas W.* Smiley—a young minister of the Gospel, who he had heard was at one time a resident of Angel's Camp. I added that, if Mr. Wheeler could tell me any thing about this Rev. Leonidas W. Smiley, I would feel under many obligations to him.

Simon Wheeler backed me into a corner and blockaded me there with his chair, and then sat me down and reeled off the monotonous narrative which follows this paragraph. He never smiled, he never frowned, he never changed his voice from the gentle-flowing key to which he tuned the initial sentence, he never betrayed the slightest suspicion of enthusiasm; but all through the interminable narrative there ran a vein of impressive earnestness and sincerity, which showed me plainly that, so far from his imagining that there was any thing ridiculous or funny about his story, he regarded it as a really important matter, and admired its two heroes as men of transcendent genius in *finesse*. To me, the spectacle of a man drifting serenely along through such a queer yarn without ever smiling, was exquisitely absurd. As I said before, I asked him to tell me what he knew of Rev. Leonidas W. Smiley, and he replied as follows. I let him go on in his own way, and never interrupted him once:

There was a feller here once by the name of *Jim* Smiley, in the winter of '49— or may be it was the spring of '50—I don't recollect exactly, somehow, though what makes me think it was one or the other is because I remember the big flume wasn't finished when he first came to the camp; but any way, he was the curiosest man about always betting on any thing that turned up you ever see, if he could get any body to bet on the other side; and if he couldn't, he'd change sides. Any way that suited the other man would suit him—any way just so's he got a bet, *he* was satisfied. But still he was lucky, uncommon lucky; he most always come out winner. He was always ready and laying for a chance; there couldn't be no solitary thing mentioned but that feller'd offer to bet on it, and take any side you please, as I was just telling you. If there was a horse-race, you'd find him flush, or you'd find him busted at the end of it; if there was a dog-fight, he'd bet on it; if there was a cat-fight, he'd bet on it; if there was a chicken-fight, he'd bet on it; why, if there was two birds setting on a fence, he would bet you which one would fly first; or if there was a camp-meeting, he would be there reg'lar, to bet on Parson Walker, which he judged to be the best exhorter about here, and so he was, too, and a good man. If he even seen a straddle-bug start to go anywheres, he would bet you how long it would take him to get wherever he was going to, and if you took him up, he would foller that straddle-bug to Mexico but what he would find out where he was bound for and how long he was on the road. Lots of the boys here has seen that Smiley, and can tell you about him. Why, it never made no difference to *him*—he would bet on *any* thing—the dangdest feller. Parson Walker's wife laid very sick once, for a good while, and it seemed as if they warn't going to save her; but one morning he come in, and Smiley asked how she was, and he said she was considerable better—thank the Lord for his inf'nit mercy—and coming on so smart that, with the blessing of Prov'dence, she'd get well yet; and Smiley, before he thought, says, "Well, I'll risk two-and-a-half that she don't, any way."

Thish-yer Smiley had a mare—the boys called her the fifteen-minute nag, but that was only in fun, you know, because, of course, she was faster than that—and he used to win money on that horse, for all she was so slow and always had the asthma, or the distemper, or the consumption, or something of that kind. They used to give her two or three hundred yards start, and then pass her under way; but always at the fag-end of the race she'd get excited and desperate-like, and come cavorting and straddling up, and scattering her legs around limber, sometimes in the air, and some times out to one side amongst the fences, and kicking up m-o-r-e dust, and raising m-o-r-e racket with her coughing and sneezing and blowing her nose—and always fetch up at the stand just about a neck ahead, as near as you could cipher it down.

And he had a little small bull pup, that to look at him you'd think he wan't worth a cent, but to set around and look ornery, and lay for a chance to steal something. But as soon as money was up on him, he was a different dog; his under-jaw'd begin to stick out like the fo'castle of a steamboat, and his teeth would uncover, and shine savage like the furnaces. And a dog might tackle him, and bully-rag him, and bite him, and throw him over his shoulder two or three times, and Andrew Jackson—which was the name of the pup—Andrew Jackson would never let on but what *he* was satisfied, and hadn't expected nothing else—and the bets being doubled and doubled on the other side all the time, till the money was all up; and then all of a sudden he would grab that other dog jest by the j'int of his hind leg and freeze to it—not chaw, you understand, but only jest grip and hang on till they throwed up the sponge, if it was a year. Smiley always come out winner on that pup, till he harnessed a dog once that didn't have no hind legs, because they'd been sawed off by a circular saw, and when the thing had gone along far enough, and the money was all up, and he come to make a snatch for his pet holt, he saw in a minute how he'd been imposed on, and how the other dog had him in the door, so to speak, and he 'peared surprised, and then he looked sorter discouraged-like, and didn't try no more to win the fight, and so he got shucked out bad. He give Smiley a look, as much as to say his heart was broke, and it was *his* fault, for putting up a dog that hadn't no hind legs for him to take holt of, which was his main dependence in a fight, and then he limped off a piece and laid down and died. It was a good pup, was that Andrew Jackson, and would have made a name for hisself if he'd lived, for the stuff was in him, and he had genius—I know it, because he hadn't had no opportunities to speak of, and it don't stand to reason that a dog could make such a fight as he could under them circumstances, if he hadn't no talent. It always makes me feel sorry when I think of that last fight of his'n, and the way it turned out.

Well, thish-yer Smiley had rat-tarriers, and chicken cocks, and tom-cats, and all them kind of things, till you couldn't rest, and you couldn't fetch nothing for him to bet on but he'd match you. He ketched a frog one day, and took him home, and said he cal'klated to edercate him; and so he never done nothing for three months but set in his back yard and learn that frog to jump. And you bet you he *did* learn him, too. He'd give him a little punch behind, and the next minute you'd see that frog whirling in the air like a doughnut—see him turn one summerset, or may be a couple, if he got a good start, and come down flat-footed and all right, like a cat. He got him up so in the matter of catching flies, and kept him in practice so constant, that he'd nail a fly every time as far as he could see him. Smiley said all a frog wanted was education, and he could do most any thing—and I believe him. Why, I've seen him set Dan'l Webster down here on this floor—Dan'l Webster was the name of the frog—and sing out, "Flies, Dan'l, flies!" and quicker'n you could wink, he'd spring straight up, and snake a fly off'n the counter there, and flop down on the floor again as solid as a gob of mud, and fall to scratching the side of his head with his hind foot as indifferent as if he hadn't no idea he'd been doin' any more'n any frog might do. You never see a frog so modest and straightfor'ard as he was, for all he was so gifted. And when it come to fair and square jumping on a dead level, he could get over more ground at one straddle than any animal of his breed you ever see. Jumping on a dead level was his strong suit, you understand; and when it come to that, Smiley would ante up money on him as long as he had a red. Smiley was monstrous proud of his frog, and well he might be, for fellers that had traveled and been everywheres, all said he laid over any frog that ever *they* see.

Well, Smiley kept the beast in a little lattice box, and he used to fetch him down town sometimes and lay for a bet. One day a feller—a stranger in the camp, he was—come across him with his box, and says:

"What might it be that you've got in the box?"

And Smiley says, sorter indifferent like, "It might be a parrot, or it might be a canary, may be, but it an't—it's only just a frog."

And the feller took it, and looked at it careful, and turned it round this way and that, and says, "H'm—so 'tis. Well, what's *he* good for?"

"Well," Smiley says, easy and careless, "He's good enough for *one* thing, I should judge—he can outjump ary frog in Calaveras county."

The feller took the box again, and took another long, particular look, and give it back to Smiley, and says, very deliberate, "Well, I don't see no p'ints about that frog that's any better'n any other frog."

"May be you don't," Smiley says. "May be you understand frogs, and may be you don't understand 'em; may be you've had experience, and may be you an't only a amature, as it were. Anyways, I've got *my* opinion, and I'll risk forty dollars that he can outjump any frog in Calaveras county."

And the feller studied a minute, and then says, kinder sad like, "Well, I'm only a stranger here, and I an't got no frog; but if I had a frog, I'd bet you."

And then Smiley says, "That's all right—that's all right—if you'll hold my box a minute, I'll go and get you a frog." And so the feller took the box, and put up his forty dollars along with Smiley's, and set down to wait.

So he set there a good while thinking and thinking to hisself, and then he got the frog out and prized his mouth open and took a teaspoon and filled him full of quail shot—filled him pretty near up to his chin—and set him on the floor. Smiley he went to the swamp and slopped around in the mud for a long time, and finally he ketched a frog, and fetched him in, and give him to this feller, and says:

"Now, if you're ready, set him alongside of Dan'l, with his fore-paws just even with Dan'l, and I'll give the word." Then he says, "One—two—three—jump!" and him and the feller touched up the frogs from behind, and the new frog hopped off, but Dan'l give a heave, and hysted up his shoulders—so—like a Frenchman, but it wan't no use—he couldn't budge; he was planted as solid as an anvil, and he couldn't no more stir than if he was anchored out. Smiley was a good deal surprised, and he was disgusted too, but he didn't have no idea what the matter was, of course.

The feller took the money and started away; and when he was going out at the door, he sorter jerked his thumb over his shoulders—this way—at Dan'l, and says again, very deliberate, "Well, I don't see no p'ints about that frog that's any better'n any other frog."

Smiley he stood scratching his head and looking down at Dan'l a long time, and at last he says, "I do wonder what in the nation that frog throw'd off for—I wonder if there an't something the matter with him—he 'pears to look mighty baggy, somehow." And he ketched Dan'l by the nap of the neck, and lifted him up and says, "Why, blame my cats, if he don't weigh five pound!" and turned him upside down, and he belched out a double handful of shot. And then he see how it was, and he was the maddest man—he set the frog down and took out after that feller, but he never ketched him. And—

[Here Simon Wheeler heard his name called from the front yard, and got up to see what was wanted.] And turning to me as he moved away, he said: "Just set where you are, stranger, and rest easy—I an't going to be gone a second."

But, by your leave, I did not think that a continuation of the history of the enterprising vagabond *Jim* Smiley would be likely to afford me much information concerning the Rev. *Leonidas W.* Smiley, and so I started away.

At the door I met the sociable Wheeler returning, and he buttonholed me and recommenced:

"Well, thish-yer Smiley had a yaller one-eyed cow that didn't have no tail, only jest a short stump like a bannanner, and—"

"Oh! hang Smiley and his afflicted cow!" I muttered, good-naturedly, and bidding the old gentleman good-day, I departed.

"Back From 'Yurrup'" (1869)

Have you ever seen a family of geese just back from Europe—or Yurrup, as they pronounce it? They never talk *to* you, of course, being strangers, but they talk to each other and *at* you till you are pretty nearly distracted with their clatter; till you are sick of their ocean experiences; their mispronounced foreign names; their dukes and emperors; their trivial adventures; their pointless reminiscences; till you are sick of their imbecile faces and their relentless clack, and wish it had pleased Providence to leave the clapper out of their empty skulls.

I traveled with such a family one eternal day, from New York to Boston, last week. They had spent just a year in "Yurrup," and were returning home to Boston. Papa said little, and looked bored—he had simply been down in New York to receive and cart home his cargo of traveled imbecility. Sister Angeline, aged 23, sister Augusta, aged 25, and brother Charles, aged 33, did the conversational drivel, and mamma purred and admired, and threw in some help when occasion offered, in the way of remembering some French barber's—I should say some French count's—name, when they pretended to have forgotten it. They occupied the choice seats in the parlor of the drawing-room car, and for twelve hours I sat opposite to them—was their *vis-a-vis*, as they would have said in their charming French way.

Augusta.—"Plague that nahsty (nasty) steamer! I've the headache yet, she rolled so the fifth day out."

Angeline.—"And well you may. *I* never saw such a nahsty old tub. I never want to go in the *Ville de Paris* again. Why *didn't* we go over to London and come in the *Scotia*?"

Augusta.—"Because we were fools."

[Endorsed that sentiment.]

Angeline.—"Gustie, what made Count Nixkumarouse drive off looking so blue, that last Thursday in Pairy? (Paris she meant.) Ah, own up, now!" (tapping her arm *so* roguishly with her ivory fan.)

Augusta.—"Now, Angie, how you talk! I *told* the nahsty creature I would not receive his attentions any longer. And the old duke his father kept boring me about him and his two million francs a year till I sent *him* off with a flea in his ear."

Chorus.—"Ke-he-he! Ha-ha-ha!"

Charles.—[Pulling a small silken cloak to pieces.] "Angie, where'd you get this cheap thing?"

Angeline.—"You Cholly, let that alone! Cheap! Well, how could I help it? There we were, tied up in Switzerland—just down from Mon Blong (Mont Blanc, doubtless)—couldn't buy anything in those nahsty shops so far away from Pairy. I had to put up with that slimpsy forty-dollar rag—but bless you, I couldn't go naked!"

Chorus.—"Ke-he-he!"

Augusta.—"Guess who I was thinking of? Those ignorant persons we saw first in Rome and afterwards in Venice—those—"

Angeline.—"Oh, ha-ha-ha! He-he-he! It *was* so funny! Papa, one of them called the Santa della Spiggiola the Santa della Spizziola! Ha-ha-ha! And she thought it was Canova that did Michael Angelo's Moses! Only *think* of it! Canova a sculptor and Moses a picture! I thought I should die! I guess I let them see by the way I laughed, that they'd made fools of themselves, because they blushed and sneaked off."

[Papa laughed faintly, but not with the easy grace of a man who was certain he knew what he was laughing about.]

Augusta.—"Why Cholly! Where did you get those nahsty Beaumarchais gloves? Well, I *wouldn't*, if I were you!"

Mamma.—[With uplifted hands.] "Beaumarchais, my son!"

Angeline.—"Beaumarchais! Why how can you! Nobody in Pairy wears those nahsty things but the commonest people."

Charles.—"They *are* a rum lot, but then Tom Blennerhasset gave 'em to me—he wanted to do something or other to curry favor, I s'pose."

Angeline.—"Tom Blennerhasset!"

Augusta.—"Tom Blennerhasset!"

Mamma.—"Tom Blennerhasset! And have you been associating with *him*?"

Papa.—[Suddenly interested.] "Heavens, what has the son of an honored and honorable old friend been doing?"

Chorus.—"Doing! Why his father has endorsed himself bankrupt for friends—that's what's the matter!"

Angeline.—"Oh, mon Dieu, j'ai faim! Avez-vous quelque chose de bon, en votre poche, mon cher frere? Excuse me for speaking French, for, to tell the truth, I haven't spoken English for so long that it comes dreadful awkward. Wish we were back in Yurrup—c'est votre desire aussi, n'est-ce pas, mes cheres?"

And from that moment they lapsed into barbarous French and kept it up for an hour—hesitating, gasping for words, stumbling head over heels through adverbs and participles, floundering among adjectives, working miracles of villainous pronunciation—and neither one of them by any chance ever understanding what another was driving at.

By that time some new comers had entered the car, and so they lapsed into English again and fell to holding everything American up to scorn and contumely in order that they might thus let those newcomers know they were just home from "Yurrup." To use their pet and best beloved phrase, they were a "nahsty" family of American snobs, and there ought to be a law against allowing such to go to Europe and misrepresent the nation. It will take these insects five years, without doubt, to get done turning their noses at everything American, and making damaging comparisons between their own country and "Yurrup." Let us pity their waiting friends in Boston in their affliction.

"Jim Baker's Bluejay Yarn" from *A Tramp Abroad* (1880)

Animals talk to each other, of course. There can be no question about that; but I suppose there are very few people who can understand them. I never knew but one man who could. I knew he could, however, because he told me so himself. He was a middle-aged, simple-hearted miner who had lived in a lonely corner of California, among the woods and mountains, a good many years, and had studied the ways of his only neighbors, the beasts and the birds, until he believed he could accurately translate any remark which they made. This was Jim Baker. According to Jim Baker, some animals have only a limited education, and use only very simple words, and scarcely ever a comparison or a flowery figure; whereas, certain other animals have a large vocabulary, a fine command of language and a ready and fluent delivery; consequently these latter talk a great deal; they like it; they are conscious of their talent, and they enjoy "showing off." Baker said, that after long and careful observation, he had come to the conclusion that the bluejays were the best talkers he had found among birds and beasts. Said he:

"There's more *to* a bluejay than any other creature. He has got more moods, and more different kinds of feelings than other creatures; and, mind you, whatever a bluejay feels, he can put into language. And no mere commonplace language, either, but rattling, out-and-out book-talk—and bristling with metaphor, too—just bristling! And as for command of language—why *you* never see a bluejay get stuck for a word. No man ever did. They just boil out of him! And another thing: I've noticed a good deal, and there's no bird, or cow, or anything that uses as good grammar as a bluejay. You may say a cat uses good grammar. Well, a cat does—but you let a cat get excited once; you let a cat get to pulling fur with another cat on a shed, nights, and you'll hear grammar that will give you the lockjaw. Ignorant people think it's the *noise* which fighting cats make that is so aggravating, but it ain't so; it's the sickening grammar they use. Now I've never heard a jay use bad grammar but very seldom; and when they do, they are as ashamed as a human; they shut right down and leave.

"You may call a jay a bird. Well, so he is, in a measure—because he's got feathers on him, and don't belong to no church, perhaps; but otherwise he is just as much a human as you be. And I'll tell you for why. A jay's gifts, and instincts, and feelings, and interests, cover the whole ground. A jay hasn't got any more principle than a Congressman. A jay will lie, a jay will steal, a jay will deceive, a jay will betray; and four times out of five, a jay will go back on his solemnest promise. The sacredness of an obligation is a thing which you can't cram into no bluejay's head. Now, on top of all this, there's another thing; a jay can out-swear any gentleman in the mines. You think a cat can swear. Well, a cat can; but you give a bluejay a subject that calls for his reserve-powers, and where is your cat? Don't talk to *me*—I know too much about this thing. And there's yet another thing; in the one little particular of scolding—just good, clean, out-and-out scolding—a bluejay can lay over anything, human or divine. Yes, sir, a jay is everything that a man is. A jay can cry, a jay can laugh, a jay can feel shame, a jay can reason and plan and discuss, a jay likes gossip and scandal, a jay has got a sense of humor, a jay knows when he is an ass just as well as you do—maybe better. If a jay ain't human, he better take in his sign, that's all. Now I'm going to tell you a perfectly true fact about some bluejays." . . .

"When I first began to understand jay language correctly, there was a little incident happened here. Seven years ago, the last man in this region but me moved away. There stands his house,—been empty ever since; a log house, with a plank roof—just one big room, and no more; no ceiling—nothing between the rafters and the floor. Well, one Sunday morning I was sitting out here in front of my cabin, with my cat, taking the sun, and looking at the blue hills, and listening to the leaves rustling so lonely in the trees, and thinking of the home away yonder in the states, that I hadn't heard from in thirteen years, when a bluejay lit on that house, with an acorn in his mouth, and says, 'Hello, I reckon I've struck something.' When he spoke, the acorn dropped out of his mouth and rolled down the roof, of course, but he didn't care; his mind was all on the thing he had struck. It was a knot-hole in the roof. He cocked his head to one side, shut one eye and put the other one to the hole, like a 'possum looking down a jug; then he glanced up with his bright eyes, gave a wink or two with his wings—which signifies gratification, you understand,—and says, 'It looks like a hole, it's located like a hole,—blamed if I don't believe it *is* a hole!'

"Then he cocked his head down and took another look; he glances up perfectly joyful, this time; winks his wings and his tail both, and says, 'Oh, no, this ain't no fat thing, I reckon! If I ain't in luck!—why it's a perfectly elegant hole!' So he flew down and got that acorn, and fetched it up and dropped it in, and was just tilting his head back, with the heavenliest smile on his face, when all of a sudden he was paralyzed into a listening attitude and that smile faded gradually out of his countenance like breath off'n a razor, and the queerest look of surprise took its place. Then he says, 'Why, I didn't hear it fall!' He cocked his eye at the hole again, and took a long look; raised up and shook his head; stepped around to the other side of the hole and took another look from that side; shook his head again. He studied a while, then he just went into the details—walked round and round the hole and spied into it from every point of the compass. No use. Now he took a thinking attitude on the comb of the roof and scratched the back of his head with his right foot a minute, and finally says, 'Well, it's too many for *me*, that's certain; must be a mighty long hole; however, I ain't got no time to fool around here, I got to 'tend to business; I reckon it's all right—chance it, anyway.'

"So he flew off and fetched another acorn and dropped it in, and tried to flirt his eye to the hole quick enough to see what become of it, but he was too late. He held his eye there as much as a minute; then he raised up and sighed, and says, 'Confound it, I don't seem to understand this thing, no way; however, I'll tackle her again.' He fetched another acorn, and done his level best to see what become of it, but he couldn't. He says, "Well, *I* never struck no such a hole as this before; I'm of the opinion it's a totally new kind of a hole.' Then he begun to get mad. He held in for a spell, walking up and down the comb of the roof and shaking his head and muttering to himself; but his feelings got the upper hand of him, presently, and he broke loose and cussed himself black in the face. I never see a bird take on so about a little thing. When he got through he walks to the hole and looks in again for half a minute; then he says, 'Well, you're a long hole, and a deep hole, and a mighty singular hole altogether—but I've started in to fill you, and I'm d—d if I *don't* fill you, if it takes a hundred years!'

"And with that, away he went. You never see a bird work so since you was born. He laid into his work . . . , and the way he hove acorns into that hole for about two hours and a half was one of the most exciting and astonishing spectacles I ever struck. He never stopped to take a look any more—he just hove 'em in and went for more. Well, at last he could hardly flop his wings, he was so tuckered out. He comes a-drooping down, once more, sweating like an ice-pitcher, drops his acorn in and says, '*Now* I guess I've got the bulge on you by this time!' So he bent down for a look. If you'll believe me, when his head come up again he was just pale with rage. He says, 'I've shoveled acorns enough in there to keep the family thirty years, and if I can see a sign of one of 'em I wish I may land in a museum with a belly full of sawdust in two minutes!'

"He just had strength enough to crawl up on to the comb and lean his back agin the chimbly, and then he collected his impressions and begun to free his mind. I see in a second that what I had mistook for profanity in the mines was only just the rudiments, as you may say.

"Another jay was going by, and heard him doing his devotions, and stops to inquire what was up. The sufferer told him the whole circumstance, and says, 'Now yonder's the hole, and if you don't believe me, go and look for yourself.' So this fellow went and looked, and comes back and says, 'How many did you say you put in there?' 'Not any less than two tons,' says the sufferer. The other jay went and looked again. He couldn't seem to make it out, so he raised a yell, and three more jays come. They all examined the hole, they all made the sufferer tell it over again, then they all discussed it, and got off as many leather-headed opinions about it as an average crowd of humans could have done.

"They called in more jays; then more and more, till pretty soon this whole region 'peared to have a blue flush about it. There must have been five thousand of them; and such another jawing and disputing and ripping and cussing, you never heard. Every jay in the whole lot put his eye to the hole and delivered a more chuckle-headed opinion about the mystery than the jay that went there before him. They examined the house all over, too. The door was standing half open, and at last one old jay happened to go and light on it and look in. Of course, that knocked the mystery galley-west in a second. There lay the acorns, scattered all over the floor. He flopped his wings and raised a whoop. 'Come here!' he says, 'Come here, everybody; hang'd if this fool hasn't been trying to fill up a house with acorns!' They all came a-swooping down like a blue cloud, and as each fellow lit on the door and took a glance, the whole absurdity of the contract that that first jay had tackled hit him home and he fell over backwards suffocating with laughter, and the next jay took his place and done the same.

"Well, sir, they roosted around here on the housetop and the trees for an hour, and guffawed over that thing like human beings. It ain't any use to tell me a bluejay hasn't got a sense of humor, because I know better. And memory, too. They brought jays here from all over the United States to look down that hole, every summer for three years. Other birds, too. And they could all see the point, except an owl that come from Nova Scotia to visit the Yo Semite, and he took this thing in on his way back. He said he couldn't see anything funny in it. But then he was a good deal disappointed about Yo Semite, too."

"Concerning the American Language"* (1882)

There was an Englishman in our compartment, and he complimented me on— on what? But you would never guess. He complimented me on my English. He said Americans in general did not speak the English language as correctly as I did. I said I was obliged to him for his compliment, since I knew he meant it for one, but that I was not fairly entitled to it, for I didn't speak English at all,—I only spoke American.

---

* Being part of a chapter which was crowded out of "A Tramp Abroad."—M.T.

He laughed, and said it was a distinction without a difference. I said no, the difference was not prodigious, but still it was considerable. We fell into a friendly dispute over the matter. I put my case as well as I could, and said,—

"The languages were identical several generations ago, but our changed conditions and the spread of our people far to the south and far to the west have made many alterations in our pronunciation, and have introduced new words among us and changed the meanings of many old ones. English people talk through their noses; we do not. We say *know*, English people say *näo*; we say *cow*, the Briton says *käow*; we—"

"Oh, come! that is pure Yankee; everybody knows that."

"Yes, it is pure Yankee; that is true. One cannot hear it in America outside of the little corner called New England, which is Yankee land. The English themselves planted it there, two hundred and fifty years ago, and there it remains; it has never spread. But England talks through her nose yet; the Londoner and the backwoods New-Englander pronounce 'know' and 'cow' alike, and then the Briton unconsciously satirizes himself by making fun of the Yankee's pronunciation."

We argued this point at some length; nobody won; but no matter, the fact remains,—Englishmen say *näo* and *käow* for "know" and "cow," and that is what the rustic inhabitant of a very small section of America does.

"You conferred your *a* upon New England, too, and there it remains; it has not travelled out of the narrow limits of those six little States in all these two hundred and fifty years. All England uses it, New England's small population— say four millions—use it, but we have forty-five millions who do not use it. You say 'glahs of wawtah,' so does New England; at least, New England says *glahs*. America at large flattens the *a*, and says 'glass of water.' These sounds are pleasanter than yours; you may think they are not right,—well, in English they are *not* right, but in 'American' they are. You say *flahsk*, and *bahsket*, and *jackahss*; we say 'flask,' 'basket,' 'jackass,'—sounding the *a* as it is in 'tallow,' 'fallow,' and so on. Up to as late as 1847 Mr. Webster's Dictionary had the impudence to still pronounce 'basket' *bahsket*, when he knew that outside of his little New England all America shortened the *a* and paid no attention to his English broadening of it. However, it called itself an English Dictionary, so it was proper enough that it should stick to English forms, perhaps. It still calls itself an English Dictionary to-day, but it has quietly ceased to pronounce 'basket' as if it were spelt *bahsket*. In the American language the *h* is respected; the *h* is not dropped or added improperly."

"The same is the case in England,—I mean among the educated classes, of course."

"Yes, that is true; but a nation's language is a very large matter. It is not simply a manner of speech obtaining among the educated handful; the manner obtaining among the vast uneducated multitude must be considered also. Your uneducated masses speak English, you will not deny that; our uneducated masses speak American,—it won't be fair for you to deny that, for you can see, yourself, that when your stable-boy says, 'It isn't the 'unting that 'urts the 'orse, but the 'ammer, 'ammer, 'ammer on the 'ard 'ighway,' and our stable-boy makes the same remark without suffocating a single *h*, these two people are manifestly talking two different languages. But if the signs are to be trusted, even your educated classes used to drop the *h*. They say *humble*, now, and *heroic*, and *historic*, etc., but I judge that they used to drop those *h*'s because your writers still keep up the fashion of putting *an* before those words, instead of *a*. This is what Mr. Darwin might call a 'rudimentary' sign that that *an* was justifiable once, and useful,—when your educated classes used to say *'umble*, and *'eroic*, and *'istorical*. Correct writers of the American language do not put *an* before those words."

The English gentleman had something to say upon this matter, but never mind what he said,—I'm not arguing his case. I have him at a disadvantage, now. I proceeded:—

"In England you encourage an orator by exclaiming 'H'yaah! h'yaah!' We pronounce it *heer* in some sections, 'h'*yer*' in others, and so on; but our whites do not say 'h'yaah,' pronouncing the *a*'s like the *a* in *ah*. I have heard English ladies say 'don't you'—making two separate and distinct words of it; your Mr. Bernand has satirized it. But we always say 'dontchu.' This is much better. Your ladies say, 'Oh, it's *o*ful nice!" Ours say, 'Oh, it's *aw*ful nice!' We say, '*Four* hundred,' you say '*For*'—as in the word *or*. Your clergymen speak of 'the Lawd,' ours of 'the Lord'; yours speak of 'the gawds of the heathen,' ours of 'the gods of the heathen.' When you are exhausted, you say you are 'knocked up.' We don't. When you say you will do a thing 'directly,' you mean 'immediately'; in the American language—generally speaking—the word signifies 'after a little.' When you say 'clever,' you mean 'capable'; with us the word used to mean 'accommodating,' but I don't know what it means now. Your word 'stout' means 'fleshy'; our word 'stout' usually means 'strong.' Your words, 'gentleman' and 'lady' have a very restricted meaning; with us they include the bar-maid, butcher, burglar, harlot, and horse-thief. You say, 'I haven't *got* any stockings on,' 'I haven't *got* any memory,' 'I haven't *got* any money in my purse'; we usually say, 'I haven't any stockings on,' 'I haven't any memory,' 'I haven't any money in my purse.' You say 'out of window'; we always put in a *the*. If one asks, 'How old is that man?' the Briton answers, 'He will be about forty'; in the American language, we should say, 'He *is* about forty.' However, won't tire you, sir; but if I wanted to, I could pile up differences here until I not only convinced you that English and American are separate languages, but that when I speak my native tongue in its utmost purity an Englishman can't understand me at all."

"I don't wish to flatter you, but it is about all I can do to understand you *now*."

That was a very pretty compliment, and it put us on the pleasantest terms directly,—I use the word in the English sense.

[*Later*—1882. Æsthetes in many of our schools are now beginning to teach the pupils to broaden the *a*, and to say, "don't you," in the elegant foreign way.]

"On Foreign Critics" (1890)

After Dinner Speech

If I look harried and worn, it is not from an ill conscience. It is from sitting up nights to worry about the foreign critic. He won't concede that we have a civilization—a "real" civilization. Five years ago, he said we had never contributed anything to the betterment of the world. And now comes Sir Lepel Griffin, whom I had not suspected of being in the world at all, and says, "There is no country calling itself civilized where one would not rather live than in America, except Russia." That settles it. That is, it settles it for Europe; but it doesn't make me any more comfortable than I was before.

What is "real" civilization? Nobody can answer that conundrum. They have all tried. Then suppose we try to get at what it is not, and then subtract the what it is not from the general sum, and call the remainder "real" civilization—so as to have a place to stand on while we throw bricks at these people. Let us say, then, in broad terms, that any system which has in it any one of these things—to wit, human slavery, despotic government, inequality, numerous and brutal punishments for crime, superstition almost universal, ignorance almost universal, and dirt and poverty almost universal—is not a real civilization, and any system which has none of them is. If you grant these terms, one may then consider this conundrum: How old is real civilization? The answer is easy and unassailable. A century ago it had not appeared anywhere in the world during a single instant since the world was made. If you grant these terms—and I don't see why it shouldn't be fair, since civilization must surely be fair, since civilization must surely mean the humanizing of a people, not a class—there is to-day but one real civilization in the world, and it is not yet thirty years old. We made the trip and hoisted its flag when we disposed of our slavery.

However, there are some partial civilizations scattered around over Europe—pretty lofty civilizations they are, too—but who begot them? What is the seed from which they sprang? Liberty and intelligence. What planted that seed? There are dates and statistics which suggest that it was the American Revolution that planted it. When that revolution began, monarchy had been on trial some thousands of years, over there, and was a distinct and convicted failure, every time. It had never produced anything but a vast, a nearly universal savagery, with a thin skim of civilization on top, and the main part of that was nickel plate and tinsel. The French, imbruted and impoverished by centuries of oppression and official robbery, were a starving nation clothed in rags, slaves of an aristocracy and smirking dandies clad in unearned silks and velvet. It makes one's cheek burn to read of the laws of the time and realize that they were for human beings; realize that they originated in this world and not in hell. Germany was unspeakable. In the Scotch lowlands the people lived in sties and were human swine; in the highlands drunkenness was general and it hardly smirched a young girl to have a family of her own. In England there was a sham liberty, and not much of that; crime was general; ignorance the same; poverty and misery were widespread; London fed a tenth of her population by charity; the law awarded the death-penalty to almost every conceivable offense; what was called medical science by courtesy stood where it had stood for two thousand years; Tom Jones and Squire Western were gentlemen.

The printer's art had been known in Germany and France three and a quarter centuries, and in England three. In all that time there had not been a newspaper in Europe that was worthy the name. Monarchies had no use for that sort of dynamite. When we hoisted the banner of revolution and raised the first genuine shout for human liberty that had ever been heard, this was a newspaperless globe. Eight years later there were six daily journals in London to proclaim to all the nations the greatest birth this world had ever seen. Who woke that printing press out of its trance of three hundred years? Let us be permitted to consider that we did it. Who summoned the French slaves to rise and set the nation free? We did it. What resulted in England and on the Continent? Crippled liberty took up its bed and walked. From that day to this its march has not halted, and please God it never will. We are called the nation of inventors. And we are. We could still claim that title and wear its loftiest honors if we had stopped with the first thing we ever invented—which was human liberty. Out of that invention has come the Christian world's great civilization. Without it it was impossible—as the history of all the centuries has proved. Well, then, who invented civilization? Even Sir Lepel Griffin ought to be able to answer that question. It looks easy enough. *We* have contributed *nothing*! Nothing hurts me like ingratitude.

"How to Tell a Story" (1895)

The Humorous Story an American Development.—Its Difference from Comic and Witty Stories

I do not claim that I can tell a story as it ought to be told. I only claim to know how a story ought to be told, for I have been almost daily in the company of the most expert story-tellers for many years.

There are several kinds of stories; but only one difficult kind—the humorous. I will talk mainly about that one. The humorous story is American, the comic story is English, the witty story is French. The humorous story depends for its effect upon the *manner* of the telling; the comic story and the witty story upon the *matter*.

The humorous story may be spun out to great length, and may wander around as much as it pleases, and arrive nowhere in particular; but the comic and witty stories must be brief and end with a point. The humorous story bubbles gently along, the others burst.

The humorous story is strictly a work of art—high and delicate art—and only an artist can tell it; but no art is necessary in telling the comic and the witty story; anybody can do it. The art of telling a humorous story—understand, I mean by word of mouth, not print—was created in America, and has remained at home.

The humorous story is told gravely; the teller does his best to conceal the fact that he even dimly suspects that there is anything funny about it; but the teller of the comic story tells you beforehand that it is one of the funniest things he has ever heard, then tells it with eager delight, and is the first person to laugh when he gets through. And sometimes, if he has had good success, he is so glad and happy that he will repeat the "nub" of it and glance around from face to face, collecting applause, and then repeat it again. It is a pathetic thing to see.

Very often, of course, the rambling and disjointed humorous story finishes with a nub, point, snapper, or whatever you like to call it. Then the listener must be alert, for in many cases the teller will divert attention from that nub by dropping it in a carefully casual and indifferent way, with the pretence that he does not know it is a nub.

Artemus Ward used that trick a good deal; then, when the belated audience presently caught the joke he would look up with innocent surprise, as if wondering what they had found to laugh at. Dan Setchell used it before him, Nye and Riley and others use it to-day.

But the teller of the comic story does not slur the nub; he shouts it at you—every time. And when he prints it, in England, France, Germany, and Italy, he italicizes it, puts some whooping exclamation-points after it, and sometimes explains it in a parenthesis. All of which is very depressing, and makes one want to renounce joking and lead a better life.

Let me set down an instance of the comic method, using an anecdote which has been popular all over the world for twelve or fifteen hundred years. The teller tells it in this way:

THE WOUNDED SOLDIER

In the course of a certain battle a soldier whose leg had been shot off appealed to another soldier who was hurrying by to carry him to the rear, informing him at the same time of the loss which he had sustained; whereupon the generous son of Mars, shouldering the unfortunate, proceeded to carry out his desire. The bullets and cannon-balls were flying in all directions, and presently one of the latter took the wounded man's head off—without, however, his deliverer being aware of it. In no long time he was hailed by an officer, who said:

"Where are you going with that carcass?"

"To the rear, sir—he's lost his leg!"

"His leg, forsooth?" responded the astonished officer; "you mean his head, you booby."

Whereupon the soldier dispossessed himself of his burden, and stood looking down upon it in great perplexity. At length he said:

"It is true, sir, just as you have said." Then after a pause he added, "*But he* TOLD *me* IT WAS HIS LEG! ! ! ! !"

Here the narrator bursts into explosion after explosion of thunderous horse-laughter, repeating that nub from time to time through his gaspings and shriekings and suffocatings.

It takes only a minute and a half to tell that in its comic-story form; and isn't worth the telling, after all. Put into the humorous-story form it takes ten minutes, and is about the funniest thing I have ever listened to—as James Whitcomb Riley tells it.

He tells it in the character of a dull-witted old farmer who has just heard it for the first time, thinks it is unspeakably funny, and is trying to repeat it to a neighbor. But he can't remember it; so he gets all mixed up and wanders helplessly round and round, putting in tedious details that don't belong in the tale and only retard it; taking them out conscientiously and putting in others that are just as useless; making minor mistakes now and then and stopping to correct them and explain how he came to make them; remembering things which he forgot to put in in their proper place and going back to put them in there; stopping his narrative a good while in order to try to recall the name of the soldier that was hurt, and finally remembering that the soldier's name was not mentioned, and remarking placidly that the name is of no real importance, anyway—better, of course, if one knew it, but not essential, after all—and so on, and so on, and so on.

The teller is innocent and happy and pleased with himself, and has to stop every little while to hold himself in and keep from laughing outright; and does hold in, but his body quakes in a jelly-like way with interior chuckles; and at the end of the ten minutes the audience have laughed until they are exhausted, and the tears are running down their faces.

The simplicity and innocence and sincerity and unconsciousness of the old farmer are perfectly simulated, and the result is a performance which is thoroughly charming and delicious. This is art—and fine and beautiful, and only a master can compass it; but a machine could tell the other story.

To string incongruities and absurdities together in a wandering and sometimes purposeless way, and seem innocently unaware that they are absurdities, is the basis of the American art, if my position is correct. Another feature is the slurring of the point. A third is the dropping of a studied remark apparently without knowing it, as if one were thinking aloud. The fourth and last is the pause.

Artemus Ward dealt in numbers three and four a good deal. He would begin to tell with great animation something which he seemed to think was wonderful; then lose confidence, and after an apparently absent-minded pause add an incongruous remark in a soliloquizing way; and that was the remark intended to explode the mine—and it did.

For instance, he would say eagerly, excitedly, "I once knew a man in New Zealand who hadn't a tooth in his head"—here his animation would die out; a silent, reflective pause would follow, then he would say dreamily, and as if to himself, "and yet that man could beat a drum better than any man I ever saw."

The pause is an exceedingly important feature in any kind of story, and a frequently recurring feature, too. It is a dainty thing, and delicate, and also uncertain and treacherous; for it must be exactly the right length—no more and no less—or it fails of its purpose and makes trouble. If the pause is too short the impressive point is passed, and the audience have had time to divine that a surprise is intended—and then you can't surprise them, of course.

On the platform I used to tell a negro ghost story that had a pause in front of the snapper on the end, and that pause was the most important thing in the whole story. If I got it the right length precisely, I could spring the finishing ejaculation with effect enough to make some impressible girl deliver a startled little yelp and jump out of her seat—and that was what I was after. This story was called "The

Golden Arm," and was told in this fashion. You can practise with it yourself—and mind you look out for the pause and get it right.

THE GOLDEN ARM

Once 'pon a time dey wuz a monsus mean man, en he live 'way out in de prairie all 'lone by hisself, 'cep'n he had a wife. En bimeby she died, en he tuck en toted her way out dah in de prairie en buried her. Well, she had a golden arm— all solid gold, fum de shoulder down. He wuz pow'ful mean—pow'ful; en dat night he couldn't sleep, caze he want dat golden arm so bad.

When it come midnight he couldn't stan' it no mo'; so he git up, he did, en tuck his lantern en shoved out thoo de storm en dug her up en got de golden arm; en he bent his head down 'gin de win', en plowed en plowed en plowed thoo de snow. Den all on a sudden he stop (make a considerable pause here, and look startled, and take a listening attitude) en say: "My *lan'*, what's dat!"

En he listen—en listen—en de win' say (set your teeth together and imitate the wailing and wheezing singsong of the wind), "Bzzz-z-zzz"—en den, way back yonder whah de grave is, he hear a *voice!*—he hear a voice all mix' up in de win'— can't hardly tell 'em 'part—"Bzzz-zzz—W-h-o—g-o-t—m-y—g-o-l-d-e-n *arm?* —zzz—zzz—W-h-o g-o-t m-y g-o-l-d-e-n *arm?* (You must begin to shiver violently now.)

En he begin to shiver en shake, en say, "Oh, my! *Oh*, my lan'!" en de win' blow de lantern out, en de snow en sleet blow in his face en mos' choke him, en he start a-plowin' knee-deep towards home mos' dead, he so sk'yerd—en pooty soon he hear de voice agin, en (pause) it 'us comin' *after* him! "Bzzz— zzz—zzz—W-h-o—g-o-t—m-y—g-o-l-d-e-n—*arm?*"

When he git to de de pasture he hear it agin—closter now, en a-*comin'!*— a-comin' back dah in de dark en de storm—(repeat the wind and the voice). When he git to de house he rush up-stairs en jump in de bed en kiver up, head and years, en lay dah shiverin' en shakin'—en den way out dah he hear it *agin!*—en a-*comin'!* En bimeby he hear (pause—awed, listening attitude)— pat—pat—pat—*hit's a-comin' up-stairs!* Den he hear de latch, en he *know* it's in de room!

Den pooty soon he know it's a-*stannin' by de bed!* (Pause.) Den—he know it's a-*bendin' down over him*—en he cain't skasely git his breath! Den—den—he seem to feel someth'n *c-o-l-d*, right down 'most agin his head! (Pause.)

Den de voice say, *right at his year*—"W-h-o—g-o-t—m-y—g-o-l-d-e-n *arm?*" (You must wail it out very plaintively and accusingly; then you stare steadily and impressively into the face of the farthest-gone auditor—a girl, preferably—and let that awe-inspiring pause begin to build itself in the deep hush. When it has reached exactly the right length, jump suddenly at that girl and yell, "*You've* got it!"

If you've got the *pause* right, she'll fetch a dear little yelp and spring right out of her shoes. But you *must* get the pause right; and you will find it the most troublesome and aggravating and uncertain thing you ever undertook.)

4–4
Bret Harte (1836–1902)

BRET HARTE (Francis Brett Harte) (1836–1902) wrote stories about the California Gold Rush, that exciting period when every 'forty-niner' panning for gold thought he would strike it rich. Born Francis Brett Harte, in Albany, New York, he came west to California at the peak of the rush to try his hand at a number of jobs. After several years as a journalist, he turned to writing fiction, creating stories about colorful characters in the camps whose luck more often than not ran out. Harte served as the influential editor of the *Overland Monthly* in the 1860s, nurturing some of the greatest talent from the West, including Mark Twain and Ambrose Bierce. Harte helped create a distinctively western brand of regional realism, influencing and drawing from other writers of the American Southwest and West, mixing raw frontier humor with realism.

≈ ≈ ≈

"The Luck of Roaring Camp" (1869)

There was commotion in Roaring Camp. It could not have been a fight, for in 1850 that was not novel enough to have called together the entire settlement. The ditches and claims were not only deserted, but "Tuttle's grocery" had contributed its gamblers, who, it will be remembered, calmly continued their game the day that French Pete and Kanaka Joe shot each other to death over the bar in the front room. The whole camp was collected before a rude cabin on the outer edge of the clearing. Conversation was carried on in a low tone, but the name of a woman was frequently repeated. It was a name familiar enough in the camp,—"Cherokee Sal."

Perhaps the less said of her the better. She was a coarse, and, it is to be feared, a very sinful woman. But at that time she was the only woman in Roaring Camp, and was just then lying in sore extremity, when she most needed the ministration of her own sex. Dissolute, abandoned, and irreclaimable, she was yet suffering a martyrdom hard enough to bear even when veiled by sympathizing womanhood, but now terrible in her loneliness. The primal curse had come to her in that original isolation which must have made the punishment of the first transgression so dreadful. It was, perhaps, part of the expiation of her sin, that, at a moment when she most lacked her sex's intuitive tenderness and care, she met only the half-contemptuous faces of her masculine associates. Yet a few of the spectators were, I think, touched by her sufferings. Sandy Tipton thought it was "rough on Sal," and, in the contemplation of her condition, for a moment rose superior to the fact that he had an ace and two bowers in his sleeve.

It will be seen, also, that the situation was novel. Deaths were by no means uncommon in Roaring Camp, but a birth was a new thing. People had been dismissed from the camp effectively, finally, and with no possibility of return; but this was the first time that anybody had been introduced *ab initio*. Hence the excitement.

"You go in there, Stumpy," said a prominent citizen known as "Kentuck," addressing one of the loungers. "Go in there, and see what you kin do. You've had experience in them things."

Perhaps there was a fitness in the selection. Stumpy, in other climes, had been the putative head of two families; in fact, it was owing to some legal informality in these proceedings that Roaring Camp—a city of refuge—was indebted to his company. The crowd approved the choice, and Stumpy was wise enough to bow to the majority. The door closed on the extempore surgeon and midwife, and Roaring Camp sat down outside, smoked its pipe, and awaited the issue.

The assemblage numbered about a hundred men. One or two of these were actual fugitives from justice, some were criminal, and all were reckless. Physically, they exhibited no indication of their past lives and character. The greatest scamp had a Raphael face, with a profusion of blond hair; Oakhurst, a gambler, had the melancholy air and intellectual abstraction of a Hamlet; the coolest and most courageous man was scarcely over five feet in height, with a soft voice and an embarrassed, timid manner. The term "roughs" applied to them was a distinction rather than a definition. Perhaps in the minor details of fingers, toes, ears, etc., the camp may have been deficient, but these slight omissions did not detract from their aggregate force. The strongest man had but three fingers on his right hand; the best shot had but one eye.

Such was the physical aspect of the men that were dispersed around the cabin. The camp lay in a triangular valley, between two hills and a river. The only outlet was a steep trail over the summit of a hill that faced the cabin, now illuminated by the rising moon. The suffering woman might have seen it from the rude bunk whereon she lay,—seen it winding like a silver thread until it was lost in the stars above.

A fire of withered pine-boughs added sociability to the gathering. By degrees the natural levity of Roaring Camp returned. Bets were freely offered and taken regarding the result. Three to five that "Sal would get through with it"; even, that the child would survive; side bets as to the sex and complexion of the coming stranger. In the midst of an excited discussion an exclamation came from those nearest the door, and the camp stopped to listen. Above the swaying and moaning of the pines, the swift rush of the river, and the crackling of the fire, rose a sharp, querulous cry,—a cry unlike anything heard before in the camp. The pines stopped moaning, the river ceased to rush, and the fire to crackle. It seemed as if Nature had stopped to listen too.

The camp rose to its feet as one man! It was proposed to explode a barrel of gunpowder, but, in consideration of the situation of the mother, better counsels prevailed, and only a few revolvers were discharged; for, whether owing to the rude surgery of the camp, or some other reason, Cherokee Sal was sinking fast. Within an hour she had climbed, as it were, that rugged road that led to the stars, and so passed out of Roaring Camp, its sin and shame forever. I do not think that the announcement disturbed them much, except in speculation as to the fate of the child. "Can he live now?" was asked of Stumpy. The answer was doubtful. The only other being of Cherokee Sal's sex and maternal condition in the settlement was an ass. There was some conjecture as to fitness, but the experiment was tried. It was less problematical than the ancient treatment of Romulus and Remus, and apparently as successful.

When these details were completed, which exhausted another hour, the door was opened, and the anxious crowd of men who had already formed themselves into a queue, entered in single file. Beside the low bunk or shelf, on which the figure of the mother was starkly outlined below the blankets stood a pine table. On this a candle-box was placed, and within it, swathed in staring red flannel, lay the last arrival at Roaring Camp. Beside the candle-box was placed a hat. Its use was soon indicated. "Gentlemen," said Stumpy, with a singular mixture of authority and *ex officio* complacency,—"Gentlemen will please pass in at the front door, round the table, and out at the back door. Them as wishes to contribute anything toward the orphan will find a hat handy." The first man entered with his hat on; he uncovered, however, as he looked about him, and so, unconsciously, set an example to the next. In such communities good and bad actions are catching. As the procession filed in, comments were audible,—criticisms addressed, perhaps, rather to Stumpy, in the character of showman,—"Is that him?" "mighty small specimen"; "hasn't mor'n got the color"; "ain't bigger nor a derringer." The contributions were as characteristic: A silver tobacco-box; a doubloon; a navy revolver, silver mounted; a gold specimen; a very beautifully embroidered lady's handkerchief (from Oakhurst the gambler); a diamond breastpin; a diamond ring (suggested by the pin, with the remark from the giver that he "saw that pin and went two diamonds better"); a slung shot; a Bible (contributor not detected); a golden spur; a silver teaspoon (the initials, I regret to say, were not the giver's); a pair of surgeon's shears; a lancet; a Bank of England note for £5; and about $200 in loose gold and silver coin. During these proceedings Stumpy maintained a silence as impassive as the dead on his left, a gravity as inscrutable as that of the newly born on his right. Only one incident occurred to break the monotony of the curious procession. As Kentuck bent over the candle-box half curiously, the child turned, and, in a spasm of pain, caught at his groping finger, and held it fast for a moment. Kentuck looked foolish and embarrassed. Something like a blush tried to assert itself in his weather-beaten cheek. "The d—d little cuss!" he said, as he extricated his finger, with, perhaps, more tenderness and care than he might have been deemed capable of showing. He held that finger a little apart from its fellows as he went out, and examined it curiously. The examination provoked the same original remark in regard to the child. In fact, he seemed to enjoy repeating it. "He rastled with my finger," he remarked to Tipton, holding up the member, "the d—d little cuss!"

It was four o'clock before the camp sought repose. A light burnt in the cabin where the watchers sat, for Stumpy did not go to bed that night. Nor did Kentuck. He drank quite freely, and related with great gusto his experience, invariably ending with his characteristic condemnation of the new-comer. It seemed to relieve him of any unjust implication of sentiment, and Kentuck had the weaknesses of the nobler sex. When everybody else had gone to bed, he walked down to the river, and whistled reflectingly. Then he walked up the gulch, past the cabin, still whistling with demonstrative unconcern. At a large redwood tree he paused and retraced his steps, and again passed the cabin. Half-way down to the river's bank he again paused, and then returned and knocked at the door. It was opened by Stumpy. "How goes it?" said Kentuck, looking past Stumpy toward the candle-box. "All serene," replied Stumpy. "Anything up?" "Nothing." There was a pause—an embarrassing one—Stumpy still holding the door. Then Kentuck had recourse to his finger, which he held up to Stumpy. "Rastled with it,—the d—d little cuss," he said, and retired.

The next day Cherokee Sal had such rude sepulture as Roaring Camp afforded. After her body had been committed to the hillside, there was a formal meeting of the camp to discuss what should be done with her infant. A resolution to adopt it was unanimous and enthusiastic. But an animated discussion in regard to the manner and feasibility of providing for its wants at once sprung up. It was remarkable that the argument partook of none of those fierce personalities with which discussions were usually conducted at Roaring Camp. Tipton proposed that they should send the child to Red Dog,—a distance of forty miles,—where female attention could be procured. But the unlucky suggestion met with fierce and unanimous opposition. It was evident that no plan which entailed parting from their new acquisition would for a moment be entertained. "Besides," said Tom Ryder, "them fellows at Red Dog would swap it, and ring in somebody else on us." A disbelief in the honesty of other camps prevailed at Roaring Camp as in other places.

The introduction of a female nurse in the camp also met with objection. It was argued that no decent woman could be prevailed to accept Roaring Camp as her home, and the speaker urged that "they didn't want any more of the other kind." This unkind allusion to the defunct mother, harsh as it may seem, was the first spasm of propriety,—the first symptom of the camp's regeneration. Stumpy advanced nothing. Perhaps he felt a certain delicacy in interfering with the selection of a possible successor in office. But when questioned, he averred stoutly that he and "Jinny"—the mammal before alluded to—could manage to rear the child. There was something original, independent, and heroic about the plan that pleased the camp. Stumpy was retained. Certain articles were sent for to Sacramento. "Mind," said the treasurer, as he pressed a bag of gold-dust into the expressman's hand, "the best that can be got,—lace, you know, and filigree-work and frills,—d—m the cost!"

Strange to say, the child thrived. Perhaps the invigorating climate of the mountain camp was compensation for material deficiencies. Nature took the foundling to her broader breast. In that rare atmosphere of the Sierra foothills,—that air pungent with balsamic odor, that ethereal cordial at once bracing and exhilarating,—he may have found food and nourishment, or a subtle chemistry that transmuted asses' milk to lime and phosphorous. Stumpy inclined to the belief that it was the latter and good nursing. "Me and that ass," he would say, "has been father and mother to him. Don't you," he would add, apostrophizing the helpless bundle before him, "never go back on us."

By the time he was a month old, the necessity of giving him a name became apparent. He had generally been known as "the Kid," "Stumpy's boy," "the Cayote" (an allusion to his vocal powers), and even by Kentuck's endearing diminutive of "the d—d little cuss." But these were felt to be vague and unsatisfactory, and were at last dismissed under another influence. Gamblers and adventurers are generally superstitious, and Oakhurst one day declared that the baby had brought "the luck" to Roaring Camp. It was certain that of late they had been successful. "Luck" was the name agreed upon, with the prefix of Tommy for greater convenience. No allusion was made to the mother, and the father was unknown. "It's better," said the philosophical Oakhurst, "to take a fresh deal all round. Call him Luck, and start him fair." A day was accordingly set apart for the christening. What was meant by this ceremony the reader may imagine, who has already gathered some idea of the reckless irreverence of Roaring Camp. The master of ceremonies was one "Boston," a noted wag, and the occasion seemed to promise the greatest facetiousness. This ingenious satirist had spent two days in preparing a burlesque of the church service, with pointed local allusions. The choir was properly trained, and Sandy Tipton was to stand godfather. But after the procession had marched to the grove with music and banners, and the child had been deposited before a mock altar, Stumpy stepped before the expectant crowd. "It ain't my style to spoil fun, boys," said the little man, stoutly, eyeing the faces around him, "but it strikes me that this thing ain't exactly on the squar. It's playing it pretty low down on this yer baby to ring in fun on him that he ain't going to understand. And ef there's going to be any godfathers round, I'd like to see who's got any better rights than me." A silence followed Stumpy's speech. To the credit of all humorists be it said, that the first man to acknowledge its justice was the satirist, thus stopped of his fun. "But," said Stumpy, quickly, following up his advantage, "we're here for a christening, and we'll have it. I proclaim you Thomas Luck, according to the laws of the United States and the State of California, so help me God." It was the first time that the name of the Deity had been uttered otherwise than profanely in the camp. The form of christening was perhaps even more ludicrous than the satirist had conceived; but, strangely enough, nobody saw it and nobody laughed. "Tommy" was christened as seriously as he would have been under a Christian roof, and cried and was comforted in as orthodox fashion.

And so the work of regeneration began in Roaring Camp. Almost imperceptibly a change came over the settlement. The cabin assigned to "Tommy Luck"—or "The Luck," as he was more frequently called—first showed signs of improvement. It was kept scrupulously clean and whitewashed. Then it was boarded, clothed, and papered. The rosewood cradle—packed eighty miles by mule—had, in Stumpy's way of putting it, "sorter killed the rest of the furniture." So the rehabilitation of the cabin became a necessity. The men who were in the habit of lounging in at Stumpy's to see "how The Luck got on" seemed to appreciate the change, and, in self-defence, the rival establishment of "Tuttle's grocery" bestirred itself, and imported a carpet and mirrors. The reflections of the latter on the appearance of Roaring Camp tended to produce stricter habits of personal cleanliness. Again, Stumpy imposed a kind of quarantine upon those who aspired to the honor and privilege of holding "The Luck." It was a cruel mortification to Kentuck—who, in the carelessness of a large nature and the habits of frontier life, had begun to regard all garments as a second cuticle, which, like a snake's, only sloughed off through decay—to be debarred this privilege from certain prudential reasons. Yet such was the subtle influence of innovation that he thereafter appeared regularly every afternoon in a clean shirt, and face still shining from his ablutions. Nor were moral and social sanitary laws neglected. "Tommy," who was supposed to spend his whole existence in a persistent attempt to repose, must not be disturbed by noise. The shouting and yelling which had gained the camp its infelicitous title were not permitted within hearing distance of Stumpy's. The men conversed in whispers, or smoked with Indian gravity. Profanity was tacitly given up in these sacred precincts, and throughout the camp a popular form of expletive, known as "D—n the luck!" and "Curse the luck!" was abandoned, as having a new personal bearing. Vocal music was not interdicted, being supposed to have a soothing, tranquillizing quality, and one song, sung by "Man-o'-War Jack," an English sailor, from her Majesty's Australian colonies, was quite popular as a lullaby. It was a lugubrious recital of the exploits of "the Arethusa, Seventy-four," in a muffled minor, ending with a prolonged dying fall at the burden of each verse, "On b-o-o-o-ard of the Arethusa." It was a fine sight to see Jack holding The Luck, rocking from side to side as if with the motion of a ship, and crooning forth this naval ditty. Either through the peculiar rocking of Jack or the length of his song,—it contained ninety stanzas, and was continued with conscientious deliberation to the bitter end,—the lullaby generally had the desired effect. At such times the men would lie at full length under the trees, in the soft summer twilight, smoking their pipes and drinking in the melodious utterances. An indistinct idea that this was pastoral happiness pervaded the camp. "This 'ere kind o' think," said the Cockney Simmons, meditatively reclining on his elbow, "is 'evingly." It reminded him of Greenwich.

On the long summer days The Luck was usually carried to the gulch, from whence the golden store of Roaring Camp was taken. There, on a blanket spread over pine-boughs, he would lie while the men were working in the ditches below. Latterly, there was a rude attempt to decorate this bower with flowers and sweet-smelling shrubs, and generally some one would bring him a cluster of wild honeysuckles, azaleas, or the painted blossoms of Las Mariposas. The men had suddenly awakened to the fact that there were beauty and significance in these trifles, which they had so long trodden carelessly beneath their feet. A flake of glittering mica, a fragment of variegated quartz, a bright pebble from the bed of the creek, became beautiful to eyes thus cleared and strengthened, and were invariably put aside for "The Luck." It was wonderful how many treasures the woods and hillsides yielded that "would do for Tommy." Surrounded by playthings such as never child out of fairy-land had before, it is to be hoped that Tommy was content. He appeared to be securely happy albeit there was an infantine gravity about him, a contemplative light in his round gray eyes, that sometimes worried Stumpy. He was always tractable and quiet, and it is recorded that once, having crept beyond his "corral,"—a hedge of tessellated pine-boughs, which surrounded his bed,—he dropped over the bank on his head in the soft earth, and remained with his mottled legs in the air in that position for at least five minutes with unflinching gravity. He was extricated without a murmur. I hesitate to record the many other instances of his sagacity, which rest, unfortunately, upon the statements of prejudiced friends. Some of them were not without a tinge of superstition. "I crep' up the bank just now," said Kentuck one day, in a breathless state of excitement, "and dern my skin if he wasn't a talking to a jaybird as was a sittin' on his lap. There they was, just as free and sociable as anything you please, a jawin' at each other just like two cherry-bums." Howbeit, whether creeping over the pine-boughs or lying lazily on his back blinking at the leaves above him, to him the birds sang, the squirrels chattered, and the flowers bloomed. Nature was his nurse and playfellow. For him she would let slip between the leaves golden shafts of sunlight that fell just within his grasp; she would send wandering breezes to visit him with the balm of bay and resinous gums; to him the tall red-woods nodded familiarly and sleepily, the bumble-bees buzzed, and the rooks cawed a slumbrous accompaniment.

Such was the golden summer of Roaring Camp. They were "flush times,"— and the Luck was with them. The claims had yielded enormously. The camp was jealous of its privileges and looked suspiciously on strangers. No encouragement was given to immigration, and, to make their seclusion more perfect, the land on either side of the mountain wall that surrounded the camp they duly preempted. This, and a reputation for singular proficiency with the revolver, kept the reserve of Roaring Camp inviolate. The expressman—their only connecting link with the surrounding world—sometimes told wonderful stories of the camp. He would say, "They've a street up there in 'Roaring,' that would lay over any street in Red Dog. They've got vines and flowers round their houses, and they wash themselves twice a day. But they're mighty rough on strangers, and they worship an Ingin baby."

With the prosperity of the camp came a desire for further improvement. It was proposed to build a hotel in the following spring, and to invite one or two decent families to reside there for the sake of "The Luck,"—who might perhaps profit by female companionship. The sacrifice that this concession to the sex cost these men, who were fiercely sceptical in regard to its general virtue and usefulness, can only be accounted for by their affection for Tommy. A few still held out. But the resolve could not be carried into effect for three months, and the minority meekly yielded in the hope that something might turn up to prevent it. And it did.

The winter of 1851 will long be remembered in the foot-hills. The snow lay deep on the Sierras, and every mountain creek became a river, and every river a lake. Each gorge and gulch was transformed into a tumultuous water-course that descended the hillsides, tearing down giant trees and scattering its drift and débris along the plain. Red Dog had been twice under water, and Roaring Camp had been forewarned. "Water put the gold into them gulches," said Stumpy. "It's been here once and will be here again!" And that night the North Fork suddenly leaped over its banks, and swept up the triangular valley of Roaring Camp.

In the confusion of rushing water, crushing trees, and crackling timber, and the darkness which seemed to flow with the water and blot out the fair valley, but little could be done to collect the scattered camp. When the morning broke, the cabin of Stumpy nearest the river-bank was gone. Higher up the gulch they found the body of its unlucky owner; but the pride, the hope, the joy, the Luck, of Roaring Camp had disappeared. They were returning with sad hearts, when a shout from the bank recalled them.

It was a relief-boat from down the river. They had picked up, they said, a man and an infant, nearly exhausted, about two miles below. Did anybody know them, and did they belong here?

It needed but a glance to show them Kentuck lying there, cruelly crushed and bruised, but still holding the Luck of Roaring Camp in his arms. As they bent over the strangely assorted pair, they saw that the child was cold and pulseless. "He is dead," said one. Kentuck opened his eyes. "Dead?" he repeated feebly. "Yes, my man, and you are dying too." A smile lit the eyes of the expiring Kentuck. "Dying," he repeated, "he's a taking me with him,—tell the boys I've got the Luck with me now"; and the strong man, clinging to the frail babe as a drowning man is said to cling to a straw, drifted away into the shadowy river that flows forever to the unknown sea.

4–5
Joaquín Miller (Cincinnatus Heine Miller) (1837–1913)

Born CINCINNATUS HEINE (OR HINER) MILLER, JOAQUIN MILLER (1837–1913) was born in Indiana but by the end of his life was known as the "Poet of the Sierras." Miller was a newspaperman, essayist, and poet, reportedly adopting his pseudonym in honor of Joaquin Murieta. Miller created a persona of the Westerner that evinced an honest appreciation for his adopted home, but he also used the created identity as a type of brand. His first real popularity came in England, where his appearance in buckskin at poetry recitations appealed to an audience hungry for what seemed like Western authenticity. "The Sierras from the Sea" (1897) shows Miller at his best: romantic and with an artist's view of the landscape.

≋ ≋ ≋

"The Sierras from the Sea"

I

Like fragments of an uncompleted world,
From bleak Alaska, bound in ice and spray,
To where the peaks of Darien lie curl'd
In clouds, the broken lands loom bold and gray.
The seamen nearing San Francisco Bay
Forget the compass here; with sturdy hand
They seize the wheel, look up, then bravely lay
The ship to shore by rugged peaks that stand
The stern and proud patrician fathers of the land.

II

They stand white stairs of heaven,—stand a line
Of lifting, endless, and eternal white.
They look upon the far and flashing brine,
Upon the boundless plains, the broken height
Of Kamiakin's battlements. The flight
Of time is underneath their untopp'd towers.
They seem to push aside the moon at night,
To jostle and to loose the stars. The flowers
Of heaven fall about their brows in shining showers.

III

They stand in line of lifted snowy isles
High held above the toss'd and tumbled sea,—
A sea of wood in wild unmeasured miles:
White pyramids of Faith where man is free;
White monuments of Hope that yet shall be
The mounts of matchless and immortal song. . . .
I look far down the hollow days; I see
The bearded prophets, simple-soul'd and strong,
That strike the sounding harp and thrill the heeding throng.

IV

Serene and satisfied! supreme! as lone
As God, they loom like God's archangels churl'd;
They look as cold as kings upon a throne;
The mantling wings of night are crush'd and curl'd
As feathers curl. The elements are hurl'd
From off their bosoms, and are bidden go,
Like evil spirits, to an under-world.
They stretch from Cariboo to Mexico,
A line of battle-tents in everlasting snow.

"Vaquero"

His broad-brimm'd hat push'd back with careless air,
The proud vaquero sits his steed as free
As winds that toss his black abundant hair.
No rover ever swept a lawless sea
With such a haught and heedless air as he
Who scorns the path, and bounds with swift disdain
Away, a peon born, yet born to be
A splendid king; behold him ride, and reign.

How brave he takes his herds in branding days,
On timber'd hills that belt about the plain;
He climbs, he wheels, he shouts through winding ways
Of hiding ferns and hanging fir; the rein
Is loose, the rattling spur drives swift; the mane
Blows free; the bullocks rush in storms before;
They turn with lifted heads, they rush again,
Then sudden plunge from out the wood, and pour

A cloud upon the plain with one terrific roar.

Now sweeps the tawny man on stormy steed,
His gaudy trappings toss'd about and blown
About the limbs as lithe as any reed;
The swift long lasso twirl'd above is thrown
From flying hand; the fall, the fearful groan
Of bullock toil'd and tumbled in the dust—
The black herds onward sweep, and all disown
The fallen, struggling monarch that has thrust
His tongue in rage and roll'd his red eyes in disgust.

"Crossing the Plains"

What great yoked brutes with briskets low,
With wrinkled necks like buffalo,
With round, brown, liquid, pleading eyes,
That turn'd so slow and sad to you,
That shone like love's eyes soft with tears,
That seem'd to plead, and make replies,
The while they bow'd their necks and drew
The creaking load; and look'd at you.
Their sable briskets swept the ground,
Their cloven feet kept solemn sound.

Two sullen bullocks led the line,
Their great eyes shining bright like wine;
Two sullen captive kings were they,
That had in time held herds at bay,
And even now they crush'd the sod
With stolid sense of majesty,
And stately stepp'd and stately trod,
As if 'twere something still to be
Kings even in captivity.

"Don't Stop at the Station Despair"

We must trust the Conductor, most surely;
Why, millions of millions before
Have made this same journey securely

And come to that ultimate shore.
And we, we will reach it in season;
And ah, what a welcome is there!
Reflect then, how out of all reason
To stop at the Station Despair.

Ay, midnights and many a potion
Of bitter black water have we
As we journey from ocean to ocean—
From sea unto ultimate sea—
To that deep sea of seas, and all silence
Of passion, concern and of care—
That vast sea of Eden-set Islands—
Don't stop at the Station Despair!

Go forward, whatever may follow,
Go forward, friend-led, or alone;
Ah me, to leap off in some hollow
Or fen, in the night and unknown—
Leap off like a thief; try to hide you
From angels, all waiting you there!
Go forward; whatever betide you
Don't stop at the Station Despair!

4–6
William Dean Howells (1837–1920)

WILLIAM DEAN HOWELLS (1837–1920) was one of the great men of letters of the nineteenth century; his influence was wide and sweeping. From Ohio, Howells followed his father in writing for newspapers. He got his first break writing a biography of Abraham Lincoln for his 1860 campaign, which opened doors in New England, where he mixed with the literary greats of the time like Nathaniel Hawthorne. After the Civil War, he became a writer and editor of literary magazines. A novelist who wrote of social problems, especially of the middle class, and of rags-to-riches/riches-to-rags tycoons, Howells touted American realism; as a critic and reviewer, he promoted emerging European writers, American women writers like Sarah Orne Jewett, and African American writers like Charles Chesnutt. "Editha" (1904) represents Howells' disapproval of the Spanish-American War, the conflict between the United States and Spain over Cuba, Puerto Rico, and the Philippines, which he regarded as Manifest Destiny.

≈ ≈ ≈

"Editha" (1904)

The air was thick with the war feeling, like the electricity of a storm which has not yet burst. Editha sat looking out into the hot spring afternoon, with her lips parted, and panting with the intensity of the question whether she could let him go. She had decided that she could not let him stay, when she saw him at the end of the still leafless avenue, making slowly up toward the house, with his head down, and his figure relaxed. She ran impatiently out on the veranda, to the edge of the steps, and imperatively demanded greater haste of him with her will before she called aloud to him, "George!"

He had quickened his pace in mystical response to her mystical urgence, before he could have heard her; now he looked up and answered, "Well?"

"Oh, how united we are!" she exulted, and then she swooped down the steps to him. "What is it?" she cried.

"It's war," he said, and he pulled her up to him, and kissed her.

She kissed him back intensely, but irrelevantly, as to their passion, and uttered from deep in her throat, "How glorious!"

"It's war," he repeated, without consenting to her sense of it; and she did not know just what to think at first. She never knew what to think of him; that made his mystery, his charm. All through their courtship, which was contemporaneous with the growth of the war feeling, she had been puzzled by his want of seriousness about it. He seemed to despise it even more than he abhorred it. She could have understood his abhorring any sort of bloodshed; that would have been a survival of his old life when he thought he would be a minister, and before he changed and took up the law. But making light of a cause so high and noble seemed to show a want of earnestness at the core of his being. Not but that she felt herself able to cope with a congenital defect of that sort, and make his love for her save him from himself. Now perhaps the miracle was already wrought in him. In the presence of the tremendous fact that he announced, all triviality seemed to have gone out of him; she began to feel that. He sank down on the top step, and wiped his forehead with his handkerchief, while she poured out upon him her question of the origin and authenticity of his news.

All the while, in her duplex emotioning, she was aware that now at the very beginning she must put a guard upon herself against urging him, by any word or act, to take the part that her whole soul willed him to take, for the completion of her ideal of him. He was very nearly perfect as he was, and he must be allowed to perfect himself. But he was peculiar, and he might very well be reasoned out of his peculiarity. Before her reasoning went her emotioning: her nature pulling upon his nature, her womanhood upon his manhood, without her knowing the means she was using to the end she was willing. She had always supposed that the man who won her would have done something to win her; she did not know what, but something. George Gearson had simply asked her for her love, on the way home from a concert, and she gave her love to him, without, as it were, thinking. But now, it flashed upon her, if he could do something worthy to *have* won her—be a hero, *her* hero—it would be even better than if he had done it before asking her; it would be grander. Besides, she had believed in the war from the beginning.

"But don't you see, dearest," she said, "that it wouldn't have come to this, if it hadn't been in the order of Providence? And I call any war glorious that is for the liberation of people who have been struggling for years against the cruelest oppression. Don't you think so too?"

"I suppose so," he returned, languidly. "But war! Is it glorious to break the peace of the world?"

"That ignoble peace! It was no peace at all, with that crime and shame at our very gates." She was conscious of parroting the current phrases of the newspapers, but it was no time to pick and choose her words. She must sacrifice anything to the high ideal she had for him, and after a good deal of rapid argument she ended with the climax: "But now it doesn't matter about the how or why. Since the war has come, all that is gone. There are no two sides, any more. There is nothing now but our country."

He sat with his eyes closed and his head leant back against the veranda, and he said with a vague smile, as if musing aloud, "Our country—right or wrong."

"Yes, right or wrong!" she returned fervidly. "I'll go and get you some lemonade." She rose rustling, and whisked away; when she came back with two tall glasses of clouded liquid, on a tray, and the ice clucking in them, he still sat as she had left him, and she said as if there had been no interruption: "But there is no question of wrong in this case. I call it a sacred war. A war for liberty, and humanity, if ever there was one. And I know you will see it just as I do, yet."

He took half the lemonade at a gulp, and he answered as he set the glass down: "I know you always have the highest ideal. When I differ from you, I ought to doubt myself."

A generous sob rose in Editha's throat for the humility of a man, so very nearly perfect, who was willing to put himself below her.

Besides, she felt, more subliminally, that he was never so near slipping through her finger; as when he took that meek way.

"You shall not say that! Only, for once I happen to be right." She seized his hand in her two hands, and poured her soul from her eyes into his. "Don't you think so?" she entreated him.

He released his hand and drank the rest of his lemonade, and she added, "Have mine, too," but he shook his hand in answering, "I've no business to think so, unless I act so, too."

Her heart stopped a beat before it pulsed on with leaps that she felt in her neck. She had noticed that strange thing in men; they seemed to feel bound to do what they believed, and not think a thing was finished when they said it, as girls did. She knew what was in his mind, but she pretended not, and she said, "Oh, I am not sure," and then faltered.

He went on as if to himself without apparently heeding her, "There's only one way of proving one's faith in a thing like this."

She could not say that she understood, but she did understand.

He went on again. "If I believed—if I felt as you do about this war—Do you wish me to feel as you do?"

Now she was really not sure; so she said, "George, I don't know what you mean."

He seemed to muse away from her as before. "There is a sort of fascination in it. I suppose that at the bottom of his heart every man would like at times to have his courage tested; to see how he would act."

"How can you talk in that ghastly way!"

"It *is* rather morbid. Still, that's what it comes to, unless you're swept away by ambition, or driven by conviction. I haven't the conviction or the ambition, and the other thing is what it comes to with me. I ought to have been a preacher, after all; then I couldn't have asked it of myself, as I must, now I'm a lawyer. And you believe it's a holy war, Editha?" he suddenly addressed her. "Oh, I know you do! But you wish me to believe so, too?"

She hardly knew whether he was mocking or not, in the ironical way he always had with her plainer mind. But the only thing was to be outspoken with him.

"George, I wish you to believe whatever you think is true, at any and every cost. If I've tried to talk you into anything, I take it all back."

"Oh, I know that, Editha. I know how sincere you are, and how—I wish I had your undoubting spirit! I'll think it over; I'd like to believe as you do. But I don't, now; I don't, indeed. It isn't this war alone; though this seems peculiarly wanton and needless; but it's every war—so stupid; it makes me sick. Why shouldn't this thing have been settled reasonably?"

"Because," she said, very throatily again, "God meant it to be war."

"You think it was God? Yes, I suppose that is what people will say."

"Do you suppose it would have been war if God hadn't meant it?"

"I don't know. Sometimes it seems as if God had put this world into men's keeping to work it as they pleased."

"Now, George, that is blasphemy."

"Well, I won't blaspheme. I'll try to believe in your pocket Providence," he said, and then he rose to go.

"Why don't you stay to dinner?" Dinner at Balcom's Works was at one o'clock.

"I'll come back to supper, if you'll let me. Perhaps I shall bring you a convert."

"Well, you may come back, on that condition."

"All right. If I don't come, you'll understand."

He went away without kissing her, and she felt it a suspension of their engagement. It all interested her intensely; she was undergoing a tremendous experience, and she was being equal to it. While she stood looking after him, her mother came out through one of the long windows, on to the veranda, with a catlike softness and vagueness.

"Why didn't he stay to dinner?"

"Because—because—war has been declared," Editha pronounced, without turning.

Her mother said, "Oh, my!" and then said nothing more until she had sat down in one of the large Shaker chairs, and rocked herself for some time. Then she closed whatever tacit passage of thought there had been in her mind with the spoken words, "Well, I hope *he* won't go."

"And *I* hope he *will*," the girl said, and confronted her mother with a stormy exaltation that would have frightened any creature less unimpressionable than a cat.

Her mother rocked herself again for an interval of cogitation. What she arrived at in speech was, "Well, I guess you've done a wicked thing, Editha Balcom."

The girl said, as she passed indoors through the same window her mother had come out by, "I haven't done anything—yet."

In her room, she put together all her letters and gifts from Gearson, down to the withered petals of the first flower he had offered, with that timidity of his veiled in that irony of his. In the heart of the packet she enshrined her engagement ring which she had restored to the pretty box he had brought it her in. Then she sat down, if not calmly yet strongly, and wrote:

> "GEORGE: I understood—when you left me. But I think we had better emphasize your meaning that if we cannot be one in everything we had better be one in nothing. So I am sending these things for your keeping till you have made up your mind.
>
> "I shall always love you, and therefore I shall never marry any one else. But the man I marry must love his country first of all, and be able to say to me,
>
> > 'I could not love thee, dear, so much,
> > Loved I not honor more.'*
>
> "There is no honor above America with me. In this great hour there is no other honor.
>
> "Your heart will make my words clear to you. I had never expected to say so much, but it has come upon me that I must say the utmost. EDITHA."

She thought she had worded her letter well, worded it in a way that could not be bettered; all had been implied and nothing expressed.

She had it ready to send with the packet she had tied with red, white, and blue ribbon, when it occurred to her that she was not just to him, that she was not giving him a fair chance. He had said he would go and think it over, and she was not waiting. She was pushing, threatening, compelling. That was not a woman's part. She must leave him free, free, free. She could not accept for her country or herself a forced sacrifice.

In writing her letter she had satisfied the impulse from which it sprang; she could well afford to wait till he had thought it over. She put the packet and the letter by, and rested serene in consciousness of having done what was laid upon her by her love itself to do, and yet used patience, mercy, justice.

She had her reward. Gearson did not come to tea, but she had given him till morning, when, late at night there came up from the village the sound of a fife and drum with a tumult of voices, in shouting, singing, and laughing. The noise drew nearer and nearer; it reached the street end of the avenue; there it silenced itself, and one voice, the voice she knew best, rose over the silence. It fell; the air was filled with cheers; the fife and drum struck up, with the

---

* [From Richard Lovelace's "To Lucasta, Going to the Wars."—E.J.D. and J.B.F.]

shouting, singing, and laughing again, but now retreating; and a single figure came hurrying up the avenue.

She ran down to meet her lover and clung to him. He was very gay, and he put his arm round her with a boisterous laugh. "Well, you must call me Captain, now; or Cap, if you prefer; that's what the boys call me. Yes, we've had a meeting at the town hall, and everybody has volunteered; and they selected me for captain, and I'm going to the war, the big war, the glorious war, the holy war ordained by the pocket Providence that blesses butchery. Come along; let's tell the whole family about it. Call them from their downy beds, father, mother, Aunt Hitty, and all the folks!"

But when they mounted the veranda steps he did not wait for a larger audience; he poured the story upon Editha alone.

"There was a lot of speaking, and then some of the fools set up a shout for me. It was all going one way, and I thought it would be a good joke to sprinkle a little cold water on them. But you can't do that with a crowd that adores you. The first thing I knew I was sprinkling hell-fire on them. 'Cry havoc, and let slip the dogs of war.' That was the style. Now that it had come to the fight, there were no two parties; there was one country, and the thing was to fight the fight to a finish as quick as possible. I suggested volunteering then and there, and I wrote my name first of all on the roster. Then they elected me—that's all. I wish I had some ice-water!"

She left him walking up and down the veranda, while she ran for the ice-pitcher and a goblet, and when she came back he was still walking up and down, shouting the story he had told her to her father and mother, who had come out more sketchily dressed than they commonly were by day. He drank goblet after goblet of the ice-water without noticing who was giving it, and kept on talking, and laughing through his talk wildly. "It's astonishing," he said, "how well the worse reason looks when you try to make it appear the better. Why, I believe I was the first convert to the war in that crowd to-night! I never thought I should like to kill a man; but now, I shouldn't care; and the smokeless powder lets you see the man drop that you kill. It's all for the country! What a thing it is to have a country that *can't* be wrong, but if it is, is right anyway!"

Editha had a great, vital thought, an inspiration. She set down the ice-pitcher on the veranda floor, and ran up-stairs and got the letter she had written him. When at last he noisily bade her father and mother, "Well, good night. I forgot I woke you up; I sha'n't want any sleep myself," she followed him down the avenue to the gate. There, after the whirling words that seemed to fly away from her thoughts and refuse to serve them, she made a last effort to solemnize the moment that seemed so crazy, and pressed the letter she had written upon him.

"What's this?" he said. "Want me to mail it?"

"No, no. It's for you. I wrote it after you went this morning. Keep it—keep it—and read it sometime—" She thought, and then her inspiration came: "Read it if ever you doubt what you've done, or fear that I regret your having done it. Read it after you've started."

They strained each other in embraces that seemed as ineffective as their words, and he kissed her face with quick, hot breaths that were so unlike him, that made her feel as if she had lost her old lover and found a stranger in his place. The stranger said, "What a gorgeous flower you are, with your red hair, and your blue eyes that look black now, and your face with the color painted out by the white moonshine! Let me hold you under my chin, to see whether I love blood, you tiger-lily!" Then he laughed Gearson's laugh, and released her, scared and giddy. Within her wilfulness she had been frightened by a sense of subtler force in him, and mystically mastered as she had never been before.

She ran all the way back to the house, and mounted the steps panting. Her mother and father were talking of the great affair. Her mother said: "Wa'n't Mr. Gearson in rather of an excited state of mind? Didn't you think he acted curious?"

"Well, not for a man who'd just been elected captain and had to set 'em up for the whole of Company A," her father chuckled back.

"What in the world do you mean, Mr. Balcom? Oh! There's Editha!" She offered to follow the girl indoors.

"Don't come, mother!" Editha called, vanishing.

Mrs. Balcom remained to reproach her husband. "I don't see much of anything to laugh at."

"Well, it's catching. Caught it from Gearson. I guess it won't be much of a war, and I guess Gearson don't think so, either. The other fellows will back down as soon as they see we mean it. I wouldn't lose any sleep over it. I'm going back to bed, myself."

Gearson came again next afternoon, looking pale, and rather sick, but quite himself, even to his languid irony. "I guess I'd better tell you, Editha, that I consecrated myself to your god of battles last night by pouring too many libations to him down my own throat. But I'm all right, now. One has to carry off the excitement, somehow."

"Promise me," she commanded, "that you'll never touch it again!"

"What! Not let the cannikin clink? Not let the soldier drink? Well, I promise."

"You don't belong to yourself now; you don't even belong to *me*. You belong to your country, and you have a sacred charge to keep yourself strong and well for your country's sake. I have been thinking, thinking all night and all day long."

"You look as if you had been crying a little, too," he said with his queer smile.

"That's all past. I've been thinking, and worshipping *you*. Don't you suppose I know all that you've been through, to come to this? I've followed you every step from your old theories and opinions."

"Well, you've had a long row to hoe."

"And I know you've done this from the highest motives—"

"Oh, there won't be much pettifogging to do till this cruel war is—"

"And you haven't simply done it for my sake. I couldn't respect you if you had."

"Well, then we'll say I haven't. A man that hasn't got his own respect intact wants the respect of all the other people he can corner. But we won't go into that. I'm in for the thing now, and we've got to face our future. My idea is that this isn't going to be a very protracted struggle; we shall just scare the enemy to death before it comes to a fight at all. But we must provide for contingencies, Editha. If anything happens to me—"

"Oh, George!" She clung to him sobbing.

"I don't want you to feel foolishly bound to my memory. I should hate that, wherever I happened to be."

"I am yours, for time and eternity—time and eternity." She liked the words; they satisfied her famine for phrases.

"Well, say eternity; that's all right; but time's another thing; and I'm talking about time. But there is something! My mother! If anything happens—"

She winced, and he laughed. "You're not the bold soldier-girl of yesterday!" Then he sobered. "If anything happens, I want you to help my mother out. She won't like my doing this thing. She brought me up to think war a fool thing as well as a bad thing. My father was in the civil war; all through it; lost his arm in it." She thrilled with the sense of the arm round her; what if that should be lost? He laughed as if divining her: "Oh, it doesn't run in the family, as far as I know!" Then he added, gravely, "He came home with misgivings about war, and they grew on him. I guess he and mother agreed between them that I was to be brought up in his final mind about it; but that was before my time. I only knew him from my mother's report of him and his opinions; I don't know whether they were hers first; but they were hers last. This will be a blow to her. I shall have to write and tell her—"

He stopped, and she asked, "Would you like me to write too, George?"

"I don't believe that would do. No, I'll do the writing. She'll understand a little if I say that I thought the way to minimize it was to make war on the largest possible scale at once—that I felt I must have been helping on the war somehow if I hadn't helped keep it from coming, and I knew I hadn't; when it came, I had no right to stay out of it."

Whether his sophistries satisfied him or not, they satisfied her. She clung to his breast, and whispered, with closed eyes and quivering lips, "Yes, yes, yes!"

"But if anything should happen, you might go to her, and see what you could do for her. You know? It's rather far off; she can't leave her chair—"

"Oh, I'll go, if it's the ends of the earth! But nothing will happen! Nothing *can!* I—"

She felt herself lifted with his rising, and Gearson was saying, with his arm still round her, to her father: "Well, we're off at once, Mr. Balcom. We're to be formally accepted at the capital, and then bunched up with the rest somehow, and sent into camp somewhere, and got to the front as soon as possible. We all want to be in the van, of course; we're the first company to report to the Governor. I came to tell Editha, but I hadn't got round to it."

She saw him again for a moment at the capital, in the station, just before the train started southward with his regiment. He looked well, in his uniform, and very soldierly, but somehow girlish, too, with his clean-shaven face and slim figure. The manly eyes and the strong voice satisfied her, and his preoccupation with some unexpected details of duty flattered her. Other girls were weeping and bemoaning themselves, but she felt a sort of noble distinction in the abstraction, the almost unconsciousness, with which they parted. Only at the last moment he said, "Don't forget my mother. It mayn't be such a walk-over as I supposed," and he laughed at the notion.

He waved his hand to her, as the train moved off—she knew it among a score of hands that were waved to other girls from the platform of the car, for it held a letter which she knew was hers. Then he went inside the car to read it, doubtless, and she did not see him again. But she felt safe for him through the strength of what she called her love. What she called her God, always speaking the name in a deep voice and with the implication of a mutual understanding, would watch over him and keep him and bring him back to her. If with an empty sleeve, then he should have three arms instead of two, for both of hers should be his for life. She did not see, though, why she should always be thinking of the arm his father had lost.

There were not many letters from him, but they were such as she could have wished, and she put her whole strength into making hers such as she imagined he could have wished, glorifying and supporting him. She wrote to his mother glorifying him as their hero, but the brief answer she got was merely to the effect that Mrs. Gearson was not well enough to write herself, and thanking her for her letter by the hand of some one who called herself "Yrs truly, Mrs. W. J. Andrews."

Editha determined not to be hurt, but to write again quite as if the answer had been all she expected. But before it seemed as if she could have written, there came news of the first skirmish, and in the list of the killed which was telegraphed as a trifling loss on our side, was Gearson's name. There was a frantic time of trying to make out that it might be, must be, some other Gearson; but the name, and the company and the regiment, and the State were too definitely given.

Then there was a lapse into depths out of which it seemed as if she never could rise again; then a lift into clouds far above all grief, black clouds, that blotted out the sun, but where she soared with him, with George, George! She had the fever that she expected of herself, but she did not die in it; she was not even delirious, and it did not last long. When she was well enough to leave her bed, her one thought was of George's mother, of his strangely worded wish that she should go to her and see what she could do for her. In the exaltation of the duty laid upon her—it buoyed her up instead of burdening her—she rapidly recovered.

Her father went with her on the long railroad journey from northern New York to western Iowa; he had business out at Davenport, and he said he could just as well go then as any other time; and he went with her to the little country town where George's mother lived in a little house on the edge of illimitable corn-fields, under trees pushed to a top of the rolling prairie. George's father had settled there after the civil war, as so many other old soldiers had done; but they were Eastern people, and Editha fancied touches of the East in the June rose overhanging the front door, and the garden with early summer flowers stretching from the gate of the paling fence.

It was very low inside the house, and so dim, with the closed blinds, that they could scarcely see one another: Editha tall and black in her crapes which filled the air with the smell of their dyes; her father standing decorously apart with his hat on his forearm, as at funerals; a woman rested in a deep armchair, and the woman who had let the strangers in stood behind the chair.

The seated woman turned her head round and up, and asked the woman behind her chair, "*Who* did you say?"

Editha, if she had done what she expected of herself, would have gone down on her knees at the feet of the seated figure and said, "I am George's Editha," for answer.

But instead of her own voice she heard that other woman's voice, saying, "Well, I don't know as I *did* get the name just right. I guess I'll have to make a little more light in here," and she went and pushed two of the shutters ajar.

Then Editha's father said in his public will-now-address-a-few-remarks tone, "My name is Balcom, ma'am; Junius H. Balcom, of Balcom's Works, New York; my daughter—"

"Oh!" The seated woman broke in, with a powerful voice, the voice that always surprised Editha from Gearson's slender frame. "Let me see you! Stand round where the light can strike on your face," and Editha dumbly obeyed. "So, you're Editha Balcom," she sighed.

"Yes," Editha said, more like a culprit than a comforter.

"What did you come for?" Mrs. Gearson asked.

Editha's face quivered, and her knees shook. "I came—because—because George—" She could go no farther.

"Yes," the mother said, "he told me he had asked you to come if he got killed. You didn't expect that, I suppose, when you sent him."

"I would rather have died myself than done it!" Editha said with more truth in her deep voice than she ordinarily found in it. "I tried to leave him free—"

"Yes, that letter of yours, that came back with his other things, left him free." Editha saw now where George's irony came from.

"It was not to be read before—unless—until—I told him so," she faltered.

"Of course, he wouldn't read a letter of yours, under the circumstances, till he thought you wanted him to. Been sick?" the woman abruptly demanded.

"Very sick," Editha said, with self-pity.

"Daughter's life," her father interposed, "was almost despaired of, at one time."

Mrs. Gearson gave him no heed. "I suppose you would have been glad to die, such a brave person as you! I don't believe *he* was glad to die. He was always a timid boy, that way; he was afraid of a good many things; but if he was afraid he did what he made up his mind to. I suppose he made up his mind to go, but I knew what it cost him, by what it cost me when I heard of it. I had been through *one* war before. When you sent him you didn't expect he would get killed."

The voice seemed to compassionate Editha, and it was time. "No," she huskily murmured.

"No, girls don't; women don't, when they give their men up to their country. They think they'll come marching back, somehow, just as gay as they went, or if it's an empty sleeve, or even an empty pantaloon, it's all the more glory, and they're so much the prouder of them, poor things."

The tears began to run down Editha's face; she had not wept till then; but it was now such a relief to be understood that the tears came.

"No, you didn't expect him to get killed," Mrs. Gearson repeated in a voice which was startlingly like George's again. "You just expected him to kill someone else, some of those foreigners, that weren't there because they had any say about it, but because they had to be there, poor wretches—conscripts, or whatever they call 'em. You thought it would be all right for my George, *your* George, to kill the sons of those miserable mothers and the husbands of those girls that you would never see the faces of." The woman lifted her powerful voice in a psalmlike note. "I thank my God he didn't live to do it! I thank my God they killed him first, and that he ain't livin' with their blood on his hands!" She dropped her eyes which she had raised with her voice, and glared at Editha. "What you got that black on for?" She lifted herself by her powerful arms so high that her helpless body seemed to hang limp its full length. "Take it off, take it off, before I tear it from your back!"

The lady who was passing the summer near Balcom's Works was sketching Editha's beauty, which lent itself wonderfully to the effects of a colorist. It had come to that confidence which is rather apt to grow between artist and sitter, and Editha had told her everything.

"To think of your having such a tragedy in your life!" the lady said. She added: "I suppose there are people who feel that way about war. But when you consider the good this war has done—how much it has done for the country! I can't understand such people, for my part. And when you had come all the way out there to console her—got up out of a sick bed! Well!"

"I think," Editha said, magnanimously, "she wasn't quite in her right mind; and so did papa."

"Yes," the lady said, looking at Editha's lips in nature and then at her lips in art, and giving an empirical touch to them in the picture. "But how dreadful of her! How perfectly—excuse me—how *vulgar!*"

A light broke upon Editha in the darkness which she felt had been without a gleam of brightness for weeks and months. The mystery that had bewildered her was solved by the word; and from that moment she rose from grovelling in shame and self-pity, and began to live again in the ideal.

4–7

Alexander Edwin Sweet (1841–1901) and J. Armoy Knox (1851–1906)

ALEXANDER EDWIN SWEET (1841–1901) was born in Canada, moved with his family to Texas shortly after statehood, fought in the Texas Cavalry during the Civil War, and became famous first in Texas and later internationally as the author of humorous newspaper articles about his adopted state. Sweet worked as a reporter in San Antonio, Galveston, and Austin before starting his humor magazine *Texas Siftings* in 1881. Irish-born J. ARMOY KNOX (1851–1906) co-wrote the *Siftings*. *On a Mexican Mustang, through Texas, from the Gulf to the Rio Grande* (1883) appeared first in that magazine as installments. The articles were later collected, published in several editions, and translated into German—the vogue for all things Western and Texan being strong there. The excerpt here, sections from the first and last chapter, offers a taste of the narrator's Texas travels.

≋ ≋ ≋

From *On a Mexican Mustang, through Texas, from the Gulf to the Rio Grande* (1883)

Chapter 1

They called him a desperado and a gambler.

They said that he "always went heeled, toted a derringer, and was a bad crowd generally." It was rumored that he had killed five, eight, some said ten men during his short career; yet no one would have thought, to look at the well-dressed young man, mild of manner, and careful as to the parting of his hair, that he was the fire-eater he was reputed to be.

He was as unlike the gory desperado of "the villain-still-pursued-her" style of literature as a divinity student is unlike the life-insurance agent of real life. Tottering under the responsibility of a copious diamond breastpin, and carrying a small cane in his gloved hand, he might have been taken for a hotel clerk, were it not for his conciliatory and gentlemanly manners.

When Phil Parker was pointed out to strangers as a gambler, and a man who had checked several of his acquaintances through to the other world, it was always added that he was a gentleman for all that, and was never known to take an unfair advantage of any of his victims, nor to go back on a friend.

This high-toned and honorable desperado "operated" in one of the inland cities of Texas two years ago. He was one of the chief features of the place. He was a character so associated with the city, that to speak of it without mentioning Phil Parker would be like writing a description of Sheffield without alluding to the matter of cutlery.

A stranger stopping a few days in the city where Parker lived, would be apt to leave with the impression that the place consisted of a wretchedly poor jail, a very handsome court-house, and of Phil Parker and several thousand other inhabitants.

Unlike most professional gamblers, he was seldom "broke." When, in the language of the fraternity, he "struck it rich," and was in funds, he would sometimes celebrate the occasion by a free use of the flowing bowl. This made him enthusiastic on the subject of shooting; his enthusiasm culminating in a visit to some friend's saloon, where he would exhibit his proficiency in the use of the revolver by shattering mirrors, lamp-chimneys, bottles, and other fragile articles, concluding with the laconic remark to the bar-keeper, "Them's mine: put 'em on the slate."

His right to indulge in such mild eccentricities was seldom disputed, for two reasons,—first, to do so would be a risk of the class that insurance companies term extra-hazardous; and, secondly, Phil always dropped in after he became sober, and paid for all the damage done. On several occasions the glass of every lamp on the square was shattered by pistol-bullets fired by some person or persons unknown.

In connection with this, it is a noteworthy fact, that, on every one of these occasions, Phil Parker was in town, and also, that, strange to say, the intelligent and ever-vigilant policeman had just stepped around the corner to obtain a clew from a man regarding a case that was being "worked up" by that lynx-eyed officer (the man wore an apron, and furnished the clew in a tumbler). Thus it was that the unfortunate absence of the peace-officer at the critical moment prevented him from seeing or arresting the offender.

The subject of this sketch was very much respected wherever he was known, especially by the police.

. . .

Two years after the date of the occurrence described above, I spent six days in a little town in one of the New-England States with Phil Parker. I did not know then, nor for some time afterwards, who he was. During those six days I knew him only as "the man from Texas."

When I first met "the man from Texas," he wore a wide-brimmed black *sombrero*, ornamented with a silver cord and tassel. His long boots of alligator-skin reached to his knees; and between the crown of the one and the soles of the others there was six feet two inches of a man whose equal was not in

Warren County on the day the train went through the bridge. Before the accident, he was sitting in the smoking-car, with his feet out of the window. His coat was off, and he was smoking cigarettes; the train rushing along at the rate of thirty miles an hour, panting through cuttings, rattling over trestles, and shooting around curves, like a house on fire. It was a sad accident. . . .

I stopped in the same town for the purpose of having some slight injuries which I had received attended to. "The man from Texas" and I stopped at the same hotel. We soon became acquainted; but, while he staid in the town, no one found out what his name was. On the hotel register he had written what the passengers on the wrecked train called him,—"the man from Texas."

I was very much interested by his tales of frontier life. Without a trace of boastfulness in his tone, he spoke of his twelve thousand head of horned cattle, his herd of eight hundred horses, and his army of *vaqueros* and herders who attended to his stock. He described the pleasures of hunting antelope and buffalo on the plains, of landing four-pound trout on the banks of the beautiful San Marcos, and of shooting alligators in the bayous and lagoons of Eastern Texas. He gave me a cordial invitation to "come and stay a month or two" at his ranch on the Rio Frio.

I had purposed taking a holiday of six months, and spending it in travel through Europe; but I changed my intention when I had listened for a few hours to descriptions of life in the Lone Star State from the lips of "the man from Texas." And when he spoke of the health to be found on the Western prairies, the clear air, the pure water, and the beneficial influence of exercise derived from a travelling copartnership with a Texas or Mexican pony, I at once decided to change the intended route of travel, and instead of walking, knapsack on back, over the beaten tracks of Europe, to take a trip through the comparatively unknown wilds of Texas on board of a Mexican mustang.

"The man from Texas" did not tell me his name; but he described the location of his ranch, and told me how to reach it. I accepted his invitation; and, although I met him afterwards, I never saw his ranch. I subsequently discovered that it was identical with the location of his castle in Spain.

The result of my acceptance of his invitation was to me three months of a vagabond life on the western frontier of Texas, thirteen weeks of Bedouin-like meanderings among the cattle on a thousand hills, out of reach of the newsboy's cry, and far from the sound of the street-car bells.

. . .

Chapter 20

A few years ago the people of Texas gave themselves a constitution, one of the sections of which reads as follows: "The Legislature shall have no power to appropriate any of the public money for the establishment and maintenance of a bureau of immigration, or for any purpose of bringing immigrants to this State."

It is currently believed that the framers of the Texas constitution had moss two feet in length growing on their backs.

That such a provision as that quoted is to be found in the constitution of the State, is a disgrace to the people of Texas, and a painful commentary on their intelligence. I was gratified to learn that fifty-six thousand voters cast their votes against the adoption of the constitution containing the anti-immigration clause.

Texas needs immigration,—there can be no question about that,—and the kind of immigrants Texas wants are men who will produce something,—men who will add to the intrinsic value of the land by cultivating and improving it,—men who will get up early in the morning, and work six days in the week, and who will not think it too much trouble to milk a cow, that they may have cream for their coffee,—men who will not be content merely to scratch the ground, and make a bare living, but who will plough deep, and cultivate the land as the rich and productive soil of Texas should be cultivated. Texas wants these men to bring with them money enough to buy land, fence it, and put it in cultivation, and wants them to have ambition enough to aspire to something better in the future than a "corn-bread and fry" diet.

Texas wants any number of strong, able-bodied men who can plough and dig, and sow and reap,—men who are willing to accept reasonable wages, and who are neither ashamed nor afraid to labor on a farm, drive a team, or work on a cattle or sheep ranch,—men who will rent a farm, and who will live economically for a year or two, content to use molasses now, that they may have butter after a while.

Texas wants capitalists,—men who have energy and enterprise to utilize the irrigation facilities that most of the rivers and streams afford,—men with money to build cotton and woollen mills, to run saw-mills, to make leather, to build narrow-gauge railroads, to utilize the immense water-power, and to develop the mineral resources of the country.

Texas wants the farmer, because there are sixty-five million acres of land that need cultivating. Texas wants to add to her wealth by having cotton, corn, wheat, etc., raised on the sixty-five million acres that are now unproductive.

. . .

My last night in Texas was spent in lower berth No. 7, in a Pullman car, between Hearne and the gate-city of Texas,—Denison.

I was lying in my berth, looking out at the moonlit landscape, trying to picture to myself the future of the great State of Texas; the man in upper No. 6 was snoring with the regularity of a death-watch; the porter was turning down the lights; the passenger in the berth above had just retired; and the wheels of the car were reciting that monotonous and soothing lullaby, "rickety-clack, rick, rack,"—when the wand of Morpheus touched me. The noise of the wheels, as they jolted and bumped over the worn-out rails of the Central Railroad, became more and more indistinct, until I ceased to be conscious of its existence.

Then there appeared to me the spirit that presides over dreams and visions. He invested me with supernatural power of vision and of intuition; and then, taking me by the hand, he carried me up above the earth, and, with that absurd incongruity that characterizes dreams and visions, time and distance had no measure. In a few moments we passed over the whole length and breadth of Texas; not the Texas I had known before, but the Texas of the year 1950,—Texas with fifteen thousand miles of railroads,—Texas with seventy-five million acres of corn, cotton, and sugar fields,—Texas with fifteen million inhabitants. I saw cities and towns that had sprung up since the century's birth, and become great manufacturing and commercial centres. In these cities and towns I heard the whir of innumerable cotton-spindles; the purring sound of molten metal, as it was poured into mould and matrix; the clatter of hundreds of sewing-machines, as they made into garments the cotton and woollen fabrics manufactured on Texas looms. I passed by great buildings, noisy with the rattle of machinery that manufactured all manner of articles fashioned of iron and steel, and brass and copper. In one city the manufacture of pottery and glass was the principal industry: in another, it was paper, leather, and agricultural implements.

We stopped for a moment on the magnificent monument erected on Capitol Hill, Austin, in 1895, by the State of Texas, to commemorate the heroic deeds done at the Alamo. From the summit of this imposing pile, we looked down upon the capital of the largest, richest, and politically the most powerful, State in the Union.

4–8

Sidney Lanier (1842–1881)

Accomplishing much in his tragically short life, SIDNEY LANIER (1842–1881) was a soldier, a poet, a concert flutist, a professor of English literature, and a noted essayist. Lanier was born in Georgia and spent most of his life in the South. He served in the Civil War on the Confederate side. "The Marshes of Glynn" (1878) is his most important and successful poem, and in it one can see the importance of the natural world to Lanier.

As an essayist, Lanier is at his best when engaged in the description of the natural and social world, as in his description of San Antonio.

≋ ≋ ≋

From "San Antonio de Bexar" (1899)

If peculiarities were quills, San Antonio de Bexar would be a rare porcupine. Over all the round of aspects in which a thoughtful mind may view a city, it bristles with striking idiosyncrasies and *bizarre* contrasts. Its history, population, climate, location, architecture, soil, water, customs, costumes, horses, cattle, all attract the stranger's attention, either by force of intrinsic singularity or of odd juxtapositions. It was a puling infant for a century and a quarter, yet has grown to a pretty vigorous youth in a quarter of a century; its inhabitants are so varied that the "go slow" directions over its bridges are printed in three languages, and the religious services in its churches held in four; the thermometer, the barometer, the vane, the hygrometer, oscillate so rapidly, so frequently, so lawlessly, and through so wide a meteorological range, that the climate is simply indescribable, yet it is a growing resort for consumptives; it stands with all its gay prosperity just in the edge of a lonesome, untilled belt of land one hundred and fifty miles wide, like *Mardi Gras* on the austere brink of Lent; it has no Sunday laws, and that day finds its bar-rooms and billiard-saloons as freely open and as fully attended as its churches; its buildings, ranging from the Mexican *jacal* to the San Fernando Cathedral, represent all the progressive stages of man's architectural progress in edifices of mud, of wood, of stone, of iron, and of sundry combinations of those materials; its soil is in wet weather an inky-black cement, but in dry a floury-white powder; it is built along both banks of two limpid streams, yet it drinks rain-water collected in cisterns; its horses and mules are from Lilliput, while its oxen are from Brobdingnag.

San Antonio de Bexar, Texas, had its birth in 1715. It was, indeed, born before its time, in consequence of a sudden fright into which its mother-Spain was thrown by the menacing activities of certain Frenchmen, who, upon other occasions besides this one, were in those days very much what immortal Mrs. Gamp has declared to Mrs. Harris "these steam-ingines is in our business,"—a frequent cause of the premature development of projects. For Spain had not intended to allow any settlements, as yet, in that part of her province of the New Philippines which embraced what is now called Texas. In the then situation of her affairs, this policy was not without some reasons to support it. She had valuable possessions in New Mexico: between these possessions and the French settlements to the eastward, intervened an enormous breadth of country, whose obstacles against intruders, appalling enough in themselves, were yet magnified by the shadowy terrors that haunt an unknown land. Why not fortify her New Mexican silver-mines with these sextuple barriers, droughts, deserts, mountains, rivers, savages, and nameless fears? Surely, if inclosure could be made impregnable, this would seem to be so; and accordingly the Spanish Government had finally determined, in 1694, not to revive the feeble posts and missions which had been established four years previously with a view to make head against the expedition of La Salle, but which had been abandoned already by soldier and friar, in consequence of the want of food and the ferocity of the savages.

But in 1712, Anthony Crozat, an enterprising French merchant, obtained from Louis XIV. a conditional grant to the whole of the French province of Louisiana. Crozat believed that a lucrative trade might be established with the northeastern provinces of Mexico, and that mines might exist in his territory. To test these beliefs, young Huchereau St. Denis, acting under instructions from Cadillac, who had been appointed Governor of Louisiana by Crozat's influence, started westward, left a nucleus of a settlement at Natchitoches, and proceeded across the country to the Rio Grande, where his explorations, after romantic adventures too numerous to be related here, came to an inglorious suspension with his seizure and imprisonment by the Spanish vice-regal authorities in Mexico.

It was this expedition which produced the premature result hereinbefore alluded to. Spain saw that instead of surrounding New Mexico with inhospitable wastes and ferocious savages, she was in reality but leaving France free to occupy whatever coigns of vantage might be found in that prodigious Debatable Land, which was claimed by both and was held by neither.

Perhaps this consideration was heightened by Spain's consciousness that the flimsiness of her title to that part of the "New Philippines" which lay east of the Rio Grande really required an actual occupation in order to bolster it up. Pretty much all that she could prove in support of her claim was, that in 1494 Pope Alexander VI., acting as arbitrator between Portugal and Spain, had assigned to the latter all of the American possessions that lay west of a meridian running three hundred and seventy miles west of the Azores; that De Leon, De Ayllon, De Narvaez, and De Soto, in voyages made between the years 1512 and 1538, had sailed from Cape Florida to Cape Catorce; and that Philip II. had denounced the penalty of extermination against any foreigner who should enter the Gulf of Mexico or any of the lands bordering thereupon.

These were, to say the least, but indefinite muniments of title; and to them France could oppose the unquestionable fact that La Salle had coasted the shore of Texas westward to Corpus Christi inlet, had returned along the same route, had explored bays and rivers and named them, and had finally built Fort St. Louis on the Lavaca River in 1685. Here now, in 1714, to crown all, was the daring young Lord Huchereau St. Denis traversing the whole land from Natchitoches to the Rio Grande, and thrusting in his audacious face like an apparition of energy upon the sleepy routines of post-life and mission-life at San Juan Bautista.

This was alarming; and in 1715 the Duke of Linares, Viceroy of Mexico, despatched Don Domingo Ramon to Texas with a party of troops and some Franciscan friars, to take steps for the permanent occupation of the country. Ramon established several forts and missions; among others he located a fort, or *presidio* (Spanish, "a garrison"), on the western bank of the San Pedro River, a small stream flowing through the western suburbs of the present city of San Antonio de Bexar, about three fourths of a mile from the present Main Plaza. This *presidio* was called San Antonio de Valero. In May, 1718, certain Alcantarine Franciscans, of the College of Queretaro, established a mission under the protection of the *presidio*, calling it by the same invocation, San Antonio de Valero. It was this mission whose Church of the Alamo afterwards shed so red a glory upon the Texan revolution. It had been founded fifteen years before, in the valley of the Rio Grande, under the invocation of San Francisco Solano; had been removed to San Ildefonso in 1708, and again removed back to the Rio Grande in 1710 under the new invocation of San José. It had not indeed yet reached the end of its wanderings. In 1722, both the *presidio* and mission of San Antonio de Valero were removed to what is now known as the Military Plaza, and a permanent system of improvements begun.

Here then, with sword and crozier, Spain set to work at once to reduce her wild claim into possession, and to fulfil the condition upon which Pope Alexander had granted her the country—of christianizing its natives. One cannot but lean one's head on one's hand to dream out, for a moment, this old Military Plaza—most singular spot on the wide expanse of the lonesome Texan prairies—as it was a hundred and fifty years ago. The rude buildings, the church, the hospital, the soldiers' dwellings, the brethren's lodgings, the huts for the converted Indians (*Yndios Reducidos*) stand ranged about the large level quadrangle, so placed upon the same theory of protection which "parks" the wagon-train that will camp this night on the plains. Ah, here they come, the inhabitants of San Antonio, from the church-door; vespers is over; the big-thighed, bow-legged, horse-riding Apache steps forth, slowly, for he is yet in a maze—the burning candles, the shrine, the genuflexions, the chants, are all yet whirling in his memory; the lazy soldier slouches by, leering at him, yet observing a certain care not to be seen therein, for Señor Soldado is not wholly free from fear of this great-thewed Señor Apache; the soldiers' wives, the squaws, the catechumens, the children, all wend their ways across the plaza. Here advances Brother Juan, bare-footed, in a gown of serge, with his knotted scourge a-dangle from his girdle; he accosts the Indian, he draws him on to talk of Manitou, his grave pale face grows intense and his forehead wrinkles as he spurs his brain on to the devising of arguments that will convince this wild soul before him of the fact of the God of Adam, of Peter, and of Francis. Yonder is a crowd: alas, it is stout Brother Antonio, laying shrewd stripes with unsparing arm upon the back of a young Indian—so hard to convince these dusky youths and maidens of the wide range and ramifications of that commandment which they seem most prone to break. Ha! there behind the church, if you look, goes on another flagellation: Brother Francis has crept back there, slipped his woollen gown from his shoulders, and fallen to with his knotted scourge upon his own bare back, for that a quick vision did, by instigation of the devil, cross his mind even in the very midst of vespers,—a vision of a certain señorita as his wife, of a warm all-day sunned *hacienda*, of children playing, of fruits, of friends, of laughter—"O blessed St. Francis of Assisi, fend off Sathanas!" he cries, and raises a heavier welt.

Presently, as evening draws on, the Indians hold meetings, males in one place, females in another; reciting prayers, singing canticles. Finally it is bedtime; honest Brother Antonio goes round and locks the unmarried young male Indians into their sleeping apartments on one side, the maidens on the other side into theirs, casts a glance mayhap towards Mexico, breathes a prayer, gets him to his pallet, and the Plaza of San Antonio de Valero is left in company of the still sentinel, the stream of the San Pedro purling on one side, that of the San Antonio whispering on the other, under the quiet stars, midst of the solemn prairie, in whose long grass yonder (by all odds) crouches some keen-eyed Apache *bravo*,* who has taken a fancy that he will ride Don Ramon's charger.

The infant settlement soon begins to serve in that capacity which gives it a "bad eminence" among the other Texan settlements for the next hundred years: to wit, as the point to which, or from which, armies are retreating or advancing, or in which armies are fighting. Already, in 1719, before the removal to the Military Plaza, the scenes of war have been transacting themselves in the young San Antonio de Valero. On a certain day in the spring of that year, the peaceful people are astonished to behold all their Spanish brethren who belong to the settlements eastward of theirs, come crowding into the town: monks, soldiers, women, and all.

---

* Sp. *Yndios Bravos*: unconverted Indians.

In the confusion they quickly learn that in the latter part of the year before, France has declared war against Spain; that the Frenchmen at Natchitoches, as soon as they have heard the news, have rushed to arms with Gallic impetuosity, and led by La Harpe and St. Denis, have advanced westward, have put to flight all the Spanish at Adaes, at Orquizaco, at Aes, and at Nacogdoches; and that these are they who are here now, disturbing the peaceful mission with unwonted sights and sounds, and stretching its slender hospitalities to repletion. The French do not attack, however, but return towards Natchitoches. In a short time enter from the opposite side of the stage, that is to say from Mexico, the Marquis de Aguayo, Governor-General of New Estremadura and the New Philippines, with five hundred mounted men. These march through, take with them the men of Orquizaco, of Adaes and Aes, reestablish those settlements, and pursue the French until they hear that the latter are in Natchitoches; De Aguayo then returns to San Antonio and sets on foot plans for its permanent improvement.

. . .

For several years after the permanent location round the Military Plaza, no important events seem to be recorded as happening in San Antonio; but the quiet work of post and mission goes on, and the probable talk on the Plaza is of the three new missions which De Aguayo establishes on the San Antonio River, below the town, under the protection of its garrison; or of the tales which come slowly floating from the northward concerning the dreadful fate of a Spanish expedition which has been sent to attack the French settlements on the Upper Mississippi, and which, mistaking the hostile Missouris on the way for friendly Osages, distributes fifteen hundred muskets, together with sabres and pistols, to the said Missouris to be used against the French, whereupon the Missouris next morning at day-break fall upon the unsuspecting Spaniards, butcher them all (save the priest, whom they keep for a "magpie," as they call him, to laugh at), and march off into the French fort arrayed in great spoils, their chief wearing the chasuble and bearing the paten before him for a breast-plate; or of Governor De Aguayo's recommendation to the home government to send colonists instead of soldiers if it would help the friars to win the Indians; or of the appointment of a separate governor for Texas in 1727; or of the withdrawal of ten soldiers in 1729, leaving only forty-three in garrison at San Antonio. About 1731, however, an important addition is made to the town. Under the auspices of the home government—which seems to have accepted De Aguayo's ideas—thirteen families and two single men arrive, pure Spaniards from the Canary Islands, also some Tlascalans, and a party from Monterey. These set to work around a Plaza (the "Plaza of the Constitution," or "Main Plaza") just eastward of and adjoining the Military Plaza, and commence a town which they call San Fernando. They are led, it seems, to this location by the same facility of irrigation which had recommended the Military Plaza to their neighbors. The new colonists impart vigor to affairs. The missions prosper, Indians are captured and brought in to be civilized whether or no, and on the 5th of March, 1731, the foundation is laid of the Mission of *La Purísima Concepcion de Acuña*, on the San Antonio River, a mile or so below the town.

Meantime a serious conspiracy against the welfare of San Antonio and San Fernando is hatched in the northeast. The Natchez Indians wish to revenge themselves upon the French, who have driven them from their home on the Mississippi. They resolve to attack St. Denis at Natchitoches, and to prevent the Spaniards from helping him (the French and Spanish are now friends, having united against England), they procure the Apaches to assail San Antonio. St. Denis, however, surprises and defeats the Natchez; and the Apaches appear to have made no organized attack, but to have confined themselves to murdering and thieving in parties. These Apaches, indeed, were dreadful scourges in these days to San Antonio and its environs. The people of the *presidio* of San Fernando and of the missions on the river complained repeatedly (says the *Testimonio de un Parecer*[*] in the archives of Bexar) that they cannot expand (*sin poder estenderse*) on account of "*las frequienttes hosttilidades que experimenttan de los Yndios Apaches.*" This great tribe had headquarters about the Pass of Bandera, some fifty miles to the northwestward, from which they forayed, not only up to Antonio, but even as far as to Coahuila. Moreover, they manage (says the *Testimonio*) horses, firearms, and arrows *con mucha desttreza y agilidad*. Finally the men of San Antonio and San Fernando get tired of it, and after some minor counter-forays, they organize an expedition in 1732 which conquers comparative peace from the Apaches for a few years.

Nothing of special interest is recorded as happening in San Antonio from this time until 1736. In September of that year arrives Don Carlos de Franquis, who immediately proceeds to throw the town into a very pretty ferment. Franquis had come out from Spain to Mexico to be Governor of Tlascala. On arriving, he finds that some one else is already Governor of Tlascala. Vizarron, Archbishop of Mexico, and acting Viceroy since Casa Fuerte's death, disposes of him—it is likely he made trouble enough till that was done—by sending him off to Texas to supersede Governor Sandoval, a fine old veteran, who has been for two years governing the Province with such soldierly fidelity as has won him great favor among the inhabitants. Franquis begins by insulting the priests, and follows this up with breaking open people's letters. Presently

---

[*] Testimony of a witness: this document is hereinafter described.

he arrests Sandoval, has him chained, and causes criminal proceedings to be commenced against him, charging him with treacherous complicity in certain movements of St. Denis at Natchitoches. It seems that St. Denis, having found a higher and drier location, has removed his garrison and the French Mission of St. John the Baptist some miles further from Red River towards the Texas territory, and built a new fort and settlements; that Sandoval, hearing of it, has promptly called him to account as an intruder on Spanish ground; and that a correspondence has ensued between St. Denis and Sandoval, urging the rights of their respective governments in the premises, which has just been brought to the point of a flat issue upon which to go to the jury of war when Sandoval is ousted by Franquis. The Viceroy sends the Governor of New Leon to investigate the trouble; and the famous lawsuit of Franquis *versus* Sandoval is fairly commenced. The Governor of New Leon seems to find against Franquis, who is sent back to the *presidio* on the Rio Grande. He gets away, however, and off to the Viceroy. But Sandoval is not satisfied, naturally, for he has been mulcted in some three thousand four hundred dollars, costs of the investigating commission. He pays, and in 1738 files his petition against Franquis for redress of his injuries. Franquis, thus attacked in turn, strengthens his position with a new line of accusations. He now, besides the French business, charges Sandoval with living at San Antonio instead of at Adaes, the official residence; with being irregular in his accounts with the San Antonio garrison; and with peculation in the matter of the salaries of certain paid missionaries, whom Sandoval is alleged to have discharged and then pocketed their stipends. The papers go to the Viceroy, and from the Viceroy to Attorney-General Vedoya. In 1740 Vedoya decides Sandoval guilty of living at San Antonio, though it was his duty to be there to defend it against the Apaches; guilty of irregular book-keeping, though through memoranda it is found that there is a balance in his favor of thirteen hundred dollars; not guilty of stealing the missionary money. Upon the French matter Vedoya will not decide without further evidence. With poor Sandoval it is pay again; he is fined five hundred dollars for his "guilt." Meantime, some months afterward, an order is made that testimony be taken in Texas with regard to the French affair, said testimony to embrace an account of pretty much everything in, about, and concerning Texas. The testimony being taken and returned, the Attorney-General, in November, 1741, entirely acquits Sandoval. But alas for the stout old soldier! this is in Mexico, where from of old, if one is asked who rules now, one must reply with the circumspection of that Georgia judge, who, being asked the politics of his son, made answer that *he knew not, not having seen the creature since breakfast.* Vizarron has gone out; the Duke de la Conquista has come into the Viceroyalty; and Sandoval has hardly had time to taste his hard-earned triumph before, through machinations of Franquis, he finds himself in prison by order of the new Viceroy. Finally, however, the rule works the other way; in December, 1743, a new Viceroy, Count Fuenclara, gets hold of the papers in the case, acquits Sandoval, and enjoins Franquis from proceeding further in the matter.

It was in the course of this litigation—a copy of the proceedings in which, "filling thirty volumes of manuscript," was transmitted to Spain—that the old document hereinbefore referred to as the *Testimonio de un Parecer* had its origin. In this paper San Antonio is called *San Antonio de Vejar ó Valero*, Vejar being the Spanish orthography of the Mexican *Bexar* (pronounced Váy-har). This name, San Antonio de Bexar, seems to have attached itself particularly to the military post, or *presidio*; its origin is not known. The town of San Fernando was still so called at this time; and the town and mission of San Antonio de Valero bore that name. In 1744 this latter extended itself to the eastward, or rather the extension had probably gone on before that time and was only evidenced then. At any rate, on the 8th of May, 1744, the first stone of the present Church of the Alamo was laid and blessed. The site of this church is nearly a quarter of a mile to the eastward of the Military Plaza, where the mission to which it belonged had been located in 1722. From an old record-book purporting to contain the baptisms in "the Parish of the Pueblo of *San José del Alamo*," it would seem that there must have been also a settlement of that name. San Antonio de Bexar, therefore—the modern city—seems to be a consolidation of the *presidio* of San Antonio de Bexar, the mission and *pueblo* (or villa) of San Antonio de Valero, and the *pueblos* of San Fernando and San José del Alamo.

For the next forty years after the foundation of the Alamo in 1744, the colonists and missionaries seem to have pursued the ordinary round of their labors without unusual events; in point of material prosperity San Antonio seems to have led but a struggling existence. Yoakum[*] estimates the whole European population of Texas in 1744 to have been fifteen hundred, which, together with about the same number of converted Indians, "was divided mostly between Adaes and San Antonio." The same author again[†] estimates the population of Adaes and San Antonio in 1765 to have been "hardly five hundred" Europeans, besides converted Indians, of whom he adds that there were only about seven hundred and fifty in the whole province of Texas. It was impossible indeed during these years that any legitimate prosperity could have been attained. Up to the year 1762, when France, to save Louisiana from the clutches of England,

---

[*] *History of Texas*, vol, i., p. 87.
[†] Vol. i., p. 97.

ceded it to Spain, trade had been prohibited by the latter between her Texan colonists and the French settlers in Louisiana, though some intercourse always went on in a smuggling way between the two, whenever they could get a Spanish official to wink his eye or turn his back; and even after the cession of Louisiana matters were little better in point of commercial activity. There were also restrictions even upon the agricultural energies of the colonists; they were, it is said, prohibited from cultivating the vine and the olive, and also from the manufacture of many articles. Indeed, the immediate necessity of settlements having passed away with the removal of the danger of French occupation, the old policy of Spain seems to have been resumed in full force,—that of keeping her provinces around New Mexico and Mexico impenetrable wastes, as barriers against enterprising neighbors.

Nor was the spiritual prosperity much greater. The arduous toils and sublime devotions of the Franciscan brethren bore but moderate fruit. Father Marest had declared in 1712 that the conversion of the Indians was "a miracle of the Lord's mercy," and that it was "necessary first to transform them into men, and afterward to labor to make them Christians." These noble brothers too had reason to believe in the inhumanity of the Indians. They could remember the San Saba Mission, where, in 1758, the Indians had fallen upon the people and massacred every human being, lay and clerical; and here, in 1785, they could see for themselves the company of San Carlos de Parras driven by the fierce Camanches to place their quarters within the enclosure of the Alamo.

In 1783–5 San Antonio de Valero ceased to be a mission. For some reason it had become customary to send whatever captive Indians were brought in to the missions below the town for christianization. The town, however, which had been built up about the mission buildings, remained, having a separate alcalde, and an organization politically and religiously distinct from that of San Antonio de Bexar and San Fernando for some years longer. In 1790 the population around the Alamo was increased by the addition of the people from the Presidio de los Adaes; this post was abandoned, and its inhabitants were provided with lands which had been the property of the mission of San Antonio de Valero, lying in the neighborhood of the Alamo, to the north. "The upper *labor* of the Alamo," says Mr. Giraud, the present mayor of the city, in an interesting note which constitutes Appendix IV. of Yoakum's *History of Texas*, ". . . is still commonly called by the old inhabitants the *labor de los Adaeseños*." These mission lands about the Alamo seem to have ceased to be such about this time, and to have been divided off to the mission-people, each of whom received a

---

* *Labor*: a Spanish land-measure of about one hundred and seventy-seven acres.

portion, with fee-simple title. In 1793 the distinct religious organization of the Mission of San Antonio de Valero terminated, and it was aggregated to the curacy of the town of San Fernando and the *presidio* of San Antonio de Bexar . . .

In the year 1800 San Antonio began to see a new sort of prisoners brought in. Instead of captive Indians, here arrived a party of eleven Americans* in irons, who were the remainder of a company with which Philip Nolan, a trader between Natchez and San Antonio, had started out, and who, after a sharp fight with one hundred and fifty Spanish soldiers, in which Nolan was killed, had been first induced to return to Nacogdoches, and there were treacherously manacled and sent to prison at San Antonio. Again, in 1805, three Americans are brought in under guard. In this year, too, matters begin to be a little more lively in the town. Spain's neighbor on the east is not now France; for in 1803 Louisiana has been formally transferred to the United States. There is already trouble with the latter about the boundary line betwixt Louisiana and Texas. Don Antonio Cordero, the new Governor of Texas, has brought on a lot of troops through the town, and fixed his official residence here; and troops continue to march through *en route* to Natchitoches, where the American General Wilkinson is menacing the border. Again, in 1807, Lieutenant Zebulon M. Pike, of the United States army, passes through town in charge of an escort. Lieutenant Pike has been sent to explore the Arkansas and Red rivers, and to treat with the Camanches, has been apprehended by the Spanish authorities in New Mexico, carried to Santa Fé, and is now being escorted home.

At this time there are four hundred troops in San Antonio, in quarters near the Alamo. Besides these, the town has about two thousand inhabitants, mostly Spaniards and Creoles, the remainder Frenchmen, Americans, civilized Indians, and half-breeds. New settlers have come in; and what with army officers, the Governor's people, the clergy, and prominent citizens, society begins to form and to enjoy itself. The Governor, Father McGuire, Colonel Delgado, Captain Ugarte, Doctor Zerbin, dispense hospitalities and adorn social meetings. There are, in the evenings, levees at the Governor's; sometimes Mexican dances on the Plaza, at which all assist; and frequent and prolonged card-parties.

But these peaceful scenes do not last long. In 1811 the passers across the San Antonio River between the Alamo and the Main Plaza behold a strange sight: it is the head of a man stuck on a pole, there, in bloody menace against rebels. This head but yesterday was on the shoulders of Colonel Delgado, a flying adherent of Hidalgo in Mexico: Hidalgo, initiator of how long a train

---

* Americans, *i.e.* United States people; in which sense, to avoid the awkwardness of the only other equivalent terms, I shall hereafter use the word.

of Mexican revolutions! having been also put to death in Chihuahua. It was not long before this blood was (as from of old) washed out with other blood. Bernardo Gutierrez, a fellow-rebel of the unfortunate Delgado, escaped to Natchitoches, and met young Magee, an officer of the United States army. In a short time the two had assembled a mixed force of American adventurers and rebellious Mexican republicans, had driven the Spanish troops from Nacogdoches, marched into Texas, captured the fort and supplies at La Bahia, enlisted its garrison, and sustained a siege there which the enemy was finally compelled to abandon with loss. It was in March, 1813, that the Spanish besieging force set out on its retreat up the river to San Antonio. Gutierrez—Magee having committed suicide in consequence of mortification at the indignant refusal of the troops to accept a surrender which he had negotiated soon after the beginning of the siege—determined to pursue. On the 28th of March he crossed the Salado, *en route* to San Antonio, with a force consisting of eight hundred Americans under Colonel Kemper, one hundred and eighty Mexicans led by Manchaco,* under Colonel James Gaines, three hundred Lipan and Twowokana Indians, and twenty-five Cooshattie Indians. Marching along the bank of the San Antonio River, with the left flank protected by the stream, this motley army arrived within nine miles of San Antonio, when the riflemen on the right suddenly discovered the enemy ambushed in the chaparral on the side of a ridge. Here the whole force that Governor Salcedo could muster had been posted; consisting of about fifteen hundred regular troops and a thousand militia. To gain time to form, the Indians were ranged to receive the opening charge of the Spanish cavalry; the enemy meantime having immediately formed along the crest of the ridge, with twelve pieces of artillery in the centre. The Indians broke at the first shock; only the Cooshatties and a few others stood their ground. These received two other charges, in which they lost two killed and several wounded. The Americans had now made their dispositions, and proceeded to execute them with matchless coolness. They charged up the hill, stopped at thirty yards of the enemy's line, fired three rounds, loaded, then charged again, and straightway the slope towards San Antonio was dotted with Spanish fugitives, whom the Indians pursued and butchered regardless of quarter. The Spanish commander, who had pledged sword and head to Governor Salcedo that he would kill and capture the American army, could not endure the sting of his misfortune. He spurred his horse upon the American ranks, attacked Major Ross, then Colonel Kemper, and while in the act of

---

* A prominent Mexican, of Texas, of strong but uncultivated intellect.

striking the latter was shot by private William Owen. The Spanish loss is said to have been near a thousand killed and wounded.

Next day the Americans advanced to the outskirts of San Antonio and demanded a surrender. Governor Salcedo desired to parley, to delay. A second demand was made—peremptory. Governor Salcedo then marched out with his staff. He presented his sword to Captain Taylor; Taylor refused, and referred him to Colonel Kemper. Presenting to Colonel Kemper, he was in turn referred to Gutierrez. No, not to that rebel! Salcedo thrust his sword into the ground, whence Gutierrez drew it. The victors got stores, arms, and treasure. Seventeen American prisoners in the Alamo were released and armed. The troops were paid,—receiving a bonus of fifteen dollars each in addition to wages,—clothed and mounted out of the booty. The Indians were not forgotten in the distribution; they "were supplied," says Yoakum, "with two dollars' worth of vermilion, together with presents of the value of a hundred and thirty dollars, and sent away rejoicing."

And now flowed the blood that must answer that which dripped down the pole from poor Colonel Delgado's head. Shortly after the victory, Captain Delgado, a son of the executed rebel, falls upon his knees before Gutierrez, and demands vengeance upon the prisoner, Governor Salcedo, who apprehended and executed his father. Gutierrez arrays his army, informs them that it would be safe to send Salcedo and staff to New Orleans, and that it so happens that vessels are about to sail for that port from Matagorda Bay. The army consents (we are so fearfully and wonderfully republican in these days: *the army* consents) that the prisoners be sent off as proposed. Captain Delgado, with a company of Mexicans, starts in charge, ostensibly *en route* for Matagorda Bay. There are fifteen of the distinguished captives: Governor Salcedo of Texas, Governor Herrera of New Leon, Ex-Governor Cordero, whom we last saw holding levees in San Antonio, several Spanish and Mexican officers, and one citizen. Delgado gets his prisoners a mile and a half from town, halts them on the bank of the river, strips them, ties them, and cuts the throat of every man: "some of the assassins," says Colonel Navarro, whetting "their knives upon the soles of their shoes in presence of their victims."

The town of San Antonio must have been anything but a pleasant place for peaceful citizens during the next two months. Colonel Kemper, who was really the commanding officer of the American army, refused further connection with those who could be guilty of such barbarity, and left, with other American officers. Their departure left in the town an uncontrolled body of troops who feared neither God nor man; and these immediately proceeded to avail themselves of the situation by indulging in all manner of riotous and lawless pleasures. With the month of June, however, came Don Elisondo from Mexico with an army of royalists, consisting of about three thousand men, half of whom were regular troops. His advance upon San Antonio seems to have been a complete surprise, and to have been only learned by the undisciplined republican army in the town together with the fact that he had captured their horses, which had been out grazing, and killed part of the guard which was protecting the *caballada*. If Elisondo had marched straight on into town, his task would probably have been an easy one. But he committed the fatal mistake of encamping a short distance from the suburbs, where he threw up two bastions with a curtain between, on a ridge near the river Alozon.

Meantime the republican army in the town recovered from the confusion into which they had been thrown by the first intelligence of Elisondo's proximity, and organized themselves under Gutierrez and Captain Perry. It was determined to anticipate the enemy's attack. Ingress and egress were prohibited, the sentinels doubled, and all the cannon spiked except four field-pieces. In the darkness of the night of June 4th the Americans marched quietly out of town, by file, to within hearing of the enemy's pickets, and remained there until the enemy was heard at matins. The signal to charge being given—a cheer from the right of companies—the Americans advanced, surprised and captured the pickets in front, mounted the enemy's work, lowered his flag and hoisted their own, before they were fairly discovered through the dim dawn. The enemy struggled hard, however, and compelled the Americans to abandon the works. The latter charged again, and this time routed the enemy completely. The royalist loss is said to have been about a thousand in killed, wounded and prisoners; and that of the Americans, ninety-four killed and mortally wounded.

For some reason Gutierrez was now dismissed from the leadership of the army (we republican soldiers decapitate our commanders very quickly if they please us not!), and shortly afterwards troops and citizens went forth in grand procession to welcome Don José Alvarez Toledo, a distinguished republican Cuban who had been forwarding recruits from Louisiana to San Antonio; and having escorted him into town with much ceremony, elected him commander-in-chief of the Republican Army of the North. Toledo immediately organized a government; but the people of San Antonio enjoyed the unaccustomed blessing of civil law only a little while.

In a few days enter, from over the Mexican border, General Arredondo with the remnant of Elisondo's men and some fresh troops, about four thousand in all, *en route* for San Antonio. Toledo marches out to meet him with about twenty-five hundred men, one third of whom are Americans, the balance Mexicans under Manchaco; and on the 18th of August, 1813, they come together. Arredondo decoys him into an ingenious *cul de sac* which he has thrown up just south of the Medina River, and has concealed by cut bushes; and pours such a murderous fire of cannon and small arms upon him, that in spite of the gallantry of the right wing, where the Americans are, the retreat which Toledo has ordered too late becomes a mere rout, and the republican army is butchered without mercy. One batch of seventy or eighty fugitives is captured by the pursuing royalists, tied, set by tens upon a log laid across a great grave, and shot!

On the 20th, Arredondo enters San Antonio in great triumph, and straight-way proceeds to wreak fearful vengeance upon the unhappy town for the massacre of his brother governors. Seven hundred citizens are thrown into prison. During the night of the 20th eighteen die of suffocation out of three hundred who are confined in one house. These only anticipate the remainder, who are shot, without trial, in detachments. Five hundred republican women are imprisoned in a building on the present site of the post-office, derisively termed the *Quinta*, and compelled to make up twenty-four bushels of corn into *tortillas* every day for the royalist army. Having thus sent up a sweet savor of revenge to the spirits of the murdered Salcedo, Cordero, Herrera, and the others, Arredondo finally gathers their bones together and buries them. In all this blood the prosperity of San Antonio was drowned. To settlers it offered no inducements; to most of its former citizens it held out nothing but terror; and it is described as almost entirely abandoned in 1816.

In December, 1820, arrived a person in San Antonio who, though not then known as such, was really a harbinger of better times. This was Moses Austin, of Connecticut. He came to see Governor Martinez, with a view of bringing a colony to Texas. The two, with the Baron de Bastrof, put in train the pre-liminary application for permission to Arredondo, Commandant-General at Monterey. Austin, it is true, died soon afterwards; but he left his project to his son Stephen F., who afterwards carried it out with a patience that amounted to genius and a fortitude that was equivalent to the favor of Heaven.

On the 24th of August, 1821, Don Juan O'Donojú and Iturbide entered into the Treaty of Córdova, which substantially perfected the separation of Mexico from the mother-country. When the intelligence of this event had spread, the citizens of San Antonio returned. Moreover, about this time a tide of emigra-tion began to set towards Texas. The Americans who had composed part of the army of Gutierrez had circulated fair reports of the country. In 1823 San Antonio is said to have had five thousand inhabitants; though the Camanches appear still to have had matters all their own way when they came into town, as they frequently did, to buy beads and other articles with skins of deer and buffalo. One would find this difficult to believe, but reasoning *a priori*, it is rendered probable by the fact that in the decree of the Federal Congress of Mexico of the 24th of August, 1826, to provide for raising troops to serve in Coahuila and Texas as frontier defenders, it is ordered that out of the gross levies there shall be first preferred for military service *"los vagos y mal entretenídos,"* vagrant and evil-disposed persons; and *a posteriori*, it is quite confirmed by the experience of Olmsted in San Fernando (a considerable town west of the Rio Grande) so late as 1854, where he found the Indians "lounging in and out of every house . . . with such an air as indicated they were masters of the town. They entered every door," adds Olmsted, "fell on every neck, patted the women on the cheek, helped themselves to whatever suited their fancy, and distributed their scowls or grunts of pleasure according to their sensations."

In the year 1824 a lot of French merchants passed through San Antonio *en route* to Santa Fé on a trading expedition. Some distance from town their pack-animals were all stolen by Indians; but they managed to get carts and oxen from San Antonio, and so conveyed their goods finally to Santa Fé, where they sold them at an immense profit. In 1831 the Bowie brothers, Rezin P., and James, organized in San Antonio their expedition in search of the old reputed silver mines at San Saba Mission. In the course of this unlucky venture occurred their famous Indian fight, where the two Bowies, with nine others, fought a pitched battle with one hundred and sixty-four Indians who had attacked them with arrow, with rifle, and with fire from sundown to sunset, killing and wounding eighty-four. They then fortified their position during the night, maintained it for eight days afterwards, and finally returned to San Antonio with their horses and three wounded comrades, leaving one man killed.

It is related that in 1832 a Camanche Indian attempted to abduct a Shawnee woman in San Antonio. She escaped him, joined a party of her people who were staying some thirty-five miles from town, and informed them where the Camanches (of whom five hundred had been in town for some purpose) would probably camp. The Shawnees ambushed themselves at the spot indicated. The Camanches came on and stopped as expected: the Shawnees poured a fire into them, and repeated it as they continually rallied, until the Camanches abandoned the contest with a loss of one hundred and seventy-five dead.

Early in 1833 (or perhaps late in December, 1832) arrives in San Antonio for the first time one who is to be called the father of his country. This is Sam Houston. He comes in company with the famous James Bowie, son-in-law of Vice-Governor Veramendi, and holds a consultation with the Camanche chiefs here to arrange a meeting at Cantonment Gibson with a view to a treaty of peace. Meantime trouble is brewing. Young Texas does not get on well with his mother. What seems to hurt most is the late union of Texas with Coahuila. This we cannot stand. Stephen F. Austin goes to the City of Mexico with a memorial on the subject to the federal government. He writes from there to the municipality of San Antonio, Oct. 2d, 1833, informing the people that their request is likely to be refused, and advising them to make themselves ready for that emergency. The municipality hand this letter over to Vice-President Farias, who, already angry with Austin on an old account, arrests him on his way home and throws him into prison, back in the City of Mexico.

In October, 1834, certain people in San Antonio hold what Yoakum calls "the first strictly revolutionary meeting in Texas"; for Santa Ana has *pronounced*, and got to be at the head of affairs, and he refuses to separate Texas from Coahuila. So, through meetings all over the State; through conferences of citizen deputations with Colonel Ugartochea, Mexican Commandant at San Antonio, for the purpose of explaining matters; through confused arguments and resolutions of the peace party and the war party; through confused rumors of the advance of Mexican General Cos with an army; through squabbling and wrangling and final fighting over the cannon that had been lent by the Post of Bexar to the people of Gonzalez; through all manner of civic trouble consequent upon the imprisonment of Governor Viesca of Texas by Santa Ana, and the suspension of the progress of the civil law machine,—we come to the time when the committee of San Felipe boldly cry: "*Let us take Bexar and drive the Mexican soldiery out of Texas!*" and presently here, on the 28th of October, 1835, is General Cos with his army in San Antonio, fortifying for dear life, while yonder is Austin with a thousand Texans, at Mission Concepcion, a mile and a half down the river below town, where Fannin and Bowie with ninety men in advance have a few hours before waged a brilliant battle with four hundred Mexicans, capturing their field-piece, killing and wounding a hundred or more, and driving the rest back to town.

General Austin believes, it seems, that Cos will surrender without a battle; and so remains at Concepcion till November 2d, then marches up past the town on the east side, encamps four or five days, marches down on the west side, displays his forces on a hillside *in terrorem*, sends in a demand for surrender—and is flatly answered *no*. He resolves to lay siege. The days pass slowly; the enemy will not come out, though allured with all manner of military enticements, and the army has no "fun," with the exception of one small skirmish, until the 26th, when "Deaf" Smith* discovers a party of a hundred Mexican troops, who have been sent out to cut prairie-grass for the horses in

* One of the most celebrated and efficient scouts of the revolution.

town, and reporting them in camp, brings on what is known as the "grass-fight." Col. James Bowie attacks with a hundred mounted men; both sides are quickly reinforced, and a sharp running fight is kept up until the enemy get back to town; the Texans capturing seventy horses and killing some fifty of the enemy, with a loss of but two wounded and one missing. Meantime discontents arise. On the day before the "grass-fight" Austin resigns, having been appointed Commissioner to the United States, and Edward Burleson is elected by the army to the command. General Burleson, for some reason, seems loth to storm. Moreover, one Dr. James Grant seduces a large party with a wild project to leave San Antonio and attack Matamoros, when he declares that the whole of Mexico will rise and overwhelm Santa Ana; and on the 29th of November it is actually announced that two hundred and twenty-five men are determined to start the next morning.

But they do not start. It is whispered the town will be stormed. On the 3d of December, Smith, Holmes, and Maverick escape from San Antonio, and give the Texan commander such information as apparently determines him to storm. Volunteers are called for to attack early next morning; all day and all night of that December 3d the men make themselves ready, and long for the moment to advance: when here comes word from the General's quarters that the attack is put off! Chagrin and indignation prevail on all sides. On the morning of the 4th there is open disobedience of orders; whole companies refuse to parade. Finally, when on the same afternoon orders are issued to abandon camp and march for La Bahia at seven o'clock, the tumult is terrible, and it seems likely that these wild energetic souls, failing the Mexicans, will end by exterminating each other.

Midst of the confusion here arrives Mexican Lieutenant Vuavis, a deserter, and declares that the projected attack is *not* known (as had been assigned for reason of postponing), and that the garrison in town is in as bad order and discontent as the besiegers. At this critical moment a brave man suddenly crystallizes the loose mass of discordant men and opinions into one compact force and one keen purpose. It is late in the morning, Col. Benjamin R. Milam steps forth among the men, and cries aloud: "Who will go with old Ben Milam into San Antonio?" Three hundred and one men will go.

A little before daylight on the 5th they "go," General Burleson agreeing to hold his position until he hears from them. Milam marches into and along Acequia Street with his party; Johnson with his along Soledad Street. Where these debouch into the Main Plaza, Cos has thrown up breastworks and placed raking batteries. The columns march parallel along the quiet streets. Presently, as Johnson gets near the Veramendi House (which he is to occupy, while

Milam is to gain De la Ganza's house), a Mexican sentinel fires. Deaf Smith shoots the sentinel. The Mexicans prick up their ears, prick into their cannon-cartridges; the Plaza batteries open, the Alamo batteries join in; spade, crow-bar, rifle, escopet, all are plied, and the storming of Bexar is begun.

But it would take many such papers as this to give even meagre details of all the battles that have been fought in and around San Antonio, and one must pass over the four days of this thrilling conflict with briefest mention. It is novel fighting; warfare intramural, one might say. The Texans advance inch by inch by piercing through the stone walls of the houses, pecking loopholes with crowbars for their rifles as they gain each room, picking off the enemy from his house-tops; from around his cannon, even from behind his own loopholes. On the night of the 5th with great trouble and risk the two columns succeed in opening communication with each other. On the 6th they advance a little beyond the Ganza house. On the 7th brave Karnes steps forth with a crowbar and breaks into a house midway between the Ganza house and the Plaza; brave Milam is stricken by a rifle ball just as he is entering the yard of the Veramendi house and falls instantly dead; and the Navarro house, one block from the Main Plaza, is gained. On the 8th they take the "Zambrano Row" of buildings, driving the enemy from it room by room; the enemy endeavor to produce a diversion with fifty men, and do, in a sense, for Burleson finds some diversion in driving them back precipitately with a six-pounder; at night those in the Zambrano Row are reinforced, and the "Priest's House" is gained amid heavy fighting.

This last is the stroke of grace. The Priest's House commands the Plaza. Early on the morning of the 9th General Cos sends a flag of truce, asking to surrender, and on the 10th agrees with General Burleson upon formal and honorable articles of capitulation.

The poor citizens of San Antonio de Bexar, however, do not yet enjoy the blessings of life in quiet; these wild soldiers who have stormed the town cannot remain long without excitement. Presently Dr. Grant revives his old Matamoros project, and soon departs, carrying with him most of the troops that had been left at Bexar for its defence, together with great part of the garrison's winter supply of clothing, ammunition, and provisions, and in addition "pressing" such property of the citizens as he needs, insomuch that Colonel Neill, at that time in command at Bexar, writes to the Governor of Texas that the place is left destitute and defenceless. Soon afterward Colonel Neill is ordered to destroy the Alamo walls and other fortifications, and bring off the artillery, since no head can be made there in the present crisis against the enemy, who is reported marching in force upon San Antonio. Having no teams, Colonel

Neill is unable to obey the order, and presently retires, his unpaid men having dropped off until but eighty remain, of whom Col. Wm. B. Travis assumes command. Colonel Travis promptly calls for more troops, but gets none as yet, for the Governor and Council are at deadly quarrel, and the soldiers are all pressing towards Matamoros. Travis has brought thirty men with him; about the middle of February he is joined by Colonel Bowie with thirty others, and these, with the eighty already in garrison, constitute the defenders of San Antonio de Bexar. On the 23d of February appears General Santa Ana at the head of a well-appointed army of some four thousand men, and marches straight on into town. The Texans retire before him slowly, and finally shut themselves up in the Alamo; here straightway begins that bloodiest, smokiest, grimiest tragedy of this century. William B. Travis, James Bowie, and David Crockett, with their hundred and forty-five effective men, are enclosed within a stone rectangle one hundred and ninety feet long and one hundred and twenty-two feet wide, having the old church of the Alamo in the southeast corner, in which are their quarters and magazine. They have a supply of water from the ditches that run alongside the walls, and by way of provision they have about ninety bushels of corn and thirty beef-cattle, their entire stock, all collected since the enemy came in sight. The walls are unbroken, with no angles from which to command besieging lines. They have fourteen pieces of artillery mounted, with but little ammunition.

Santa Ana demands unconditional surrender. Travis replies with a cannon-shot, and the attack commences, the enemy running up a blood-red flag in town. Travis dispatches a messenger with a call to his countrymen for reinforcements, which concludes: "Though this call may be neglected, I am determined to sustain myself as long as possible, and die like a soldier who never forgets what is due to his own honor and that of his country. Victory or death!" Meantime the enemy is active. On the 25th Travis has a sharp fight to prevent him from erecting a battery raking the gate of the Alamo. At night it is erected, with another a half-mile off at the *Garita*, or powder-house, on a sharp eminence at the extremity of the present main street of the town. On the 26th there is skirmishing with the Mexican cavalry. In the cold—for a norther has commenced to blow and the thermometer is down to thirty-nine—the Texans make a sally successfully for wood and water; and that night they burn some old houses on the northeast that might afford cover for the enemy. So amid the enemy's constant rain of shells and balls, which miraculously hurt no one, the Texans strengthen their works and the siege goes on. On the 28th Fannin starts from Goliad with three hundred troops and four pieces of artillery, but for lack of teams and provisions quickly returns, and the little garrison is left to its fate. On the morning of the 1st of March there is doubtless a wild shout of welcome in the Alamo; Capt. John W. Smith has managed to convey thirty-two men from Gonzales into the fort. These join the heroes, and the attack and defence go on. On the 3d a single man, Moses Rose, escapes from the fort. His account of that day* must entitle it to consecration as one of the most pathetic days of time.

"About two hours before sunset on the 3d of March, 1836, the bombardment suddenly ceased, and the enemy withdrew an unusual distance. . . . Colonel Travis paraded all his effective men in a single file, and taking his position in front of the centre, he stood for some moments apparently speechless from emotion; then nerving himself for the occasion, he addressed them substantially as follows:—

"'My brave companions: stern necessity compels me to employ the few moments afforded by this probably brief cessation of conflict, in making known to you the most interesting, yet the most solemn, melancholy, and unwelcome fact that humanity can realize. . . . Our fate is sealed. Within a very few days, perhaps a very few hours, we must all be in eternity! I have deceived you long by the promise of help; but I crave your pardon, hoping that after hearing my explanation you will not only regard my conduct as pardonable, but heartily sympathize with me in my extreme necessity. . . . I have continually received the strongest assurances of help from home. Every letter from the Council, and every one that I have seen from individuals at home, has teemed with assurances that our people were ready, willing, and anxious to come to our relief. . . . These assurances I received as facts. . . . In the honest and simple confidence of my heart I have transmitted to you these promises of help and my confident hope of success. But the promised help has not come, and our hopes are not to be realized. I have evidently confided too much in the promises of our friends; but let us not be in haste to censure them. . . . Our friends were evidently not informed of our perilous condition in time to save us. Doubtless they would have been here by this time had they expected any considerable force of the enemy. . . . My calls on Colonel Fannin remain unanswered, and my messengers have not returned. The probabilities are that his whole command has fallen into the hands of the enemy, or been cut to pieces, and that our couriers have been cut off. [So does the brave simple soul refuse to feel any bitterness

---

* As transmitted by the Zuber family, whose residence was the first place at which poor Rose had dared to stop, and with whom he remained some weeks, healing the festered wounds made on his legs by the cactus-thorns during the days of his fearful journey. The account from which these extracts are taken, is contributed to the Texas Almanac for 1873, by W.P. Zuber, and his mother, Mary Ann Zuber.

in the hour of death.] . . . Then we must die. . . . Our business is not to make a fruitless effort to save our lives, but to choose the manner of our death. But three modes are presented to us; let us choose that by which we may best serve our country. Shall we surrender and be deliberately shot without taking the life of a single enemy? Shall we try to cut our way out through the Mexican ranks and be butchered before we can kill twenty of our adversaries? I am opposed to either method. . . . Let us resolve to withstand our adversaries to the last, and at each advance to kill as many of them as possible. And when at last they shall storm our fortress, let us kill them as they come! kill them as they scale our wall! kill them as they leap within! kill them as they raise their weapons and as they use them! kill them as they kill our companions! and continue to kill them as long as one of us shall remain alive! . . . But I leave every man to his own choice. Should any man prefer to surrender . . . or to attempt an escape . . . he is at liberty to do so. My own choice is to stay in the fort and die for my country, fighting as long as breath shall remain in my body. This will I do, even if you leave me alone. Do as you think best; but no man can die with me without affording me comfort in the hour of death!'

"Colonel Travis then drew his sword, and with its point traced a line upon the ground extending from the right to the left of the file. Then resuming his position in front of the centre, he said, 'I now want every man who is determined to stay here and die with me to come across this line. Who will be first? March!' The first respondent was Tapley Holland, who leaped the line at a bound, exclaiming, 'I am ready to die for my country!' His example was instantly followed by every man in the file with the exception of Rose. . . . Every sick man that could walk, arose from his bunk and tottered across the line. Colonel Bowie, who could not leave his bed, said, 'Boys, I am not able to come to you, but I wish some of you would be so kind as to remove my cot over there.' Four men instantly ran to the cot, and each lifting a corner, carried it across the line. Then every sick man that could not walk made the same request, and had his bunk removed in the same way.

"Rose too was deeply affected, but differently from his companions. He stood till every man but himself had crossed the line. . . . He sank upon the ground, covered his face, and yielded to his own reflections. . . . A bright idea came to his relief; he spoke the Mexican dialect very fluently, and could he once get safely out of the fort, he might easily pass for a Mexican and effect an escape. . . . He directed a searching glance at the cot of Colonel Bowie. . . . Col. David Crockett was leaning over the cot, conversing with its occupant in an undertone. After a few seconds Bowie looked at Rose and said, 'You seem not to be willing to die with us, Rose.' 'No,' said Rose; 'I am not prepared to die, and shall not do so if I can avoid it.' Then Crockett also looked at him, and said, 'You may as well conclude to die with us, old man, for escape is impossible.' Rose made no reply, but looked at the top of the wall. 'I have often done worse than to climb that wall,' thought he. Suiting the action to the thought, he sprang up, seized his wallet of unwashed clothes, and ascended the wall. Standing on its top, he looked down within to take a last view of his dying friends. They were all now in motion, but what they were doing he heeded not; overpowered by his feelings, he looked away and saw them no more. . . . He threw down his wallet and leaped after it. . . . He took the road which led down the river around a bend to the ford, and through the town by the church. He waded the river at the ford and passed through the town. He saw no person . . . but the doors were all closed, and San Antonio appeared as a deserted city.

"After passing through the town he turned down the river. A stillness as of death prevailed. When he had gone about a quarter of a mile below the town, his ears were saluted by the thunder of the bombardment, which was then renewed. That thunder continued to remind him that his friends were true to their cause, by a continual roar with but slight intervals until a little before sunrise on the morning of the 6th, when it ceased and he heard it no more."*

And well may it "cease" on that morning of that 6th; for after that thrilling 3d the siege goes on, the enemy furious, the Texans replying calmly and slowly. Finally Santa Ana determines to storm. Some hours before daylight on the morning of the 6th the Mexican infantry, provided with scaling-ladders, and backed by the cavalry to keep them up to the work, surround the doomed fort. At daylight they advance and plant their ladders, but give back under a deadly fire from the Texans. They advance again, and again retreat. A third time—Santa Ana threatening and coaxing by turns—they plant their ladders. Now they mount the walls. The Texans are overwhelmed by sheer weight of numbers and exhaustion of continued watching and fighting. The Mexicans swarm into the fort. The Texans club their guns; one by one they fall fighting— now Travis yonder by the western wall, now Crockett here in the angle of the church-wall, now Bowie butchered and mutilated in his sick-cot, breathe quick and pass away; and presently every Texan lies dead, while there in horrid heaps are stretched five hundred and twenty-one dead Mexicans and as many more wounded! Of the human beings that were in the fort five remain alive: Mrs. Dickinson and her child, Colonel Travis' negro-servant, and two Mexican women. The conquerors endeavored to get some more revenge out of the

---

* Rose succeeded in making his escape, and reached the house of the Zubers, as before stated, in fearful condition. After remaining here some weeks, he started for his home in Nacogdoches, but on the way his thorn-wounds became inflamed anew, and when he reached home "his friends thought that he could not live many months." This was "the last" that the Zubers "heard of him."

dead, and close the scene with raking together the bodies of the Texans, amid insults, and burning them.

The town did not long remain in the hands of the Mexicans. Events followed each other rapidly until the battle of San Jacinto, after which the dejected Santa Ana wrote his famous letter of captivity under the tree, which for a time relieved the soil of Texas from hostile footsteps. San Antonio was nevertheless not free from bloodshed, though beginning to drive a sharp trade with Mexico and to make those approaches towards the peaceful arts which necessarily accompany trade. The Indians kept life from stagnating, and in the year 1840 occurred a bloody battle with them in the very midst of the town. Certain Camanche chiefs, pending negotiations for a treaty of peace, had promised to bring in all the captives they had; and on the 19th of March, 1840, met the Texan Commissioners in the Council-house in San Antonio to redeem their promise. Leaving twenty warriors and thirty-two women and children outside, twelve chiefs entered the council-room and presented the only captive they had brought—a little white girl—declaring that they had no others. This statement the little girl pronounced false, asserting that it was made solely for the purpose of extorting greater ransoms, and that she had but recently seen other captives in their camp. An awkward pause followed. Presently one of the chiefs inquired, How the Commissioners liked it. By way of reply, the company of Captain Howard, who had been sent for, filed into the room, and the Indians were told that they would be held prisoners until they should send some of their party outside after the rest of the captives. The Commissioners then rose and left the room. As they were in the act of leaving, however, one of the Indian chiefs attempted to rush through the door, and being confronted by the sentinel, stabbed him. Seeing the sentinel hurt, and Captain Howard also stabbed, the other chiefs sprang forward with knives and bows and arrows, and the fight raged until they were all killed. Meantime the warriors outside began to fight, and engaged the company of Captain Read; but, taking shelter in a stone-house, were surrounded and killed. Still another detachment of the Indians managed to continue the fight until they had reached the other side of the river, when they were finally despatched. Thirty-two Indian warriors and five Indian women and children were slain, and the rest of the women and children were made prisoners. The savages fought desperately, for seven Texans were killed and eight wounded.

The war between Texas and Mexico had now languished for some years. The project of annexation was much discussed in the United States; one great objection to it was that the United States would embroil itself with a nation with which it was at peace—Mexico—by annexing Texas, then at war. The war, however, seemed likely to die away; and to prevent the removal of the obstacle to annexation in that way, Mexico made feeble efforts to keep up such hostilities as might at least give color to the assertion that the war had not ended. Accordingly in the year 1842 a Mexican army again invested San Antonio. After a short parley, Colonel Hays withdrew with his small force, and the Mexicans, numbering about seven hundred men under General Vasquez, took possession of the place and formally reorganized it as a Mexican town. They remained, however, only two days, and conducted themselves, officially, with great propriety, though the citizens are said to have lost a great deal of valuable property by unauthorized depredations of private soldiers and of Mexican citizens who accompanied the army on its departure.

Again on the 11th of September, 1842, a Mexican army of twelve hundred men under General Woll, sent probably by the same policy which had despatched the other, surprised the town of San Antonio, and after having a few killed and wounded, took possession, the citizens having capitulated. General Woll captured the entire bar of lawyers in attendance on the District Court, then in session, and held them as prisoners of war. He did not escape, however, so easily as General Vasquez. The Texans gathered rapidly, and by the 17th had assembled two hundred and twenty men on the Salado, some six miles from town. Captain Hays with fifty men decoyed General Woll forth, and a battle ensued from which the enemy withdrew at sunset with a loss of sixty killed and about the same number wounded, the Texans losing one killed and nine wounded. It is easy to believe that the honest citizens of San Antonio got little sleep on that night of the 17th of September, 1842. General Woll was busy making preparations for retreat; and the Mexican citizens who intended to accompany him were also busy gathering up plunder right and left to take with them. At daylight they all departed. This was the last time that San Antonio de Bexar was ever in Mexican hands.

After annexation, in 1845, the town began to improve. The trade from certain portions of Mexico—Chihuahua and the neighboring States—seems always to have eagerly sought San Antonio as a point of supplies whenever peace gave it the opportunity. Presently, too, the United States government selected San Antonio as the base for the frontier army below El Paso, and the large quantities of money expended in connection with the supply and transportation of all *matériel* for so long a line of forts have contributed very materially to the prosperity of the town. From a population of about 3500 in 1850, it increased to 10,000 in 1856, and has now about 15,000.

4–9
Elizabeth Bacon Custer (1842–1933)

The widow of famed general George Armstrong Custer, ELIZABETH BACON CUSTER (1842–1933) traveled with his army for many of his expeditions. Born in Michigan, Elizabeth Bacon met her future husband during the Civil War. After their marriage, her unique attitude toward army life became apparent, for she insisted on traveling with her husband to his various billets, affecting an attire that was an adaptation of the Union Army uniform, including a billed cap. She accompanied her husband to his commands in Texas, Kansas, and to his final appointment with the Black Hills Expedition, which ended with the Battle of Little Bighorn (1876) in Montana Territory and the annihilation of Custer's command. "Libbie," as she was known, survived her husband by half a century, preserving and defending her husband's memory in public speeches and writings. Her enthusiasm for Western and camp life is as apparent as her attention to detail in her works like *Boots and Saddles* (1885), *Tenting on the Plains, or General Custer in Kansas and Texas* (1887), and *Following the Guidon* (1890). This excerpt describes the couple's travels through postbellum Central Texas and things witnessed— the institutions for the hearing impaired in Austin, the extenuation of slavery after Emancipation, and Texas hill-country homes.

≈ ≈ ≈

From *Tenting on the Plains, or General Custer in Kansas and Texas* (1887)

Chapter 7

The march to Austin was varied by fording. All the streams and rivers were crossed in that manner, except one, where we used the ponton bridge. The Colorado we found too high to ford, and so made a détour of some miles. The citizens were not unfriendly, while there was a total cessation of work on the part of the negroes until our column went by. They sat on the fences like a row of black crows, and with their usual politeness made an attempt to answer questions the troops put to them, which were unanswerable, even in the ingenious brain of the propounder. "Well, uncle, how far is it ten miles down the road from here?" If their feelings were hurt by such irrepressible fun, they were soon healed by the lively trade they kept up in chickens, eggs and butter.

The citizens sometimes answered the General's salute, and his interested questions about the horse they rode, by joining us for a short distance on the march. The horse-flesh of Texas was a delight to him; but I could not be so interested in the fine points as to forget the disfiguring brands that were often upon the fore-shoulder, as well as the flank. They spoke volumes for the country where a man has to sear a thoroughbred with a hot iron to ensure his keeping possession. Father Custer used to say, "What sort of country is this, anyhow, when a man, in order to keep his property, has got to print the whole constitution of the United States on his horse?" The whole get up of the Texans was rather cumbersome, it seemed to me, though they rode perfectly. They frequently had a Mexican saddle, heavily ornamented with silver on the high pommel, and everywhere else that it could be added. Even the design of the stamped leather, for which Mexico is famous, was embroidered with silver bullion. The stirrup had handsome leather covers, while a fringe of thongs fell almost to the ground, to aid in pushing their way through the tall prairie grass. Sometimes the saddle-cloth, extending to the crupper, was of fur. The bridle and bit were rich with silver also. On the massive silver pommel hung an incongruous coil of horse-hair rope, disfiguring and ugly. There was an iron picket-pin attached to the lariat, which we soon learned was of inestimable value in the long rides that the Texans took. If a man made a halt, he encircled himself with this prickly lariat and lay down securely, knowing that no snake could cross that barrier. In a land of venomous serpents, it behooved a man to carry his own abatis everywhere. The saddle was also secured by a cinch or girth of cow's hair, which hard riders found a great help in keeping the saddle firm. The Texan himself, though not often wearing the high-crowned, silver-embroidered Mexican sombrero, wore usually a wide-brimmed felt hat, on which the General afterward doted, as the felt was of superior quality. If the term "dude" had been invented then, it would often have applied to a Texan horseman. The hair was frequently long, and they wore no waistcoat, I concluded, because they could better display the vast expanse of shirt-front. While the General and his casual companion in our march talked horse, too absorbed to notice anything else, I used to lose myself in the contemplation of the maze of tucks, puffs and embroidery of this cambric finery, ornamented with three old-fashioned bosom-pins. The wearer seemed to me to represent two epochs: the fine linen, side-saddle and blooded horse belonged to "befo' the war"; while the ragged elbows of the coat-sleeves, and the worn boots, were decidedly "since the war." If the shirt-front was intricate in its workmanship, the boots were ignored by the placid owner.

They usually had the Mexican serape strapped to the back of the saddle, or, if it was cold, as it was in our late November march, they put their head through the opening in the middle, so woven for that purpose, and flung the end across their breast and over one shoulder in a picturesque manner. The bright hues of the blanket, dyed by the Indians from the juice of the prickly pear, its soft, flexible folds having been woven in a hand-loom, made a graceful and attractive bit of color, which was not at all out of place in that country. These blankets were valuable possessions. They were so pliable and perfectly water-proof, that they protected one from every storm. We had a pair, which we used through every subsequent campaign, and when the cold in Kansas and Dakota became almost unbearable, sometimes, after the long trial of a journey in the wagon, my husband used to say, "We will resort to extreme measures, Libbie, and wrap you in the Mexican blankets." They were the warmest of all our wraps. Nothing seemed to fade them, and even when burnt with Tom's cigarette ashes, or stuck through with the General's spurs, they did not ravel, as do other fabrics. They have hung as portières in my little home, and the design and coloring are so like the Persian rug on the floor, that it seems to be an argument to prove that Mr. Ignatius Donnelly, in his theory of Atlantis, is right, and that we once had a land highway between the East and Mexico, and that the reason the Aztec now uses the designs on his pottery and in his weaving is, that his ancestors brought over the first sketches on papyrus.*

A Texan travels for comfort and safety rather than for style. If a norther overtakes him, he dismounts and drives the picket-pin into the ground, thus tethering his horse, which turns his back, the better to withstand the oncoming wind. The master throws himself face down in the long grass, buried in his blanket, and thus awaits the termination of the fury with which the storm sweeps a Texas prairie.

Sometimes one of the planters, after riding a distance with us, talking the county over, and taking in every point of our horses as he rode, made his adieus and said he was now at his own place, where he turned in. The General followed his fine thoroughbred with longing eyes, and was more than astonished to find in what stables they kept these valuable and delicate animals. No

---

* In a town of Mexico last year I saw these small looms with blankets in them, in various stages of progress, in many cottages. Among the Indians the rude loom is carried about in the mountain villages, and with some tribes there is a superstition about finishing the blankets in the same place where they were begun. A squaw will sometimes have one half done, and if an order is given her she will not break over her rule to finish it if a move is made in the midst of her work. She waits until the next year, when her people return to the same camp, as is the custom when the Indian seeks certain game or grazing, or to cut longer poles.

matter if the house was habitable, the stable was usually in a state of careless dilapidation. Doors swung on one hinge, and clap-boards were torn off here and there, while the warped roof was far from weather-proof. Even though Texas is in the "Sunny South," the first sharp norther awakens one to the knowledge that it is not always summer. Sometimes these storms are quickly over, but frequently they last three days. This carelessness about stabling stock was not owing to the depredations of an invading army. We were the first "Yankees" they had seen. It was the general shiftlessness that creeps into one's veins. We were not long there ourselves before climatic influence had its effect on even the most active among us.

Before we reached Austin, several citizens sent out invitations for us to come to their houses; but I knew the General would not accept, and, cold as the nights were, I felt unwilling to lose a day of camp life. We pitched our tents on rolling ground in the vicinity of Austin, where we overlooked a pretty town of stuccoed houses that appeared summery in the midst of the live-oak's perennial green. The State House, Land Office, and governor's mansion looked regal to us, so long bivouacking in the forest and on uncultivated prairies. The governor offered for our headquarters the Blind Asylum, which had been closed during the war. This possessed one advantage that we were glad to improve: there was room enough for all the staff, and a long saloon parlor and dining-room for our hops during the winter. By this time two pretty, agreeable women, wives of staff-officers, were added to our circle. Still, I went into the building with regret. The wagon in which the wind had rocked me to sleep so often, and which had proved such a stronghold against the crawling foes of the country, was consigned to the stable with a sigh. Camp life had more pleasures than hardships.

There were three windows in our room, which we opened at night; but, notwithstanding the air that circulated, the feeling, after having been so long out of doors, was suffocating. The ceiling seemed descending to smother us. There was one joy: reveillé could ring out on the dawning day, and there was no longer imperative necessity to spring from a warm bed and make ablutions in ice-water. There is a good deal of that sort of mental snapping of the fingers on the part of campaigners when they are again stationary and need not prepare for a march. Civilization and a looking-glass must now be assumed, as it would no longer do to rough it and ignore appearances, after we had moved into a house, and were to live like "folks." Besides, we soon began to be invited by the townspeople to visit them. Refined, agreeable and well-dressed women came to see us, and, woman-like, we ran our eyes over their dresses. They were embroidered and trimmed richly with lace, "befo' the war" finery or from the cargo of a blockade runner; but it was all strange enough in such an isolated State. Almost everything was then brought from the terminus of the Brenham Railroad to Austin, 150 miles, by ox-team. We had been anxiously expected for some time, and there was no manner of doubt that the arrival of the Division was a great relief to the reputable of both sides. They said so frankly—the returned Confederate officers and the "stay-at-home rangers," as well as the newly appointed Union governor.

Texas was then a "go-as-you-please" State, and the lawlessness was terrible. The returned Confederate soldiers were poor, and did not know how to set themselves to work, and in many instances preferred the life of a freebooter. It was so easy, if a crime was committed, to slip into Mexico, for though it was inaccessible except by stage or on horseback, a Texan would not mind a forced march over the country to the Rio Grande. There were then but one or two short railroads in operation. The one from Galveston to Brenham was the principal one, while telegraph lines were not in use. The stage to Brenham was our one means of communication with the outside world.

It was hard for the citizens who had remained at home to realize that war was over, and some were unwilling to believe there ever had been an emancipation proclamation. In the northern part of the State they were still buying and selling slaves. The lives of the newly appointed United States officers were threatened daily, and it was an uneasy head that wore the gubernatorial crown. I thought them braver men than many who had faced the enemy in battle. The unseen, lurking foe that hides under cover of darkness was their terror. They held themselves valiantly; but one wife and daughter were on my mind night after night, as from dark till dawn they slept uneasily, and started from their rooms out into the halls at every strange sound. The General and I thought the courageous daughter had enough brave, devoted blood in her veins to distill a portion into the heart of many a soldier who led a forlorn hope. They told us that in the early part of the war the girl had known of a Union flag in the State House, held in derision and scornfully treated by the extremists. She and her younger brother climbed upon the roof of a wing of the building, after dark, entered a window of the Capitol, found the flag, concealed it in the girl's clothing, and made their perilous descent safely. The father of such a daughter might well prize her watchfulness of his safety, as she vigilantly kept it up during our stay, and was equal to a squadron of soldiers. She won our admiration; and our bachelor officers paid the tribute that brave men always pay to courageous, unselfish women, for she danced, rode and walked with them, and when she was not so engaged, their orderlies held their horses before the official door, while they improved every hour allowed them within the hospitable portal.

It was a great relief to find a Southern State that was not devastated by the war. The homes destroyed in Virginia could not fail to move a woman's heart, as it was women and children that suffered from such destruction. In Texas nothing seemed to have been altered. I suppose some profited, for blockade-running could be carried on from the ports of that great State, and there was always Mexico from which to draw supplies.

In our daily rides we found the country about Austin delightful. The roads were smooth and the surface rolling. Indeed, there was one high hill, called Mount Brunnel, where we had picnics and enjoyed the fine view, far and near, taking one of the bands of the regular regiments from the North that joined us soon after our arrival. Mount Brunnel was so steep we had to dismount and climb a part of the distance. The band played the "Anvil Chorus," and the sound descended through the valley grandly. The river, filled with sand-bars and ugly on close examination, looked like a silver ribbon. At that height, the ripened cotton, at certain seasons of the year, looked like fields of foam. The thermometer was over eighty before we left the lowlands; but at the altitude to which we climbed the air was cool. We even went once to the State Insane Asylum, taking the band, when the attendants asked if dancing music might be played, and we watched with wonder the quadrille of an insane eight.

The favorite ride for my husband was across the Colorado, to the Deaf and Dumb Asylum. There seemed to be a fascination for him in the children, who were equally charmed with the young soldier that silently watched their pretty, pathetic exhibitions of intelligent speech by gesture. My husband riveted his gaze on their speaking eyes, and as their instructor spelt the passions of love, hatred, remorse and reverence on his fingers, one little girl represented them by singularly graceful gestures, charming him, and filling his eyes with tears, which he did not seek to hide. The pupils were from ten to sixteen years of age. Their supple wrists were a delight to us, and the tiny hands of a child of the matron, whom the General held, talked in a cunning way to its playmates, who, it knew, could not comprehend its speech. It was well that the Professor was hospitality itself, and did not mind a cavalcade dashing up the road to his house. My husband, when he did not openly suggest going, used some subterfuge as trivial as going for water-cress, that grew in a pond near the Asylum. The children knew him, and welcomed him with lustrous, eloquent eyes, and went untiringly through their little exhibitions, learning to bring him their compositions, examples and maps, for his commendation. How little we thought then that the lessons he was taking, in order to talk with the children he learned to love, would soon come into use while sitting round a camp-fire and making himself understood by Indians. Of course, their sign-language is wholly their own, but it is the same method of using the simplest signs as expressive of thought. It was a long, pleasant ride; its only drawback to me being the fording of the river, which had quicksands and a rapid current. The Colorado was low, but the river-bed was wide and filled with sand-bars. The mad torrent that the citizens told us of in freshets, we did not see. If I followed my husband, as Custis Lee had learned to do, I found myself guided safely, but it sometimes happened that our party entered the river, laughing and talking so earnestly, noisily and excitedly that we forgot caution. One lesson was enough; the sensation of the sinking of the horse's hind legs in quicksands is not to be forgotten. The loud cry of the General to "saw on the bit" or whip my horse, excited, frightened directions from the staff to turn to the right or the left, Custis Lee trembling and snorting with fear, but responding to a cruel cut of my whip (for I rarely struck him), and we plunged on to a firmer soil, wiser for all the future on account of that moment of serious peril. . . .

. . . Fortunately, our now well-disciplined Division and the regular cavalry kept everything in a better condition; but there were constantly individual cases of outrageous conduct, and often of crime, among whites and blacks, high and low. Texas had so long been looked upon as a sort of "city of refuge" by outlaws, that those whom the other States refused to harbor came to that locality. A country reached only by sea from the south or by a wagon-train from the north, and through which no telegraph lines ran until after we came, would certainly offer an admirable hiding-place for those who leave their country for their country's good. I have read somewhere that Texas derived its name from a group of rascals, who, sitting round a fire on their arrival on the soil that was to protect them, composed this couplet:

"If every other land forsakes us,

This is the land that freely takes us (Texas)."

As story after story reached us, I began to think the State was well named. There were a great many excellent, law-abiding citizens, but not enough to leaven the lump at that chaotic period. Even the women learned to defend themselves, as the war had deprived them of their natural protectors, who had gone either in the Northern or the Southern army—for Texas had a cavalry regiment of refugees in our service. One woman, while we were there, found a teamster getting into her window, and shot him fatally. Fire-arms were so constantly about—for the men did not dress without a pistol in their belts—that women grew accustomed to the sight of weapons. There was a lady of whom I constantly heard, rich and refined, but living out of town on a plantation that seemed to be fit only for negroes. She rode fearlessly, and diverted her monotonous life by hunting. The planters frequently met her with game slung upon her saddle, and once she lassoed and brought in a wolf alone. Finally this woman came to see me, but curiosity made me hardly civil for a few moments, as I was trying to reconcile myself to the knowledge, that the quiet, graceful woman before me, with rich dress, jewels and a French hat, could take her gun and dogs, mount a fiery horse, and go hunting alone. We found, on returning the visit, that, though they were rich, owning blooded horses, a plantation and a mill, their domicile was anything but what we at the North would call comfortable. It was a long, one-storied, log building, consisting of a parlor, dining-room, bedroom and two small "no-'count" rooms, as the servants said, all opening into one another and upon the porch. The first surprise on entering was, that the roof did not fit down snugly on the side wall. A strip of the blue sky was visible on three sides, while the partition of the dining-room only came up part way. There seemed to be no sort of provision for "Caudle lectures." The walls were roughly plastered, but this space just under the roof was for ventilation, and I fancied they would get enough of it during a norther.

I am reminded of a story that one of the witty Southern women told me, after repeating some very good comic verses, in which they excel. She said the house I described was not uncommon in Texas, and that once she was traveling over a portion of the State, on a journey of great suffering, as she was accompanying her husband's remains to a family burial-ground. They assisted her from her carriage into one of the rooms of a long log house, used as a wayside inn, and the landlady kindly helped her into bed, as she was prostrated with suffering and fatigue. After she left her, the landlady seemed to forget that the partition did not extend to the rafters, and began questioning her servant as to what was the matter, etc. Hearing that the lady had lost her husband, the old dame exclaimed, sympathetically, "Poor thing! Poor thing! I know how it is; I've lost three of 'em."

. . .

The lawlessness of the State was much diminished by the troops scattered through the country. General Custer was much occupied in answering communications that came from distant parts of Texas, describing the demoralized state of the country, and asking for troops. These appeals were from all sides. It was felt more and more that the presence of the troops was absolutely necessary, and it was certainly agreeable to us that we were not looked upon as invaders. The General then had thirteen regiments of infantry and as many of cavalry, scattered in every part of the State comprised in his district. The regular troops arriving, brought their wives and daughters, and it was a great addition, as we had constant entertainments, in which the civilians, so long cut off from all gayety, were glad to participate. The staff assisted me greatly in my preparations. We dressed the long parlors in evergreens, made canopies of flags, arranged wax-lights in impromptu wooden sconces, and with the waxed floor it was tempting enough to those who cared for dancing. The soldiers soon organized a string band, and a sergeant called off the quadrilles. Sometimes my husband planned and arranged the suppers alone, but usually the staff divided the duty of preparing the refreshments. Occasionally we attempted a dinner, and, as we wanted to invite our own ladies as well as some from the regular regiments, the table was a subject of study; for when twenty came, the dishes gave out. The staff dined early, so that we could have theirs, and the Southern woman who occupied two rooms in the building lent everything she had. Uncle Charley, our cook, who now had found a colored church in which to preach on Sunday, did up all his religion on that day, and swore all the week, but the cellar-kitchen was distant, and, besides, my husband used to argue that it was just as well to endure placidly the evils right about us, but not to seek for more. The swearing did not interfere with the cooking, and Charley thought it necessary to thus clear the kitchen, as our yard at that time was black with the colored race. Each officer's servant had his circle of friends, and they hovered round us like a dark cloud. The dishes that Uncle Charley sent up were excellent. The Texas beef and poultry were of superior quality, and we even had a respite from condensed milk, as a citizen had lent us a cow. . . .

4–10

Sarah Winnemucca (Thocmentony) (ca. 1844–1891)

SARAH WINNEMUCCA (ca. 1844–1891), also known as THOCMENTONY or TOCMETONE, the Paiute word for "SHELL FLOWER," was born in what is today Nevada. Winnemucca came of age in a place that was rapidly changing, particularly after gold and silver were discovered in Nevada, bringing many miners who hoped to strike it rich. Her tribe was frequently in conflict with the settlers, and occasionally at war with them. She often served as a translator and mediator between the groups. Winnemucca also became an activist, eloquently speaking out for the rights of her tribe in the work *Life among the Piutes: Their Wrongs and Claims* (1883), from which this selection is taken. This excerpt challenges Rachel Parker Plummer's captivity narrative.

≈ ≈ ≈

From *Life among the Piutes: Their Wrongs and Claims* (1883)

Chapter 1. First Meeting of Piutes and Whites

I was born somewhere near 1844, but am not sure of the precise time. I was a very small child when the first white people came into our country. They came like a lion, yes, like a roaring lion, and have continued so ever since, and I have never forgotten their first coming. My people were scattered at that time over nearly all the territory now known as Nevada. My grandfather was chief of the entire Piute nation, and was camped near Humboldt Lake, with a small portion of his tribe, when a party travelling eastward from California was seen coming. When the news was brought to my grandfather, he asked what they looked like? When told that they had hair on their faces, and were white, he jumped up and clasped his hands together, and cried aloud,—

"My white brothers—my long-looked for white brothers have come at last!"

He immediately gathered some of his leading men, and went to the place where the party had gone to camp. Arriving near them, he was commanded to halt in a manner that was readily understood without an interpreter. Grandpa at once made signs of friendship by throwing down his robe and throwing up his arms to show them he had no weapons; but in vain,—they kept him at a distance. He knew not what to do. He had expected so much pleasure in welcoming his white brothers to the best in the land, that after looking at them sorrowfully for a little while, he came away quite unhappy. But he would not give them up so easily. He took some of his most trustworthy men and followed them day after day, hoping in this way to gain their confidence. But he was disappointed, poor dear old soul!

I can imagine his feelings, for I have drank deeply from the same cup. When I think of my past life, and the bitter trials I have endured, I can scarcely believe I live, and yet I do; and, with the help of Him who notes the sparrow's fall, I mean to fight for my down-trodden race while life lasts.

Seeing they would not trust him, my grandfather left them, saying, "Perhaps they will come again next year." Then he summoned his whole people, and told them this tradition:—

"In the beginning of the world there were only four, two girls and two boys. Our forefather and mother were only two, and we are their children. You all know that a great while ago there was a happy family in this world. One girl and one boy were dark and the others were white. For a time they got along together without quarrelling, but soon they disagreed, and there was trouble. They were cross to one another and fought, and our parents were very much grieved. They prayed that their children might learn better, but it did not do any good; and afterwards the whole household was made so unhappy that the father and mother saw that they must separate their children; and then our father took the dark boy and girl, and the white boy and girl, and asked them, 'Why are you so cruel to each other?' They hung down their heads, and would not speak. They were ashamed. He said to them, 'Have I not been kind to you all, and given you everything your hearts wished for? You do not have to hunt and kill your own game to live upon. You see, my dear children, I have power to call whatsoever kind of game we want to eat; and I also have the power to separate my dear children, if they are not good to each other.' So he separated his children by a word. He said, 'Depart from each other, you cruel children;— go across the mighty ocean and do not seek each other's lives.'

"So the light girl and boy disappeared by that one word, and their parents saw them no more, and they were grieved, although they knew their children were happy. And by-and-by the dark children grew into a large nation; and we believe it is the one we belong to, and that the nation that sprung from the white children will some time send some one to meet us and heal all the old trouble. Now, the white people we saw a few days ago must certainly be our white brothers, and I want to welcome them. I want to love them as I love all of you. But they would not let me; they were afraid. But they will come again, and I want you one and all to promise that, should I not live to welcome them myself, you will not hurt a hair on their heads, but welcome them as I tried to do."

How good of him to try and heal the wound, and how vain were his efforts! My people had never seen a white man, and yet they existed, and were a strong race. The people promised as he wished, and they all went back to their work.

The next year came a great emigration, and camped near Humboldt Lake. The name of the man in charge of the trains was Captain Johnson, and they stayed three days to rest their horses, as they had a long journey before them without water. During their stay my grandfather and some of his people called upon them, and they all shook hands, and when our white brothers were going away they gave my grandfather a white tin plate. Oh, what a time they had over that beautiful gift,—it was so bright! They say that after they left, my grandfather called for all his people to come together, and he then showed them the beautiful gift which he had received from his white brothers. Everybody was so pleased; nothing like it was ever seen in our country before. My grandfather thought so much of it that he bored holes in it and fastened it on his head, and wore it as his hat. He held it in as much admiration as my white sisters hold their diamond rings or a sealskin jacket. So that winter they talked of nothing but their white brothers. The following spring there came great news down the Humboldt River, saying that there were some more of the white brothers coming, and there was something among them that was burning all in a blaze. My grandfather asked them what it was like. They told him it looked like a man; it had legs and hands and a head, but the head had quit burning, and it was left quite black. There was the greatest excitement among my people everywhere about the men in a blazing fire. They were excited because they did not know there were any people in the world but the two—that is, the Indians and the whites; they thought that was all of us in the beginning of the world, and, of course, we did not know where the others had come from, and we don't know yet. Ha! ha! oh, what a laughable thing that was! It was two negroes wearing red shirts!

The third year more emigrants came, and that summer Captain Fremont, who is now General Fremont.

My grandfather met him, and they were soon friends. They met just where the railroad crosses Truckee River, now called Wadsworth, Nevada. Captain Fremont gave my grandfather the name of Captain Truckee, and he also called the river after him. Truckee is an Indian word; it means *all right*, or *very well*. A party of twelve of my people went to California with Captain Fremont. I do not know just how long they were gone.[*]

. . .

When my grandfather went to California he helped Captain Fremont fight the Mexicans. When he came back he told the people what a beautiful country California was. Only eleven returned home, one having died on the way back.

. . .

That same fall, after my grandfather came home, he told my father to take charge of his people and hold the tribe, as he was going back to California with as many of his people as he could get to go with him. So my father took his place as Chief of the Piutes, and had it as long as he lived. Then my grandfather started back to California again with about thirty families. That same fall, very late, the emigrants kept coming. It was this time that our white brothers first came amongst us. They could not get over the mountains, so they had to live with us. It was on Carson River, where the great Carson City stands now. You call my people bloodseeking. My people did not seek to kill them, nor did they steal their horses,—no, no, far from it. During the winter my people helped them. They gave them such as they had to eat. They did not hold out their hands and say:—

"You can't have anything to eat unless you pay me." No,—no such word was used by us savages at that time; and the persons I am speaking of are living yet; they could speak for us if they choose to do so.

[*] [Grandfather and some of the tribe travel back and forth from Nevada and California. —E.J.D. and J.B.F.]

The following spring, before my grandfather returned home, there was a great excitement among my people on account of fearful news coming from different tribes, that the people whom they called their white brothers were killing everybody that came in their way, and all the Indian tribes had gone into the mountains to save their lives. So my father told all his people to go into the mountains and hunt and lay up food for the coming winter. Then we all went into the mountains. There was a fearful story they told us children. Our mothers told us that the whites were killing everybody and eating them. So we were all afraid of them. Every dust that we could see blowing in the valleys we would say it was the white people. In the late fall my father told his people to go to the rivers and fish, and we all went to Humboldt River, and the women went to work gathering wild seed, which they grind between the rocks. The stones are round, big enough to hold in the hands. The women did this when they got back, and when they had gathered all they could they put it in one place and covered it with grass, and then over the grass mud. After it is covered it looks like an Indian wigwam.

Oh, what a fright we all got one morning to hear some white people were coming. Every one ran as best they could. My poor mother was left with my little sister and me. Oh, I never can forget it. My poor mother was carrying my little sister on her back, and trying to make me run; but I was so frightened I could not move my feet, and while my poor mother was trying to get me along my aunt overtook us, and she said to my mother: "Let us bury our girls, or we shall all be killed and eaten up." So they went to work and buried us, and told us if we heard any noise not to cry out, for if we did they would surely kill us and eat us. So our mothers buried me and my cousin, planted sage bushes over our faces to keep the sun from burning them, and there we were left all day.

Oh, can anyone imagine my feelings *buried alive*, thinking every minute that I was to be unburied and eaten up by the people that my grandfather loved so much? With my heart throbbing, and not daring to breathe, we lay there all day. It seemed that the night would never come. Thanks be to God! the night came at last. Oh, how I cried and said: "Oh, father, have you forgotten me? Are you never coming for me?" I cried so I thought my very heartstrings would break.

At last we heard some whispering. We did not dare to whisper to each other, so we lay still. I could hear their footsteps coming nearer and nearer. I thought my heart was coming right out of my mouth. Then I heard my mother say, "'Tis right here!" Oh, can any one in this world ever imagine what were my feelings when I was dug up by my poor mother and father? My cousin and

I were once more happy in our mothers' and fathers' care, and we were taken to where all the rest were.

I was once buried alive; but my second burial shall be for ever, where no father or mother will come and dig me up. It shall not be with throbbing heart that I shall listen for coming footsteps. I shall be in the sweet rest of peace,—I, the chieftain's weary daughter.

Well, while we were in the mountains hiding, the people that my grandfather called our white brothers came along to where our winter supplies were. They set everything we had left on fire. It was a fearful sight. It was all we had for the winter, and it was all burnt during that night. My father took some of his men during the night to try and save some of it, but they could not; it had burnt down before they got there.

These were the last white men that came along that fall. My people talked fearfully that winter about those they called our white brothers. My people said they had something like awful thunder and lightning, and with that they killed everything that came in their way.

This whole band of white people perished in the mountains, for it was too late to cross them. We could have saved them, only my people were afraid of them. We never knew who they were, or where they came from. So, poor things, they must have suffered fearfully, for they all starved there. The snow was too deep.

Early in the following spring, my father told all his people to go to the mountains, for there would be a great emigration that summer. He told them he had had a wonderful dream, and wanted to tell them all about it.

He said, "Within ten days come together at the sink of Carson, and I will tell you my dream."

The sub-chiefs went everywhere to tell their people what my father had told them to say; and when the time came we all went to the sink of Carson.

Just about noon, while we were on the way, a great many of our men came to meet us, all on their horses. Oh, what a beautiful song they sang for my father as they came near us! We passed them, and they followed us, and as we came near to the encampment, every man, woman, and child were out looking for us. They had a place all ready for us. Oh, how happy everybody was! One could hear laughter everywhere, and songs were sung by happy women and children.

My father stood up and told his people to be merry and happy for five days. It is a rule among our people always to have five days to settle anything. My father told them to dance at night, and that the men should hunt rabbits and fish, and some were to have games of football, or any kind of sport or playthings they wished, and the women could do the same, as they had nothing else to do. My people were so happy during the five days,—the women ran races, and the men ran races on foot and on horses.

My father got up very early one morning, and told his people the time had come,—that we could no longer be happy as of old, as the white people we called our brothers had brought a great trouble and sorrow among us already. He went on and said,—

"These white people must be a great nation, as they have houses that move. It is wonderful to see them move along. I fear we will suffer greatly by their coming to our country; they come for no good to us, although my father said they were our brothers, but they do not seem to think that we are like them. What do you all think about it? Maybe I am wrong. My dear children, there is something telling me that I am not wrong, because I am sure they have minds like us, and think as we do; and I know that they were doing wrong when they set fire to our winter supplies. They surely knew it was our food."

And this was the first wrong done to us by our white brothers.

Now comes the end of our merrymaking.

Then my father told his people his fearful dream, as he called it. He said,—

"I dreamt this same thing three nights,—the very same. I saw the greatest emigration that has yet been through our country. I looked North and South and East and West, and saw nothing but dust, and I heard a great weeping. I saw women crying, and I also saw men shot down by the white people. They were killing my people with something that made a great noise like thunder and lightning, and I saw the blood streaming from the mouths of my men that lay all around me. I saw it as if it was real. Oh, my dear children! You may all think it is only a dream,—nevertheless, I feel that it will come to pass. And to avoid bloodshed, we must all go to the mountain during the summer, or till my father comes back from California. He will then tell us what to do. Let us keep away from the emigrant roads and stay in the mountains all summer. There are to be a great many pine-nuts this summer, and we can lay up great supplies for the coming winter, and if the emigrants don't come too early, we can take a run down and fish for a month, and lay up dried fish. I know we can dry a great many in a month, and young men can go into the valleys on hunting excursions, and kill as many rabbits as they can. In that way we can live in the mountains all summer and all winter too."

So ended my father's dream. During that day one could see old women getting together talking over what they had heard my father say. They said,—

"It is true what our great chief has said, for it was shown to him by a higher power. It is not a dream. Oh, it surely will come to pass. We shall no longer be a happy people, as we now are; we shall no longer go here and there as of old; we shall no longer build our big fires as a signal to our friends, for we shall always be afraid of being seen by those bad people."

"Surely they don't eat people?"

"Yes, they do eat people, because they ate each other up in the mountains last winter."

This was the talk among the old women during the day.

"Oh, how grieved we are! Oh, where will it end?" . . .

4–11

Sarah Orne Jewett (1849–1909)

SARAH ORNE JEWETT (1849–1909) spent her life in Maine; she is considered a regional writer, her ear close to nature and culture around her. Jewett was schooled at home as a child and at a local academy as an adolescent. Lore has it that she followed her father, a country doctor and obstetrician, on house calls. Inspired by Stowe's New England stories, Jewett built on the tradition of Local Colorists, those writers who have a strong sense of place, focus on ordinary folk, and appreciate realistic fiction. She was first published at age twenty in the *Atlantic Monthly*; and within a dozen years her work was "discovered" by William Dean Howells. Willa Cather, the great Nebraska writer, would later point to Jewett as a powerful influence on her writing. "A White Heron" is a treasure, superbly capturing the innocence of a child and our indwelling connection to nature, just as New England is shifting from country to city.

≈ ≈ ≈

"A White Heron" (1886)

I

The woods were already filled with shadows one June evening, just before eight o'clock, though a bright sunset still glimmered faintly among the trunks of the trees. A little girl was driving home her cow, a plodding, dilatory, provoking creature in her behavior, but a valued companion for all that. They were going away from whatever light there was, and striking deep into the woods, but their feet were familiar with the path, and it was no matter whether their eyes could see it or not.

There was hardly a night the summer through when the old cow could be found waiting at the pasture bars; on the contrary, it was her greatest pleasure to hide herself away among the huckleberry bushes, and though she wore a loud bell she had made the discovery that if one stood perfectly still it would not ring. So Sylvia had to hunt for her until she found her, and call Co'! Co'! with never an answering Moo, until her childish patience was quite spent. If the creature had not given good milk and plenty of it, the case would have seemed very different to her owners. Besides, Sylvia had all the time there was, and very little use to make of it. Sometimes in pleasant weather it was a consolation to look upon the cow's pranks as an intelligent attempt to play hide and seek, and as the child had no playmates she lent herself to this amusement with a good deal of zest. Though this chase had been so long that the wary animal herself had given an unusual signal of her whereabouts, Sylvia had only laughed when she came upon Mistress Moolly at the swampside, and urged her affectionately homeward with a twig of birch leaves. The old cow was not inclined to wander farther, she even turned in the right direction for once as they left the pasture, and stepped along the road at a good pace. She was quite ready to be milked now, and seldom stopped to browse. Sylvia wondered what her grandmother would say because they were so late. It was a great while since she had left home at half-past five o'clock, but everybody knew the difficulty of making this errand a short one. Mrs. Tilley had chased the hornéd torment too many summer evenings herself to blame any one else for lingering, and was only thankful as she waited that she had Sylvia, nowadays, to give such valuable assistance. The good woman suspected that Sylvia loitered occasionally on her own account; there never was such a child for straying about out-of-doors since the world was made! Everybody said that it was a good change for a little maid who had tried to grow for eight years in a crowded manufacturing town, but, as for Sylvia herself, it seemed as if she never had been alive at all before she came to live at the farm. She thought often with wistful compassion of a wretched geranium that belonged to a town neighbor.

"'Afraid of folks,'" old Mrs. Tilley said to herself, with a smile, after she had made the unlikely choice of Sylvia from her daughter's houseful of children, and was returning to the farm. "'Afraid of folks,' they said! I guess she won't be troubled no great with 'em up to the old place!" When they reached the door of the lonely house and stopped to unlock it, and the cat came to purr loudly, and rub against them, a deserted pussy, indeed, but fat with young robins, Sylvia whispered that this was a beautiful place to live in, and she never should wish to go home.

The companions followed the shady wood road, the cow taking slow steps and the child very fast ones. The cow stopped long at the brook to drink, as if the pasture were not half a swamp, and Sylvia stood still and waited, letting her bare feet cool themselves in the shoal water, while the great twilight moths struck softly against her. She waded on through the brook as the cow moved away, and listened to the thrushes with a heart that beat fast with pleasure. There was a stirring in the great boughs overhead. They were full of little birds and beasts that seemed to be wide awake, and going about their world, or else saying good-night to each other in sleepy twitters. Sylvia herself felt sleepy as she walked along. However, it was not much farther to the house, and the air was soft and sweet. She was not often in the woods so late as this, and it made her feel as if she were a part of the gray shadows and the moving leaves. She was just thinking how long it seemed since she first came to the farm a year ago, and wondering if everything went on in the noisy town just the same as when she was there; the thought of the great red-faced boy who used to chase and frighten her made her hurry along the path to escape from the shadow of the trees.

Suddenly this little woods-girl is horror-stricken to hear a clear whistle not very far away. Not a bird's-whistle, which would have a sort of friendliness, but a boy's whistle, determined, and somewhat aggressive. Sylvia left the cow to whatever sad fate might await her, and stepped discreetly aside into the brush-es, but she was just too late. The enemy had discovered her, and called out in a very cheerful and persuasive tone, "Halloa, little girl, how far is it to the road?" and trembling Sylvia answered almost inaudibly, "A good ways."

She did not dare to look boldly at the tall young man, who carried a gun over his shoulder, but she came out of her bush and again followed the cow, while he walked alongside.

"I have been hunting for some birds," the stranger said kindly, "and I have lost my way, and need a friend very much. Don't be afraid," he added gallantly. "Speak up and tell me what your name is, and whether you think I can spend the night at your house, and go out gunning early in the morning."

Sylvia was more alarmed than before. Would not her grandmother consid-er her much to blame? But who could have foreseen such an accident as this? It did not seem to be her fault, and she hung her head as if the stem of it were broken, but managed to answer "Sylvy," with much effort when her companion again asked her name.

Mrs. Tilley was standing in the doorway when the trio came into view. The cow gave a loud moo by way of explanation.

"Yes, you'd better speak up for yourself, you old trial! Where'd she tucked herself away this time, Sylvy?" But Sylvia kept an awed silence; she knew by instinct that her grandmother did not comprehend the gravity of the situation. She must be mistaking the stranger for one of the farmer-lads of the region.

The young man stood his gun beside the door, and dropped a lumpy game-bag beside it; then he bade Mrs. Tilley good-evening, and repeated his wayfar-er's story, and asked if he could have a night's lodging.

"Put me anywhere you like," he said. "I must be off early in the morning, before day; but I am very hungry, indeed. You can give me some milk at any rate, that's plain."

"Dear sakes, yes," responded the hostess, whose long slumbering hospitali-ty seemed to be easily awakened. "You might fare better if you went out to the main road a mile or so, but you're welcome to what we've got. I'll milk right off, and you make yourself at home. You can sleep on husks or feathers," she proffered graciously. "I raised them all myself. There's good pasturing for geese just below here towards the ma'sh. Now step round and set a plate for the gen-tleman, Sylvy!" And Sylvia promptly stepped. She was glad to have something to do, and she was hungry herself.

It was a surprise to find so clean and comfortable a little dwelling in this New England wilderness. The young man had known the horrors of its most primitive housekeeping, and the dreary squalor of that level of society which does not rebel at the companionship of hens. This was the best thrift of an old-fashioned farmstead, though on such a small scale that it seemed like a hermit-age. He listened eagerly to the old woman's quaint talk, he watched Sylvia's pale face and shining gray eyes with ever growing enthusiasm, and insisted that this was the best supper he had eaten for a month, and afterward the new-made friends sat down in the door-way together while the moon came up.

Soon it would be berry-time, and Sylvia was a great help at picking. The cow was a good milker, though a plaguy thing to keep track of, the hostess gossiped frankly, adding presently that she had buried four children, so Sylvia's mother, and a son (who might be dead) in California were all the children she had left. "Dan, my boy, was a great hand to go gunning," she explained sadly. "I never wanted for pa'tridges or gray squer'ls while he was to home. He's been a great wand'rer, I expect, and he's no hand to write letters. There, I don't blame him, I'd ha' seen the world myself if it had been so I could."

"Sylvy takes after him," the grandmother continued affectionately, after a minute's pause. "There ain't a foot o' ground she don't know her way over, and the wild creaturs counts her one o' themselves. Squer'ls she'll tame to come an' feed right out o' her hands, and all sorts o' birds. Last winter she got the jay-birds to bangeing here, and I believe she'd 'a' scanted herself of her own meals to have plenty to throw out amongst 'em, if I hadn't kep' watch. Anything but crows, I tell her, I'm willin' to help support—though Dan he had a tamed one o' them that did seem to have reason same as folks. It was round here a good spell after he went away. Dan an' his father they didn't hitch,—but he never held up his head ag'in after Dan had dared him an' gone off."

The guest did not notice this hint of family sorrows in his eager interest in something else.

"So Sylvy knows all about birds, does she?" he exclaimed, as he looked round at the little girl who sat, very demure but increasingly sleepy, in the moonlight. "I am making a collection of birds myself. I have been at it ever since I was a boy." (Mrs. Tilley smiled.) "There are two or three very rare ones I have been hunting for these five years. I mean to get them on my own ground if they can be found."

"Do you cage 'em up?" asked Mrs. Tilley doubtfully, in response to this enthusiastic announcement.

"Oh no, they're stuffed and preserved, dozens and dozens of them," said the ornithologist, "and I have shot or snared every one myself. I caught a glimpse of a white heron a few miles from here on Saturday, and I have followed it in this direction. They have never been found in this district at all. The little white heron, it is," and he turned again to look at Sylvia with the hope of discovering that the rare bird was one of her acquaintances.

But Sylvia was watching a hop-toad in the narrow footpath.

"You would know the heron if you saw it," the stranger continued eagerly. "A queer tall white bird with soft feathers and long thin legs. And it would have a nest perhaps in the top of a high tree, made of sticks, something like a hawk's nest."

Sylvia's heart gave a wild beat; she knew that strange white bird, and had once stolen softly near where it stood in some bright green swamp grass, away over at the other side of the woods. There was an open place where the sunshine always seemed strangely yellow and hot, where tall, nodding rushes grew, and her grandmother had warned her that she might sink in the soft black mud underneath and never be heard of more. Not far beyond were the salt marshes just this side the sea itself, which Sylvia wondered and dreamed much about, but never had seen, whose great voice could sometimes be heard above the noise of the woods on stormy nights.

"I can't think of anything I should like so much as to find that heron's nest," the handsome stranger was saying. "I would give ten dollars to anybody who could show it to me," he added desperately, "and I mean to spend my whole vacation hunting for it if need be. Perhaps it was only migrating, or had been chased out of its own region by some bird of prey."

Mrs. Tilley gave amazed attention to all this, but Sylvia still watched the toad, not divining, as she might have done at some calmer time, that the creature wished to get to its hole under the door-step, and was much hindered by the unusual spectators at that hour of the evening. No amount of thought, that night, could decide how many wished-for treasures the ten dollars, so lightly spoken of, would buy.

The next day the young sportsman hovered about the woods, and Sylvia kept him company, having lost her first fear of the friendly lad, who proved to be most kind and sympathetic. He told her many things about the birds and what they knew and where they lived and what they did with themselves. And he gave her a jack-knife, which she thought as great a treasure as if she were a desert-islander. All day long he did not once make her troubled or afraid except when he brought down some unsuspecting singing creature from its bough. Sylvia would have liked him vastly better without his gun; she could not understand why he killed the very birds he seemed to like so much. But as the day waned, Sylvia still watched the young man with loving admiration. She had never seen anybody so charming and delightful; the woman's heart, asleep in the child, was vaguely thrilled by a dream of love. Some premonition of that great power stirred and swayed these young creatures who traversed the solemn woodlands with soft-footed silent care. They stopped to listen to a bird's song; they pressed forward again eagerly, parting the branches—speaking to each other rarely and in whispers; the young man going first and Sylvia following, fascinated, a few steps behind, with her gray eyes dark with excitement.

She grieved because the longed-for white heron was elusive, but she did not lead the guest, she only followed, and there was no such thing as speaking first. The sound of her own unquestioned voice would have terrified her—it was hard enough to answer yes or no when there was need of that. At last evening began to fall, and they drove the cow home together, and Sylvia smiled with pleasure when they came to the place where she heard the whistle and was afraid only the night before.

II

Half a mile from home, at the farther edge of the woods, where the land was highest, a great pine-tree stood, the last of its generation. Whether it was left for a boundary mark, or for what reason, no one could say; the woodchoppers who had felled its mates were dead and gone long ago, and a whole forest of sturdy trees, pines and oaks and maples, had grown again. But the stately head of this old pine towered above them all and made a landmark for sea and shore miles and miles away. Sylvia knew it well. She had always believed that whoever climbed to the top of it could see the ocean; and the little girl had often laid her hand on the great rough trunk and looked up wistfully at those dark boughs that the wind always stirred, no matter how hot and still the air might be below. Now she thought of the tree with a new excitement, for why, if one climbed it at break of day could not one see all the world, and easily discover from whence the white heron flew, and mark the place, and find the hidden nest?

What a spirit of adventure, what wild ambition! What fancied triumph and delight and glory for the later morning when she could make known the secret! It was almost too real and too great for the childish heart to bear.

All night the door of the little house stood open and the whippoorwills came and sang upon the very step. The young sportsman and his old hostess were sound asleep, but Sylvia's great design kept her broad awake and watching. She forgot to think of sleep. The short summer night seemed as long as the winter darkness, and at last when the whippoorwills ceased, and she was afraid the morning would after all come too soon, she stole out of the house and followed the pasture path through the woods, hastening toward the open ground beyond, listening with a sense of comfort and companionship to the drowsy twitter of a half-awakened bird, whose perch she had jarred in passing. Alas, if the great wave of human interest which flooded for the first time this dull little life should sweep away the satisfactions of an existence heart to heart with nature and the dumb life of the forest!

There was the huge tree asleep yet in the paling moonlight, and small and silly Sylvia began with utmost bravery to mount to the top of it, with tingling, eager blood coursing the channels of her whole frame, with her bare feet and fingers, that pinched and held like bird's claws to the monstrous ladder reaching up, up, almost to the sky itself. First she must mount the white oak tree that grew alongside, where she was almost lost among the dark branches and the green leaves heavy and wet with dew; a bird fluttered off its nest, and a red squirrel ran to and fro and scolded pettishly at the harmless housebreaker. Sylvia felt her way easily. She had often climbed there, and knew that higher still one of the oak's upper branches chafed against the pine trunk, just where its lower boughs were set close together. There, when she made the dangerous pass from one tree to the other, the great enterprise would really begin.

She crept out along the swaying oak limb at last, and took the daring step across into the old pine-tree. The way was harder than she thought; she must reach far and hold fast, the sharp dry twigs caught and held her and scratched her like angry talons, the pitch made her thin little fingers clumsy and stiff as she went round and round the tree's great stem, higher and higher upward. The sparrows and robins in the woods below were beginning to wake and twitter to the dawn, yet it seemed much lighter there aloft in the pine-tree, and the child knew she must hurry if her project were to be of any use.

The tree seemed to lengthen itself out as she went up, and to reach farther and farther upward. It was like a great main-mast to the voyaging earth; it must truly have been amazed that morning through all its ponderous frame as it felt this determined spark of human spirit wending its way from higher branch to branch. Who knows how steadily the least twigs held themselves to advantage this light, weak creature on her way! The old pine must have loved his new dependent. More than all the hawks, and bats, and moths, and even the sweet voiced thrushes, was the brave, beating heart of the solitary gray-eyed child. And the tree stood still and frowned away the winds that June morning while the dawn grew bright in the east.

Sylvia's face was like a pale star, if one had seen it from the ground, when the last thorny bough was past, and she stood trembling and tired but wholly triumphant, high in the treetop. Yes, there was the sea with the dawning sun making a golden dazzle over it, and toward that glorious east flew two hawks with slow-moving pinions. How low they looked in the air from that height when one had only seen them before far up, and dark against the blue sky. Their gray feathers were as soft as moths; they seemed only a little way from the tree, and Sylvia felt as if she too could go flying away among the clouds. Westward, the woodlands and farms reached miles and miles into the distance; here and there were church steeples, and white villages, truly it was a vast and awesome world!

The birds sang louder and louder. At last the sun came up bewilderingly bright. Sylvia could see the white sails of ships out at sea, and the clouds that were purple and rose-colored and yellow at first began to fade away. Where was the white heron's nest in the sea of green branches, and was this wonderful sight and pageant of the world the only reward for having climbed to such a giddy height? Now look down again, Sylvia, where the green marsh is set among the shining birches and dark hemlocks; there where you saw the white heron once you will see him again; look, look! a white spot of him like a single floating feather comes up from the dead hemlock and grows larger, and rises, and comes close at last, and goes by the landmark pine with steady sweep of wing and outstretched slender neck and crested head. And wait! wait! do not move a foot or a finger, little girl, do not send an arrow of light and conscious-ness from your two eager eyes, for the heron has perched on a pine bough not far beyond yours, and cries back to his mate on the nest and plumes his feathers for the new day!

The child gives a long sigh a minute later when a company of shouting cat-birds comes also to the tree, and vexed by their fluttering and lawlessness the solemn heron goes away. She knows his secret now, the wild, light, slender bird that floats and wavers, and goes back like an arrow presently to his home in the green world beneath. Then Sylvia, well satisfied, makes her perilous way down again, not daring to look far below the branch she stands on, ready to cry sometimes because her fingers ache and her lamed feet slip. Wondering over and over again what the stranger would say to her, and what he would think when she told him how to find his way straight to the heron's nest.

"Sylvy, Sylvy!" called the busy old grandmother again and again, but nobody answered, and the small husk bed was empty and Sylvia had disappeared.

The guest waked from a dream, and remembering his day's pleasure hurried to dress himself that might it sooner begin. He was sure from the way the shy little girl looked once or twice yesterday that she had at least seen the white heron, and now she must really be made to tell. Here she comes now, paler than ever, and her worn old frock is torn and tattered, and smeared with pine pitch. The grandmother and the sportsman stand in the door together and question her, and the splendid moment has come to speak of the dead hemlock-tree by the green marsh.

But Sylvia does not speak after all, though the old grandmother fretfully rebukes her, and the young man's kind, appealing eyes are looking straight in her own. He can make them rich with money; he has promised it, and they are poor now. He is so well worth making happy, and he waits to hear the story she can tell.

No, she must keep silence! What is it that suddenly forbids her and makes her dumb? Has she been nine years growing and now, when the great world for the first time puts out a hand to her, must she thrust it aside for a bird's sake? The murmur of the pine's green branches is in her ears, she remembers how the white heron came flying through the golden air and how they watched the sea and the morning together, and Sylvia cannot speak; she cannot tell the heron's secret and give its life away.

Dear loyalty, that suffered a sharp pang as the guest went away disappointed later in the day, that could have served and followed him and loved him as a dog loves! Many a night Sylvia heard the echo of his whistle haunting the pasture path as she came home with the loitering cow. She forgot even her sorrow at the sharp report of his gun and the sight of thrushes and sparrows dropping silent to the ground, their songs hushed and their pretty feathers stained and wet with blood. Were the birds better friends than their hunter might have been,—who can tell? Whatever treasures were lost to her, woodlands and summer-time, remember! Bring your gifts and graces and tell your secrets to this lonely country child!

4–12
Emma Lazarus (1849–1887)

"Give me your tired, your poor, your huddled masses yearning to breathe free," begins one of the most famous American poems, "The New Colossus" (1883). EMMA LAZARUS (1849–1887) was born into a wealthy Jewish family in New York City. Privately tutored, she mastered several foreign languages and published a volume of her early translations of poetry. She identified with the German poet Heine, also Jewish, and translated his poetry as well as dedicated a poem to him. Lazarus' "The New Colossus" was written to raise funds for the pedestal of the Statue of Liberty. So identified was the poem with the statue that it was engraved on the pedestal itself in 1903. "In Exile" illustrates how the role of America as a haven for oppressed people, in this case Jews suffering from Tsarist pogroms, was helping to create a new identity for the growing country.

≋ ≋ ≋

"The New Colossus" (1883)

Not like the brazen giant of Greek fame,
With conquering limbs astride from land to land,
Here at our sea-washed, sunset gates shall stand
A mighty woman, with a torch, whose flame
Is the imprisoned lightning, and her name
Mother of Exiles. From her beacon-hand
Glows world-wide welcome; her mild eyes command
The air-bridged harbor that twin-cities frame.

"Keep, ancient lands, your storied pomp!" cries she,
With silent lips. "Give me your tired, your poor,
"Your huddled masses, yearning to breathe free;
"The wretched refuse of your teeming shore—
"Send these, the homeless, tempest-tost to me—
"I lift my lamp beside the golden door!"

"In Exile: Extract from a Letter of a Russian Refugee in Texas" (1888)

"Since that day till now our life is one unbroken paradise. We live a true brotherly life. Every evening after supper we take a seat under the mighty oak and sing our songs."—*Extract from a letter of a Russian refugee in Texas*

Twilight is here, soft breezes bow the grass,
Day's sounds of various toil break slowly off,
The yoke-freed oxen low, the patient ass
Dips his dry nostril in the cool, deep trough.
Up from the prairie the tanned herdsman pass
With frothy pails, guiding with voices rough
Their udder-lightened kine. Fresh smells of earth,
The rich, black furrows of the glebe send forth.

After the Southern day of heavy toil,
How good to lie, with limbs relaxed, brows bare
To evening's fan, and watch the smoke-wreaths coil
Up from one's pipe-stem through the rayless air.
So deem these unused tillers of the soil,
Who stretched beneath the shadowing oak-tree, stare
Peacefully on the star-unfolding skies,
And name their life unbroken paradise.

The hounded stag that has escaped the pack,
And pants at ease within a thick-leaved dell;
The unimprisoned bird that finds the track
Through sun-bathed space, to where his fellows dwell;
The martyr, granted respite from the rack,
The death-doomed victim pardoned from his cell.—
Such only know the joy these exiles gain,—
Life's sharpest rapture is surcease of pain.

Strange faces theirs, wherethrough the Orient sun
Gleams from the eyes and glows athwart the skin.
Grave lines of studious thought and purpose run
From curl-crowned forehead to dark-bearded chin.
And over all the seal is stamped thereon
Of anguish branded by a world of sin,
In fire and blood through ages on their name,
Their seal of glory and the Gentiles' shame.

Freedom to love the law that Moses brought,
To sing the songs of David, and to think
The thoughts Gabirol to Spinoza taught,
Freedom to dig the common earth, to drink
The universal air—for this they sought
Refuge o'er wave and continent, to link

Egypt to Texas in their mystic chain,
And truth's perpetual lamp forbid to wane.

Hark! through the quiet evening air, their song
Floats forth with wild sweet rhythm and glad refrain.
They sing the conquest of the spirit strong,
The soul that wrests the victory from pain;
The noble joys of manhood that belong
To comrades and to brothers. In their strain
Rustle of palms and Eastern streams one hears,
And the broad prairie melts in mist of tears.

5 :: Naturalism

5–1

Kate Chopin (1850–1904)

KATE CHOPIN (1850–1904), née Katherine O'Flaherty, heralded from St. Louis, Missouri, and an Irish Catholic family, though the setting and subject matter of her fiction was distinctly Louisiana Creole. Educated in a Catholic girls' school, Chopin developed a strong affinity for nineteenth-century French writers Gustave Flaubert and Guy de Maupassant. She married at age nineteen, had six children, and spent her married life in New Orleans and western Louisiana, on the Natchitoches River. When her husband died insolvent in 1884, Chopin returned to her mother's house in St. Louis; there she wrote to support herself and her children. Chopin produced three novels and over one hundred short stories. Her most famous novel, *The Awakening* (1899), brought about a storm of criticism for its modern themes of women's sexuality. "Désirée's Baby" (first published in 1893) is set in the antebellum South, on a Creole plantation. The complicated connections between race and kinship erupt, resulting in the destruction of a family.

≈ ≈ ≈

"Désirée's Baby" (1893)

As the day was pleasant, Madame Valmondé drove over to L'Abri to see Désirée and the baby.

It made her laugh to think of Désirée with a baby. Why, it seemed but yesterday that Désirée was little more than a baby herself; when Monsieur in riding through the gateway of Valmondé had found her lying asleep in the shadow of the big stone pillar.

The little one awoke in his arms and began to cry for "Dada." That was as much as she could do or say. Some people thought she might have strayed there of her own accord, for she was of the toddling age. The prevailing belief was that she had been purposely left by a party of Texans, whose canvas-covered wagon, late in the day, had crossed the ferry that Coton Maïs kept, just below the plantation. In time Madame Valmondé abandoned every speculation but the one that Désirée had been sent to her by a beneficent Providence to be the child of her affection, seeing that she was without child of the flesh. For the girl grew to be beautiful and gentle, affectionate and sincere,—the idol of Valmondé.

It was no wonder, when she stood one day, against the stone pillar in whose shadow she had lain asleep, eighteen years before, that Armand Aubigny riding by and seeing her there, had fallen in love with her. That was the way all the Aubignys fell in love, as if struck by a pistol shot. The wonder was that he had not loved her before; for he had known her since his father brought him home from Paris, a boy of eight, after his mother died there. The passion that awoke in him that day, when he saw her at the gate, swept along like an avalanche, or like a prairie fire, or like anything that drives headlong over all obstacles.

Monsieur Valmondé grew practical and wanted things well considered: that is, the girl's obscure origin. Armand looked into her eyes and did not care. He was reminded that she was nameless. What did it matter about a name when he could give her one of the oldest and proudest in Louisiana? He ordered the *corbeille* from Paris, and contained himself with what patience he could until it arrived; then they were married.

Madame Valmondé had not seen Désirée and the baby for four weeks. When she reached L'Abri she shuddered at the first sight of it, as she always did. It was a sad looking place, which for many years had not known the gentle presence of a mistress, old Monsieur Aubigny having married and buried his wife in France, and she having loved her own land too well ever to leave it. The roof came down steep and black like a cowl, reaching out beyond the wide galleries that encircled the yellow stuccoed house. Big, solemn oaks grew close to it, and their thick-leaved, far-reaching branches shadowed it like a pall. Young Aubigny's rule was a strict one, too, and under it his negroes had forgotten how to be gay, as they had been during the old master's easy-going and indulgent lifetime.

The young mother was recovering slowly, and lay full length, in her soft white muslins and laces, upon a couch. The baby was beside her, upon her arm, where he had fallen asleep, at her breast. The yellow nurse woman sat beside a window fanning herself.

Madame Valmondé bent her portly figure over Désirée and kissed her, holding her an instant tenderly in her arms. Then she turned to the child.

"This is not the baby!" she exclaimed, in startled tones. French was the language spoken at Valmondé in those days.

"I knew you would be astonished," laughed Désirée, "at the way he has grown. The little *cochon de lait!* Look at his legs, mamma, and his hands and finger-nails,—real finger-nails. Zandrine had to cut them this morning. Isn't it true, Zandrine?"

The woman bowed her turbaned head majestically, "Mais si, Madame."

"And the way he cries," went on Désirée, "is deafening. Armand heard him the other day as far away as La Blanche's cabin."

Madame Valmondé had never removed her eyes from the child. She lifted it and walked with it over to the window that was lightest. She scanned the baby narrowly, then looked as searchingly at Zandrine, whose face was turned to gaze across the fields.

"Yes, the child has grown, has changed"; said Madame Valmondé, slowly, as she replaced it beside its mother. "What does Armand say?"

Désirée's face became suffused with a glow that was happiness itself.

"Oh, Armand is the proudest father in the parish, I believe, chiefly because it is a boy, to bear his name; though he says not,—that he would have loved a girl as well. But I know it isn't true. I know he says that to please me. And mamma," she added, drawing Madame Valmondé's head down to her, and speaking in a whisper, "he hasn't punished one of them—not one of them—since baby is born. Even Négrillon, who pretended to have burnt his leg that he might rest from work—he only laughed, and said Négrillon was a great scamp. Oh, mamma, I'm so happy; it frightens me."

What Désirée said was true. Marriage, and later the birth of his son, had softened Armand Aubigny's imperious and exacting nature greatly. This was what made the gentle Désirée so happy, for she loved him desperately. When he frowned she trembled, but loved him. When he smiled, she asked no greater blessing of God. But Armand's dark, handsome face had not often been disfigured by frowns since the day he fell in love with her.

When the baby was about three months old, Désirée awoke one day to the conviction that there was something in the air menacing her peace. It was at first too subtle to grasp. It had only been a disquieting suggestion; an air of mystery among the blacks; unexpected visits from far-off neighbors who could hardly account for their coming. Then a strange, an awful change in her husband's manner, which she dared not ask him to explain. When he spoke to her, it was with averted eyes, from which the old love-light seemed to have gone out. He absented himself from home; and when there, avoided her presence and that of her child, without excuse. And the very spirit of Satan seemed suddenly to take hold of him in his dealings with the slaves. Désirée was miserable enough to die.

She sat in her room, one hot afternoon, in her *peignoir*, listlessly drawing through her fingers the strands of her long, silky brown hair that hung about her shoulders. The baby, half naked, lay asleep upon her own great mahogany bed, that was like a sumptuous throne, with its satin-lined half-canopy. One of La Blanche's little quadroon boys—half naked too—stood fanning the child slowly with a fan of peacock feathers. Désirée's eyes had been fixed absently and sadly upon the baby, while she was striving to penetrate the threatening mist that she felt closing about her. She looked from her child to the boy who stood beside him, and back again; over and over. "Ah!" It was a cry that she could not help; which she was not conscious of having uttered. The blood turned like ice in her veins, and a clammy moisture gathered upon her face.

She tried to speak to the little quadroon boy; but no sound would come, at first. When he heard his name uttered, he looked up, and his mistress was pointing to the door. He laid aside the great, soft fan, and obediently stole away, over the polished floor, on his bare tiptoes.

She stayed motionless, with gaze riveted upon her child, and her face the picture of fright.

Presently her husband entered the room, and without noticing her, went to a table and began to search among some papers which covered it.

"Armand," she called to him, in a voice which must have stabbed him, if he was human. But he did not notice. "Armand," she said again. Then she rose and tottered towards him. "Armand," she panted once more, clutching his arm, "look at our child. What does it mean? tell me."

He coldly but gently loosened her fingers from about his arm and thrust the hand away from him. "Tell me what it means!" she cried despairingly.

"It means," he answered lightly, "that the child is not white; it means that you are not white."

A quick conception of all that this accusation meant for her nerved her with unwonted courage to deny it. "It is a lie; it is not true, I am white! Look at my hair, it is brown; and my eyes are gray, Armand, you know they are gray. And my skin is fair," seizing his wrist. "Look at my hand; whiter than yours, Armand," she laughed hysterically.

"As white as La Blanche's," he returned cruelly; and went away leaving her alone with their child.

When she could hold a pen in her hand, she sent a despairing letter to Madame Valmondé.

"My mother, they tell me I am not white. Armand has told me I am not white. For God's sake tell them it is not true. You must know it is not true. I shall die. I must die. I cannot be so unhappy, and live!"

The answer that came was as brief:

"My own Désirée: Come home to Valmondé; back to your mother who loves you. Come with your child."

When the letter reached Désirée she went with it to her husband's study, and laid it open upon the desk before which he sat. She was like a stone image: silent, white, motionless after she placed it there.

In silence he ran his cold eyes over the written words. He said nothing. "Shall I go, Armand?" she asked in tones sharp with agonized suspense.

"Yes, go."

"Do you want me to go?"

"Yes, I want you to go."

He thought Almighty God had dealt cruelly and unjustly with him; and felt, somehow, that he was paying Him back in kind when he stabbed thus into his wife's soul. Moreover he no longer loved her, because of the unconscious injury she had brought upon his home and his name.

She turned away like one stunned by a blow, and walked slowly towards the door, hoping he would call her back.

"Good-by, Armand," she moaned.

He did not answer her. That was his last blow at fate.

Désirée went in search of her child. Zandrine was pacing the sombre gallery with it. She took the little one from the nurse's arms with no word of explanation, and descending the steps, walked away, under the live-oak branches.

It was an October afternoon; the sun was just sinking. Out in the still fields the negroes were picking cotton.

Désirée had not changed the thin white garment nor the slippers which she wore. Her hair was uncovered and the sun's rays brought a golden gleam from its brown meshes. She did not take the broad, beaten road which led to the far-off plantation of Valmondé. She walked across a deserted field, where the stubble bruised her tender feet, so delicately shod, and tore her thin gown to shreds.

She disappeared among the reeds and willows that grew thick along the banks of the deep, sluggish bayou; and she did not come back again.

Some weeks later there was a curious scene enacted at L'Abri. In the centre of the smoothly swept back yard was a great bonfire. Armand Aubigny sat in the wide hallway that commanded a view of the spectacle; and it was he who dealt out to a half dozen negroes the material which kept this fire ablaze.

A graceful cradle of willow, with all its dainty furbishings, was laid upon the pyre, which had already been fed with the richness of a priceless *layette*. Then there were silk gowns, and velvet and satin ones added to these; laces, too, and embroideries; bonnets and gloves; for the *corbeille* had been of rare quality.

The last thing to go was a tiny bundle of letters; innocent little scribblings that Désirée had sent to him during the days of their espousal. There was the remnant of one back in the drawer from which he took them. But it was not Désirée's; it was part of an old letter from his mother to his father. He read it. She was thanking God for the blessing of her husband's love:—

"But, above all," she wrote, "night and day, I thank the good God for having so arranged our lives that our dear Armand will never know that his mother, who adores him, belongs to the race that is cursed with the brand of slavery."

5–2
Ernest Francisco Fenollosa (Kano Eitan Masanobu) (1853–1908)

ERNEST FRANCISCO FENOLLOSA [KANO EITAN MASANOBU] (1853–1908) did more than any American of his generation to bring Eastern aesthetics to the West. Raised in Salem, Massachusetts, by a Spanish father, Fenollosa attended Harvard and art school in Boston. At age twenty-five, he traveled to Tokyo where he taught at university and studied Japanese religious temples, shrines, and artifacts. Fenollosa remained in Japan for most of his life, converting to Buddhism and changing his name. He became the foremost Western scholar of the classical Japanese drama Noh, drafted laws to preserve Asian art and architecture, wrote several important works on Asian art, and directed Tokyo's first art museum. Ezra Pound translated Fenollosa's notes on Chinese haiku and Japanese Noh, published as *Cathay* (1915). *East and West* (1893), Fenollosa's book of poetry, shows the influence of Eastern poetry on American modernism.

≈ ≈ ≈

From *East and West* (1893)

"Part II, The Separated East"

O wing of the Empress of mountains!
So sang thy last poet at Kásŭga's fountains.
The chant of the vestals had ceased.
The moon was awake in the East.
The love-locked pine-branches o'er us
Tinkled their bells in sympathetic chorus;
And the willow wept
Where the violet smiled as she slept.
My heart too was swelling
With the tears of a love past telling.
But I said:—
"O blossom of life in a dew-starred bed,
Thou art too sweet for this earth,
Too exquisite to linger;
Like the peace of a blest babe who dies at birth,
Like the agony of tears
When the young mother robbed of its prayed-for years
Kisses the listless finger.
Say, on the feminine curves of thy plain
Rises no rock for a counter-strain?
Are there no trumpets to shriek
In the sleeping ear of the meek?
No comet to threaten the sun?"
Yes, there was one;—
One priest white-robed who seemed to glide*
Like a ghost from the rock at my side,
With a smile that pierced like a sword

---

* His Reverence the Archbishop Keitoku, of the Tendai sect at Miidera temple on Lake Biwa, I still look up to as my most inspired and devoutly liberal teacher in matters religious. Precious were the days and nights I had the privilege of spending with him in the vicinities of Kioto, Nara, and Nikko. He was a lofty living exemplar of the spiritual knighthood. He passed from the visible form in 1889.

And a soul-compelling word.
And I heard him say,
As we fell on our knees to pray:—

"The fire of combat flashes
'Neath the grass-grown slopes of the ashes.
The planets are held in their places
By the struggles of mighty races.
Choice souls have forever come
To be trained for their martyrdom
Since the days when Kukai hurled
His dart from the Chinese world.*
What can the dreaming people know
Of the tempest surging below,
Of the devils storming the very
Fort of the monastery?
He who would strangle an elf
Must first of all conquer himself;
The true knight
With his own heart fight,
Antagony
Of untold agony!
On no external god relying,
Self-armed, heaven and hell alike defying,
Lonely,
With bare will only,
Biting his bitter blood-stained sod;—
This for the *world*, as for Japan,†
This is to be a man!
This is to be a god!"

---

* Kukai, or Kobo Daishi, one of the three great founders of Esoteric Buddhism in Japan,
spent many years of his youth in study at a famous Chinese monastery. About to return to
his native country early in the ninth century, he meditated long concerning the site of his
projected temple. Leaving the decision to the powers of heaven, he is said to have thrown
his *vagra*, or metal mace, into the air in the direction of Japan, whither it was borne by
divine means, and lodged in a tall tree on the top of Koya mountain. Here after his return
it was found by the Daishi, and here he built the splendid monastery of Koyasan, which
remains to this day the patriarchal seat of the Shingon sect in Japan.

† The Archbishop Keitoku believed that the Western spirit was nearly ripe to receive the
lofty doctrine which Eastern guardians have preserved for its precious legacy.

5–3
José Martí (1853–1895)

JOSÉ MARTÍ (1853–1895), a Cuban poet, essayist, journalist, and activist, gave his life to the cause of Cuban liberation from Spanish colonial rule. Like José Maria Heredia, Martí spent years in exile, traveling, speaking, writing, and founding newspapers abroad to promote Cuban independence. Arrested at age sixteen for seditious writing, Martí was imprisoned and deported to Spain. He studied law in Spain and continued his activism; he traveled to Mexico and Central America, lecturing, publishing, and organizing for freedom against Spanish rule. For the last dozen years of his life, Martí lived in New York City, Tampa, Florida, and Key West, galvanizing Cuban émigrés in the United States. *Simple Verses* (1891) written while in New York, contains Martí's best poems, such as the highly popular "Guantanamera," made into a 1920s folk song and revived by the Weavers during the 1960s counterculture movement. Martí died as he lived, leading the charge of the revolutionary Cubans against the Spanish forces at the Battle of Dos Rios.

≈ ≈ ≈

"Our America" (1891)

The conceited villager believes that the whole world is his village. He considers the universal order favorable, as long as he remains in charge, can pay back the rival that stole his girlfriend, and is accumulating wealth. He is oblivious to the giants with the seven-league stride that can squash him under their boots and to the battle of the comets in the sky that sail through the still air devouring worlds. What remains of the village in America must wake up. These are not times for lying down with a handkerchief over the head, but with weapons under the pillow, like Juan de Castellanos's men: the weapons of good sense, which conquer other weapons. Trenches of ideas are worth more than trenches of stone.

There is no prow that can cut through a cloud of ideas. A vigorous idea, set ablaze at the right time before the world, can stop—like the mystic banner of the final judgment—a squadron of battleships. The peoples that don't know each other must hurry to do so, as those who will fight side by side. Those who brandish their fists at each other, like jealous brothers who both want the same land, or the man with a small house that envies the man with a better house, must join hands, that they may be one. As for those who claim the shelter of a criminal tradition to seize the land of their conquered brother with the saber darkened by the blood of his own veins, if they don't want to be called thieves, let them return the lands to their brother, for the punishment is greater than he deserves. The honorable do not charge debts of honor in money, as if each slap were worth so much. We can no longer be people resembling leaves, living in the air, laden with flowers bursting open and quivering, as light unexpectedly strikes them, or thrashed and torn by storms; the trees must line up so that the giant with the seven-league stride may not pass! It's time for a head count, for the united march, and we must proceed in tight formation, like veins of silver at the base of the Andes.

Those who have no faith in their land are premature men, lacking in courage. Because they lack courage, they deny it to everyone else. The tree is out of reach of their feeble arm with painted fingernails and bracelet, the arm of Madrid or of Paris, and they say that the tree is inaccessible. The ships must be rife with those harmful insects that gnaw to the bone the land that nourishes them. If they are Parisians or natives of Madrid, let them go stand under the streetlights of the Prado or enjoy a sorbet at Tortoni's. These carpenter's sons, ashamed that their father is a carpenter! These men born in America, ashamed of the mother that raised them because they wear an Indian apron, who reject her and abandon her while she is bedridden with sickness (the scoundrels)! Who is a man, then? The one who stays with his mother to cure her sickness, or the one who puts her to work where no one can see her, and lives on her sustenance in corrupt lands, cursing the womb that bore him, wearing ridiculous ties and the sign of traitor on the back of his paper dress coat? These sons of our America, which will be saved by the Indians and is improving; these deserters that wield rifles in the armies of North America, which drowns its Indians in blood and is deteriorating! These effeminate people—men who don't want to do the work of men! Did Washington, who made this land for them, go to live with the English in the years of their assault on his own land? These *incroyables* of honor, that drag it through foreign soil—like the *incroyables* of the French Revolution, dancing and gloating—had exaggerated speech.

And in what country can a man have more pride than in our afflicted republics of America, erected among the mute masses of Indians upon the bloody arms of a hundred apostles, at the sound of battle between the book and the candlestick? Never have such advanced and compact nations been created of factors so disjointed in so short a period of time. The proud person believes that the land was made as a pedestal for him because he has an easy pen or florid speech. He accuses his native republic of being incompetent and beyond help, because its untouched rainforests do not give him a way to travel throughout the world like a prince, guiding Persian ponies and pouring champagne. The incompetence is not in the nascent country, which seeks appropriate forms and a grandeur that is useful, but in those who want to govern original nations of a singular and violent composition, with laws inherited from four centuries of free practice in the United States, from nineteen centuries of monarchy in France. A decree of Hamilton cannot stop the charge of the plainsman's horse. A phrase of Sieyès cannot revitalize the sluggish blood of the Indian race. In governing, one must pay attention in order to govern well; and the good governor in America is not the one who knows how the German or the Frenchman governs, but the one who knows what elements make up his country, and how he can go about guiding the people as a whole, in order to arrive—by methods and institutions born from the country itself—at the desirable state wherein each man knows and exerts himself, and everyone enjoys the abundance that Nature gave to all those that contribute with their work and defend with their lives. The government must be born from the country itself. The spirit of government must be that of the country! The form of government must go hand in hand with the constitution of the country. The government is nothing more than the balance between the country's natural elements.

For that reason, the imported book has been conquered in America by the natural man. Natural men have conquered the artificial learned ones. The indigenous mestizo has conquered the exotic Creole. There is no battle between civilization and barbarism, but between false erudition and nature. The natural man is good. He respects and rewards superior intelligence, as long as no one takes malicious advantage of his submission or offends him by disregarding him, which the natural man—ready to recover by force the respect of anyone who hurts his sensitivity or harms his interests—will not forgive. The tyrants of America have risen to power by conforming to the scorned natural elements and fallen as soon as they betrayed them. The republics have purged from tyrannies their inability to identify the country's true elements, to derive from them the form of their government, and to govern accordingly. Governor, in a new nation, means creator.

In nations made up of learned and unlearned elements, wherever the learned don't learn the art of government, the unlearned will govern, by their habit of assaulting and resolving doubts by force. The unlearned masses are lazy and timid in matters of intelligence, and they want to be governed well; but if the government hurts them, they shake it off and govern themselves. How can the universities produce governors, if there is no university in America where even the basics of the art of government—which is the analysis of the peculiar elements of the American peoples—are not taught? The young graduates will most likely come out into the world, wearing Yankee or French glasses, and aspire to lead a people they don't know. Entry into a political career should be refused to those who don't understand the basics of politics. The prize in literary competitions need not be for the best poem but for the best study of the qualities of the country in which one lives. In the newspaper, in the university, in schools, the study of the country's real qualities should be carried forward. To know them truly and simply is enough; for whoever sets aside—willingly or out of ignorance—one part of the truth, falls headlong by reason of disregarding the truth, which grows in spite of negligence and overturns what is erected without her. Solving a problem after knowing its elements is easier than solving a problem without knowing them. The natural man comes, indignant and strong, and overturns the system of law established by the book because it is not administered in accordance with the patent necessities of the country. To know is to solve. To know the country, and to govern it according to knowledge, is the only way to free it from tyranny. The European university must give way to the American university. The history of America from the Incas until now must be taught thoroughly, even if the history of the Greek archons is not. Our Greece is preferable to the Greece that is not ours. National politicians must replace foreign politicians. Let the world be grafted into our republics, but our republics must be the trunk of the tree. And let the conquered pedant be silent, for there is no land in which man can have more pride than in our afflicted American republics.

Standing on the rosary, with white head and the mottled skin of the Indian or the Creole, we came boldly to the world of nations. With the standard of the Virgin we set out for the conquest of freedom. A priest, a few lieutenants, and a woman set up the republic in Mexico on the shoulders of the Indians. A Spanish clergyman, shrouded in his cape, schooled a few excellent youths in French liberty, and they fought against Spain under a Spanish general they named chief of Central America. With their monarchic habits, and the sun as their banner, Venezuelans in the north and Argentines in the south began to liberate nations. When the two heroes met, and the continent was about to tremble, one of them (not the lesser) turned back. And just as heroism is most rare in peace, because it is less glorious than heroism in war, so also for man it is easier to die with honor than to think with order. Similarly, to govern with exalted and unanimous sentiments is more feasible than to manage the diverse, arrogant, exotic, or ambitious thoughts that arise after battle. The powers crushed in the bygone epic, with the feline caution of their species and the weight of reality, sabotaged the edifice in both the crude, strange regions of our mestizo America and the towns of bare legs and Parisian dress coats, which had been erected under the flag of peoples nourished by the vitality that accompanies the continual practice of reason and liberty. Just as the hierarchical institution of the colonies resisted the democratic organization of the republic; just as the capital cities with their bow ties left the rural towns with their horsehide boots in the vestibule; just as the book-smart redeemers did not understand that the revolution that triumphed with the soul of the land, freed by the savior's voice, had to govern in a way befitting the soul of the land, not against her or without her—America began to suffer, and still suffers, from the fatigue of trying to accommodate the discordant and hostile elements she inherited from a despotic and hostile colonizer and the imported forms and ideas that have ended up delaying logical government, for lack of correspondence to local realities. The continent, disjointed for three centuries due to an authority that denied man the right to exercise his reason, instituted a government with reason as its foundation, disregarding and ignoring the ignorant people that had contributed to its redemption. Everyone's reason, not the academic reason of one over the rustic reason of others, should have been the decisive factor in what concerned everyone. The problem of independence was not the change of forms, but the change of spirit.

It was necessary to make common cause with the oppressed in order to secure the system opposed to the authoritarian interests and habits of the oppressors. The tiger, fearing the explosion, returns at night to the prey's dwelling. He dies with flames dancing in his eyes and his claws drawn. No one hears him come, for he walks on velvet paws. When the prey wakes up, the tiger is upon him. The colony continued living in the republic; and our America is saving itself from its great errors—from the pride of the capital cities, from the blind triumph of scorned peasants, from the excessive importation of foreign ideas and formulas, from the cruel and impolitic scorn for the indigenous race—by the superior virtue (prepared necessarily with blood) of the republic that fights against the colony. The tiger waits behind every tree, crouching in every corner. He will die with claws drawn and flames dancing in his eyes.

But "these countries will be saved," as the Argentine Rivadavia announced, the one who sinned by living in luxury in hard times; a silk sheath doesn't go well with a machete, nor can the spear be cast aside in a country that owes its victory to the spear, because it becomes angry and stands in the door of Iturbide's Congress urging that "the fair-haired one be made emperor." These countries will be saved because—with the genius of moderation that seems to be prevailing, by the peaceful harmony of Nature, in the continent of light, and by the influx of critical literature that has taken place in Europe instead of the speculative and esoteric literature in which the previous generation was steeped—the real man is being born to America in these real times.

We were a sight to see, with an athlete's chest, a dandy's hands, and a child's forehead. We wore a disguise: English trousers, Parisian vests, North American short coat, and Spanish hat. The Indian looked in silence upon this strange ensemble and went to the mountains to baptize his children. The black man, looking on, sang into the night the music of his heart, lonely and strange, among the waves and wild beasts. The man of the country—the creator—rose up, blind with indignation, against the scornful city, against his creature. We wore epaulets and togas, in countries that came to the world with rope sandals and headbands. The genius would have been in uniting, with the charity of heart and the daring of our founders, the headband and the toga; in freeing the Indian; in making a place for the fit black man; in fitting freedom to the body of those who rose up and conquered in her name. What remained to us were the judge, the general, the intellectual, and the prebendary. Angelic youth, like the arms of an octopus, threw up its head, crowned with clouds, to Heaven, only to fall with sterile glory. The natural nation, impelled by instinct and blinded by its triumph, overturned the golden staffs. Neither the European nor the Yankee book could solve the Hispanic-American enigma. Hatred was tried, and each year the countries declined. Weary of fruitless hatred, of the resistance of the book against the spear, of reason against religious teaching, of the city against the country, of the impossible rule of divided urban castes over the natural nation, at once tempestuous or lifeless, we begin, nigh unwittingly, to try love. Peoples stand up and greet each other. "What are we like?" they ask; and they tell each other what they are like. When a problem arises in Cojímar, they don't go to Dantzig to find the solution. Frock coats still come from France, but thought is beginning to be American. The young people of America roll their sleeves up to the elbow, sink their hands in the dough, and leaven it with their own sweat. They understand that they imitate too much, and that salvation is in creating. Create is the password of this generation. Our wine, made from plantains: even if it comes out sour, it is our wine! We understand that a country's forms of government must be fitted to the country's natural elements; that absolute ideas, to avoid failing due to an error of form, must be put into relative forms; that freedom, in order to be viable, must be sincere and full; that if the republic doesn't open its arms to all and move forward with all, it dies. The tiger, whether from within or without, enters through the crevice. The general does not let the cavalry march beyond the infantry, for if he leaves the infantry behind, the enemy surrounds the cavalry. Strategy is politics. Nations must be always critical of themselves because this is a sign of health, but they must do so with one heart and one mind. Oh, to descend to the unfortunate and raise them up in our arms! To thaw frozen America with the fire of the heart! To let the natural blood of the country flow racing and pulsing through her veins! On foot, with the happy eyes of workers, new American men of one nation greet those of another. Natural statesmen arise from direct study of Nature. They read in order to apply, but not to copy. Economists study problems at their root. The orators become more serious. Playwrights bring native characters to the scene. Academies discuss viable topics. Poetry sheds its affectation and hangs its red vest on the glorious tree. Prose, with vitality and discernment, is laden with ideas. Governors in the Indian republics learn Indian.

America is being saved from all her dangers. The octopus slumbers over some republics. Others, by the law of equilibrium, rush on foot right into the sea, to recover, with mad and sublime haste, the lost centuries. Others, forgetting that Juárez rode in a coach drawn by a mule, make a soap bubble the driver of their coach drawn by the wind; poisonous luxury, the enemy of freedom, corrupts the frivolous man and opens the door to the foreigner. Others solidify their vigorous character with the epic spirit of threatened independence. Others, in savage wars against their neighbor, rear the very soldiers that can devour them. But another danger, perhaps, threatens our America, coming not from within, but from the difference of origins, methods, and interests between the two parts of the continent. The hour is near when an enterprising and thriving people will come and demand intimate relations with America, not knowing but scorning her. And just as powerful nations—that have established themselves with the shotgun and the law—love (and only love) powerful nations; just as the time of excess and ambition, from which North America may possibly be freed by the predominance of the purest of its blood, or into which her vengeful and sordid masses, the tradition of conquest, and the selfishness of a clever leader could propel her, is not so close even to the eyes of the most fearful that there is no time to reveal the resolute and equable pride that could challenge her and lead her astray. Just as her republican decorum puts before North America, within view of the watchful towns of the Universe, an obstacle that will not be removed either by the childish provocation, the ostentatious arrogance, or the murderous discord of our America, the urgent duty of our America is to teach herself what she is, one in soul and intent, rapid conqueror of a suffocating past, stained only with the blood of hands struggling through the ruins and that of veins pierced by our masters. Our America's greatest danger is the scorn of her formidable neighbor that doesn't know her; and it is urgent that this neighbor get to know her, and soon, that he may not scorn her, for the day of the visit is near. Out of ignorance he would perhaps direct his greed against her. Out of respect, after he gets to know her, he would take his hands off her. One must have faith in the best of man and distrust the worst in him. It is necessary to give occasion to the best so that it be revealed and prevail over the worst. If not, the worst prevails. The nations should have a pillory for whoever pressures them to useless hatreds, and another for whoever doesn't tell them the truth on time.

There is no hatred of races, because there are no races. The weak thinkers, the merely abstract thinkers, only shuffle briefly through studies of races. Nature's justice does not reveal these races (the fair traveler and the polite observer seek them there to no avail) but displays the universal identity of man in its victorious love and turbulent appetite. The soul emanates, equal and eternal, from bodies diverse in shape and color. He that foments and propagates opposition and racial hatred sins against Humanity. But in the medley of peoples in proximity with other diverse peoples, there is a gathering of peculiar and active characters, of ideas and habits, of expansion and acquisition, of vanity and of greed, that could, in a period of internal disorder or of the decline of the accumulated character of the country, morph from the latent state of national worries into a grave threat for neighboring lands, isolated and weak, that the strong country pronounces perishable and inferior. To think is to serve. No one need suppose, out of boorish antipathy, that the fair-haired people of the continent possess an innate and terrible evil because they don't speak our language or see the home as we see it or resemble us politically; one does not highly value the bilious and mulatto men, nor look charitably from his eminence (though it hardly be secure) upon those who with less of History's favor walk the way of the republics by heroic strides; neither need anyone hide the patent facts of the problem that can be solved—for a peace lasting centuries— with timely study and the tacit and urgent union of the continental soul. For the unanimous hymn is already sounding; the present generation carries the weight of hardworking America on the path blazed by the sublime fathers. From the Rio Grande to the Magellan Strait, seated on the backbone of the Condor mountain, the Great Spirit watered the seed of New America resting in the romantic nations of the continent and the afflicted islands of the sea!

5–4
Nat Love (1854–1921)

An ex-slave who became a rodeo performer, a porter, and an autobiographer, NAT LOVE (1854–1921) was one of the great African American cowboys of Texas. After the end of the Civil War, Love left Tennessee to drive cattle and horses over Texas and the West—as far north as the Dakotas. Later in life, he bragged of his exploits, calling himself "Deadwood Dick," and in the days of the dime novel, a genre akin to an airport adventure novel, Love decided to pen his story. The following two chapters from his autobiography (1907) speak to his ability as a wonderful chronicler of the life of the Texas cowboy in the 1870s before fences, trains, and roads curtailed the cattle drive.

≈ ≈ ≈

From *The Life and Adventures of Nat Love* (1907)

Chapter 6. The World Is before Me. I Join the Texas Cowboys. Red River Dick. My First Outfit. My First Indian Fight. I Learn to Use My Gun.

It was on the tenth day of February, 1869, that I left the old home, near Nashville, Tennessee. I was at that time about fifteen years old, and though while young in years the hard work and farm life had made me strong and hearty, much beyond my years, and I had full confidence in myself as being able to take care of myself and making my way.

I at once struck out for Kansas of which I had heard something. And believing it was a good place in which to seek employment. It was in the west, and it was the great west I wanted to see, and so by walking and occasional lifts from farmers going my way and taking advantage of every thing that promised to assist me on my way, I eventually brought up at Dodge City, Kansas, which at that time was a typical frontier city, with a great many saloons, dance halls, and gambling houses, and very little of anything else. When I arrived the town was full of cow boys from the surrounding ranches, and from Texas and other parts of the west. As Kansas was a great cattle center and market, the wild cow boy, prancing horses of which I was very fond, and the wild life generally, all had their attractions for me, and I decided to try for a place with them. Although it seemed to me I had met with a bad outfit, at least some of them, going around among them I watched my chances to get to speak with them, as I wanted to find some one whom I thought would give me a civil answer to the questions I wanted to ask, but they all seemed too wild around town, so the next day I went out where they were in camp.

Approaching a party who were eating their breakfast, I got to speak with them. They asked me to have some breakfast with them, which invitation I gladly accepted. During the meal I got a chance to ask them many questions. They proved to be a Texas outfit, who had just come up with a herd of cattle and having delivered them they were preparing to return. There were several colored cow boys among them, and good ones too. After breakfast I asked the camp boss for a job as cow boy. He asked me if I could ride a wild horse. I said "yes sir." He said if you can I will give you a job. So he spoke to one of the colored cow boys called Bronko Jim, and told him to go out and rope old Good Eye, saddle him and put me on his back. Bronko Jim gave me a few pointers and told me to look out for the horse was especially bad on pitching. I told Jim I was a good rider and not afraid of him. I thought I had rode pitching horses before, but from the time I mounted old Good Eye I knew I had not learned what pitching was. This proved the worst horse to ride I had ever mounted in my life, but I stayed with him and the cow boys were the most surprised outfit you ever saw, as they had taken me for a tenderfoot, pure and simple. After the horse got tired and I dismounted the boss said he would give me a job and pay me $30.00 per month and more later on. He asked what my name was and I answered Nat Love, he said to the boys we will call him Red River Dick. I went by this name for a long time.

The boss took me to the city and got my outfit, which consisted of a new saddle, bridle and spurs, chaps, a pair of blankets and a fine 45 Colt revolver. Now that the business which brought them to Dodge City was concluded, preparations were made to start out for the Pan Handle country in Texas to the home ranch. The outfit of which I was now a member was called the Duval outfit, and their brand was known as the Pig Pen brand. I worked with this outfit for over three years. On this trip there were only about fifteen of us riders, all excepting myself were hardy, experienced men, always ready for anything that might turn up, but they were as jolly a set of fellows as one could find in a long journey. There now being nothing to keep us longer in Dodge City, we prepared for the return journey, and left the next day over the old

Dodge and Sun City lonesome trail, on a journey which was to prove the most eventful of my life up to now.

A few miles out we encountered some of the hardest hailstorms I ever saw, causing discomfort to man and beast, but I had no notion of getting discouraged but I resolved to be always ready for any call that might be made on me, of whatever nature it might be, and those with whom I have lived and worked will tell you I have kept that resolve. Not far from Dodge City on our way home we encountered a band of the old Victoria tribe of Indians and had a sharp fight.

These Indians were nearly always harrassing travelers and traders and the stock men of that part of the country, and were very troublesome. In this band we encountered there were about a hundred painted bucks all well mounted. When we saw the Indians they were coming after us yelling like demons. As we were not expecting Indians at this particular time, we were taken somewhat by surprise.

We only had fifteen men in our outfit, but nothing daunted we stood our ground and fought the Indians to a stand. One of the boys was shot off his horse and killed near me. The Indians got his horse, bridle and saddle. During this fight we lost all but six of our horses, our entire packing outfit and our extra saddle horses, which the Indians stampeded, then rounded them up after the fight and drove them off. And as we only had six horses left us, we were unable to follow them, although we had the satisfaction of knowing we had made several good Indians out of bad ones.

This was my first Indian fight and likewise the first Indians I had ever seen. When I saw them coming after us and heard their blood curdling yell, I lost all courage and thought my time had come to die. I was too badly scared to run, some of the boys told me to use my gun and shoot for all I was worth. Now I had just got my outfit and had never shot off a gun in my life, but their words brought me back to earth and seeing they were all using their guns in a way that showed they were used to it, I unlimbered my artillery and after the first shot I lost all fear and fought like a veteran.

We soon routed the Indians and they left, taking with them nearly all we had, and we were powerless to pursue them. We were compelled to finish our journey home almost on foot, as there were only six horses left to fourteen of us. Our friend and companion who was shot in the fight, we buried on the plains, wrapped in his blanket with stones piled over his grave. After this engagement with the Indians I seemed to lose all sense as to what fear was and thereafter during my whole life on the range I never experienced the least feeling of fear, no matter how trying the ordeal or how desperate my position.

The home ranch was located on the Palo Duro river in the western part of the Pan Handle, Texas, which we reached in the latter part of May, it taking us considerably over a month to make the return journey home from Dodge City. I remained in the employ of the Duval outfit for three years, making regular trips to Dodge City every season and to many other places in the surrounding states with herds of horses and cattle for market and to be delivered to other ranch owners all over Texas, Wyoming and the Dakotas. By strict attention to business, born of a genuine love of the free and wild life of the range, and absolute fearlessness, I became known throughout the country as a good all around cow boy and a splendid hand in a stampede.

After returning from one of our trips north with a bunch of cattle in the fall of 1872, I received and accepted a better position with the Pete Gallinger company, whose immense range was located on the Gila River in southern Arizona. So after drawing the balance of my pay from the Duval company and bidding good bye to the true and tried companions of the past three years, who had learned me the business and been with me in many a trying situation, it was with genuine regret that I left them for my new position, one that meant more to me in pay and experience. I stayed with Pete Gallinger company for several years and soon became one of their most trusted men, taking an important part in all the big round-ups and cuttings throughout western Texas, Arizona and other states where the company had interests to be looked after, sometimes riding eighty miles a day for days at a time over the trails of Texas and the surrounding country and naturally I soon became well known among the cowboys, rangers, scouts and guides it was my pleasure to meet in my wanderings over the country, in the wake of immense herds of the long horned Texas cattle and large bands of range horses. Many of these men who were my companions on the trail and in camp, have since become famous in story and history, and a braver, truer set of men never lived than these wild sons of the plains whose home was in the saddle and their couch, mother earth, with the sky for a covering. They were always ready to share their blanket and their last ration with a less fortunate fellow companion and always assisted each other in the many trying situations that were continually coming up in a cowboy's life.

When we were not on the trail taking large herds of cattle or horses to market or to be delivered to other ranches we were engaged in range riding, moving large numbers of cattle from one grazing range to another, keeping them together, and hunting up strays which, despite the most earnest efforts of the range riders would get away from the main herd and wander for miles over the plains before they could be found, overtaken and returned to the main herd.

Then the Indians and the white outlaws who infested the country gave us no end of trouble, as they lost no opportunity to cut out and run off the choicest part of a herd of long horns, or the best of a band of horses, causing the cowboys a ride of many a long mile over the dusty plains in pursuit, and many are the fierce engagements we had, when after a long chase of perhaps hundreds of miles over the ranges we overtook the thieves. It then became a case of "to the victor belongs the spoils," as there was no law respected in this wild country, except the law of might and the persuasive qualities of the 45 Colt pistol.

Accordingly it became absolutely necessary for a cowboy to understand his gun and know how to place its contents where it would do the most good, therefore I in common with my other companions never lost an opportunity to practice with my 45 Colts and the opportunities were not lacking by any means and so in time I became fairly proficient and able in most cases to hit a barn door providing the door was not too far away, and was steadily improving in this as I was in experience and knowledge of the other branches of the business which I had chosen as my life's work and which I had begun to like so well, because while the life was hard and in some ways exacting, yet it was free and wild and contained the elements of danger which my nature craved and which began to manifest itself when I was a pugnacious youngster on the old plantation in our rock battles and the breaking of the wild horses. I gloried in the danger, and the wild and free life of the plains, the new country I was continually traversing, and the many new scenes and incidents continually arising in the life of a rough rider.

Chapter 7. I Learn to Speak Spanish and Am Made Chief Brand Reader. The Big Round-ups. Riding the 7-Y-L Steer. Long Rides. Hunting Strays.

Having now fairly begun my life as a cowboy, I was fast learning the many ins and outs of the business, while my many roamings over the range country gave me a knowledge of it not possessed by many at that time. Being of a naturally observant disposition, I noticed many things to which others attached no significance. This quality of observance proved of incalculable benefit to me in many ways during my life as a range rider in the western country. My employment with the Pete Gallinger company took me all over the Pan Handle country, Texas, Arizona, and New Mexico with herds of horses and cattle for market and to be delivered to other ranch owners and large cattle breeders. Naturally I became very well acquainted with all the many different trails and grazing ranges located in the stretch of country between the north of Montana and the Gulf of Mexico, and between the Missouri state line and the Pacific

ocean. This whole territory I have covered many times in the saddle, sometimes at the rate of eighty or one hundred miles a day. These long rides and
much traveling over the country were of great benefit to me, as it enabled me
to meet so many different people connected with the cattle business and also
to learn the different trails and the lay of the country generally.

Among the other things that I picked up on my wanderings, was a knowledge of the Spanish language, which I learned to speak like a native. I also became very well acquainted with the many different brands scattered over this
stretch of country, consequently it was not long before the cattle men began
to recognize my worth and the Gallinger company made me their chief brand
reader, which duties I performed for several years with honor to myself and
satisfaction to my employers. In the cattle country, all the large cattle raisers
had their squad of brand readers whose duty it was to attend all the big round-
ups and cuttings throughout the country, and to pick out their own brands and
to see that the different brands were not altered or counterfeited. They also had
to look to the branding of the young stock.

During the big round-ups it was our duty to pick out our brand, and then
send them home under the charge of our cowboys, likewise the newly branded
stock. After each brand was cut out and started homeward, we had to stay with
the round up to see that strays from the different herds from the surrounding country did not again get mixed up, until the different home ranges were
reached. This work employed a large number of cowboys, who lived, ate and
often slept in the saddle, as they covered many hundreds of miles in a very
short space of time. This was made possible as every large cattleman had relays
of horses sent out over the country where we might be expected to touch, and
so we could always count on finding a fresh horse awaiting us at the end of
a twenty-five or a fifty mile ride. But for us brand readers there was no rest,
we merely changed our saddles and outfit to a fresh horse and were again on
the go. After the general round up was over, cowboy sports and a good time
generally was in order for those engaged in it. The interest of nearly all of us
centered in the riding of what was known as the 7 Y-L steer. A big long horn
wild steer, generally the worst in the herd, was cut out and turned loose on the
open prairie. The cow boy who could rope and ride him would get the steer
as his reward, and let me assure you dear reader, that it was not so easy as it
sounds, as the steer separated from its fellows would become extremely ferocious and wild, and the man who attempted to rope and ride him would be in
momentary danger of losing his life, if he relaxed in the least his vigilance and
caution, because a wild steer is naturally ferocious. Even in cutting them out of
the round up I have known them to get mad and attack the cowboys who only
saved themselves by the quickness of their horses, or the friendly intervention

of a comrade who happened to be near to rope the maddened long horn, and thus divert his attention to other things. But in the case of the 7 Y-L steer such intervention is against the rules, and the cowboy who attempts to rope and ride the steer must at all times look out for himself. I have seen two horses and their riders gored to death in this sport, and I have had to shoot more than one steer to save myself and horse after my horse had fallen with me and placed himself as well as me at the maddened beast's mercy. At such times it takes a cool head and a steady hand as no random shot will stop a wild steer. The bullet must be placed in a certain spot, the center of the forehead, to accomplish its mission. The last time I had a horse fall with me in roping the 7 Y-L steer, he fell as the steer was but a few feet away, falling in such a way that my leg caught under the saddle, holding me fast. Quick as I could I gave the steer a bullet in the head and he stumbled and fell dead on top of my horse and me, so that the boys had to interfere to the extent of dragging the steer and horse off of my leg.

The cowboy who is successful in roping the steer must then mount and ride him. If he does that successfully the steer becomes his personal property to do with as he will, only a slight reward for the risking of his life and the trouble of accomplishing the feat. But it is done more for sport's sake than anything else, and the love of showing off, a weakness of all cow boys more or less. But really it takes a high class of horsemanship to ride a long horn, to get on his back and stay there as he runs, jumps, pitches side ways, backwards, forward, up and down, then over the prairie like a streak of lightning. I have had the experience and I can assure you it is no child's play. More than one 7 Y-L steer has fallen to my lot, but I had to work for it, and work hard. After all it was only part of the general routine of the cow boy's life, in which danger plays so important a part. It is seldom thought of being merely a matter of course, and none of us would have foregone the sport, had we known that sure death awaited us as the result, because above all things, the test of a cow boy's worth is his gameness and his nerve. He is not supposed to know what fear means, and I assure you there are very few who know the meaning of that word.

Most of my readers no doubt have heard of the great round ups and cuttings, connected with the cattle raiser's life. But not one in a hundred has any idea as to how an immense herd of wild cattle are handled in a big round up. My many years of experience has given me unusual knowledge on the subject, and you may bring any cattleman or boss to me, and I will guarantee to answer any question he can ask me about the cattle business. The first general round up occurs about the first of April. This round up is to run in all the near cattle belonging to each man, and head them toward our respective ranges. If we find any other brand mixed up with ours we head them toward their own range, and keep our own together. Every cow boy does the same and in this way every cattleman is enabled to get his own brand together on his own range, so that when the next general round up occurs he will have most of his near cattle together on the home range. In order to get the cattle together in the first general round up, we would have to ride for hundreds of miles over the country in search of the long horn steers and old cows that had drifted from the home range during the winter and were now scattered to the four winds of heaven. As soon as they were found they were started off under the care of cow boys for the place agreed upon for the general round up, whether they belonged to us or not, while the rest of us continued the search. All the cow boys from the many different outfits working this way enabled us to soon get all the strays rounded up in one great herd in which the cattle of a dozen different owners were mixed up together. It then became our duty to cut out our different herds and start them homewards. Then we had to brand the young stock that had escaped that ordeal at the hands of the range riders. On finding the strays and starting them homewards, we had to keep up the search, because notwithstanding the fact that we had done range riding or line riding all winter, a large number of cattle would manage to evade the vigilance of the cow boys and get away. These must all be accounted for at the great round up, as they stood for dollars and cents, profit and loss to the great cattle kings of the west. In going after these strayed and perhaps stolen cattle we boys always provided ourselves with everything we needed, including plenty of grub, as sometimes we would be gone for nearly two months and sometimes much longer. It was not an uncommon occurrence for us to have shooting trouble over our different brands. In such disputes the boys would kill each other if others did not interfere in time to prevent it, because in those days on the great cattle ranges there was no law but the law of might, and all disputes were settled with a forty-five Colt pistol. In such cases the man who was quickest on the draw and whose eye was the best, pretty generally got the decision. Therefore it was of the greatest importance that the cow boy should understand his gun, its capabilities and its shooting qualities. A cow boy would never carry anything but the very best gun obtainable, as his life depended on it often. After securing a good gun the cow boy had to learn how to use it, if he did not already know how. In doing so no trouble or expense was spared, and I know there were very few poor shots on the ranges over which we rode and they used the accomplishment to protect themselves and their employer's cattle from the Indian thiefs and the white desperadoes who infested the cattle country, and who lost no opportunity to stampede the herds and run off large numbers of them. Whenever this happened it generally resulted in a long chase and a fierce fight in which someone was sure to get hurt, and hurt badly. But that fact did not bother us in the least. It was all simply our duty and our business for which we were paid and paid good, and so we accepted things as they came, always ready for it whatever it might be, and always taking pride in our work in which we always tried to excel.

Christmas, Dec. 25, 1872, is a day in my memory which time cannot blot out. I and a number of friends were in a place called Holbrook, Ariz. A dispute started over a saddle horse with the following result. Arizona Bob drew his forty-five Colt revolver, but before he had time to fire he was instantly killed by A. Jack. Then a general fight ensued in which five horses and three men were killed.

It was a sad thing for me to see my friends dead in a corral on a Christmas morning, but I helped bury the dead and took care of the wounded. The names were A. Jack, Wild Horse Pete and Arizona Bill.

5–5
Booker T. Washington (1856–1915)

Booker T. (Taliaferro) Washington (1856–1915), from West Virginia, began life in obscurity, a slave, without a birthdate, a last name, or a father who claimed him. Washington worked from the age of nine in a variety of jobs involving hard labor—in the salt mines, the coal mines, as a janitor—but always with his mind resolute on earning an education. His determination to read and write, and later to graduate from Hampton Normal and Agricultural Institute, a school to prepare African Americans to teach—remains one of the great stories of the American work ethic, as well as a tribute to the belief that education is opportunity. His career led to his leadership at Tuskegee Institute in Alabama, a school that prepared African Americans in mechanical trade, agriculture, and teaching. In 1895, Washington delivered the Atlanta Compromise, promoting education for African Americans while deferring equal rights. A chapter from his autobiography describes his postbellum childhood.

≈≈ ≈≈ ≈≈

From *Up from Slavery* (1901)

Chapter 2. Boyhood Days

After the coming of freedom there were two points upon which practically all the people on our place were agreed, and I find that this was generally true throughout the South: that they must change their names, and that they must leave the old plantation for at least a few days or weeks in order that they might really feel sure that they were free.

In some way a feeling got among the coloured people that it was far from proper for them to bear the surname of their former owners, and a great many of them took other surnames. This was one of the first signs of freedom. When they were slaves, a coloured person was simply called "John" or "Susan." There was seldom occasion for more than the use of the one name. If "John" or "Susan" belonged to a white man by the name of "Hatcher," sometimes he was called "John Hatcher," or as often "Hatcher's John." But there was a feeling that "John Hatcher" or "Hatcher's John" was not the proper title by which to denote a freeman; and so in many cases "John Hatcher" was changed to "John S. Lincoln" or "John S. Sherman," the initial "S" standing for no name, it being simply a part of what the coloured man proudly called his "entitles."

As I have stated, most of the coloured people left the old plantation for a short while at least, so as to be sure, it seemed, that they could leave and try their freedom on to see how it felt. After they had remained away for a time, many of the older slaves, especially, returned to their old homes and made some kind of contract with their former owners by which they remained on the estate.

My mother's husband, who was the stepfather of my brother John and myself, did not belong to the same owners as did my mother. In fact, he seldom came to our plantation. I remember seeing him there perhaps once a year, that being about Christmas time. In some way, during the war, by running away and following the Federal soldiers, it seems, he found his way into the new state of West Virginia. As soon as freedom was declared, he sent for my mother to come to the Kanawha Valley, in West Virginia. At that time a journey from Virginia over the mountains to West Virginia was rather a tedious and in some cases a painful undertaking. What little clothing and few household goods we had were placed in a cart, but the children walked the greater portion of the distance, which was several hundred miles.

I do not think any of us ever had been very far from the plantation, and the taking of a long journey into another state was quite an event. The parting from our former owners and the members of our own race on the plantation was a serious occasion. From the time of our parting till their death we kept up a correspondence with the older members of the family, and in later years we have kept in touch with those who were the younger members. We were several weeks making the trip, and most of the time we slept in the open air and did our cooking over a log fire out-of-doors. One night I recall that we camped near an abandoned log cabin, and my mother decided to build a fire in that for cooking, and afterward to make a "pallet" on the floor for our sleeping. Just as the fire had gotten well started a large black snake fully a yard and a half long dropped down the chimney and ran out on the floor. Of course we at once abandoned that cabin. Finally we reached our destination—a little town called Malden, which is about five miles from Charleston, the present capital of the state.

At that time salt-mining was the great industry in that part of West Virginia, and the little town of Malden was right in the midst of the salt-furnaces. My stepfather had already secured a job at a salt-furnace, and he had also secured a little cabin for us to live in. Our new house was no better than the one we had left on the old plantation in Virginia. In fact, in one respect it was worse. Notwithstanding the poor condition of our plantation cabin, we were at all times sure of pure air. Our new home was in the midst of a cluster of cabins crowded closely together, and as there were no sanitary regulations, the filth about the cabins was often intolerable. Some of our neighbours were coloured people, and some were the poorest and most ignorant and degraded white people. It was a motley mixture. Drinking, gambling, quarrels, fights, and shockingly immoral practices were frequent. All who lived in the little town were in one way or another connected with the salt business. Though I was a mere child, my stepfather put me and my brother at work in one of the furnaces. Often I began work as early as four o'clock in the morning.

The first thing I ever learned in the way of book knowledge was while working in this salt-furnace. Each salt-packer had his barrels marked with a certain number. The number allotted to my stepfather was "18." At the close of the day's work the boss of the packers would come around and put "18" on each of our barrels, and I soon learned to recognize that figure wherever I saw it, and after a while got to the point where I could make that figure, though I knew nothing about any other figures or letters.

From the time that I can remember having any thoughts about anything, I recall that I had an intense longing to learn to read. I determined, when quite a small child, that, if I accomplished nothing else in life, I would in some way get enough education to enable me to read common books and newspapers. Soon after we got settled in some manner in our new cabin in West Virginia, I induced my mother to get hold of a book for me. How or where she got it I do not know, but in some way she procured an old copy of Webster's "blue-back" spelling-book, which contained the alphabet, followed by such meaningless words as "ab," "ba," "ca," "da." I began at once to devour this book, and I think that it was the first one I ever had in my hands. I had learned from somebody that the way to begin to read was to learn the alphabet, so I tried in all the ways I could think of to learn it,—all of course without a teacher, for I could find no one to teach me. At that time there was not a single member of my race anywhere near us who could read, and I was too timid to approach any of the white people. In some way, within a few weeks, I mastered the greater portion of the alphabet. In all my efforts to learn to read my mother shared fully my ambition, and sympathized with me and aided me in every way that she could. Though she was totally ignorant, so far as mere book knowledge was concerned, she had high ambitions for her children, and a large fund of good, hard, common sense which seemed to enable her to meet and master every situation. If I have done anything in life worth attention, I feel sure that I inherited the disposition from my mother.

In the midst of my struggles and longing for an education, a young coloured boy who had learned to read in the state of Ohio came to Malden. As soon as the coloured people found out that he could read, a newspaper was secured, and at the close of nearly every day's work this young man would be surrounded by a group of men and women who were anxious to hear him read the news contained in the papers. How I used to envy this man! He seemed to me to be the one young man in all the world who ought to be satisfied with his attainments.

About this time the question of having some kind of a school opened for the coloured children in the village began to be discussed by members of the race. As it would be the first school for Negro children that had ever been opened in that part of Virginia, it was, of course, to be a great event, and the discussion excited the widest interest. The most perplexing question was where to find a teacher. The young man from Ohio who had learned to read the papers was considered, but his age was against him. In the midst of the discussion about a teacher, another young coloured man from Ohio, who had been a soldier, in some way found his way into town. It was soon learned that he possessed considerable education, and he was engaged by the coloured people to teach their first school. As yet no free schools had been started for coloured people in that section, hence each family agreed to pay a certain amount per month, with the understanding that the teacher was to "board 'round"—that is, spend a day with each family. This was not bad for the teacher, for each family tried to provide the very best on the day the teacher was to be its guest. I recall that I looked forward with an anxious appetite to the "teacher's day" at our little cabin.

This experience of a whole race beginning to go to school for the first time, presents one of the most interesting studies that has ever occurred in connection with the development of any race. Few people who were not right in the midst of the scenes can form any exact idea of the intense desire which the people of my race showed for an education. As I have stated, it was a whole race trying to go to school. Few were too young, and none too old, to make the attempt to learn. As fast as any kind of teachers could be secured, not only were day-schools filled, but night-schools as well. The great ambition of the older people was to try to learn to read the Bible before they died. With this end in view, men and women who were fifty or seventy-five years old would often be found in the night-school. Sunday-schools were formed soon after freedom, but the principal book studied in the Sunday-school was the spelling-book. Day-school, night-school, Sunday-school, were always crowded, and often many had to be turned away for want of room.

The opening of the school in the Kanawha Valley, however, brought to me one of the keenest disappointments that I ever experienced. I had been working in a salt-furnace for several months, and my stepfather had discovered that I had a financial value, and so, when the school opened, he decided that he could not spare me from my work. This decision seemed to cloud my every ambition. The disappointment was made all the more severe by reason of the fact that my place of work was where I could see the happy children passing to and from school, mornings and afternoons. Despite this disappointment, however, I determined that I would learn something, anyway. I applied myself with greater earnestness than ever to the mastering of what was in the "blue-back" speller.

My mother sympathized with me in my disappointment, and sought to comfort me in all the ways she could, and to help me find a way to learn. After a while I succeeded in making arrangements with the teacher to give me some lessons at night, after the day's work was done. These night lessons were so welcome that I think I learned more at night than the other children did during the day. My own experiences in the night-school gave me faith in the night-school idea, with which, in after years, I had to do both at Hampton and Tuskegee. But my boyish heart was still set upon going to the day-school, and I let no opportunity slip to push my case. Finally I won, and was permitted to go to the school in the day for a few months, with the understanding that I was to rise early in the morning and work in the furnace till nine o'clock, and return immediately after school closed in the afternoon for at least two more hours of work.

The schoolhouse was some distance from the furnace, and as I had to work till nine o'clock, and the school opened at nine, I found myself in a difficulty. School would always be begun before I reached it, and sometimes my class had recited. To get around this difficulty I yielded to a temptation for which most people, I suppose, will condemn me; but since it is a fact, I might as well state it. I have great faith in the power and influence of facts. It is seldom that anything is permanently gained by holding back a fact. There was a large clock in a little office in the furnace. This clock, of course, all the hundred or more workmen depended upon to regulate their hours of beginning and ending the day's work. I got the idea that the way for me to reach school on time was to move the clock hands from half-past eight up to the nine o'clock mark. This I found myself doing morning after morning, till the furnace "boss" discovered that something was wrong, and locked the clock in a case. I did not mean to inconvenience anybody. I simply meant to reach that schoolhouse in time.

When, however, I found myself at the school for the first time, I also found myself confronted with two other difficulties. In the first place, I found that all of the other children wore hats or caps on their heads, and I had neither hat nor cap. In fact, I do not remember that up to the time of going to school I had ever worn any kind of covering upon my head, nor do I recall that either I or anybody else had even thought anything about the need of covering for my head. But, of course, when I saw how all the other boys were dressed, I began to feel quite uncomfortable. As usual, I put the case before my mother, and she explained to me that she had no money with which to buy a "store hat," which was a rather new institution at that time among the members of my race and was considered quite the thing for young and old to own, but that she would find a way to help me out of the difficulty. She accordingly got two pieces of "homespun" (jeans) and sewed them together, and I was soon the proud possessor of my first cap.

The lesson that my mother taught me in this has always remained with me, and I have tried as best I could to teach it to others. I have always felt proud, whenever I think of the incident, that my mother had strength of character enough not to be led into the temptation of seeming to be that which she was not—of trying to impress my schoolmates and others with the fact that she was able to buy me a "store hat" when she was not. I have always felt proud that she refused to go into debt for that which she did not have the money to pay for. Since that time I have owned many kinds of caps and hats, but never one of which I have felt so proud as of the cap made of the two pieces of cloth sewed together by my mother. I have noted the fact, but without satisfaction, I need not add, that several of the boys who began their careers with "store hats" and who were my schoolmates and used to join in the sport that was made of me because I had only a "homespun" cap, have ended their careers in the penitentiary, while others are not able now to buy any kind of hat.

My second difficulty was with regard to my name, or rather *a* name. From the time when I could remember anything, I had been called simply "Booker." Before going to school it had never occurred to me that it was needful or appropriate to have an additional name. When I heard the school-roll called, I noticed that all of the children had at least two names, and some of them indulged in what seemed to me the extravagance of having three. I was in deep perplexity, because I knew that the teacher would demand of me at least two names, and I had only one. By the time the occasion came for the enrolling of my name, an idea occurred to me which I thought would make me equal to the situation; and so, when the teacher asked me what my full name was, I calmly told him "Booker Washington," as if I had been called by that name all my life; and by that name I have since been known. Later in my life I found that my mother had given me the name of "Booker Taliaferro" soon after I was born, but in some way that part of my name seemed to disappear and for a long while was forgotten, but as soon as I found out about it I revived it, and made my full name "Booker Taliaferro Washington." I think there are not many men in our country who have had the privilege of naming themselves in the way that I have.

More than once I have tried to picture myself in the position of a boy or man with an honoured and distinguished ancestry which I could trace back through a period of hundreds of years, and who had not only inherited a name, but fortune and a proud family homestead; and yet I have sometimes had the feeling that if I had inherited these, and had been a member of a more popular race, I should have been inclined to yield to the temptation of depending upon my ancestry and my colour to do that for me which I should do for myself. Years ago I resolved that because I had no ancestry myself I would leave a record of which my children would be proud, and which might encourage them to still higher effort.

The world should not pass judgment upon the Negro, and especially the Negro youth, too quickly or too harshly. The Negro boy has obstacles, discouragements, and temptations to battle with that are little known to those not situated as he is. When a white boy undertakes a task, it is taken for granted that he will succeed. On the other hand, people are usually surprised if the Negro boy does not fail. In a word, the Negro youth starts out with the presumption against him.

The influence of ancestry, however, is important in helping forward any individual or race, if too much reliance is not placed upon it. Those who constantly direct attention to the Negro youth's moral weaknesses, and compare his advancement with that of white youths, do not consider the influence of the memories which cling about the old family homesteads. I have no idea, as I have stated elsewhere, who my grandmother was. I have, or have had, uncles and aunts and cousins, but I have no knowledge as to where most of them are.

My case will illustrate that of hundreds of thousands of black people in every part of our country. The very fact that the white boy is conscious that, if he fails in life, he will disgrace the whole family record, extending back through many generations, is of tremendous value in helping him to resist temptations. The fact that the individual has behind and surrounding him proud family history and connection serves as a stimulus to help him to overcome obstacles when striving for success.

The time that I was permitted to attend school during the day was short, and my attendance was irregular. It was not long before I had to stop attending day-school altogether, and devote all of my time again to work. I resorted to the night-school again. In fact, the greater part of the education I secured in my boyhood was gathered through the night-school after my day's work was done. I had difficulty often in securing a satisfactory teacher. Sometimes, after I had secured some one to teach me at night, I would find, much to my disappointment, that the teacher knew but little more than I did. Often I would have to walk several miles at night in order to recite my night-school lessons. There was never a time in my youth, no matter how dark and discouraging the days might be, when one resolve did not continually remain with me, and that was a determination to secure an education at any cost.

Soon after we moved to West Virginia, my mother adopted into our family, notwithstanding our poverty, an orphan boy, to whom afterward we gave the name of James B. Washington. He has ever since remained a member of the family.

After I had worked in the salt-furnace for some time, work was secured for me in a coal-mine which was operated mainly for the purpose of securing fuel for the salt-furnace. Work in the coal-mine I always dreaded. One reason for this was that any one who worked in a coal-mine was always unclean, at least while at work, and it was a very hard job to get one's skin clean after the day's work was over. Then it was fully a mile from the opening of the coal-mine to the face of the coal, and all, of course, was in the blackest darkness. I do not believe that one ever experiences anywhere else such darkness as he does in a coal-mine. The mine was divided into a large number of different "rooms" or departments, and, as I never was able to learn the location of all these "rooms," I many times found myself lost in the mine. To add to the horror of being lost, sometimes my light would go out, and then, if I did not happen to have a match, I would wander about in the darkness until by chance I found some one to give me a light. The work was not only hard, but it was dangerous. There was always the danger of being blown to pieces by a premature explosion of powder, or of being crushed by falling slate. Accidents from one or the other of these causes were frequently occurring, and this kept me in constant fear. Many children of the tenderest years were compelled then, as is now true, I fear, in most coal-mining districts, to spend a large part of their lives in these coal-mines, with little opportunity to get an education; and, what is worse, I have often noted that, as a rule, young boys who begin life in a coal-mine are often physically and mentally dwarfed. They soon lose ambition to do anything else than to continue as a coal-miner.

In those days, and later as a young man, I used to try to picture in my imagination the feelings and ambitions of a white boy with absolutely no limit placed upon his aspirations and activities. I used to envy the white boy who had no obstacles placed in the way of his becoming a Congressman, Governor, Bishop, or President by reason of the accident of his birth or race. I used to picture the way that I would act under such circumstances; how I would begin at the bottom and keep rising until I reached the highest round of success.

In later years, I confess that I do not envy the white boy as I once did. I have learned that success is to be measured not so much by the position that one has reached in life as by the obstacles which he has overcome while trying to succeed. Looked at from this standpoint, I almost reach the conclusion that often the Negro boy's birth and connection with an unpopular race is an advantage, so far as real life is concerned. With few exceptions, the Negro youth must work harder and must perform his tasks even better than a white youth in order to secure recognition. But out of the hard and unusual struggle through which he is compelled to pass, he gets a strength, a confidence, that one misses whose pathway is comparatively smooth by reason of birth and race.

From any point of view, I had rather be what I am, a member of the Negro race, than be able to claim membership with the most favoured of any other race. I have always been made sad when I have heard members of any race claiming rights and privileges, or certain badges of distinction, on the ground simply that they were members of this or that race, regardless of their own individual worth or attainments. I have been made to feel sad for such persons because I am conscious of the fact that mere connection with what is known as a superior race will not permanently carry an individual forward unless he has individual worth, and mere connection with what is regarded as an inferior race will not finally hold an individual back if he possesses intrinsic, individual merit. Every persecuted individual and race should get much consolation out of the great human law, which is universal and eternal, that merit, no matter under what skin found, is, in the long run, recognized and rewarded. This I have said here, not to call attention to myself as an individual, but to the race to which I am proud to belong.

Chapter 14. The Atlanta Exposition Address

The Atlanta Exposition* at which I had been asked to make an address as a representative of the Negro race . . . was opened with a short address from Governor Bullock. . . . Governor Bullock introduced me with the words, "We have with us to-day a representative of Negro enterprise and Negro civilization."

When I arose to speak, there was considerable cheering, especially from the coloured people. As I remember it now, the thing that was uppermost in my mind was the desire to say something that would cement the friendship of the races and bring about hearty coöperation between them. So far as my outward surroundings were concerned, the only thing that I recall distinctly now is that when I got up, I saw thousands of eyes looking intently into my face. The following is the address which I delivered:—

> Mr. President and Gentlemen of the Board of Directors and Citizens,
>
> One-third of the population of the South is of the Negro race. No enterprise seeking the material, civil, or moral welfare of this section can disregard this element of our population and reach the highest success. I but convey to you, Mr. President and Directors, the sentiment of the masses of my race when I say that in no way have the value and manhood of the American Negro been more fittingly and generously recognized than by the managers of this magnificent Exposition at every stage of its progress. It is a recognition that will do more to cement the friendship of the two races than any occurrence since the dawn of our freedom.
>
> Not only this, but the opportunity here afforded will awaken among us a new era of industrial progress. Ignorant and inexperienced, it is not strange that in the first years of our new life we began at the top instead of at the bottom; that a seat in Congress or the state legislature was more sought than real estate or industrial skill; that the political convention or stump speaking had more attractions than starting a dairy farm or truck garden.
>
> A ship lost at sea for many days suddenly sighted a friendly vessel. From the mast of the unfortunate vessel was seen a signal, "Water, water; we die of thirst!" The answer from the friendly vessel at once came back, "Cast down your bucket where you are." A second time the signal, "Water, water; send us water!" ran up from the distressed vessel, and was answered, "Cast down your bucket where you are." And a third and fourth signal for water was answered, "Cast down your bucket where you are." The captain of the distressed vessel, at last heeding the injunction, cast down his bucket, and it came up full of fresh, sparkling water from the mouth of the Amazon River. To those of my race who depend on bettering their condition in a

* [1895—E.J.D. and J.B.F.]

foreign land or who underestimate the importance of cultivating friendly relations with the Southern white man, who is their next-door neighbor, I would say: "Cast down your bucket where you are"—cast it down in making friends in every manly way of the people of all races by whom we are surrounded.

Cast it down in agriculture, mechanics, in commerce, in domestic service, and in the professions. And in this connection it is well to bear in mind that whatever other sins the South may be called to bear, when it comes to business, pure and simple, it is in the South that the Negro is given a man's chance in the commercial world, and in nothing is this Exposition more eloquent than in emphasizing this chance. Our greatest danger is that in the great leap from slavery to freedom we may overlook the fact that the masses of us are to live by the productions of our hands, and fail to keep in mind that we shall prosper in proportion as we learn to dignify and glorify common labour and put brains and skill into the common occupations of life; shall prosper in proportion as we learn to draw the line between the superficial and the substantial, the ornamental gewgaws of life and the useful. No race can prosper till it learns that there is as much dignity in tilling a field as in writing a poem. It is at the bottom of life we must begin, and not at the top. Nor should we permit our grievances to overshadow our opportunities.

To those of the white race who look to the incoming of those of foreign birth and strange tongue and habits for the prosperity of the South, were I permitted I would repeat what I say to my own race, "Cast down your bucket where you are." Cast it down among the eight millions of Negroes whose habits you know, whose fidelity and love you have tested in days when to have proved treacherous meant the ruin of your firesides. Cast down your bucket among these people who have, without strikes and labour wars, tilled your fields, cleared your forests, builded your railroads and cities, and brought forth treasures from the bowels of the earth, and helped make possible this magnificent representation of the progress of the South. Casting down your bucket among my people, helping and encouraging them as you are doing on these grounds, and to education of head, hand, and heart, you will find that they will buy your surplus land, make blossom the waste places in your fields, and run your factories. While doing this, you can be sure in the future, as in the past, that you and your families will be surrounded by the most patient, faithful, law-abiding, and unresentful people that the world has seen. As we have proved our loyalty to you in the past, in nursing your children, watching by the sick-bed of your mothers and fathers, and often following them with tear-dimmed eyes to their graves, so in the future, in our humble way, we shall stand by you with a devotion that no foreigner can approach, ready to lay down our lives, if need be, in defence of yours, interlacing our industrial, commercial, civil, and religious life with yours in a way that shall make the interests of both races one. In all things that are purely social we can be as separate as the fingers, yet one as the hand in all things essential to mutual progress.

There is no defence or security for any of us except in the highest intelligence and development of all. If anywhere there are efforts tending to curtail the fullest growth of the Negro, let these efforts be turned into stimulating, encouraging, and making him the most useful and intelligent citizen. Effort or means so invested will pay a thousand per cent interest. These efforts will be twice blessed—"blessing him that gives and him that takes."

There is no escape through law of man or God from the inevitable:—

> The laws of changeless justice bind
>
> Oppressor with oppressed;
>
> And close as sin and suffering joined
>
> We march to fate abreast.

Nearly sixteen millions of hands will aid you in pulling the load upward, or they will pull against you the load downward. We shall constitute one-third and more of the ignorance and crime of the South, or one-third its intelligence and progress; we shall contribute one-third to the business and industrial prosperity of the South, or we shall prove a veritable body of death, stagnating, depressing, retarding every effort to advance the body politic.

Gentlemen of the Exposition, as we present to you our humble effort at an exhibition of our progress, you must not expect overmuch. Starting thirty years ago with ownership here and there in a few quilts and pumpkins and chickens (gathered from miscellaneous sources), remember the path that has led from these to the inventions and production of agricultural implements, buggies, steam-engines, newspapers, books, statuary, carving, paintings, the management of drug-stores and banks, has not been trodden without contact with thorns and thistles. While we take pride in what we exhibit as a result of our independent efforts, we do not for a moment forget that our part in this exhibition would fall far short of your expectations but for the constant help that has come to our educational life, not only from the Southern states, but especially from Northern philanthropists, who have made their gifts a constant stream of blessing and encouragement.

The wisest among my race understand that the agitation of questions of social equality is the extremest folly, and that progress in the enjoyment of all the privileges that will come to us must be the result of severe and constant struggle rather than of artificial forcing. No race that has anything to contribute to the markets of the world is long in any degree ostracized. It is important and right that all privileges of the law be ours, but it is vastly more important that we be prepared for the exercises of these privileges. The opportunity to earn a dollar in a factory just now is worth infinitely more than the opportunity to spend a dollar in an opera-house.

In conclusion, may I repeat that nothing in thirty years has given us more hope and encouragement, and drawn us so near to you of the white race, as this opportunity offered by the Exposition; and here bending, as it were, over the altar that represents the results of the struggles of your race and mine, both starting practically empty-handed three decades ago, I pledge that in your effort to work out the great and intricate problem which God has laid at the doors of the South, you shall have at all times the patient, sympathetic help of my race; only let this be constantly in mind, that, while from representations in these buildings of the product of field, of forest, of mine, of factory, letters, and art, much good will come, yet far above and beyond material benefits will be that higher good, that, let us pray God, will come, in a blotting out of sectional differences and racial animosities and suspicions, in a determination to administer absolute justice, in a willing obedience among all classes to the mandates of law. This, coupled with our material prosperity, will bring into our beloved South a new heaven and a new earth.

5–6
Charles Waddell Chesnutt (1858–1932)

CHARLES WADDELL CHESNUTT (1858–1932), born in Ohio and raised in Fayetteville, North Carolina, was a freeborn African American, whose father served in the Union Army. His schooling through the Freedman's Bureau led him to teach and later to a career in accounting, and still later, in Cleveland, to the law. His first published short story, at age twenty-nine, was a radical retelling of the Brer Rabbit tradition. Chesnutt used folk tales, folk culture, and dialect to subvert the master/slave relationship. Trickster figures, in the tradition of Southwest Humor, are used to prank the white masters and overseers. Grandison, Colonel Owens' slave, is an excellent example of this usage.

≈ ≈ ≈

"The Passing of Grandison" (1899)

I

When it is said that it was done to please a woman, there ought perhaps to be enough said to explain anything; for what a man will not do to please a woman is yet to be discovered. Nevertheless, it might be well to state a few preliminary facts to make it clear why young Dick Owens tried to run one of his father's negro men off to Canada.

In the early fifties, when the growth of anti-slavery sentiment and the constant drain of fugitive slaves into the North had so alarmed the slaveholders of the border States as to lead to the passage of the Fugitive Slave Law, a young white man from Ohio, moved by compassion for the sufferings of a certain bondman who happened to have a "hard master," essayed to help the slave to freedom. The attempt was discovered and frustrated; the abductor was tried and convicted for slave-stealing, and sentenced to a term of imprisonment in the penitentiary. His death, after the expiration of only a small part of the sentence, from cholera contracted while nursing stricken fellow prisoners, lent to the case a melancholy interest that made it famous in anti-slavery annals.

Dick Owens had attended the trial. He was a youth of about twenty-two, intelligent, handsome, and amiable, but extremely indolent, in a graceful and gentlemanly way; or, as old Judge Fenderson put it more than once, he was lazy as the Devil,—a mere figure of speech, of course, and not one that did justice to the Enemy of Mankind. When asked why he never did anything serious, Dick would good-naturedly reply, with a well-modulated drawl, that he didn't have to. His father was rich; there was but one other child, an unmarried daughter, who because of poor health would probably never marry, and Dick was therefore heir presumptive to a large estate. Wealth or social position he did not need to seek, for he was born to both. Charity Lomax had shamed him into studying law, but notwithstanding an hour or so a day spent at old Judge Fenderson's office, he did not make remarkable headway in his legal studies.

"What Dick needs," said the judge, who was fond of tropes, as became a scholar, and of horses, as was befitting a Kentuckian, "is the whip of necessity, or the spur of ambition. If he had either, he would soon need the snaffle to hold him back."

But all Dick required, in fact, to prompt him to the most remarkable thing he accomplished before he was twenty-five, was a mere suggestion from Charity Lomax. The story was never really known to but two persons until after the war, when it came out because it was a good story and there was no particular reason for its concealment.

Young Owens had attended the trial of this slave-stealer, or martyr,—either or both,—and, when it was over, had gone to call on Charity Lomax, and, while they sat on the veranda after sundown, had told her all about the trial. He was a good talker, as his career in later years disclosed, and described the proceedings very graphically.

"I confess," he admitted, "that while my principles were against the prisoner, my sympathies were on his side. It appeared that he was of good family, and that he had an old father and mother, respectable people, dependent upon him for support and comfort in their declining years. He had been led into the matter by pity for a negro whose master ought to have been run out of the county long ago for abusing his slaves. If it had been merely a question of old Sam Briggs's negro, nobody would have cared anything about it. But father and the rest of them stood on the principle of the thing, and told the judge so, and the fellow was sentenced to three years in the penitentiary."

Miss Lomax had listened with lively interest.

"I've always hated old Sam Briggs," she said emphatically, "ever since the time he broke a negro's leg with a piece of cordwood. When I hear of a cruel deed it makes the Quaker blood that came from my grandmother assert itself. Personally I wish that all Sam Briggs's negroes would run away. As for the young man, I regard him as a hero. He dared something for humanity. I could love a man who would take such chances for the sake of others."

"Could you love me, Charity, if I did something heroic?"

"You never will, Dick. You're too lazy for any use. You'll never do anything harder than playing cards or fox-hunting."

"Oh, come now, sweetheart! I've been courting you for a year, and it's the hardest work imaginable. Are you never going to love me?" he pleaded.

His hand sought hers, but she drew it back beyond his reach.

"I'll never love you, Dick Owens, until you have done something. When that time comes, I'll think about it."

"But it takes so long to do anything worth mentioning, and I don't want to wait. One must read two years to become a lawyer, and work five more to make a reputation. We shall both be gray by then."

"Oh, I don't know," she rejoined. "It doesn't require a lifetime for a man to prove that he is a man. This one did something, or at least tried to."

"Well, I'm willing to attempt as much as any other man. What do you want me to do, sweetheart? Give me a test."

"Oh, dear me!" said Charity, "I don't care what you *do*, so you do *something*. Really, come to think of it, why should I care whether you do anything or not?"

"I'm sure I don't know why you should, Charity," rejoined Dick humbly, "for I'm aware that I'm not worthy of it."

"Except that I do hate," she added, relenting slightly, "to see a really clever man so utterly lazy and good for nothing."

"Thank you, my dear; a word of praise from you has sharpened my wits already. I have an idea! Will you love me if *I* run a negro off to Canada?"

"What nonsense!" said Charity scornfully. "You must be losing your wits. Steal another man's slave, indeed, while your father owns a hundred!"

"Oh, there'll be no trouble about that," responded Dick lightly; "I'll run off one of the old man's; we've got too many anyway. It may not be quite as difficult as the other man found it, but it will be just as unlawful, and will demonstrate what I am capable of."

"Seeing's believing," replied Charity. "Of course, what you are talking about now is merely absurd. I'm going away for three weeks, to visit my aunt in Tennessee. If you're able to tell me, when I return, that you've done something to prove your quality, I'll—well, you may come and tell me about it."

II

Young Owens got up about nine o'clock next morning, and while making his toilet put some questions to his personal attendant, a rather bright looking young mulatto of about his own age.

"Tom," said Dick.

"Yas, Mars Dick," responded the servant.

"I'm going on a trip North. Would you like to go with me?"

Now, if there was anything that Tom would have liked to make, it was a trip North. It was something he had long contemplated in the abstract, but had never been able to muster up sufficient courage to attempt in the concrete. He was prudent enough, however, to dissemble his feelings.

"I wouldn't min' it, Mars Dick, ez long ez you'd take keer er me an' fetch me home all right."

Tom's eyes belied his words, however, and his young master felt well assured that Tom needed only a good opportunity to make him run away. Having a comfortable home, and a dismal prospect in case of failure, Tom was not likely to take any desperate chances; but young Owens was satisfied that in a free State but little persuasion would be required to lead Tom astray. With a very logical and characteristic desire to gain his end with the least necessary expenditure of effort, he decided to take Tom with him, if his father did not object.

Colonel Owens had left the house when Dick went to breakfast, so Dick did not see his father till luncheon.

"Father," he remarked casually to the colonel, over the fried chicken, "I'm feeling a trifle run down. I imagine my health would be improved somewhat by a little travel and change of scene."

"Why don't you take a trip North?" suggested his father. The colonel added to paternal affection a considerable respect for his son as the heir of a large estate. He himself had been "raised" in comparative poverty, and had laid the foundations of his fortune by hard work; and while he despised the ladder by which he had climbed, he could not entirely forget it, and unconsciously manifested, in his intercourse with his son, some of the poor man's deference toward the wealthy and well-born.

"I think I'll adopt your suggestion, sir," replied the son, "and run up to New York; and after I've been there awhile I may go on to Boston for a week or so. I've never been there, you know."

"There are some matters you can talk over with my factor in New York," rejoined the colonel, "and while you are up there among the Yankees, I hope you'll keep your eyes and ears open to find out what the rascally abolitionists are saying and doing. They're becoming altogether too active for our comfort, and entirely too many ungrateful niggers are running away. I hope the conviction of that fellow yesterday may discourage the rest of the breed. I'd just like to catch any one trying to run off one of my darkeys. He'd get short shrift; I don't think any Court would have a chance to try him."

"They are a pestiferous lot," assented Dick, "and dangerous to our institutions. But say, father, if I go North I shall want to take Tom with me."

Now, the colonel, while a very indulgent father, had pronounced views on the subject of negroes, having studied them, as he often said, for a great many years, and, as he asserted oftener still, understanding them perfectly. It is scarcely worth while to say, either, that he valued more highly than if he had inherited them the slaves he had toiled and schemed for.

"I don't think it safe to take Tom up North," he declared, with promptness and decision. "He's a good enough boy, but too smart to trust among those low-down abolitionists. I strongly suspect him of having learned to read, though I can't imagine how. I saw him with a newspaper the other day, and while he pretended to be looking at a woodcut, I'm almost sure he was reading the paper. I think it by no means safe to take him."

Dick did not insist, because he knew it was useless. The colonel would have obliged his son in any other matter, but his negroes were the outward and visible sign of his wealth and station, and therefore sacred to him.

"Whom do you think it safe to take?" asked Dick. "I suppose I'll have to have a body-servant."

"What's the matter with Grandison?" suggested the colonel. "He's handy enough, and I reckon we can trust him. He's too fond of good eating, to risk losing his regular meals; besides, he's sweet on your mother's maid, Betty, and I've promised to let 'em get married before long. I'll have Grandison up, and we'll talk to him. Here, you boy Jack," called the colonel to a yellow youth in the next room who was catching flies and pulling their wings off to pass the time, "go down to the barn and tell Grandison to come here."

"Grandison," said the colonel, when the negro stood before him, hat in hand.

"Yas, marster."

"Haven't I always treated you right?"

"Yas, marster."

"Haven't you always got all you wanted to eat?"

"Yas, marster."

"And as much whiskey and tobacco as was good for you, Grandison?"

"Y-a-s, marster."

"I should just like to know, Grandison, whether you don't think yourself a great deal better off than those poor free negroes down by the plank road, with no kind master to look after them and no mistress to give them medicine when they're sick and—and"—

"Well, I sh'd jes' reckon I is better off, suh, dan dem low-down free niggers, suh! Ef anybody ax 'em who dey b'long ter, dey has ter say nobody, er e'se lie erbout it. Anybody ax me who I b'longs ter, I ain' got no 'casion ter be shame' ter tell 'em, no, suh, 'deed I ain', suh!"

The colonel was beaming. This was true gratitude, and his feudal heart thrilled at such appreciative homage. What cold-blooded, heartless monsters they were who would break up this blissful relationship of kindly protection on the one hand, of wise subordination and loyal dependence on the other! The colonel always became indignant at the mere thought of such wickedness.

"Grandison," the colonel continued, "your young master Dick is going North for a few weeks, and I am thinking of letting him take you along. I shall send you on this trip, Grandison, in order that you may take care of your young master. He will need some one to wait on him, and no one can ever do it so well as one of the boys brought up with him on the old plantation. I am going to trust him in your hands, and I'm sure you'll do your duty faithfully, and bring him back home safe and sound—to old Kentucky."

Grandison grinned. "Oh yas, marster, I'll take keer er young Mars Dick."

"I want to warn you, though, Grandison," continued the colonel impressively, "against these cussed abolitionists, who try to entice servants from their comfortable homes and their indulgent masters, from the blue skies, the green fields, and the warm sunlight of their southern home, and send them away off yonder to Canada, a dreary country, where the woods are full of wildcats and wolves and bears, where the snow lies up to the eaves of the houses for six months of the year, and the cold is so severe that it freezes your breath and curdles your blood; and where, when runaway niggers get sick and can't work, they are turned out to starve and die, unloved and uncared for. I reckon, Grandison, that you have too much sense to permit yourself to be led astray by any such foolish and wicked people."

"'Deed, suh, I wouldn' low none er dem cussed, low-down abolitioners ter come nigh me, suh. I'd—I'd—would I be 'lowed ter hit 'em, suh?"

"Certainly, Grandison," replied the colonel, chuckling, "hit 'em as hard as you can. I reckon they'd rather like it. Begad, I believe they would! It would serve 'em right to be hit by a nigger!"

"Er ef I didn't hit 'em, suh," continued Grandison reflectively, "I'd tell Mars Dick, en *he'd* fix 'em. He'd smash de face off'n 'em, suh, I jes' knows he would."

"Oh yes, Grandison, your young master will protect you. You need fear no harm while he is near."

"Dey won't try ter steal me, will dey, marster?" asked the negro, with sudden alarm.

"I don't know, Grandison," replied the colonel, lighting a fresh cigar. "They're a desperate set of lunatics, and there's no telling what they may resort to. But if you stick close to your young master, and remember always that he is your best friend, and understands your real needs, and has your true interests at heart, and if you will be careful to avoid strangers who try to talk to you, you'll stand a fair chance of getting back to your home and your friends. And if you please your master Dick, he'll buy you a present, and a string of beads for Betty to wear when you and she get married in the fall."

"Thanky, marster, thanky, suh," replied Grandison, oozing gratitude at every pore; "you is a good marster, to be sho', suh; yas, 'deed you is. You kin jes' bet me and Mars Dick gwine git 'long jes' lack I wuz own boy ter Mars Dick. En it won't be my fault ef he don' want me fer his boy all de time, w'en we come back home ag'in."

"All right, Grandison, you may go now. You needn't work any more to-day, and here's a piece of tobacco for you off my own plug."

"Thanky, marster, thanky, marster! You is de bes' marster any nigger ever had in dis worl'." And Grandison bowed and scraped and disappeared round the corner, his jaws closing around a large section of the colonel's best tobacco.

"You may take Grandison," said the colonel to his son. "I allow he's abolitionist-proof."

III

Richard Owens, Esq., and servant, from Kentucky, registered at the fashionable New York hostelry for Southerners in those days, a hotel where an atmosphere congenial to Southern institutions was sedulously maintained. But there were negro waiters in the dining-room, and mulatto bell-boys, and Dick had no doubt that Grandison, with the native gregariousness and garrulousness of his race, would foregather and palaver with them sooner or later, and Dick hoped that they would speedily inoculate him with the virus of freedom. For it was not Dick's intention to say anything to his servant about his plan to free him, for obvious reasons. To mention one of them, if Grandison should go away, and by legal process be recaptured, his young master's part in the matter would doubtless become known, which would be embarrassing to Dick, to say the least. If, on the other hand, he should merely give Grandison sufficient latitude, he had no doubt he would eventually lose him. For while not exactly skeptical about Grandison's perfervid loyalty, Dick had been a somewhat keen observer of human nature, in his own indolent way, and based his expectations upon the force of the example and argument that his servant could scarcely fail to encounter. Grandison should have a fair chance to become free by his own initiative; if it should become necessary to adopt other measures to get rid of him, it would be time enough to act when the necessity arose; and Dick Owens was not the youth to take needless trouble.

The young master renewed some acquaintances and made others, and spent a week or two very pleasantly in the best society of the metropolis, easily accessible to a wealthy, well-bred young Southerner, with proper introductions. Young women smiled on him, and young men of convivial habits pressed their hospitalities; but the memory of Charity's sweet, strong face and clear blue eyes made him proof against the blandishments of the one sex and the persuasions of the other. Meanwhile he kept Grandison supplied with pocket-money, and left him mainly to his own devices. Every night when Dick came in he hoped he might have to wait upon himself, and every morning he looked forward with pleasure to the prospect of making his toilet unaided. His hopes, however, were doomed to disappointment, for every night when he came in Grandison was on hand with a bootjack, and a nightcap mixed for his young master as the colonel had taught him to mix it, and every morning Grandison appeared with his master's boots blacked and his clothes brushed, and laid his linen out for the day.

"Grandison," said Dick one morning, after finishing his toilet, "this is the chance of your life to go around among your own people and see how they live. Have you met any of them?"

"Yas, suh, I's seen some of 'em. But I don' keer nuffin fer 'em, suh. Dey're diffe'nt f'm de niggers down ou' way. Dey 'lows dey're free, but dey ain' got sense 'nuff ter know dey ain' half as well off as dey would be down Souf, whar dey'd be 'preciated."

When two weeks had passed without any apparent effect of evil example upon Grandison, Dick resolved to go on to Boston, where he thought the atmosphere might prove more favorable to his ends. After he had been at the Revere House for a day or two without losing Grandison, he decided upon slightly different tactics.

Having ascertained from a city directory the addresses of several well-known abolitionists, he wrote them each a letter something like this:—

Dear Friend and Brother:—

A wicked slaveholder from Kentucky, stopping at the Revere House, has dared to insult the liberty-loving people of Boston by bringing his slave into their midst. Shall this be tolerated? Or shall steps be taken in the name of liberty to rescue a fellow-man from bondage? For obvious reasons I can only sign myself,

A Friend of Humanity.

That his letter might have an opportunity to prove effective, Dick made it a point to send Grandison away from the hotel on various errands. On one of these occasions Dick watched him for quite a distance down the street. Grandison had scarcely left the hotel when a long-haired, sharp-featured man came out behind him, followed him, soon overtook him, and kept along beside him until they turned the next corner. Dick's hopes were roused by this spectacle, but sank correspondingly when Grandison returned to the hotel. As Grandison said nothing about the encounter, Dick hoped there might be some self-consciousness behind this unexpected reticence, the results of which might develop later on.

But Grandison was on hand again when his master came back to the hotel at night, and was in attendance again in the morning, with hot water, to assist at his master's toilet. Dick sent him on further errands from day to day, and upon one occasion came squarely up to him—inadvertently of course—while Grandison was engaged in conversation with a young white man in clerical garb. When Grandison saw Dick approaching, he edged away from the preacher and hastened toward his master, with a very evident expression of relief upon his countenance.

"Mars Dick," he said, "dese yer abolitioners is jes' pesterin' de life out er me tryin' ter git me ter run away. I don' pay no 'tention ter 'em, but dey riles me so sometimes dat I'm feared I'll hit some of 'em some er dese days, an' dat mought git me inter trouble. I ain' said nuffin' ter you 'bout it, Mars Dick, fer I didn' wanter 'sturb yo' min'; but I don' like it, suh; no, suh, I don'! Is we gwine back home 'fo' long, Mars Dick?"

"We'll be going back soon enough," replied Dick somewhat shortly, while he inwardly cursed the stupidity of a slave who could be free and would not, and registered a secret vow that if he were unable to get rid of Grandison without assassinating him, and were therefore compelled to take him back to Kentucky, he would see that Grandison got a taste of an article of slavery that would make him regret his wasted opportunities. Meanwhile he determined to tempt his servant yet more strongly.

"Grandison," he said next morning, "I'm going away for a day or two, but I shall leave you here. I shall lock up a hundred dollars in this drawer and give you the key. If you need any of it, use it and enjoy yourself,—spend it all if you like,—for this is probably the last chance you'll have for some time to be in a free State, and you'd better enjoy your liberty while you may."

When he came back a couple of days later and found the faithful Grandison at his post, and the hundred dollars intact, Dick felt seriously annoyed. His vexation was increased by the fact that he could not express his feelings adequately. He did not even scold Grandison; how could he, indeed, find fault with one who so sensibly recognized his true place in the economy of civilization, and kept it with such touching fidelity?

"I can't say a thing to him," groaned Dick. "He deserves a leather medal, made out of his own hide tanned. I reckon I'll write to father and let him know what a model servant he has given me."

He wrote his father a letter which made the colonel swell with pride and pleasure. "I really think," the colonel observed to one of his friends, "that Dick ought to have the nigger interviewed by the Boston papers, so that they may see how contented and happy our darkeys really are."

Dick also wrote a long letter to Charity Lomax, in which he said, among many other things, that if she knew how hard he was working, and under what difficulties, to accomplish something serious for her sake, she would no longer keep him in suspense, but overwhelm him with love and admiration.

Having thus exhausted without result the more obvious methods of getting rid of Grandison, and diplomacy having also proved a failure, Dick was forced to consider more radical measures. Of course he might run away himself, and abandon Grandison, but this would be merely to leave him in the United States, where he was still a slave, and where, with his notions of loyalty, he would speedily be reclaimed. It was necessary, in order to accomplish the purpose of his trip to the North, to leave Grandison permanently in Canada, where he would be legally free.

"I might extend my trip to Canada," he reflected, "but that would be too palpable. I have it! I'll visit Niagara Falls on the way home, and lose him on the Canada side. When he once realizes that he is actually free, I'll warrant that he'll stay."

So the next day saw them westward bound, and in due course of time, by the somewhat slow conveyances of the period, they found themselves at Niagara. Dick walked and drove about the Falls for several days, taking Grandison along with him on most occasions. One morning they stood on the Canadian side, watching the wild whirl of the waters below them.

"Grandison," said Dick, raising his voice above the roar of the cataract, "do you know where you are now?"

"I's wid you, Mars Dick; dat's all I keers."

"You are now in Canada, Grandison, where your people go when they run away from their masters. If you wished, Grandison, you might walk away from me this very minute, and I could not lay my hand upon you to take you back."

Grandison looked around uneasily. "Let's go back ober de ribber, Mars Dick. I's feared I'll lose you ovuh heah, an' den I won't nebber hab no marster, an' won't nebber be able to git back home no mo'."

Discouraged, but not yet hopeless, Dick said, a few minutes later,—

"Grandison, I'm going up the road a bit, to the inn over yonder. You stay here until I return. I'll not be gone a great while."

Grandison's eyes opened wide and he looked somewhat fearful.

"Is dey any er dem dadblasted abolitioners roun' heah, Mars Dick?"

"I don't imagine that there are," replied his master, hoping there might be. "But I'm not afraid of *your* running away, Grandison. I only wish I were," he added to himself.

Dick walked leisurely down the road to where the whitewashed inn, built of stone, with true British solidity, loomed up through the trees by the roadside. Arrived there he ordered a glass of ale and a sandwich, and took a seat at a table by a window, from which he could see Grandison in the distance. For a while he hoped that the seed he had sown might have fallen on fertile ground, and that Grandison, relieved from the restraining power of a master's eye, and finding himself in a free country, might get up and walk away; but the hope was vain, for Grandison remained faithfully at his post, awaiting his master's return. He had seated himself on a broad flat stone, and, turning his eyes away from the grand and awe-inspiring spectacle that lay close at hand, was looking anxiously toward the inn where his master sat cursing his ill-timed fidelity.

By and by a girl came into the room to serve his order, and Dick very naturally glanced at her; and as she was young and pretty and remained in attendance, it was some minutes before he looked for Grandison. When he did so his faithful servant had disappeared.

To pay his reckoning and go away without the change was a matter quickly accomplished. Retracing his footsteps toward the Falls, he saw, to his great disgust, as he approached the spot where he had left Grandison, the familiar form of his servant stretched out on the ground, his face to the sun, his mouth open, sleeping the time away, oblivious alike to the grandeur of the scenery, the thunderous roar of the cataract, or the insidious voice of sentiment.

"Grandison," soliloquized his master, as he stood gazing down at his ebony encumbrance, "I do not deserve to be an American citizen; I ought not to have the advantages I possess over you; and I certainly am not worthy of Charity Lomax, if I am not smart enough to get rid of you. I have an idea! You shall yet be free, and I will be the instrument of your deliverance. Sleep on, faithful and affectionate servitor, and dream of the blue grass and the bright skies of old Kentucky, for it is only in your dreams that you will ever see them again!"

Dick retraced his footsteps towards the inn. The young woman chanced to look out of the window and saw the handsome young gentleman she had waited on a few minutes before, standing in the road a short distance away, apparently engaged in earnest conversation with a colored man employed as hostler for the inn. She thought she saw something pass from the white man to the other, but at that moment her duties called her away from the window, and when she looked out again the young gentleman had disappeared, and the hostler, with two other young men of the neighborhood, one white and one colored, were walking rapidly towards the Falls.

IV

Dick made the journey homeward alone, and as rapidly as the conveyances of the day would permit. As he drew near home his conduct in going back without Grandison took on a more serious aspect than it had borne at any previous time, and although he had prepared the colonel by a letter sent several days ahead, there was still the prospect of a bad quarter of an hour with him; not, indeed, that his father would upbraid him, but he was likely to make searching inquiries. And notwithstanding the vein of quiet recklessness that had carried Dick through his preposterous scheme, he was a very poor liar, having rarely had occasion or inclination to tell anything but the truth. Any reluctance to meet his father was more than offset, however, by a stronger force drawing him homeward, for Charity Lomax must long since have returned from her visit to her aunt in Tennessee.

Dick got off easier than he had expected. He told a straight story, and a truthful one, so far as it went.

The colonel raged at first, but rage soon subsided into anger, and anger moderated into annoyance, and annoyance into a sort of garrulous sense of injury. The colonel thought he had been hardly used; he had trusted this negro, and he had broken faith. Yet, after all, he did not blame Grandison so much as he did the abolitionists, who were undoubtedly at the bottom of it.

As for Charity Lomax, Dick told her, privately of course, that he had run his father's man, Grandison, off to Canada, and left him there.

"Oh, Dick," she had said with shuddering alarm, "what have you done? If they knew it they'd send you to the penitentiary, like they did that Yankee."

"But they don't know it," he had replied seriously; adding, with an injured tone, "you don't seem to appreciate my heroism like you did that of the Yankee; perhaps it's because I wasn't caught and sent to the penitentiary. I thought you wanted me to do it."

"Why, Dick Owens!" she exclaimed. "You know I never dreamed of any such outrageous proceeding.

"But I presume I'll have to marry you," she concluded, after some insistence on Dick's part, "if only to take care of you. You are too reckless for anything; and a man who goes chasing all over the North, being entertained by New York and Boston society and having negroes to throw away, needs some one to look after him."

"It's a most remarkable thing," replied Dick fervently, "that your views correspond exactly with my profoundest convictions. It proves beyond question that we were made for one another."

They were married three weeks later. As each of them had just returned from a journey, they spent their honeymoon at home.

A week after the wedding they were seated, one afternoon, on the piazza of the colonel's house, where Dick had taken his bride, when a negro from the yard ran down the lane and threw open the big gate for the colonel's buggy to enter. The colonel was not alone. Beside him, ragged and travel-stained, bowed with weariness, and upon his face a haggard look that told of hardship and privation, sat the lost Grandison.

The colonel alighted at the steps.

"Take the lines, Tom," he said to the man who had opened the gate, "and drive round to the barn. Help Grandison down,—poor devil, he's so stiff he can hardly move!—and get a tub of water and wash him and rub him down, and feed him, and give him a big drink of whiskey, and then let him come round and see his young master and his new mistress."

The colonel's face wore an expression compounded of joy and indignation,—joy at the restoration of a valuable piece of property; indignation for reasons he proceeded to state.

"It's astounding, the depths of depravity the human heart is capable of! I was coming along the road three miles away, when I heard some one call me from the roadside. I pulled up the mare, and who should come out of the woods but Grandison. The poor nigger could hardly crawl along, with the help of a broken limb. I was never more astonished in my life. You could have knocked me down with a feather. He seemed pretty far gone,—he could hardly talk above a whisper,—and I had to give him a mouthful of whiskey to brace him up so he could tell his story. It's just as I thought from the beginning, Dick; Grandison had no notion of running away; he knew when he was well off, and where his friends were. All the persuasions of abolition liars and runaway niggers did not move him. But the desperation of those fanatics knew no bounds; their guilty consciences gave them no rest. They got the notion somehow that Grandison belonged to a nigger-catcher, and had been brought North as a spy to help capture ungrateful runaway servants. They actually kidnaped him—just think of it!—and gagged him and bound him and threw him rudely into a wagon, and carried him into the gloomy depths of a Canadian forest, and locked him in a lonely hut, and fed him on bread and water for three weeks. One of the scoundrels wanted to kill him, and persuaded the others that it ought to be done; but they got to quarreling about how they should do it, and before they had their minds made up Grandison escaped, and, keeping his back steadily to the North Star, made his way, after suffering incredible hardships, back to the old plantation, back to his master, his friends, and his home. Why, it's as good as one of Scott's novels! Mr. Simms or some other one of our Southern authors ought to write it up."

"Don't you think, sir," suggested Dick, who had calmly smoked his cigar throughout the colonel's animated recital, "that that kidnaping yarn sounds a little improbable? Isn't there some more likely explanation?"

"Nonsense, Dick; it's the gospel truth! Those infernal abolitionists are capable of anything—everything! Just think of their locking the poor, faithful nigger up, beating him, kicking him, depriving him of his liberty, keeping him on bread and water for three long, lonesome weeks, and he all the time pining for the old plantation!"

There were almost tears in the colonel's eyes at the picture of Grandison's sufferings that he conjured up. Dick still professed to be slightly skeptical, and met Charity's severely questioning eye with bland unconsciousness.

The colonel killed the fatted calf for Grandison, and for two or three weeks the returned wanderer's life was a slave's dream of pleasure. His fame spread throughout the county, and the colonel gave him a permanent place among the house servants, where he could always have him conveniently at hand to relate his adventures to admiring visitors.

About three weeks after Grandison's return the colonel's faith in sable humanity was rudely shaken, and its foundations almost broken up. He came near losing his belief in the fidelity of the negro to his master,—the servile virtue most highly prized and most sedulously cultivated by the colonel and his kind. One Monday morning Grandison was missing. And not only Grandison, but his wife, Betty the maid; his mother, aunt Eunice; his father, uncle Ike; his brothers, Tom and John, and his little sister Elsie, were likewise absent from the plantation; and a hurried search and inquiry in the neighborhood resulted in no information as to their whereabouts. So much valuable property could not be lost without an effort to recover it, and the wholesale nature of the transaction carried consternation to the hearts of those whose ledgers were chiefly bound in black. Extremely energetic measures were taken by the colonel and his friends. The fugitives were traced, and followed from point to point, on their northward run through Ohio. Several times the hunters were close upon their heels, but the magnitude of the escaping party begot unusual vigilance on the part of those who sympathized with the fugitives, and strangely enough, the underground railroad seemed to have had its tracks cleared and signals set for this particular train. Once, twice, the colonel thought he had them, but they slipped through his fingers.

One last glimpse he caught of his vanishing property, as he stood, accompanied by a United States marshal, on a wharf at a port on the south shore of Lake Erie. On the stern of a small steamboat which was receding rapidly from the wharf, with her nose pointing toward Canada, there stood a group of familiar dark faces, and the look they cast backward was not one of longing for the fleshpots of Egypt. The colonel saw Grandison point him out to one of the crew of the vessel, who waved his hand derisively toward the colonel. The latter shook his fist impotently—and the incident was closed.

5–7
William Lawrence Chittenden (1862–1934)

WILLIAM LAWRENCE CHITTENDEN (1862–1934) heralded from New Jersey, but as the saying goes, he may have come from elsewhere but at heart he was a Texan. At age twenty-one, he arrived in Texas to work family lands west of Fort Worth, near Abilene. There he ranched, bought land, and expanded his holdings. The poet-rancher of Texas, Chittenden is known for "The Cowboys' Christmas Ball" (1890) and other songs honoring Texas life, later published in *Ranch Verses* (1893). Chittenden is one of the founders of Texas country-western music, long before Willie Nelson.

≈ ≈ ≈

"The Cowboys' Christmas Ball"

To the Ranchmen of Texas

'Way out in Western Texas, where the Clear Fork's waters flow,
Where the cattle are "a-browzin'," an' the Spanish ponies grow;
Where the Northers "come a-whistlin'" from beyond the Neutral strip;
And the prairie dogs are sneezin', as if they had "The Grip";
Where the cayotes come a-howlin' 'round the ranches after dark,
And the mocking-birds are singin' to the lovely "medder lark";
Where the 'possum and the badger, and rattlesnakes abound,
And the monstrous stars are winkin' o'er a wilderness profound;
Where lonesome, tawny prairies melt into airy streams,
While the Double Mountains slumber, in heavenly kinds of dreams;
Where the antelope is grazin' and the lonely plovers call—
It was there that I attended "The Cowboys' Christmas Ball."

The town was Anson City, old Jones's county seat,
Where they raise Polled Angus cattle, and waving whiskered wheat;
Where the air is soft and "bammy," an' dry an' full of health,
And the prairies is explodin' with agricultural wealth;
Where they print the *Texas Western*, that Hec. McCann supplies,
With news and yarns and stories, uv most amazin' size;
Where Frank Smith "pulls the badger," on knowin' tenderfeet,
And Democracy's triumphant, and mighty hard to beat;
Where lives that good old hunter, John Milsap from Lamar,

Who "used to be the Sheriff, back East, in Paris, sah!"
'Twas there, I say, at Anson, with the lively "widder Wall,"
That I went to that reception, "The Cowboys' Christmas Ball."

The boys had left the ranches and come to town in piles;
The ladies—"kinder scatterin'"—had gathered in for miles.
And yet the place was crowded, as I remember well,
'Twas got for the occasion, at "The Morning Star Hotel."
The music was a fiddle an' a lively tambourine,
And a "viol come imported," by the stage from Abilene.
The room was togged out gorgeous—with mistletoe and shawls,
And candles flickered frescoes, around the airy walls.
The "wimmin folks" looked lovely—the boys looked kinder treed,
Till their leader commenced yellin': "Whoa! fellers, let's stampede,"
And the music started sighin', an' awailin' through the hall,
As a kind of introduction to "The Cowboys' Christmas Ball."

The leader was a feller that came from Swenson's Ranch,
They called him "Windy Billy," from "little Deadman's Branch."
His rig was "kinder keerless," big spurs and high-heeled boots;
He had the reputation that comes when "fellers shoots."
His voice was like a bugle upon the mountain's height;
His feet were animated, an' a *mighty, movin' sight*,
When he commenced to holler, "Neow fellers, stake yer pen!
"Lock horns ter all them heifers, an' russle 'em like men.
"Saloot yer lovely critters; neow swing an' let 'em go,
"Climb the grape vine 'round 'em—all hands do-ce-do !
"You Mavericks, jine the round-up—Jest skip her waterfall,"
Huh! hit wuz gettin' happy, "The Cowboys' Christmas Ball!"

The boys were tolerable skittish, the ladies powerful neat,
That old bass viol's music *just got there with both feet!*
That wailin', frisky fiddle, I never shall forget;
And Windy kept a singin'—I think I hear him yet—
"O Xes, chase your squirrels, an' cut 'em to one side,
"Spur Treadwell to the centre, with Cross P Charley's bride,
"Doc. Hollis down the middle, an' twine the ladies' chain,
"Varn Andrews pen the fillies in big T Diamond's train.
"All pull yer freight tergether, neow swallow fork an' change,
"'Big Boston' lead the trail herd, through little Pitchfork's range.
"Purr 'round yer gentle pussies, neow rope 'em! Balance all!"

Huh! hit wuz gettin' active—"The Cowboys' Christmas Ball!"

The dust riz fast an' furious, we all just galloped 'round,
Till the scenery got so giddy, that Z Bar Dick was downed.
We buckled to our partners, an' told 'em to hold on,
Then shook our hoofs like lightning, until the early dawn.
Don't tell me 'bout cotillions, or germans. No sir 'ee!
That whirl at Anson City just takes the cake with me.
I'm sick of lazy shufflin's, of them I've had my fill,
Give me a frontier break-down, backed up by Windy Bill.
McAllister ain't nowhar! when Windy leads the show,
I've seen 'em both in harness, and so I sorter know—
Oh, Bill, I sha'n't forget yer, and I'll oftentimes recall,
That lively gaited sworray—"The Cowboys' Christmas Ball."

"The Cowboy Preacher's Sermon"

Said he: "You Maverick Sinners—are in an awful state
And Hell is shore to git yer—unless you Pull your Freight
Oh leave them deep hog wallers of filth and mire and sin
And hit the trail to Heaven—the Lord will let you in!
The Corrals of Salvation are free and big and fair
There's Water, Grass and Shelter—in Pastures Over There
The Boss of this hyar Outfit—I know him—all too well
Has ear marks of the Devil—His Brands are hot from Hell
His Hoss will shore out run you and ketch you with his rope
Unless you git religion and find Eternal Hope.

"Oh, if I could but tell you—how happy you would be
To quit Sin's Mires of Meanness and ride God's range with me
Thar haint no more Night herding beyond the Big Divide
And cares Stampedes is over—when God is on your side
The Hell and Hails of Trouble can't never hit you then
If you put on Christ's Slicker—and camp at his Big Pen
Old Beelzebub's chuck Wagon—hit is a hungry place
So leave hit now you fellers—for Pullman Kyars of Grace
Sin's Quick Sands of Perdition is gwine to drag you down
So git aboard Faith's Sleeper—for God's Celestial town.

"Thar haint no more barb fences and no more lines to ride
In God's green bloomin' pastures beyond the Big Divide
God's Range is full of flowers—far as the eye can see

Thar's worlds of feed and water—and all of hit is free
Thar haint no Blizzard sand storms, nor fightin' over brands
Nor Strays—Nor Jails—Nor Northers—in Love's eternal Lands
So Quit your Mires of Meanness and ride God's Range with me
I can't begin to tell you how happy you will be
Get shet of that old Devil—Get shet of him I say
And hit the Trail for Heaven—Now fellers let us pray."

5–8

O. Henry (William Sydney Porter) (1862–1910)

O. HENRY [WILLIAM SYDNEY PORTER] (1862–1910) was born in North Carolina, but came to Texas when he was twenty, living in Austin, San Antonio, and Houston for over a dozen years, where he held numerous jobs and had many adventures. In 1896, he escaped to Central America after he was charged with embezzling bank funds; this led to time in prison. A colorful character, O. Henry matched his writing to his life. "The Caballero's Way" (1907) features a fictional character O. Henry made popular; the Cisco Kid, a twenty-five-year-old desperado, pursues his Tonia on the Mexico-Texas border. The story was made into a 1914 silent film. A *caballero* has many meanings—a horseman, a knight and cavalier, and a gentleman.

≈≈ ≈≈ ≈≈

"The Caballero's Way" (1907)

The Cisco Kid had killed six men in more or less fair scrimmages, had murdered twice as many (mostly Mexicans), and had winged a larger number whom he modestly forbore to count. Therefore a woman loved him.

The Kid was twenty-five, looked twenty; and a careful insurance company would have estimated the probable time of his demise at, say, twenty-six. His habitat was anywhere between the Frio and the Rio Grande. He killed for the love of it—because he was quick-tempered—to avoid arrest—for his own amusement—any reason that came to his mind would suffice. He had escaped capture because he could shoot five-sixths of a second sooner than any sheriff or ranger in the service, and because he rode a speckled roan horse that knew every cow-path in the mesquite and pear thickets from San Antonio to Matamoras.

Tonia Perez, the girl who loved the Cisco Kid, was half Carmen, half Madonna, and the rest—oh, yes, a woman who is half Carmen and half Madonna can always be something more—the rest, let us say, was humming-bird. She lived in a grass-roofed *jacal* near a little Mexican settlement at the Lone Wolf Crossing of the Frio. With her lived a father or grandfather, a lineal Aztec, somewhat less than a thousand years old, who herded a hundred goats and lived in a continuous drunken dream from drinking *mescal*. Back of the *jacal* a tremendous forest of bristling pear, twenty feet high at its worst, crowded almost to its door. It was along the bewildering maze of this spinous thicket that the speckled roan would bring the Kid to see his girl. And once, clinging like a lizard to the ridge-pole, high up under the peaked grass roof, he had heard Tonia, with her Madonna face and Carmen beauty and humming-bird soul, parley with the sheriff's posse, denying knowledge of her man in her soft *mélange* of Spanish and English.

One day the adjutant-general of the State, who is, *ex officio*, commander of the ranger forces, wrote some sarcastic lines to Captain Duval of Company X, stationed at Laredo, relative to the serene and undisturbed existence led by murderers and desperadoes in the said captain's territory.

The captain turned the colour of brick dust under his tan, and forwarded the letter, after adding a few comments, per ranger Private Bill Adamson, to ranger Lieutenant Sandridge, camped at a water hole on the Nueces with a squad of five men in preservation of law and order.

Lieutenant Sandridge turned a beautiful *couleur de rose* through his ordinary strawberry complexion, tucked the letter in his hip pocket, and chewed off the end of his gamboge moustache.

The next morning he saddled his horse and rode alone to the Mexican settlement at the Lone Wolf Crossing of the Frio, twenty miles away.

Six feet two, blond as a Viking, quiet as a deacon, dangerous as a machine gun, Sandridge moved among the *Jacales*, patiently seeking news of the Cisco Kid.

Far more than the law, the Mexicans dreaded the cold and certain vengeance of the lone rider that the ranger sought. It had been one of the Kid's pastimes to shoot Mexicans "to see them kick": if he demanded from them moribund Terpsichorean feats, simply that he might be entertained, what terrible and extreme penalties would be certain to follow should they anger him! One and all they lounged with upturned palms and shrugging shoulders, filling the air with "*quien sabes*" and denials of the Kid's acquaintance.

But there was a man named Fink who kept a store at the Crossing—a man of many nationalities, tongues, interests, and ways of thinking.

"No use to ask them Mexicans," he said to Sandridge. "They're afraid to tell. This *hombre* they call the Kid—Goodall is his name, ain't it?—he's been in my store once or twice. I have an idea you might run across him at—but I guess I don't keer to say, myself. I'm two seconds later in pulling a gun than I used to be, and the difference is worth thinking about. But this Kid's got a half-Mexican girl at the Crossing that he comes to see. She lives in that *jacal* a hundred yards down the arroyo at the edge of the pear. Maybe she—no, I don't suppose she would, but that *jacal* would be a good place to watch, anyway."

Sandridge rode down to the *jacal* of Perez. The sun was low, and the broad shade of the great pear thicket already covered the grass-thatched hut. The goats were enclosed for the night in a brush corral near by. A few kids walked the top of it, nibbling the chaparral leaves. The old Mexican lay upon a blanket on the grass, already in a stupor from his mescal, and dreaming, perhaps, of the nights when he and Pizarro touched glasses to their New World fortunes—so old his wrinkled face seemed to proclaim him to be. And in the door of the *jacal* stood Tonia. And Lieutenant Sandridge sat in his saddle staring at her like a gannet agape at a sailorman.

The Cisco Kid was a vain person, as all eminent and successful assassins are, and his bosom would have been ruffled had he known that at a simple exchange of glances two persons, in whose minds he had been looming large, suddenly abandoned (at least for the time) all thought of him.

Never before had Tonia seen such a man as this. He seemed to be made of sunshine and blood-red tissue and clear weather. He seemed to illuminate the shadow of the pear when he smiled, as though the sun were rising again. The men she had known had been small and dark. Even the Kid, in spite of his achievements, was a stripling no larger than herself, with black, straight hair and a cold, marble face that chilled the noonday.

As for Tonia, though she sends description to the poorhouse, let her make a millionaire of your fancy. Her blue-black hair, smoothly divided in the middle and bound close to her head, and her large eyes full of the Latin melancholy, gave her the Madonna touch. Her motions and air spoke of the concealed fire and the desire to charm that she had inherited from the *gitanas* of the Basque province. As for the humming-bird part of her, that dwelt in her heart; you could not perceive it unless her bright red skirt and dark blue blouse gave you a symbolic hint of the vagarious bird.

The newly lighted sun-god asked for a drink of water. Tonia brought it from the red jar hanging under the brush shelter. Sandridge considered it necessary to dismount so as to lessen the trouble of her ministrations.

I play no spy; nor do I assume to master the thoughts of any human heart; but I assert, by the chronicler's right, that before a quarter of an hour had sped, Sandridge was teaching her how to plait a six-strand rawhide stake-rope, and Tonia had explained to him that were it not for her little English book that the peripatetic *padre* had given her and the little crippled *chivo*, that she fed from a bottle, she would be very, very lonely indeed.

Which leads to a suspicion that the Kid's fences needed repairing, and that the adjutant-general's sarcasm had fallen upon unproductive soil.

In his camp by the water hole Lieutenant Sandridge announced and reiterated his intention of either causing the Cisco Kid to nibble the black loam of the Frio country prairies or of haling him before a judge and jury. That sounded business-like. Twice a week he rode over to the Lone Wolf Crossing of the Frio, and directed Tonia's slim, slightly lemon-tinted fingers among the intricacies of the slowly growing lariata. A six-strand plait is hard to learn and easy to teach.

The ranger knew that he might find the Kid there at any visit. He kept his armament ready, and had a frequent eye for the pear thicket at the rear of the *jacal*. Thus he might bring down the kite and the humming-bird with one stone.

While the sunny-haired ornithologist was pursuing his studies the Cisco Kid was also attending to his professional duties. He moodily shot up a saloon in a small cow village on Quintana Creek, killed the town marshal (plugging him neatly in the centre of his tin badge), and then rode away, morose and unsatisfied. No true artist is uplifted by shooting an aged man carrying an old-style .38 bulldog.

On his way the Kid suddenly experienced the yearning that all men feel when wrong-doing loses its keen edge of delight. He yearned for the woman he loved to reassure him that she was his in spite of it. He wanted her to call his bloodthirstiness bravery and his cruelty devotion. He wanted Tonia to bring him water from the red jug under the brush shelter, and tell him how the *chivo* was thriving on the bottle.

The Kid turned the speckled roan's head up the ten-mile pear flat that stretches along the Arroyo Hondo until it ends at the Lone Wolf Crossing of the Frio. The roan whickered; for he had a sense of locality and direction equal to that of a belt-line street-car horse; and he knew he would soon be nibbling the rich mesquite grass at the end of a forty-foot stake rope while Ulysses rested his head in Circe's straw-roofed hut.

More weird and lonesome than the journey of an Amazonian explorer is the ride of one through a Texas pear flat. With dismal monotony and startling variety the uncanny and multiform shapes of the cacti lift their twisted trunks, and fat, bristly hands to encumber the way. The demon plant, appearing to live without soil or rain, seems to taunt the parched traveller with its lush grey greenness. It warps itself a thousand times about what look to be open and inviting paths, only to lure the rider into blind and impassable spine-defended "bottoms of the bag," leaving him to retreat, if he can, with the points of the compass whirling in his head.

To be lost in the pear is to die almost the death of the thief on the cross, pierced by nails and with grotesque shapes of all the fiends hovering about.

But it was not so with the Kid and his mount. Winding, twisting, circling, tracing the most fantastic and bewildering trail ever picked out, the good roan lessened the distance to the Lone Wolf Crossing with every coil and turn that he made.

While they fared the Kid sang. He knew but one tune and he sang it, as he knew but one code and lived it, and but one girl and loved her. He was a single-minded man of conventional ideas. He had a voice like a coyote with bronchitis, but whenever he chose to sing his song he sang it. It was a conventional song of the camps and trail, running at its beginning as near as may be to these words:

> Don't you monkey with my Lulu girl
>
> Or I'll tell you what I'll do—

and so on. The roan was inured to it, and did not mind.

But even the poorest singer will, after a certain time, gain his own consent to refrain from contributing to the world's noises. So the Kid, by the time he was within a mile or two of Tonia's *jacal*, had reluctantly allowed his song to die away—not because his vocal performance had become less charming to his own ears, but because his laryngeal muscles were aweary.

As though he were in a circus ring the speckled roan wheeled and danced through the labyrinth of pear until at length his rider knew by certain landmarks that the Lone Wolf Crossing was close at hand. Then, where the pear was thinner, he caught sight of the grass roof of the *jacal* and the hackberry tree on the edge of the arroyo. A few yards farther the Kid stopped the roan—and gazed intently through the prickly openings. Then he dismounted, dropped the roan's reins, and proceeded on foot, stooping and silent, like an Indian. The roan, knowing his part, stood still, making no sound.

The Kid crept noiselessly to the very edge of the pear thicket and reconnoitered between the leaves of a clump of cactus.

Ten yards from his hiding-place, in the shade of the *jacal*, sat his Tonia calmly plaiting a rawhide lariat. So far she might surely escape condemnation; women have been known, from time to time, to engage in more mischievous occupations. But if all must be told, there is to be added that her head reposed against the broad and comfortable chest of a tall red-and-yellow man, and that his arm was about her, guiding her nimble small fingers that required so many lessons at the intricate six-strand plait.

Sandridge glanced quickly at the dark mass of pear when he heard a slight squeaking sound that was not altogether unfamiliar. A gun-scabbard will make that sound when one grasps the handle of a six-shooter suddenly. But the sound was not repeated; and Tonia's fingers needed close attention.

And then, in the shadow of death, they began to talk of their love; and in the still July afternoon every word they uttered reached the ears of the Kid.

"Remember, then," said Tonia, "you must not come again until I send for you. Soon he will be here. A *vaquero* at the *tienda* said to-day he saw him on the Guadalupe three days ago. When he is that near he always comes. If he comes and finds you here he will kill you. So, for my sake, you must come no more until I send you the word."

"All right," said the ranger. "And then what?"

"And then," said the girl, "you must bring your men here and kill him. If not, he will kill you."

"He ain't a man to surrender, that's sure," said Sandridge. "It's kill or be killed for the officer that goes up against Mr. Cisco Kid."

"He must die," said the girl. "Otherwise there will not be any peace in the world for thee and me. He has killed many. Let him so die. Bring your men, and give him no chance to escape."

"You used to think right much of him," said Sandridge.

Tonia dropped the lariat, twisted herself around, and curved a lemon-tinted arm over the ranger's shoulder.

"But then," she murmured in liquid Spanish, "I had not beheld thee, thou great, red mountain of a man! And thou art kind and good, as well as strong. Could one choose him, knowing thee? Let him die; for then I will not be filled with fear by day and night lest he hurt thee or me."

"How can I know when he comes?" asked Sandridge.

"When he comes," said Tonia, "he remains two days, sometimes three. Gregorio, the small son of old Luisa, the *lavandera*, has a swift pony. I will write a letter to thee and send it by him, saying how it will be best to come upon him. By Gregorio will the letter come. And bring many men with thee, and have much care, oh, dear red one, for the rattlesnake is not quicker to strike than is 'El Chivato,' as they call him, to send a ball from his *pistola*."

"The Kid's handy with his gun, sure enough," admitted Sandridge, "but when I come for him I shall come alone. I'll get him by myself or not at all. The Cap wrote one or two things to me that make me want to do the trick without any help. You let me know when Mr. Kid arrives, and I'll do the rest."

"I will send you the message by the boy Gregorio," said the girl. "I knew you were braver than that small slayer of men who never smiles. How could I ever have thought I cared for him?"

It was time for the ranger to ride back to his camp on the water hole. Before he mounted his horse he raised the slight form of Tonia with one arm high from the earth for a parting salute. The drowsy stillness of the torpid summer air still lay thick upon the dreaming afternoon. The smoke from the fire in the *jacal*, where the *frijoles* blubbered in the iron pot, rose straight as a plumb-line above the clay-daubed chimney. No sound or movement disturbed the serenity of the dense pear thicket ten yards away.

When the form of Sandridge had disappeared, loping his big dun down the steep banks of the Frio crossing, the Kid crept back to his own horse, mounted him, and rode back along the tortuous trail he had come.

But not far. He stopped and waited in the silent depths of the pear until half an hour had passed. And then Tonia heard the high, untrue notes of his unmusical singing coming nearer and nearer; and she ran to the edge of the pear to meet him.

The Kid seldom smiled; but he smiled and waved his hat when he saw her. He dismounted, and his girl sprang into his arms. The Kid looked at her fondly. His thick, black hair clung to his head like a wrinkled mat. The meeting brought a slight ripple of some undercurrent of feeling to his smooth, dark face that was usually as motionless as a clay mask.

"How's my girl?" he asked, holding her close.

"Sick of waiting so long for you, dear one," she answered. "My eyes are dim with always gazing into that devil's pincushion through which you come. And I can see into it such a little way, too. But you are here, beloved one, and I will not scold. *Que mal muchacho!* not to come to see your *alma* more often. Go in and rest, and let me water your horse and stake him with the long rope. There is cool water in the jar for you."

The Kid kissed her affectionately.

"Not if the court knows itself do I let a lady stake my horse for me," said he. "But if you'll run in, *chica*, and throw a pot of coffee together while I attend to the *caballo*, I'll be a good deal obliged."

Besides his marksmanship the Kid had another attribute for which he admired himself greatly. He was *muy caballero*, as the Mexicans express it, where the ladies were concerned. For them he had always gentle words and consideration. He could not have spoken a harsh word to a woman. He might ruthlessly slay their husbands and brothers, but he could not have laid the weight of a finger in anger upon a woman. Wherefore many of that interesting division of humanity who had come under the spell of his politeness declared their disbelief in the stories circulated about Mr. Kid. One shouldn't believe everything one heard, they said. When confronted by their indignant men folk with proof of the *caballero's* deeds of infamy, they said maybe he had been driven to it, and that he knew how to treat a lady, anyhow.

Considering this extremely courteous idiosyncrasy of the Kid and the pride that he took in it, one can perceive that the solution of the problem that was presented to him by what he saw and heard from his hiding-place in the pear that afternoon (at least as to one of the actors) must have been obscured by difficulties. And yet one could not think of the Kid overlooking little matters of that kind.

At the end of the short twilight they gathered around a supper of *frijoles*, goat steaks, canned peaches, and coffee, by the light of a lantern in the *jacal*. Afterward, the ancestor, his flock corralled, smoked a cigarette and became a mummy in a grey blanket. Tonia washed the few dishes while the Kid dried them with the flour-sacking towel. Her eyes shone; she chatted volubly of the inconsequent happenings of her small world since the Kid's last visit; it was as all his other home-comings had been.

Then outside Tonia swung in a grass hammock with her guitar and sang sad *canciones de amor*.

"Do you love me just the same, old girl?" asked the Kid, hunting for his cigarette papers.

"Always the same, little one," said Tonia, her dark eyes lingering upon him.

"I must go over to Fink's," said the Kid, rising, "for some tobacco. I thought I had another sack in my coat. I'll be back in a quarter of an hour."

"Hasten," said Tonia, "and tell me—how long shall I call you my own this time? Will you be gone again to-morrow, leaving me to grieve, or will you be longer with your Tonia?"

"Oh, I might stay two or three days this trip," said the Kid, yawning. "I've been on the dodge for a month, and I'd like to rest up."

He was gone half an hour for his tobacco. When he returned Tonia was still lying in the hammock.

"It's funny," said the Kid, "how I feel. I feel like there was somebody lying behind every bush and tree waiting to shoot me. I never had mullygrubs like them before. Maybe it's one of them presumptions. I've got half a notion to light out in the morning before day. The Guadalupe country is burning up about that old Dutchman I plugged down there."

"You are not afraid—no one could make my brave little one fear."

"Well, I haven't been usually regarded as a jackrabbit when it comes to scrapping; but I don't want a posse smoking me out when I'm in your *jacal*. Somebody might get hurt that oughtn't to."

"Remain with your Tonia; no one will find you here."

The Kid looked keenly into the shadows up and down the arroyo and toward the dim lights of the Mexican village.

"I'll see how it looks later on," was his decision.

At midnight a horseman rode into the rangers' camp, blazing his way by noisy "halloes" to indicate a pacific mission. Sandridge and one or two others turned out to investigate the row. The rider announced himself to be Domingo Sales, from the Lone Wolf Crossing. He bore a letter for Señor Sandridge. Old Luisa, the *lavandera*, had persuaded him to bring it, he said, her son Gregorio being too ill of a fever to ride.

Sandridge lighted the camp lantern and read the letter. These were its words:

> *Dear One*: He has come. Hardly had you ridden away when he came out of the pear. When he first talked he said he would stay three days or more. Then as it grew later he was like a wolf or a fox, and walked about without rest, looking and listening. Soon he said he must leave before daylight when it is dark and stillest. And then he seemed to suspect that I be not true to him. He looked at me so strange that I am frightened. I swear to him that I love him, his own Tonia. Last of all he said I must prove to him I am true. He thinks that even now men are waiting to kill him as he rides from my house. To escape he says he will dress in my clothes, my red skirt and the blue waist I wear and the brown mantilla over the head, and thus ride away. But before that he says that I must put on his clothes, his *pantalones* and *camisa* and hat, and ride away on his horse from the *jacal* as far as the big road beyond the crossing and back again. This before he goes, so he can tell if I am true and if men are hidden to shoot him. It is a terrible thing. An hour before daybreak this is to be. Come, my dear one, and kill this man and take me for your Tonia. Do not try to take hold of him alive, but kill him quickly. Knowing all, you should do that. You must come long before the time and hide yourself in the little shed near the *jacal* where the wagon and saddles

are kept. It is dark in there. He will wear my red skirt and blue waist and brown mantilla. I send you a hundred kisses. Come surely and shoot quickly and straight.

Thine Own Tonia.

Sandridge quickly explained to his men the official part of the missive. The rangers protested against his going alone.

"I'll get him easy enough," said the lieutenant. "The girl's got him trapped. And don't even think he'll get the drop on me."

Sandridge saddled his horse and rode to the Lone Wolf Crossing. He tied his big dun in a clump of brush on the arroyo, took his Winchester from its scabbard, and carefully approached the Perez *jacal*. There was only the half of a high moon drifted over by ragged, milk-white gulf clouds.

The wagon-shed was an excellent place for ambush; and the ranger got inside it safely. In the black shadow of the brush shelter in front of the *jacal* he could see a horse tied and hear him impatiently pawing the hard-trodden earth.

He waited almost an hour before two figures came out of the *jacal*. One, in man's clothes, quickly mounted the horse and galloped past the wagon-shed toward the crossing and village. And then the other figure, in skirt, waist, and mantilla over its head, stepped out into the faint moonlight, gazing after the rider. Sandridge thought he would take his chance then before Tonia rode back. He fancied she might not care to see it.

"Throw up your hands," he ordered loudly, stepping out of the wagon-shed with his Winchester at his shoulder.

There was a quick turn of the figure, but no movement to obey, so the ranger pumped in the bullets—one—two—three—and then twice more; for you never could be too sure of bringing down the Cisco Kid. There was no danger of missing at ten paces even in that half moonlight.

The old ancestor, asleep on his blanket, was awakened by the shots. Listening further, he heard a great cry from some man in mortal distress or anguish, and rose up grumbling at the disturbing ways of moderns.

The tall, red ghost of a man burst into the *jacal*, reaching one hand, shaking like a *tule* reed, for the lantern hanging on its nail. The other spread a letter on the table.

"Look at this letter, Perez," cried the man. "Who wrote it?"

"*Ah, Dios!* it is Señor Sandridge," mumbled the old man, approaching. "*Pues, señor,* that letter was written by '*El Chivato,*' as he is called—by the man of Tonia. They say he is a bad man; I do not know. While Tonia slept he wrote the letter and sent it by this old hand of mine to Domingo Sales to be brought to you. Is there anything wrong in the letter? I am very old; and I did not know. *Valgame Dios!* it is a very foolish world; and there is nothing in the house to drink—nothing to drink."

Just then all that Sandridge could think of to do was to go outside and throw himself face downward in the dust by the side of his humming-bird, of whom not a feather fluttered. He was not a *caballero* by instinct, and he could not understand the niceties of revenge.

A mile away the rider who had ridden past the wagon-shed struck up a harsh, untuneful song, the words of which began:

> Don't you monkey with my Lulu girl
>
> Or I'll tell you what I'll do—

5–9
Sui Sin Far (Edith Maude Eaton) (1865–1914)

One of the first published Asian American writers, SUI SIN FAR (1865–1914) was born EDITH MAUDE EATON in England of an English father and Chinese mother. Though her father was from money, and afforded Far and her eldest siblings an education, his poor life choices and a burgeoning family of a dozen children led to fiscal disaster. Her family's many moves to Montreal and elsewhere along with alarming poverty led Far to leave home young for employment with the newspapers. By her early thirties, Far was working in Seattle and San Francisco; there during the height of the anti-Asian immigrant movement, she discovered her love of fiction writing when reporting on the Asian American community segregated in Chinatowns. Assimilation, exclusion, and racial stereotyping became themes of her works; her stories, like "Mrs. Spring Fragrance" (1912), have inspired other Asian American writers like Amy Tan.

≈ ≈ ≈

"Mrs. Spring Fragrance" (1912)

I

When Mrs. Spring Fragrance first arrived in Seattle, she was unacquainted with even one word of the American language. Five years later her husband, speaking of her, said: "There are no more American words for her learning." And everyone who knew Mrs. Spring Fragrance agreed with Mr. Spring Fragrance.

Mr. Spring Fragrance, whose business name was Sing Yook, was a young curio merchant. Though conservatively Chinese in many respects, he was at the same time what is called by the Westerners, "Americanized." Mrs. Spring Fragrance was even more "Americanized."

Next door to the Spring Fragrances lived the Chin Yuens. Mrs. Chin Yuen was much older than Mrs. Spring Fragrance; but she had a daughter of eighteen with whom Mrs. Spring Fragrance was on terms of great friendship. The daughter was a pretty girl whose Chinese name was Mai Gwi Far (a rose) and whose American name was Laura. Nearly everybody called her Laura, even her parents and Chinese friends. Laura had a sweetheart, a youth named Kai Tzu. Kai Tzu, who was American-born, and as ruddy and stalwart as any young Westerner, was noted amongst baseball players as one of the finest pitchers on the Coast. He could also sing, "Drink to me only with thine eyes," to Laura's piano accompaniment.

Now the only person who knew that Kai Tzu loved Laura and that Laura loved Kai Tzu, was Mrs. Spring Fragrance. The reason for this was that, although the Chin Yuen parents lived in a house furnished in American style, and wore American clothes, yet they religiously observed many Chinese customs, and their ideals of life were the ideals of their Chinese forefathers. Therefore, they had betrothed their daughter, Laura, at the age of fifteen, to the eldest son of the Chinese Government school-teacher in San Francisco. The time for the consummation of the betrothal was approaching.

Laura was with Mrs. Spring Fragrance and Mrs. Spring Fragrance was trying to cheer her.

"I had such a pretty walk today," said she. "I crossed the banks above the beach and came back by the long road. In the green grass the daffodils were blowing, in the cottage gardens the currant bushes were flowering, and in the air was the perfume of the wallflower. I wished, Laura, that you were with me."

Laura burst into tears. "That is the walk," she sobbed, "Kai Tzu and I so love; but never, ah, never, can we take it together again."

"Now, Little Sister," comforted Mrs. Spring Fragrance, "you really must not grieve like that. Is there not a beautiful American poem written by a noble American named Tennyson, which says:

> "'Tis better to have loved and lost,
> Than never to have loved at all?'"*

Mrs. Spring Fragrance was unaware that Mr. Spring Fragrance, having returned from the city, tired with the day's business, had thrown himself down on the bamboo settee on the veranda, and that although his eyes were engaged in scanning the pages of the *Chinese World*, his ears could not help receiving the words which were borne to him through the open window.

> "'Tis better to have loved and lost,
> Than never to have loved at all,"

repeated Mr. Spring Fragrance. Not wishing to hear more of the secret talk of women, he arose and sauntered around the veranda to the other side of the house. Two pigeons circled around his head. He felt in his pocket for a li-chi which he usually carried for their pecking. His fingers touched a little box. It contained a jadestone pendant, which Mrs. Spring Fragrance had particularly admired the last time she was down town. It was the fifth anniversary of Mr. and Mrs. Spring Fragrance's wedding day.

Mr. Spring Fragrance pressed the little box down into the depths of his pocket.

A young man came out of the back door of the house at Mr. Spring Fragrance's left. The Chin Yuen house was at his right.

"Good evening," said the young man. "Good evening," returned Mr. Spring Fragrance. He stepped down from his porch and went and leaned over the railing which separated this yard from the yard in which stood the young man.

"Will you please tell me," said Mr. Spring Fragrance, "the meaning of two lines of an American verse which I have heard?"

"Certainly," returned the young man with a genial smile. He was a star student at the University of Washington, and had not the slightest doubt that he could explain the meaning of all things in the universe.

"Well," said Mr. Spring Fragrance, "it is this:

> "'Tis better to have loved and lost,
> Than never to have loved at all."

* [Verse from the English poet Alfred, Lord Tennyson's "In Memoriam A.H.H."—*E.J.D. and J.B.F.*]

"Ah!" responded the young man with an air of profound wisdom. "That, Mr. Spring Fragrance, means that it is a good thing to love anyway—even if we can't get what we love, or, as the poet tells us, lose what we love. Of course, one needs experience to feel the truth of this teaching."

The young man smiled pensively and reminiscently. More than a dozen young maidens "loved and lost" were passing before his mind's eye.

"The truth of the teaching!" echoed Mr. Spring Fragrance, a little testily. "There is no truth in it whatever. It is disobedient to reason. Is it not better to have what you do not love than to love what you do not have?"

"That depends," answered the young man, "upon temperament."

"I thank you. Good evening," said Mr. Spring Fragrance. He turned away to muse upon the unwisdom of the American way of looking at things.

Meanwhile, inside the house, Laura was refusing to be comforted.

"Ah, no! no!" cried she. "If I had not gone to school with Kai Tzu, nor talked nor walked with him, nor played the accompaniments to his songs, then I might consider with complacency, or at least without horror, my approaching marriage with the son of Man You. But as it is—oh, as it is—!"

The girl rocked herself to and fro in heartfelt grief.

Mrs. Spring Fragrance knelt down beside her, and clasping her arms around her neck, cried in sympathy:

"Little Sister, oh, Little Sister! Dry your tears—do not despair. A moon has yet to pass before the marriage can take place. Who knows what the stars may have to say to one another during its passing? A little bird has whispered to me—"

For a long time Mrs. Spring Fragrance talked. For a long time Laura listened. When the girl arose to go, there was a bright light in her eyes.

II

Mrs. Spring Fragrance, in San Francisco on a visit to her cousin, the wife of the herb doctor of Clay Street, was having a good time. She was invited everywhere that the wife of an honorable Chinese merchant could go. There was much to see and hear, including more than a dozen babies who had been born in the families of her friends since she last visited the city of the Golden Gate. Mrs. Spring Fragrance loved babies. She had had two herself, but both had been transplanted into the spirit land before the completion of even one moon. There were also many dinners and theatre-parties given in her honor. It was at one of the theatre-parties that Mrs. Spring Fragrance met Ah Oi, a young girl who had the reputation of being the prettiest Chinese girl in San Francisco, and the naughtiest. In spite of gossip, however, Mrs. Spring Fragrance took a great fancy to Ah Oi and invited her to a tête-à-tête picnic on the following day. This invitation Ah Oi joyfully accepted. She was a sort of bird girl and never felt so happy as when out in the park or woods.

On the day after the picnic Mrs. Spring Fragrance wrote to Laura Chin Yuen thus:

> My Precious Laura,—May the bamboo ever wave. Next week I accompany Ah Oi to the beauteous town of San José. There will we be met by the son of the Illustrious Teacher, and in a little Mission, presided over by a benevolent American priest, the little Ah Oi and the son of the Illustrious Teacher will be joined together in love and harmony—two pieces of music made to complete one another.
>
> The Son of the Illustrious Teacher, having been through an American Hall of Learning, is well able to provide for his orphan bride and fears not the displeasure of his parents, now that he is assured that your grief at his loss will not be inconsolable. He wishes me to waft to you and to Kai Tzu— and the little Ah Oi joins with him—ten thousand rainbow wishes for your happiness.
>
> My respects to your honorable parents, and to yourself, the heart of your loving friend,
>
> Jade Spring Fragrance

To Mr. Spring Fragrance, Mrs. Spring Fragrance also indited a letter:

> Great and Honored Man,—Greeting from your plum blossom,* who is desirous of hiding herself from the sun of your presence for a week of seven days more. My honorable cousin is preparing for the Fifth Moon Festival, and wishes me to compound for the occasion some American "fudge," for which delectable sweet, made by my clumsy hands, you have sometimes shown a slight prejudice. I am enjoying a most agreeable visit, and American friends, as also our own, strive benevolently for the accomplishment of my pleasure. Mrs. Samuel Smith, an American lady, known to my cousin, asked for my accompaniment to a magniloquent lecture the other evening. The subject was "America, the Protector of China!" It was most exhilarating, and the effect of so much expression of benevolence leads me to beg of you to forget to remember that the barber charges you one dollar for a shave while he humbly submits to the American man a bill of fifteen cents. And murmur no more because your honored elder brother, on a visit to

---

* The plum blossom is the Chinese flower of virtue. It has been adopted by the Japanese, just in the same way as they have adopted the Chinese national flower, the chrysanthemum.

this country, is detained under the roof-tree of this great Government instead of under your own humble roof. Console him with the reflection that he is protected under the wing of the Eagle, the Emblem of Liberty. What is the loss of ten hundred years or ten thousand times ten dollars compared with the happiness of knowing oneself so securely sheltered? All of this I have learned from Mrs. Samuel Smith, who is as brilliant and great of mind as one of your own superior sex.

For me it is sufficient to know that the Golden Gate Park is most enchanting, and the seals on the rock at the Cliff House extremely entertaining and amiable. There is much feasting and merry-making under the lanterns in honor of your Stupid Thorn.

I have purchased for your smoking a pipe with an amber mouth. It is said to be very sweet to the lips and to emit a cloud of smoke fit for the gods to inhale.

Awaiting, by the wonderful wire of the telegram message, your gracious permission to remain for the celebration of the Fifth Moon Festival and the making of American "fudge," I continue for ten thousand times ten thousand years,

Your ever loving and obedient woman,

Jade

P.S. Forget not to care for the cat, the birds, and the flowers. Do not eat too quickly nor fan too vigorously now that the weather is warming.

Mrs. Spring Fragrance smiled as she folded this last epistle. Even if he were old-fashioned, there was never a husband so good and kind as hers. Only on one occasion since their marriage had he slighted her wishes. That was when, on the last anniversary of their wedding, she had signified a desire for a certain jadestone pendant, and he had failed to satisfy that desire.

But Mrs. Spring Fragrance, being of a happy nature, and disposed to look upon the bright side of things, did not allow her mind to dwell upon the jade-stone pendant. Instead, she gazed complacently down upon her bejeweled fingers and folded in with her letter to Mr. Spring Fragrance a bright little sheaf of condensed love.

III

Mr. Spring Fragrance sat on his doorstep. He had been reading two letters, one from Mrs. Spring Fragrance, and the other from an elderly bachelor cousin in

San Francisco. The one from the elderly bachelor cousin was a business letter, but contained the following postscript:

> Tsen Hing, the son of the Government schoolmaster, seems to be much in the company of your young wife. He is a good-looking youth, and pardon me, my dear cousin; but if women are allowed to stray at will from under their husbands' mulberry roofs, what is to prevent them from becoming butterflies?

"Sing Foon is old and cynical," said Mr. Spring Fragrance to himself. "Why should I pay any attention to him? This is America, where a man may speak to a woman, and a woman listen, without any thought of evil."

He destroyed his cousin's letter and re-read his wife's. Then he became very thoughtful. Was the making of American fudge sufficient reason for a wife to wish to remain a week longer in a city where her husband was not?

The young man who lived in the next house came out to water the lawn.

"Good evening," said he. "Any news from Mrs. Spring Fragrance?"

"She is having a very good time," returned Mr. Spring Fragrance.

"Glad to hear it. I think you told me she was to return the end of this week."

"I have changed my mind about her," said Mr. Spring Fragrance. "I am bidding her remain a week longer, as I wish to give a smoking party during her absence. I hope I may have the pleasure of your company."

"I shall be delighted," returned the young fellow. "But, Mr. Spring Fragrance, don't invite any other white fellows. If you do not I shall be able to get in a scoop. You know, I'm a sort of honorary reporter for the *Gleaner*."

"Very well," absently answered Mr. Spring Fragrance.

"Of course, your friend the Consul will be present. I shall call it 'A high-class Chinese stag party!'"

In spite of his melancholy mood, Mr. Spring Fragrance smiled.

"Everything is 'high-class' in America," he observed.

"Sure!" cheerfully assented the young man. "Haven't you ever heard that all Americans are princes and princesses, and just as soon as a foreigner puts his foot upon our shores, he also becomes of the nobility—I mean, the royal family."

"What about my brother in the Detention Pen?" dryly inquired Mr. Spring Fragrance.

"Now, you've got me," said the young man, rubbing his head. "Well, that is a shame—'a beastly shame,' as the Englishman says. But understand, old fellow, we that are real Americans are up against that—even more than you. It is against our principles."

"I offer the real Americans my consolations that they should be compelled to do that which is against their principles."

"Oh, well, it will all come right some day. We're not a bad sort, you know. Think of the indemnity money returned to the Dragon by Uncle Sam."

Mr. Spring Fragrance puffed his pipe in silence for some moments. More than politics was troubling his mind.

At last he spoke. "Love," said he, slowly and distinctly, "comes before the wedding in this country, does it not?"

"Yes, certainly."

Young Carman knew Mr. Spring Fragrance well enough to receive with calmness his most astounding queries.

"Presuming," continued Mr. Spring Fragrance—"presuming that some friend of your father's, living—presuming—in England—has a daughter that he arranges with your father to be your wife. Presuming that you have never seen that daughter, but that you marry her, knowing her not. Presuming that she marries you, knowing you not.—After she marries you and knows you, will that woman love you?"

"Emphatically, no," answered the young man.

"That is the way it would be in America—that the woman who marries the man like that—would not love him?"

"Yes, that is the way it would be in America. Love, in this country, must be free, or it is not love at all."

"In China, it is different!" mused Mr. Spring Fragrance.

"Oh, yes, I have no doubt that in China it is different."

"But the love is in the heart all the same," went on Mr. Spring Fragrance.

"Yes, all the same. Everybody falls in love some time or another. Some"—pensively—"many times."

Mr. Spring Fragrance arose.

"I must go down town," said he.

As he walked down the street he recalled the remark of a business acquaintance who had met his wife and had had some conversation with her: "She is just like an American woman."

He had felt somewhat flattered when this remark had been made. He looked upon it as a compliment to his wife's cleverness; but it rankled in his mind as he entered the telegraph office. If his wife was becoming as an American woman, would it not be possible for her to love as an American woman—a man to whom she was not married? There also floated in his memory the verse which his wife had quoted to the daughter of Chin Yuen. When the telegraph clerk handed him a blank, he wrote this message:

"Remain as you wish, but remember that "Tis better to have loved and lost, than never to have loved at all.""

When Mrs. Spring Fragrance received this message, her laughter tinkled like falling water. How droll! How delightful! Here was her husband quoting American poetry in a telegram. Perhaps he had been reading her American poetry books since she had left him! She hoped so. They would lead him to understand her sympathy for her dear Laura and Kai Tzu. She need no longer keep from him their secret. How joyful! It had been such a hardship to refrain from confiding in him before. But discreetness had been most necessary, seeing that Mr. Spring Fragrance entertained as old-fashioned notions concerning marriage as did the Chin Yuen parents. Strange that that should be so, since he had fallen in love with her picture before *ever* he had seen her, just as she had fallen in love with his! And when the marriage veil was lifted and each beheld the other for the first time in the flesh, there had been no disillusion— no lessening of the respect and affection, which those who had brought about the marriage had inspired in each young heart.

Mrs. Spring Fragrance began to wish she could fall asleep and wake to find the week flown, and she in her own little home pouring tea for Mr. Spring Fragrance.

IV

Mr. Spring Fragrance was walking to business with Mr. Chin Yuen. As they walked they talked.

"Yes," said Mr. Chin Yuen, "the old order is passing away, and the new order is taking its place, even with us who are Chinese. I have finally consented to give my daughter in marriage to young Kai Tzu."

Mr. Spring Fragrance expressed surprise. He had understood that the marriage between his neighbor's daughter and the San Francisco school-teacher's son was all arranged.

"So 'twas," answered Mr. Chin Yuen; "but it seems the young renegade, without consultation or advice, has placed his affections upon some untrustworthy female, and is so under her influence that he refuses to fulfil his parents' promise to me for him."

"So!" said Mr. Spring Fragrance. The shadow on his brow deepened.

"But," said Mr. Chin Yuen, with affable resignation, "it is all ordained by Heaven. Our daughter, as the wife of Kai Tzu, for whom she has long had a loving feeling, will not now be compelled to dwell with a mother-in-law and where her own mother is not. For that, we are thankful, as she is our only one and the conditions of life in this Western country are not as in China.

Moreover, Kai Tzu, though not so much of a scholar as the teacher's son, has a keen eye for business and that, in America, is certainly much more desirable than scholarship. What do you think?"

"Eh! What!" exclaimed Mr. Spring Fragrance. The latter part of his companion's remarks had been lost upon him.

That day the shadow which had been following Mr. Spring Fragrance ever since he had heard his wife quote, "'Tis better to have loved," etc., became so heavy and deep that he quite lost himself within it.

At home in the evening he fed the cat, the bird, and the flowers. Then, seating himself in a carved black chair—a present from his wife on his last birthday—he took out his pipe and smoked. The cat jumped into his lap. He stroked it softly and tenderly. It had been much fondled by Mrs. Spring Fragrance, and Mr. Spring Fragrance was under the impression that it missed her. "Poor thing!" said he. "I suppose you want her back!" When he arose to go to bed he placed the animal carefully on the floor, and thus apostrophized it:

"O Wise and Silent One, your mistress returns to you, but her heart she leaves behind her, with the Tommies in San Francisco."

The Wise and Silent One made no reply. He was not a jealous cat.

Mr. Spring Fragrance slept not that night; the next morning he ate not. Three days and three nights without sleep and food went by.

There was a springlike freshness in the air on the day that Mrs. Spring Fragrance came home. The skies overhead were as blue as Puget Sound stretching its gleaming length toward the mighty Pacific, and all the beautiful green world seemed to be throbbing with springing life.

Mrs. Spring Fragrance was never so radiant.

"Oh," she cried light-heartedly, "is it not lovely to see the sun shining so clear, and everything so bright to welcome me?"

Mr. Spring Fragrance made no response. It was the morning after the fourth sleepless night.

Mrs. Spring Fragrance noticed his silence, also his grave face.

"Everything—everyone is glad to see me but you," she declared, half seriously, half jestingly.

Mr. Spring Fragrance set down her valise. They had just entered the house.

"If my wife is glad to see me," he quietly replied, "I also am glad to see her!"

Summoning their servant boy, he bade him look after Mrs. Spring Fragrance's comfort.

"I must be at the store in half an hour," said he, looking at his watch. "There is some very important business requiring attention."

"What is the business?" inquired Mrs. Spring Fragrance, her lip quivering with disappointment.

"I cannot just explain to you," answered her husband.

Mrs. Spring Fragrance looked up into his face with honest and earnest eyes. There was something in his manner, in the tone of her husband's voice, which touched her.

"Yen," said she, "you do not look well. You are not well. What is it?"

Something arose in Mr. Spring Fragrance's throat which prevented him from replying.

"O darling one! O sweetest one!" cried a girl's joyous voice. Laura Chin Yuen ran into the room and threw her arms around Mrs. Spring Fragrance's neck.

"I spied you from the window," said Laura, "and I couldn't rest until I told you. We are to be married next week, Kai Tzu and I. And all through you, all through you—the sweetest jade jewel in the world!"

Mr. Spring Fragrance passed out of the room.

"So the son of the Government teacher and little Happy Love are already married," Laura went on, relieving Mrs. Spring Fragrance of her cloak, her hat, and her folding fan.

Mr. Spring Fragrance paused upon the doorstep.

"Sit down, Little Sister, and I will tell you all about it," said Mrs. Spring Fragrance, forgetting her husband for a moment.

When Laura Chin Yuen had danced away, Mr. Spring Fragrance came in and hung up his hat.

"You got back very soon," said Mrs. Spring Fragrance, covertly wiping away the tears which had begun to fall as soon as she thought herself alone.

"I did not go," answered Mr. Spring Fragrance. "I have been listening to you and Laura."

"But if the business is very important, do not you think you should attend to it?" anxiously queried Mrs. Spring Fragrance.

"It is not important to me now," returned Mr. Spring Fragrance. "I would prefer to hear again about Ah Oi and Man You and Laura and Kai Tzu."

"How lovely of you to say that!" exclaimed Mrs. Spring Fragrance, who was easily made happy. And she began to chat away to her husband in the friendliest and wifeliest fashion possible. When she had finished she asked him if he were not glad to hear that those who loved as did the young lovers whose secrets she had been keeping, were to be united; and he replied that indeed he was; that he would like every man to be as happy with a wife as he himself had ever been and ever would be.

"You did not always talk like that," said Mrs. Spring Fragrance slyly. "You must have been reading my American poetry books!"

"American poetry!" ejaculated Mr. Spring Fragrance almost fiercely, "American poetry is detestable, *abhorrable!*"

"Why! why!" exclaimed Mrs. Spring Fragrance, more and more surprised.

But the only explanation which Mr. Spring Fragrance vouchsafed was a jadestone pendant.

5–10
Mary Hunter Austin (1868–1934)

MARY HUNTER AUSTIN (1868–1934) moved west from Illinois at age twenty to homestead and farm the dry California San Joaquin Valley. There she farmed with her birth family and her husband until they separated, their marriage worn down from raising a developmentally delayed daughter and from fighting for and losing their water rights. Around 1900, Austin discovered her love of writing, when eco-writing about the desert was becoming popular. Environmentalists like John Muir loved an untouched landscape, but Austin shared the farmer's heart, and championed the utility of land, even if this meant the use of precious water resources for irrigation. A lover of the stark California desert, she found solace and discovered her voice in writing *The Land of Little Rain* (1903). This excerpt attests to the stunning quality of her prose and sensitivity to nature, a sensitivity also apparent in her work collecting the poetry and song of Southwest Native Americans (see *Path on the Rainbow*).

≈ ≈ ≈

From *The Land of Little Rain* (1903)

Chapter 2. Water Trails of the Ceriso

By the end of the dry season the water trails of the Ceriso are worn to a white ribbon in the leaning grass, spread out faint and fanwise toward the homes of gopher and ground rat and squirrel. But however faint to man-sight, they are sufficiently plain to the furred and feathered folk who travel them. Getting down to the eye level of rat and squirrel kind, one perceives what might easily be wide and winding roads to us if they occurred in thick plantations of trees three times the height of a man. It needs but a slender thread of barrenness to make a mouse trail in the forest of the sod. To the little people the water trails are as country roads, with scents as signboards.

It seems that man-height is the least fortunate of all heigh
study trails. It is better to go up the front of some tall hill, say
Mountain, looking back and down across the hollow of th
how long the soil keeps the impression of any continuous tr
grass has overgrown it. Twenty years since, a brief heyday of mining at ....
Mountain made a stage road across the Ceriso, yet the parallel lines that are
the wheel traces show from the height dark and well defined. Afoot in the Ceriso one looks in vain for any sign of it. So all the paths that wild creatures use
going down to the Lone Tree Spring are mapped out whitely from this level,
which is also the level of the hawks.

There is little water in the Ceriso at the best of times, and that little brackish
and smelling vilely, but by a lone juniper where the rim of the Ceriso breaks
away to the lower country, there is a perpetual rill of fresh sweet drink in the
midst of lush grass and watercress. In the dry season there is no water else for
a man's long journey of a day. East to the foot of Black Mountain, and north
and south without counting, are the burrows of small rodents, rat and squirrel
kind. Under the sage are the shallow forms of the jackrabbits, and in the dry
banks of washes, and among the strewn fragments of black rock, lairs of bobcat, fox, and coyote.

The coyote is your true water-witch, one who snuffs and paws, snuffs and
paws again at the smallest spot of moisture-scented earth until he has freed
the blind water from the soil. Many water-holes are no more than this detected
by the lean hobo of the hills in localities where not even an Indian would look
for it.

It is the opinion of many wise and busy people that the hill-folk pass the
ten-month interval between the end and renewal of winter rains, with no
drink; but your true idler, with days and nights to spend beside the water trails,
will not subscribe to it. The trails begin, as I said, very far back in the Ceriso,
faintly, and converge in one span broad, white, hard-trodden way in the gully
of the spring. And why trails if there are no travelers in that direction?

I have yet to find the land not scarred by the thin, far roadways of rabbits
and what not of furry folks that run in them. Venture to look for some seldom-
touched water-hole, and so long as the trails run with your general direction
make sure you are right, but if they begin to cross yours at never so slight an
angle, to converge toward a point left or right of your objective, no matter what
the maps say, or your memory, trust them; they *know*.

It is very still in the Ceriso by day, so that were it not for the evidence of
those white beaten ways, it might be the desert it looks. The sun is hot in the
dry season, and the days are filled with the glare of it. Now and again some

.ıseen coyote signals his pack in a long-drawn, dolorous whine that comes from no determinate point, but nothing stirs much before mid-afternoon. It is a sign when there begin to be hawks skimming above the sage that the little people are going about their business.

We have fallen on a very careless usage, speaking of wild creatures as if they were bound by some such limitation as hampers clockwork. When we say of one and another, they are night prowlers, it is perhaps true only as the things they feed upon are more easily come by in the dark, and they know well how to adjust themselves to conditions wherein food is more plentiful by day. And their accustomed performance is very much a matter of keen eye, keener scent, quick ear, and a better memory of sights and sounds than man dares boast. Watch a coyote come out of his lair and cast about in his mind where he will go for his daily killing. You cannot very well tell what decides him, but very easily that he has decided. He trots or breaks into short gallops, with very perceptible pauses to look up and about at landmarks, alters his tack a little, looking forward and back to steer his proper course. I am persuaded that the coyotes in my valley, which is narrow and beset with steep, sharp hills, in long passages steer by the pinnacles of the sky-line, going with head cocked to one side to keep to the left or right of such and such a promontory.

I have trailed a coyote often, going across country, perhaps to where some slant-winged scavenger hanging in the air signaled prospect of a dinner, and found his track such as a man, a very intelligent man accustomed to a hill country, and a little cautious, would make to the same point. Here a detour to avoid a stretch of too little cover, there a pause on the rim of a gully to pick the better way,—and it is usually the best way,—and making his point with the greatest economy of effort. Since the time of Seyavi the deer have shifted their feeding ground across the valley at the beginning of deep snows, by way of the Black Rock, fording the river at Charley's Butte, and making straight for the mouth of the cañon that is the easiest going to the winter pastures on Waban. So they still cross, though whatever trail they had has been long broken by ploughed ground; but from the mouth of Tinpah Creek, where the deer come out of the Sierras, it is easily seen that the creek, the point of Black Rock, and Charley's Butte are in line with the wide bulk of shade that is the foot of Waban Pass. And along with this the deer have learned that Charley's Butte is almost the only possible ford, and all the shortest crossing of the valley. It seems that the wild creatures have learned all that is important to their way of life except the changes of the moon. I have seen some prowling fox or coyote, surprised by its sudden rising from behind the mountain wall, slink in its increasing glow, watch it furtively from the cover of near-by brush, unprepared and half uncertain of its identity until it rode clear of the peaks, and finally make off with all the air of one caught napping by an ancient joke. The moon in its wanderings must be a sort of exasperation to cunning beasts, likely to spoil by untimely risings some fore-planned mischief.

But to take the trail again; the coyotes that are astir in the Ceriso of late afternoons, harrying the rabbits from their shallow forms, and the hawks that sweep and swing above them, are not there from any mechanical promptings of instinct, but because they know of old experience that the small fry are about to take to seed gathering and the water trails. The rabbits begin it, taking the trail with long, light leaps, one eye and ear cocked to the hills from whence a coyote might descend upon them at any moment. Rabbits are a foolish people. They do not fight except with their own kind, nor use their paws except for feet, and appear to have no reason for existence but to furnish meals for meat-eaters. In flight they seem to rebound from the earth of their own elasticity, but keep a sober pace going to the spring. It is the young watercress that tempts them and the pleasures of society, for they seldom drink. Even in localities where there are flowing streams they seem to prefer the moisture that collects on herbage, and after rains may be seen rising on their haunches to drink delicately the clear drops caught in the tops of the young sage. But drink they must, as I have often seen them mornings and evenings at the rill that goes by my door. Wait long enough at the Lone Tree Spring and sooner or later they will all come in. But here their matings are accomplished, and though they are fearful of so little as a cloud shadow or blown leaf, they contrive to have some playful hours. At the spring the bobcat drops down upon them from the black rock, and the red fox picks them up returning in the dark. By day the hawk and eagle overshadow them, and the coyote has all times and seasons for his own.

Cattle, when there are any in the Ceriso, drink morning and evening, spending the night on the warm last lighted slopes of neighboring hills, stirring with the peep o' day. In these half wild spotted steers the habits of an earlier lineage persist. It must be long since they have made beds for themselves, but before lying down they turn themselves round and round as dogs do. They choose bare and stony ground, exposed fronts of westward facing hills, and lie down in companies. Usually by the end of the summer the cattle have been driven or gone of their own choosing to the mountain meadows. One year a maverick yearling, strayed or overlooked by the vaqueros, kept on until the season's end, and so betrayed another visitor to the spring that else I might have missed. On a certain morning the half-eaten carcass lay at the foot of the black rock, and in moist earth by the rill of the spring, the foot-pads of a cougar, puma, mountain lion, or whatever the beast is rightly called. The kill must have been made early in the evening, for it appeared that the cougar had been twice to the spring; and since the meat-eater drinks little until he has eaten, he must have fed and drunk, and after an interval of lying up in the black rock, had eaten and drunk again. There was no knowing how far he had come, but if he came again the second night he found that the coyotes had left him very little of his kill.

Nobody ventures to say how infrequently and at what hour the small fry visit the spring. There are such numbers of them that if each came once between the last of spring and the first of winter rains, there would still be water trails. I have seen badgers drinking about the hour when the light takes on the yellow tinge it has from coming slantwise through the hills. They find out shallow places, and are loath to wet their feet. Rats and chipmunks have been observed visiting the spring as late as nine o'clock mornings. The larger spermophiles that live near the spring and keep awake to work all day, come and go at no particular hour, drinking sparingly. At long intervals on half-lighted days, meadow and field mice steal delicately along the trail. These visitors are all too small to be watched carefully at night, but for evidence of their frequent coming there are the trails that may be traced miles out among the crisping grasses. On rare nights, in the places where no grass grows between the shrubs, and the sand silvers whitely to the moon, one sees them whisking to and fro on innumerable errands of seed gathering, but the chief witnesses of their presence near the spring are the elf owls. Those burrow-haunting, speckled fluffs of greediness begin a twilight flitting toward the spring, feeding as they go on grasshoppers, lizards, and small, swift creatures, diving into burrows to catch field mice asleep, battling with chipmunks at their own doors, and getting down in great numbers toward the lone juniper. Now owls do not love water greatly on its own account. Not to my knowledge have I caught one drinking or bathing, though on night wanderings across the mesa they flit up from under the horse's feet along stream borders. Their presence near the spring in great numbers would indicate the presence of the things they feed upon. All night the rustle and soft hooting keeps on in the neighborhood of the spring, with seldom small shrieks of mortal agony. It is clear day before they have all gotten back to their particular hummocks, and if one follows cautiously, not to frighten them into some near-by burrow, it is possible to trail them far up the slope.

The crested quail that troop in the Ceriso are the happiest frequenters of the water trails. There is no furtiveness about their morning drink. About the time the burrowers and all that feed upon them are addressing themselves to sleep, great flocks pour down the trails with that peculiar melting motion of moving

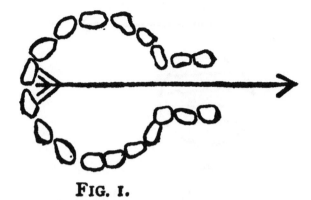

FIG. I.

quail, twittering, shoving, and shouldering. They splatter into the shallows, drink daintily, shake out small showers over their perfect coats, and melt away again into the scrub, preening and pranking, with soft contented noises.

After the quail, sparrows and ground-inhabiting birds bathe with the utmost frankness and a great deal of splutter; and here in the heart of noon hawks resort, sitting panting, with wings aslant, and a truce to all hostilities because of the heat. One summer there came a road-runner up from the lower valley, peeking and prying, and he had never any patience with the water baths of the sparrows. His own ablutions were performed in the clean, hopeful dust of the chaparral; and whenever he happened on their morning splatterings, he would depress his glossy crest, slant his shining tail to the level of his body, until he looked most like some bright venomous snake, daunting them with shrill abuse and feint of battle. Then suddenly he would go tilting and balancing down the gully in fine disdain, only to return in a day or two to make sure the foolish bodies were still at it.

Out on the Ceriso about five miles, and wholly out of sight of it, near where the immemorial foot trail goes up from Saline Flat toward Black Mountain, is a water sign worth turning out of the trail to see. It is a laid circle of stones large enough not to be disturbed by any ordinary hap, with an opening flanked by two parallel rows of similar stones, between which were an arrow placed, touching the opposite rim of the circle, thus (Fig. 1), it would point as the crow flies to the spring. It is the old, indubitable water mark of the Shoshones. One still finds it in the desert ranges in Salt Wells and Mesquite valleys, and along the slopes of Waban. On the other side of Ceriso, where the black rock begins, about a mile from the spring, is the work of an older, forgotten people. The rock hereabout is all volcanic, fracturing with a crystalline whitish surface, but

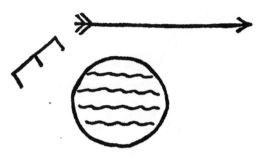

FIG. 2.

weathered outside to furnace blackness. Around the spring, where must have been a gathering place of the tribes, it is scored over with strange pictures and symbols that have no meaning to the Indians of the present day; but out where the rock begins, there is carved into the white heart of it a pointing arrow over the symbol for distance and a circle full of wavy lines (Fig. 2) reading thus: "In this direction three [units of measurement unknown] is a spring of sweet water; look for it."

5–11

Stephen Crane (1871–1900)

The fourteenth child of an aging minister, STEPHEN CRANE (1871–1900) led a peripatetic and adventure-filled life of a mere twenty-eight years. From New Jersey, Crane was eight when his father died, and he was passed off from one relative to another. College did not steady Crane; he dropped out of two universities by age twenty. For his next adventure, Crane became a journalist, covering the slums of New York City. Social realism appealed to the young writer, and under the guidance of writer Hamlin Garland, Crane began to find his voice with *Maggie, A Girl of the Streets* (1893), a novel of environmental determinism, in which a young woman is a victim of circumstance. After writing *The Red Badge of Courage*, a novel about the effects of war on a soldier, Crane took work as a reporter in the West, where he first conceived of "The Bride Comes to Yellow Sky" (1898), a story about a town marshal's return to the fictional Texas town of Yellow Sky and the end of the Old West.

≈ ≈ ≈

"The Bride Comes to Yellow Sky" (1898)

I

The great Pullman was whirling onward with such dignity of motion that a glance from the window seemed simply to prove that the plains of Texas were pouring eastward. Vast flats of green grass, dull-hued spaces of mesquit and cactus, little groups of frame houses, woods of light and tender trees, all were sweeping into the east, sweeping over the horizon, a precipice.

A newly married pair had boarded this coach at San Antonio. The man's face was reddened from many days in the wind and sun, and a direct result of his new black clothes was that his brick-colored hands were constantly performing in a most conscious fashion. From time to time he looked down respectfully at his attire. He sat with a hand on each knee, like a man waiting in a barber's shop. The glances he devoted to other passengers were furtive and shy.

The bride was not pretty, nor was she very young. She wore a dress of blue cashmere, with small reservations of velvet here and there, and with steel buttons abounding. She continually twisted her head to regard her puff-sleeves, very stiff, straight, and high. They embarrassed her. It was quite apparent that she had cooked, and that she expected to cook, dutifully. The blushes caused by the careless scrutiny of some passengers as she had entered the car were strange to see upon this plain, under-class countenance, which was drawn in placid, almost emotionless lines.

They were evidently very happy. "Ever been in a parlor-car before?" he asked, smiling with delight.

"No," she answered; "I never was. It's fine, ain't it?"

"Great! And then after a while we'll go forward to the diner, and get a big lay-out. Finest meal in the world. Charge a dollar."

"Oh, do they?" cried the bride. "Charge a dollar? Why, that's too much—for us—ain't it, Jack?"

"Not this trip, anyhow," he answered bravely. "We're going to go the whole thing."

Later, he explained to her about the train. "You see, it's a thousand miles from one end of Texas to the other; and this train runs right across it, and never stops but four times." He had the pride of an owner. He pointed out to her the dazzling fittings of the coach; and in truth her eyes opened wider as she contemplated the sea-green figured velvet, the shining brass, silver, and glass, the wood that gleamed as darkly brilliant as the surface of a pool of oil. At one end a bronze figure sturdily held a support for a separated chamber, and at convenient places on the ceiling were frescoes in olive and silver.

To the minds of the pair, their surroundings reflected the glory of their marriage that morning in San Antonio; this was the environment of their new estate; and the man's face in particular beamed with an elation that made him appear ridiculous to the negro porter. This individual at times surveyed them from afar with an amused and superior grin. On other occasions he bullied them with skill in ways that did not make it exactly plain to them that they were being bullied. He subtly used all the manners of the most unconquerable kind of snobbery. He oppressed them; but of this oppression they had small knowledge, and they speedily forgot that infrequently a number of travelers covered them with stares of derisive enjoyment. Historically there was supposed to be something infinitely humorous in their situation.

"We are due in Yellow Sky at 3:42," he said, looking tenderly into her eyes.

"Oh, are we?" she said, as if she had not been aware of it. To evince surprise at her husband's statement was part of her wifely amiability. She took from a pocket a little silver watch; and as she held it before her, and stared at it with a frown of attention, the new husband's face shone.

"I bought it in San Anton' from a friend of mine," he told her gleefully.

"It's seventeen minutes past twelve," she said, looking up at him with a kind of shy and clumsy coquetry. A passenger, noting this play, grew excessively sardonic, and winked at himself in one of the numerous mirrors.

At last they went to the dining-car. Two rows of negro waiters, in glowing white suits, surveyed their entrance with the interest, and also the equanimity, of men who had been forewarned. The pair fell to the lot of a waiter who happened to feel pleasure in steering them through their meal. He viewed them with the manner of a fatherly pilot, his countenance radiant with benevolence. The patronage, entwined with the ordinary deference, was not plain to them. And yet, as they returned to their coach, they showed in their faces a sense of escape.

To the left, miles down a long purple slope, was a little ribbon of mist where moved the keening Rio Grande. The train was approaching it at an angle, and the apex was Yellow Sky. Presently it was apparent that, as the distance from Yellow Sky grew shorter, the husband became commensurately restless. His brick-red hands were more insistent in their prominence. Occasionally he was even rather absent-minded and far-away when the bride leaned forward and addressed him.

As a matter of truth, Jack Potter was beginning to find the shadow of a deed weigh upon him like a leaden slab. He, the town marshal of Yellow Sky, a man known, liked, and feared in his corner, a prominent person, had gone to San Antonio to meet a girl he believed he loved, and there, after the usual prayers, had actually induced her to marry him without consulting Yellow Sky for any part of the transaction. He was now bringing his bride before an innocent and unsuspecting community.

Of course people in Yellow Sky married as it pleased them, in accordance with a general custom; but such was Potter's thought of his duty to his friends, or of their idea of his duty, or of an unspoken form which does not control men in these matters, that he felt he was heinous. He had committed an extraordinary crime. Face to face with this girl in San Antonio, and spurred by his sharp impulse, he had gone headlong over all the social hedges. At San Antonio he was like a man hidden in the dark. A knife to sever any friendly duty, any form, was easy to his hand in that remote city. But the hour of Yellow Sky—the hour of daylight—was approaching.

He knew full well that his marriage was an important thing to his town. It could only be exceeded by the burning of the new hotel. His friends could not forgive him. Frequently he had reflected on the advisability of telling them by telegraph, but a new cowardice had been upon him. He feared to do it. And now the train was hurrying him toward a scene of amazement, glee, and reproach. He glanced out of the window at the line of haze swinging slowly in toward the train.

Yellow Sky had a kind of brass band, which played painfully, to the delight of the populace. He laughed without heart as he thought of it. If the citizens could dream of his prospective arrival with his bride, they would parade the band at the station and escort them, amid cheers and laughing congratulations, to his adobe home.

He resolved that he would use all the devices of speed and plains-craft in making the journey from the station to his house. Once within that safe citadel, he could issue some sort of a vocal bulletin, and then not go among the citizens until they had time to wear off a little of their enthusiasm.

The bride looked anxiously at him. "What's worrying you, Jack?"

He laughed again. "I'm not worrying, girl; I'm only thinking of Yellow Sky."

She flushed in comprehension.

A sense of mutual guilt invaded their minds and developed a finer tenderness. They looked at each other with eyes softly aglow. But Potter often laughed the same nervous laugh; the flush upon the bride's face seemed quite permanent.

The traitor to the feelings of Yellow Sky narrowly watched the speeding landscape. "We're nearly there," he said.

Presently the porter came and announced the proximity of Potter's home. He held a brush in his hand, and, with all his airy superiority gone, he brushed

Potter's new clothes as the latter slowly turned this way and that way. Potter fumbled out a coin and gave it to the porter, as he had seen others do. It was a heavy and muscle-bound business, as that of a man shoeing his first horse.

The porter took their bag, and as the train began to slow they moved forward to the hooded platform of the car. Presently the two engines and their long string of coaches rushed into the station of Yellow Sky.

"They have to take water here," said Potter, from a constricted throat and in mournful cadence, as one announcing death. Before the train stopped his eye had swept the length of the platform, and he was glad and astonished to see there was none upon it but the station-agent, who, with a slightly hurried and anxious air, was walking toward the water-tanks. When the train had halted, the porter alighted first, and placed in position a little temporary step.

"Come on, girl," said Potter, hoarsely. As he helped her down, they each laughed on a false note. He took the bag from the negro, and bade his wife cling to his arm. As they slunk rapidly away, his hang-dog glance perceived that they were unloading the two trunks, and also that the station-agent, far ahead near the baggage-car, had turned and was running toward him, making gestures. He laughed, and groaned as he laughed, when he noted the first effect of his marital bliss upon Yellow Sky. He gripped his wife's arm firmly to his side, and they fled. Behind them the porter stood, chuckling fatuously.

II

The California express on the Southern Railway was due at Yellow Sky in twenty-one minutes. There were six men at the bar of the Weary Gentleman Saloon. One was a drummer, who talked a great deal and rapidly; three were Texans, who did not care to talk at that time; and two were Mexican sheep-herders, who did not talk as a general practice in the Weary Gentleman Aaloon. The barkeeper's dog lay on the board walk that crossed in front of the door. His head was on his paws, and he glanced drowsily here and there with the constant vigilance of a dog that is kicked on occasion. Across the sandy street were some vivid green grass-plots, so wonderful in appearance, amid the sands that burned near them in a blazing sun, that they caused a doubt in the mind. They exactly resembled the grass mats used to represent lawns on the stage. At the cooler end of the railway station, a man without a coat sat in a tilted chair and smoked his pipe. The fresh-cut bank of the Rio Grande circled near the town, and there could be seen beyond it a great plum-colored plain of mesquit.

Save for the busy drummer and his companions in the saloon, Yellow Sky was dozing. The new-comer leaned gracefully upon the bar, and recited many tales with the confidence of a bard who has come upon a new field.

"—and at the moment that the old man fell down-stairs with the bureau in his arms, the old woman was coming up with two scuttles of coal, and of course—"

The drummer's tale was interrupted by a young man who suddenly appeared in the open door. He cried: "Scratchy Wilson's drunk, and has turned loose with both hands." The two Mexicans at once set down their glasses and faded out of the rear entrance of the saloon.

The drummer, innocent and jocular, answered: "All right, old man. S'pose he has? Come in and have a drink, anyhow."

But the information had made such an obvious cleft in every skull in the room that the drummer was obliged to see its importance. All had become instantly solemn. "Say," said he, mystified, "what is this?" His three companions made the introductory gesture of eloquent speech; but the young man at the door forestalled them.

"It means, my friend," he answered, as he came into the saloon, "that for the next two hours this town won't be a health resort."

The barkeeper went to the door, and locked and barred it; reaching out of the window, he pulled in heavy wooden shutters, and barred them. Immediately a solemn, chapel-like gloom was upon the place. The drummer was looking from one to another.

"But say," he cried, "what is this, anyhow? You don't mean there is going to be a gun-fight?"

"Don't know whether there'll be a fight or not," answered one man, grimly; "but there'll be some shootin'—some good shootin'."

The young man who had warned them waved his hand. "Oh, there'll be a fight fast enough, if any one wants it. Anybody can get a fight out there in the street. There's a fight just waiting."

The drummer seemed to be swayed between the interest of a foreigner and a perception of personal danger.

"What did you say his name was?" he asked.

"Scratchy Wilson," they answered in chorus.

"And will he kill anybody? What are you going to do? Does this happen often? Does he rampage around like this once a week or so? Can he break in that door?"

"No; he can't break down that door," replied the barkeeper. "He's tried it three times. But when he comes you'd better lay down on the floor, stranger. He's dead sure to shoot at it, and a bullet may come through."

Thereafter the drummer kept a strict eye on the door. The time had not yet been called for him to hug the floor, but, as a minor precaution, he sidled near to the wall. "Will he kill anybody?" he said again.

The men laughed low and scornfully at the question.

"He's out to shoot, and he's out for trouble. Don't see any good in experimentin' with him."

"But what do you do in a case like this? What do you do?"

A man responded: "Why, he and Jack Potter—"

"But," in chorus the other men interrupted, "Jack Potter's in San Anton'."

"Well, who is he? What's he got to do with it?"

"Oh, he's the town marshal. He goes out and fights Scratchy when he gets on one of these tears."

"Wow!" said the drummer, mopping his brow. "Nice job he's got."

The voices had toned away to mere whisperings. The drummer wished to ask further questions, which were born of an increasing anxiety and bewilderment; but when he attempted them, the men merely looked at him in irritation and motioned him to remain silent. A tense waiting hush was upon them. In the deep shadows of the room their eyes shone as they listened for sounds from the street. One man made three gestures at the barkeeper; and the latter, moving like a ghost, handed him a glass and a bottle. The man poured a full glass of whisky, and set down the bottle noiselessly. He gulped the whisky in a swallow, and turned again toward the door in immovable silence. The drummer saw that the barkeeper, without a sound, had taken a Winchester from beneath the bar. Later he saw this individual beckoning to him, so he tiptoed across the room.

"You better come with me back of the bar."

"No, thanks," said the drummer, perspiring; "I'd rather be where I can make a break for the back door."

Whereupon the man of bottles made a kindly but peremptory gesture. The drummer obeyed it, and, finding himself seated on a box with his head below the level of the bar, balm was laid upon his soul at sight of various zinc and copper fittings that bore a resemblance to armor-plate. The barkeeper took a seat comfortably upon an adjacent box.

"You see," he whispered, "this here Scratchy Wilson is a wonder with a gun—a perfect wonder; and when he goes on the war-trail, we hunt our holes—naturally. He's about the last one of the old gang that used to hang out along the river here. He's a terror when he's drunk. When he's sober he's all right—kind of simple—wouldn't hurt a fly—nicest fellow in town. But when he's drunk—whoo!"

There were periods of stillness. "I wish Jack Potter was back from San Anton'," said the barkeeper. "He shot Wilson up once,—in the leg,—and he would sail in and pull out the kinks in this thing."

Presently they heard from a distance the sound of a shot, followed by three wild yowls. It instantly removed a bond from the men in the darkened saloon. There was a shuffling of feet. They looked at each other. "Here he comes," they said.

III

A man in a maroon-colored flannel shirt, which had been purchased for purposes of decoration, and made principally by some Jewish women on the East Side of New York, rounded a corner and walked into the middle of the main street of Yellow Sky. In either hand the man held a long, heavy, blue-black revolver. Often he yelled, and these cries rang through a semblance of a deserted village, shrilly flying over the roofs in a volume that seemed to have no relation to the ordinary vocal strength of a man. It was as if the surrounding stillness formed the arch of a tomb over him. These cries of ferocious challenge rang against walls of silence. And his boots had red tops with gilded imprints, of the kind beloved in winter by little sledding boys on the hillsides of New England.

The man's face flamed in a rage begot of whisky. His eyes, rolling, and yet keen for ambush, hunted the still doorways and windows. He walked with the creeping movement of the midnight cat. As it occurred to him, he roared menacing information. The long revolvers in his hands were as easy as straws; they were moved with an electric swiftness. The little fingers of each hand played sometimes in a musician's way. Plain from the low collar of the shirt, the cords of his neck straightened and sank, as passion moved him. The only sounds were his terrible invitations. The calm adobes preserved their demeanor at the passing of this small thing in the middle of the street.

There was no offer of fight—no offer of fight. The man called to the sky. There were no attractions. He bellowed and fumed and swayed his revolver here and everywhere.

The dog of the barkeeper of the Weary Gentleman Saloon had not appreciated the advance of events. He yet lay dozing in front of his master's door. At sight of the dog, the man paused and raised his revolver humorously. At sight of the man, the dog sprang up and walked diagonally away, with a sullen head, and growling. The man yelled, and the dog broke into a gallop. As it was about to enter an alley, there was a loud noise, a whistling, and something spat the ground directly before it. The dog screamed, and, wheeling in terror, galloped headlong in a new direction. Again there was a noise, a whistling, and sand was kicked viciously before it. Fear-stricken, the dog turned and flurried like an animal in a pen. The man stood laughing, his weapons at his hips.

Ultimately the man was attracted by the closed door of the Weary Gentleman Saloon. He went to it, and, hammering with a revolver, demanded drink.

The door remaining imperturbable, he picked a bit of paper from the walk, and nailed it to the framework with a knife. He then turned his back contemptuously upon this popular resort, and, walking to the opposite side of the street, and spinning there on his heel quickly and lithely, fired at the bit of paper. He missed it by a half-inch. He swore at himself, and went away. Later, he comfortably fusilladed the windows of his most intimate friend. The man was playing with this town; it was a toy for him.

But still there was no offer of fight. The name of Jack Potter, his ancient antagonist, entered his mind, and he concluded that it would be a glad thing if he should go to Potter's house, and by bombardment induce him to come out and fight. He moved in the direction of his desire, chanting Apache scalp-music.

When he arrived at it, Potter's house presented the same still front as had the other adobes. Taking up a strategic position, the man howled a challenge. But this house regarded him as might a great stone god. It gave no sign. After a decent wait, the man howled further challenges, mingling with them wonderful epithets.

Presently there came the spectacle of a man churning himself into deepest rage over the immobility of a house. He fumed at it as the winter wind attacks a prairie cabin in the North. To the distance there should have gone the sound of a tumult like the fighting of two hundred Mexicans. As necessity bade him, he paused for breath or to reload his revolvers.

IV

Potter and his bride walked sheepishly and with speed. Sometimes they laughed together shamefacedly and low.

"Next corner, dear," he said finally.

They put forth the efforts of a pair walking bowed against a strong wind. Potter was about to raise a finger to point the first appearance of the new home when, as they circled the corner, they came face to face with a man in a maroon-colored shirt, who was feverishly pushing cartridges into a large revolver. Upon the instant the man dropped this revolver to the ground, and, like lightning, whipped another from its holster. The second weapon was aimed at the bridegroom's chest.

There was a silence. Potter's mouth seemed to be merely a grave for his tongue. He exhibited an instinct to at once loosen his arm from the woman's grip, and he dropped the bag to the sand. As for the bride, her face had gone as yellow as old cloth. She was a slave to hideous rites, gazing at the apparitional snake.

The two men faced each other at a distance of three paces. He of the revolver smiled with a new and quiet ferocity.

"Tried to sneak up on me," he said. "Tried to sneak up on me!" His eyes grew more baleful. As Potter made a slight movement, the man thrust his revolver venomously forward. "No; don't you do it, Jack Potter. Don't you move a finger toward a gun just yet. Don't you move an eyelash. The time has come for me to settle with you, and I'm goin' to do it my own way, and loaf along with no interferin'. So if you don't want a gun bent on you, just mind what I tell you."

Potter looked at his enemy. "I ain't got a gun on me, Scratchy," he said. "Honest, I ain't." He was stiffening and steadying, but yet somewhere at the back of his mind a vision of the Pullman floated: the sea-green figured velvet, the shining brass, silver, and glass, the wood that gleamed as darkly brilliant as the surface of a pool of oil—all the glory of the marriage, the environment of the new estate. "You know I fight when it comes to fighting, Scratchy Wilson; but I ain't got a gun on me. You'll have to do all the shootin' yourself."

His enemy's face went livid. He stepped forward, and lashed his weapon to and fro before Potter's chest. "Don't you tell me you ain't got no gun on you, you whelp. Don't tell me no lie like that. There ain't a man in Texas ever seen you without no gun. Don't take me for no kid." His eyes blazed with light, and his throat worked like a pump.

"I ain't takin' you for no kid," answered Potter. His heels had not moved an inch backward. "I'm takin' you for a—fool. I tell you I ain't got a gun, and I ain't. If you're goin' to shoot me up, you'd better begin now; you'll never get a chance like this again."

So much enforced reasoning had told on Wilson's rage; he was calmer. "If you ain't got a gun, why ain't you got a gun?" he sneered. "Been to Sunday-school?"

"I ain't got a gun because I've just come from San Anton' with my wife. I'm married," said Potter. "And if I'd thought there was going to be any galoots like you prowling around when I brought my wife home, I'd had a gun, and don't you forget it."

"Married!" said Scratchy, not at all comprehending.

"Yes, married. I'm married," said Potter, distinctly.

"Married?" said Scratchy. Seemingly for the first time, he saw the drooping, drowning woman at the other man's side. "No!" he said. He was like a creature allowed a glimpse of another world. He moved a pace backward, and his arm, with the revolver, dropped to his side. "Is this the lady?" he asked.

"Yes; this is the lady," answered Potter.

There was another period of silence.

"Well," said Wilson at last, slowly, "I s'pose it's all off now."

"It's all off if you say so, Scratchy. You know I didn't make the trouble." Potter lifted his valise.

"Well, I 'low it's off, Jack," said Wilson. He was looking at the ground. "Married!" He was not a student of chivalry; it was merely that in the presence of this foreign condition he was a simple child of the earlier plains. He picked up his starboard revolver, and, placing both weapons in their holsters, he went away. His feet made funnel-shaped tracks in the heavy sand.

5—12
Paul Laurence Dunbar (1872–1906)

PAUL LAURENCE DUNBAR (1872–1906) came from Dayton, Ohio, and was a child of ex-slaves. "When Malindy Sings" is thought to be a tribute to his mother, reputedly illiterate, who encouraged her son to earn an education. Dunbar excelled in school where he was classmates with the aviators, the Wright brothers. Dunbar's dialect poems were especially popular in his lifetime and garnered the attention of William Dean Howells and others. (During the Harlem Renaissance of the 1920s and 1930s, writing in dialect was discouraged as it was perceived as playing into stereotypes.) Dunbar wrote other poetry as well, most notably "Sympathy" and "We Wear the Mask." The publication of his poetry brought him into contact with important African American leaders, such as Frederick Douglass and Booker T. Washington, who admired Dunbar's verse.

≈ ≈ ≈

"We Wear the Mask" (1895)

We wear the mask that grins and lies,
It hides our cheeks and shades our eyes,—
This debt we pay to human guile;
With torn and bleeding hearts we smile,
And mouth with myriad subtleties.

Why should the world be overwise,
In counting all our tears and sighs?
Nay, let them only see us, while
    We wear the mask.

We smile, but, O great Christ, our cries
To thee from tortured souls arise.
We sing, but oh the clay is vile

Beneath our feet, and long the mile;
But let the world dream otherwise,
    We wear the mask!

"When Malindy Sings" (1895)

G'way an' quit dat noise, Miss Lucy—
    Put dat music book away;
What's de use to keep on tryin'?
    Ef you practise twell you're gray,
You cain't sta't no notes a-flyin'
    Lak de ones dat rants and rings
F'om de kitchen to be big woods
    When Malindy sings.

You ain't got de nachel o'gans
    Fu' to make de soun' come right,
You ain't got de tu'ns an' twistin's
    Fu' to make it sweet an' light.
Tell you one thing now, Miss Lucy,
    An' I'm tellin' you fu' true,
When hit comes to raal right singin',
    'Tain't no easy thing to do.

Easy 'nough fu' folks to hollah,
    Lookin' at de lines an' dots,
When dey ain't no one kin sence it,
    An' de chune comes in, in spots;
But fu' real melojous music,
    Dat jes' strikes you' hea't and clings,
Jes' you stan' an' listen wif me
    When Malindy sings.

Ain't you nevah hyeahd Malindy?
    Blessed soul, tek up de cross!
Look hyeah, ain't you jokin', honey?
    Well, you don't know whut you los'.
Y' ought to hyeah dat gal a-wa'blin',
    Robins, la'ks, an' all dem things,
Heish dey moufs an' hides dey faces
    When Malindy sings.

Fiddlin' man jes' stop his fiddlin',
    Lay his fiddle on de she'f;

Mockin'-bird quit tryin' to whistle,
    'Cause he jes' so shamed hisse'f.
Folks a-playin' on de banjo
    Draps dey fingahs on de strings—
Bless yo' soul—fu'gits to move 'em,
    When Malindy sings.

She jes' spreads huh mouf and hollahs,
    "Come to Jesus," twell you hyeah
Sinnahs' tremblin' steps and voices,
    Timid-lak a-drawin' neah;
Den she tu'ns to "Rock of Ages,"
    Simply to de cross she clings,
An' you fin' yo' teahs a-drappin'
    When Malindy sings.

Who dat says dat humble praises
    Wif de Master nevah counts?
Heish yo' mouf, I hyeah dat music,
    Ez hit rises up an' mounts—
Floatin' by de hills an' valleys,
    Way above dis buryin' sod,
Ez hit makes its way in glory
    To de very gates of God!

Oh, hit's sweetah dan de music
    Of an edicated band;
An' hit's dearah dan de battle's
    Song o' triumph in de lan'.
It seems holier dan evenin'
    When de solemn chu'ch bell rings,
Ez I sit an' ca'mly listen
    While Malindy sings.

Towsah, stop dat ba'kin', hyeah me!
    Mandy, mek dat chile keep still;
Don't you hyeah de echoes callin'
    F'om de valley to de hill?
Let me listen, I can hyeah it,
    Th'oo de bresh of angels' wings,
Sof' an' sweet, "Swing Low, Sweet Chariot,"
    Ez Malindy sings.

"Sympathy" (1899)

I know what the caged bird feels, alas!
    When the sun is bright on the upland slopes;
When the wind stirs soft through the springing grass,
And the river flows like a stream of glass;
    When the first bird sings and the first bud opes,
And the faint perfume from its chalice steals—
I know what the caged bird feels!

I know why the caged bird beats his wing
    Till its blood is red on the cruel bars;
For he must fly back to his perch and cling
When he fain would be on the bough a-swing;
    And a pain still throbs in the old, old scars
And they pulse again with a keener sting—
I know why he beats his wing!

I know why the caged bird sings, ah me,
    When his wing is bruised and his bosom sore,—
When he beats his bars and he would be free;
It is not a carol of joy or glee,
    But a prayer that he sends from his heart's deep core,
But a plea, that upward to Heaven he flings—
I know why the caged bird sings!

5–13
Willa Cather (1873–1947)

The great writer of the Nebraska plains, WILLA CATHER (1873–1947) came west with her family from Winchester, Virginia, when she was nine. She came to love the lonely, treeless landscape, the tall grasses, and strange burrowing prairie dogs, owls, and badgers, which became the landscape where many of her best novels and stories are set. She spent hours in her childhood visiting the immigrant families from Eastern and Northern Europe who had left the Old Country to homestead the Great Plains. Educated at the University of Nebraska–Lincoln, Cather excelled at classical language, theater, and English literature, and by age twenty-three had left Nebraska permanently for Pittsburgh and later New York City, where she would write for women's magazines. She published her first collection of stories in 1905; "The Enchanted Bluff" (1909), about midwestern boys daydreaming of the Native American cliff dwellings in New Mexico, became a precursor of Tom Outland's story in Cather's later work, *The Professor's House* (1925).

≈ ≈ ≈

"The Enchanted Bluff" (1909)

We had our swim before sundown, and while we were cooking our supper the oblique rays of light made a dazzling glare on the white sand about us. The translucent red ball itself sank behind the brown stretches of corn field as we sat down to eat, and the warm layer of air that had rested over the water and our clean sand-bar grew fresher and smelled of the rank ironweed and sunflowers growing on the flatter shore. The river was brown and sluggish, like any other of the half-dozen streams that water the Nebraska corn lands. On one shore was an irregular line of bald clay bluffs where a few scrub-oaks with thick trunks and flat, twisted tops threw light shadows on the long grass. The western shore was low and level, with corn fields that stretched to the sky-line, and all along the water's edge were little sandy coves and beaches where slim cottonwoods and willow saplings flickered.

The turbulence of the river in springtime discouraged milling, and, beyond keeping the old red bridge in repair, the busy farmers did not concern themselves with the stream; so the Sandtown boys were left in undisputed possession. In the autumn we hunted quail through the miles of stubble and fodder land along the flat shore, and, after the winter skating season was over and the ice had gone out, the spring freshets and flooded bottoms gave us our great excitement of the year. The channel was never the same for two successive seasons. Every spring the swollen stream undermined a bluff to the east, or bit out a few acres of corn field to the west and whirled the soil to deposit it in spumy mud banks somewhere else. When the water fell low in midsummer, new sand-bars were thus exposed to dry and whiten in the August sun. Sometimes these were banked so firmly that the fury of the next freshet failed to unseat them; the little willow seedlings emerged triumphantly from the yellow froth, broke into spring leaf, shot up into summer growth, and with their mesh of roots bound together the moist sand beneath them against the batterings of another April. Here and there a cottonwood soon glittered among them, quivering in the low current of air that, even on breathless days when the dust hung like smoke above the wagon road, trembled along the face of the water.

It was on such an island, in the third summer of its yellow green, that we built our watch-fire; not in the thicket of dancing willow wands, but on the level terrace of fine sand which had been added that spring; a little new bit of world, beautifully ridged with ripple marks, and strewn with the tiny skeletons of turtles and fish, all as white and dry as if they had been expertly cured. We had been careful not to mar the freshness of the place, although we often swam out to it on summer evenings and lay on the sand to rest.

This was our last watch-fire of the year, and there were reasons why I should remember it better than any of the others. Next week the other boys were to file back to their old places in the Sandtown High School, but I was to go up to the Divide to teach my first country school in the Norwegian district. I was already homesick at the thought of quitting the boys with whom I had always played; of leaving the river, and going up into a windy plain that was all windmills and corn fields and big pastures; where there was nothing wilful or unmanageable in the landscape, no new islands, and no chance of unfamiliar birds—such as often followed the watercourses.

Other boys came and went and used the river for fishing or skating, but we six were sworn to the spirit of the stream, and we were friends mainly because of the river. There were the two Hassler boys, Fritz and Otto, sons of the little German tailor. They were the youngest of us; ragged boys of ten and twelve, with sunburned hair, weather-stained faces, and pale blue eyes. Otto, the elder, was the best mathematician in school, and clever at his books, but he always dropped out in the spring term as if the river could not get on without him. He and Fritz caught the fat, horned catfish and sold them about the town, and they lived so much in the water that they were as brown and sandy as the river itself.

There was Percy Pound, a fat, freckled boy with chubby cheeks, who took half a dozen boys' story-papers and was always being kept in for reading detective stories behind his desk. There was Tip Smith, destined by his freckles and red hair to be the buffoon in all our games, though he walked like a timid little old man and had a funny, cracked laugh. Tip worked hard in his father's grocery store every afternoon, and swept it out before school in the morning. Even his recreations were laborious. He collected cigarette cards and tin tobacco-tags indefatigably, and would sit for hours humped up over a snarling little scroll-saw which he kept in his attic. His dearest possessions were some little pill-bottles that purported to contain grains of wheat from the Holy Land, water from the Jordan and the Dead Sea, and earth from the Mount of Olives. His father had bought these dull things from a Baptist missionary who peddled them, and Tip seemed to derive great satisfaction from their remote origin.

The tall boy was Arthur Adams. He had fine hazel eyes that were almost too reflective and sympathetic for a boy, and such a pleasant voice that we all loved to hear him read aloud. Even when he had to read poetry aloud at school, no one ever thought of laughing. To be sure, he was not at school very much of the time. He was seventeen and should have finished the High School the year before, but he was always off somewhere with his gun. Arthur's mother was dead, and his father, who was feverishly absorbed in promoting schemes, wanted to send the boy away to school and get him off his hands; but Arthur always begged off for another year and promised to study. I remember him as a tall, brown boy with an intelligent face, always lounging among a lot of us little fellows, laughing at us oftener than with us, but such a soft, satisfied laugh that we felt rather flattered when we provoked it. In after-years people said that Arthur had been given to evil ways even as a lad, and it is true that we often saw him with the gambler's sons and with old Spanish Fanny's boy, but if he learned anything ugly in their company he never betrayed it to us. We would have followed Arthur anywhere, and I am bound to say that he led us into no worse places than the cattail marshes and the stubble fields. These, then, were the boys who camped with me that summer night upon the sand-bar.

After we finished our supper we beat the willow thicket for driftwood. By the time we had collected enough, night had fallen, and the pungent, weedy smell from the shore increased with the coolness. We threw ourselves down about the fire and made another futile effort to show Percy Pound the Little Dipper. We had tried it often before, but he could never be got past the big one.

"You see those three big stars just below the handle, with the bright one in the middle?" said Otto Hassler; "that's Orion's belt, and the bright one is the clasp." I crawled behind Otto's shoulder and sighted up his arm to the star that seemed perched upon the tip of his steady forefinger. The Hassler boys did seine-fishing at night, and they knew a good many stars.

Percy gave up the Little Dipper and lay back on the sand, his hands clasped under his head. "I can see the North Star," he announced, contentedly, pointing toward it with his big toe. "Any one might get lost and need to know that."

We all looked up at it.

"How do you suppose Columbus felt when his compass didn't point north anymore?" Tip asked.

Otto shook his head. "My father says that there was another North Star once, and that maybe this one won't last always. I wonder what would happen to us down here if anything went wrong with it?"

Arthur chuckled. "I wouldn't worry, Ott. Nothing's apt to happen to it in your time. Look at the Milky Way! There must be lots of good dead Indians."

We lay back and looked, meditating, at the dark cover of the world. The gurgle of the water had become heavier. We had often noticed a mutinous, complaining note in it at night, quite different from its cheerful daytime chuckle, and seeming like the voice of a much deeper and more powerful stream. Our water had always these two moods: the one of sunny complaisance, the other of inconsolable, passionate regret.

"Queer how the stars are all in sort of diagrams," remarked Otto. "You could do most any proposition in geometry with 'em. They always look as if they meant something. Some folks say everybody's fortune is all written out in the stars, don't they?"

"They believe so in the old country," Fritz affirmed.

But Arthur only laughed at him. "You're thinking of Napoleon, Fritzey. He had a star that went out when he began to lose battles. I guess the stars don't keep any close tally on Sandtown folks."

We were speculating on how many times we could count a hundred before the evening star went down behind the corn fields, when someone cried, "There comes the moon, and it's as big as a cart wheel!"

We all jumped up to greet it as it swam all over the bluffs behind us. It came up like a galleon in full sail; an enormous, barbaric thing, red as an angry heathen god.

"When the moon came up red like that, the Aztecs used to sacrifice their prisoners on the temple top," Percy announced.

"Go on, Perce. You got that out of *Golden Days*. Do you believe that, Arthur?" I appealed.

Arthur answered, quite seriously: "Like as not. The moon was one of their gods. When my father was in Mexico City he saw the stone where they used to sacrifice their prisoners."

As we dropped down by the fire again some one asked whether the Mound-Builders were older than the Aztecs. When we once got upon the Mound-Builders we never willingly got away from them, and we were still conjecturing when we heard a loud splash in the water.

"Must have been a big cat jumping," said Fritz. "They do sometimes. They must see bugs in the dark. Look what a track the moon makes!"

There was a long, silvery streak on the water, and where the current fretted over a big log it boiled up like gold pieces.

"Suppose there ever *was* any gold hid away in this old river?" Fritz asked. He lay like a little brown Indian, close to the fire, his chin on his hand and his bare feet in the air. His brother laughed at him, but Arthur took his suggestion seriously.

"Some of the Spaniards thought there was gold up here somewhere. Seven cities chuck full of gold, they had it, and Coronado and his men came up to hunt it. The Spaniards were all over this country once."

Percy looked interested. "Was that before the Mormons went through?"

We all laughed at this.

"Long enough before. Before the Pilgrim Fathers, Perce. Maybe they came along this very river. They always followed the watercourses."

"I wonder where this river really does begin?" Tip mused. That was an old and a favorite mystery which the map did not clearly explain. On the map the little black line stopped somewhere in western Kansas; but since rivers generally rose in mountains, it was only reasonable to suppose that ours came from the Rockies. Its destination, we knew, was the Missouri, and the Hassler boys always maintained that we could embark at Sandtown in flood-time, follow our noses, and eventually arrive at New Orleans. Now they took up their old argument. "If us boys had grit enough to try it, it wouldn't take no time to get to Kansas City and St. Joe."

We began to talk about the places we wanted to go. The Hassler boys wanted to see the stock-yards in Kansas City, and Percy wanted to see a big store in Chicago. Arthur was interlocutor and did not betray himself.

"Now it's your turn, Tip."

Tip rolled over on his elbow and poked the fire, and his eyes looked shyly out of his queer, tight little face. "My place is awful far away. My uncle Bill told me about it."

Tip's Uncle Bill was a wanderer, bitten with mining fever, who had drifted into Sandtown with a broken arm, and when it was well had drifted out again.

"Where is it?"

"Aw, it's down in New Mexico somewheres. There aren't no railroads or anything. You have to go on mules, and you run out of water before you get there and have to drink canned tomatoes."

"Well, go on, kid. What's it like when you do get there?"

Tip sat up and excitedly began his story.

"There's a big red rock there that goes right up out of the sand for about nine hundred feet. The country's flat all around it, and this here rock goes up all by itself, like a monument. They call it the Enchanted Bluff down there, because no white man has ever been on top of it. The sides are smooth rock, and straight up, like a wall. The Indians say that hundreds of years ago, before the Spaniards came, there was a village away up there in the air. The tribe that lived there had some sort of steps, made out of wood and bark, hung down over the face of the bluff, and the braves went down to hunt and carried water up in big jars swung on their backs. They kept a big supply of water and dried meat up there, and never went down except to hunt. They were a peaceful tribe that made cloth and pottery, and they went up there to get out of the wars. You see, they could pick off any war party that tried to get up their little steps. The

Indians say they were a handsome people, and they had some sort of a queer religion. Uncle Bill thinks they were Cliff-Dwellers who had got into trouble and left home. They weren't fighters, anyhow.

"One time the braves were down hunting and an awful storm came up—a kind of waterspout—and when they got back to their rock they found their little staircase had been all broken to pieces, and only a few steps were left hanging away up in the air. While they were camped at the foot of the rock, wondering what to do, a war party from the north came along and massacred 'em to a man, with all the old folks and women looking on from the rocks. Then the war party went on south and left the village to get down the best way they could. Of course they never got down. They starved to death up there, and when the war party came back on their way north, they could hear the children crying from the edge of the bluff where they had crawled out, but they didn't see a sign of a grown Indian, and nobody has ever been up there since."

We exclaimed at this dolorous legend and sat up.

"There couldn't have been many people up there," Percy demurred. "How big is the top, Tip?"

"Oh, pretty big. Big enough so that the rock doesn't look nearly as tall as it is. The top's bigger than the base. The bluff is sort of worn away for several hundred feet up. That's one reason it's so hard to climb."

I asked how the Indians got up, in the first place.

"Nobody knows how they got up or when. A hunting party came along once and saw that there was a town up there, and that was all."

Otto rubbed his chin and looked thoughtful. "Of course there must be some way to get up there. Couldn't people get a rope over someway and pull a ladder up?"

Tip's little eyes were shining with excitement. "I know a way. Me and Uncle Bill talked it all over. There's a kind of rocket that would take a rope over—life-savers use 'em—and then you could hoist a rope ladder and peg it down at the bottom and make it tight with guy-ropes on the other side. I'm going to climb that there bluff, and I've got it all planned out."

Fritz asked what he expected to find when he got up there.

"Bones, maybe, or the ruins of their town, or pottery, or some of their idols. There might be 'most anything up there. Anyhow, I want to see."

"Sure nobody else has been up there, Tip?" Arthur asked.

"Dead sure. Hardly anybody ever goes down there. Some hunters tried to cut steps in the rock once, but they didn't get higher than a man can reach. The Bluff's all red granite, and Uncle Bill thinks it's a boulder the glaciers left. It's a queer place, anyhow. Nothing but cactus and desert for hundreds of miles, and yet right under the bluff there's good water and plenty of grass. That's why the bison used to go down there."

Suddenly we heard a scream above our fire, and jumped up to see a dark, slim bird floating southward far above us—a whooping-crane, we knew by her cry and her long neck. We ran to the edge of the island, hoping we might see her alight, but she wavered southward along the rivercourse until we lost her. The Hassler boys declared that by the look of the heavens it must be after midnight, so we threw more wood on our fire, put on our jackets, and curled down in the warm sand. Several of us pretended to doze, but I fancy we were really thinking about Tip's Bluff and the extinct people. Over in the wood the ring-doves were calling mournfully to one another, and once we heard a dog bark, far away. "Somebody getting into old Tommy's melon patch," Fritz murmured, sleepily, but nobody answered him. By and by Percy spoke out of the shadow.

"Say, Tip, when you go down there will you take me with you?"

"Maybe."

"Suppose one of us beats you down there, Tip?"

"Whoever gets to the Bluff first has got to promise to tell the rest of us exactly what he finds," remarked one of the Hassler boys, and to this we all readily assented.

Somewhat reassured, I dropped off to sleep. I must have dreamed about a race for the Bluff, for I awoke in a kind of fear that other people were getting ahead of me and that I was losing my chance. I sat up in my damp clothes and looked at the other boys, who lay tumbled in uneasy attitudes about the dead fire. It was still dark, but the sky was blue with the last wonderful azure of night. The stars glistened like crystal globes, and trembled as if they shone through a depth of clear water. Even as I watched, they began to pale and the sky brightened. Day came suddenly, almost instantaneously. I turned for another look at the blue night, and it was gone. Everywhere the birds began to call, and all manner of little insects began to chirp and hop about in the willows. A breeze sprang up from the west and brought the heavy smell of ripened corn. The boys rolled over and shook themselves. We stripped and plunged into the river just as the sun came up over the windy bluffs.

When I came home to Sandtown at Christmas time, we skated out to our island and talked over the whole project of the Enchanted Bluff, renewing our resolution to find it.

Although that was twenty years ago, none of us have ever climbed the Enchanted Bluff. Percy Pound is a stockbroker in Kansas City and will go nowhere that his red touring-car cannot carry him. Otto Hassler went on the railroad and lost his foot braking; after which he and Fritz succeeded their father as the town tailors.

Arthur sat about the sleepy little town all his life—he died before he was twenty-five. The last time I saw him, when I was home on one of my college vacations, he was sitting in a steamer-chair under a cottonwood tree in a little yard behind one of the two Sandtown saloons. He was very untidy and his hand was not steady, but when he rose, unabashed, to greet me, his eyes were as clear and warm as ever. When I had talked with him for an hour and heard him laugh again, I wondered how it was that when Nature had taken such pains with a man, from his hands to the arch of his long foot, she had ever lost him in Sandtown. He joked about Tip Smith's Bluff, and declared he was going down there just as soon as the weather got cooler; he thought the Grand Cañon might be worth while, too.

I was perfectly sure when I left him that he would never get beyond the high plank fence and the comfortable shade of the cottonwood. And, indeed, it was under that very tree that he died one summer morning.

Tip Smith still talks about going to New Mexico. He married a slatternly, unthrifty country girl, has been much tied to a perambulator, and has grown stooped and gray from irregular meals and broken sleep. But the worst of his difficulties are now over, and he has, as he says, come into easy water. When I was last in Sandtown I walked home with him late one moonlight night, after he had balanced his cash and shut up his store. We took the long way around and sat down on the schoolhouse steps, and between us we quite revived the romance of the lone red rock and the extinct people. Tip insists that he still means to go down there, but he thinks now he will wait until his boy, Bert, is old enough to go with him. Bert has been let into the story, and thinks of nothing but the Enchanted Bluff.

5–14
Robert Frost (1874–1963)

A failed farmer who relished privacy, a depressive who could be cranky and self-centered, ROBERT FROST (1874–1963) seems an unlikely candidate to become one of the most loved American poets. Frost's father died of tuberculosis when Frost was eleven. This loss resulted in the family leaving California, Frost's place of birth, for Massachusetts, where he met and fell in love with Elinor White, his eventual wife. Frost's two-year stint at Harvard ended due to poor health. After nine unsuccessful years of farming in Derry, New Hampshire, he and Elinor moved to England (1912–1914), where he published *A Boy's Will* (1913) and *North of Boston* (1914). Leaving Europe at the outbreak of World War I, Frost bought a farm in Franconia, New Hampshire, and began a career of writing, teaching, and lecturing. An independent poet, Frost never associated with any school of poetry, though Ezra Pound and the Imagists helped launch his career. Instead, Frost espoused his own poetics, principally the "sound of sense," a natural cadence built on marrying syllables and sounds to create both sensation and meaning.

≈ ≈ ≈

"Mending Wall" (1914)

Something there is that doesn't love a wall,
That sends the frozen-ground-swell under it,
And spills the upper boulders in the sun;
And makes gaps even two can pass abreast.
The work of hunters is another thing:
I have come after them and made repair
Where they have left not one stone on a stone,
But they would have the rabbit out of hiding,
To please the yelping dogs. The gaps I mean,
No one has seen them made or heard them made,
But at spring mending-time we find them there.
I let my neighbour know beyond the hill;
And on a day we meet to walk the line
And set the wall between us once again.
We keep the wall between us as we go.
To each the boulders that have fallen to each.
And some are loaves and some so nearly balls
We have to use a spell to make them balance:
"Stay where you are until our backs are turned!"
We wear our fingers rough with handling them.
Oh, just another kind of out-door game,
One on a side. It comes to little more:
There where it is we do not need the wall:
He is all pine and I am apple orchard.
My apple trees will never get across
And eat the cones under his pines, I tell him.

He only says, "Good fences make good neighbours."
Spring is the mischief in me, and I wonder
If I could put a notion in his head:
"*Why* do they make good neighbours? Isn't it
Where there are cows? But here there are no cows.
Before I built a wall I'd ask to know
What I was walling in or walling out,
And to whom I was like to give offence.
Something there is that doesn't love a wall,
That wants it down." I could say "Elves" to him,
But it's not elves exactly, and I'd rather
He said it for himself. I see him there
Bringing a stone grasped firmly by the top
In each hand, like an old-stone savage armed.
He moves in darkness as it seems to me,
Not of woods only and the shade of trees.
He will not go behind his father's saying,
And he likes having thought of it so well
He says again, "Good fences make good neighbours."

"The Death of the Hired Man" (1914)

Mary sat musing on the lamp-flame at the table
Waiting for Warren. When she heard his step,
She ran on tip-toe down the darkened passage
To meet him in the doorway with the news
And put him on his guard. "Silas is back."
She pushed him outward with her through the door
And shut it after her. "Be kind," she said.
She took the market things from Warren's arms
And set them on the porch, then drew him down
To sit beside her on the wooden steps.

"When was I ever anything but kind to him?
But I'll not have the fellow back," he said.
"I told him so last haying, didn't I?
'If he left then,' I said, 'that ended it.'
What good is he? Who else will harbour him
At his age for the little he can do?
What help he is there's no depending on.
Off he goes always when I need him most.

'He thinks he ought to earn a little pay,
Enough at least to buy tobacco with,
So he won't have to beg and be beholden.'
'All right,' I say, 'I can't afford to pay
Any fixed wages, though I wish I could.'
'Someone else can.' 'Then someone else will have to.'
I shouldn't mind his bettering himself
If that was what it was. You can be certain,
When he begins like that, there's someone at him
Trying to coax him off with pocket-money,—
In haying time, when any help is scarce.
In winter he comes back to us. I'm done."

"Sh! not so loud: he'll hear you," Mary said.

"I want him to: he'll have to soon or late."

"He's worn out. He's asleep beside the stove.
When I came up from Rowe's I found him here,
Huddled against the barn-door fast asleep,
A miserable sight, and frightening, too—
You needn't smile—I didn't recognise him—
I wasn't looking for him—and he's changed.
Wait till you see."

        "Where did you say he'd been?"

"He didn't say. I dragged him to the house,
And gave him tea and tried to make him smoke.
I tried to make him talk about his travels.
Nothing would do: he just kept nodding off."

"What did he say? Did he say anything?"

"But little."

        "Anything? Mary, confess
He said he'd come to ditch the meadow for me."

"Warren!"

        "But did he? I just want to know."

"Of course he did. What would you have him say?
Surely you wouldn't grudge the poor old man

Some humble way to save his self-respect.
He added, if you really care to know,
He meant to clear the upper pasture, too.
That sounds like something you have heard before?
Warren, I wish you could have heard the way
He jumbled everything. I stopped to look
Two or three times—he made me feel so queer—
To see if he was talking in his sleep.
He ran on Harold Wilson—you remember—
The boy you had in haying four years since.
He's finished school, and teaching in his college.
Silas declares you'll have to get him back.
He says they two will make a team for work:
Between them they will lay this farm as smooth!
The way he mixed that in with other things.
He thinks young Wilson a likely lad, though daft
On education—you know how they fought
All through July under the blazing sun,
Silas up on the cart to build the load,
Harold along beside to pitch it on."

"Yes, I took care to keep well out of earshot."

"Well, those days trouble Silas like a dream.
You wouldn't think they would. How some things linger!
Harold's young college boy's assurance piqued him.
After so many years he still keeps finding
Good arguments he sees he might have used.
I sympathise. I know just how it feels
To think of the right thing to say too late.
Harold's associated in his mind with Latin.
He asked me what I thought of Harold's saying
He studied Latin like the violin
Because he liked it—that an argument!
He said he couldn't make the boy believe
He could find water with a hazel prong—
Which showed how much good school had ever done him.
He wanted to go over that. But most of all
He thinks if he could have another chance

To teach him how to build a load of hay—"

"I know, that's Silas' one accomplishment.
He bundles every forkful in its place,
And tags and numbers it for future reference,
So he can find and easily dislodge it
In the unloading. Silas does that well.
He takes it out in bunches like big birds' nests.
You never see him standing on the hay
He's trying to lift, straining to lift himself."

"He thinks if he could teach him that, he'd be
Some good perhaps to someone in the world.
He hates to see a boy the fool of books.
Poor Silas, so concerned for other folk,
And nothing to look backward to with pride,
And nothing to look forward to with hope,
So now and never any different."

Part of a moon was falling down the west,
Dragging the whole sky with it to the hills.
Its light poured softly in her lap. She saw
And spread her apron to it. She put out her hand
Among the harp-like morning-glory strings,
Taut with the dew from garden bed to eaves,
As if she played unheard the tenderness
That wrought on him beside her in the night.
"Warren," she said, "he has come home to die:
"You needn't be afraid he'll leave you this time."

"Home," he mocked gently.

        "Yes, what else but home?
It all depends on what you mean by home.
Of course he's nothing to us, any more
Than was the hound that came a stranger to us
Out of the woods, worn out upon the trail."

"Home is the place where, when you have to go there,
They have to take you in."

        "I should have called it
Something you somehow haven't to deserve."

Warren leaned out and took a step or two,
Picked up a little stick, and brought it back

And broke it in his hand and tossed it by.
"Silas has better claim on us you think
Than on his brother? Thirteen little miles
As the road winds would bring him to his door.
Silas has walked that far no doubt to-day.
Why didn't he go there? His brother's rich,
A somebody—director in the bank."

"He never told us that."

        "We know it though."

"I think his brother ought to help, of course.
I'll see to that if there is need. He ought of right
To take him in, and might be willing to—
He may be better than appearances.
But have some pity on Silas. Do you think
If he'd had any pride in claiming kin
Or anything he looked for from his brother,
He'd keep so still about him all this time?"

"I wonder what's between them."

        "I can tell you.
Silas is what he is—we wouldn't mind him—
But just the kind that kinsfolk can't abide.
He never did a thing so very bad.
He don't know why he isn't quite as good
As anyone. He won't be made ashamed
To please his brother, worthless though he is."

"*I* can't think Si ever hurt anyone."

"No, but he hurt my heart the way he lay
And rolled his old head on that sharp-edged chair-back.
He wouldn't let me put him on the lounge.
You must go in and see what you can do.
I made the bed up for him there to-night.
You'll be surprised at him—how much he's broken.
His working days are done; I'm sure of it."

"I'd not be in a hurry to say that."

"I haven't been. Go, look, see for yourself.
But, Warren, please remember how it is:
He's come to help you ditch the meadow.

He has a plan. You mustn't laugh at him.
He may not speak of it, and then he may.
I'll sit and see if that small sailing cloud
Will hit or miss the moon."

It hit the moon.
Then there were three there, making a dim row,
The moon, the little silver cloud, and she.
Warren returned—too soon, it seemed to her,
Slipped to her side, caught up her hand and waited.

"Warren," she questioned.

"Dead," was all he answered.

5—15
Folk Ballad, author unknown (ca. 1900)

"THE BALLAD OF GREGORIO CORTEZ," by an unknown author, tells the life of Gregorio Cortez (1875–1916), a farmer from South Texas. In 1901, according to one version of the legend, Gregorio's brother Roman outconned a notorious horse dealer. Consequently, the swindler returned with the authorities. A translator's poor interpretation of Spanish resulted in the brothers being wrongfully accused of horse stealing. During the dispute, the sheriff killed Roman, and Gregorio killed the sheriff; he fled, eluding the Texas Rangers for four hundred miles. Gregorio was caught, charged, and sentenced to prison for life, but was pardoned in 1913. The *corrido*, or border ballad, like "The Ballad of Gregorio Cortez," focuses on a popular Mexican legend, set to music. The scholar Américo Paredes first collected the many variants of the ballad and wrote a history entitled *Pistol in His Hand: A Border Ballad and Its Hero*. The ballad inspired a 1982 film with Edward James Olmos.

≋ ≋ ≋

"The Ballad of Gregorio Cortez"*

In Carmen County
Look at what has happened,

---

* Variant A. This *corrido* is the first extant ballad of the legend of Gregorio Cortez, who in 1901 killed a sheriff along the lower Rio Grande border.

the Major Sheriff died,
leaving Román wounded.

Another day in the morning,
when the people came,
they said one to another:
—No one knows who to blame.

They went around investigating;
three hours they spent,
and found out that the culprit
was Gregorio Cortez.

They declared Cortez a fugitive
all throughout the land,
to catch him alive or dead,
for several had died by his hand.

Said Gregorio Cortez
with his pistol in his hand:
—I'm not sorry for killing him,
I have pity only for my brother.

Said Gregorio Cortez,
fired up in his soul:
—I'm not sorry for killing him,
I'm allowed to defend myself.

The Americans were coming,
flying on the wind;
the three thousand pesos they were promised
they were coming to win.

He set out toward Gonzales,
and though several sheriffs saw,
they wouldn't follow him,
for fear held them in awe.

The hounds were coming;
they were following his trail,
but chasing after Cortez
was like following a star.

Said Gregorio Cortez:
—What good are all your schemes

if even with those hounds
you can't catch me?

The Americans said:
—If we catch him what will we do?
If we come at him straight on,
those of us who escape will be few.

He went from Brownsville to the ranch;
they managed to surround him,
little more than three hundred men,
and there he jumped the fence.

Over by El Encinal,
so around here it's said,
they got into a gunfight,
and another of their sheriffs died.

Said Gregorio Cortez
with his pistol in his hand:
—Don't mess around, cowardly rangers,
with a lone Mexican.

He set out toward Laredo
with no fear in his breast:
—Follow me, cowardly rangers,
I am Gregorio Cortez.

Gregorio says to Juan
on the Cypress Ranch:
—Tell me what's new,
I am Gregorio Cortez.

Gregorio says to Juan:
—Very soon you'll see;
go and tell the sheriffs
to come and get me.

When the sheriffs arrived,
there appeared Gregorio:
—You can take me if I let you,
but otherwise you won't.

They grabbed Cortez,
and the matter was resolved;

his poor family pines,
bearing the burden of his loss.

And with this I bid farewell
from the shade of the cypress tree;
here ends the song
of Cortez and his tragedy.

5–16
Jack London (John Griffith Chaney) (1876–1916)

Like Stephen Crane, with whom he shared a journalistic style and a fascination with environmental determinism, JACK LONDON [JOHN GRIFFITH CHANEY] (1876–1916) lived a bold and risk-filled life. Lacking a parental figure—an absent father and an emotionally disordered mother—London was taken in by an African American woman, once a slave, in the San Francisco area. According to one story, London wrote his putative father for confirmation of his identity; when this man denied fatherhood, and besmirched his mother's reputation, the distraught young man left California for Alaska and the Klondike Gold Rush. The adventure cost London physically—he developed scurvy and lost his front teeth—but he gained much fodder for storytelling. "To Build a Fire," *The Call of the Wild*, and *White Fang*—arguably his best fiction—all resulted from his years in Alaska. Ever eager for adventure, London became a war correspondent during the Russo-Japanese War, which ended after three arrests by the Japanese. "Koolau the Leper" (1909), the story of the leader of a leper colony who refuses to move to forced encampment, was inspired by the actual rebellion and ensuing Leper War of Kaua'i in 1893.

≈ ≈ ≈

"Koolau the Leper" (1909)
"Because we are sick they take away our liberty. We have obeyed the law. We have done no wrong. And yet they would put us in prison. Molokai is a prison. That you know. Niuli, there, his sister was sent to Molokai seven years ago. He has not seen her since. Nor will he ever see her. She must stay there until she dies. This is not her will. It is not Niuli's will. It is the will of the white men who rule the land. And who are these white men?

"We know. We have it from our fathers and our fathers' fathers. They came like lambs, speaking softly. Well might they speak softly, for we were many and strong, and all the islands were ours. As I say, they spoke softly. They were of two kinds. The one kind asked our permission, our gracious permission, to preach to us the word of God. The other kind asked our permission, our gracious permission, to trade with us. That was the beginning. To-day all the islands are theirs, all the land, all the cattle—everything is theirs. They that preached the word of God and they that preached the word of Rum have foregathered and become great chiefs. They live like kings in houses of many rooms, with multitudes of servants to care for them. They who had nothing have everything, and if you, or I, or any Kanaka be hungry, they sneer and say, 'Well, why don't you work? There are the plantations.'"

Koolau paused. He raised one hand, and with gnarled and twisted fingers lifted up the blazing wreath of hibiscus that crowned his black hair. The moonlight bathed the scene in silver. It was a night of peace, though those who sat about him and listened had all the seeming of battle-wrecks. Their faces were leonine. Here a space yawned in a face where should have been a nose, and there an arm-stump showed where a hand had rotted off. They were men and women beyond the pale, the thirty of them, for upon them had been placed the mark of the beast.

They sat, flower-garlanded, in the perfumed, luminous night, and their lips made uncouth noises and their throats rasped approval of Koolau's speech. They were creatures who once had been men and women. But they were men and women no longer. They were monsters—in face and form grotesque caricatures of everything human. They were hideously maimed and distorted, and had the seeming of creatures that had been racked in millenniums of hell. Their hands, when they possessed them, were like harpy-claws. Their faces were the misfits and slips, crushed and bruised by some mad god at play in the machinery of life. Here and there were features which the mad god had smeared half away, and one woman wept scalding tears from twin pits of horror, where her eyes once had been. Some were in pain and groaned from their chests. Others coughed, making sounds like the tearing of tissue. Two were idiots, more like huge apes marred in the making, until even an ape were an angel. They mowed and gibbered in the moonlight, under crowns of drooping, golden blossoms. One, whose bloated ear-lobe flapped like a fan upon his shoulder, caught up a gorgeous flower of orange and scarlet and with it decorated the monstrous ear that flip-flapped with his every movement.

And over these things Koolau was king. And this was his kingdom,—a flower-throttled gorge, with beetling cliffs and crags, from which floated the blattings of wild goats. On three sides the grim walls rose, festooned in fantastic draperies of tropic vegetation and pierced by cave-entrances—the rocky lairs of Koolau's subjects. On the fourth side the earth fell away into a tremendous abyss, and, far below, could be seen the summits of lesser peaks and crags, at whose bases foamed and rumbled the Pacific surge. In fine weather a boat could land on the rocky beach that marked the entrance of Kalalau Valley, but the weather must be very fine. And a cool-headed mountaineer might climb from the beach to the head of Kalalau Valley, to this pocket among the peaks where Koolau ruled; but such a mountaineer must be very cool of head, and he must know the wild-goat trails as well. The marvel was that the mass of human wreckage that constituted Koolau's people should have been able to drag its helpless misery over the giddy goat-trails to this inaccessible spot.

"Brothers," Koolau began.

But one of the mowing, apelike travesties emitted a wild shriek of madness, and Koolau waited while the shrill cachination was tossed back and forth among the rocky walls and echoed distantly through the pulseless night.

"Brothers, is it not strange? Ours was the land, and behold, the land is not ours. What did these preachers of the word of God and the word of Rum give us for the land? Have you received one dollar, as much as one dollar, any one of you, for the land? Yet it is theirs, and in return they tell us we can go to work on the land, their land, and that what we produce by our toil shall be theirs. Yet in the old days we did not have to work. Also, when we are sick, they take away our freedom."

"Who brought the sickness, Koolau?" demanded Kiloliana, a lean and wiry man with a face so like a laughing faun's that one might expect to see the cloven hoofs under him. They were cloven, it was true, but the cleavages were great ulcers and livid putrefactions. Yet this was Kiloliana, the most daring climber of them all, the man who knew every goat-trail and who had led Koolau and his wretched followers into the recesses of Kalalau.

"Ay, well questioned," Koolau answered. "Because we would not work the miles of sugar-cane where once our horses pastured, they brought the Chinese slaves from over seas. And with them came the Chinese sickness—that which we suffer from and because of which they would imprison us on Molokai. We were born on Kauai. We have been to the other islands, some here and some there, to Oahu, to Maui, to Hawaii, to Honolulu. Yet always did we come back to Kauai. Why did we come back? There must be a reason. Because we love Kauai. We were born here. Here we have lived. And here shall we die—unless—unless—there be weak hearts amongst us. Such we do not want. They are fit for Molokai. And if there be such, let them not remain. To-morrow the soldiers land on the shore. Let the weak hearts go down to them. They will be sent swiftly to Molokai. As for us, we shall stay and fight. But know that we will not die. We have rifles. You know the narrow trails where men must creep, one by one. I, alone, Koolau, who was once a cowboy on Niihau, can hold the trail against a thousand men. Here is Kapalei, who was once a judge over men and a man with honor, but who is now a hunted rat, like you and me. Hear him. He is wise."

Kapalei arose. Once he had been a judge. He had gone to college at Punahou. He had sat at meat with lords and chiefs and the high representatives of alien powers who protected the interests of traders and missionaries. Such had been Kapalei. But now, as Koolau had said, he was a hunted rat, a creature outside the law, sunk so deep in the mire of human horror that he was above the law as well as beneath it. His face was featureless, save for gaping orifices and for the lidless eyes that burned under hairless brows.

"Let us not make trouble," he began. "We ask to be left alone. But if they do not leave us alone, then is the trouble theirs, and the penalty. My fingers are gone, as you see." He held up his stumps of hands that all might see. "Yet have I the joint of one thumb left, and it can pull a trigger as firmly as did its lost neighbor in the old days. We love Kauai. Let us live here, or die here, but do not let us go to the prison of Molokai. The sickness is not ours. We have not sinned. The men who preached the word of God and the word of Rum brought the sickness with the coolie slaves who work the stolen land. I have been a judge. I know the law and the justice, and I say to you it is unjust to steal a man's land, to make that man sick with the Chinese sickness, and then to put that man in prison for life."

"Life is short, and the days are filled with pain," said Koolau. "Let us drink and dance and be happy as we can."

From one of the rocky lairs calabashes were produced and passed around. The calabashes were filled with the fierce distillation of the root of the *ti*-plant; and as the liquid fire coursed through them and mounted to their brains, they forgot that they had once been men and women, for they were men and women once more. The woman who wept scalding tears from open eye-pits was indeed a woman apulse with life as she plucked the strings of an *ukulele* and lifted her voice in a barbaric love-call such as might have come from the dark forest-depths of the primeval world. The air tingled with her cry, softly imperious and seductive. Upon a mat, timing his rhythm to the woman's song, Kiloliana danced. It was unmistakable. Love danced in all his movements, and, next, dancing with him on the mat, was a woman whose heavy hips and generous breast gave the lie to her disease-corroded face. It was a dance of the living dead, for in their disintegrating bodies life still loved and longed. Ever the woman whose sightless eyes ran scalding tears chanted her love-cry, ever the dancers danced of love in the warm night, and ever the calabashes went around till in all their brains were maggots crawling of memory and desire. And with the woman on the mat danced a slender maid whose face was beautiful and unmarred, but whose twisted arms that rose and fell marked the disease's ravage. And the two idiots, gibbering and mouthing strange noises, danced apart, grotesque, fantastic, travestying love as they themselves had been travestied by life.

But the woman's love-cry broke midway, the calabashes were lowered, and the dancers ceased, as all gazed into the abyss above the sea, where a rocket flared like a wan phantom through the moonlit air.

"It is the soldiers," said Koolau. "Tomorrow there will be fighting. It is well to sleep and be prepared."

The lepers obeyed, crawling away to their lairs in the cliff, until only Koolau remained, sitting motionless in the moonlight, his rifle across his knees, as he gazed far down to the boats landing on the beach.

The far head of Kalalau Valley had been well chosen as a refuge. Except Kiloliana, who knew back-trails up the precipitous walls, no man could win to the gorge save by advancing across a knife-edged ridge. This passage was a hundred yards in length. At best, it was a scant twelve inches wide. On either side yawned the abyss. A slip, and to right or left the man would fall to his death. But once across he would find himself in an earthly paradise. A sea of vegetation laved the landscape, pouring its green billows from wall to wall, dripping from the cliff-lips in great vinemasses, and flinging a spray of ferns and air-plants into the multitudinous crevices. During the many months of Koolau's rule, he and his followers had fought with this vegetable sea. The choking jungle, with its riot of blossoms, had been driven back from the bananas, oranges, and mangoes that grew wild. In little clearings grew the wild arrowroot; on stone terraces, filled with soil scrapings, were the *taro* patches and the melons; and in every open space where the sunshine penetrated, were *papaia* trees burdened with their golden fruit.

Koolau had been driven to this refuge from the lower valley by the beach. And if he were driven from it in turn, he knew of gorges among the jumbled peaks of the inner fastnesses where he could lead his subjects and live. And now he lay with his rifle beside him, peering down through a tangled screen of foliage at the soldiers on the beach. He noted that they had large guns with them, from which the sunshine flashed as from mirrors. The knife-edged passage lay directly before him. Crawling upward along the trail that led to it he could see tiny specks of men. He knew they were not the soldiers, but the police. When they failed, then the soldiers would enter the game.

He affectionately rubbed a twisted hand along his rifle barrel and made sure that the sights were clean. He had learned to shoot as a wild-cattle hunter on Niihau, and on that island his skill as a marksman was unforgotten. As the toiling specks of men grew nearer and larger, he estimated the range, judged the deflection of the wind that swept at right angles across the line of fire, and calculated the chances of overshooting marks that were so far below his level. But he did not shoot. Not until they reached the beginning of the passage did he make his presence known. He did not disclose himself, but spoke from the thicket.

"What do you want?" he demanded.

"We want Koolau, the leper," answered the man who led the native police, himself a blue-eyed American.

"You must go back," Koolau said.

He knew the man, a deputy sheriff, for it was by him that he had been harried out of Niihau, across Kauai, to Kalalau Valley, and out of the valley to the gorge.

"Who are you?" the sheriff asked.

"I am Koolau, the leper," was the reply.

"Then come out. We want you. Dead or alive, there is a thousand dollars on your head. You cannot escape."

Koolau laughed aloud in the thicket.

"Come out!" the sheriff commanded, and was answered by silence.

He conferred with the police, and Koolau saw that they were preparing to rush him.

"Koolau," the sheriff called. "Koolau, I am coming across to get you."

"Then look first and well about you at the sun and sea and sky, for it will be the last time you behold them."

"That's all right, Koolau," the sheriff said soothingly. "I know you're a dead shot. But you won't shoot me. I have never done you any wrong."

Koolau grunted in the thicket.

"I say, you know, I've never done you any wrong, have I?" the sheriff persisted.

"You do me wrong when you try to put me in prison," was the reply. "And you do me wrong when you try for the thousand dollars on my head. If you will live, stay where you are."

"I've got to come across and get you. I'm sorry. But it is my duty."

"You will die before you get across."

The sheriff was no coward. Yet was he undecided. He gazed into the gulf on either side, and ran his eyes along the knife-edge he must travel. Then he made up his mind.

"Koolau," he called.

But the thicket remained silent.

"Koolau, don't shoot. I am coming."

The sheriff turned, gave some orders to the police, then started on his perilous way. He advanced slowly. It was like walking a tight rope. He had nothing to lean upon but the air. The lava rock crumbled under his feet, and on either side the dislodged fragments pitched downward through the depths. The sun blazed upon him, and his face was wet with sweat. Still he advanced, until the halfway point was reached.

"Stop!" Koolau commanded from the thicket. "One more step and I shoot."

The sheriff halted, swaying for balance as he stood poised above the void. His face was pale, but his eyes were determined. He licked his dry lips before he spoke.

"Koolau, you won't shoot me. I know you won't."

He started once more. The bullet whirled him half about. On his face was an expression of querulous surprise as he reeled to the fall. He tried to save himself by throwing his body across the knife-edge; but at that moment he knew death. The next moment the knife-edge was vacant. Then came the rush, five policemen, in single file, with superb steadiness, running along the knife-edge. At the same instant the rest of the posse opened fire on the thicket. It was madness. Five times Koolau pulled the trigger, so rapidly that his shots constituted a rattle. Changing his position and crouching low under the bullets that were biting and singing through the bushes, he peered out. Four of the police had followed the sheriff. The fifth lay across the knife-edge, still alive. On the farther side, no longer firing, were the surviving police. On the naked rock there was no hope for them. Before they could clamber down Koolau could have picked off the last man. But he did not fire, and, after a conference, one of them took off a white undershirt and waved it as a flag. Followed by another, he advanced along the knife-edge to their wounded comrade. Koolau gave no sign, but watched them slowly withdraw and become specks as they descended into the lower valley.

Two hours later, from another thicket, Koolau watched a body of police trying to make the ascent from the opposite side of the valley. He saw the wild goats flee before them as they climbed higher and higher, until he doubted his judgment and sent for Kiloliana who crawled in beside him.

"No, there is no way," said Kiloliana.

"The goats?" Koolau questioned.

"They come over from the next valley, but they cannot pass to this. There is no way. Those men are not wiser than goats. They may fall to their deaths. Let us watch."

"They are brave men," said Koolau. "Let us watch."

Side by side they lay among the morning-glories, with the yellow blossoms of the *hau* dropping upon them from overhead, watching the motes of men toil upward, till the thing happened, and three of them, slipping, rolling, sliding, dashed over a cliff-lip and fell sheer half a thousand feet.

Kiloliana chuckled.

"We will be bothered no more," he said.

"They have war guns," Koolau made answer. "The soldiers have not yet spoken."

In the drowsy afternoon, most of the lepers lay in their rock dens asleep. Koolau, his rifle on his knees, fresh-cleaned and ready, dozed in the entrance to his own den. The maid with the twisted arm lay below in the thicket and kept watch on the knife-edge passage. Suddenly Koolau was startled wide awake by the sound of an explosion on the beach. The next instant the atmosphere was incredibly rent asunder. The terrible sound frightened him. It was as if all the gods had caught the envelope of the sky in their hands and were ripping it apart as a woman rips apart a sheet of cotton cloth. But it was such an immense ripping, growing swiftly nearer. Koolau glanced up apprehensively, as if expecting to see the thing. Then high up on the cliff overhead the shell burst in a fountain of black smoke. The rock was shattered, the fragments falling to the foot of the cliff.

Koolau passed his hand across his sweaty brow. He was terribly shaken. He had had no experience with shell-fire, and this was more dreadful than anything he had imagined.

"One," said Kapahei, suddenly bethinking himself to keep count.

A second and a third shell flew screaming over the top of the wall, bursting beyond view. Kapahei methodically kept the count. The lepers crowded into the open space before the caves. At first they were frightened, but as the shells continued their flight overhead the leper folk became reassured and began to admire the spectacle. The two idiots shrieked with delight, prancing wild antics as each air-tormenting shell went by. Koolau began to recover his confidence. No damage was being done. Evidently they could not aim such large missiles at such long range with the precision of a rifle.

But a change came over the situation. The shells began to fall short. One burst below in the thicket by the knife-edge. Koolau remembered the maid who lay there on watch, and ran down to see. The smoke was still rising from the bushes when he crawled in. He was astounded. The branches were splintered and broken. Where the girl had lain was a hole in the ground. The girl herself was in shattered fragments. The shell had burst right on her.

First peering out to make sure no soldiers were attempting the passage, Koolau started back on the run for the caves. All the time the shells were moaning, whining, screaming by, and the valley was rumbling and reverberating with the explosions. As he came in sight of the caves, he saw the two idiots cavorting about, clutching each other's hands with their stumps of fingers. Even as he ran, Koolau saw a spout of black smoke rise from the ground, near to the idiots. They were flung apart bodily by the explosion. One lay motionless, but the other was dragging himself by his hands toward the cave. His legs trailed out helplessly behind him, while the blood was pouring from his body. He seemed bathed in blood, and as he crawled he cried like a little dog. The rest of the lepers, with the exception of Kapahei, had fled into the caves.

"Seventeen," said Kapahei. "Eighteen," he added.

This last shell had fairly entered into one of the caves. The explosion caused all the caves to empty. But from the particular cave no one emerged. Koolau crept in through the pungent, acrid smoke. Four bodies, frightfully mangled, lay about. One of them was the sightless woman whose tears till now had never ceased.

Outside, Koolau found his people in a panic and already beginning to climb the goat trail that led out of the gorge and on among the jumbled heights and chasms. The wounded idiot, whining feebly and dragging himself along on the ground by his hands, was trying to follow. But at the first pitch of the wall his helplessness overcame him and he fell back.

"It would be better to kill him," said Koolau to Kapahei, who still sat in the same place.

"Twenty-two," Kapahei answered. "Yes, it would be a wise thing to kill him. Twenty-three—twenty-four."

The idiot whined sharply when he saw the rifle leveled at him. Koolau hesitated, then lowered the gun.

"It is a hard thing to do," he said.

"You are a fool, twenty-six, twenty-seven," said Kapahei. "Let me show you."

He arose and, with a heavy fragment of rock in his hand, approached the wounded thing. As he lifted his arm to strike, a shell burst full upon him, relieving him of the necessity of the act and at the same time putting an end to his count.

Koolau was alone in the gorge. He watched the last of his people drag their crippled bodies over the brow of the height and disappear. Then he turned and went down to the thicket where the maid had been killed. The shell-fire still continued, but he remained; for far below he could see the soldiers climbing up. A shell burst twenty feet away. Flattening himself into the earth, he heard the rush of the fragments above his body. A shower of *hau* blossoms rained upon him. He lifted his head to peer down the trail, and sighed. He was very much afraid. Bullets from rifles would not have worried him, but this shell-fire was abominable. Each time a shell shrieked by he shivered and crouched; but each time he lifted his head again to watch the trail.

At last the shells ceased. This, he reasoned, was because the soldiers were drawing near. They crept along the trail in single file, and he tried to count them until he lost track. At any rate, there were a hundred or so of them—all come after Koolau the leper. He felt a fleeting prod of pride. With war guns and rifles, police and soldiers, they came for him, and he was only one man, a crippled wreck of a man at that. They offered a thousand dollars for him, dead or alive. In all his life he had never possessed that much money. The thought was a bitter one. Kapahei had been right. He, Koolau, had done no wrong. Because the *haoles* wanted labor with which to work the stolen land, they had brought in the Chinese coolies, and with them had come the sickness. And now, because he had caught the sickness, he was worth a thousand dollars—but not to himself. It was his worthless carcass, rotten with disease or dead from a bursting shell, that was worth all that money.

When the soldiers reached the knife-edged passage, he was prompted to warn them. But his gaze fell upon the body of the murdered maid, and he kept silent. When six had ventured on the knife-edge, he opened fire. Nor did he cease when the knife-edge was bare. He emptied his magazine, reloaded, and emptied it again. He kept on shooting. All his wrongs were blazing in his brain, and he was in a fury of vengeance. All down the goat trail the soldiers were firing, and though they lay flat and sought to shelter themselves in the shallow inequalities of the surface, they were exposed marks to him. Bullets whistled and thudded about him, and an occasional ricochet sang sharply through the air. One bullet ploughed a crease through his scalp, and a second burned across his shoulder-blade without breaking the skin.

It was a massacre, in which one man did the killing. The soldiers began to retreat, helping along their wounded. As Koolau picked them off he became aware of the smell of burnt meat. He glanced about him at first, and then discovered that it was his own hands. The heat of the rifle was doing it.

The leprosy had destroyed most of the nerves in his hands. Though his flesh burned and he smelled it, there was no sensation.

He lay in the thicket, smiling, until he remembered the war guns. Without doubt they would open up on him again, and this time, upon the very thicket from which he had inflicted the damage. Scarcely had he changed his position to a nook behind a small shoulder of the wall where he had noted that no shells fell, than the bombardment recommenced. He counted the shells. Sixty more were thrown into the gorge before the war-guns ceased. The tiny area was pitted with their explosions, until it seemed impossible that any creature could have survived. So the soldiers thought, for, under the burning afternoon sun, they climbed the goat trail again. And again the knife-edged passage was disputed, and again they fell back to the beach.

For two days longer Koolau held the passage, though the soldiers contented themselves with flinging shells into his retreat. Then Pahau, a leper boy, came to the top of the wall at the back of the gorge and shouted down to him that Kiloliana, hunting goats that they might eat, had been killed by a fall, and that the women were frightened and knew not what to do. Koolau called the boy down and left him with a spare gun with which to guard the passage. Koolau found his people disheartened. The majority of them were too helpless to forage food for themselves under such forbidding circumstances, and all were starving. He selected two women and a man who were not too far gone with the disease, and sent them back to the gorge to bring up food and mats. The rest he cheered and consoled until even the weakest took a hand in building rough shelters for themselves.

But those he had dispatched for food did not return, and he started back for the gorge. As he came out on the brow of the wall, half a dozen rifles cracked. A bullet tore through the fleshy part of his shoulder, and his cheek was cut by a sliver of rock where a second bullet smashed against the cliff. In the moment that this happened, and he leaped back, he saw that the gorge was alive with soldiers. His own people had betrayed him. The shell-fire had been too terrible, and they had preferred the prison of Molokai.

Koolau dropped back and unslung one of his heavy cartridge-belts. Lying among the rocks, he allowed the head and shoulders of the first soldier to rise clearly into view before pulling trigger. Twice this happened, and then, after some delay, in place of a head and shoulders a white flag was thrust above the edge of the wall.

"What do you want?" he demanded.

"I want you, if you are Koolau the leper," came the answer.

Koolau forgot where he was, forgot everything, as he lay and marvelled at the strange persistence of these *haoles* who would have their will though the sky fell in. Aye, they would have their will over all men and all things, even though they died in getting it. He could not but admire them, too, what of that will in them that was stronger than life and that bent all things to their bidding. He was convinced of the hopelessness of his struggle. There was no gainsaying that terrible will of the *haoles*. Though he killed a thousand, yet would they rise like the sands of the sea and come upon him, ever more and more. They never knew when they were beaten. That was their fault and their virtue. It was where his own kind lacked. He could see, now, how the handful of the preachers of God and the preachers of Rum had conquered the land. It was because—

"Well, what have you got to say? Will you come with me?"

It was the voice of the invisible man under the white flag. There he was, like any *haole*, driving straight toward the end determined.

"Let us talk," said Koolau.

The man's head and shoulders arose, then his whole body. He was a smooth-faced, blue-eyed youngster of twenty-five, slender and natty in his captain's uniform. He advanced until halted, then seated himself a dozen feet away:—

"You are a brave man," said Koolau wonderingly. "I could kill you like a fly."

"No, you couldn't," was the answer.

"Why not?"

"Because you are a man, Koolau, though a bad one. I know your story. You kill fairly."

Koolau grunted, but was secretly pleased.

"What have you done with my people?" he demanded. "The boy, the two women, and the man?"

"They gave themselves up, as I have now come for you to do."

Koolau laughed incredulously.

"I am a free man," he announced. "I have done no wrong. All I ask is to be left alone. I have lived free, and I shall die free. I will never give myself up."

"Then your people are wiser than you," answered the young captain. "Look—they are coming now."

Koolau turned and watched the remnant of his band approach. Groaning and sighing, a ghastly procession, it dragged its wretchedness past. It was given to Koolau to taste a deeper bitterness, for they hurled imprecations and insults at him as they went by; and the panting hag who brought up the rear halted, and with skinny, harpy-claws extended, shaking her snarling death's head from side to side, she laid a curse upon him. One by one they dropped over the lip-edge and surrendered to the hiding soldiers.

"You can go now," said Koolau to the captain. "I will never give myself up. That is my last word. Good-by."

The captain slipped over the cliff to his soldiers. The next moment, and without a flag of truce, he hoisted his hat on his scabbard, and Koolau's bullet tore through it. That afternoon they shelled him out from the beach, and as he retreated into the high inaccessible pockets beyond, the soldiers followed him.

For six weeks they hunted him from pocket to pocket, over the volcanic peaks and along the goat trails. When he hid in the lantana jungle, they formed lines of beaters, and through lantana jungle and guava scrub they drove him like a rabbit. But ever he turned and doubled and eluded. There was no cornering him. When pressed too closely, his sure rifle held them back and they carried their wounded down the goat trails to the beach. There were times when they did the shooting as his brown body showed for a moment through the underbrush. Once, five of them caught him on an exposed goat trail between pockets. They emptied their rifles at him as he limped and climbed along his dizzy way. Afterward they found blood-stains and knew that he was wounded. At the end of six weeks they gave up. The soldiers and police returned to Honolulu, and Kalalau Valley was left to him for his own, though head-hunters ventured after him from time to time and to their own undoing.

Two years later, and for the last time, Koolau crawled into a thicket and lay down among the *ti*-leaves and wild ginger blossoms. Free he had lived, and free he was dying. A slight drizzle of rain began to fall, and he drew a ragged blanket about the distorted wreck of his limbs. His body was covered with an oilskin coat. Across his chest he laid his Mauser rifle, lingering affectionately for a moment to wipe the dampness from the barrel. The hand with which he wiped had no fingers left upon it with which to pull the trigger.

He closed his eyes, for, from the weakness in his body and the fuzzy turmoil in his brain, he knew that his end was near. Like a wild animal he had crept into hiding to die. Half-conscious, aimless and wandering, he lived back in his life to his early manhood on Niihau. As life faded and the drip of the rain grew dim in his ears, it seemed to him that he was once more in the thick of the horse-breaking, with raw colts rearing and bucking under him, his stirrups tied together beneath, or charging madly about the breaking corral and driving the helping cowboys over the rails. The next instant, and with seeming naturalness, he found himself pursuing the wild bulls of the upland pastures, roping them and leading them down to the valleys. Again the sweat and dust of the branding pen stung his eyes and bit his nostrils.

All his lusty, whole-bodied youth was his, until the sharp pangs of impending dissolution brought him back. He lifted his monstrous hands and gazed at them in wonder. But how? Why? Why should the wholeness of that wild youth of his change to this? Then he remembered, and once again, and for a moment, he was Koolau, the leper. His eyelids fluttered wearily down and the drip of the rain ceased in his ears. A prolonged trembling set up in his body. This, too, ceased. He half-lifted his head, but it fell back. Then his eyes opened, and did not close. His last thought was of his Mauser, and he pressed it against his chest with his folded, fingerless hands.

6 :: Early Modernism

6–1

Susan Glaspell (1876–1948)

SUSAN GLASPELL (1876–1948), a native of Davenport, Iowa, began a career in journalism in Des Moines, later pursuing writing and the theater, publishing numerous novels, short stories, and plays. Glaspell and her spouse cofounded the Provincetown Players in Cape Cod, where they encouraged innovative playwrights including Eugene O'Neill; Glaspell wrote, directed, and performed in plays by Provincetown Players between 1916 and 1922. In the 1930s, she returned to theater at Chicago's Federal Theater. *Alison's House* (1931), based on a fictional Emily Dickinson, earned her the Pulitzer Prize for Drama. The following story, set in rural Iowa around 1900, was first written as a one-act play, *Trifles* (1916); it speaks to Glaspell's favorite subjects: women's issues—the harsh rural world of the downtrodden housewife—and female friendship.

≈ ≈ ≈

"A Jury of Her Peers" (1917)

When Martha Hale opened the storm-door and got a cut of the north wind, she ran back for her big woolen scarf. As she hurriedly wound that round her head her eye made a scandalized sweep of her kitchen. It was no ordinary thing that called her away—it was probably farther from ordinary than anything that had ever happened in Dickson County. But what her eye took in was that her kitchen was in no shape for leaving: her bread all ready for mixing, half the flour sifted and half unsifted.

She hated to see things half done; but she had been at that when the team from town stopped to get Mr. Hale, and then the sheriff came running in to say his wife wished Mrs. Hale would come too—adding, with a grin, that he guessed she was getting scarey and wanted another woman along. So she had dropped everything right where it was.

"Martha!" now came her husband's impatient voice. "Don't keep folks waiting out here in the cold."

She again opened the storm-door, and this time joined the three men and the one woman waiting for her in the big two-seated buggy.

After she had the robes tucked around her she took another look at the woman who sat beside her on the back seat. She had met Mrs. Peters the year before at the county fair, and the thing she remembered about her was that she didn't seem like a sheriff's wife. She was small and thin and didn't have a strong voice. Mrs. Gorman, sheriff's wife before Gorman went out and Peters came in, had a voice that somehow seemed to be backing up the law with every word. But if Mrs. Peters didn't look like a sheriff's wife, Peters made it up in looking like a sheriff. He was to a dot the kind of man who could get himself elected sheriff—a heavy man with a big voice, who was particularly genial with the law-abiding, as if to make it plain that he knew the difference between criminals and non-criminals. And right there it came into Mrs. Hale's mind, with a stab, that this man who was so pleasant and lively with all of them was going to the Wrights' now as sheriff.

"The country's not very pleasant this time of year," Mrs. Peters at last ventured, as if she felt they ought to be talking as well as the men.

Mrs. Hale scarcely finished her reply, for they had gone up a little hill and could see the Wright place now, and seeing it did not make her feel like talking. It looked very lonesome this cold March morning. It had always been a lonesome-looking place. It was down in a hollow, and the poplar trees around it were lonesome-looking trees. The men were looking at it and talking about what had happened. The county attorney was bending to one side of the buggy, and kept looking steadily at the place as they drew up to it.

"I'm glad you came with me," Mrs. Peters said nervously, as the two women were about to follow the men in through the kitchen door.

Even after she had her foot on the door-step, her hand on the knob, Martha Hale had a moment of feeling she could not cross that threshold. And the reason it seemed she couldn't cross it now was simply because she hadn't crossed it before. Time and time again it had been in her mind, "I ought to go over and see Minnie Foster"—she still thought of her as Minnie Foster, though for twenty years she had been Mrs. Wright. And then there was always something to do and Minnie Foster would go from her mind. But *now* she could come.

The men went over to the stove. The women stood close together by the door. Young Henderson, the county attorney, turned around and said, "Come up to the fire, ladies."

Mrs. Peters took a step forward, then stopped. "I'm not—cold," she said.

And so the two women stood by the door, at first not even so much as looking around the kitchen.

The men talked for a minute about what a good thing it was the sheriff had sent his deputy out that morning to make a fire for them, and then Sheriff Peters stepped back from the stove, unbuttoned his outer coat, and leaned his hands on the kitchen table in a way that seemed to mark the beginning of official business. "Now, Mr. Hale," he said in a sort of semi-official voice, "before we move things about, you tell Mr. Henderson just what it was you saw when you came here yesterday morning."

The county attorney was looking around the kitchen.

"By the way," he said, "has anything been moved?" He turned to the sheriff. "Are things just as you left them yesterday?"

Peters looked from cupboard to sink; from that to a small worn rocker a little to one side of the kitchen table.

"It's just the same."

"Somebody should have been left here yesterday," said the county attorney.

"Oh—yesterday," returned the sheriff, with a little gesture as of yesterday having been more than he could bear to think of. "When I had to send Frank to Morris Center for that man who went crazy—let me tell you, I had my hands full *yesterday*. I knew you could get back from Omaha by to-day, George, and as long as I went over everything here myself—"

"Well, Mr. Hale," said the county attorney, in a way of letting what was past and gone go, "tell just what happened when you came here yesterday morning."

Mrs. Hale, still leaning against the door, had that sinking feeling of the mother whose child is about to speak a piece. Lewis often wandered along and got things mixed up in a story. She hoped he would tell this straight and plain, and not say unnecessary things that would just make things harder for Minnie Foster. He didn't begin at once, and she noticed that he looked queer—as if standing in that kitchen and having to tell what he had seen there yesterday morning made him almost sick.

"Yes, Mr. Hale?" the county attorney reminded.

"Harry and I had started to town with a load of potatoes," Mrs. Hale's husband began.

Harry was Mrs. Hale's oldest boy. He wasn't with them now, for the very good reason that those potatoes never got to town yesterday and he was taking them this morning, so he hadn't been home when the sheriff stopped to say he wanted Mr. Hale to come over to the Wright place and tell the county attorney his story there, where he could point it all out. With all Mrs. Hale's other emotions came the fear now that maybe Harry wasn't dressed warm enough—they hadn't any of them realized how that north wind did bite.

"We come along this road," Hale was going on, with a motion of his hand to the road over which they had just come, "and as we got in sight of the house I says to Harry, 'I'm goin' to see if I can't get John Wright to take a telephone.' You see," he explained to Henderson, "unless I can get somebody to go in with me they won't come out this branch road except for a price *I* can't pay. I'd spoke to Wright about it once before; but he put me off, saying folks talked too much anyway, and all he asked was peace and quiet—guess you know about how much he talked himself. But I thought maybe if I went to the house and talked about it before his wife, and said all the women-folks liked the telephones, and that in this lonesome stretch of road it would be a good thing—well, I said to Harry that that was what I was going to say—though I said at the same time that I didn't know as what his wife wanted made much difference to John—"

Now, there he was!—saying things he didn't need to say. Mrs. Hale tried to catch her husband's eye, but fortunately the county attorney interrupted with:

"Let's talk about that a little later, Mr. Hale. I do want to talk about that, but I'm anxious now to get along to just what happened when you got here."

When he began this time, it was very deliberately and carefully:

"I didn't see or hear anything. I knocked at the door. And still it was all quiet inside. I knew they must be up—it was past eight o'clock. So I knocked again, louder, and I thought I heard somebody say, 'Come in.' I wasn't sure—I'm not sure yet. But I opened the door—this door," jerking a hand toward the door by which the two women stood, "and there, in that rocker"—pointing to it—"sat Mrs. Wright."

Every one in the kitchen looked at the rocker. It came into Mrs. Hale's mind that that rocker didn't look in the least like Minnie Foster—the Minnie Foster of twenty years before. It was a dingy red, with wooden rungs up the back, and the middle rung was gone, and the chair sagged to one side.

"How did she—look?" the county attorney was inquiring.

"Well," said Hale, "she looked—queer."

"How do you mean—queer?"

As he asked it he took out a note-book and pencil. Mrs. Hale did not like the sight of that pencil. She kept her eye fixed on her husband, as if to keep him from saying unnecessary things that would go into that note-book and make trouble.

Hale did speak guardedly, as if the pencil had affected him too.

"Well, as if she didn't know what she was going to do next. And kind of—done up."

"How did she seem to feel about your coming?"

"Why, I don't think she minded—one way or other. She didn't pay much attention. I said, 'Ho' do, Mrs. Wright? It's cold, ain't it?' And she said, 'Is it?'—and went on pleatin' at her apron.

"Well, I was surprised. She didn't ask me to come up to the stove, or to sit down, but just set there, not even lookin' at me. And so I said: 'I want to see John.'

"And then she—laughed. I guess you would call it a laugh.

"I thought of Harry and the team outside, so I said, a little sharp, 'Can I see John?' 'No,' says she—kind of dull like. 'Ain't he home?' says I. Then she looked at me. 'Yes,' says she, 'he's home.' 'Then why can't I see him?' I asked her, out of patience with her now. ''Cause he's dead,' says she, just as quiet and dull—and fell to pleatin' her apron. 'Dead?' says I, like you do when you can't take in what you've heard.

"She just nodded her head, not getting a bit excited, but rockin' back and forth.

"'Why—where is he?' says I, not knowing *what* to say.

"She just pointed upstairs—like this"—pointing to the room above.

"I got up, with the idea of going up there myself. By this time I—didn't know what to do. I walked from there to here; then I says: 'Why, what did he die of?'

"'He died of a rope round his neck,' says she; and just went on pleatin' at her apron."

Hale stopped speaking, and stood staring at the rocker, as if he were still seeing the woman who had sat there the morning before. Nobody spoke; it was as if every one were seeing the woman who had sat there the morning before.

"And what did you do then?" the county attorney at last broke the silence.

"I went out and called Harry. I thought I might—need help. I got Harry in, and we went upstairs." His voice fell almost to a whisper. "There he was—lying over the—"

"I think I'd rather have you go into that upstairs," the county attorney interrupted, "where you can point it all out. Just go on now with the rest of the story."

"Well, my first thought was to get that rope off. It looked—"

He stopped, his face twitching.

"But Harry, he went up to him, and he said, 'No, he's dead all right, and we'd better not touch anything.' So we went downstairs.

"She was still sitting that same way. 'Has anybody been notified?' I asked. 'No,' says she, unconcerned.

"'Who did this, Mrs. Wright?' said Harry. He said it businesslike, and she stopped pleatin' at her apron. 'I don't know,' she says. 'You don't *know*?' says Harry. 'Weren't you sleepin' in the bed with him?' 'Yes,' says she, 'but I was on the inside.' 'Somebody slipped a rope round his neck and strangled him, and you didn't wake up?' says Harry. 'I didn't wake up,' she said after him.

"We may have looked as if we didn't see how that could be, for after a minute she said, 'I sleep sound.'

"Harry was going to ask her more questions, but I said maybe that weren't our business; maybe we ought to let her tell her story first to the coroner or the sheriff. So Harry went fast as he could over to High Road—the Rivers' place, where there's a telephone."

"And what did she do when she knew you had gone for the coroner?" The attorney got his pencil in his hand all ready for writing.

"She moved from that chair to this one over here"—Hale pointed to a small chair in the corner—"and just sat there with her hands held together and looking down. I got a feeling that I ought to make some conversation, so I said I had come in to see if John wanted to put in a telephone; and at that she started to laugh, and then she stopped and looked at me—scared."

At the sound of a moving pencil the man who was telling the story looked up.

"I dunno—maybe it wasn't scared," he hastened; "I wouldn't like to say it was. Soon Harry got back, and then Dr. Lloyd came, and you, Mr. Peters, and so I guess that's all I know that you don't."

He said that last with relief, and moved a little, as if relaxing. Everyone moved a little. The county attorney walked toward the stair door.

"I guess we'll go upstairs first—then out to the barn and around there."

He paused and looked around the kitchen.

"You're convinced there was nothing important here?" he asked the sheriff. "Nothing that would—point to any motive?"

The sheriff too looked all around, as if to re-convince himself.

"Nothing here but kitchen things," he said, with a little laugh for the insignificance of kitchen things.

The county attorney was looking at the cupboard—a peculiar, ungainly structure, half closet and half cupboard, the upper part of it being built in the wall, and the lower part just the old-fashioned kitchen cupboard. As if its queerness attracted him, he got a chair and opened the upper part and looked in. After a moment he drew his hand away sticky.

"Here's a nice mess," he said resentfully.

The two women had drawn nearer, and now the sheriff's wife spoke.

"Oh—her fruit," she said, looking to Mrs. Hale for sympathetic understanding. She turned back to the county attorney and explained: "She worried about that when it turned so cold last night. She said the fire would go out and her jars might burst."

Mrs. Peters' husband broke into a laugh.

"Well, can you beat the women! Held for murder, and worrying about her preserves!"

The young attorney set his lips.

"I guess before we're through with her she may have something more serious than preserves to worry about."

"Oh, well," said Mrs. Hale's husband, with good-natured superiority, "women are used to worrying over trifles."

The two women moved a little closer together. Neither of them spoke. The county attorney seemed suddenly to remember his manners—and think of his future.

"And yet," said he, with the gallantry of a young politician, "for all their worries, what would we do without the ladies?"

The women did not speak, did not unbend. He went to the sink and began washing his hands. He turned to wipe them on the roller towel—whirled it for a cleaner place.

"Dirty towels! Not much of a housekeeper, would you say, ladies?"

He kicked his foot against some dirty pans under the sink.

"There's a great deal of work to be done on a farm," said Mrs. Hale stiffly.

"To be sure. And yet"—with a little bow to her—"I know there are some Dickson County farm-houses that do not have such roller towels." He gave it a pull to expose its full length again.

"Those towels get dirty awful quick. Men's hands aren't always as clean as they might be."

"Ah, loyal to your sex, I see," he laughed. He stopped and gave her a keen look. "But you and Mrs. Wright were neighbors. I suppose you were friends, too."

Martha Hale shook her head.

"I've seen little enough of her of late years. I've not been in this house—it's more than a year."

"And why was that? You didn't like her?"

"I liked her well enough," she replied with spirit. "Farmers' wives have their hands full, Mr. Henderson. And then—" She looked around the kitchen.

"Yes?" he encouraged.

"It never seemed a very cheerful place," said she, more to herself than to him.

"No," he agreed; "I don't think anyone would call it cheerful. I shouldn't say she had the home-making instinct."

"Well, I don't know as Wright had, either," she muttered.

"You mean they didn't get on very well?" he was quick to ask.

"No; I don't mean anything," she answered, with decision. As she turned a little away from him, she added: "But I don't think a place would be any the cheerfuler for John Wright's bein' in it."

"I'd like to talk to you about that a little later, Mrs. Hale," he said. "I'm anxious to get the lay of things upstairs now."

He moved toward the stair door, followed by the two men.

"I suppose anything Mrs. Peters does'll be all right?" the sheriff inquired. "She was to take in some clothes for her, you know—and a few little things. We left in such a hurry yesterday."

The county attorney looked at the two women whom they were leaving alone there among the kitchen things.

"Yes—Mrs. Peters," he said, his glance resting on the woman who was not Mrs. Peters, the big farmer woman who stood behind the sheriff's wife. "Of course Mrs. Peters is one of us," he said, in a manner of entrusting responsibility. "And keep your eye out, Mrs. Peters, for anything that might be of use. No telling; you women might come upon a clue to the motive—and that's the thing we need."

Mr. Hale rubbed his face after the fashion of a show man getting ready for a pleasantry.

"But would the women know a clue if they did come upon it?" he said; and, having delivered himself of this, he followed the others through the stair door.

The women stood motionless and silent, listening to the footsteps, first upon the stairs, then in the room above them.

Then, as if releasing herself from something strange, Mrs. Hale began to arrange the dirty pans under the sink, which the county attorney's disdainful push of the foot had deranged.

"I'd hate to have men comin' into my kitchen," she said testily—"snoopin' round and criticizin.'"

"Of course it's no more than their duty," said the sheriff's wife, in her manner of timid acquiescence.

"Duty's all right," replied Mrs. Hale bluffly; "but I guess that deputy sheriff that come out to make the fire might have got a little of this on." She gave the roller towel a pull. "Wish I'd thought of that sooner! Seems mean to talk about her for not having things slicked up, when she had to come away in such a hurry."

She looked around the kitchen. Certainly it was not "slicked up." Her eye was held by a bucket of sugar on a low shelf. The cover was off the wooden bucket, and beside it was a paper bag—half full.

Mrs. Hale moved toward it.

"She was putting this in there," she said to herself—slowly.

She thought of the flour in her kitchen at home—half sifted, half not sifted. She had been interrupted, and had left things half done. What had interrupted Minnie Foster? Why had that work been left half done? She made a move as if to finish it,—unfinished things always bothered her,—and then she glanced around and saw that Mrs. Peters was watching her—and she didn't want Mrs. Peters to get that feeling she had got of work begun and then—for some reason—not finished.

"It's a shame about her fruit," she said, and walked toward the cupboard that the county attorney had opened, and got on the chair, murmuring: "I wonder if it's all gone."

It was a sorry enough looking sight, but "Here's one that's all right," she said at last. She held it toward the light. "This is cherries, too." She looked again. "I declare I believe that's the only one."

With a sigh, she got down from the chair, went to the sink, and wiped off the bottle.

"She'll feel awful bad, after all her hard work in the hot weather. I remember the afternoon I put up my cherries last summer."

She set the bottle on the table, and, with another sigh, started to sit down in the rocker. But she did not sit down. Something kept her from sitting down in that chair. She straightened—stepped back, and, half turned away, stood looking at it, seeing the woman who had sat there "pleatin' at her apron."

The thin voice of the sheriff's wife broke in upon her: "I must be getting those things from the front room closet." She opened the door into the other room, started in, stepped back. "You coming with me, Mrs. Hale?" she asked nervously. "You—you could help me get them."

They were soon back—the stark coldness of that shut-up room was not a thing to linger in.

"My!" said Mrs. Peters, dropping the things on the table and hurrying to the stove.

Mrs. Hale stood examining the clothes the woman who was being detained in town had said she wanted.

"Wright was close!" she exclaimed, holding up a shabby black skirt that bore the marks of much making over. "I think maybe that's why she kept so much to herself. I s'pose she felt she couldn't do her part; and then, you don't enjoy things when you feel shabby. She used to wear pretty clothes and be lively—when she was Minnie Foster, one of the town girls, singing in the choir. But that—oh, that was twenty years ago."

With a carefulness in which there was something tender, she folded the shabby clothes and piled them at one corner of the table. She looked up at Mrs. Peters, and there was something in the other woman's look that irritated her.

"She don't care," she said to herself. "Much difference it makes to her whether Minnie Foster had pretty clothes when she was a girl."

Then she looked again, and she wasn't so sure; in fact, she hadn't at any time been perfectly sure about Mrs. Peters. She had that shrinking manner, and yet her eyes looked as if they could see a long way into things.

"This all you was to take in?" asked Mrs. Hale.

"No," said the sheriff's wife; "she said she wanted an apron. Funny thing to want," she ventured in her nervous little way, "for there's not much to get you dirty in jail, goodness knows. But I suppose just to make her feel more natural. If you're used to wearing an apron—. She said they were in the bottom drawer of this cupboard. Yes—here they are. And then her little shawl that always hung on the stair door."

She took the small gray shawl from behind the door leading upstairs, and stood a minute looking at it.

Suddenly Mrs. Hale took a quick step toward the other woman.

"Mrs. Peters!"

"Yes, Mrs. Hale?"

"Do you think she—did it?"

A frightened look blurred the other thing in Mrs. Peters' eyes.

"Oh, I don't know," she said, in a voice that seemed to shrink away from the subject.

"Well, I don't think she did," affirmed Mrs. Hale stoutly. "Asking for an apron, and her little shawl. Worryin' about her fruit."

"Mr. Peters says—." Footsteps were heard in the room above; she stopped, looked up, then went on in a lowered voice: "Mr. Peters says—it looks bad for her. Mr. Henderson is awful sarcastic in a speech, and he's going to make fun of her saying she didn't—wake up."

For a moment Mrs. Hale had no answer. Then, "Well, I guess John Wright didn't wake up—when they was slippin' that rope under his neck," she muttered.

"No, it's *strange*," breathed Mrs. Peters. "They think it was such a—funny way to kill a man."

She began to laugh; at sound of the laugh, abruptly stopped.

"That's just what Mr. Hale said," said Mrs. Hale, in a resolutely natural voice. "There was a gun in the house. He says that's what he can't understand."

"Mr. Henderson said, coming out, that what was needed for the case was a motive. Something to show anger—or sudden feeling."

"Well, I don't see any signs of anger around here," said Mrs. Hale. "I don't—"

She stopped. It was as if her mind tripped on something. Her eye was caught by a dish-towel in the middle of the kitchen table. Slowly she moved toward the table. One half of it was wiped clean, the other half messy. Her eyes made a slow, almost unwilling turn to the bucket of sugar and the half empty bag beside it. Things begun—and not finished.

After a moment she stepped back, and said, in that manner of releasing herself:

"Wonder how they're finding things upstairs? I hope she had it a little more red up up there. You know,"—she paused, and feeling gathered,—"it seems kind of *sneaking*: locking her up in town and coming out here to get her own house to turn against her!"

"But, Mrs. Hale," said the sheriff's wife, "the law is the law."

"I s'pose 'tis," answered Mrs. Hale shortly.

She turned to the stove, saying something about that fire not being much to brag of. She worked with it a minute, and when she straightened up she said aggressively:

"The law is the law—and a bad stove is a bad stove. How'd you like to cook on this?"—pointing with the poker to the broken lining. She opened the oven door and started to express her opinion of the oven; but she was swept into her own thoughts, thinking of what it would mean, year after year, to have that stove to wrestle with. The thought of Minnie Foster trying to bake in that oven—and the thought of her never going over to see Minnie Foster—.

She was startled by hearing Mrs. Peters say: "A person gets discouraged—and loses heart."

The sheriff's wife had looked from the stove to the sink—to the pail of water which had been carried in from outside. The two women stood there silent, above them the footsteps of the men who were looking for evidence against the woman who had worked in that kitchen. That look of seeing into things, of seeing through a thing to something else, was in the eyes of the sheriff's wife now. When Mrs. Hale next spoke to her, it was gently:

"Better loosen up your things, Mrs. Peters. We'll not feel them when we go out."

Mrs. Peters went to the back of the room to hang up the fur tippet she was wearing. A moment later she exclaimed, "Why, she was piecing a quilt," and held up a large sewing basket piled high with quilt pieces.

Mrs. Hale spread some of the blocks out on the table.

"It's log-cabin pattern," she said, putting several of them together. "Pretty, isn't it?"

They were so engaged with the quilt that they did not hear the footsteps on the stairs. Just as the stair door opened Mrs. Hale was saying:

"Do you suppose she was going to quilt it or just knot it?"

The sheriff threw up his hands.

"They wonder whether she was going to quilt it or just knot it!"

There was a laugh for the ways of women, a warming of hands over the stove, and then the county attorney said briskly:

"Well, let's go right out to the barn and get that cleared up."

"I don't see as there's anything so strange," Mrs. Hale said resentfully, after the outside door had closed on the three men—"our taking up our time with little things while we're waiting for them to get the evidence. I don't see as it's anything to laugh about."

"Of course they've got awful important things on their minds," said the sheriff's wife apologetically.

They returned to an inspection of the block for the quilt. Mrs. Hale was looking at the fine, even sewing, and preoccupied with thoughts of the woman who had done that sewing, when she heard the sheriff's wife say, in a queer tone:

"Why, look at this one."

She turned to take the block held out to her.

"The sewing," said Mrs. Peters, in a troubled way. "All the rest of them have been so nice and even—but—this one. Why, it looks as if she didn't know what she was about!"

Their eyes met—something flashed to life, passed between them; then, as if with an effort, they seemed to pull away from each other. A moment Mrs. Hale sat there, her hands folded over that sewing which was so unlike all the rest of the sewing. Then she had pulled a knot and drawn the threads.

"Oh, what are you doing, Mrs. Hale?" asked the sheriff's wife, startled.

"Just pulling out a stitch or two that's not sewed very good," said Mrs. Hale mildly.

"I don't think we ought to touch things," Mrs. Peters said, a little helplessly.

"I'll just finish up this end," answered Mrs. Hale, still in that mild, matter-of-fact fashion.

She threaded a needle and started to replace bad sewing with good. For a little while she sewed in silence. Then, in that thin, timid voice, she heard:

"Mrs. Hale!"

"Yes, Mrs. Peters?"

"What do you suppose she was so—nervous about?"

"Oh, *I* don't know," said Mrs. Hale, as if dismissing a thing not important enough to spend much time on. "I don't know as she was—nervous. I sew awful queer sometimes when I'm just tired."

She cut a thread, and out of the corner of her eye looked up at Mrs. Peters. The small, lean face of the sheriff's wife seemed to have tightened up. Her eyes had that look of peering into something. But next moment she moved, and said in her thin, indecisive way:

"Well, I must get those clothes wrapped. They may be through sooner than we think. I wonder where I could find a piece of paper—and string."

"In that cupboard, maybe," suggested Mrs. Hale, after a glance around.

One piece of the crazy sewing remained unripped. Mrs. Peters' back turned, Martha Hale now scrutinized that piece, compared it with the dainty, accurate sewing of the other blocks. The difference was startling. Holding this block made her feel queer, as if the distracted thoughts of the woman who had perhaps turned to it to try and quiet herself were communicating themselves to her.

Mrs. Peters' voice roused her.

"Here's a bird-cage," she said. "Did she have a bird, Mrs. Hale?"

"Why, I don't know whether she did or not." She turned to look at the cage Mrs. Peters was holding up. "I've not been here in so long." She sighed. "There was a man round last year selling canaries cheap—but I don't know as she took one. Maybe she did. She used to sing real pretty herself."

Mrs. Peters looked around the kitchen.

"Seems kind of funny to think of a bird here." She half laughed—an attempt to put up a barrier. "But she must have had one—or why would she have a cage? I wonder what happened to it."

"I suppose maybe the cat got it," suggested Mrs. Hale, resuming her sewing.

"No; she didn't have a cat. She's got that feeling some people have about cats—being afraid of them. When they brought her to our house yesterday, my cat got in the room, and she was real upset and asked me to take it out."

"My sister Bessie was like that," laughed Mrs. Hale.

The sheriff's wife did not reply. The silence made Mrs. Hale turned round. Mrs. Peters was examining the bird-cage.

"Look at this door," she said slowly. "It's broke. One hinge has been pulled apart."

Mrs. Hale came nearer.

"Looks as if some one must have been—rough with it."

Again their eyes met—startled, questioning, apprehensive. For a moment neither spoke nor stirred. Then Mrs. Hale, turning away, said brusquely:

"If they're going to find any evidence, I wish they'd be about it. I don't like this place."

"But I'm awful glad you came with me, Mrs. Hale." Mrs. Peters put the bird-cage on the table and sat down. "It would be lonesome for me—sitting here alone."

"Yes, it would, wouldn't it?" agreed Mrs. Hale, a certain determined naturalness in her voice. She had picked up the sewing, but now it dropped in her lap, and she murmured in a different voice: "But I tell you what I *do* wish, Mrs. Peters. I wish I had come over sometimes when she was here. I wish—I had."

"But of course you were awful busy, Mrs. Hale. Your house—and your children."

"I could've come," retorted Mrs. Hale shortly. "I stayed away because it weren't cheerful—and that's why I ought to have come. I"—she looked around—"I've never liked this place. Maybe because it's down in a hollow and you don't see the road. I don't know what it is, but it's a lonesome place, and always was. I wish I had come over to see Minnie Foster sometimes. I can see now—" She did not put it into words.

"Well, you mustn't reproach yourself," counseled Mrs. Peters. "Somehow, we just don't see how it is with other folks till—something comes up."

"Not having children makes less work," mused Mrs. Hale, after a silence, "but it makes a quiet house—and Wright out to work all day—and no company when he did come in. Did you know John Wright, Mrs. Peters?"

"Not to know him. I've seen him in town. They say he was a good man."

"Yes—good," conceded John Wright's neighbor grimly. "He didn't drink, and kept his word as well as most, I guess, and paid his debts. But he was a hard man, Mrs. Peters. Just to pass the time of day with him—." She stopped, shivered a little. "Like a raw wind that gets to the bone." Her eye fell upon the cage on the table before her, and she added, almost bitterly: "I should think she would've wanted a bird!"

Suddenly she leaned forward, looking intently at the cage. "But what do you s'pose went wrong with it?"

"I don't know," returned Mrs. Peters; "unless it got sick and died."

But after she said it she reached over and swung the broken door. Both women watched it as if somehow held by it.

"You didn't know—her?" Mrs. Hale asked, a gentler note in her voice.

"Not till they brought her yesterday," said the sheriff's wife.

"She—come to think of it, she was kind of like a bird herself. Real sweet and pretty, but kind of timid and—fluttery. How—she—did—change."

That held her for a long time. Finally, as if struck with a happy thought and relieved to get back to everyday things, she exclaimed:

"Tell you what, Mrs. Peters, why don't you take the quilt in with you? It might take up her mind."

"Why, I think that's a real nice idea, Mrs. Hale," agreed the sheriff's wife, as if she too were glad to come into the atmosphere of a simple kindness. "There couldn't possibly be any objection to that, could there? Now, just what will I take? I wonder if her patches are in here—and her things."

They turned to the sewing basket.

"Here's some red," said Mrs. Hale, bringing out a roll of cloth. Underneath that was a box. "Here, maybe her scissors are in here—and her things." She held it up. "What a pretty box! I'll warrant that was something she had a long time ago—when she was a girl."

She held it in her hand a moment; then, with a little sigh, opened it.

Instantly her hand went to her nose.

"Why—!"

Mrs. Peters drew nearer—then turned away.

"There's something wrapped up in this piece of silk," faltered Mrs. Hale.

"This isn't her scissors," said Mrs. Peters, in a shrinking voice.

Her hand not steady, Mrs. Hale raised the piece of silk. "Oh, Mrs. Peters!" she cried. "It's—"

Mrs. Peters bent closer.

"It's the bird," she whispered.

"But, Mrs. Peters!" cried Mrs. Hale. "*Look* at it! Its *neck*—look at its neck! It's all—other side *to*."

She held the box away from her.

The sheriff's wife again bent closer.

"Somebody wrung its neck," said she, in a voice that was slow and deep.

And then again the eyes of the two women met—this time clung together in a look of dawning comprehension, of growing horror. Mrs. Peters looked from the dead bird to the broken door of the cage. Again their eyes met. And just then there was a sound at the outside door.

Mrs. Hale slipped the box under the quilt pieces in the basket, and sank into the chair before it. Mrs. Peters stood holding to the table. The county attorney and the sheriff came in from outside.

"Well, ladies," said the county attorney, as one turning from serious things to little pleasantries, "have you decided whether she was going to quilt it or knot it?"

"We think," began the sheriff's wife in a flurried voice, "that she was going to—knot it."

He was too preoccupied to notice the change that came in her voice on that last.

"Well, that's very interesting, I'm sure," he said tolerantly. He caught sight of the bird-cage. "Has the bird flown?"

"We think the cat got it," said Mrs. Hale in a voice curiously even.

He was walking up and down, as if thinking something out.

"Is there a cat?" he asked absently.

Mrs. Hale shot a look up at the sheriff's wife.

"Well, not *now*," said Mrs. Peters. "They're superstitious, you know; they leave."

She sank into her chair.

The county attorney did not heed her. "No sign at all of any one having come in from the outside," he said to Peters, in the manner of continuing an interrupted conversation. "Their own rope. Now let's go upstairs again and go over it, piece by piece. It would have to have been some one who knew just the—"

The stair door closed behind them and their voices were lost.

The two women sat motionless, not looking at each other, but as if peering into something and at the same time holding back. When they spoke now it was as if they were afraid of what they were saying, but as if they could not help saying it.

"She liked the bird," said Martha Hale, low and slowly. "She was going to bury it in that pretty box."

"When I was a girl," said Mrs. Peters, under her breath, "my kitten—there was a boy took a hatchet, and before my eyes—before I could get there—" She covered her face an instant. "If they hadn't held me back I would have—" she caught herself, looked upstairs where footsteps were heard, and finished weakly—"hurt him."

Then they sat without speaking or moving.

"I wonder how it would seem," Mrs. Hale at last began, as if feeling her way over strange ground—"never to have had any children around?" Her eyes made a slow sweep of the kitchen, as if seeing what that kitchen had meant through all the years. "No, Wright wouldn't like the bird," she said after that— "a thing that sang. She used to sing. He killed that too." Her voice tightened.

Mrs. Peters moved uneasily.

"Of course we don't know who killed the bird."

"I knew John Wright," was Mrs. Hale's answer.

"It was an awful thing was done in this house that night, Mrs. Hale," said the sheriff's wife. "Killing a man while he slept—slipping a thing round his neck that choked the life out of him."

Mrs. Hale's hand went out to the bird-cage.

"His neck. Choked the life out of him."

"We don't *know* who killed him," whispered Mrs. Peters wildly. "We don't *know*."

Mrs. Hale had not moved. "If there had been years and years of—nothing, then a bird to sing to you, it would be awful—still—after the bird was still."

It was as if something within her not herself had spoken, and it found in Mrs. Peters something she did not know as herself.

"I know what stillness is," she said in a queer, monotonous voice. "When we homesteaded in Dakota, and my first baby died—after he was two years old— and me with no other then—"

Mrs. Hale stirred.

"How soon do you suppose they'll be through looking for the evidence?"

"I know what stillness is," repeated Mrs. Peters, in just that same way. Then she too pulled back. "The law has got to punish crime, Mrs. Hale," she said in her tight little way.

"I wish you'd seen Minnie Foster," was the answer, "when she wore a white dress with blue ribbons, and stood up there in the choir and sang."

The picture of that girl, the fact that she had lived neighbor to that girl for twenty years, and had let her die for lack of life, was suddenly more than she could bear.

"Oh, I *wish* I'd come over here once in a while!" she cried. "That was a crime! That was a crime! Who's going to punish that?"

"We mustn't take on," said Mrs. Peters, with a frightened look toward the stairs.

"I might 'a' *known* she needed help! I tell you, it's *queer*, Mrs. Peters. We live close together, and we live far apart. We all go through the same things—it's all just a different kind of the same thing! If it weren't—why do you and I *understand*? Why do we *know*—what we know this minute?"

She dashed her hand across her eyes. Then, seeing the jar of fruit on the table, she reached for it and choked out:

"If I was you I wouldn't *tell* her her fruit was gone! Tell her it *ain't*. Tell her it's all right—all of it. Here—take this in to prove it to her! She—she may never know whether it was broke or not."

She turned away.

Mrs. Peters reached out for the bottle of fruit as if she were glad to take it—as if touching a familiar thing, having something to do, could keep her from something else. She got up, looked about for something to wrap the fruit in, took a petticoat from the pile of clothes she had brought from the front room, and nervously started winding that round the bottle.

"My!" she began, in a high, false voice, "it's a good thing the men couldn't hear us! Getting all stirred up over a little thing like a—dead canary." She hurried over that. "As if that could have anything to do with—with—My, wouldn't they *laugh*?"

Footsteps were heard on the stairs.

"Maybe they would," muttered Mrs. Hale—"maybe they wouldn't."

"No, Peters," said the county attorney incisively; "it's all perfectly clear, except the reason for doing it. But you know juries when it comes to women. If there was some definite thing—something to show. Something to make a story about. A thing that would connect up with this clumsy way of doing it."

In a covert way Mrs. Hale looked at Mrs. Peters. Mrs. Peters was looking at her. Quickly they looked away from each other. The outer door opened and Mr. Hale came in.

"I've got the team round now," he said. "Pretty cold out there."

"I'm going to stay here awhile by myself," the county attorney suddenly announced. "You can send Frank out for me, can't you?" he asked the sheriff. "I want to go over everything. I'm not satisfied we can't do better."

Again, for one brief moment, the two women's eyes found one another.

The sheriff came up to the table.

"Did you want to see what Mrs. Peters was going to take in?"

The county attorney picked up the apron. He laughed.

"Oh, I guess they're not very dangerous things the ladies have picked out."

Mrs. Hale's hand was on the sewing basket in which the box was concealed. She felt that she ought to take her hand off the basket. She did not seem able to. He picked up one of the quilt blocks which she had piled on to cover the box. Her eyes felt like fire. She had a feeling that if he took up the basket she would snatch it from him.

But he did not take it up. With another little laugh, he turned away, saying:

"No; Mrs. Peters doesn't need supervising. For that matter, a sheriff's wife is married to the law. Ever think of it that way, Mrs. Peters?"

Mrs. Peters was standing beside the table. Mrs. Hale shot a look up at her; but she could not see her face. Mrs. Peters had turned away. When she spoke, her voice was muffled.

"Not—just that way," she said.

"Married to the law!" chuckled Mrs. Peters' husband. He moved toward the door into the front room, and said to the county attorney:

"I just want you to come in here a minute, George. We ought to take a look at these windows."

"Oh—windows," said the county attorney scoffingly.

"We'll be right out, Mr. Hale," said the sheriff to the farmer, who was still waiting by the door.

Hale went to look after the horses. The sheriff followed the county attorney into the other room. Again—for one final moment—the two women were alone in that kitchen.

Martha Hale sprang up, her hands tight together, looking at that other woman, with whom it rested. At first she could not see her eyes, for the sheriff's wife had not turned back since she turned away at that suggestion of being married to the law. But now Mrs. Hale made her turn back. Slowly, unwillingly, Mrs. Peters turned her head until her eyes met the eyes of the other woman. There was a moment when they held each other in a steady, burning look in which there was no evasion nor flinching. Then Martha Hale's eyes pointed the way to the basket in which was hidden the thing that would make certain the conviction of the other woman—that woman who was not there and yet who had been there with them all through that hour.

For a moment Mrs. Peters did not move. And then she did it. With a rush forward, she threw back the quilt pieces, got the box, tried to put it in her handbag. It was too big. Desperately she opened it, started to take the bird out. But there she broke—she could not touch the bird. She stood there helpless, foolish.

There was the sound of a knob turning in the inner door. Martha Hale snatched the box from the sheriff's wife, and got it in the pocket of her big coat just as the sheriff and county attorney came back into the kitchen.

"Well, Henry," said the county attorney facetiously, "at least we found out that she was not going to quilt it. She was going to—what is it you call it, ladies?"

Mrs. Hale's hand was against the pocket of her coat.

"We call it—knot it, Mr. Henderson."

6–2

Zitkala-Ša (Gertrude Simmons Bonnin) (1876–1938)

ZITKALA-ŠA [GERTRUDE SIMMONS BONNIN] (1876–1936), a Yankton Sioux from South Dakota, was a storyteller, memoirist, speaker, and activist for native peoples. Born as the Sioux were forced from tribal ground to the reservation, Zitkala-Ša (pronounced "sha") witnessed the assault on long-held rituals, language, and tradition. She was sent to missionary school in Indiana where, she would later write, her hair—and her spirit—were "gnawed away." The "land of big red apples"—the promised paradise—never materialized; but out of this experience grew Zitkala-Ša's voice. As an adult, she married a fellow Sioux, and together they worked to secure rights for native peoples. A violinist with exceptional musical talent, she wrote the libretto *Sun Dance Opera*. *American Indian Stories* (1921), from which the following story comes, speaks to the passing of the old and the coming of the new, of cultures clashing, and of the spirit world of her childhood.

≋ ≋ ≋

"The Trial Path" (1921)

It was an autumn night on the plain. The smoke-lapels of the cone-shaped tepee flapped gently in the breeze. From the low night sky, with its myriad fire points, a large bright star peeped in at the smoke-hole of the wigwam between its fluttering lapels, down upon two Dakotas talking in the dark. The mellow stream from the star above, a maid of twenty summers, on a bed of sweetgrass, drank in with her wakeful eyes. On the opposite side of the tepee, beyond the centre fireplace, the grandmother spread her rug. Though once she had lain down, the telling of a story has aroused her to a sitting posture.

Her eyes are tight closed. With a thin palm she strokes her wind-shorn hair.

"Yes, my grandchild, the legend says the large bright stars are wise old warriors, and the small dim ones are handsome young braves," she reiterates, in a high, tremulous voice.

"Then this one peeping in at the smoke-hole yonder is my dear old grandfather," muses the young woman, in long-drawn-out words.

Her soft rich voice floats through the darkness within the tepee, over the cold ashes heaped on the centre fire, and passes into the ear of the toothless old woman, who sits dumb in silent reverie. Thence it flies on swifter wing over many winter snows, till at last it cleaves the warm light atmosphere of her grandfather's youth. From there her grandmother made answer:

"Listen! I am young again. It is the day of your grandfather's death. The elder one, I mean, for there were two of them. They were like twins, though they were not brothers. They were friends, inseparable! All things, good and bad, they shared together, save one, which made them mad. In that heated frenzy the younger man slew his most intimate friend. He killed his elder brother, for long had their affection made them kin."

The voice of the old woman broke. Swaying her stooped shoulders to and fro as she sat upon her feet, she muttered vain exclamations beneath her breath. Her eyes, closed tight against the night, beheld behind them the light of bygone days. They saw again a rolling black cloud spread itself over the land. Her ear heard the deep rumbling of a tempest in the west. She bent low a cowering head, while angry thunder-birds shrieked across the sky. "Heyä! heyä!" (No! no!) groaned the toothless grandmother at the fury she had awakened. But the glorious peace afterward, when yellow sunshine made the people glad, now lured her memory onward through the storm.

"How fast, how loud my heart beats as I listen to the messenger's horrible tale!" she ejaculates. "From the fresh grave of the murdered man he hurried to our wigwam. Deliberately crossing his bare shins, he sat down unbidden beside my father, smoking a long-stemmed pipe. He had scarce caught his breath when, panting, he began:

"'He was an only son, and a much-adored brother.'

"With wild, suspecting eyes he glanced at me as if I were in league with the man-killer, my lover. My father, exhaling sweet-scented smoke, assented— 'How.' Then interrupting the 'Eya' on the lips of the round-eyed tale-bearer, he asked, 'My friend, will you smoke?' He took the pipe by its red-stone bowl, and pointed the long slender stem toward the man. 'Yes, yes, my friend,' replied he, and reached out a long brown arm.

"For many heart-throbs he puffed out the blue smoke, which hung like a cloud between us. But even through the smoke-mist I saw his sharp black eyes glittering toward me. I longed to ask what doom awaited the young murderer, but dared not open my lips, lest I burst forth into screams instead. My father plied the question. Returning the pipe, the man replied: 'Oh, the chieftain and his chosen men have had counsel together. They have agreed it is not safe to allow a man-killer loose in our midst. He who kills one of our tribe is an enemy, and must suffer the fate of a foe.'

"My temples throbbed like a pair of hearts!

"While I listened, a crier passed by my father's tepee. Mounted, and swaying with his pony's steps, he proclaimed in a loud voice these words (hark! I hear them now!): 'Ho-po! Give ear, all you people. A terrible deed is done. Two friends—ay, brothers in heart—have quarreled together. Now one lies buried on the hill, while the other sits, a dreaded man-killer, within his dwelling.' Says our chieftain: 'He who kills one of our tribe commits the offense of an enemy. As such he must be tried. Let the father of the dead man choose the mode of torture or taking of life. He has suffered livid pain, and he alone can judge how great the punishment must be to avenge his wrong.' It is done.

"'Come, every one, to witness the judgment of a father upon him who was once his son's best friend. A wild pony is now lassoed. The man-killer must mount and ride the ranting beast. Stand you all in two parallel lines from the centre tepee of the bereaved family to the wigwam opposite in the great outer ring. Between you, in the wide space, is the given trialway. From the outer circle the rider must mount and guide his pony toward the centre tepee. If, having gone the entire distance, the man-killer gains the centre tepee still sitting on the pony's back, his life is spared and pardon given. But should he fall, then he himself has chosen death.'

"The crier's words now cease. A lull holds the village breathless. Then hurrying feet tear along, swish, swish, through the tall grass. Sobbing women hasten toward the trialway. The muffled groan of the round camp-ground is unbearable. With my face hid in the folds of my blanket, I run with the crowd toward the open place in the outer circle of our village. In a moment the two long files of solemn-faced people mark the path of the public trial. Ah! I see strong men trying to lead the lassoed pony, pitching and rearing, with white foam flying from his mouth. I choke with pain as I recognize my handsome lover desolately alone, striding with set face toward the lassoed pony. 'Do not fall! Choose life and me!' I cry in my breast, but over my lips I hold my thick blanket.

"In an instant he has leaped astride the frightened beast, and the men have let go their hold. Like an arrow sprung from a strong bow, the pony, with extended nostrils, plunges halfway to the centre tepee. With all his might the rider draws the strong reins in. The pony halts with wooden legs. The rider is thrown forward by force, but does not fall. Now the maddened creature pitches, with flying heels. The line of men and women sways outward. Now it is back in place, safe from the kicking, snorting thing.

"The pony is fierce, with its large black eyes bulging out of their sockets. With humped back and nose to the ground, it leaps into the air. I shut my eyes. I can not see him fall.

"A loud shout goes up from the hoarse throats of men and women. I look. So! The wild horse is conquered. My lover dismounts at the doorway of the centre wigwam. The pony, wet with sweat and shaking with exhaustion, stands like a guilty dog at his master's side. Here at the entranceway of the tepee sit the bereaved father, mother, and sister. The old warrior father rises. Stepping forward two long strides, he grasps the hand of the murderer of his only son. Holding it so the people can see, he cries, with compassionate voice, 'My son!' A murmur of surprise sweeps like a puff of sudden wind along the lines.

"The mother, with swollen eyes, with her hair cut square with her shoulders, now rises. Hurrying to the young man, she takes his right hand. 'My son!' she greets him. But on the second word her voice shook, and she turned away in sobs.

"The young people rivet their eyes upon the young woman. She does not stir. With bowed head, she sits motionless. The old warrior speaks to her. 'Shake hands with the young brave, my little daughter. He was your brother's friend for many years. Now he must be both friend and brother to you.'

"Hereupon the girl rises. Slowly reaching out her slender hand, she cries, with twitching lips, 'My brother!' The trial ends."

"Grandmother!" exploded the girl on the bed of sweet-grass. "Is this true?"

"Tosh!" answered the grandmother, with a warmth in her voice. "It is all true. During the fifteen winters of our wedded life many ponies passed from our hands, but this little winner, Ohiyesa, was a constant member of our family. At length, on that sad day your grandfather died, Ohiyesa was killed at the grave."

Though the various groups of stars which move across the sky, marking the passing of time, told how the night was in its zenith, the old Dakota woman ventured an explanation of the burial ceremony.

"My grandchild, I have scarce ever breathed the sacred knowledge in my heart. Tonight I must tell you one of them. Surely you are old enough to understand.

"Our wise medicine-man said I did well to hasten Ohiyesa after his master. Perchance on the journey along the ghostpath your grandfather will weary, and in his heart wish for his pony. The creature, already bound on the spirit-trail, will be drawn by that subtle wish. Together master and beast will enter the next camp-ground."

The woman ceased her talking. But only the deep breathing of the girl broke the quiet, for now the night wind had lulled itself to sleep.

"Hinnu! hinnu! Asleep! I have been talking in the dark, unheard. I did wish the girl would plant in her heart this sacred tale," muttered she, in a querulous voice.

Nestling into her bed of sweet-scented grass, she dozed away into another dream. Still the guardian star in the night sky beamed compassionately down upon the little tepee on the plain.

6–3
Dorothy Scarborough (1878–1935)

DOROTHY SCARBOROUGH (1878–1935), born in East Texas, raised in Sweetwater and Waco, and educated at Baylor University, wrote novels, collected folklore, and researched Texas cultures. After earning her master's at Baylor, Scarborough taught in Baylor's English Department; in 1915, she left Texas for New York City and Columbia University, where she would earn her doctorate and teach creative writing. Her novel, *The Wind* (1925), and the 1928 silent film of the same title, depicted the harsh climate of West Texas, stirring controversy among local farmers and ranchers unhappy with her portrait of the Lone Star State. *Fugitive Verses* (1912) reflects her love of Central Texas; however, her prose work *In the Land of Cotton* (1923) reveals a more critical eye toward postbellum Central Texas, an economy based on corn, cattle, and cotton, and a society based on segregation and unjust labor practices for African Americans.

≋ ≋ ≋

"Carroll Chapel and Library" (1912)

To the memory of F. L. and Sara Carroll

When I pass by the building beautiful
    That bears your name so greatly loved, there rush
A troop of memories ineffable
    That touch my spirit with a tender hush.

I think of your two joinéd lives that till
    The even-time walked ever side by side
In faithful love that through earth's changes still,
    Through toil and time, did steadfastly abide.

You cared not for the pomp and pageantry
    Of social show nor for the glare of fame;
You spent your days in helpful ministry
    And left the world a noble, stainless name.

You gave to Texas children you had taught
    In simple truth and in God's love and fear;
Immortal, you still live in them and naught
    Can dim the crowns of glory that you wear.

You did not care to hoard your wealth, nor spent
    It lavish on yourselves; what God had given
You rendered back to Him, and nobly lent
    To others that for which you'd patient striven.

Your lives were silent prayers that like incense
    Rose up to God, and since you went away
We still are molded by your influence
    And still your memory cherish day by day.

Rich gifts of toil and loving sacrifice
    You gave to Baylor through the years, and now
In pure and simple grandeur there doth rise
    This building that through centuries shall show

Young men and women wisdom's ways and light
    Them to the ever-lasting Life and Truth.
O immortality of glory bright,—
    O power unceasing of eternal youth!

For even when the mordant tooth of time
    Shall bring these milky marbles to decay,
When brick on brick shall crumble, still sublime
    Your mission shall go to endless day!

"The Passing of the Prairie" (1912)

Gone are our prairies known of old!—
Gone, gone those plains,
Those vast, empyrial, sunset-haunted sweeps
Of distance measureless,
Those soundless, tideless seas of gray-waved grass
Whose undulations never break on any beach
Or near or far.
Gone are those winter whitenesses, wide wastes of snow
Soft-patterned by the wind in flakes and wreaths
Of fairy-filigree all exquisite,
Fore-doomed to melt unseen by eye of man,
Unscarred by any trace

Save where the hungry cattle huddle up for warmth
Or a lone coyote skulks across the snow.
Gone are those Irised pampas of the spring,
Those level and illimitable fields of flowers
Whose myriad forms and colors follow each
In bright, bewildering sequences of bloom
As if the prodigal year
Were crowding all her sweets in one brief ecstasy.
Gone those unmeasured meadows
Where the riot of lupin's blue and white
Reflect the far sky with its trailing, fleecy clouds!

Across those plains the buffaloes once roamed
And untamed, wind-swift horses raced and fled,
While Indians waged their unrecorded, passionate
Pursuits of love and war.
Now all is changed,—all, all!
Gone are the camp-fires and the wigwams, gone,
Of wild Comanches, the fierce Arabs of the prairies,
Of Caranchuas, the Apaches and the Wacoes
And all the kindred nomad bands of hunters.
Their ancient trails are now obliterated quite.
No more is heard their wild, unearthly war-cry
Nor their wailing song of death.
No more is seen their scalp-dance
Nor their painted gauds of war.
They left no trace behind them but a few lone mounds,
Some scattered arrow-heads that "pale-face" children wonder at.
And is that eager life,
That savage lust for strife, that haughty strength,
That hate undying and that faithful love
Now altogether nothing and forgot?
This was the Indians' land,
Their primal home.
They loved it with a fierce, unreasoning rapture
And yet we
Desired and wrestled it from them.
We called them savages;
What ones we did not slay we sent afar
Into a mournful banishment

To eat their hearts out in their home-sick grief
Or fall before the evils of the town,
While we grow rich upon the land we stole
And smugly teach our children patriotism in the schools!
Ah, yes, the march of civilization must go on,—
But could we not have dwelt at peace
With these brown brothers,
Sons of God as well as we?

But they are gone—their land knows them no more.
Where once they roamed rise schools and factories
To teach of arts they never dreamed of.
Where the thundering tread
Of buffalo once shook the earth
The fierce steam-dragon with his eye of fire
Now tears his way.
Where once the gracile form
Of antelope, the sinuous cougar and the wild,
Complaining coyote roamed at will
The click of reapers and the din of mills is heard.
The bear-grass and the cactus, the wild sage
Have been upturned for rows
On limitless rows of cotton
And vast standing ranks of corn.
Mesquite trees with their lace-like, tender leaves
And creamy, perfumed plumes
That grew at vagrant wish upon the plains
Have given place
To orchards orderly and even and well-kept.
The racing motor-cars now wheel and flee
Where once the prairie schooners
Sought their trackless way across the plains.
Where once the cow-boy on his lonely watch
Pillowed his head upon his saddle and gazed up
Into the wide and starry silences
Now gleam the unwinking lights of city streets.
The dug-out has become the lordly home.

Soon, too, shall go the round-up and the fetes,
The orgies of the jocund branding-time.
Soon shall the dogy and the maverick be gone

As now the Indian and the buffalo!
The broncho shall be trained to pull the plow;
The valiant cow-boy with his world all changed
Must sadly fold his lariat and depart.
The rattle-snake that erst was wont to lie
Coiled in the sun,
In sullen stillness brooding o'er his immemorial wrongs
Till sharp and suddenly
He waking, raised his head to hiss and strike,
Must go!
The sovreign eagle floating in the dim,
Blue distance knows his kingdom is divided now,
His reign is o'er.
All, all is changed!

Ah, true, we ill could spare these fertile farms,
These pleasant homes.
World's progress must go on,
No matter what the cost.
Yet now that we are narrowed down
To little, tidy grass-plots and tilled fields
Shall not our natures be contracted, too?
Do not our souls need their unfencéd ranges, wild and free?
How shall we know again
Such wide, illimitable space to dream and grow?
Where shall we see again such wind-swept distances,
Such epic, star-sown nights,
Such lyric dawns?

6–4

Wallace Stevens (1879–1955)

Known as America's first businessman-lawyer-poet, WALLACE STEVENS (1879–1955) represents modernism both in life and subject. He spent his days defending Hartford Accident and Indemnity Company against litigation, and his nights and vacations creating his art. Connecticut born and Harvard educated, Stevens summered in the Keys, where he met Ernest Hemingway and Robert Frost, among others. *Harmonium* (1923), his first book of poetry, contains many of his most famous poems. His urbanity and wit, elegant style and complex allusions, and critique of faith and truth, play with imagination and reality, making him a true modernist poet.

≋ ≋ ≋

"Disillusionment of Ten O'Clock" (1915)

The houses are haunted
By white night-gowns.
None are green,
Or purple with green rings,
Or green with yellow rings,
Or yellow with blue rings.
None of them are strange,
With socks of lace
And beaded ceintures.
People are not going
To dream of baboons and periwinkles.
Only, here and there, an old sailor,
Drunk and asleep in his boots,
Catches tigers
In red weather.

"Thirteen Ways of Looking at a Blackbird" (1917)

I

Among twenty snowy mountains,
The only moving thing
Was the eye of the black bird.

II

I was of three minds,
Like a tree
In which there are three blackbirds.

III

The blackbird whirled in the autumn winds.
It was a small part of the pantomime.

IV

A man and a woman
Are one.
A man and a woman and a blackbird
Are one.

V

I do not know which to prefer,
The beauty of inflections
Or the beauty of innuendoes,
The blackbird whistling
Or just after.

VI

Icicles filled the long window
With barbaric glass.
The shadow of the blackbird
Crossed it, to and fro.
The mood
Traced in the shadow
An indecipherable cause.

VII

O thin men of Haddam,
Why do you imagine golden birds?
Do you not see how the blackbird
Walks around the feet
Of the women about you?

VIII

I know noble accents
And lucid, inescapable rhythms;
But I know, too,
That the blackbird is involved
In what I know.

IX

When the blackbird flew out of sight,
It marked the edge
Of one of many circles.

X

At the sight of blackbirds
Flying in a green light,
Even the bawds of euphony
Would cry out sharply.

XI

He rode over Connecticut
In a glass coach.
Once, a fear pierced him,
In that he mistook
The shadow of his equipage
For blackbirds.

XII

The river is moving.
The blackbird must be flying.

XIII

It was evening all afternoon.
It was snowing
And it was going to snow.
The blackbird sat
In the cedar-limbs.

"Anecdote of the Jar" (1919)

I placed a jar in Tennessee,
And round it was, upon a hill.
It made the slovenly wilderness
Surround that hill.

The wilderness rose up to it,
And sprawled around, no longer wild.
The jar was round upon the ground
And tall and of a port in air.

It took dominion everywhere.
The jar was gray and bare.
It did not give of bird or bush,
Like nothing else in Tennessee.

"The Emperor of Ice-Cream" (1922)

Call the roller of big cigars,
The muscular one, and bid him whip
In kitchen cups concupiscent curds.
Let the wenches dawdle in such dress
As they are used to wear, and let the boys

Bring flowers in last month's newspapers.
Let be be finale of seem.
The only emperor is the emperor of ice-cream.

Take from the dresser of deal,
Lacking the three glass knobs, that sheet
On which she embroidered fantails once
And spread it so as to cover her face.
If her horny feet protrude, they come
To show how cold she is, and dumb.
Let the lamp affix its beam.
The only emperor is the emperor of ice-cream.

6–5
Anzia Yezierska (1882?–1970)

ANZIA YEZIERSKA [HARRIET MAYER] (1882?–1970) was born an Orthodox Jew in a Russian-Polish shtetl, or village. Her father, a Talmudic scholar, emigrated with his large family to Manhattan's Lower East Side around 1890 to escape the pogroms (religious and ethnic persecution). Her semi-autobiographical writing focuses largely on injustice related to immigration, ethnicity and religion, and women's issues. In the city, Yezierska struggled to escape poverty, sweatshop labor, and the ghetto, to achieve autonomy from her Old-World father, and to earn an education. *Hungry Hearts* (1920), a collection of short stories, was her first success, and was made into a 1922 silent film. The collection evokes a passion for America and the freedom it offered, the "democracy of beauty"—yet addresses the problems for women and ethnic and religious minorities in achieving the American dream. Baylor University's copy, dated 1920, is inscribed by Yezierska for Texas writer Dorothy Scarborough, whom she thanked for "invaluable criticism of many of these stories."

≋ ≋ ≋

"Soap and Water" (1920)
What I so greatly feared, happened! Miss Whiteside, the dean of our college, withheld my diploma. When I came to her office, and asked her why she did not pass me, she said that she could not recommend me as a teacher because of my personal appearance.

She told me that my skin looked oily, my hair unkempt, and my finger-nails sadly neglected. She told me that I was utterly unmindful of the little niceties of the well-groomed lady. She pointed out that my collar did not set evenly, my belt was awry, and there was a lack of freshness in my dress. And she ended with: "Soap and water are cheap. Any one can be clean."

In those four years while I was under her supervision, I was always timid and diffident. I shrank and trembled when I had to come near her. When I had to say something to her, I mumbled and stuttered, and grew red and white in the face with fear.

Every time I had to come to the dean's office for a private conference, I prepared for the ordeal of her cold scrutiny, as a patient prepares for a surgical operation. I watched her gimlet eyes searching for a stray pin, for a spot on my dress, for my unpolished shoes, for my uncared-for finger-nails, as one strapped on the operating table watches the surgeon approaching with his tray of sterilized knives.

She never looked into my eyes. She never perceived that I had a soul. She did not see how I longed for beauty and cleanliness. How I strained and struggled to lift myself from the dead toil and exhaustion that weighed me down. She could see nothing in people like me, except the dirt and the stains on the outside.

But this last time when she threatened to withhold my diploma, because of my appearance, this last time when she reminded me that "Soap and water are cheap. Any one can be clean," this last time, something burst within me.

I felt the suppressed wrath of all the unwashed of the earth break loose within me. My eyes blazed fire. I didn't care for myself, nor the dean, nor the whole laundered world. I had suffered the cruelty of their cleanliness and the tyranny of their culture to the breaking point. I was too frenzied to know what I said or did. But I saw clean, immaculate, spotless Miss Whiteside shrivel and tremble and cower before me, as I had shriveled and trembled and cowered before her for so many years.

Why did she give me my diploma? Was it pity? Or can it be that in my outburst of fury, at the climax of indignities that I had suffered, the barriers broke, and she saw into the world below from where I came?

Miss Whiteside had no particular reason for hounding and persecuting me. Personally, she didn't give a hang if I was clean or dirty. She was merely one of the agents of clean society, delegated to judge who is fit and who is unfit to teach.

While they condemned me as unfit to be a teacher, because of my appearance, I was slaving to keep them clean. I was slaving in a laundry from five to eight in the morning, before going to college, and from six to eleven at night, after coming from college. Eight hours of work a day, outside my studies. Where was the time and the strength for the "little niceties of the well-groomed lady"?

At the time when they rose and took their morning bath, and put on their fresh-laundered linen that somebody had made ready for them, when they were being served with their breakfast, I had already toiled for three hours in a laundry.

When college hours were over, they went for a walk in the fresh air. They had time to rest, and bathe again, and put on fresh clothes for dinner. But I, after college hours, had only time to bolt a soggy meal, and rush back to the grind of the laundry till eleven at night.

At the hour when they came from the theater or musicale, I came from the laundry. But I was so bathed in the sweat of exhaustion that I could not think of a bath of soap and water. I had only strength to drag myself home, and fall down on the bed and sleep. Even if I had had the desire and the energy to take a bath, there were no such things as bathtubs in the house where I lived.

Often as I stood at my board at the laundry, I thought of Miss Whiteside, and her clean world, clothed in the snowy shirt-waists I had ironed. I was thinking—I, soaking in the foul vapors of the steaming laundry, I, with my dirty, tired hands, I am ironing the clean, immaculate shirt-waists of clean, immaculate society. I, the unclean one, am actually fashioning the pedestal of their cleanliness, from which they reach down, hoping to lift me to the height that I have created for them.

I look back at my sweatshop childhood. One day, when I was about sixteen, some one gave me Rosenfeld's poem, "The Machine," to read. Like a spark thrown among oily rags, it set my whole being aflame with longing for self-expression. But I was dumb. I had nothing but blind, aching feeling. For days I went about with agonies of feeling, yet utterly at sea how to fathom and voice those feelings—birth-throes of infinite worlds, and yet dumb.

Suddenly, there came upon me this inspiration. I can go to college! There I shall learn to express myself, to voice my thoughts. But I was not prepared to go to college. The girl in the cigar factory, in the next block, had gone first to a preparatory school. Why shouldn't I find a way, too?

Going to college seemed as impossible for me, at that time, as for an ignorant Russian shopgirl to attempt to write poetry in English. But I was sixteen then, and the impossible was a magnet to draw the dreams that had no outlet. Besides, the actual was so barren, so narrow, so strangling, that the dream of the unattainable was the only air in which the soul could survive.

The ideal of going to college was like the birth of a new religion in my soul. It put new fire in my eyes, and new strength in my tired arms and fingers.

For six years I worked daytimes and went at night to a preparatory school. For six years I went about nursing the illusion that college was a place where I should find self-expression, and vague, pent-up feelings could live as thoughts and grow as ideas.

At last I came to college. I rushed for it with the outstretched arms of youth's aching hunger to give and take of life's deepest and highest, and I came against the solid wall of the well-fed, well-dressed world—the frigid whitewashed wall of cleanliness.

Until I came to college I had been unconscious of my clothes. Suddenly I felt people looking at me at arm's length, as if I were crooked or crippled, as if I had come to a place where I didn't belong, and would never be taken in.

How I pinched, and scraped, and starved myself, to save enough to come to college! Every cent of the tuition fee I paid was drops of sweat and blood from underpaid laundry work. And what did I get for it? A crushed spirit, a broken heart, a stinging sense of poverty that I never felt before.

The courses of study I had to swallow to get my diploma were utterly barren of interest to me. I didn't come to college to get dull learning from dead books. I didn't come for that dry, inanimate stuff that can be hammered out in lectures. I came because I longed for the larger life, for the stimulus of intellectual associations. I came because my whole being clamored for more vision, more light. But everywhere I went I saw big fences put up against me, with the brutal signs: "No trespassing. Get off the grass."

I experienced at college the same feeling of years ago when I came to this country, when after months of shut-in-ness, in dark tenements and stifling sweatshops, I had come to Central Park for the first time. Like a bird just out from a cage, I stretched out my arms, and then flung myself in ecstatic abandon on the grass. Just as I began to breathe in the fresh-smelling earth, and lift up my eyes to the sky, a big, fat policeman with a club in his hand, seized me, with: "Can't you read the sign? Get off the grass!" Miss Whiteside, the dean of the college, the representative of the clean, the educated world, for all her external refinement, was to me like that big, brutal policeman, with the club in his hand, that drove me off the grass.

The death-blows to all aspiration began when I graduated from college and tried to get a start at the work for which I had struggled so hard to fit myself. I soon found other agents of clean society, who had the power of giving or withholding the positions I sought, judging me as Miss Whiteside judged me. One glance at my shabby clothes, the desperate anguish that glazed and dulled my eyes and I felt myself condemned by them before I opened my lips to speak.

Starvation forced me to accept the lowest-paid substitute position. And because my wages were so low and so unsteady, I could never get the money for the clothes to make an appearance to secure a position with better pay. I was tricked and foiled. I was considered unfit to get decent pay for my work because of my appearance, and it was to the advantage of those who used me that my appearance should damn me, so as to get me to work for the low wages I was forced to accept. It seemed to me the whole vicious circle of society's injustices was thrust like a noose around my neck to strangle me.

The insults and injuries I had suffered at college had so eaten into my flesh that I could not bear to get near it. I shuddered with horror whenever I had to pass the place blocks away. The hate which I felt for Miss Whiteside spread like poison inside my soul, into hate for all clean society. The whole clean world was massed against me. Whenever I met a well-dressed person, I felt the secret stab of a hidden enemy.

I was so obsessed and consumed with my grievances that I could not get away from myself and think things out in the light. I was in the grip of that blinding, destructive, terrible thing—righteous indignation. I could not rest. I wanted the whole world to know that the college was against democracy in education, that clothes form the basis of class distinctions, that after graduation the opportunities for the best positions are passed out to those who are best-dressed, and the students too poor to put up a front are pigeon-holed and marked unfit and abandoned to the mercy of the wind.

A wild desire raged in the corner of my brain. I knew that the dean gave dinners to the faculty at regular intervals. I longed to burst in at one of those feasts, in the midst of their grand speech-making, and tear down the fine clothes from these well-groomed ladies and gentlemen, and trample them under my feet, and scream like a lunatic: "Soap and water are cheap! Soap and water are cheap! Look at me! See how cheap it is!"

There seemed but three avenues of escape to the torments of my wasted life, madness, suicide, or a heart-to-heart confession to some one who understood. I had not energy enough for suicide. Besides, in my darkest moments of despair, hope clamored loudest. Oh, I longed so to live, to dream my way up on the heights, above the unreal realities that ground me and dragged me down to earth.

Inside the ruin of my thwarted life, the *unlived* visionary immigrant hungered and thirsted for America. I had come a refugee from the Russian pogroms, aflame with dreams of America. I did not find America in the sweatshops, much less in the schools and colleges. But for hundreds of years the persecuted races all over the world were nurtured on hopes of America. When a little baby in my mother's arms, before I was old enough to speak, I saw all around me weary faces light up with thrilling tales of the far-off "golden country." And so, though my faith in this so-called America was shattered, yet underneath, in the sap and roots of my soul, burned the deathless faith that America is, must be, somehow, somewhere. In the midst of my bitterest hates and rebellions, visions of America rose over me, like songs of freedom of an oppressed people.

My body was worn to the bone from overwork, my footsteps dragged with exhaustion, but my eyes still sought the sky, praying, ceaselessly praying, the dumb, inarticulate prayer of the lost immigrant: "America! Ach, America! Where is America?"

It seemed to me if I could only find some human being to whom I could unburden my heart, I would have new strength to begin again my insatiable search for America.

But to whom could I speak? The people in the laundry? They never understood me. They had a grudge against me because I left them when I tried to work myself up. Could I speak to the college people? What did these icebergs of convention know about the vital things of the heart?

And yet, I remembered, in the freshman year, in one of the courses in chemistry, there was an instructor, a woman, who drew me strangely. I felt she was the only real teacher among all the teachers and professors I met. I didn't care for the chemistry, but I liked to look at her. She gave me life, air, the unconscious emanation of her beautiful spirit. I had not spoken a word to her, outside the experiments in chemistry, but I knew her more than the people around her who were of her own class. I felt in the throb of her voice, in the subtle shading around the corner of her eyes, the color and texture of her dreams.

Often in the midst of our work in chemistry I felt like crying out to her: "Oh, please be my friend. I'm so lonely." But something choked me. I couldn't speak. The very intensity of my longing for her friendship made me run away from her in confusion the minute she approached me. I was so conscious of my shabbiness that I was afraid maybe she was only trying to be kind. I couldn't bear kindness. I wanted from her love, understanding, or nothing.

About ten years after I left college, as I walked the streets bowed and beaten with the shame of having to go around begging for work, I met Miss Van Ness. She not only recognized me, but stopped to ask how I was, and what I was doing.

I had begun to think that my only comrades in this world were the homeless and abandoned cats and dogs of the street, whom everybody gives another kick, as they slam the door on them. And here was one from the clean world human enough to be friendly. Here was one of the well-dressed, with a look in her eyes and a sound in her voice that was like healing oil over the bruises of my soul. The mere touch of that woman's hand in mine so overwhelmed me, that I burst out crying in the street.

The next morning I came to Miss Van Ness at her office. In those ten years she had risen to a professorship. But I was not in the least intimidated by her high office. I felt as natural in her presence as if she were my own sister. I heard myself telling her the whole story of my life, but I felt that even if I had not said a word she would have understood all I had to say as if I had spoken. It was all so unutterable, to find one from the other side of the world who was so simply and naturally that miraculous thing—a friend. Just as contact with Miss Whiteside had tied and bound all my thinking processes, so Miss Van Ness unbound and freed me and suffused me with light.

I felt the joy of one breathing on the mountain-tops for the first time. I looked down at the world below. I was changed and the world was changed. My past was the forgotten night. Sunrise was all around me.

I went out from Miss Van Ness's office, singing a song of new life: "America! I found America."

6–6

William Carlos Williams (1883–1963)

WILLIAM CARLOS WILLIAMS (1883–1963), a pediatrician, lived most of his life in Rutherford, New Jersey. Culture and class influenced Williams; while he received an elite education and came from a privileged English and European background, he identified with the working class and his mother's Puerto Rican heritage. A friend of Ezra Pound and H. D. from their university days, Williams entered the poetry scene in 1917 with *Al Que Quiere!* (loosely, "To Him Who Wants It"). *Spring and All* (1923) contains several of Williams' best-known verses. Williams prized concrete, local, colloquial language, social issues and realistic topics, and a more egalitarian, pragmatic approach to human experience. *Al Que Quiere!* opens with an epigraph to Rafael Arévalo Martínez, the Guatemalan writer who wrote a satirical story, "El hombre que parecía un caballo" (1914), or "The Man Who Resembled a Horse."

≈≈ ≈≈ ≈≈

"Pastoral" (1915)

The little sparrows
hop ingenuously
about the pavement
quarreling
with sharp voices
over those things
that interest them.
But we who are wiser
shut ourselves in
on either hand
and no one knows
whether we think good
or evil.
        Meanwhile,
the old man who goes about
gathering dog-lime
walks in the gutter
without looking up
and his tread
is more majestic than
that of the Episcopal minister
approaching the pulpit
of a Sunday.
        These things
astonish me beyond words.

"Apology" (1916)

Why do I write today?

The beauty of
the terrible faces
of our nonentities
stirs me to it:

colored women
day workers—
old and experienced—
returning home at dusk
in cast off clothing

faces like
old Florentine oak.

Also

the set pieces
of your faces stir me—
leading citizens—
but not
in the same way.

"Libertad! Igualdad! Fraternidad!" (1917)

You sullen pig of a man
you force me into the mud
with your stinking ash-cart!

Brother!
        —if we were rich
we'd stick our chests out
and hold our heads high!

It is dreams that have destroyed
    us.

There is no more pride
in horses or in rein holding.
We sit hunched together brooding
our fate.
        Well—
all things turn bitter in the end
whether you choose the right or
the left way
        and—
dreams are not a bad thing.

"El Hombre" (1918)

It's a strange courage
you give me ancient star:

Shine alone in the sunrise
toward which you lend no part!

"The Widow's Lament in Springtime" (1921)

Sorrow is my own yard
where the new grass
flames as it has flamed
often before but not
with the cold fire
that closes round me this year.
Thirtyfive years
I lived with my husband.
The plumtree is white today
with masses of flowers.
Masses of flowers
load the cherry branches
and color some bushes
yellow and some red
but the grief in my heart
is stronger than they
for though they were my joy
formerly, today I notice them
and turn away forgetting.
Today my son told me
that in the meadows,
at the edge of the heavy woods
in the distance, he saw
trees of white flowers.
I feel that I would like
to go there
and fall into those flowers
and sink into the marsh near them.

"The Great Figure" (1921)

Among the rain
and lights
I saw the figure 5
in gold
on a red
firetruck
moving
with weight and urgency
tense
unheeded
to gong clangs
siren howls
and wheels rumbling
through the dark city.

"The Red Wheelbarrow" (1923)

so much depends
upon

a red wheel
barrow

glazed with rain
water

beside the white
chickens

6–7

Ezra Pound (1885–1972)

EZRA POUND (1885–1972), born in Idaho and raised in Pennsylvania, determined at an early age to know more than any human alive about poetry. Arguably, he succeeded. Friends from university days with the poets H. D. and William Carlos Williams, Pound studied languages and literature, earning a master's. After a brief, failed venture as a college professor, he boarded a boat for Europe, his home for most of his remaining life. He settled in London between 1908 and 1920, in Paris after World War I, and in Italy in 1924, and like the nineteenth-century writer William Dean Howells, became the friend and advocate of many young writers. Pound's interest in "Imagism"—free verse that focuses intently on a single image—is represented in the poetry included here. "Vorticism," a second movement to which Pound subscribed, focused even more intently on an image—on a "vortex, from which, and through which, and into which ideas are constantly rushing," as Pound himself described it in his 1916 book *Gaudier-Brzeska: A Memoir* (New York: John Lane, 1916), p. 106.

≋ ≋ ≋

"The Seafarer" (1911)

(from the early Anglo-Saxon text)

May I for my own self song's truth reckon,
Journey's jargon, how I in harsh days
Hardship endured oft.
Bitter breast-cares have I abided,
Known on my keel many a care's hold,
And dire sea-surge, and there I oft spent
Narrow nightwatch nigh the ship's head
While she tossed close to cliffs. Coldly afflicted,
My feet were by frost benumbed.
Chill its chains are; chafing sighs
Hew my heart round and hunger begot
Mere-weary mood. Lest man know not
That he on dry land loveliest liveth,

List how I, care-wretched, on ice-cold sea,
Weathered the winter, wretched outcast
Deprived of my kinsmen;
Hung with hard ice-flakes, where hailscur flew,
There I heard naught save the harsh sea
And ice-cold wave, at whiles the swan cries,
Did for my games the gannet's clamour,
Sea-fowls' loudness was for me laughter,
The mews' singing all my mead-drink.
Storms, on the stone-cliffs beaten, fell on the stern
In icy feathers; full oft the eagle screamed
With spray on his pinion.

                 Not any protector
May make merry man faring needy.
This he little believes, who aye in winsome life
Abides 'mid burghers some heavy business,
Wealthy and wine-flushed, how I weary oft
Must bide above brine.
Neareth nightshade, snoweth from north,
Frost froze the land, hail fell on earth then,
Corn of the coldest. Nathless there knocketh now
The heart's thought that I on high streams
The salt-wavy tumult traverse alone.
Moaneth away my mind's lust
That I fare forth, that I afar hence
Seek out a foreign fastness.
For this there's no mood-lofty man over earth's midst,
Not though he be given his good, but will have in his youth greed;
Nor his deed to the daring, nor his king to the faithful
But shall have his sorrow for sea-fare
Whatever his lord will.
He hath not heart for harping, nor in ring-having
Nor winsomeness to wife, nor world's delight
Nor any whit else save the wave's slash,
Yet longing comes upon him to fare forth on the water.
Bosque taketh blossom, cometh beauty of berries,
Fields to fairness, land fares brisker,
All this admonisheth man eager of mood,

The heart turns to travel so that he then thinks
On flood-ways to be far departing.
Cuckoo calleth with gloomy crying,
He singeth summerward, bodeth sorrow,
The bitter heart's blood. Burgher knows not—
He the prosperous man—what some perform
Where wandering them widest draweth.
So that but now my heart burst from my breastlock,
My mood 'mid the mere-flood,
Over the whale's acre, would wander wide.
On earth's shelter cometh oft to me,
Eager and ready, the crying lone-flyer,
Whets for the whale-path the heart irresistibly,
O'er tracks of ocean; seeing that anyhow
My lord deems to me this dead life
On loan and on land, I believe not
That any earth-weal eternal standeth
Save there be somewhat calamitous
That, ere a man's tide go, turn it to twain.
Disease or oldness or sword-hate
Beats out the breath from doom-gripped body.
And for this, every earl whatever, for those speaking after—
Laud of the living, boasteth some last word,
That he will work ere he pass onward,
Frame on the fair earth 'gainst foes his malice,
Daring ado, . . .
So that all men shall honour him after
And his laud beyond them remain 'mid the English,
Aye, for ever, a lasting life's-blast,
Delight mid the doughty.
                              Days little durable,
And all arrogance of earthen riches,
There come now no kings nor Cæsars
Nor gold-giving lords like those gone.
Howe'er in mirth most magnified,
Whoe'er lived in life most lordliest,
Drear all this excellence, delights undurable!
Waneth the watch, but the world holdeth.
Tomb hideth trouble. The blade is layed low.

Earthly glory ageth and seareth.
No man at all going the earth's gait,
But age fares against him, his face paleth,
Grey-haired he groaneth, knows gone companions,
Lordly men are to earth o'ergiven,
Nor may he then the flesh-cover, whose life ceaseth,
Nor eat the sweet nor feel the sorry,
Nor stir hand nor think in mid heart,
And though he strew the grave with gold,
His born brothers, their buried bodies
Be an unlikely treasure hoard.

"In a Station of the Metro" (1913)

The apparition   of these faces   in the crowd :
Petals   on a wet, black   bough .

"A Pact" (1913)

I make truce with you, Walt Whitman—
I have detested you long enough.
I come to you as a grown child
Who has had a pig-headed father;
I am old enough now to make friends.
It was you that broke the new wood,
Now is a time for carving.
We have one sap and one root—
Let there be commerce between us.

"The River-Merchant's Wife: A Letter" (1915)

(from Li Po)*

While my hair was still cut straight across my forehead
I played about the front gate, pulling flowers.
You came by on bamboo stilts, playing horse,
You walked about my seat, playing with blue plums.

* [The poem is an adaptation of Li Po, the Chinese poet, named Rihaku by the Japanese. Pound inherited Fenollosa's papers, and the Chinese poet's work was among them. —E.J.D. and J.B.F.]

And we went on living in the village of Chokan:
Two small people, without dislike or suspicion.

At fourteen I married My Lord you.
I never laughed, being bashful.
Lowering my head, I looked at the wall.
Called to, a thousand times, I never looked back.

At fifteen I stopped scowling,
I desired my dust to be mingled with yours
Forever and forever and forever.
Why should I climb the look out?

At sixteen you departed,
You went into far Ku-to-Yen, by the river of swirling eddies,
And you have been gone five months.
The monkeys make sorrowful noise overhead.
You dragged your feet when you went out.
By the gate now, the moss is grown, the different mosses,
Too deep to clear them away!
The leaves fall early this autumn, in wind.
The paired butterflies are already yellow with August
Over the grass in the West garden;
They hurt me.
I grow older.
If you are coming down through the narrows of the river Kiang,
Please let me know beforehand,
And I will come out to meet you
                    As far as Cho-fu-Sa.

6–8

H. D. (Hilda Doolittle) (1886–1961)

Friends with Ezra Pound and William Carlos Williams, H. D. [HILDA
DOOLITTLE] (1886–1961) met the two students while her father ran the
observatory at the University of Pennsylvania. After a brief time at Bryn
Mawr College, H. D. would head to London; her lifelong passions—
for poetry, language and culture; mysticism as a result of her Moravian
(German Protestant) upbringing; and astronomy—followed her. She
would spend much of her life, like Pound, in London, with shorter stays

in Switzerland and Austria. Always fascinated with the unknown, H. D. underwent analysis with Sigmund Freud, and would later help the great psychoanalyst escape the Nazis. The influence of Imagism is evident in these early poems; H. D.'s poetry depends on vivid, sensuous images and pretty turns of phrase—yet it builds on a womanist perspective and a strong sense of mystery.

≈≈ ≈≈ ≈≈

"Oread" (1914)

Whirl up, sea—
Whirl your pointed pines,
Splash your great pines
On our rocks,
Hurl your green over us,
Cover us with your pools of fir.

"Sea Iris" (1915)

I

Weed, moss-weed,
root tangled in sand,
sea-iris, brittle flower,
one petal like a shell
is broken,
and you print a shadow
like a thin twig.

Fortunate one,
scented and stinging,
rigid myrrh-bud,
camphor-flower,
sweet and salt—you are wind
in our nostrils.

II

Do the murex-fishers
drench you as they pass?
Do your roots drag up colour
from the sand?

Have they slipped gold under you;
rivets of gold?

Band of iris-flowers
above the waves,
You are painted blue,
painted like a fresh prow
stained among the salt weeds.

"Sea Rose" (1915)

Rose, harsh rose,
marred and with stint of petals,
meagre flower, thin,
sparse of leaf,

more precious
than a wet rose,
single on a stem—
you are caught in the drift.

Stunted, with small leaf,
you are flung on the sands,
you are lifted
in the crisp sand
that drives the wind.

Can the spice-rose
drip such acrid fragrance
hardened in a leaf?

6–9

Katherine Anne Porter (1890–1980)

KATHERINE ANNE PORTER (1890–1980) hailed from Indian Creek in West Texas. After her mother died, her father moved the family to her grandmother's in Kyle, Texas. While her grandmother was born into the antebellum world of the Southern planter and privilege, by 1900 that world had radically changed. Porter's own formal education was scant, her health poor, her family's finances depleted. She eloped at age sixteen, a disastrous first love that ended in divorce, and began a life of travel and writing. Porter would write only a small canon in her life-time and yet hers is some of the finest prose of American modernism. She worked briefly as a journalist, and in the 1920s as a writer for a magazine in Mexico. There, in Mexico, where some of her best fiction is set, Porter wrote about the land, people, and culture in the period directly after the Mexican Revolution. In "Maria Concepción" (1922), a young pregnant Mexican woman, betrayed by her spouse, rejects Span-ish Catholic cultural norms and returns to indigenous folkways.

≈ ≈ ≈

"María Concepción" (1922)

Maria Concepción walked carefully, keeping to the middle of the white, dusty road, where the maguey thorns and the treacherous curved spines of organa cactus had not gathered so profusely. She would have enjoyed resting for a mo-ment in the dark shade by the roadside, but she had no time to waste drawing cactus needles from her feet. Juan and his *jefe* would be waiting for their food in the damp trenches of the buried city.

She carried about a dozen living fowls slung over her right shoulder, their feet fastened together. Half of them fell upon the flat of her back, the balance dangled uneasily over her breast. They wriggled their benumbed and swol-len legs against her neck, they twisted their stupefied, half-blind eyes upward, seeming to peer into her face inquiringly. She did not see them or think of them. Her left arm was a trifle tired with the weight of the food basket, and she was hungry after her long morning's work.

Under her clean bright-blue cotton rebozo her straight back outlined itself strongly. Instinctive serenity softened her black eyes, shaped like almonds set far apart, and tilted a bit endwise. She walked with the free, natural, yet guard-ed, ease of the primitive woman carrying an unborn child. The shape of her body was easy, the swelling life was not a distortion, but the right, inevitable proportions of a woman. She was entirely contented, calmly filled with a sense of the goodness of life.

Her small house was half-way up a shallow hill, under a clump of peru-trees, a wall of organa cactus inclosing it on the side nearest the road. Now she came down into the valley, divided by the narrow spring, and crossed a bridge of loose stones near the hut where Maria Rosa the bee-keeper lived with her old godmother, Lupe, the medicine-woman. Maria Concepción had no faith in the charred owl bones, the singed rabbit fur, the messes and ointments sold by Lupe to the ailing of the village. She was a good Christian, and bought her remedies, bottled, with printed directions that she could not read, at the drugstore near the city market, where she went almost daily with her fowls. But she often purchased a jar of honey from young Maria Rosa, a pretty, shy child only fifteen years old.

Maria Concepción and her husband, Juan Villegas, were each a little past their eighteenth year. She had a good reputation with the neighbors as an energetic, religious woman. It was commonly known that if she wished to buy a new rebozo for herself or a shirt for Juan, she could bring out a sack of hard silver pesos for the purpose.

She had paid for the license, nearly a year ago, the potent bit of stamped paper which permits people to be married in the church. She had given money to the priest before she and Juan walked together up to the altar the Monday after Holy Week. It had been the adventure of the villagers to go, three Sundays one after another, to hear the banns called by the priest for Juan de Dios Villegas and Maria Concepción Guiterrez. After the wedding she had called herself Maria Concepción Guiterrez de Villegas, as though she owned a whole hacienda.

She paused on the bridge and dabbled her feet in the water, her eyes resting themselves from the sun-rays in a fixed, dreaming gaze to the far-off mountains, deeply blue under their hanging drift of clouds. It came to her that she would like a fresh crust of honey. The delicious aroma of bees, their slow, thrilling hum poured upon her, awakening a pleasant desire for a crisp flake of sweetness in her mouth.

"If I do not eat it now, I shall mark my child," she thought, peering through the crevices in the thick hedge of cactus that sheered up nakedly, like prodigious bared knife-blades cast protectingly around the small clearing. The place was so silent that she doubted if Maria Rosa and Lupe were at home.

The leaning *jacal* of dried rush-withes and corn-sheaves, bound to tall saplings thrust into the earth, roofed with yellowed maguey-leaves flattened and overlapping like shingles, sat drowsy and fragrant in the warmth of noonday. The hives, similarly constructed, were scattered toward the back of the clearing, like small mounds of clean vegetable refuse. Over each mound there hung a dusty golden shimmer of bees.

A light, gay scream of laughter rose from behind the hut; a man's short laugh joined in. "Ah, Maria Rosa has a *novio!*" Maria Concepción stopped short, smiling, shifted her burden slightly, bending forward to see more clearly through the hedge spaces, shading her eyes.

Maria Rosa ran, dodging between beehives, parting two stunted jasmine bushes as she came, lifting her knees in swift leaps, looking over her shoulder and laughing in a quivering, excited way. A heavy jar, swung by the handle to her wrist, knocked against her thighs as she ran. Her toes pushed up sudden spurts of dust, her half-unbraided hair showered around her shoulders in long crinkled wisps.

Juan Villegas ran after her, also laughing strangely, his teeth set, both rows gleaming behind the small, soft black beard growing sparsely on his lips, his chin, leaving his brown cheeks girl-smooth. When he seized her, he clenched so hard that her chemise gave way and slipped off her shoulder. Frightened, she stopped laughing, pushed him away, and stood silent, trying to pull up the ripped sleeve with one hand. Her pointed chin and dark-red mouth moved in an uncertain way, as if she wished to laugh again; her long black lashes flickered with the tiny quick-moving lights in her half-hidden eyes.

Maria Concepción realized that she had not stirred or breathed for some seconds. Her forehead was cold, and yet boiling water seemed to be pouring slowly along her spine. An unaccountable pain was in her knees, as though pieces of ice had got into them. She was afraid Juan and Maria Rosa would feel her eyes fixed upon them, and find her there, unable to move. But they did not pass beyond the inclosure, or even glance toward the gap in the wall opening upon the road.

Juan lifted one of Maria Rosa's half-bound braids and slapped her neck with it, playfully. She smiled with soft, expectant shyness. Together they moved back through the hives of honey-comb. Juan flourished his wide hat back and forth, walking very proudly. Maria Rosa balanced her jar on one hip, and swung her long, full petticoats with every step.

Maria Concepción came out of the heavy darkness which seemed to enwrap her head and bind her at the throat, and found herself walking onward, keeping the road by instinct, feeling her way delicately, her ears strumming as if all Maria Rosa's bees had hived in them. Her careful sense of duty kept her moving toward the buried city where Juan's chief, the American archæologist, was taking his midday rest, waiting for his dinner.

Juan and Maria Rosa! She burned all over now, as if a layer of those tiny fig-cactus bristles, as insidious and petty-cruel as spun glass, had crawled under her skin. She wished to sit down quietly and wait for her death without finishing what she had set out to do, remembering no more those two strange people, Juan and Maria Rosa, laughing and kissing in the sweet-smelling sunshine. Once, years before, when she was a young girl, she had returned from market to find her *jacal* burned to a pile of ash and her few pesos gone. An incredibly lost and empty feeling had possessed her; she had kept moving about the place, unbelieving, somehow expecting it all to take shape again before her eyes, restored unchanged. But it was all gone. And now here was a worse thing.

This was something that could not happen. But it was true. Maria Rosa, that sinful girl, shameless!

She heard herself saying a harsh, true word about Maria Rosa, saying it aloud as if she expected some one to answer, "Yes, you are right." At this moment the gray, untidy head of Givens appeared over the edges of the newest trench he had caused to be dug in his field of excavations. The long, deep crevasses, in which a man might stand without being seen, lay crisscrossed like orderly gashes of a giant scalpel. Nearly all the men of the small community were employed by Givens in this work of uncovering the lost city of their ancestors. They worked all the year through and prospered, digging all day for those small clay heads and bits of pottery for which there was no use on earth, they being all broken and covered with earth. They themselves could make better ones, perfectly stout and new. But the unearthly delight of the *jefe* in finding these things was an endless puzzle. He would fairly roar for joy at times, waving a shattered pot or a human rib-bone above his head, shouting for his photographer to come and make a picture of this!

Now he emerged, and his young enthusiast's eyes welcomed Maria Concepción from his old-man face, covered with hard wrinkles, burned to the color of red earth under the countless suns of his explorer's life.

"I hope you've brought me a nice fat one." He selected a fowl from the bunch dangling nearest him as Maria Concepción, wordless, leaned over the trench. "Dress it for me, there's a good girl. I'll broil it."

Maria Concepción took the fowl by the head, and silently, swiftly drew the knife across the throat, twisting off the head with the casual firmness one might use with the top of a beet.

"*Dios*, woman, but you have valor!" said Givens, watching her. "I can't do that. It makes me creep."

"My home country is Guadalajara," answered Maria Concepción, without bravado. "There we have valor for everything."

She stood and regarded Givens condescendingly, that diverting white man who had no woman to cook for him, and, moreover, appeared not to feel any loss of dignity in preparing his own food. He knelt now, eyes squinted tightly, nose wrinkled, trying to avoid the smoke, turning the roasting fowl busily on a stick. Juan's *jefe*, therefore to be humored, to be placated.

"The tortillas are fresh and hot, Señor," she murmured. "By permission, I will now go to market."

"Yes, yes, run along; bring me another to-morrow." Givens turned his head to look at her again. Her grand manner reminded him of royalty in exile. He noticed her unnatural paleness. "The sun is too hot, eh?" he asked.

"*Si*, Señor. Pardon me, but Juan will be here soon?"

"He should be, the scamp. Leave his food. The others will eat it."

She moved away; the blue of her rebozo became a dancing spot in the heat vibrations that appeared to rise from the gray-red soil. Givens considered her exceptionally intelligent. He liked to tell stories of Juan's escapades also, of how often he had saved him, within the last five years, from going to jail, or even from being shot, for his varied and highly imaginative misdemeanors.

"I am never a minute too soon," he would say indulgently. "Well, why not? He is a good worker. He never intentionally did harm in his life."

After Juan was married, he used to twit him, with exactly the right shade of condescension, on his many infidelities to Maria Concepción. He was fond of saying, "She'll discover you yet, young demon!" which would please Juan immensely.

Maria Concepción did not think of telling Juan she had found him out, but she kept saying to herself, "If I had been a young girl like Maria Rosa, and a man had caught hold of me so, I would have broken my jar over his head." Her anger was all against Maria Rosa because she had not done this.

Less than a week after this the two culprits went away to war, Juan as a common soldier, Maria Rosa as his *soldadera*. She bowed her neck under a heavy and onerous yoke of duties: she carried the blankets and the cooking pots, she slept on stones or dry branches, she marched ahead of the troops, with the battalion of experienced women of war, in search of provisions. She ate with them what was left after the men had eaten. After battles she went out on the field with the others to salvage clothing and guns and ammunition from the slain before they should begin to spoil in the heat.

This was the life the little bee-keeper found at the end of her runaway journey. There was no particular scandal in the village. People shrugged. It was far better for every one that they were gone. There was a popular belief among her neighbors that Maria Concepción was not so mild as she seemed.

When she learned about her man and that shameless girl she did not weep. Later, when the baby was born, and died within four days, she did not weep. "She is mere stone," said old Lupe, who had offered all her charms for the preservation of the little life, and had been rebuffed with a ferocity that appalled her.

If Maria Concepción had not gone so regularly to church, lighting candles before the saints and receiving holy communion at the altar every month, there might have been talk of her being devil-possessed, her face was so changed and blind-looking. But this was impossible when, after all, she had been married by the priest. It must be, they reasoned, that she was being punished for her pride. They decided this was the true reason: she was altogether too proud.

During the two years that Juan and Maria Rosa were gone Maria Concepción sold her fowls and looked after her house, and her sack of hard pesos grew. Lupe had no talent for bees, and the hives did not prosper. She used to see Maria Concepción in the market or at church, and afterward she always said that no one could tell by looking that she was a woman who had such a heavy grief.

"I pray God everything goes well with Maria Concepción from this out," she would say, "for she has had her share of trouble."

When some idle person repeated this to the deserted woman, she went down to Lupe's house and stood within the clearing, and called to the medicine-woman, who sat in her doorway stirring a jar of fresh snake's grease and rabbit blood, a cure for sores:

"Keep your prayers to yourself, Lupe, or offer them for others who need them. I will ask God for what I want in this world."

"And will you get it, you think, Maria Concepción?" asked Lupe, tittering cruelly, and smelling the mixture clinging to the wooden spoon. "Did you pray for what you have now?"

Afterward every one noticed that Maria Concepción went more often to church, and less to the village to talk with the other women as they sat along the curb, eating fruit and nursing their infants, at the end of the market-day.

"After all, she is wrong to take us for her enemies," said grave old Soledad, who always thought such things out. "All women have these troubles. Well, we should suffer together."

But Maria Concepción lived alone. She was thin, as if something was gnawing her away inside, her eyes were sunken, and she spoke no more than was necessary. She worked harder than ever, and her butchering knife was scarcely ever out of her hand.

Juan and Maria Rosa, tired of military life, came home one day without asking permission of any authority whatever. The field of war had unrolled itself, a long scroll of vexations, until the end had frayed out within twenty miles of Juan's village. So he and his *soldadera*, now as lean as a wolf, and burdened with a child daily expected, set out with no ostentation and walked home.

They arrived one morning about daybreak. Juan was picked up on sight by a group of military police from the small *cuartel* on the edge of town, who told him with impersonal cheerfulness that he would add one to a group of ten waiting to be shot next morning as deserters.

Maria Rosa, screaming, and falling on her face in the road, was taken under the armpits by two guards and helped briskly to her own *jacal*, now sadly run down. She was received with professional calm by Lupe, who hastily set about the business obviously in hand.

Limping with foot weariness, a layer of dust concealing his fine new clothes, got mysteriously from somewhere, Juan appeared before the captain of the *cuartel*. The captain recognized him as the chief digger for his good friend Givens. He despatched a note in haste to that kindly and eccentric person.

Shortly afterward, Givens showed up at the *cuartel*, and Juan was delivered to him, with the urgent request that nothing be made public about so humane and sensible an operation on the part of military authority.

Juan walked out of the rather stifling atmosphere of the drumhead court, a definite air of swagger about him. His hat, incredibly huge and embroidered with silver thread, hung over one eyebrow, secured at the back by a cord of silver dripping with cobalt-blue tassels. His shirt was of a checkerboard pattern in green and black, his white cotton trousers were bound by a belt of yellow leather tooled in red. His feet were bare, the beautifully arched and muscled feet of the Indian, with long, flexible toes.

He removed his cigarette from the corner of his full-lipped, wide mouth. He removed the splendid hat. His black hair, pressed damply to his forehead, sprang up suddenly in a cloudy thatch on his crown.

"You young devil," said Givens, a trifle shaken, "some day I shall be five minutes too late!"

Juan bowed to the officer, who appeared to be gazing at a vacuum. He swung his arm wide in a free circle upsoaring toward the prison window, where forlorn heads poked over the window-sill, hot eyes following the lucky departing one. Two or three of them flipped a hand in response, with a gallant effort to imitate his own casual and heady manner.

He kept up this insufferable pantomime until they rounded the first sheltering clump of fig-cactus. Then he seized Givens's hand, and his eyes blazed adoration and gratitude.

"With all my life, all my life, I thank thee!" he said. "It is nothing to be shot, *mi jefe*,—certainly you know I was not afraid,—but to be shot in a drove of deserters, against a cold wall, by order of that—"

Glittering epithets tumbled over one another like explosions of a rocket. All the scandalous analogies from the animal and vegetable worlds were applied in a vivid, unique, and personal way to the life, loves, and family history of the harmless young officer who had just set him free. But Juan cared nothing for this; his gratitude to his *jefe* excluded all other possible obligations.

"What will Maria Concepción say to all this?" asked Givens. "You are very informal, Juan, for a man who was married in the church."

Juan put on his hat.

"Oh, Maria Concepción! That's nothing! Look you, *mi jefe*, to be married in the church is a great misfortune to a man. After that he is not himself any more. How can that woman complain when I do not drink, not even on days of fiesta, more than a glass of pulque? I do not beat her; never, never. We were always at peace. I say to her, 'Come here,' and she comes straight. I say, 'Go there,' and she goes quickly. Yet sometimes I looked at her and thought, 'Now I am married to that woman in the church,' and I felt a sinking inside, as if something were lying heavy on my stomach. With Maria Rosa it is all different. She is not silent; she talks. When she talks too much, I slap her and say, 'Silence, thou simpleton!' and she weeps. She is just a girl with whom I do as I please. You know how she used to keep those clean little bees in their hives? She always smelt of their honey. I swear it. I would not harm Maria Concepción because I am married to her in the church; but also, *mi jefe*, I will not leave Maria Rosa, because she pleases me more than any other woman."

"Let me tell you, Juan, Maria Concepción will some day take your head off with that sharp knife she uses on the fowls. Then you will remember what I have said."

Juan's expression was the proper blend of sentimental triumph and melancholy. It was pleasant to think of himself in the rôle of romantic hero to two such desirable women. His present situation was ineffably perfect. He had just escaped from the threat of a disagreeable end. His clothes were new and handsome. He was on his way to work and civilian life with his patient *jefe*. He was little more than twenty years old. Life tasted good, for a certainty. He fairly smacked his lips on its savor.

The early sunshine, the light, clear air, full of the good smell of ripening cactus-figs, peaches, and melons, of pungent pepper-berries dangling in bright red clusters on the peru-trees, the very smell of his cigarette, shook him with a merry ecstasy of good-will for all life, whatever it was.

"Señor,"—he addressed his friend handsomely, as one man to another,— "women are good things, but not at this moment. By your permission, I will now go to the village and eat. To-morrow morning very early I will come to the buried city and work. Let us forget Maria Concepción and Maria Rosa. Each one in her place. I will manage them when the time comes."

News of Juan's adventure soon got abroad, and Juan found many friends about him during the morning. They frankly commended his leaving the army. *Por Dios!* a man could do no better thing than that! The new hero ate a great deal and drank a little, the occasion being better than a feast-day. It was almost noon before he returned to visit Maria Rosa.

He found her sitting on a straw mat, rubbing oil on her three-hour-old son. Before this felicitous vision Juan's emotions so twisted him that he returned to the village and invited every man in the "Death and Resurrection" *pulqueria* to drink with him.

Having thus taken leave of his balance, he found himself unaccountably back in his own house after his long absence, attempting to beat Maria Concepción by way of reëstablishing himself in his legal household.

Maria Concepción, knowing what had happened in the withe hut of her enemy, knowing all the events of that unhappy day, refused to be beaten by Juan drunk when Juan sober had never thought of such a thing. She did not scream; she stood her ground and resisted; she even struck at him.

Juan, amazed, only half comprehending his own actions, stepped back and gazed at her questioningly through a leisurely whirling film which seemed to have lodged behind his eyes. Certainly here was a strange thing. He had not intended to touch her. Oh, well, no harm done. He gave up, turned away. Sleep was better. He lay down amiably in a shadowed corner and floated away dreamlessly.

Maria Concepción, seeing that Juan was quiet, began automatically to bind the legs of her fowls. It was market-day, and she would be late.

Her movements were quick and rigid, like a doll jerked about on strings. She fumbled and tangled the bits of cord in her haste, and set off across the plowed, heavy fields instead of taking the accustomed road. She ran grotesquely, in uneven, jolting leaps between furrows, a crazy panic in her head, in her stumbling legs. She seemed not to know her directions. Now and then she would stop and look about, trying to place herself, then proceed a few steps.

At once, with an inner quivering, she came to her senses completely, recognized the thing that troubled her so terribly, was certain of what she wanted. She sat down quietly under a sheltering thorny bush and gave herself over to her long and devouring sorrow; flinched and shuddered away for the first time from that pain in the heart that pressed and pressed intolerably, until she wished to tear out the heart with her hands to be eased of it. The thing which had for so long squeezed her whole body into a tight, dumb knot of suffering suddenly broke with painful and shocking violence. She jerked with the involuntary recoil of one who receives a blow, and the tears poured from her eyes as if the wounds of her whole life were shedding their salt ichor. Drawing her rebozo over her head, she bowed her forehead on her arms, folded upon her updrawn knees, and wept.

After a great while she sat up, throwing the rebozo off her face, and leaned against the clustered saplings of the bush, arms relaxed at her sides, her face still, her eyes swollen, the lids closed and heavy. She sat there in deadly silence and immobility, the tears still forming steadily under the lashes, as if poured from an inexhaustible, secret, slow-moving river. She seemed to be crying in her sleep. From time to time she would lift the corner of her rebozo to wipe her face dry; and silently the tears would run again, streaking her face, drenching the front of her chemise. She had that complete and horrifying realization of calamity which is not a thing of the mind, but a physical experience as sharp and certain as the bite of thorns. All her being was a dark, confused memory of an endless loss, of grief burning in the heart by night, of deadly baffled anger eating at her by day, until her feet were as heavy as if she were mired in the muddy roads during the time of rains.

Juan awakened slowly, with long yawns and grumblings, alternated with short relapses into sleep full of visions and clamorous noises. A blur of orange light seared his eyeballs when he tried to unseal his lids. There came from somewhere a rapid confusion of words, a low voice weeping without tears, speaking awful meaningless phrases over and over. He began to listen. He strained and tugged at the leash of his stupor, he sweated to grasp those words which should have fearful meanings, yet somehow he could not comprehend them. Then he came awake with frightening suddenness, sitting up, eyes straining at the long, lashing streak of gilded light piercing the corn-husk walls from the level, disappearing sun.

Maria Concepción stood in the doorway, looming colossally tall to his shocked eyes. She was talking quickly, calling to him. Then he saw her clearly.

"*Por Dios!*" thought Juan, frozen with amazement, "here I am facing my death!" for the long knife she wore habitually at her belt was in her hand. But instead, she threw it away, clear from her, and got down on her knees, crawling toward him as he had seen her crawl toward the shrine at Guadalupe many times. Never had she knelt before him! He watched her approach with superstitious horror. Falling forward upon her face, she kissed his feet. She huddled upon his knees, lips moving urgently in a thrilling whisper. Her words became clear, and Juan understood them all.

For a second he could not speak. He sat immovable. Then he took her head between both his hands, and supported her somewhat in this way, saying swiftly, anxiously reassuring, almost in a babble:

"Oh, thou poor creature! Oh, thou dear woman! Oh, my Maria Concepción, unfortunate! Listen! do not fear! Hear me! I will hide thee away, I, thy own man, will protect thee! Quiet! Not a sound!"

Trying to collect himself, he held and soothed her as they sat together in the new darkness. Maria Concepción bent over, face almost upon his knees, her feet folded under her, seeking security of him. For the first time in his careless, utterly unafraid existence Juan was aware of danger. This was danger. Maria Concepción would be dragged away between two gendarmes, with him helpless and unarmed, to spend her days in Belem Prison, maybe. Danger! The night was peopled with tangible menaces. He stood up, dragging the woman to her feet with him. She was silent now, perfectly rigid, holding to him with resistless strength, her hands frozen on his arms.

"Get me the knife," he told her in a whisper. She obeyed, her feet slipping along the hard earth floor, her shoulders straight, her arms stiffened downward. He lighted a candle. Maria Concepción held the knife out to him. It was stained and dark even to the end of the handle, a thick stain with a viscous gleam.

He frowned at her harshly, noting the same stains on her chemise and hands. "Take off thy clothes and wash thy hands," he ordered. He washed the knife carefully, and threw the water wide of the doorway. She watched him, and did likewise with the bowl where she had bathed.

"Light thy brasero and cook food for me," he told her in the same peremptory tone. He took her garments and went out. When he returned, she was wearing an old soiled dress, and was fanning the fire in the charcoal-burner. Seating himself cross-legged near her, he stared at her as at a creature unknown to him, who bewildered him utterly, for whom there was no possible explanation. She did not turn her head, but kept an oblivious silence and stillness, save for the movement of her strong hands fanning the blaze which cast sparks and small jets of white smoke, flaring and dying rhythmically with the motion of the fan, lighting her face and leaving it in darkness by turns.

"*Tu mujer*,"—Juan's voice barely disturbed the silence,—"listen now to me carefully, and answer my questions as I ask them, and later, when the gendarmes come here for us, thou shalt have nothing to fear. But there will be something to settle between us afterward."

She turned her head slowly at this. The light from the fire cast small red sparks into the corners of her eyes; a yellow phosphorescence glimmered behind the dark iris.

"For me it is all settled, *Juanito mio*," she answered, without fear, in a tone so tender, so grave, so heavy with sorrow, that Juan felt his vitals contract. He wished to weep openly not as a man, but as a very small child. He could not fathom this woman, or the mysterious fortunes of life grown so instantly tangled where all had seemed so gay and simple. He felt, too, that she had become unique and invaluable, a woman without an equal in a million women, and he could not tell why. He drew an enormous sigh that rattled in his chest.

"*Sí, Sí*, it is all settled. I shall not go away again. We shall stay here together, you and I, forever."

In whispers he questioned her, and she answered whispering, and he instructed her over and over until she had her lesson by heart. The profound blackness of the night encroached upon them, flowing over the narrow threshold, invading their hearts. It brought with it sighs and murmurs, the pad of ghostly feet in the near-by road, the sharp staccato whimper of wind through the cactus leaves. All these familiar cadences were now invested with sinister terrors; a dread, formless and uncontrollable, possessed them both.

"Light another candle," said Juan, aloud, suddenly, in too resolute, in too hard a tone. "Let us eat now."

They sat facing each other and ate from the same dish, after their old habit. Neither tasted what they ate. With food half-way to his mouth, Juan listened. The sound of voices grew, spread, widened at the turn of the road, along the organa wall. A spray of lantern-light filtered through the hedge, a single voice slashed the blackness, literally ripped the fragile layer of stillness which hovered above the hut.

"Juan Villegas!"

"Pass, friends!" Juan cried cheerfully. They stood in the doorway, simple, cautious gendarmes from the village, partly Indian themselves, personally known to all the inhabitants. They flashed their lanterns almost apologetically upon the pleasant, harmless scene of a man eating supper with his wife.

"Pardon, Brother," said the leader. "Some one has killed the woman Maria Rosa, and we must ask questions of all her neighbors and friends." He paused, and added with an attempt at severity, "Naturally!"

"Naturally," agreed Juan. "I was a good friend of Maria Rosa. I regret her bad fortune."

They all went away together, the men walking in a group, Maria Concepción following a trifle to one side, a few steps in the rear, but near Juan. This was the custom. There was no thought of changing it even for such an important occasion.

The two points of candle-light at Maria Rosa's head fluttered uneasily; the shadows shifted and dodged on the stained, darkened walls. To Maria Concepción everything in the smothering, inclosing room shared an evil restlessness. The watchful faces of those called as witnesses, those familiar faces of old friends, were made alien by that look of speculation in the eyes. The ridges of the rose-colored silk rebozo thrown over the body varied continually, as though the thing it covered was not perfectly in repose. Her eyes swerved over the body from the candle-tips at the head to the feet, jutting up thinly, the small, scarred soles protruding, freshly washed, a mass of crooked, half-healed wounds, thorn-pricks and cuts of sharp stones. Her gaze went back to the candle-flare, to Juan's eyes warning her, to the gendarmes talking among themselves. Her eyes would not be controlled.

With a leap that shook her her gaze settled upon the face of Maria Rosa. Instantly, her blood ran smoothly again: there was nothing to fear. Even the restless light could not give a look of life to that fixed countenance. She was dead. Maria Concepción felt her muscles give way softly; her heart began beating without effort. She knew no more rancor against that pitiable thing, lying indifferently on its new mat under the fine silk rebozo. The mouth drooped sharply at the corners in a grimace of weeping arrested half-way. The brows were strangely distressed; the dead could not cast off some dark, final obsession of terror. It was all finished. Maria Rosa had eaten too much honey and had had too much love. Now she must sit in hell, crying over her sins and her hard death forever and ever.

Old Lupe's cackling voice arose. She had spent the morning helping Maria Rosa. The child had spat blood the moment it was born, a bad sign. She thought then that bad luck would come to the house. Well, about sunset she was in the yard at the back of the house grinding tomatoes and pepper. She had left mother and babe asleep. She heard a strange noise in the house, a choking and smothered calling, like some one in the nightmare. Well, such a thing is only natural. But there followed a light, quick, thudding sound—

"Like the blows of a fist?" interrupted the officer.

"No, not at all like such a thing."

"How do you know?"

"I am acquainted with that sound, Señor," retorted Lupe. "This noise was something else."

But she was at a loss to describe it exactly. Immediately, there was a slight rattle of pebbles rolling and slipping under feet; then she knew some one had been there and was running away.

"Why did you wait so long before going to see?"

"I am old and hard in the joints," said Lupe; "I cannot run after people. I walked as fast as I could to the organa hedge, for it is only by this way that any one can enter. There was no one in the road, Señor, no one. Three cows, with a dog driving them; nothing else. When I got to Maria Rosa, she was lying all tangled up, and from her neck to her middle she was full of knife-holes. It was a sight to move the Blessed Image Himself! Her mouth and eyes were—"

"Never mind. Who came oftenest to her house? Who were her enemies?"

The old face congealed, closed. Her spongy skin drew into a network of secretive wrinkles. She turned withdrawn and expressionless eyes upon the gendarmes.

"I am an old woman; I do not see well; I cannot hurry on my feet. I did not see any one leave the clearing."

"You did not hear splashing in the spring near the bridge?"

"No, Señor."

"Why, then, do our dogs follow a scent there and lose it?"

"*Solo Dios sabe*, Señor. I am an old wo—"

"How did the footfalls sound?" broke in the officer, hastily.

"Like the tread of an evil spirit!" intoned Lupe in a swelling oracular tone startling to the listeners. The Indians stirred among themselves, watchfully. To them the medicine-woman was an incalculable force. They half expected her to pronounce a charm that would produce the evil spirit among them at once.

The gendarme's politeness began to wear thin.

"No, poor fool; I mean, were they heavy or light? The footsteps of a man or of a woman? Was the person shod or barefoot?"

A glance at the listening circle assured Lupe of their thrilled attention. She enjoyed the prominence, the menacing importance, of her situation. What she had not seen she could not describe, thank God! No one could harm her because her knees were stiff and she could not run even to seize a murderer. As for knowing the difference between footfalls, shod or bare, man or woman, nay, even as between devil and human, who ever heard of such madness?

"My ears are not eyes, Señor," she ended grandly; "but upon my heart I swear those footsteps fell as the tread of the spirit of evil!"

"*Loca!*" yapped the gendarme in a shrill voice. "Take her away somebody! Juan Villegas, tell me—"

Juan told him everything he knew, patiently, several times over. He had returned to his wife that day. She had gone to market as usual. He had helped her prepare her fowls. She had returned about mid-afternoon, they had talked, she had cooked, they had eaten. Nothing was amiss. Then the gendarmes came. That was all. Yes, Maria Rosa had gone away with him, but there had been no bad blood on this account between him and his wife or Maria Rosa. Everybody knew that his wife was a quiet woman.

Maria Concepción heard her own voice answering without a break. It was true at first she was troubled when her husband went away, but after that she had not cared. It was the way of men, she believed. Well, he had come home, thank God! She had gone to market, but had returned early, because now she had her man to cook for. That was all.

Other voices followed. A toothless old man said, "But she is a woman of good repute among us, and Maria Rosa was not." A smiling young mother, Anita, baby at breast, said: "But if no one thinks so, how can you accuse her? Should not a woman's own husband know best where she was at all times?" Another: "Maria Rosa had a strange life, apart from us. How do we know who may have wished her evil?"

Maria Concepción suddenly felt herself guarded, surrounded, upborne by her faithful friends. They were all about her, speaking for her, defending her, refusing to admit ill of her. The forces of life were ranged invincibly with her against the vanquished dead. Maria Rosa had forfeited her share in their loyalty. What did they really believe? How much had old Lupe seen? She looked from one to the other of the circling faces. Their eyes gave back reassurance, understanding, a secret and mighty sympathy.

The gendarmes were at a loss. They, too, felt that sheltering wall cast impenetrably around the woman they had meant to accuse of murder. They watched her closely. They questioned several people over again. There was no prying open the locked doors of their defenses.

A small bundle lying against the wall at the head of the body squirmed like an eel. A wail, a mere sliver of sound, issued. Maria Concepción took the almost forgotten son of Maria Rosa in her arms.

"He is mine," she said clearly; "I will take him with me."

No one assented in words, but she felt an approving nod, a bare breath of friendly agreement, run around the tight, hot room.

The gendarmes gave up. Nobody could be accused; there was not a shred of true evidence. Well, then, good night to everybody. Many pardons for having intruded. Good health!

Maria Concepción, carrying the child, followed Juan from the clearing. The hut was left with its lighted candles and a group of old women who would sit up all night, drinking coffee and smoking and relating pious tales of horror.

Juan's exaltation had burned down. There was not an ember of excitement left in him. He was tired; the high sense of adventure was faded. Maria Rosa was vanished, to come no more forever. Their days of marching, of eating, of fighting, of making love, were all over. To-morrow he would go back to dull and endless labor, he would descend into the trenches of the buried city as Maria Rosa would go into her grave. He felt his veins fill up with bitterness, with black and unendurable melancholy. *O Dios!* what strange fortunes overtake a man!

Well, there was no way out of it. For the moment he craved to forget in sleep. He found himself so drowsy he could hardly guide his feet. The occasional light touch of the woman at his elbow was unreal, as ghostly as the brushing of a leaf against his face. Having secured her safety, compelled by an instinct he could not in the least comprehend, he forgot her. There survived in him only a vast blind hurt like a covered wound.

He entered the *jacal*, and, without waiting to light a candle, threw off his clothing, sitting just within the door. He moved with lagging, half-awake hands, seeking to strip his outwearied body of its heavy finery. With a long groaning sigh of relief he fell straight back on the floor, almost instantly asleep, his arms flung up and out in the simple attitude of exhaustion.

Maria Concepción, a small clay jar in her hand, approached the gentle little mother goat tethered to a sapling, which gave and yielded as she pulled at the rope's-end after the farthest reaches of grass about her. The kid, tied up a few yards away, rose bleating, its feathery fleece shivering in the fresh wind. Sitting on her heels, holding his tether, she allowed him to suckle a few moments. Afterward—all her movements very deliberate and even—she drew a supply of milk for the child.

She sat against the wall of her house, near the doorway. The child, fed and asleep, was cradled in the hollow of her crossed legs. The silence overfilled the world, the skies flowed down evenly to the rim of the valley, the stealthy moon crept slantwise to the shelter of the mountains. She felt soft and warm all over; she dreamed that the newly born child was her own, and she was resting deliciously.

Maria Concepción could hear Juan's breathing. The sound vapored from the low doorway, calmly; the house seemed to be resting after a burdensome day. She breathed, too, very slowly and quietly, each inspiration saturating her with repose. The child's light, faint breath was a mere shadowy moth of sound flitting in the silver air. The night, the earth under her, seemed to swell and recede together with a vast, unhurried, benign breathing. She drooped and closed her eyes, feeling the slow rise and fall within her own body. She did not know what it was, but it eased her all through. Even as she was falling asleep, head bowed over the child, she was still aware of a strange, wakeful happiness.

6–10

F. Scott Fitzgerald (1896–1940)

A key writer of the "Lost Generation," F. SCOTT FITZGERALD [FRANCIS SCOTT FITZGERALD] (1896–1940), had midwestern origins—like Christopher Newman of Henry James' *The American*. In his stories and novels of American modernism, midwestern values—hard work, frugality, practicality—confront the big city life, a world of excess and waste. "Dissipation," a favorite word of Fitzgerald's, overtakes his characters, and they lose control of their youthful, resplendent dreams. Fitzgerald grew up as an insider-outsider to the world of privilege. When his father failed at his business, Fitzgerald's extended family cobbled together the resources to send him to Princeton, where he failed at football and academics, but succeeded in being liked by those destined for high society. Handsome, charming, and penniless, he sought and won the hand of Alabama Southern belle Zelda Sayre—but only after proving himself by publishing *This Side of Paradise* (1920). *The Great Gatsby* (1925), written in the Jazz Age, followed, exposing changing social mores for men and women. A witty comedy of manners, "Bernice Bobs Her Hair" (1921) centers on midwestern satire, adolescent pecking order, peer pressure and popularity, and flappers as "mean girls."

≈ ≈ ≈

"Bernice Bobs Her Hair" (1921)

I

After dark on Saturday night one could stand on the first tee of the golf-course and see the country-club windows as a yellow expanse over a very black and wavy ocean. The waves of this ocean, so to speak, were the heads of many curious caddies, a few of the more ingenious chauffeurs, the golf professional's deaf sister—and there were usually several stray, diffident waves who might have rolled inside had they so desired. This was the gallery.

The balcony was inside. It consisted of the circle of wicker chairs that lined the wall of the combination clubroom and ballroom. At these Saturday-night dances it was largely feminine; a great babel of middle-aged ladies with sharp eyes and icy hearts behind lorgnettes and large bosoms. The main function of the balcony was critical. It occasionally showed grudging admiration, but never approval, for it is well known among ladies over thirty-five that when the younger set dance in the summer-time it is with the very worst intentions in the world, and if they are not bombarded with stony eyes stray couples will dance weird barbaric interludes in the corners, and the more popular, more dangerous, girls will sometimes be kissed in the parked limousines of unsuspecting dowagers.

But, after all, this critical circle is not close enough to the stage to see the actors' faces and catch the subtler byplay. It can only frown and lean, ask questions and make satisfactory deductions from its set of postulates, such as the one which states that every young man with a large income leads the life of a hunted partridge. It never really appreciates the drama of the shifting, semi-cruel world of adolescence. No; boxes, orchestra-circle, principals, and chorus are represented by the medley of faces and voices that sway to the plaintive African rhythm of Dyer's dance orchestra.

From sixteen-year-old Otis Ormonde, who has two more years at Hill School, to G. Reece Stoddard, over whose bureau at home hangs a Harvard law diploma; from little Madeleine Hogue, whose hair still feels strange and uncomfortable on top of her head, to Bessie MacRae, who has been the life of the party a little too long—more than ten years—the medley is not only the centre of the stage but contains the only people capable of getting an unobstructed view of it.

With a flourish and a bang the music stops. The couples exchange artificial, effortless smiles, facetiously repeat "*la*-de-*da-da* dum-*dum*," and then the clatter of young feminine voices soars over the burst of clapping.

A few disappointed stags caught in midfloor as they had been about to cut in subsided listlessly back to the walls, because this was not like the riotous Christmas dances—these summer hops were considered just pleasantly warm and exciting, where even the younger marrieds rose and performed ancient waltzes and terrifying fox trots to the tolerant amusement of their younger brothers and sisters.

Warren McIntyre, who casually attended Yale, being one of the unfortunate stags, felt in his dinner-coat pocket for a cigarette and strolled out onto the wide, semidark veranda, where couples were scattered at tables, filling the lantern-hung night with vague words and hazy laughter. He nodded here and there at the less absorbed and as he passed each couple some half-forgotten fragment of a story played in his mind, for it was not a large city and every one was Who's Who to every one else's past. There, for example, were Jim Strain and Ethel Demorest, who had been privately engaged for three years. Every one knew that as soon as Jim managed to hold a job for more than two months she would marry him. Yet how bored they both looked, and how wearily Ethel regarded Jim sometimes, as if she wondered why she had trained the vines of her affection on such a wind-shaken poplar.

Warren was nineteen and rather pitying with those of his friends who hadn't gone East to college. But, like most boys, he bragged tremendously about the girls of his city when he was away from it. There was Genevieve Ormonde, who regularly made the rounds of dances, house-parties, and football games at Princeton, Yale, Williams, and Cornell; there was black-eyed Roberta Dillon, who was quite as famous to her own generation as Hiram Johnson or Ty Cobb; and, of course, there was Marjorie Harvey, who beside having a fairylike face and a dazzling, bewildering tongue was already justly celebrated for having turned five cart-wheels in succession during the last pump-and-slipper dance at New Haven.

Warren, who had grown up across the street from Marjorie, had long been "crazy about her." Sometimes she seemed to reciprocate his feelings with a faint gratitude, but she had tried him by her infallible test and informed him gravely that she did not love him. Her test was that when she was away from him she forgot him and had affairs with other boys. Warren found this discouraging, especially as Marjorie had been making little trips all summer, and for the first two or three days after each arrival home he saw great heaps of mail on the Harveys' hall table addressed to her in various masculine handwritings. To make matters worse, all during the month of August she had been visited by her cousin Bernice from Eau Claire, and it seemed impossible to see her alone. It was always necessary to hunt round and find some one to take care of Bernice. As August waned this was becoming more and more difficult.

Much as Warren worshipped Marjorie, he had to admit that Cousin Bernice was sorta hopeless. She was pretty, with dark hair and high color, but she was no fun on a party. Every Saturday night he danced a long arduous duty dance with her to please Marjorie, but he had never been anything but bored in her company.

"Warren"—a soft voice at his elbow broke in upon his thoughts, and he turned to see Marjorie, flushed and radiant as usual. She laid a hand on his shoulder and a glow settled almost imperceptibly over him.

"Warren," she whispered, "do something for me—dance with Bernice. She's been stuck with little Otis Ormonde for almost an hour."

Warren's glow faded.

"Why—sure," he answered half-heartedly.

"You don't mind, do you? I'll see that you don't get stuck."

"'Sall right."

Marjorie smiled—that smile that was thanks enough.

"You're an angel, and I'm obliged loads."

With a sigh the angel glanced round the veranda, but Bernice and Otis were not in sight. He wandered back inside, and there in front of the women's dressing-room he found Otis in the centre of a group of young men who were convulsed with laughter. Otis was brandishing a piece of timber he had picked up, and discoursing volubly.

"She's gone in to fix her hair," he announced wildly. "I'm waiting to dance another hour with her."

Their laughter was renewed.

"Why don't some of you cut in?" cried Otis resentfully. "She likes more variety."

"Why, Otis," suggested a friend, "you've just barely got used to her."

"Why the two-by-four, Otis?" inquired Warren, smiling.

"The two-by-four? Oh, this? This is a club. When she comes out I'll hit her on the head and knock her in again."

Warren collapsed on a settee and howled with glee.

"Never mind, Otis," he articulated finally. "I'm relieving you this time."

Otis simulated a sudden fainting attack and handed the stick to Warren.

"If you need it, old man," he said hoarsely.

No matter how beautiful or brilliant a girl may be, the reputation of not being frequently cut in on makes her position at a dance unfortunate. Perhaps boys prefer her company to that of the butterflies with whom they dance a dozen times an evening, but youth in this jazz-nourished generation is temperamentally restless, and the idea of fox-trotting more than one full fox trot with the same girl is distasteful, not to say odious. When it comes to several dances and the intermissions between she can be quite sure that a young man, once relieved, will never tread on her wayward toes again.

Warren danced the next full dance with Bernice, and finally, thankful for the intermission, he led her to a table on the veranda. There was a moment's silence while she did unimpressive things with her fan.

"It's hotter here than in Eau Claire," she said.

Warren stifled a sigh and nodded. It might be for all he knew or cared. He wondered idly whether she was a poor conversationalist because she got no attention or got no attention because she was a poor conversationalist.

"You going to be here much longer?" he asked, and then turned rather red. She might suspect his reasons for asking.

"Another week," she answered, and stared at him as if to lunge at his next remark when it left his lips.

Warren fidgeted. Then with a sudden charitable impulse he decided to try part of his line on her. He turned and looked at her eyes.

"You've got an awfully kissable mouth," he began quietly.

This was a remark that he sometimes made to girls at college proms when they were talking in just such half dark as this. Bernice distinctly jumped. She turned an ungraceful red and became clumsy with her fan. No one had ever made such a remark to her before.

"Fresh!"—the word had slipped out before she realized it, and she bit her lip. Too late she decided to be amused, and offered him a flustered smile.

Warren was annoyed. Though not accustomed to have that remark taken seriously, still it usually provoked a laugh or a paragraph of sentimental banter. And he hated to be called fresh, except in a joking way. His charitable impulse died and he switched the topic.

"Jim Strain and Ethel Demorest sitting out as usual," he commented.

This was more in Bernice's line, but a faint regret mingled with her relief as the subject changed. Men did not talk to her about kissable mouths, but she knew that they talked in some such way to other girls.

"Oh, yes," she said, and laughed. "I hear they've been mooning round for years without a red penny. Isn't it silly?"

Warren's disgust increased. Jim Strain was a close friend of his brother's, and anyway he considered it bad form to sneer at people for not having money. But Bernice had had no intention of sneering. She was merely nervous.

II

When Marjorie and Bernice reached home at half after midnight they said good night at the top of the stairs. Though cousins, they were not intimates. As a matter of fact Marjorie had no female intimates—she considered girls stupid. Bernice on the contrary all through this parent-arranged visit had rather longed to exchange those confidences flavored with giggles and tears that she considered an indispensable factor in all feminine intercourse. But in this respect she found Marjorie rather cold; felt somehow the same difficulty in talking to her that she had in talking to men. Marjorie never giggled, was never frightened, seldom embarrassed, and in fact had very few of the qualities which Bernice considered appropriately and blessedly feminine.

As Bernice busied herself with tooth-brush and paste this night she wondered for the hundredth time why she never had any attention when she was away from home. That her family were the wealthiest in Eau Claire; that her mother entertained tremendously, gave little dinners for her daughter before all dances and bought her a car of her own to drive round in, never occurred to her as factors in her home-town social success. Like most girls she had been brought up on the warm milk prepared by Annie Fellows Johnston and on novels in which the female was beloved because of certain mysterious womanly qualities, always mentioned but never displayed.

Bernice felt a vague pain that she was not at present engaged in being popular. She did not know that had it not been for Marjorie's campaigning she would have danced the entire evening with one man; but she knew that even in Eau Claire other girls with less position and less pulchritude were given a much bigger rush. She attributed this to something subtly unscrupulous in those girls. It had never worried her, and if it had her mother would have assured her that the other girls cheapened themselves and that men really respected girls like Bernice.

She turned out the light in her bathroom, and on an impulse decided to go in and chat for a moment with her aunt Josephine, whose light was still on. Her soft slippers bore her noiselessly down the carpeted hall, but hearing voices inside she stopped near the partly opened door. Then she caught her own name, and without any definite intention of eavesdropping lingered—and the thread of the conversation going on inside pierced her consciousness sharply as if it had been drawn through with a needle.

"She's absolutely hopeless!" It was Marjorie's voice. "Oh, I know what you're going to say! So many people have told you how pretty and sweet she is, and how she can cook! What of it? She has a bum time. Men don't like her."

"What's a little cheap popularity?"

Mrs. Harvey sounded annoyed.

"It's everything when you're eighteen," said Marjorie emphatically. "I've done my best. I've been polite and I've made men dance with her, but they just won't stand being bored. When I think of that gorgeous coloring wasted on such a ninny, and think what Martha Carey could do with it—oh!"

"There's no courtesy these days."

Mrs. Harvey's voice implied that modern situations were too much for her. When she was a girl all young ladies who belonged to nice families had glorious times.

"Well," said Marjorie, "no girl can permanently bolster up a lame-duck visitor, because these days it's every girl for herself. I've even tried to drop her hints about clothes and things, and she's been furious—given me the funniest looks. She's sensitive enough to know she's not getting away with much, but I'll bet she consoles herself by thinking that she's very virtuous and that I'm too gay and fickle and will come to a bad end. All unpopular girls think that way. Sour grapes! Sarah Hopkins refers to Genevieve and Roberta and me as gardenia girls! I'll bet she'd give ten years of her life and her European education to be a gardenia girl and have three or four men in love with her and be cut in on every few feet at dances."

"It seems to me," interrupted Mrs. Harvey rather wearily, "that you ought to be able to do something for Bernice. I know she's not very vivacious."

Marjorie groaned.

"Vivacious! Good grief! I've never heard her say anything to a boy except that it's hot or the floor's crowded or that she's going to school in New York next year. Sometimes she asks them what kind of car they have and tells them the kind she has. Thrilling!"

There was a short silence, and then Mrs. Harvey took up her refrain:

"All I know is that other girls not half so sweet and attractive get partners. Martha Carey, for instance, is stout and loud, and her mother is distinctly common. Roberta Dillon is so thin this year she looks as though Arizona were the place for her. She's dancing herself to death."

"But, mother," objected Marjorie impatiently, "Martha is cheerful and awfully witty and an awfully slick girl, and Roberta's a marvellous dancer. She's been popular for ages!"

Mrs. Harvey yawned.

"I think it's that crazy Indian blood in Bernice," continued Marjorie. "Maybe she's a reversion to type. Indian women all just sat round and never said anything."

"Go to bed, you silly child," laughed Mrs. Harvey. "I wouldn't have told you that if I'd thought you were going to remember it. And I think most of your ideas are perfectly idiotic," she finished sleepily.

There was another silence, while Marjorie considered whether or not convincing her mother was worth the trouble. People of forty can seldom be permanently convinced of anything. At eighteen our convictions are hills from which we look; at forty-five they are caves in which we hide.

Having decided this, Marjorie said good night. When she came out into the hall it was quite empty.

III

While Marjorie was breakfasting late next day Bernice came into the room with a rather formal good morning, sat down opposite, stared intently over and slightly moistened her lips.

"What's on your mind?" inquired Marjorie, rather puzzled.

Bernice paused before she threw her hand-grenade.

"I heard what you said about me to your mother last night."

Marjorie was startled, but she showed only a faintly heightened color and her voice was quite even when she spoke.

"Where were you?"

"In the hall. I didn't mean to listen—at first."

After an involuntary look of contempt Marjorie dropped her eyes and became very interested in balancing a stray corn-flake on her finger.

"I guess I'd better go back to Eau Claire—if I'm such a nuisance." Bernice's lower lip was trembling violently and she continued on a wavering note: "I've tried to be nice, and—and I've been first neglected and then insulted. No one ever visited me and got such treatment."

Marjorie was silent.

"But I'm in the way, I see. I'm a drag on you. Your friends don't like me." She paused, and then remembered another one of her grievances. "Of course I was furious last week when you tried to hint to me that that dress was unbecoming. Don't you think I know how to dress myself?"

"No," murmured Marjorie less than half-aloud.

"What?"

"I didn't hint anything," said Marjorie succinctly. "I said, as I remember, that it was better to wear a becoming dress three times straight than to alternate it with two frights."

"Do you think that was a very nice thing to say?"

"I wasn't trying to be nice." Then after a pause: "When do you want to go?"

Bernice drew in her breath sharply.

"Oh!" It was a little half-cry.

Marjorie looked up in surprise.

"Didn't you say you were going?"

"Yes, but—"

"Oh, you were only bluffing!"

They stared at each other across the breakfast table for a moment. Misty waves were passing before Bernice's eyes, while Marjorie's face wore that rather hard expression that she used when slightly intoxicated undergraduates were making love to her.

"So you were bluffing," she repeated as if it were what she might have expected.

Bernice admitted it by bursting into tears. Marjorie's eyes showed boredom.

"You're my cousin," sobbed Bernice. "I'm v-v-visiting you. I was to stay a month, and if I go home my mother will know and she'll wah-wonder—"

Marjorie waited until the shower of broken words collapsed into little sniffles.

"I'll give you my month's allowance," she said coldly, "and you can spend this last week anywhere you want. There's a very nice hotel—"

Bernice's sobs rose to a flute note, and rising of a sudden she fled from the room.

An hour later, while Marjorie was in the library absorbed in composing one of those non-committal, marvellously elusive letters that only a young girl can write, Bernice reappeared, very red-eyed and consciously calm. She cast no glance at Marjorie but took a book at random from the shelf and sat down as if to read. Marjorie seemed absorbed in her letter and continued writing. When the clock showed noon Bernice closed her book with a snap.

"I suppose I'd better get my railroad ticket."

This was not the beginning of the speech she had rehearsed up-stairs, but as Marjorie was not getting her cues—wasn't urging her to be reasonable; it's all a mistake—it was the best opening she could muster.

"Just wait till I finish this letter," said Marjorie without looking round. "I want to get it off in the next mail."

After another minute, during which her pen scratched busily, she turned round and relaxed with an air of "at your service." Again Bernice had to speak.

"Do you want me to go home?"

"Well," said Marjorie, considering, "I suppose if you're not having a good time you'd better go. No use being miserable."

"Don't you think common kindness—"

"Oh, please don't quote 'Little Women'!" cried Marjorie impatiently. "That's out of style."

"You think so?"

"Heavens, yes! What modern girl could live like those inane females?"

"They were the models for our mothers."

Marjorie laughed.

"Yes, they were—not! Besides, our mothers were all very well in their way, but they know very little about their daughters' problems."

Bernice drew herself up.

"Please don't talk about my mother."

Marjorie laughed.

"I don't think I mentioned her."

Bernice felt that she was being led away from her subject.

"Do you think you've treated me very well?"

"I've done my best. You're rather hard material to work with."

The lids of Bernice's eyes reddened.

"I think you're hard and selfish, and you haven't a feminine quality in you."

"Oh, my Lord!" cried Marjorie in desperation. "You little nut! Girls like you are responsible for all the tiresome colorless marriages; all those ghastly inefficiencies that pass as feminine qualities. What a blow it must be when a man with imagination marries the beautiful bundle of clothes that he's been building ideals round, and finds that she's just a weak, whining, cowardly mass of affectations!"

Bernice's mouth had slipped half open.

"The womanly woman!" continued Marjorie. "Her whole early life is occupied in whining criticisms of girls like me who really do have a good time."

Bernice's jaw descended farther as Marjorie's voice rose.

"There's some excuse for an ugly girl whining. If I'd been irretrievably ugly I'd never have forgiven my parents for bringing me into the world. But you're starting life without any handicap—" Marjorie's little fist clinched. "If you expect me to weep with you you'll be disappointed. Go or stay, just as you like." And picking up her letters she left the room.

Bernice claimed a headache and failed to appear at luncheon. They had a matinée date for the afternoon, but the headache persisting, Marjorie made explanation to a not very downcast boy. But when she returned late in the afternoon she found Bernice with a strangely set face waiting for her in her bedroom.

"I've decided," began Bernice without preliminaries, "that maybe you're right about things—possibly not. But if you'll tell me why your friends aren't—aren't interested in me I'll see if I can do what you want me to."

Marjorie was at the mirror shaking down her hair.

"Do you mean it?"

"Yes."

"Without reservations? Will you do exactly what I say?"

"Well, I—"

"Well nothing! Will you do exactly as I say?"

"If they're sensible things."

"They're not! You're no case for sensible things."

"Are you going to make—to recommend—"

"Yes, everything. If I tell you to take boxing-lessons you'll have to do it. Write home and tell your mother you're going to stay another two weeks."

"If you'll tell me—"

"All right—I'll just give you a few examples now. First, you have no ease of manner. Why? Because you're never sure about your personal appearance. When a girl feels that she's perfectly groomed and dressed she can forget that part of her. That's charm. The more parts of yourself you can afford to forget the more charm you have."

"Don't I look all right?"

"No; for instance you never take care of your eyebrows. They're black and lustrous, but by leaving them straggly they're a blemish. They'd be beautiful if you'd take care of them in one-tenth the time you take doing nothing. You're going to brush them so that they'll grow straight."

Bernice raised the brows in question.

"Do you mean to say that men notice eyebrows?"

"Yes—subconsciously. And when you go home you ought to have your teeth straightened a little. It's almost imperceptible, still—"

"But I thought," interrupted Bernice in bewilderment, "that you despised little dainty feminine things like that."

"I hate dainty minds," answered Marjorie. "But a girl has to be dainty in person. If she looks like a million dollars she can talk about Russia, ping-pong, or the League of Nations and get away with it."

"What else?"

"Oh, I'm just beginning! There's your dancing."

"Don't I dance all right?"

"No, you don't—you lean on a man; yes, you do—ever so slightly. I noticed it when we were dancing together yesterday. And you dance standing up straight instead of bending over a little. Probably some old lady on the sideline once told you that you looked so dignified that way. But except with a very small girl it's much harder on the man, and he's the one that counts."

"Go on." Bernice's brain was reeling.

"Well, you've got to learn to be nice to men who are sad birds. You look as if you'd been insulted whenever you're thrown with any except the most popular boys. Why, Bernice, I'm cut in on every few feet—and who does most of it? Why, those very sad birds. No girl can afford to neglect them. They're the big part of any crowd. Young boys too shy to talk are the very best conversational practice. Clumsy boys are the best dancing practice. If you can follow them and yet look graceful you can follow a baby tank across a barb-wire sky-scraper."

Bernice sighed profoundly, but Marjorie was not through.

"If you go to a dance and really amuse, say, three sad birds that dance with you; if you talk so well to them that they forget they're stuck with you, you've done something. They'll come back next time, and gradually so many sad birds will dance with you that the attractive boys will see there's no danger of being stuck—then they'll dance with you."

"Yes," agreed Bernice faintly. "I think I begin to see."

"And finally," concluded Marjorie, "poise and charm will just come. You'll wake up some morning knowing you've attained it, and men will know it too."

Bernice rose.

"It's been awfully kind of you—but nobody's ever talked to me like this before, and I feel sort of startled."

Marjorie made no answer but gazed pensively at her own image in the mirror.

"You're a peach to help me," continued Bernice.

Still Marjorie did not answer, and Bernice thought she had seemed too grateful.

"I know you don't like sentiment," she said timidly.

Marjorie turned to her quickly.

"Oh, I wasn't thinking about that. I was considering whether we hadn't better bob your hair."

Bernice collapsed backward upon the bed.

IV

On the following Wednesday evening there was a dinner-dance at the country club. When the guests strolled in Bernice found her place-card with a slight feeling of irritation. Though at her right sat G. Reece Stoddard, a most desirable and distinguished young bachelor, the all-important left held only Charley Paulson. Charley lacked height, beauty, and social shrewdness, and in her new enlightenment Bernice decided that his only qualification to be her partner was that he had never been stuck with her. But this feeling of irritation left with the last of the soup-plates, and Marjorie's specific instruction came to her. Swallowing her pride she turned to Charley Paulson and plunged.

"Do you think I ought to bob my hair, Mr. Charley Paulson?"

Charley looked up in surprise.

"Why?"

"Because I'm considering it. It's such a sure and easy way of attracting attention."

Charley smiled pleasantly. He could not know this had been rehearsed. He replied that he didn't know much about bobbed hair. But Bernice was there to tell him.

"I want to be a society vampire, you see," she announced coolly, and went on to inform him that bobbed hair was the necessary prelude. She added that she wanted to ask his advice, because she had heard he was so critical about girls.

Charley, who knew as much about the psychology of women as he did of the mental states of Buddhist contemplatives, felt vaguely flattered.

"So I've decided," she continued, her voice rising slightly, "that early next week I'm going down to the Sevier Hotel barber-shop, sit in the first chair, and get my hair bobbed." She faltered, noticing that the people near her had paused in their conversation and were listening; but after a confused second Marjorie's coaching told, and she finished her paragraph to the vicinity at large. "Of course I'm charging admission, but if you'll all come down and encourage me I'll issue passes for the inside seats."

There was a ripple of appreciative laughter, and under cover of it G. Reece Stoddard leaned over quickly and said close to her ear: "I'll take a box right now."

She met his eyes and smiled as if he had said something surpassingly brilliant.

"Do you believe in bobbed hair?" asked G. Reece in the same undertone.

"I think it's unmoral," affirmed Bernice gravely. "But, of course, you've either got to amuse people or feed 'em or shock 'em." Marjorie had culled this from Oscar Wilde. It was greeted with a ripple of laughter from the men and a series of quick, intent looks from the girls. And then as though she had said nothing of wit or moment Bernice turned again to Charley and spoke confidentially in his ear.

"I want to ask you your opinion of several people. I imagine you're a wonderful judge of character."

Charley thrilled faintly—paid her a subtle compliment by overturning her water.

Two hours later, while Warren McIntyre was standing passively in the stag line abstractedly watching the dancers and wondering whither and with whom Marjorie had disappeared, an unrelated perception began to creep slowly upon him—a perception that Bernice, cousin to Marjorie, had been cut in on several times in the past five minutes. He closed his eyes, opened them and looked again. Several minutes back she had been dancing with a visiting boy, a matter easily accounted for; a visiting boy would know no better. But now she was dancing with some one else, and there was Charley Paulson headed for her with enthusiastic determination in his eye. Funny—Charley seldom danced with more than three girls an evening.

Warren was distinctly surprised when—the exchange having been effected—the man relieved proved to be none other than G. Reece Stoddard himself. And G. Reece seemed not at all jubilant at being relieved. Next time Bernice danced near, Warren regarded her intently. Yes, she was pretty, distinctly pretty; and to-night her face seemed really vivacious. She had that look that no woman, however histrionically proficient, can successfully counterfeit—she looked as if she were having a good time. He liked the way she had her hair arranged, wondered if it was brilliantine that made it glisten so. And that dress was becoming—a dark red that set off her shadowy eyes and high coloring. He remembered that he had thought her pretty when she first came to town, before he had realized that she was dull. Too bad she was dull—dull girls were unbearable—certainly pretty though.

His thoughts zigzagged back to Marjorie. This disappearance would be like other disappearances. When she reappeared he would demand where she had been—would be told emphatically that it was none of his business. What a pity she was so sure of him! She basked in the knowledge that no other girl in town interested him; she defied him to fall in love with Genevieve or Roberta.

Warren sighed. The way to Marjorie's affections was a labyrinth indeed. He looked up. Bernice was again dancing with the visiting boy. Half unconsciously he took a step out from the stag line in her direction, and hesitated. Then he said to himself that it was charity. He walked toward her—collided suddenly with G. Reece Stoddard.

"Pardon me," said Warren.

But G. Reece had not stopped to apologize. He had again cut in on Bernice.

That night at one o'clock Marjorie, with one hand on the electric-light switch in the hall, turned to take a last look at Bernice's sparkling eyes.

"So it worked?"

"Oh, Marjorie, yes!" cried Bernice.

"I saw you were having a gay time."

"I did! The only trouble was that about midnight I ran short of talk. I had to repeat myself—with different men of course. I hope they won't compare notes."

"Men don't," said Marjorie, yawning, "and it wouldn't matter if they did—they'd think you were even trickier."

She snapped out the light, and as they started up the stairs Bernice grabbed the banister thankfully. For the first time in her life she had been danced tired.

"You see," said Marjorie at the top of the stairs, "one man sees another man cut in and he thinks there must be something there. Well, we'll fix up some new stuff to-morrow. Good night."

"Good night."

As Bernice took down her hair she passed the evening before her in review. She had followed instructions exactly. Even when Charley Paulson cut in for the eighth time she had simulated delight and had apparently been both interested and flattered. She had not talked about the weather or Eau Claire or automobiles or her school, but had confined her conversation to me, you, and us.

But a few minutes before she fell asleep a rebellious thought was churning drowsily in her brain—after all, it was she who had done it. Marjorie, to be sure, had given her her conversation, but then Marjorie got much of her conversation out of things she read. Bernice had bought the red dress, though she had never valued it highly before Marjorie dug it out of her trunk—and her own voice had said the words, her own lips had smiled, her own feet had danced. Marjorie nice girl—vain, though—nice evening—nice boys—like Warren—Warren—Warren—what's-his-name—Warren—

She fell asleep.

V

To Bernice the next week was a revelation. With the feeling that people really enjoyed looking at her and listening to her came the foundation of self-confidence. Of course there were numerous mistakes at first. She did not know, for instance, that Draycott Deyo was studying for the ministry; she was unaware that he had cut in on her because he thought she was a quiet, reserved girl. Had she known these things she would not have treated him to the line which began "Hello, Shell Shock!" and continued with the bathtub story—"It takes a frightful lot of energy to fix my hair in the summer—there's so much of it—so I always fix it first and powder my face and put on my hat; then I get into the bathtub, and dress afterward. Don't you think that's the best plan?"

Though Draycott Deyo was in the throes of difficulties concerning baptism by immersion and might possibly have seen a connection, it must be admitted that he did not. He considered feminine bathing an immoral subject, and gave her some of his ideas on the depravity of modern society.

But to offset that unfortunate occurrence Bernice had several successes to her credit. Little Otis Ormonde pleaded off from a trip East and elected instead to follow her with a puppylike devotion, to the amusement of his crowd and to the irritation of G. Reece Stoddard, several of whose afternoon calls Otis completely ruined by the disgusting tenderness of the glances he bent on Bernice. He even told her the story of the two-by-four and the dressing-room to show her how frightfully mistaken he and every one else had been in their first judgment of her. Bernice laughed off that incident with a slight sinking sensation.

Of all Bernice's conversation perhaps the best known and most universally approved was the line about the bobbing of her hair.

"Oh, Bernice, when you goin' to get the hair bobbed?"

"Day after to-morrow maybe," she would reply, laughing. "Will you come and see me? Because I'm counting on you, you know."

"Will we? You know! But you better hurry up."

Bernice, whose tonsorial intentions were strictly dishonorable, would laugh again.

"Pretty soon now. You'd be surprised."

But perhaps the most significant symbol of her success was the gray car of the hypercritical Warren McIntyre, parked daily in front of the Harvey house. At first the parlor-maid was distinctly startled when he asked for Bernice instead of Marjorie; after a week of it she told the cook that Miss Bernice had gotta holda Miss Marjorie's best fella.

And Miss Bernice had. Perhaps it began with Warren's desire to rouse jealousy in Marjorie; perhaps it was the familiar though unrecognized strain of

Marjorie in Bernice's conversation; perhaps it was both of these and something of sincere attraction besides. But somehow the collective mind of the younger set knew within a week that Marjorie's most reliable beau had made an amazing face-about and was giving an indisputable rush to Marjorie's guest. The question of the moment was how Marjorie would take it. Warren called Bernice on the 'phone twice a day, sent her notes, and they were frequently seen together in his roadster, obviously engrossed in one of those tense, significant conversations as to whether or not he was sincere.

Marjorie on being twitted only laughed. She said she was mighty glad that Warren had at last found some one who appreciated him. So the younger set laughed, too, and guessed that Marjorie didn't care and let it go at that.

One afternoon when there were only three days left of her visit Bernice was waiting in the hall for Warren, with whom she was going to a bridge party. She was in rather a blissful mood, and when Marjorie—also bound for the party—appeared beside her and began casually to adjust her hat in the mirror, Bernice was utterly unprepared for anything in the nature of a clash. Marjorie did her work very coldly and succinctly in three sentences.

"You may as well get Warren out of your head," she said coldly.

"What?" Bernice was utterly astounded.

"You may as well stop making a fool of yourself over Warren McIntyre. He doesn't care a snap of his fingers about you."

For a tense moment they regarded each other—Marjorie scornful, aloof; Bernice astounded, half-angry, half-afraid. Then two cars drove up in front of the house and there was a riotous honking. Both of them gasped faintly, turned, and side by side hurried out.

All through the bridge party Bernice strove in vain to master a rising uneasiness. She had offended Marjorie, the sphinx of sphinxes. With the most wholesome and innocent intentions in the world she had stolen Marjorie's property. She felt suddenly and horribly guilty. After the bridge game, when they sat in an informal circle and the conversation became general, the storm gradually broke. Little Otis Ormonde inadvertently precipitated it.

"When you going back to kindergarten, Otis?" some one had asked.

"Me? Day Bernice gets her hair bobbed."

"Then your education's over," said Marjorie quickly. "That's only a bluff of hers. I should think you'd have realized."

"That a fact?" demanded Otis, giving Bernice a reproachful glance.

Bernice's ears burned as she tried to think up an effectual come-back. In the face of this direct attack her imagination was paralyzed.

"There's a lot of bluffs in the world," continued Marjorie quite pleasantly. "I should think you'd be young enough to know that, Otis."

"Well," said Otis, "maybe so. But gee! With a line like Bernice's—"

"Really?" yawned Marjorie. "What's her latest bon mot?"

No one seemed to know. In fact, Bernice, having trifled with her muse's beau, had said nothing memorable of late.

"Was that really all a line?" asked Roberta curiously.

Bernice hesitated. She felt that wit in some form was demanded of her, but under her cousin's suddenly frigid eyes she was completely incapacitated.

"I don't know," she stalled.

"Splush!" said Marjorie. "Admit it!"

Bernice saw that Warren's eyes had left a ukulele he had been tinkering with and were fixed on her questioningly.

"Oh, I don't know!" she repeated steadily. Her cheeks were glowing.

"Splush!" remarked Marjorie again.

"Come through, Bernice," urged Otis. "Tell her where to get off."

Bernice looked round again—she seemed unable to get away from Warren's eyes.

"I like bobbed hair," she said hurriedly, as if he had asked her a question, "and I intend to bob mine."

"When?" demanded Marjorie.

"Any time."

"No time like the present," suggested Roberta.

Otis jumped to his feet.

"Good stuff!" he cried. "We'll have a summer bobbing party. Sevier Hotel barber-shop, I think you said."

In an instant all were on their feet. Bernice's heart throbbed violently.

"What?" she gasped.

Out of the group came Marjorie's voice, very clear and contemptuous.

"Don't worry—she'll back out!"

"Come on, Bernice!" cried Otis, starting toward the door.

Four eyes—Warren's and Marjorie's—stared at her, challenged her, defied her. For another second she wavered wildly.

"All right," she said swiftly, "I don't care if I do."

An eternity of minutes later, riding down-town through the late afternoon beside Warren, the others following in Roberta's car close behind, Bernice had all the sensations of Marie Antoinette bound for the guillotine in a tumbrel. Vaguely she wondered why she did not cry out that it was all a mistake. It was all she could do to keep from clutching her hair with both hands to protect it from the suddenly hostile world. Yet she did neither. Even the thought of her mother was no deterrent now. This was the test supreme of her sportsmanship; her right to walk unchallenged in the starry heaven of popular girls.

Warren was moodily silent, and when they came to the hotel he drew up at the curb and nodded to Bernice to precede him out. Roberta's car emptied a laughing crowd into the shop, which presented two bold plate-glass windows to the street.

Bernice stood on the curb and looked at the sign, Sevier Barber-Shop. It was a guillotine indeed, and the hangman was the first barber, who, attired in a white coat and smoking a cigarette, leaned nonchalantly against the first chair. He must have heard of her; he must have been waiting all week, smoking eternal cigarettes beside that portentous, too-often-mentioned first chair. Would they blind-fold her? No, but they would tie a white cloth round her neck lest any of her blood—nonsense—hair—should get on her clothes.

"All right, Bernice," said Warren quickly.

With her chin in the air she crossed the sidewalk, pushed open the swinging screen-door, and giving not a glance to the uproarious, riotous row that occupied the waiting bench, went up to the first barber.

"I want you to bob my hair."

The first barber's mouth slid somewhat open. His cigarette dropped to the floor.

"Huh?"

"My hair—bob it!"

Refusing further preliminaries, Bernice took her seat on high. A man in the chair next to her turned on his side and gave her a glance, half lather, half amazement. One barber started and spoiled little Willy Schuneman's monthly haircut. Mr. O'Reilly in the last chair grunted and swore musically in ancient Gaelic as a razor bit into his cheek. Two bootblacks became wide-eyed and rushed for her feet. No, Bernice didn't care for a shine.

Outside a passer-by stopped and stared; a couple joined him; half a dozen small boys' noses sprang into life, flattened against the glass; and snatches of conversation borne on the summer breeze drifted in through the screen-door.

"Lookada long hair on a kid!"

"Where'd yuh get 'at stuff? 'At's a bearded lady he just finished shavin'."

But Bernice saw nothing, heard nothing. Her only living sense told her that this man in the white coat had removed one tortoise-shell comb and then another; that his fingers were fumbling clumsily with unfamiliar hairpins; that this hair, this wonderful hair of hers, was going—she would never again feel its long voluptuous pull as it hung in a dark-brown glory down her back. For a second she was near breaking down, and then the picture before her swam mechanically into her vision—Marjorie's mouth curling in a faint ironic smile as if to say:

"Give up and get down! You tried to buck me and I called your bluff. You see you haven't got a prayer."

And some last energy rose up in Bernice, for she clinched her hands under the white cloth, and there was a curious narrowing of her eyes that Marjorie remarked on to some one long afterward.

Twenty minutes later the barber swung her round to face the mirror, and she flinched at the full extent of the damage that had been wrought. Her hair was not curly, and now it lay in lank lifeless blocks on both sides of her suddenly pale face. It was ugly as sin—she had known it would be ugly as sin. Her face's chief charm had been a Madonna-like simplicity. Now that was gone and she was—well, frightfully mediocre—not stagy; only ridiculous, like a Greenwich Villager who had left her spectacles at home.

As she climbed down from the chair she tried to smile—failed miserably. She saw two of the girls exchange glances; noticed Marjorie's mouth curved in attenuated mockery—and that Warren's eyes were suddenly very cold.

"You see"—her words fell into an awkward pause—"I've done it."

"Yes, you've—done it," admitted Warren.

"Do you like it?"

There was a half-hearted "Sure" from two or three voices, another awkward pause, and then Marjorie turned swiftly and with serpent-like intensity to Warren.

"Would you mind running me down to the cleaners?" she asked. "I've simply got to get a dress there before supper. Roberta's driving right home and she can take the others."

Warren stared abstractedly at some infinite speck out the window. Then for an instant his eyes rested coldly on Bernice before they turned to Marjorie.

"Be glad to," he said slowly.

VI

Bernice did not fully realize the outrageous trap that had been set for her until she met her aunt's amazed glance just before dinner.

"Why, Bernice!"

"I've bobbed it, Aunt Josephine."

"Why, child!"

"Do you like it?"

"Why, Ber-nice!"

"I suppose I've shocked you."

"No, but what'll Mrs. Deyo think to-morrow night? Bernice, you should have waited until after the Deyos' dance—you should have waited if you wanted to do that."

"It was sudden, Aunt Josephine. Anyway, why does it matter to Mrs. Deyo particularly?"

"Why, child," cried Mrs. Harvey, "in her paper on 'The Foibles of the Younger Generation' that she read at the last meeting of the Thursday Club she devoted fifteen minutes to bobbed hair. It's her pet abomination. And the dance is for you and Marjorie!"

"I'm sorry."

"Oh, Bernice, what'll your mother say? She'll think I let you do it."

"I'm sorry."

Dinner was an agony. She had made a hasty attempt with a curling-iron, and burned her finger and much hair. She could see that her aunt was both worried and grieved, and her uncle kept saying, "Well, I'll be darned!" over and over in a hurt and faintly hostile tone. And Marjorie sat very quietly, intrenched behind a faint smile, a faintly mocking smile.

Somehow she got through the evening. Three boys called; Marjorie disappeared with one of them, and Bernice made a listless unsuccessful attempt to entertain the two others—sighed thankfully as she climbed the stairs to her room at half past ten. What a day!

When she had undressed for the night the door opened and Marjorie came in.

"Bernice," she said, "I'm awfully sorry about the Deyo dance. I'll give you my word of honor I'd forgotten all about it."

"'Sall right," said Bernice shortly. Standing before the mirror she passed her comb slowly through her short hair.

"I'll take you down-town to-morrow," continued Marjorie, "and the hairdresser'll fix it so you'll look slick. I didn't imagine you'd go through with it. I'm really mighty sorry."

"Oh, 'sall right!"

"Still it's your last night, so I suppose it won't matter much."

Then Bernice winced as Marjorie tossed her own hair over her shoulders and began to twist it slowly into two long blond braids until in her cream-colored negligée she looked like a delicate painting of some Saxon princess. Fascinated, Bernice watched the braids grow. Heavy and luxurious they were, moving under the supple fingers like restive snakes—and to Bernice remained this relic and the curling-iron and a to-morrow full of eyes. She could see G.

Reece Stoddard, who liked her, assuming his Harvard manner and telling his dinner partner that Bernice shouldn't have been allowed to go to the movies so much; she could see Draycott Deyo exchanging glances with his mother and then being conscientiously charitable to her. But then perhaps by to-morrow Mrs. Deyo would have heard the news; would send round an icy little note requesting that she fail to appear—and behind her back they would all laugh and know that Marjorie had made a fool of her; that her chance at beauty had been sacrificed to the jealous whim of a selfish girl. She sat down suddenly before the mirror, biting the inside of her cheek.

"I like it," she said with an effort. "I think it'll be becoming."

Marjorie smiled.

"It looks all right. For heaven's sake, don't let it worry you!"

"I won't."

"Good night, Bernice."

But as the door closed something snapped within Bernice. She sprang dynamically to her feet, clinching her hands, then swiftly and noiselessly crossed over to her bed and from underneath it dragged out her suitcase. Into it she tossed toilet articles and a change of clothing. Then she turned to her trunk and quickly dumped in two drawerfuls of lingerie and summer dresses. She moved quietly, but with deadly efficiency, and in three-quarters of an hour her trunk was locked and strapped and she was fully dressed in a becoming new travelling suit that Marjorie had helped her pick out.

Sitting down at her desk she wrote a short note to Mrs. Harvey, in which she briefly outlined her reasons for going. She sealed it, addressed it, and laid it on her pillow. She glanced at her watch. The train left at one, and she knew that if she walked down to the Marborough Hotel two blocks away she could easily get a taxicab.

Suddenly she drew in her breath sharply and an expression flashed into her eyes that a practised character reader might have connected vaguely with the set look she had worn in the barber's chair—somehow a development of it. It was quite a new look for Bernice—and it carried consequences.

She went stealthily to the bureau, picked up an article that lay there, and turning out all the lights stood quietly until her eyes became accustomed to the darkness. Softly she pushed open the door to Marjorie's room. She heard the quiet, even breathing of an untroubled conscience asleep.

She was by the bedside now, very deliberate and calm. She acted swiftly. Bending over she found one of the braids of Marjorie's hair, followed it up with her hand to the point nearest her head, and then holding it a little slack so the sleeper would feel no pull, she reached down with the shears and severed it.

With the pigtail in her hand she held her breath. Marjorie muttered something in her sleep. Bernice deftly amputated the other braid, paused for an instant, and then flitted swiftly and silently back to her own room.

Down-stairs she opened the big front door, closed it carefully behind her, and feeling oddly happy and exuberant stepped off the porch into the moon-light, swinging her heavy grip like a shopping-bag. After a minute's brisk walk she discovered that her left hand still held the two blond braids. She laughed unexpectedly—had to shut her mouth hard to keep from emitting an absolute peal. She was passing Warren's house now, and on the impulse she set down her baggage, and swinging the braids like pieces of rope flung them at the wooden porch, where they landed with a slight thud. She laughed again, no longer restraining herself.

"Huh!" she giggled wildly. "Scalp the selfish thing!"

Then picking up her suitcase she set off at a half-run down the moonlit street.

6–11

Langston Hughes (1902–1967)

LANGSTON HUGHES [JAMES MERCER LANGSTON HUGHES] (1902–1967) wrote his first published poem, "The Negro Speaks of Rivers" (1921), allegedly as he crossed the Mississippi by train en route to Mexico. Hughes was born in Joplin, Missouri. His parents separated when he was a boy, and his father moved to Cuba and later Mexico to escape racism, leaving Hughes behind to be raised in Kansas by his grandmother. He attended Columbia University for one year and would later graduate from Lincoln University, a classmate of Thurgood Marshall. Hughes traveled consider-ably, with a spell as a merchant seaman and time in London and Paris, returning to New York at the height of the Harlem Renaissance. Similar to Chesnutt's and Dunbar's use of dialect, Hughes' signature style takes from the oral tradition; his poetry imitates colloquial speech and the cadence of improvisational jazz, while it simultaneously challenges racial stereotypes.

≈ ≈ ≈

"The Negro Speaks of Rivers" (1921)

I've known rivers:
I've known rivers ancient as the world and older than the flow of
human blood in human veins.

My soul has grown deep like the rivers.

I bathed in the Euphrates when dawns were young.
I built my hut near the Congo and it lulled me to sleep.
I looked upon the Nile and raised the pyramids above it.
I heard the singing of the Mississippi when Abe Lincoln went down to
    New Orleans, and I've seen its muddy bosom turn all golden in the
    sunset.

I've known rivers;
Ancient, dusky rivers.

My soul has grown deep like the rivers.

"Mother to Son" (1922)

Well, son, I'll tell you:
Life for me ain't been no crystal stair.
It's had tacks in it,
And splinters,
And boards torn up,
And places with no carpet on the floor—
Bare;
But all the time
I'se been a-climbin' on,
And reachin' landin's,
And turnin' corners,
And sometimes goin' in the dark,
Where there ain't been no light.
So boy, don't you turn back,
Don't you sit down on the steps,
'Cause you finds it's kinder hard;
Don't you fall now—
For I'se still goin', honey,
I'se still climbin',
And life for me ain't been no crystal stair.

6—12

Federal Writers' Project: Slave Narratives Collection

THE FEDERAL WRITERS' PROJECT, a project funded by the Works Progress Administration (WPA), was established to put writers to work during the Great Depression. The largest of these projects was the

SLAVE NARRATIVES COLLECTION, which sent hundreds of unemployed interviewers—some famous like Zora Neale Hurston, who collected interviews in her home state of Florida—across seventeen states to collect over two thousand interviews and five hundred photographs of exslaves. Charges of bias and poor methodology have dogged the project. Still, historians view the collection as valuable, if for smaller inquiries. Included here are interviews from Central Texas, collected between 1936 and 1938. Denson and Little were among those to celebrate the first Juneteenth.

≈ ≈ ≈

Interview—Nelsen Denson

Nelsen Denson, 90, was born near Hamburg, Arkansas, a slave of Jim Nelson, who sold Nelsen and his family to Felix Grundy. Nelsen's memory is poor, but he managed to recall a few incidents. He now lives in Waco, Texas.

"I'll be ninety years old this December. (1937). I was born in Arkansas, up in Ashley County, and it was the twenty-second day of December in 1847. My mammy was from Virginny and pappy was from old Kentucky, and I was one of they eight chillen. Our owner, Marse Jim Densen,* brung us to Texas and settled near Marlin, but got in debt and sold us all to Marse Felix Grundy, and he kep' us till freedom, and most of us worked for him after that.

"Marse Jim Densen had a easy livin' in Arkansas, but folks everywhere was comin' to Texas and he 'cides to throw in his fortunes. It wasn't so long after that war with Mexico and folks come in a crowd to 'tect theyselves 'gainst Indians and wild animals. The wolves was the worst to smell cookin' and sneak into camp, but Indians come up and makes the peace sign and has a pow wow with the white folks. Marse git beads or cloth and trade for leather breeches and things.

"I want to tell how we crosses the Red River on de Red River Raft. Back in them days the Red River was near closed up by dis timber raft and de big boats couldn't git up de river at all. We gits a li'l boat, and a Caddo Indian to guide us. Dis Red River raft dey say was centuries old. De driftwood floatin' down de river stops in de still waters and makes a bunch of trees and de dirt 'cumulates, and broomstraws and willows and brush grows out dis rich dirt what cover de driftwood. Dis raft growed 'bout a mile a year and de oldes' timber rots and breaks away, but dis not fast 'nough to keep de river clear. We found bee trees on de raft and had honey.

---

* [The interviews with the ex-slaves were transcribed quickly, with interviewers traveling on back roads from one small town to the next to collect stories from their subjects; errors are common. Densen and Jensen are probably the same white man.—E.J.D. and J.B.F.]

"It was long time after us come to Texas when de gov'ment opens up de channel. Dat am in 1873. 'Fore dat, a survey done been made and dey found de raft am a hundred and twenty-eight miles long. When we was on dat raft it am like a big swamp, with trees and thick brush and de driftwood and logs all wedge up tight 'tween everything.

"'Fore Texas secedes, Marse Jensen done sell us all to Marse Felix Grundy, and he goes to war in General Hardeman's Brigade and is with him for bodyguard. When de battle of Mansfield come I'm sixteen years old. We was camped on the Sabine River, on the Texas side, and the Yanks on the other side a li'l ways. I 'member the night 'fore the battle, how the campfires looked, and a quiet night and the whippoorwills callin' in the weeds. We was 'spectin' a 'tack and sings to keep cheerful. The Yanks sings the 'Battle Cry of Freedom' when they charges us. They come on and on and, Lawd, how they fit! I stays clost to Marse Grundy and the rebels wins and takes 'bout a thousand Yanks.

"Most the slaves was happy, the ones I knowed. They figgers the white men fightin' for some principle, but lots of them didn't care nothin' 'bout bein' free. I s'pose some was with bad white folks, but not round us. We had more to eat and now I'm so old I wouldn't feel bad if I had old marse to look after me 'gain."

Interview—Annie Little

Annie Little, 81, was born a slave of Bill Gooden, in Springfield, Missouri. Her master owned a plantation in Mississippi, and sent Annie's family there while she was a baby. Annie now lives in Mart, Texas.

"I's first a baby in Springfield. Dat in Missouri and dere am where I's birthed in January, 1856. My daddy and mammy was Howard and Annie and dey 'longed to Massa Bill Gooden. He have de plantation in Missipp' and send us dere while I's still de li'l baby. Dat am what dey call de Delta now, and de cotton so high I clumb up in de trees to reach de top of de stalks, and de corn so high a man on he mule only have de top he hat showin'.

"If us mind massa and missus, dey good to us, but if da hands lazy and not work den de overseer whop dem. When dey run 'way he sot de bloodhounds on dem and dey clumb de tree. I's heared dem hounds bayin' de nigger up a tree jes' lots of times. Massa never sold none my family and we stays with him till he wife die and he die, too.

"In de cold days de women spin and weave de cloth on looms. I stands by and pick up de shuttle when dey fall. Us niggers all wore de clothes make on de spinnin' wheel, but de white folks wore dresses from de store. Dey have to pay fifty and seventy-five cents de yard for calico den.

"Den de war come. I 'member how massa come home on de furlough and when word come he on de way, us all git ready for de big cel'bration. Dey kilt de yearlin' or hawg and all us niggers cook for de big feast. Sometimes iffen he stay a week, we jes' do nothin' but eat and cook.

"Dem de good old days, but dey didn't last, for de war am over to sot de slaves free and old massa ask if we'll stay or go. My folks jes' stays till I's a growed gal and gits married and has a home of my own. Den my old man tell me how de Yankees stoled him from de fields. Dey some cavalry sojers and dey make him take care of de hosses. He's 'bout twict as old as me, and he say he was in de Bull Run Battle. He's capture in one battle and run 'way and 'scape by the holp of a Southern regiment and fin'ly come back to Mississip'. He like de war songs like 'Marchin' Through Georgia,' but bes' of all he like dis song:

"'I ain't gwine study war no more,
I gwine lay down my burden,
Down by de river side,
Down by de river side.

"'Gwine lay down my sword and shield
Down by de riverside,
Down by de riverside.

"'I ain't gwine study war no more,
Gwine try on my starry crown,
Down by de river side,
Down by de river side.'

"Well, he done lay he burden down and quit dis world in 1916.

"Do I 'member any hant stories? Well, we'd sit around de fire in de wintertime and tell ghos' stories till us chillen 'fraid to go to bed at night. Iffen I can 'lect, I'll tell you one. Dis story am 'bout a old, haunted house, a big, old house with two front rooms down and two front rooms up and a hall runnin' from back to front. In back am de li'l house where Alex, massa's boy what kep' he hoss, stay.

"Dis big house face de river. Old Massa go to war and never come back no more. Old missy jes' wait and wait, till fin'ly dey all say she am weak in de head. Every day she tell de niggers to kill de pig, dat massa be home today. Every day she fix up in de Sunday best and wait for him. It go on like dat for years and years, till old miss am gone to be with old massa, and de niggers all left and dere am jes' de old house left.

"One day long time after freedom, Alex come back, and he hair turned white. He go up de river to de old plantation to tell Old Miss dat Old Massa gone to he Heavenly Home, and won't be back to the old place. He come up to de old house and de front gate am offen de hinges and de grass high as he head, and de blinds all hangin' sideways and rattle with de wind. Dey ain't no lightnin' bug and no crickets on de fireplace, jes' de old house and de wind a-blowin' through de window blinds and moanin' through de trees.

"Old Alex so broke up he jes' sot down on de steps and 'fore he knowed it he's asleep. He saw Old Massa and hisself gwine to war and Old Massa am on he white hoss and he new gray uniform what de women make for him, and de band am playin' Dixie. Old Alex seed hisself ridin' he li'l roan pony by Old Massa's side. Den he dream o after the battle when he look for Old Massa and finds him and he hoss lyin' side by side, done gone to where dere ain't no more war. He buries him, and—den de thunder and lightnin' make Alex wake up and he look in Old Miss' room and dere she am, jes' sittin' in her chair, waitin' for Old Massa. Old Alex go to talk to her and she fade 'way. Alex stay in he li'l old cabin waitin' to tell Old Miss, and every time it come rain and lightnin' she allus sot in her chair and go 'way 'fore he git in her room. So Old Alex fin'ly goes to sleep forever, but he never left he place of watchin' for Old Miss."

Source List

1 :: Contact and Conflict

1–1 | Southwestern Native American Poetry and Song

Troyer, Carlos, transcribed and harmonized. "Sunset Song: Ceremonial Thanks Offering to the Sun." *Traditional Songs of the Zuñi Indians.* Philadelphia: Theodore Presser Co., 1912. 3–6.

Songs from *The Path on the Rainbow: An Anthology of Songs and Chants from the Indians of North America.* Edited by George W. Cronyn. With an introduction by Mary Austin. New York: Boni and Liveright, 1918.

"Early Moon." Translated by Carl Sandburg. Front matter.

"Hunting Songs" (Dakota). Translated by Stephen Return Riggs. 47.

"Songs of the Ghost-Dance Religion" (Arapaho), "Songs of Life Returning" (Paiute), and "Judgment" (Kiowa). Translated by James Mooney. 62–68.

"War Songs" (Zuñi). Translated by Matilda Coxe Stevenson. 73–74.

"Rain Song of the Giant Society" (Sia). Translated by Matilda Coxe Stevenson. 76–77.

"Magpie Song" (Navajo). Translated by Washington Matthews. 80.

"Protection Song ("To Be Sung on Going into Battle.") and "Song of Spirits" (Wintu). Translated by Washington Matthews. 97–98, 151.

"Songs of the Kumastamxo" (Yuma). Translated by John Peabody Harrington. 152–53.

"Songs to the Mesa" and "Mother Corn Reasserts Leadership" (Pawnee). Translated by Alice Fletcher. 271–73.

Songs from *Ancient Nahuatl Poetry, Containing the Nahuatl Text of XXVII Ancient Mexican Poems.* Brinton's Library of Aboriginal

American Literature No. 7. Edited and Translated by Daniel G. Brinton. Philadelphia: D. G. Brinton, 1887.

"Song at the Beginning." 55–57.

"Another Plain Song, to the Same Tune." 61–63.

"An Otomi Song of the Mexicans." 65.

"XIV." 87.

"XIX." 109.

"XXV." 123.

1–2 | Slafter, Rev. Edmund F., ed. *Voyages of the Northmen to America including extracts from Icelandic sagas relating to western voyages by north-men in the tenth and eleventh centuries in an English translation by North Ludlow Beamish with a synopsis of the historical evidence and the opinion of Professor Rafn as to the places visited by the Scandinavians on the coast of America.* Boston: The Prince Society, 1877. 48–59.

1–3 | Cabeza de Vaca, Álvar Núñez. *The Journey of Álvar Núñez Cabeza de Vaca and His Companions from Florida to the Pacific, 1528–1536. Translated from his own narrative by Fanny Bandelier together with the report of Father Marcos of Nizza and a letter from the Viceroy Mendoza.* Edited and with introduction by Ad. F. Bandelier. Translated by Fanny Bandelier. New York: Allerton Book Co., 1922. 56–68, 76, 77, 78–90, 104–15.

1–4 | Reyes de Castañeda, Pedro. *The Journey of Coronado: 1540–1542; from the City of Mexico to the Grand Canyon of the Colorado and the Buffalo Plains of Texas, Kansas, and Nebraska, as told by himself and his followers.* Translated and edited with an introduction by George Parker Winship. New York: A. S. Barnes & Co., 1904. 109–16. Available online at http://hdl.handle.net/2027/hvd.32044019636018.

1–5 | Lazo de la Vega, Luis. "History of the Miraculous Apparition." Translated from *Álbum de la coronación de la Sma. Virgen de Guadalupe.* Mexico: V. Agüeros, 1895. 17–23. English translation by Hannah M. Dyar, © Baylor University Press.

1–6 | Williams, Roger. *A Key into the Language of America, or an Help to the Language of the Natives in that Part of America called New-England; together with briefe observations of the customes, manners, and worships, &c. of the aforesaid Natives, in peace and warre, in life and death. On all which are added, spirituall observations generall and particular, by the author, of chiefe and speciall use (upon all occasions) to all the English inhabiting those parts; yet pleasant and profitable to the view of all men.* London: Gregory Dexter, 1643. In *Collections of the Rhode-Island Historical Society.* Vol 1. Reprinted. Providence: John Miller, 1827. 17–24, 25–26, 27–29, 29–32.

1–7 | Bradstreet, Anne. *The Works of Anne Bradstreet in Prose and Verse*. Edited by John Harvard Ellis. Charlestown: Abram E. Cutter, 1867.
    "By Night When Others Soundly Slept." 11.
    "Before the Birth of One of Her Children." 393–94.
    "To My Dear and Loving Husband." 394.

2 :: Colonial Literature and the Road to Revolution

2–1 | Sáenz of San Antonio, Brother Matías. "Lord, if the Shepherd Does Not Give Heed." Translated from *Señor, si el pastor no escucha*. Madrid?: n.p., 1724. 6 numbered leaves. Original Spanish text available through the Recovering the U.S. Hispanic Literary Heritage program and Arte Público Press, University of Houston. English translation by Hannah M. Dyar, © Baylor University Press.

2–2 | Franklin, Benjamin. The image of the rattlesnake in this section is available through the Library of Congress and is titled "Benjamin Franklin's warning to the British colonies in America 'join or die' exhorting them to unite against the French and the Natives, shows a segmented snake, 'S.C., N.C., V., M., P., N.J., N.Y., [and] N.E.'" Illustrated in *The Pennsylvania Gazette*, May 9, 1754. Woodcut, item number LC-USZC4-5315 (color film copy transparency), https://www.loc.gov/pictures/item/2002695523/.
    "The Rattle-Snake as a Symbol of America." *Pennsylvania & Weekly Journal*. December 27, 1775.
    "Information to Those Who Would Remove to America." *The Writings of Benjamin Franklin*. Collected and edited with a life and introduction by Albert Henry Smyth. Vol. 8, 1780–1782. New York: Macmillan, 1906. 603–14.
    "Remarks Concerning the Savages of North America." *The Writings of Benjamin Franklin*. Collected and edited with a life and introduction by Albert Henry Smyth. Vol. 10, 1789–1790. New York: Macmillan, 1907. 97–105.

2–3 | Paine, Thomas. "The Liberty Tree." *American Poetry*. Edited by Percy H. Boynton. New York: Charles Scribner's Sons, 1918. 66.

2–4 | Equiano, Olaudah. *The Interesting Narrative of the Life of Olaudah Equiano, or Gustavus Vassa, the African, written by himself*. Two volumes in one. Boston: Isaac Knapp, 1837. 7–10, 13–14, 16–17, 18–19, 20–21, 22–23, 30–33, 37–38, 39–41, 43–46, 47–48, 50–52.

2–5 | Stone, William L. *The Life and Times of Red-Jacket or Sa-Go-Ye-Wat-Ha; Being the Sequel to the History of the Six Nations. By William L. Stone*. New York: Wiley and Putnam, 1841. 189–93.

2–6 | Wheatley, Phillis. Portrait of Wheatley from *Poems on Various Subjects, Religious and Moral,* by Phillis Wheatley, Negro servant to Mr. John Wheatley, of Boston, in New England. London: Printed for A. Bell, bookseller, Aldgate, and sold by Messrs. Cox and Berry, King-Street, Boston, M DCC LXXIII [1773].
> *Memoir and Poems of Phillis Wheatley, A Native African and a Slave. Also Poems by a Slave.* 3rd ed. Boston: Isaac Knapp, 1838.
> "On Being Brought from Africa to America." 48.
> "To the University of Cambridge, in New-England." 48–49.
> "On the Death of the Rev. Mr. George Whitefield—1770." 52–54.

3 :: Romanticism

3–1 | Holley, Mary Austin. *Texas: Observations, Historical, Geographical and Descriptive, in a Series of Letters, Written during a Visit to Austin's Colony.* Lexington, Ky.: J. Clarke & Co., 1836. 127–39, 141–48. Available online at https://catalog.hathitrust.org/Record/011923924.

3–2 | Poetry of Early Texas. *Early Texas Verse, 1835–1850, Collected from the Original Newspapers and Edited.* Authors unknown. Edited by Philip Graham. Austin, Tex.: The Steck Co., 1936.
> "Lines to the San Antonio River" (1838). 92.
> "Storm on the Prairie" (1841). 99–100.

3–3 | Audubon, John James. "The Prairie." Chapter in *Ornithological Biography, Or an Account of the Habits of the Birds of the United States of America; Accompanied by Descriptions of the Objects Represented in the Work Entitled The Birds of America, and Interspersed with Delineations of American Scenery and Manners.* Philadelphia: E. L. Carey and A. Hart, 1832. 81–84.

3–4 | Catlin, George. Letter 42, "Great Camanche Village." *Letters and Notes on the Manners, Customs and Conditions of the North American Indians, Written during Eight Years' Travel amongst the Wildest Tribes of Indians in North America.* 3rd ed. 2 vols. London: Tilt and Bogue, 1842. 2:64–69.

3–5 | Truth, Sojourner. Speech to the Women's Rights Convention in Akron, Ohio. From Elizabeth Cady Stanton, Susan B. Anthony, and Matilda Joslyn Gage, eds. *History of Woman Suffrage.* Vol. 1, *1848–1861.* Rochester, N.Y., 1881, 1886. 114–17. Available online at https://archive.org/details/historyofwomansu01stanuoft/page/116/mode/2up. Portrait of Truth from *Narrative of Sojourner Truth: A northern slave, emancipated from bodily servitude by the state of New York, in 1828, with a portrait.* Introduction by Harriet Beecher Stowe. New York: Published for the author, 1853. https://hdl.handle.net/2027/mdp.39015071140142.

3–6 | Apess, William. "An Indian's Looking-Glass for the White Man." *The Experiences of Five Christian Indians of the Pequod Tribe: Or the Indian's Looking-Glass for the White Man*. Boston: James B. Dow, 1833. 53–60.

3–7 | Smith, Richard Penn, supposed author. *Col. Crockett's Exploits and Adventures in Texas: Wherein is Contained a Full Account of His Journey from Tennessee to the Red River and Natchitoches, and Thence across Texas to San Antonio; Including His Many Hair-Breadth Escapes; Together with a Topographical, Historical, and Political View of Texas. Written by Himself*. Philadelphia: T. K. and P. G. Collins, 1836. 23–25, 25, 27–29, 29–32, 90–95. Available online at http://hdl.handle.net/2027/loc.ark:/13960/t3qv3t57f.

3–8 | Heredia, José María. *The Literary History of Spanish America*. By Alfred Lester Coester. Translated by William Cullen Bryant. New York: Macmillan, 1916.
 "Niagara." 94–98.
 "Hurricane." 99–100.

3–9 | Commuck, Thomas. *Indian Melodies*. Harmonized by Thomas Hastings. New York: G. Lane & C. B. Tippett, 1845. iii–vi, 17, 20, 26, 30–31, 37, 40, 47, 83.

3–10 | Hawthorne, Nathaniel. "The Birthmark." *Mosses from an Old Manse*. Vol. 1. Boston: Houghton Mifflin Company, 1900. 48–77.

3–11 | Tocqueville, Alexis de. "Literary Characteristics of Democratic Ages." *Democracy in America*. Translated by Henry Reeve with special introductions by Hon. John T. Morgan and Hon. John J. Ingalls. Revised ed. Vol. 2. New York: The Co-operative Publication Society, 1900. 58–63.

3–12 | Longfellow, Henry Wadsworth. *The Song of Hiawatha. The Complete Poetical Works of Henry Wadsworth Longfellow*. Cambridge ed. Boston: Houghton, Mifflin and Company, 1893. 119–21, 160–62.

3–13 | Poe, Edgar Allan. *Poems and Tales of Edgar Allan Poe*. Selected and edited by Alphonso G. Newcomer. Revised edition with helps to study. Chicago: Scott, Foresman and Company, 1920.
 "To Helen." 33.
 "The Raven." 37–44.
 "The Masque of the Red Death." 175–85.

3–14 | Holmes, Oliver Wendell, Sr. "The Chambered Nautilus." *The Complete Works of Oliver Wendell Holmes*. Poems, Vol. 2. University ed. New York: Sully and Kleinteich, Houghton Mifflin Company, 1908. 107–8.

3–15 | Stowe, Harriet Beecher. "The Two Altars; or, Two Pictures in One." *Dred, A Tale of the Great Dismal Swamp together with Anti-slavery Tales and Papers, and Life in Florida after the War*. In *The Writings of Harriet Beecher*

Stowe. Vol. 2. Riverside ed. Boston: Houghton, Mifflin and Company, 1896. 249–64.

3–16 | Jacobs, Harriet. *Incidents in the Life of a Slave Girl By Mrs. Harriet Brent Jacobs. Written by herself.* Edited by L. Maria Child. Boston: Published for the author, 1861.
    "Preface by the Author and Introduction by the Editor." 5–8.
    "Childhood." Chapter 1. 11–16.
    "The Trials of Girlhood." Chapter 5. 44–48.
    "A Perilous Passage in the Slave Girl's Life." Chapter 10. 82–89.
    "The Loophole of Retreat." Chapter 21. 173–78.

3–17 | Duval, John C. *The Adventures of Big-Foot Wallace, the Texas Ranger and Hunter.* Philadelphia: Claxton, Remsen & Haffelfinger, 1871. 58–64, 137–42, 255–62.

3–18 | Thoreau, Henry David. "Walking." *The Writings of Henry David Thoreau.* Vol. 5. *Excursions and Poems.* Boston: Houghton, Mifflin & Co., 1906. 205–8, 210–13, 213, 216–18, 219–21, 222, 222–25, 226–27, 228–30, 231–34, 237–38, 239–41, 241–44, 244–48.

3–19 | Plummer, Rachel. *Narrative of the Capture and Subsequent Sufferings of Mrs. Rachel Plummer, during a Captivity of Twenty-One Months among the Cumanche Indians, with a Sketch of Their Manners, Customs, Laws, & with a Short Description of the Country over Which She Travelled whilst with the Indians. Written by Herself.* 1839. 3, 5–16, 20–21, 27–28, 28–29, 29–30, 31–32, 32–33.

3–20 | Whitman, Walt. *Leaves of Grass.* With an introduction by Stuart P. Sherman. New York: Charles Scribner's Sons, 1922.
    "To Foreign Lands." 213.
    "Passage to India." 447–57.

3–21 | Ridge, John Rollin [Cheesquatalawny]. *The Life and Adventures of Joaquin Murieta, the Celebrated California Bandit.* 3rd ed. Rev. and enl. by the author. In *The Lives of Joaquin Murieta and Tiburcio Vasquez.* San Francisco: Fred'k MacCrellish & Co., Publishers, 1874. 5, 5–12, 12–13, 13–14.

3–22 | Dickinson, Emily. *The Complete Poems of Emily Dickinson.* With an introduction by her niece Martha Dickinson Bianchi. Boston: Little, Brown, and Company, 1924.
    "1: Success Is Counted Sweetest." 3.
    "15: A Route of Evanescence." 86.
    "19: I Started Early, Took My Dog." 88–89.
    "34: Nature Is What We See." 268–69.

"49: They Dropped like Flakes." 206.

"64: This Is the Land the Sunset Washes." 116.

4 :: Realism

4-1 | Jackson, Helen Hunt. "Cheyenne Mountain." *Poems by Helen Jackson*. Boston: Little, Brown, and Company, 1902. 258.

4-2 | Ruiz de Burton, María Amparo [C. Loyal]. "The Don in His Broad Acres." Chapter 5 in *The Squatter and the Don: A Novel Descriptive of Contemporaneous Occurrences in California*. San Francisco, 1885. 48–59.

4-3 | Twain, Mark [Samuel L. Clemens]. The portrait of Twain is from *Literary Essays*. Illustrated. New York: Harper & Brothers Publishers, 1899. Front matter.

"The Celebrated Jumping Frog of Calaveras County." *The Celebrated Jumping Frog of Calaveras County, and Other Sketches*. Edited by John Paul. New York: C. H. Webb, Publisher, 1867. 7–19.

"Back from 'Yurrup.'" *Mark Twain's Sketches*. Number One. Authorized ed. With illustrations by R. T. Sperry. New York: American News Company, 1874. 17–19.

A Tramp Abroad. Vol. 1. New York: Harper & Brothers Publishers, 1907.

"Jim Baker." 24–26.

"Baker's Blue Jay Yarn." 27–32.

"Concerning the American Language." *The Stolen White Elephant Etc.* Boston: James R. Osgood and Company, 1882. 265–69.

"On Foreign Critics." *Mark Twain's Speeches*. With an introduction by Albert Bigelow Paine and an appreciation by William Dean Howells. New York: Harper & Brothers Publishers, 1923. 150–53.

"How to Tell a Story." *Literary Essays*. Illustrated. New York: Harper & Brothers Publishers, 1899. 7–14.

4-4 | Harte, Bret. "The Luck of Roaring Camp." *The Luck of Roaring Camp, and Other Sketches*. Boston: Houghton Mifflin Company, 1869. 1–18.

4-5 | Miller, Joaquin [Cincinnatus Heine Miller]. *The Complete Poetical Works of Joaquin Miller*. San Francisco: The Whitaker & Ray Co. (Incorporated), 1897.

"The Sierras from the Sea." 163–64.

"Vaquero." 166.

"Crossing the Plains." 184–85.

"Don't Stop at the Station Despair." 221.

4-6 | Howells, William Dean. "Editha." *Harper's Monthly Magazine*, December 1, 1904. 214–24.

4–7 | Sweet, Alexander Edwin and J. Armoy Knox. Selections from chapters 1 and 20 in *On a Mexican Mustang, through Texas, from the Gulf to the Rio Grande*. Illustrated. Chicago: Rand, McNally & Company, Publishers, 1883. 15–21, 284–88.

4–8 | Lanier, Sidney. "San Antonio de Bexar." *Retrospects and Prospects: Descriptive and Historical Essays*. New York: Charles Scribner's Sons, 1899. 34–41, 43–50, 51–76.

4–9 | Custer, Elizabeth Bacon. Chapter 7 in *Tenting on the Plains, or General Custer in Kansas and Texas*. New York: Charles L. Webster & Company, 1889. 210–23, 224–27, 229–30.

4–10 | Winnemucca, Sarah [Thocmentony]. "First Meeting of Piutes and Whites." Chapter 1 in *Life among the Piutes: Their Wrongs and Claims*. Edited by Mrs. Horace Mann and printed for the author. New York: G. P. Putnam's Sons, 1883. 5–9, 9, 10–15.

4–11 | Jewett, Sarah Orne. "A White Heron." *A White Heron and Other Stories*. Boston: Houghton, Mifflin and Company, 1886. 1–22.

4–12 | Lazarus, Emma.
"The New Colossus." In *Catalogue of the Pedestal Fund Art Loan Exhibition*. Published in conjunction with the exhibit "Pedestal Fund Art Loan Exhibition" shown at the National Academy of Design, New York, December 1883.
"In Exile." *The Poems of Emma Lazarus*. Vol. 2. Jewish Poems: Translations. Boston: Houghton, Mifflin and Company, 1888. 5–7.

5 :: Naturalism

5–1 | Chopin, Kate. "Désirée's Baby." *Bayou Folk*. Boston: Houghton Mifflin Company, 1894. 147–58.

5–2 | Fenollosa, Ernest Francisco [Kano Eitan Masanobu]. "Part II, The Separated East." *East and West: The Discovery of America and Other Poems*. New York: Thomas Y. Crowell and Company, 1893. 26–28, 211–12.

5–3 | Martí, José. "Our America." Translated from *Nuestra América*, edited by Gonzalo de Quesada, 2 vols. Havana: Imprenta y Papelería de Rambla y Bouza, 1909–1910. 2:79–91. English translation by Hannah M. Dyar, © Baylor University Press.

5–4 | Love, Nat. Chapters 6 and 7 in *The Life and Adventures of Nat Love, Better Known in the Cattle Country as "Deadwood Dick," by Himself. A true history of slavery days, life on the great cattle ranges and on the plains of the "wild and woolly" west, based on facts, and personal experiences of the author.* Los Angeles: Nat Love, Author, 1907. 40–45, 46–51.

5-5 | Washington, Booker T. Chapters 2 ("Boyhood Days") and 14 ("Atlanta Exposition Address") in *Up from Slavery, An Autobiography*. New York: The Association Press, 1900, 1901. 23–41, 217–25.

5-6 | Chesnutt, Charles Waddell. "The Passing of Grandison." *The Wife of His Youth and Other Stories of the Color Line*. With illustrations by Clyde O. De Land. Boston: Houghton, Mifflin and Company, 1901. 168–202.

5-7 | Chittenden, William Lawrence. *Ranch Verses*. Illustrated. Fifteenth ed. enlarged. Montclair ed. New York: G. P. Putnam's Sons, 1921.
   "The Cowboys' Christmas Ball." 12–17.
   "The Cowboy Preacher's Sermon." 209–11.

5-8 | Henry, O. [William Sydney Porter]. "The Caballero's Way." *Heart of the West*. New York: Doubleday, Page & Company, 1904. 187–204.

5-9 | Far, Sui Sin [Edith Maude Eaton]. "Mrs. Spring Fragrance." *Mrs. Spring Fragrance*. Chicago: A. C. McClurg & Co., 1912. 1–21.

5-10 | Austin, Mary Hunter. "Water Trails of the Ceriso." Chapter 2 in *The Land of Little Rain*. Boston: Houghton, Mifflin and Company, 1903. 25–43.

5-11 | Crane, Stephen. "The Bride Comes to Yellow Sky." *The Open Boat and Other Tales of Adventure*. New York: Doubleday & McClure Co., 1898. 183–211.

5-12 | Dunbar, Paul Laurence. *The Complete Poems of Paul Laurence Dunbar*. With the Introduction to "Lyrics of Lowly Life" by W. D. Howells. [no place of publication]: Dodd, Mead & Company, 1913.
   "We Wear the Mask." 112–13.
   "When Malindy Sings." 131–34.
   "Sympathy." 162–63.

5-13 | Cather, Willa. "The Enchanted Bluff." *Harper's Monthly Magazine*. Vol. 118, no. 607 (April 1909): 774–81.

5-14 | Frost, Robert. *North of Boston*. New York: Henry Holt and Company, 1917.
   "Mending Wall." 11–13.
   "The Death of the Hired Man." 14–23.

5-15 | "The Ballad of Gregorio Cortez." Author unknown. Translated from a transcription of a Spanish recording (vocalion record number SA 283 8351 by "Los Trovadores Regionales") of the ballad "El Corrido de Gregorio Cortez," included in Américo Paredes, *"With His Pistol in His Hand": A Border Ballad and Its Hero*. Austin: University of Texas Press, 1958. 158–61. English translation by Hannah M. Dyar, © Baylor University Press.

5–16 | London, Jack [John Griffith Chaney]. "Koolau the Leper." *The House of Pride and Other Tales of Hawaii*. New York: Macmillan, 1912. 47–91.

6 :: Early Modernism

6–1 | Glaspell, Susan. "A Jury of Her Peers." *The Best Short Stories of 1917 and the Yearbook of the American Short Story*. Edited by Edward J. O'Brien. Boston: Small, Maynard & Company, 1918. 256–82.

6–2 | Zitkala-Ša [Gertrude Simmons Bonnin, Dakota Sioux Indian]. "The Trial Path." *American Indian Stories*. Washington: Hayworth Publishing House, 1921. 127–35.

6–3 | Scarborough, Dorothy. *Fugitive Verses*. Waco: Baylor University Press, 1912.
"Carroll Chapel and Library." 19–20.
"The Passing of the Prairie." 98–102.

6–4 | Stevens, Wallace. *Harmonium*. New York: Alfred A. Knopf, 1923.
"Disillusionment of Ten O'Clock." 99.
"Thirteen Ways of Looking at a Blackbird." 135–37.
"Anecdote of the Jar." 112.
"The Emperor of Ice-Cream." 95.

6–5 | Yezierska, Anzia [Harriet Mayer]. "Soap and Water." *Hungry Hearts*. Boston: Houghton Mifflin Company, 1920. 163–177.

6–6 | Williams, William Carlos.
A Book of Poems, Al Que Quiere! Boston: The Four Seas Company, 1917.
"Pastoral." 23–24.
"Apology." 22–23.
"Libertad! Igualdad! Fraternidad!" 32–33.
"El Hombre." 31.
Sour Grapes, A Book of Poems. Boston: The Four Seas Company, 1921.
"The Widow's Lament in Springtime." 73.
"The Great Figure." 78.
Spring and All. Dijon, France: Maurice Darantière [Contact Publishing Company, copyright by author], 1923.
"The Red Wheelbarrow." 74.

6–7 | Pound, Ezra.
Lustra of Ezra Pound with Earlier Poems. New York: Alfred A. Knopf, 1917.
"The Seafarer" (from the Anglo-Saxon). 161–65.
"The River-Merchant's Wife: A Letter" (from Li Po). 77–79.
Poetry: A Magazine of Verse. Vol. 2, no. 1 (April 1913)
"In a Station of the Metro." 12.
"A Pact." 11–12.

6–8 | H. D. [Hilda Doolittle]. *Some Imagist Poets: An Anthology*. Boston: Houghton Mifflin Company, 1915.
    "Oread." 28.
    "Sea Iris." 25–26.
    "Sea Rose." 27.

6–9 | Porter, Katherine Anne. "Maria Concepción." *The Century Magazine*. Vol. 105, no. 2 (December 1922): 224–39.

6–10 | Fitzgerald, F. Scott."Bernice Bobs Her Hair." *Flappers and Philosophers*. New York: Charles Scribner's Sons, 1921. 155–93.

6–11 | Hughes, Langston.
    "The Negro Speaks of Rivers." *The Crisis*. Vol. 22, no. 2 (June 1921): 71.
    "Mother to Son." *The Crisis*. Vol 25, no. 2 (December 1922): 87.

6–12 | Federal Writers' Project: Slave Narratives Collection, vol. 16, Texas, part 1 and part 3. Interviews collected 1936–1938. United States Works Progress Administration (WPA). Available online at https://www.loc.gov/collections/slave-narratives-from-the-federal-writers-project-1936-to-1938/about-this-collection/.
    Nelsen Denson. Vol. 16, part I, 305–7.
    Annie Little. Vol. 16, part III, 20–22.